American Military
Communities in
West Germany

American Military Communities in West Germany

Life in the Cold War Badlands, 1945–1990

John W. Lemza

McFarland & Company, Inc., Publishers
Jefferson, North Carolina

LIBRARY OF CONGRESS CATALOGUING-IN-PUBLICATION DATA

Names: Lemza, John W., 1954–
Title: American military communities in West Germany :
life in the Cold War Badlands, 1945–1990 / John W. Lemza.
Description: Jefferson, North Carolina : McFarland & Company, Inc.,
Publishers, 2016 | Includes bibliographical references and index.
Identifiers: LCCN 2016014657 | ISBN 9781476664163
(softcover : acid free paper) ∞
Subjects: LCSH: United States—Armed Forces—Germany (West)—History. |
Americans—Germany (West)—Social conditions. | Families of military personnel—
United States—History—20th century. | Military bases, American—Social
aspects—Germany (West) | United States—Armed Forces—Military life—History—
20th century. | Sociology, Military—United States—History—20th century. | Germany
(West)—Social conditions—20th century. | Cold War—Social aspects—Germany
(West) | Germany (West)—Relations—United States. | United States—
Relations—Germany (West)
Classification: LCC UA26.G3 L46 2016 | DDC 355.1/208913043—dc23
LC record available at https://lccn.loc.gov/2016014657

BRITISH LIBRARY CATALOGUING DATA ARE AVAILABLE

ISBN (print) 978-1-4766-6416-3
ISBN (ebook) 978-1-4766-2410-5

© 2016 John W. Lemza. All rights reserved

*No part of this book may be reproduced or transmitted in any form
or by any means, electronic or mechanical, including photocopying
or recording, or by any information storage and retrieval system,
without permission in writing from the publisher.*

Front cover: Photograph of Mark Twain Village,
Heidelberg, Germany, in 2007

Printed in the United States of America

*McFarland & Company, Inc., Publishers
Box 611, Jefferson, North Carolina 28640
www.mcfarlandpub.com*

To my wife Laura,
my children Nick and Kate,
my parents and grandparents,
and those Americans who lived in the far flung
overseas communities of the Cold War

Table of Contents

Acronyms and Abbreviations — viii
Preface — 1
Introduction — 3

One. From First Arrivals to Established Network (1946–1967) — 11
Two. The Footprint of American Culture and Consumerism (1946–1967) — 38
Three. Religion, Race, Stereotyping and the Media (1946–1967) — 55
Four. Anti-Communism and Nuclear Concerns (1946–1967) — 82
Five. Challenge to American Economic Dominance (1946–1967) — 108
Six. Fast Food, Violence, Crime and Drugs (1967–1990) — 122
Seven. Race, Feminism and Media Manipulation (1967–1990) — 146
Eight. Testing German-American Bonds (1967–1990) — 172
Nine. Economic Challenges (1967–1990) — 202

Conclusion — 226
Chapter Notes — 233
Bibliography — 279
Index — 285

Acronyms and Abbreviations

AAFES	Army-Air Force Exchange System
AFN	Armed Forces Network
AFRTS	Armed Forces Radio and Television Service
AMZON	American Zone
BPE	Bremerhaven Port of Entry
COLA	Cost of Living Adjustment
DM	Deutsche mark
DOD	Department of Defense
DODDS	Department of Defense Dependent Schools
EES	European Exchange System
EUCOM	European Command
GYA	German Youth Activities
HICOG	High Commissioner of Germany
Milcom	Military Community
MPC	Military Payment Certificate
NATO	North Atlantic Treaty Organization
NEO	Non-Combatant Evacuation Operation
PX	Post Exchange
RAF	Red Army Faction
REFORGER	Return of Forces to Germany
SMLM	Soviet Military Liaison Mission
SOFA	Status of Forces Agreement
USAFE	U.S. Airforce, Europe
USAREUR	U.S. Army Europe
VAT	Value Added Tax
WAC	Women's Army Corps

Preface

On a sunny afternoon in July 2013, I stood on a sidewalk along Römerstrasse in the Südstadt section of Heidelberg, Germany, peering through the gates of Campbell Barracks, former Headquarters of the United States Army, Europe (USAREUR). More than 20 years had passed since my last visit there when military police guarded the wide open gates and waved pedestrians, cyclists and vehicular traffic through a maze of concrete security baffles after verifying individual identity cards. In the 1980s, Campbell Barracks had been a vibrant and busy place, the beating heart of a military force of nearly 500,000 including service members, civilians and dependent families. By the summer of 2013 it stood silent and empty, rows of windows in the buildings offering blank stares and knee-high weeds taking the place of long gone military sentries. In both directions, north and south along Römerstrasse and across the way, former housing areas also stood empty with tall weeds crowding the abandoned gardens, living spaces and parking lots. Playground equipment sat motionless, fading in the sun, waiting for children who would never again return. The Americans were gone. They were gone from Heidelberg and from hundreds of other cities, towns, villages and remote sites throughout Germany.[1]

Before I turned to leave the gate at Campbell Barracks, chained shut against trespassers, I glanced up toward the top of the brown sandstone gate post. There, affixed with rusting bolts was a metal USAREUR shield; but immediately behind it, barely covered and still visible at an angle, was a carved symbol of the Third Reich. That juxtaposition struck me as a visual signifier of the passage of time and changing political, social, cultural and economic realities. The Americans had arrived in Germany on the heels of the Nazi defeat and stayed for nearly five decades, first as conquerors and protectors against Soviet aggression, then as economic, military and political partners, and finally as awkward guests. By 2013 new geo-political circumstances had forced the remaining few Americans into a handful of clustered enclaves, these new places serving as vague reminders of a once extensive, thriving network of military facilities, housing areas, schools and training sites that had spread from the port of Bremerhaven on the North Sea to the southern Bavarian town of Garmisch-Partenkirchen, an area encompassing nearly 100,000 square miles. Now, all that remained were the ghosts and memories of those communities established 70 years ago.

Thoughts about how this extensive network came into existence, the Americans who lived there and their interaction with their German neighbors framed the development of this study. Much has been written from the perspective of the conquered European nation struggling to find a new identity amid the postwar rubble while bearing the imposition of a foreign occupation army. Much less exists to tell the story of the American service personnel, civilians, and their families, who arrived on the beam of victory's light to fill those communities along the Cold War's frontier, worked to accomplish their mission and sometimes struggled to maintain the routine of daily existence. Perhaps the fresher perspective offered here will help readers rethink their assumptions about the Americans' presence, how they thought about themselves, how they interacted with their German hosts and how changing global dynamics affected their lives and missions, and challenged their identity.

I wish to gratefully acknowledge the support of faculty, family and friends whose guidance and encouragement made the completion of this study possible. I want to thank Dr. Meredith Lair and the other members of my dissertation committee, Dr. Marion Deshmukh and Dr. Sam Lebovic, for their inspiration and guidance of the work while still in the conceptual phase and their patient support and mentorship during the research and writing phases. The example of their fine scholarship set the standard for research and analytical interpretation I hoped to emulate in this work. I am grateful to the scholars of the Department of History and Art History at George Mason University who cultivated an academic enthusiasm for historical studies among their students by sharing their own time, knowledge and experiences. Thanks especially to Dr. Cynthia Kierner, Dr. Michael O'Malley, Dr. Rosemarie Zagarri, Dr. Jane Censer and Dr. Steven Barnes. I am grateful also for the generous financial support provided by the department and university that made travel in pursuit of knowledge through research possible. I also want to acknowledge the guidance and support of those scholars who shaped many of my early ideas and thoughts about history and stoked my intellectual fires, Dr. Joseph Bendersky, Dr. John Kneebone and Dr. Melvin I. Urofsky. Many individuals, American and German, also willingly shared their memories, personal experiences and photographs from the period explored in this study. Their words breathed life into the narrative. In that regard I am especially grateful to those who graciously opened their homes and offered advice and friendship to me during my travels in Germany, Larry Applebaum, Dr. Arthur G. Volz and Eric Gerencser. Again, warm and loving thanks to my family, who tolerated the brooding thunderheads of scholarship that often gathered during the passion of writing, knew when to steer clear of the storm and still provided a constant safe harbor.

Introduction

> The American position is, therefore, entirely exceptional and it is quite possible that no democratic nation will ever be similarly placed.—*Alexis de Tocqueville*

> From the very inception of the American Republic, the United States has constantly supposed that it had a message for the world, even a mission to perform in the world. That message, we were convinced, was democracy; that mission, the exemplification to all the world of the merit of democratic institutions—even the propagation of such institutions.—*David M. Potter*

> As a representative of the American people, we have a big job to do in Germany. Our speech and actions, more than anything the United States policy could devise, will make Germans respect and demand democracy or decide that, after all, democracy is not what it's cracked up to be. For this reason, whether or not you like the Germans you meet, you must watch your behavior carefully.—*A Pocket Guide to Germany*, March 1950

By the end of the war in 1945, American troops bore a banner of triumphalism proclaiming their fresh victory over the dark designs of fascism. Although the proximate energy feeding that attitude was the Allies' recent military success, the course of those feelings was traceable to the evolution of an exceptional identity that characterized the early postwar Americans. At its heart was a consensus that had its roots in a historic tradition of ideals that gained shape over time and produced an amalgam of prevailing characteristics.[1] These represented an ideology that resonated throughout early postwar American society shaping its social, cultural and political behaviors and attitudes during that period.[2]

Collectively, that exceptional slate of prescribed and insinuated attributes melded together the concepts of anti-statism, anti-socialism, anti-communism, anti-colonialism, populism and individualism, a rejection of class consciousness, educational and economic opportunity, and meritocracy. Blended in were other contemporary ideas such as a belief in assigned gender roles and the centrality of both a traditional American home and religion.[3] At the same time, Americans viewed Europe through a long telescopic lens believing that a wide gulf of historical experience separated the two continents and that America was essentially different from Europe. In that view, Americans were born with a revolutionary spirit and were free of the past chains of a European-style feudal system and the yoke of a socialist future. Altogether these distinctions suggest that by 1945 Americans felt a separation from European politics, society and culture, believing instead that they had little to learn or gain from the Continent regardless of past historical connections or existing associations.[4]

Campbell Barracks, Heidelberg, circa 1945. Note the lack of fencing and security measures which only began appearing as terrorist threats emerged in the 1970s and again after 9/11. Image source: "Campbell Barracks," *US Army*, accessed July 6, 2015, https://en.wikipedia.org/wiki/Campbell_Barracks.

Fused together, all of these concepts, attitudes and thoughts about what it meant to be an American emerged as a paradigm of behavior and attitudes by the dawn of the postwar period. It was a consensus that gained energy from that sense of victory and served as a lens through which Americans, especially those overseas in the armed forces and living in military communities, viewed themselves. At the hands of the U.S military this exceptional American way of life became a "redemptive pedagogy" of sorts for the occupied nations by offering healing through example.[5] In that context this existing consensus of attitude lent its dynamism to a parochial "sense of superiority amongst many Americans: we've won the war, now we're going to reorganize Europe our way."[6] Seizing the moment, various conservative groups in the U.S., many who were associates of the Eisenhower Administration, also sought to insinuate their beliefs into the culture of the armed forces.[7] Combined, they contributed to the core of an imagined identity that Washington elites expected the military communities to accept, and in turn project, as overseas representatives of America.

By the time the official American occupation of West Germany had ended in 1949, and that nation's relationship with the U.S. began to change, so did the role of the military communities (Milcom).[8] No longer were they simple enclaves of American goodwill ambassadors functioning under prescribed guidance to represent their country. By 1950 they became deliberate conduits for a directed American identity that was the product of a series of focused initiatives that sought to craft a national will and underscore defining national characteristics. Within two decades however, Milcom members began struggling to come to terms with troubling internal contradictions of exceptionalist behaviors. These became evident through tensions wrought from the dynamics of contemporary cultural, social, political and economic discourses that occurred back home in the U.S., in the German host nation and around the globe. These included issues such as changing perspectives on the international counter-culture movement, the war in Vietnam, race relations, an emerging drug culture, the place of violence in society, gender rights, a weakening dollar and even West German political re-engagement with the East. An understanding of how these tensions challenged that consensus of an exceptional America in the Milcoms is integral to the purpose of this study that traces change over time within the overseas communities from their inception to diminished role and to eventual abandonment.

Also tested by those tensions was the very identity of the Milcoms that the consensus had informed and shaped. As a result, Milcom members, as individuals and as members of a community, faced the decision to either endorse existing prescribed ideals broadcast by the U.S government or accept a rescripting of the exceptional narrative that was sensitive to the influence of changing times. These decisions affected how they presented themselves to the German community, how the host nation interacted with the Milcom and how its members reconceptualized and articulated what it meant to be an American. This study addresses those cross boundary interactions between Milcom and host nation members that at once influenced and reflected those changes and shaped the identities of both communities.

But gaining a deeper appreciation for the evolution of the overseas Milcom as an imagined community, understanding the reactions of its members to tensions within the exceptionalist paradigm, and appreciating their negotiated interactions across existing social and cultural boundaries with the German host community, requires a grassroots level perspective.[9] This approach, which is essential to this work by capturing experiences and lost voices, provides a means to examine those places where Americans and Germans shared points of contact along the lines of four thematic threads: culture, society, politics and economics. It follows those courses by narrowing its scope to focus its investigation on those events, issues and concerns that most affected contemporary life in the Milcoms and interprets the members' reactions and interactions with one another and their German neighbors. It also considers those actions in the reflective mirror of the host nation. Some of the points of contact this study examines are the hiring of local nationals, the fluctuating Deutsche Mark rate, debates on the deployment of nuclear-ready missiles and a common terrorist threat.

That approach gives further form to the narrative that is at once thematic as well as chronological. Within that structure there is a division to the work that separates it into two sections: 1946 to 1967, and 1967 to 1990. As it reveals in the first five chapters, through 1967, the behaviors of the general American population and most members of the Milcoms hewed closely to the described tenets of the prescribed consensus. After that time, the changing global dynamics acted as catalysts to influence transformations within the belief system of American ideals among the community members. A number of significant events that occurred during the mid–1960s delineate that time as a logical caesura between the two sections. Among them was the 1968 Tet offensive in Vietnam, which many histories suggest turned American public opinion against the war. Also significant were a series of anti-war, anti-establishment and anti-authoritarian protests that erupted in 1968 around the globe in cities such as Paris, Mexico City, Peking, London and Berlin. That same summer, Soviet troops rolled into the city of Prague to put down a quasi-democratic movement and anti-establishment protests, and riots disrupted the Democratic National Convention in Chicago. That year also gained dark notoriety in the U.S. for the assassination of the key political and civil rights figures Robert F. Kennedy and Martin Luther King, Jr. Also, in West Germany, that generation known as the '68ers [*68er Bewegung*], born during World War II, came of age in the mid–1960s and rejected the values of the previous generations.[10] They added their voices to the growing chorus of global protest against the war in Vietnam and against authoritarianism that seemed too similar to their recent national past. This collection of influences, which unleased energies that affected Milcom members' thoughts about the American ideals, provides context for the latter half of the study.

The utilization of first person experiences provides the most information from the grass-roots perspective and offers evidence of exceptional attitudes and changing behaviors over time. In addition, they include German-American interactions along the cultural and social boundary and German perceptions of American actions. Integral to this are individual histories and shared experiences, letters to the editors of newspapers, reports of individual experiences and printed memoirs. The individual histories and shared experiences come from a variety of sources including existing university archives. In a similar manner, this study gathered information from a wide spectrum of former Milcom members: military members of all ranks, civilians and their family members who lived and worked in the communities during the timeframe of the study. Included in this group are the shared experiences of several German civilians who interacted with Americans during this period.[11] Letters to the editor of *Stars and Stripes* were another source of individual responses to the impact of current events in the Milcoms as were featured articles that included the impressions and reactions of individual service members, civilians, and dependents.[12] Also important as first person sources were compilations of personal letters and memories in bound form.[13] The value of these eye-witness sources rests in the immediacy of impressions that did not have to stand the vicissitudes of time and memory. Taken together, the value of all these varied sources of first hand perspectives is inestimable.

Chapter One of this work recounts the origins of the military communities in West Germany starting with the decision to deploy family members to Europe as a means to raise the morale of American occupation troops and to still restless urges that service members manifested in acts of ill-discipline such as excessive drinking, fighting, black marketing and fraternization. This establishes the chronological beginning of the study that then follows decisions by the U.S. government to exploit the coalescing network of Milcoms as a vehicle to sell American ideals at a time when there was hard competition with the Soviets to win the hearts and minds of people in occupied lands. It also introduces exceptionalist ideals as the prevailing set of tenets that American elites used as a template to direct Milcom members' behaviors and attitudes. This chapter also unpacks ideas about segmentation by shedding new light on the barriers that prevented early engagement of the German and American cultures and societies. These included physical separation between the groups, differences in nourishment and health, and the demands of daily life in the Milcoms for military personnel and their family members.

Chapter Two follows the first of four thematic threads and investigates the impact of American culture in Germany during the early postwar decades leading up to 1967. It examines the ways that the Germans negotiated accommodation and resistance to the exceptional cultural imprint that Americans presented through the dynamics of consumerism as well as through the artifacts of popular culture such as music, film and automobiles. In doing so, Germans gained a familiarity with their occupiers and came to terms with the visual and physical signifiers of Americanism present in cultural form.

Chapter Three examines the second thematic thread as it explores those dimensions of American society that served as a foundation to an exceptional consensus but also provided contested grounds within the public sphere. Ideas such as racial equality, gender roles and freedom of speech were among the concepts that were central to a postwar American identity but were also fraught with challenges. These difficulties came to light within the Milcoms and dictated how the members interacted with one another in the early postwar years. It also notes how their German neighbors evaluated the credibility of the exceptional credo by observing life within the segmented American communities.

Chapter Four explores the third thematic thread by studying the influence of two powerful postwar engines that drove American politics and political strategy: anti-communism and nuclear armament. It analyzes how Milcom members engaged with contemporary politics and unlike their counterparts back home lived in easy striking distance of the Soviet Bloc's nuclear weapons. In examining those dynamics this study reveals how the political energies of those days offered points of commonality and friction between the Americans and their German partners. It shows that for many Americans, especially those living in the West German Milcoms, the nuclear threat generated fears and tensions between the potential consequences of confrontation with the East and the responsibility to do their duty. On one hand, West Germans began to view American presence and the reliance on nuclear defense through a dark lens and this evolved into a political wedge between the nations, suggesting that their unity on the issue was perhaps illusory. On the other hand, a staunch defiance of communist influence continued to serve as a bond between the Germans and their Milcom neighbors.

Chapter Five follows the fourth thematic thread analyzing the effect of the German economic miracle [*Wirtschaftswunder*] that brought the nation out of the rubble of the postwar and proved to be an essential ingredient in shaping a strong, new anti-communist partner for the West. Adding to existing histories this chapter illuminates the impact that the *Wirtschaftswunder* had on the lives of Germans and how that trajectory of economic success had three points of contact with the American Milcoms that affected their relationship with the host nation: employment of the local populace, a changing Deutsche Mark rate and local taxes. It addresses the extant and emerging challenges of black marketeering and loss of buying power that confronted the Americans and heralded the beginning of the end of the halcyon days of unchallenged economic advantage for Milcom members.

The last four chapters of this study address the period that witnessed the greatest change in thinking about American ideals within the Milcoms subsequent to the political, cultural, social and economic tumult of the mid–1960s. Chapter Six addresses a new American cultural imprint that arrived via the Milcoms that the Germans both welcomed and eschewed. Unlike earlier decades it did not include an overt fascination with the physical manifestations of Americana such as automobiles, washing machines and blue jeans, or other cultural artifacts such as music and print media. Instead, this second wave of American culture introduced the popular dining fad of fast food and the dark triumvirate of violence, crime and drugs. The latter intersected at the Milcom and shaped Americans' opinions of their culture and their

Campbell Barracks' shuttered gate. By 2013 the former USAREUR headquarters lay dormant and quiet, the dynamic energies of the Cold War having dissipated. Weeds and small flocks of birds filled the empty spaces once busy with sentries, troops, couriers and vehicles. Image source: the author.

interactions with one another. Together, the fast food phenomenon and the collections of problems also informed West Germans' continued assessment of the U.S. by providing a lens to study the troubling complexity of contemporary modern American culture.

Chapter Seven explores how by the mid–1960s the societal issues of race, feminism, and media manipulation emerged as increasingly contested grounds within the public sphere for most Americans. It was during this period, in this environment, that the Milcom members encountered a newly energized struggle for racial equality that had gained strength from an organized civil rights movement that had developed a threatening radical edge. Here, also, a blossoming feminist movement confronted service members, civilian workers, their spouses and families, with new challenges as well as opportunities. Finally, the familiar media outlets, Armed Forces Network (AFN) and *Stars and Stripes*, which had for decades provided almost all non-military news and information, would fall under renewed scrutiny for improper manipulation and censorship. It was a time of change and opportunity for Milcom members that offered challenges to come to terms with the failures of American society and to negotiate new ways to relate to one another and their German neighbors. In that context this study explores how the usefulness of consensual thinking and identity, such as that of exceptionalism, became limited and its value reduced in light of those troubling inconsistencies. But that process also demonstrated to Americans that the resiliency of their society lay in its continued openness and its ability to meet societal challenges head-on and work together to find solutions.

Chapter Eight addresses the effects of post–1967 politics on the Milcoms by exploring how contemporary political dissent and protest, as well as the growing malignancy of terrorism, informed the lives of the Milcom members and shaped their behaviors. It also offers a unique perspective of Americans who were among some of the first to live in the shadow of fear cast by terrorism and felt its initial sting, and who, unlike their fellow citizens back home, confronted anti–American antagonists not through second-hand news sources but at the very gates of the places they lived, worked and played. The Milcoms felt the effects in a series of three distinct events that tested the bonds of the German-American political relations: the conflict in Vietnam, the Pershing Missile protests and terrorist attacks. The first two provided points of tension but the third, much like early postwar concerns of a communist threat, drew Germans and Americans closer as both groups eschewed violence as a viable form of political protest.

Chapter Nine analyzes changes on the global economic game board that had an impact on life in the military communities. As in earlier postwar years the economics of the Milcom again intersected those of the host nation at key points of contact such as a changing Deutsche Mark rate, fuel prices, taxes and hiring of local nationals. But as this work reveals, unlike previous times, emerging economic realities presented different and often troubling crises for American service members, civilians, dependents and retirees living overseas. Beginning in the 1970s, and through most of the 1980s, Germans would recognize Milcom members as the "rich uncles from times past [who had become] the poor devils from overseas" as they struggled with challenges that often seemed to eclipse the more mundane demands of their assigned mission overseas.[14]

USAREUR Shield. The juxtaposition of the metal shield covering the original swastika symbol of the Third Reich suggests the significance of the passage of time and the changing political, social, cultural and economic realities that affected the military communities and the German nation. Image source: the author.

As this work reveals, the tenets of American exceptionalism were not immutable but changed with the times, causing members of the military communities to reinterpret their meaning and renegotiate their interactions with one another and the host nation. Throughout the four-and-a-half decade process, the German nation rebuilt its economy and sculpted a new national identity just as the Milcoms experienced a reframing of American ideals that included greater inclusion, equality and opportunity. The result is a new understanding of what it meant to be an American that challenges and redefines the earlier prewar consensus. But as much as this is an account of ideological change it is also fundamentally a narrative about the lives of Americans and their families, military and civilian, active duty and retired, who populated those overseas communities and their very human reactions to the dynamics of change.

One

From First Arrivals to Established Network (1946–1967)

The First Arrivals

On April 28, 1946, a small group of 379 wives and children disembarked from the U.S. Army transport ship *Thomas Barry* onto Columbus Quay at the port of Bremerhaven, West Germany. Among the mix of passengers, which included families of all ranks, were Mrs. Lucius D. Clay, Mrs. Mark W. Clark and the wives of 12 other generals.[1] As an Army band played "*Stars and Stripes* Forever," these military family members were ushered onto buses and trains that would eventually bring them to reunions with fathers, husbands, and fiancés serving in the postwar American occupation force in western Germany. News accounts of the day noted that although soldiers at pier-side hailed them with remarks such as "You'll be sorry!" the new arrivals, flushed with excitement, chortled back, "No we won't."[2]

The months following the first arrivals witnessed thousands more family members making the same trans–Atlantic journey.[3] In evidence, periodic news of arriving transport ships appeared in the pages of the military's *Stars and Stripes* newspaper so servicemen could track the arrival of their loved ones. The reports offered the date of arrival, the name of the ship and passenger lists reflecting the first and last name of the family members and their final destination by German town or military community (Milcom).[4] For many it was an unpleasant voyage that preceded a pleasant reunion. Jane Mulvihill remembers her journey in 1962 aboard the transport ship USS *United States* also as a "rough trip." Three months pregnant, she shared a windowless cabin with three other women and their toddlers. Only stop-overs in Dover and LaHavre broke the monotony of her ten day passage.[5] Terry Dean, who crossed the ocean as a young dependent remembers, "We traveled across the North Atlantic over Christmas to get there [Germany] aboard the USS *Upshur*, an old troop ship…. I was 9, and I remember being sick every morning."[6] Tim Gilbert crossed over as a dependent child in 1952 aboard the USS *Patch*, a retrofitted World War II troop ship. The voyage, he recalls, was a rough trip consisting of five days on wintery seas.[7] Ironically, an article that later appeared in a woman's magazine noted military ocean travel with a cheery difference, "Here's a service that takes away the pain of separation and adds the pleasure of a sea voyage." It described the accommodations as "a comfortable living space with bath, upper and lower bunks, writing desk, and miscellaneous other furniture."[8]

Regardless of the circumstances of their travel these family members formed the vanguard of a successful initiative sponsored by the American government to solve a plethora of problems. These included fraternization with locals, sagging morale, failing retention rates, high rates of violent crime, a burgeoning black market and widespread venereal disease among the American troops.[9] As one German worker confided, "The *Ami* [American] is great, as long as he isn't drunk, because then he fights with anyone who gets in his way, just for the fun of fighting."[10] American authorities hoped that the presence of families would still these urges of ill-discipline among the soldiers and thus calm a growing anxiety among the German populace that "gave rise to a strain of anti–American sentiment" that regarded the recalcitrant *Amis* as "poor examples of democracy and equality."[11]

This was an enterprise that owed its impetus and success in no small measure to the actions of a protest group of twenty angry wives who in January 1946 confronted General Eisenhower while on his way to a Congressional hearing.[12] In the presence of reporters and photographers they laid their demands for increasing the tempo of demobilization at his feet and appealed for the earliest return home of their husbands and relations who remained in postwar Germany. Among their concerns was a need to alleviate the financial burden on military families of maintaining dual households, one in Germany and one in the States. That same month Representative Margaret Chase Smith of Maine, ever an advocate for the welfare of service members, assumed the political lead and petitioned Secretary of War Henry Stimson to allow both wives and fiancées to join service members "in Europe on tours lasting a minimum of one year."[13] Earlier, in November 1945, the new military governor of the American Zone, General Lucius Clay, had added his voice to the growing chorus of military and political leaders who advocated normalizing the situation by forming "military communities [of families] with units of approximately regimental size as the nucleus."[14] The solution, they hoped, to the collective problems of troop ill-discipline, a disgruntled German citizenry, and protesting spouses, would be the reunion of soldiers and their families.

The success of this initiative became apparent within a year of the arrival of the first group of wives and children at the port of Bremerhaven as troop discipline improved significantly, postwar crimes rates declined, and relations with the German public had improved.[15] These changes were important, as both American and German leaders "praised the beneficial effects of the family presence in stabilizing the occupation environment."[16] Contemporary issues of *Stars and Stripes* newspaper carried periodic articles that reflected the positive change. A piece in the February 11, 1948, edition noted, "Two units of the Nuremberg Military Post have received commendations from Gen. Lucius Clay, EC [European Command] commander, for their record of six consecutive months without a case of venereal disease."[17] As the newspaper archives reveal, units often competed for this distinction, with passes and time off as coveted rewards.

A December 1949 survey sponsored by the U.S. High Commissioner of Germany (HICOG) revealed that a majority of West Germans queried "described the conduct of American occupation troops as good, with an additional six percent in AMZON [the American Zone] saying they thought it was very good" and that the "soldiers' behavior had improved since the end of the war."[18] Whether there was a direct correlation between the arrival of the families and the positive changes, or a combination of family presence and separate incentive, or all were simply coincidental, the changes were still timely and important for stabilizing the postwar situation. Just as important, these military families formed the seeds of a system of inter-connected Milcoms that increased rapidly in number and spread across the devastated West German landscape.[19]

Within a short time the number of resident American family members had grown significantly.[20] By 1948 there were over 3,000 wives and children in the West Berlin community alone.[21] Numerous sources such as the U.S. Census Bureau, the Defense Manpower Data Center (DMDC), the Center for Military History (CMH) and the Heritage Foundation all provide some variances in the exact number of American family members residing overseas in West Germany. Still, all agree that the successive yearly increases in the population of dependents in the first three postwar decades were considerable.[22] By 1970, the 143,932 service-related dependents in West Germany accounted for 45.26 percent of the world-wide total of family members residing overseas.[23] Consistently, that nation remained home to the largest number of overseas American military families throughout the entire Cold War period.[24] By 1990, that included 47 major military communities and 800 satellite localities.[25] In comparison, the number of dependents in Japan, which also hosted a large American presence, remained a distant second.[26]

American Resolve

It was however, not the dominating American physical presence alone but rather its confluence with Cold War politics and the exigencies of U.S.-Soviet tensions, which made the impact of the system of Milcoms in West Germany resonate with the American leadership. That early realization transpired when Soviet forces, under instructions from Moscow, played a typically dangerous game of Cold War brinksmanship and sealed off all land and water routes of ingress and egress to the Western Allied sectors of Berlin on June 19, 1948. As contemporary histories note, the Soviet's gambit was a reaction to perceptions of Western intransigence in negotiating a settlement of economic issues for the divided halves of Germany. The intention of their action was to prove their resolve and starve the French, British and American allies into a capitulation of their claims to sectors of the former capital that was located 100 miles deep in Soviet-controlled eastern Germany. For Germans living in the AMZON that summer of 1948 the situation seemed dire. One young diarist recorded, "Everybody believes the Americans will give up Berlin.... For many people suicide seems the only way out."[27]

As decision-makers in Washington struggled to find various options, General Clay observed, "The evacuation of [American] family members from Berlin would lead to a hysterical reaction and drive the Germans in droves into the supposed safety of Communism." He added, "We must not destroy their confidence by any indication of departure from Berlin. I still do not believe our dependents should be evacuated. Once again we have to sweat it out, come what may."[28] The die was cast when President Truman agreed, "We stay in Berlin. Period."[29]

Heroic efforts to resupply the city via an air bridge created from round-the-clock sorties of Allied military aircraft eventually lifted the year-long siege in May 1949.[30] Sensing the gravity of the moment, General Clay understood that the plight of the 3,000 American military family members in Berlin provided the world with an opportunity to form a strong negative opinion of the Soviets, while underscoring America's own resolve in the face of a determined threat. It was a propitious moment and his estimation proved correct. Years later he would recall, "I do not believe that our families were ever as content as during the blockade when they felt themselves as part of the effort of Western Democracies."[31] Clay also proudly added, "There was no nervousness or tenseness evidenced by any of the Americans in Berlin."[32]

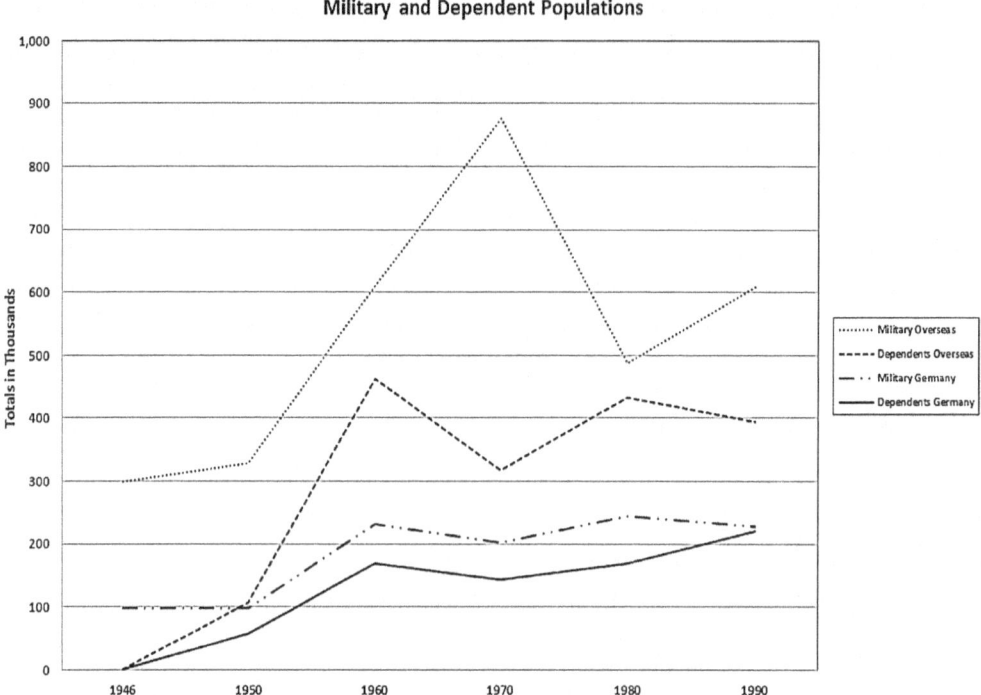

Military and Dependent Populations, 1945–1990. The statistical increase of "Military Overseas" from 1965 to 1970 resulted from the large deployment of unaccompanied service personnel to Southeast Asia. The drop in "Dependents Overseas" during that period reflects those corresponding families remaining in CONUS. Data sources: Heritage Foundation, Center of Military History, Office of the Secretary of Defense-Defense Manpower Data Center (OSD-DMDC), the U.S. Census Bureau, and *Stars and Stripes* newspaper (European Edition).

Their patriotic solidarity seemed especially vibrant as the soldiers and families of that isolated outpost enjoyed a special Christmas show performed by Bob Hope, Irving Berlin, and Tex McCrary. By comparison, the uniqueness of the relationship between Americans and West Berliners also appeared solid because after that moment, "West Berlin wanted to become more modern and more American than any other place in Germany."[33]

The American leadership in Washington understood that the propaganda value of the Berlin success was inestimable. Just as the end of the war in 1945 had been the *Stunde Null* [Zero Hour] for a new Germany, the Berlin Airlift marked a figurative "zero hour" for the Milcom's emerging role as an instrument of foreign policy. As the frequency of daily interactions between Milcom members and German nationals increased with the easing of postwar non-fraternization policies and the expansion of the Milcom network so did the U.S. government's realization that these communities could provide a vehicle to extend the reach and effectiveness of American person-to-person "soft power" contact across the Atlantic.[34]

Milcoms and the Propaganda War

By the end of the 1940s the U.S. and the Soviet Union found themselves in the grips of a revised Cold War. No longer was direct military confrontation, with the potential for world-

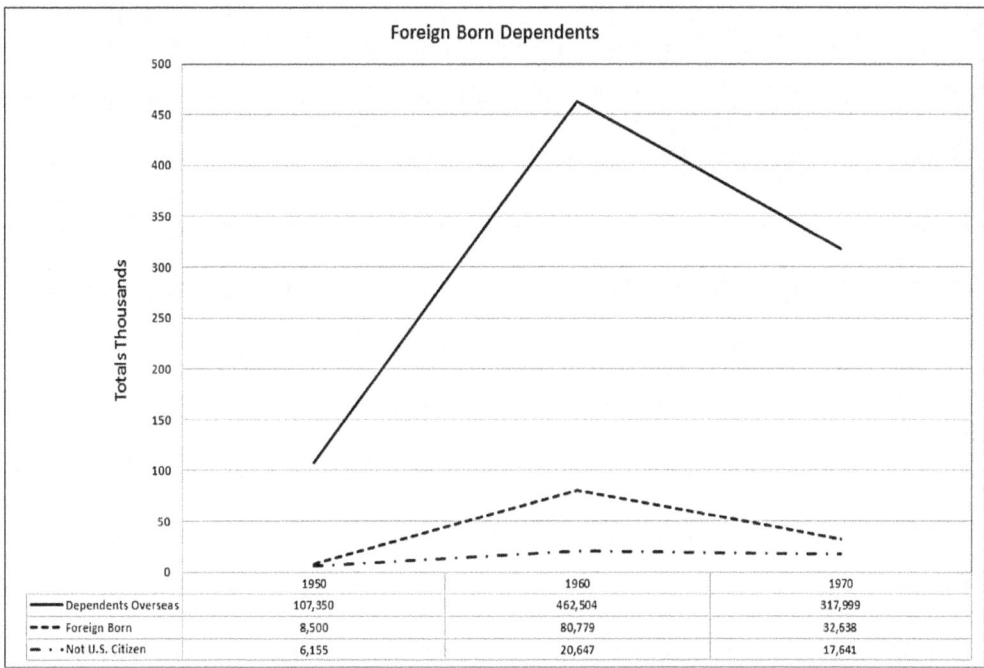

Foreign Born Dependents. (Includes all ages.) These numbers contributed to the total overseas dependent population. In 1950, foreign-born dependents represented 7.8 percent of the Dependents Overseas total. Of that group, 72 percent were not U.S. citizens. Of the Dependents Overseas total 5.7 percent were not U.S. citizens. By 1960, foreign-born dependents represented 17.4 percent of the Dependents Overseas total. Of that group, 25.5 percent were not U.S. citizens. Of the Dependents Overseas total 4.4 percent were not U.S. citizens. By 1970, foreign born dependents represented 10.6 percent of the Dependents Overseas total. Of that group, 54.0 percent were not U.S. citizens. Of the Dependents Overseas total 5.5 percent were not U.S. citizens. Data source: U.S. Census Bureau.

wide nuclear annihilation, an acceptable option in the cut and thrust arena of diplomatic maneuverings between the two hegemons. In that context it was President Eisenhower, following in the footsteps of his predecessor Truman, who first gave weight to the concept of psychological warfare as a suitable alternative. Eisenhower determined that American leadership and dominance in the postwar world depended on the skillful application of psychological forces. In his estimation it was a battle for the hearts and minds of people in other lands. But it would require a different set of weapons and skills that went beyond those of official propaganda agencies. Instead, it must include a comprehensive strategy that tied together diplomacy, economic assistance, trade, person-to-person contacts, and ideas. In essence, it challenged Americans "to prove their peaceful intentions, and to persuade others of the ideological and cultural superiority of the American way of life."[35]

Between December 1947 and April 1950, a succession of National Security Council (NSC) documents captured and reflected the President's thinking.[36] These laid out the designs for appraising the threat to national security and developing means to confront the Soviets. Using these documents as a foundation, the Eisenhower administration moved forward with a Cold War strategy that located both covert and overt psychological warfare at the center. The government created, then modified over time, an alphabet soup of agencies to plan and implement these new policies and programs. They included offices such as the PSB, OCB, OPC, USIS, and the USIA, and programs such as People-to-People, which worked to involve private businesses, non-government organizations (NGO) and the military services.[37] All of these initiatives understood the importance of contact at the personal grassroots level and provided generous budget allocations for effecting necessary programs.[38] A key factor in the formula was a realization of the availability of the overseas Milcoms and their prime location in Germany to favorably affect the opinion of West Europeans in the war of words and ideas with the Soviet East. The military communities would find themselves on the frontline of this psychological war.

Some of the first salvoes were fired with the start of the Korean War when disturbing reports regarding American POW behavior began appearing in the media. A flurry of articles by news outlets, including *Stars and Stripes*, described American GIs' susceptibility to enemy interrogation pressures. The contemporary public's perception was that American servicemen had been easy subjects for North Korean brainwashing because, as one military psychiatrist claimed, the behavior of "too many of our soldiers in [North Korean] prison fell far short of the historical American standards of honor, character, loyalty, courage and personal integrity."[39] Some journalists' reports alleged that, unlike in previous wars, Americans had become soft and quickly collaborated, even refusing to escape, and died at an alarming rate from "a morale malady called 'give-up-itis.'"[40] The cause one Army report noted was that "parental training failed to provide them with moral values and Yankee resourcefulness."[41] These reports alarmed the public and drove the administration to take action.

Fearing that service personnel no longer understood the foundational principles of American freedoms or why they were fighting, President Eisenhower charged Defense Secretary Charles Wilson to develop a Code of Conduct. The six articles of the Code would serve as a manifesto of American ideals and recommit the serviceman to a dedication of "the principles which made [our] country free." Furthermore, it encouraged them to "trust in [our] God and in the United States of America."[42] All the Services readily accepted the Code, which was incorporated it into training programs around the world with the assistance of specially prepared programs and films. Among those affected were the Milcoms in Germany. *Stars and Stripes* European edition announced the implementation of the Code in September 1955 under a headline that read "Army Adopts Education Program to Back-Up New Conduct Code." The text emphasized that the new guidelines called for development in each soldier of "a firm conviction that the principles of American democracy and freedom are sound and correct so that he is willing to fight and preserve them."[43]

In an interesting parallel, a redrafted version of the military's code appeared in the February 1956 issue of *U.S. Lady*, a popular contemporary magazine for military spouses.[44] It featured a full-page illustration of a well-dressed military wife and young child standing before a globe. It was easy to see in the illustration that the U.S. was at the center of the globe and the world seemed to be their exclusive domain. To the right of the image is a printed listing that delineated the responsibilities and duties of the military spouse. Jean Andrew, an Army wife, was the author. Among the charges: "Wherever she lives in the world itself, she represents America and its women," as a dependent spouse she serves "as part of a bigger defense team," her responsibilities include "civic duties of voting absentee, thereby exercising her rights and duties of citizenship," most important, her world "centers in the spot where her husband and children are."[45] With this distaff endorsement the editors of *U.S. Lady* ensured their consonance with the military's intent behind the code and shaped Milcom members' thinking about their commitment to the American way of life.

Heeding the clarion call for action, individual Milcom newspapers also took up the challenge to bolster American service members' faith in the American way of life. The December 2, 1950, issue of the *Stuttgart Post News* featured an article titled "Soldier! Why are you Here?" The text, which included excerpts from the Secretary of State, referred to the communist aggressions in Korea observing, "The fate of the entire world is in the balance" and that the "United States is assigned a leading role; ideologically the battle is between democracy and communism."[46] More important, it noted, "The U.S. is so certain that the democratic ideal, the American way of life, is important that no effort to preserve our way of life can be considered too much."[47] Casting back with historical reference it called on the "spirit of man" to demand his heritage citing the storming of the Bastille in France as an example of that spirit of freedom and liberty.

In parallel to these efforts President Eisenhower courted several conservative organizations to develop, define, and promulgate American ideals within the military and to a wider public audience. One such group, the Freedoms Foundation, established in 1949 by a duo of advertising executives, sought to re-establish the nation's Christian heritage and believed like Eisenhower that the country was in a battle for the minds of men with the Soviet East. This came at a time of widespread conservative anti-communist backlash in America that included the "red scare" tactics of Senator Joseph McCarthy who in 1950 claimed, "Today we are engaged in a final, all-out battle between communistic atheism and Christianity."[48]

The foundation incorporated its ideas into an "American Credo" which included many of the tenets of Americanism and expanded them with a broad spiritual basis and an abiding belief in a Christian God.[49] They were among the first conservative groups to begin working closely with the Department of Defense Office of Armed Forces Information and Education (AFI&E) and the Armed Forces Radio and Television Service (AFRTS). Their intention was to disseminate anti-communist and conservative political and economic views to civilians as well as service personnel and their family members, at home and overseas. Captivated by this initiative, especially the spiritual aspect, Eisenhower consistently lent his support while still in uniform, then as a college president, and later when he occupied the Oval Office. The foundation was active in transmitting its message of the centrality of spirituality for more than five decades and its charter included joining with the armed forces to develop a set of national core values that would inspire an ideological and spiritual reawakening in America.[50]

A favorite vehicle of the foundation was the annual writing contest. It challenged all applicants, servicemen and women, as well as family members, to craft an essay in response to a patriotic topic such as "Freedom—My Heritage, My Responsibility" and "My Hopes for America's Future."[51] The winners received $1,000, the foundation's George Washington Honor medal and recognition in *Stars and Stripes* newspaper. On at least one occasion, in February 1951, the Foundation also invited German youth to participate. The subject was "The Free Way of Life." The requirements explained that their work had to adhere to the Freedoms Foundation's Americanist credo: "A fundamental belief in God, recognition of a constitutional government designed to serve the people, and an indivisible collection of personal, economic, and political freedoms."[52] Winners of this competition, which ran during the entire Cold War period, were usually junior enlisted service personnel, but included Milcom family members, students in the Department of Defense Dependent School system (DODDS) and officers.

Various organizations within the Defense Department were also recipients of Freedoms Foundation awards. As the February 24, 1956, issue of *Stars and Stripes* noted, one winner was the Armed Forces Information and Education Division for its efforts in disseminating pro–American material. Eventually, the foundation also recognized eight European AFRTS stations with awards of the Washington Honor Medal for their achievements in producing "outstanding programs which focus attention on the American way of life."[53] During the early years of the Cold War, the Freedoms Foundation, with support of the military leadership in Washington, cast its net wide to reach the American public and service personnel and broadcast messages of an exceptional America.

Just as energetic, but less successful, were other initiatives such as the Militant Liberty program, which initially followed the same trajectory as the Freedoms Foundation.[54] It provided a basis for evaluating and assessing the availability of liberties and freedoms in any global society. In November 1954, Admiral Radford encouraged the Secretary of Defense, Charles E. Wilson, to release a government publication titled: *Militant Liberty: A Program of Evaluation and Assessment of Freedom*. It was a comprehensive booklet that the military leadership intended to serve as guide for the Armed Forces to enable them to better understand the ideals of the American way of life and to better educate foreign audiences.[55] A November 1955 European edition of *Stars and Stripes* announced the unveiling of the program "for instructing servicemen in 'militant liberty' to enable them to combat 'militant communism' in the war for men's minds." The article, "Yank Classes on 'Militant Liberty' Set" outlined the goal, which was to allow service personnel to "understand ideals of liberty which people should strive for."[56] Some interest in the program remained beyond 1957 when *Stars and Stripes* announced that "Pentagon Tests 'Liberty' Plan" with the release of "100 kits of motion picture footage, recordings and pamphlets" aimed at "educating servicemen in the advantages of the American way."[57] While there is no way to determine the exact number of overseas troops exposed to the program, it is certain that Militant Liberty did reach the service personnel in the West German Milcoms and offered yet another vehicle for shaping their thoughts and attitudes about American ideals. By 1956 the Militant Liberty initiative was dead, the victim of budget restraints and departmental infighting.[58]

Another initiative to instill American ideals in Milcom members that went awry was that of Major General Edwin Walker. In September 1959, as he assumed command of the U.S. Army's 24th Infantry Division stationed in Augsburg, West Germany, he instituted his own "Pro-Blue" program for his troops.[59] It was a mandatory anti-communist indoctrination program that included reading materials from the John Birch Society and the evangelist Billy James Hargis.[60] In a message carried by the unit newspaper, the *Taro Leaf*, Walker decried the "criminal conspiracy of atheistic communism" and explained to his soldiers that, "If Americans gave to the battle of ideas one-tenth of the thought and sacrifices that it deserves, our country would be unchallenged."[61] He added that they "should be psychologically better prepared to defend [their] freedom than any other soldiers in the Army."[62] Walker's opinions and actions drew both criticism and support.

Accusations of the general's heavy-handed control of political thinking by some unit members led to a series of articles in the privately owned English language newspaper, the *Overseas Weekly*, which had a limited circulation among Milcom members. Charges by critics centered on reports that Walker attempted to manipulate the opinions of soldiers and family member during the 1962 congressional elections by distributing copies of the *Conservative Voting Index*.[63] This drew the attention of both President Kennedy and the Secretary of Defense, Robert McNamara, who relieved him of his command pending further investigation by the Senate Armed Service Committee. A front page *Stars and Stripes* article noted that the committee determined Walker had improperly used his position for political purposes in violation of the Hatch Act, and that he would receive an official admonition.[64] It also quoted McNamara as saying that the general "had conducted an indoctrination program which violated Army regulations and made inflammatory and derogatory remarks about public officials including President Truman."[65] Under this firestorm of criticism, Walker eventually resigned his commission on November 2, 1961. Conservative Congressional supporters of Walker were just as vocal but failed to secure his reinstatement.[66]

Operating in parallel to the efforts of programs such as Militant Liberty and Pro-Blue were those of Christian evangelicals who had been establishing a presence in the military since the National Security Act of 1947. That evangelical movement evolved within the armed forces' Chaplain's Corps and placed a number of proponents of American civil-military religion in key positions of power. This opened the door for the inclusion of evangelical Christianity into service-directed character education.[67] It was not uncommon for exceptional themes to lace the homilies of military chaplains. That resonated overseas and was apparent at the dedication of the new Neckarsulm Milcom chapel in December 1952. Chaplain (Lt Col) Aubrey J. O'Reilly commented that the "value of religion is in making the complete soldier" and that the "greatest force against communism today [sic] is the American way of life based upon the four great freedoms."[68] Evidence of the spreading impact of the incorporation of American civil-military religious imagery appeared in a number of venues from homilies to stained glass windows in Milcom chapels.[69] One example was the "Airlift Memorial Window" located in the Rhein-Main Air Base chapel.[70]

Films such as the Army's *Of Soldiers and Altars*, also reflected this influence. Created to describe the "extensive religious activities and facilities provided by [the] US Army Chaplaincy in CONUS and overseas for members the Army and their dependents" the film's narrator emphasized "the Founding Fathers' dependency on a divine creator."[71] Maintaining that perspective the script described the "protection of divine providence" that has graced America's past and the "deep religious principles" that will guide its future endeavors.[72]

The Eisenhower administration endorsed this evangelical movement and saw it as another piece in the bulwark against the spread of communist dogma. In that context the President enlisted the support of evangelicals such as Billy Graham, whose influence found resonance in the Milcoms.[73] Eisenhower saw him as a strong advocate of an "American civil-military religion" and the Reverend Graham did not disappoint.[74] Travelling the globe between the White House and the Milcoms he preached a mixture of conservative Christian tenets strongly laced with American ideals. As early as 1954 the reverend had proclaimed that "if you would be a true patriot, then become a Christian, if you would be a loyal American, then become a loyal Christian."[75] Readers of *Stars and Stripes* followed his journeys for decades through articles that traced scheduled sermons at locations such as the Army's Christ Chapel in Frankfurt and at the Vogelweh Milcom chapel.[76] During those years, *Stars and Stripes* provided preferential coverage that exposed Milcom members to the evangelical religious-military connection framing an exceptional American vision. Periodically, large features and spreads in *Stars and Stripes* reflected a growing national acceptance of Graham's agenda and his influence in military communities.[77]

The Chief of Chaplains, Major General Ivan L. Bennett, also often traveled to the overseas Milcoms covering much of the same ground as Graham. On one occasion, during a brief visit with the staff of *Stars and Stripes*, he expressed his satisfaction with their work and appreciation for the many pages of religious service schedules that were printed "each Easter, Thanksgiving, and Christmas, as well as the schedules for the Jewish holidays."[78] The newspaper also carried daily listings under the "Dial Day" column for AFN radio listeners to tune into the "0730 Catholic Devotional," "0845 Hymns," or the "1445 Winged Victory Chorus."[79] The influence of the evangelical right had insinuated itself into the lives of Milcom members from the pulpit, in training and through print media, radio and television with its message of anti-communism and American ideals. By the 1980s, AFNTV-Germany also provided Milcom audiences with regular anti-communist pro-free enterprise broadcasts of Robert Schuller's Sunday morning "Hour of Power" sermons issued from his 10,000-member congregation in the Crystal Cathedral.[80] The particular fear of communist infiltration of American life and culture served as an engine for propagation and insinuation of evangelical Christianity into the Milcoms and ensured its acceptance.[81]

Family members also participated in the evangelical initiative. Aside from regular meetings of local wives' clubs, the women of the Milcoms came together through religious groups such as the European Council of Protestant Women (COPW) and the Military Council of Catholic Women (MCCW), to discuss religious matters and charity. For example a gathering that numbered at least 450 MCCW delegates met at a military recreation hotel in Berchtesgaden in 1966 to discuss "Joy in Leadership" and "Women in World Leadership."[82] Articles in *Stars and Stripes* consistently addressed annual autumn rallies for both the COPW and MCCW conventions. As the newspaper noted, these ladies' groups met regularly during the first three postwar decades to deliberate the best ways to maintain an essentially American core of spirituality within their family lives and continue good works in the German community. The behaviors of religious participation, discussion and expressions of spirituality were central to contemporary life in the Milcoms. They also maintained links through affiliation with the global churches. An example was the frequent presence of a speaker from the American church in Rome at MCCW conventions.[83] Within the context of the American tenet of religious freedom these behaviors served to shape members' thoughts about their own identity particularly as models of spiritual morality not unlike John Winthrop's "city upon a hill."[84]

Prescribing Proper Behavior

Within that cycle of conceptualizing a strategy of American ideals the administration continued to mold the thinking of service families living overseas. Central to those early efforts was the encouragement of good behavior, by reminding dependents that Americans abroad had responsibilities as spokespersons for the U.S. In a memorandum issued to members of the armed forces serving abroad, President Eisenhower charged that an essential part of their mission was building good will for our country. Orientation programs for military family members included Department of Defense motion pictures, which reminded them of their "responsibilities as person-to-person ambassadors."[85] These Army orientation briefings challenged spouses and children stationed in the AMZON to remember "you are serving your country while here" and that "every American man, woman, and child in the European Theater has the power to do either good or harm to our foreign relations, depending on his contacts with Europeans."[86] Not only were American dependents unofficial ambassadors, they were told they were "part of an army in the field." Their proper behavior contributed to the advancement of "U.S aims by exercising soft power, influencing what non–Americans thought of them—and by extension, the U.S. military presence, and even American values." All of these goals were consistent with the Administration's prescriptive directives including the concepts reflected in the NSC papers.

Printed materials produced specifically for families preparing for overseas deployment to Germany tended to reinforce the themes of goodwill and American values, but were sometimes fraught with unintentional contradictions. Publications such as *An Introduction to Germany for Occupation Families* and *A Pocket Guide to Germany* couched their guidance in comfortable, easily readable text that resembled the glossy pages of a travel brochure.[87] Contents included pictures and drawing of castles along the Rhine and pastoral landscapes, as well as descriptions of the climate, foods and local customs. Woven throughout the narratives there were gentle reminders that "above all considerations, you are to be resident in an occupied land as a representative of the United States ... your good example can help guide them [the Germans] along the road to democracy, economic recovery, and peace."[88] Photographs of smiling Americans and Germans engaged in expressions of *bonhomie* laced both publications.

Still, within those pages that encouraged fellowship and recommended weekend getaways to the Chiemsee lakeside resort and recreational skiing on the Zugspitze there was a harder edge. The *Introduction to Germany*, penned just two years after the Axis defeat, recalled America's failure to act in time to forestall the Second World War. It quoted General Eisenhower's determined view, which also reflected the charge from JCS Directive 1067 that "our duty extends beyond to [sic] seeing that it doesn't happen again."[89] The pamphlet explained, "That is why you are in Germany. That is why you, as a member of one of the Occupation families, are to make your home in this land for the next year or so."[90] The *Introduction* as well as the *Pocket Guide* also provided subtle comparisons that showed various dimensions of America's superiority: Germany "is smaller than the state of Montana alone," "You may compare the old-fashioned German equipment unfavorably with the modern machinery used on American farms" and "They [rural Germans] are a plodding folk of peasant stock, moving on foot, pulling their heavy loads in small carts."[91] Political comparisons were similar, as depicted by such condemning comments in the *Pocket Guide* as "It should be apparent that, although liberal elements have risen in Germany upon occasion, the basic tendency has been to 'follow the leader' in an autocratic, all-powerful central government."[92] Following that same tone at least one orientation video, "Your Job in Germany," reminded the first arriving soldiers and families "by your conduct and attitude you can lay the groundwork for peace." But it also cautioned viewers "you are in enemy country," to "be alert ... suspicious of everyone" and to "guard particularly against.... German youth."[93]

Another technique that the Department of Defense employed to ensure dissemination of guidelines beyond print media was the production of films. Three particular examples were *Defense against Enemy Propaganda*, *The Code of Conduct* and *Challenge of Ideas*. The scripts of each were prepared to offer viewers some knowledge of the foundational ideas and values that the screenwriters believed made America exceptional, as well as to cultivate in the audience an understanding of how to best deflect Soviet criticisms. The writers laced the narratives with warnings of Soviet "propaganda and its danger to the American way of life" and boasts that "Red countries cannot stand comparison in the light of day" and "the fact is: every free nation of the world looks to America as the bulwark of liberty."[94] A *New York Times* review considered these films "a simple but thoughtful depiction of the attitudes and aspirations that are commonly believed to have shaped the American character."[95] As film narrator Edward R. Murrow noted, the battle of ideologies "touches not only members of the armed forces and their families but everyone who supports the mission of the armed forces," including every American taxpayer.[96]

These three films were only one part of a series of over 700 that formed thea propaganda program initiated by the Army in 1950 titled "The Big Picture."[97] The official claim provided by the regular narrator at the start of each show was that "The Big Picture is the official television report by the U.S. Army to its members and the American people."[98] The 28-minute segments offered viewers a look at Army units at various locations around the globe during peacetime training, wartime operations (the Korean and Vietnam conflicts) and off-duty activities. Big Picture "Army Newsreel Number One" alerted military family members that it "highlighted events of their lives month by month, day by day."[99] Overseas, Milcom theaters showed the films together with feature presentations, and European Command AFN television regularly aired them by1958. Time listings for the Big Picture episodes appeared in *Stars and Stripes*. Viewers found them under "Dial A Day," and later "AFNTV in Germany," nestled among popular shows such as "Wild Kingdom," "Mayberry RFD" and "Doris Day." Viewing times were generally during the dinner hours when families normally gathered. Regardless of the Big Picture subject however, the voice-over narratives consistently provided patriotic, American-centric overtones to the scripts.[100]

Also included in the catalogue of Big Picture films were a number of special feature editions that were unique to America's presence in West Germany. Among them were *Information and Education Overseas* and *People-to-People*, which addressed specific government programs and activities. The first highlighted the efforts of the Army's education program and its initiatives to provide access to education, an exceptional American value. It addressed the importance of the soldier's "chance to raise [their] mental standards through education," as well as the educational opportunities available for dependent children through the DODDS system. As the narrator confidently concludes, "There is something solidly American here in this school system that embraces the whole world."[101] The Big Picture "People-to-People" film explained how service personnel and their families in Germany were participating in that Presidential initiative and were especially "situated to play a major role in the job of winning friends for America." It mentioned how American soldiers "could not ignore the appeal" of German children, who after the war "were hungry for food, gentleness, and recognition." Narration also addressed spiritual worship as a common cultural ground with the Germans noting, "The spiritual fabric of Germany also needed a rebuilding."[102] The visual evidence was black and white footage showing military units rebuilding churches and using cranes to lift recast bells up to newly raised steeples.

The object of another Germany-specific film, *Operation Friendly Hand*, intended to tug at heart strings and encourage an emotional tie with the German people. It featured Sergeant Arthur Dames and his family of the Vogelweh Milcom, who sponsored a poor German girl for a month's vacation. Although framed as an inter-cultural exchange, a discriminating viewer could see that the German youth was more the beneficiary of American largesse and consumer wealth as she enjoyed plenty to eat, new clothing, bubble gum, a bubble bath, Saturday afternoon movies, a new hairdo and cosmetics. While the obvious message to audiences was the strengthening of the bonds of friendship through kindness, the subtext highlighted

American economic superiority and beneficence. In 1953, Milcom families participating in Operation Friendly Hand hosted 150 West German children. That number rose to 600 in 1954.[103]

Two additional films focused on Germany: *The West Berlin Struggle* and *Germany Today*. Each was a record of America's commitment to "hold back the tide of Communism in Germany and the free world" and to show the "face of West Germany today re-carved in the image of freedom." Central to both films was a discussion of American efforts to save Berlin during the desperate days of the Airlift and the city's "place as a symbol of the West's freedom."[104] Like the other Big Picture productions about Germany, it seemed that the Department of the Army crafted these films to accomplish four things: to underscore America's unity with that nation as a bulwark against Communism; to showcase America's economic, cultural and political superiority; to sell American ideals to the world; and as a vehicle to further imprint the American ideals on service members and their families in the Milcoms.

Other efforts of the Big Picture series to define and demonstrate American ideals in action were the films *Ottumwa, U.S.A.* and the *American Way of Life* collection. A narrator's voice-over in the first production introduces the film by explaining that Americans "must be able to explain liberty and freedom" in order to remain free. This is important he notes because communists "know what they believe and can explain it in understandable terms" unlike most Americans "who lack the ability to explain or defend what liberty is." The second production was a series that included previous Big Picture productions *Ottumwa, U.S.A.*, *People-to-People* and *Eisenhower the Soldier* to offer scenarios of those American ideals in action, such as a lack of social distinction between classes and an opportunity for education. The film also addressed other contemporary American liberties that were widely held such as the freedom to elect leaders, equality and fair play for all, and the right to worship as one pleases. Not neglected was the presence of the town's friendly Army recruiter and the knowledge that the "biggest responsibility young men face is military duty."[105] Most important, the *American Way of Life* highlighted the recognition the Big Picture series received from the Freedoms Foundation for achievement in bringing about a better understanding of the "American way of life" to both military and civilian viewers.[106]

Hard Physical Realities

Just as the printed word and scripted films made an impression on the early arrivals to the AMZON, so too did the physical realities of life in devastated postwar Germany.[107] These contributed to an atmosphere that encouraged a special, exceptional feeling among the Americans. Military authorities often forewarned the first cohorts of dependent adults arriving in Germany to guard against consumer shortages and "bring a year's supply of clothing" with them for their families.[108] In a similar manner they conveyed warnings of shortages of fresh vegetables, fruits, eggs and milk, and the rationing of cigarettes, gasoline and liquor. These hardships cultivated among some Milcom members feelings that they were among "a new generation of American pioneers" setting out to carve an existence in an alien land, which offered physical as well as cultural obstacles and dangers.[109] Although this attitude began early after the establishment of the Milcoms it did resonate through later decades. As Scott Hambric recalls:

> The 11th ACR issued border certificates to the troopers and to their spouses at the conclusion of their assignments. In the case of the trooper, he was credited with serving "on the frontiers of freedom" and enrolled in the Border Legion. Also commended was the wife who "followed her trooper to the farthest outpost of our forces in Germany and has in frontier communities, under adverse conditions, and resolutely established a home, confident that her post was at her husband's side." She was thereby designated a Border Belle. Children who were born in the border communities also received border certificates. Our daughter's certificate pointed out that she was "…born under adventurous circumstances…."[110]

Some of those pioneering hardships were also evident in letters sent back home to relatives in the U.S. One from a teenager to his grandparents contained a list of family needs they should send as soon as possible. Among them were hard-to-get items such as Scotch tape, Ipana toothpaste and chewing gum, "only Chicklets, Dentyne, or Beechnut."[111] Also included was a listing of various garden seeds to begin a vegetable garden that would supplement their lacking diet.[112] Another letter home included a request for his infant brother, "Will you send some nipples over, please, we can't buy them here except what is gotten from the States."[113] Still another letter home recounted the perils of souvenir hunting by American boys among the ruins of buildings and forests and their discovery of helmets, pistols and unexploded ordnance. These dangerous practices occurred despite the fact that "it was against the rules to pick-up souvenirs in the bombed-out areas of Germany or to enter bombed buildings."[114] The expectation for many newly arrived American dependents was that their hardy and exceptional frontier spirit would naturally in time overcome these many trials. These challenges aside, the immediate and longer-lasting concern among recent arrivals was shelter.

As family members began pouring into Germany by 1946, the first available places to live were usually those most readily accessible. For any local population near a coalescing American Milcom, it often meant their private homes or property.[115] Residences as well as furniture were often "requisitioned" as the occupation authorities forced the German owners to relocate, sometimes on short notice. An associated complication of the unexpected relocation was the Germans' inability to bring along large items of furniture or personal libraries because of the shortage of available postwar transportation. Although there was some degree of remuneration for requisitioned property, it was "paid for at German rates" through a system that combined "some American dollar support along with a heavy contribution in marks."[116] By June 1946, the U.S. military had taken control of more than 30,000 properties.[117] In some instances the military requisitioned entire sections of towns to create an "American enclave."[118] An *Introduction to Germany* provides several pages of lighthearted comments describing the interior features of German homes and with an almost conspiratorial wink notes that "they [Germans] left pianos—mostly out of tune but with excellent tone once tuning is accomplished."[119] Acquisition of wartime spoils appeared acceptable and normalized.

An example of one such requisitioning of a home was the settlement of Major Sam Kale's family into a substantial German house overlooking the city of Würzburg. Because he was an American Army officer, "with a large family, the military appropriated him a large house." The military authorities forced the German owner, a wealthy department store proprietor and his family to move down the hill on the same grounds and reside throughout the occupation period in a much smaller caretaker's house.[120] Hank Johnson remembers those early days as a military "brat" in the Nüremberg military community.[121] He recalls, "There were no housing areas" initially, "but that turned out to be the best time for kids. Brats were rare; and we lived in houses seized from the Nazis (our house had been the Furth Gauleiter's home).[122] My playmates were all German kids, but our friendships were very guarded. The good news?

I picked up fluent German in no time."¹²³ Stories such as these were commonplace during the early postwar years in Germany. Norman Kappes recalls that:

> We arrived in November of 1946 (I was 9 years old, my brother 5 1/2 and my sister 9 months old). They housed us in the suburbs of Frankfurt, Neu Isenburg. Only a few bombs fell on the town so the houses were undamaged. I'm not sure how the military did it but they made the German families move out of 2 sections of Neu Isenburg and American families moved into their houses. These sections were called "compounds." The Germans had to fend for themselves. We had a beautiful 3 story house on 12 *Zeppelin Strasse* with a big backyard. Our compound, the North Compound, was 4 square blocks and surrounded by barbed wire fences. The military provided each family with a maid to cook and take care of the house. Also a "fireman" who made sure the furnace was always full of coal. We became very friendly with our maid, Anna, and kept in touch after we left Germany. We all loved her—she took care of us kids.¹²⁴

Occasionally, military families also rented shelter out of necessity when adequate housing was not available. Such was the case for Terry Dean's family:

> There were shortages and waiting lists for government quarters, so my dad had to rent a 4-room first floor of a 2-story house in Finthen. There was a coal stove for heat, and a coal stove for cooking, and the hot water heater was also coal fired. It took about 30 minutes to get lukewarm hot water, and that was only for the tub. There was no refrigerator, but it was winter, and we would lower the rouladen [external window shutters] and put our cold storage items on the sill between the window and the rouladen. And we had an outhouse. Life was not good there, and we moved after 6 months to a modern apartment downtown Mainz.¹²⁵

When it was not possible to requisition or rent housing for American Milcom families it was constructed. American officials working with German counterparts and companies organized major projects in the early 1950s that provided military families with permanent quarters. Very often they sported American names. Places with such titles as Alvin York Village in Bad Nauheim, Lincoln Village in Darmstadt, George C. Marshall Village in Giessen and MacArthur Village in Friedberg became home to thousands of Milcom members who travelled streets named Patton Avenue, Grant Avenue and Clay Alley on their way to work, school, or shopping. Often, they drove to those places in American cars, always conspicuous by design, which also sported special license plates identifying the owners as U.S. citizens.¹²⁶

Those structures, which rose close to most major American military locations, were "built with German deutschmarks by German contractors."¹²⁷ Very often this included the labor of German POWs still under postwar Allied control.¹²⁸ The works projects also raised other infrastructure and facilities exclusive to American use alongside these new quarters. They included schools for Milcom children, commissaries, post exchanges (PX), barber shops, movie theaters and even bowling alleys.¹²⁹ Much like the *kasernes* [military barracks] where military units and equipment were located these living areas and support facilities were sometimes encompassed by walls, fences and access-controlled gates monitored by American military police (MP).

Local Germans often referred to these isolated clusters, which impressed them as small replicas of American suburban life, as "Little Americas."¹³⁰ Other Germans applied the *bon mot*, "Golden Ghettos."¹³¹ Some Milcom members residing in the clusters likened them to a "51st state."¹³² Their locations separated American military families from German neighbors in physical environments that often encouraged daily socialization only with other Americans. Very often these islands of exclusivity rendered most direct relationships with Germans superficial. This limited many Milcom residents to only casual contacts such as shopping on the local economy, dining out, or vacationing. For many Americans it was the perception of a sequestered lifestyle that identified them as unique and separate from the host nation populace. One service member wryly observed, "There's a new form of segregation here. All of us Americans—Negroes, Puerto Ricans, Hawaiians, Mexicans, whites, Nisei—live in those big apartment houses on the hill above the town, all one big happy family, all cut off from the German community."[133] Joe Kiely who served as an Air Force officer in the early 1950s offers a similar perspective of those early days:

> Most of the social life at Ramstein was with fellow Americans. It was a close knit, self-contained community with everything needed for work and entertainment at the Officers' Club, Chapel and theatre. In one instance I even won $1,000 at Bingo at the Officers Club. Our limited contact with German people was pretty much limited to the employees who worked with us and the help in restaurants.[134]

The need for military bases and training areas by the Americans created similar challenges. Often, displaced persons already occupied the most obvious structures, such as former Wehrmacht facilities. Through the early 1950s the U.S. continued negotiations with the German government to find suitable locations. One case study of the town of Wildflecken notes the displacement of 957 Germans from homes and farms surrounding the rural community. Examples such as this also contributed to existing feelings of separation and brewing resentment.[135]

Other realities contributed to "exceptional" feelings among the Americans. Milcom members could, unlike their German neighbors, enjoy unrestricted travel within the AMZON and ride for free on German trains.[136] They could take their leisure at a variety of exclusive year-round Recreation Service sites and during the early occupation years they existed largely outside German civil law. The Status of Forces Agreement (SOFA) protected Americans from arrest by the West German police who referred any *Ami* charged with traffic violations to the nearest American MP substation for legal action.[137] Americans also enjoyed listening to the exclusive Armed Forces Network (AFN), radio and later television, which broadcast European and Stateside news, sports, entertainment and music to the Milcoms.[138] Additionally, Milcom members had access to reading materials in the new American libraries as well as the widely circulating English-language *Stars and Stripes* newspaper.[139] However, as one contemporary German journalist bemoaned, "only 8 percent of the American civilian employees spoke German fluently, 20 percent could speak if necessary" and "of the nearly three thousand books in a PX library only two were German."[140]

Still, the print media also played an important role. Principal among the materials available to the Milcoms were the magazine *U.S. Lady* and *Stars and Stripes* and each offered a venue for display of American ideals and attitudes. Aside from the *U.S. Lady* Code of Conduct, many other features in the magazine contributed to parochial images of Americanism among Milcom wives. One sign of their exceptional roles appeared in the nominations for the magazine's "U.S. Lady of the Month" award. Paramount among the requirements for selection to the honor was evidence of the nominee's "selfless devotion to her family, service, her community and country."[141] One example of an exceptional selectee for the honor was Nancy Lynam, a Milcom wife, who as a flight instructor had broken the sound barrier in 1962.[142] Other monthly winners exhibited the traits expected of the ideal Milcom wife: good relations with the host community, patriotism, dedication to her family, charitable works and extraordinarily humanitarian gestures, such as adopting war orphans and providing them with the benefits of an American upbringing. This was the case with Aurelia Richards, *U.S. Lady's* first "Lady of the Month" in October 1955, who with her husband received recognition for adopting several war orphans from both Europe and Asia.[143] The February 1956 issue also featured a letter from a Milcom wife who encouraged others to maintain appropriate dress and deportment while abroad to help deflect stereotypes of Americans as luxury-corrupted. Political and military elites, as well as conservative publishers, considered Milcom wives as central to the project of an American ideal.

Those feelings and attitudes of Americanism also resonated in letters to *Stars and Stripes* editor. Prior to 1968 the newspaper maintained a column titled the "B-Bag."[144] The vast majority of B-Bag letters normally addressed daily concerns that service personnel faced: shortages of consumer goods, slow promotion rates, reimbursement for travel and questions about command policies. But the B-Bag also occasionally carried letters that expressed pro–American views, particularly after the establishment of the Milcoms in 1946. One letter written in May 1948 recounted with patriotic zeal that during two V-E Day anniversary parades the author "Saw Freedom on the March."[145] Another letter penned in December 1950 endorsed a German tourist's observations that "in every respect the foreigner enjoys just as much freedom as the American citizen."[146] Still another, from November 1956, glowed with nationalistic pride after viewing a "Veterans' Day Program."[147] Grassroots Milcom acceptance of exceptional American attitudes during the early postwar years appeared to go largely unchallenged prior to the early 1950s.

Articles in *Stars and Stripes* contributed to enforcement of that perspective. One January 1948 printed piece recorded a rebuke to a group of Russian correspondents by the military governor of Hesse, who crowed "the Americans would not use force [like the Soviets] to collect food from farmers because such police state methods were not in line with American democratic ideals."[148] A statement of new Department of Defense personnel policies, carried by the newspaper in March 1951, emphasized as an objective the importance for commanders to provide their soldiers "information on citizenship, American ideals and current events, to the end that each man realizes his personal responsibility for the general welfare."[149] An April 1951 feature spoke of how the State Department's American *Kreis* [state] resident officers served as liaisons whose "principal task is to cultivate, within the framework of Germany's own culture, American ideals of democracy."[150] Central to the article was the stunning success of a program that introduced American political and business philosophies and procedures to German culture. A separate column that appeared in August 1954 offered a refreshing balance to concerns of POW brainwashing at the hands of North Korean captors. It told how two former captives "actively and openly defied the Communists despite inhuman punishments." It provided an excerpt from their award citation that read that the "desire to remain true to American ideals was source of inspiration to others."[151] Collectively, these journalistic pieces served the military hierarchy as a controllable and manageable vehicle to prescribe and demonstrate expected behaviors to residents in the Milcoms. How controlling and manipulative of the print media and other outlets the military hierarchy really was however, would be a subject of great debate in the years to come.[152]

Another visual signifier of American supremacy was the display of military prowess. Beginning as early in the occupation period as 1948, Milcoms and their associated military *Kasernes* hosted annual "open houses." These events, which grew grander over the years, were usually well-attended by the local German citizens who visited the nearby American garrison, viewed displays of military equipment, toured facilities and even sample American foods.[153] U.S. Air Force bases in Germany, such as that located at Ramstein, often included fly-overs of military aircraft and demonstrations of aerobatics. The European Command (EC) scheduled the open house events to coincide with annual "Armed Forces Day" celebrations which in the words of President Eisenhower were set to "pay suitable honor to the members of our

Armed Forces" who were "engaged in combat against ruthless aggression and despotism."[154] Although the military command designed the events "to show European citizens the strength of U.S. military men and equipment," they also afforded an opportunity to develop good community relations and demonstrate partnership with the Germans as a bulwark against Soviet Bloc aggression.[155] Still, as Jack Cipolla, a former GI stationed in Berlin in 1953 observed, the Germans respected the exhibitions of military might and it seemed as if "they loved the expression of power" by the Americans.[156]

In many ways, Americans could see themselves as the new Caesars arriving in Germany as both "conquerors and custodians," and the "United States could easily be seen as a reincarnation of Rome."[157] In that context early postwar official policy also dictated that the Milcom families maintain a German maid or servants:

> German civilians for household help are supplied on the following basis: one maid for each enlisted man's family plus a gardener shared by a second family; one maid and one gardener for each company grade officer's family; two maids and one gardener for each family of a field grade officer or a general.[158]

Charles Millstein, who in 1954 was a young dependent, remembers that:

> Like other families, especially major and up, we had a German maid. Ours was hired in an unusual but fortuitous way. The night our household goods arrived there was a knock on the door. A man I came to know as "Onkel" asked if we were interested in hiring a maid. He spoke some English and said his wife was looking for work. Mom, always the practical one, asked when she could start and he said "right now," and that is how "Ammie" joined our overseas family.[159]

An account from Army Major Sam Kale to relatives back home reflects on his wife's behavior, "Jewel certainly is going to be spoiled when we return to the States as we have a housemaid, laundress, cook and gardener." He also notes, "You would be surprised as to the amount of German she understands—she can't talk it but understands it quite a lot."[160] Collectively, these American behaviors and attitudes suggest an existence that was at least similar to one experienced by occupying Romans.

But the Americans' existence overseas, and in particular Germany, was rife with complications. These arose in part from the difficulties Milcom members had in coming to terms with the duality described in a "conquerors and custodians" motif that would haunt Milcom members' lives by shaping and informing their behaviors and attitudes during the postwar decades. In that context, these tensions grew out of a paradox of realities and expectations. On one hand there was the reality of an exceptional existence derived from physical circumstances, such as segregated living arrangements and special treatment, combined with associated postwar triumphal attitudes. On the other, there was the expectation of Washington's prescriptive directives that called for Americans to eschew overt displays of condescending behavior and serve as unofficial Cold War goodwill ambassadors. The result was an existence deep with complicated and troubling contradictions that Milcom members faced on a daily basis. For example, charity and relief work were extensions of munificence, yet they also underscored the overwhelming wealth and abundance of the Americans over the defeated and needy Germans. These in turn conjured images of *noblesse oblige* where "American aristocrats" gave "succor to the pitiful masses of Germany."[161] This stemmed from the idea that some Milcom members considered their way of life superior to others. The contrast between being a goodwill ambassador and haughty attitudes was a tension that ran through Milcom life. Elites in Washington inadvertently encouraged this from the beginning when they saw the Milcoms as something more than just a palliative for the social ills of occupation troops.[162]

But it is also possible to interpret the tensions between the Milcoms and the host communities by viewing them through a framework of newer interpretations. These fresher explanations exist within the context of contemporary realities that have been unexplored by recent histories. They include reduced sustenance levels, disease prevention, conduct of daily routines and existing early postwar attitudes. The first treatment focuses on the hard reality of reduced sustenance levels during the period 1945–1949. As the destructive outcome of war had reduced Germany's manufacturing and transportation capabilities, so too had it significantly reduced its agricultural production.[163] The Western Allied military governments struggled to feed the indigenous population of Germans, plus 10 million displaced persons (DPs) from the east, as well as large numbers of remaining Polish, Czech, and Jewish forced laborers.[164] This challenge required the setting of standards by the OMGUS for the per-person daily caloric allocation in the occupied zone.[165] At times this suffered complications because of special needs, such as a late 1940s a demand by Jewish DPs for kosher foods.[166] Nevertheless, allied authorities worked to set and enforce standards of sustenance. In the AMZON General Clay and his advisors periodically adjusted a standard that was contingent on harvests, the weather, transportation capabilities and aid shipments from the U.S.[167] At best, it attempted to sustain life and stave off starvation; at worst it served as yet another wedge between the Germans and the Americans who received a much superior caloric allocation through a robust PX and com-

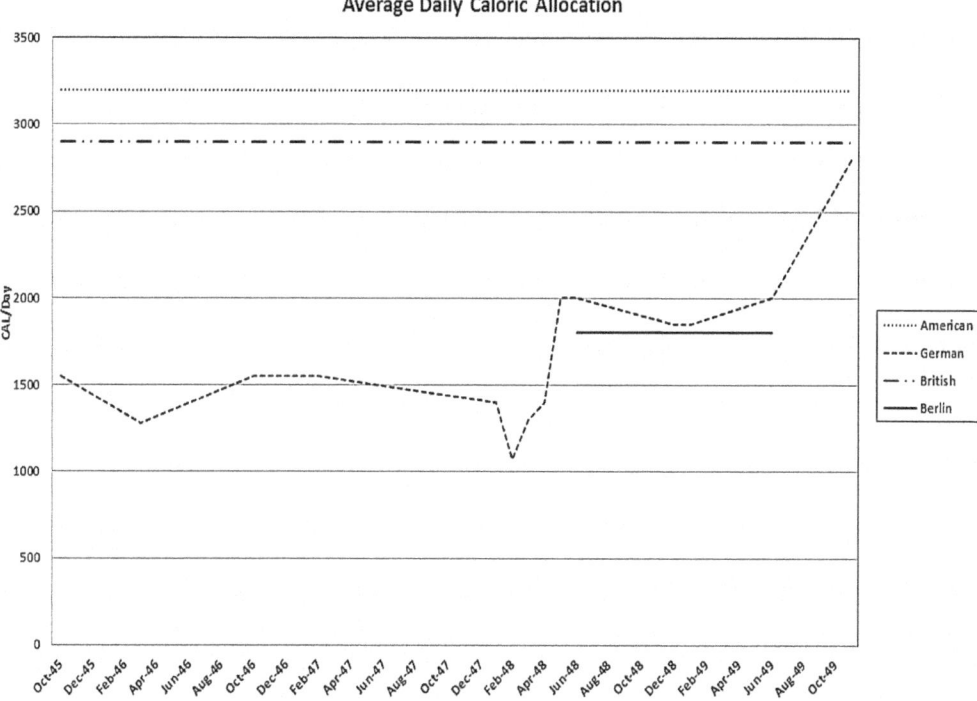

Average Daily Caloric Allocation, October 1945–November 1949. Legend entry "Berlin" refers to the period of the Berlin Blockade, June 1948 to May 1949, and applies only to German residents of that city. Data sources: the *New York Times*, *Stars and Stripes* newspaper (European Edition), Detlef Junker, ed., *The United States and Germany in the Era of the Cold War, 1945–1990: A Handbook, Volume 1: 1945–1968* and Richard Reeves, *Daring Young Men: The Heroism and Triumph of the Berlin Airlift, June 1948–May 1949.*

missary system.[168] As a result, newly arrived Milcom members were warned "Germany cannot grow even enough food for herself," so "don't try to eat in German restaurants or buy German-grown produce."[169] Regardless, tensions arose at the grass-roots level when unthinking Milcom ladies' clubs usurped local community garden plots, which often served as a ready source of produce for hungry Germans.

Until 1949 the scarcity of food was the subject of studies such as Herbert Hoover's 1947 mission to Germany, budgetary debates in Congress and German activism, which inspired the hunger strikes of February 1948.[170] Eventually, increased aid shipments and agricultural production, as well as improved distribution, reduced the size of the caloric wedge separating the Germans and the Americans. By November 1949, the allocation for Germans had at last reached the level of the Britons.[171] Still, the haunting specter of hunger remained ever present throughout the early postwar years.

Disease loomed as yet another barrier that stood between West Germans and Americans during the first two postwar decades. The press in the U.S. began offering notices as early as May 1946, with warnings that called the rise of tuberculosis in Germany rampant.[172] General Clay's concern for the American sector in Berlin showed in a monthly report for July 1947 that noted, "About 14,500 cases of open, infectious tuberculosis [German civilians] are walking the streets because hospital facilities are unavailable."[173] American medical authorities showed their concern by periodically placing warnings and announcements for Milcom members in the pages of *Stars and Stripes*. A February 1949 column in the *Washington Post* reflected such a notice and placed the number of deaths at 130.[174] A March 1949 notice announced, "The spread of tuberculosis has reached epidemic proportions in Europe with more than 100 dying daily."[175] Both articles listed Greece, Austria, Germany, Czechoslovakia, Hungary, and Italy following Yugoslavia in order of severity. A January 1951 *Stars and Stripes* article informed Milcom readers that the "breakdown of then existing anti-tuberculosis organizations, resulted for a time in a state of affairs bordering on an acute tuberculosis epidemic" in Europe.[176] By the mid-1950s medical authorities still considered it the world's "No. 1 Enemy."[177] But tuberculosis was not the only widespread illness that Milcom members needed to fear. A February 1950 article included a warning from the Frankfurt Milcom surgeon that, "Among the German population, cases of chicken pox, measles, whooping cough and diphtheria are sufficiently on the rise to warrant the taking of preventative measures by parents of U.S. children."[178] The prudent measure to be sure, was separation of American children from German playmates and classmates.

More upsetting to American Milcom parents, however, were measles and polio. These two diseases were present everywhere American service members and families lived in the European theater and they tracked them very closely. During the 1940s and 1950s, *Stars and Stripes* regularly reported outbreaks in Germany, France, Turkey, and Greenland. A 1949 report warned readers that 44 percent of German grammar school children in a Munich suburb had the measles, another in 1952 reported an outbreak in a Berlin refugee camp and a 1954 report warned of a measles outbreak near the Göppingen Milcom.[179] Between 1948 and 1949 the state of Bavaria announced hundreds of cases of polio that required the closing of schools and public swimming pools. *Stars and Stripes* carried the reports of deaths including those of American children.[180] Until a vaccine was available, separation from those with the illness or in danger of carrying it, was still the best preventative measure.

During the first two postwar decades Milcom parents continued to fear the specter of measles. By the early 1960s they anxiously scanned the pages of *Stars and Stripes* or community newsletters searching for the arrival of relief in announcements.[181] When that occurred, they flocked to Milcom clinics to take advantage of newly available vaccinations. But German children were not as fortunate and like most other European youth their nations' healthcare systems still suffered from the ravages of war. Most required assistance from outside agencies such as the Danish Red Cross to keep up with the basic needs of preventative medicine for their populations. Certain modified behaviors by Milcom members reflected their very real concerns regarding this discrepancy between the ability of Americans and their West German hosts to deal with disease control and protection. For example, American authorities often barred Germans from attending Milcom movie theaters during periods of outbreaks. In January 1948 "all Germans had already been barred from American movies and plays because of Berlin's polio epidemic" and only GIs who were immune to childhood illnesses could visit orphanages during outbreaks.[182]

A third interpretation of the segmentation between American Milcom members and their German neighbors exists in the context of everyday routine. Many members of the armed forces and their families devoted long hours each day to their respective daily duties and responsibilities, including school attendance, after-school activities and household chores. That daily pattern was not unusual for the majority of middle-class Americans whose lives consisted of similar routines that kept them occupied most of the work week.[183] Bill Hanne, who served as an Army lieutenant at Coleman Barracks in the Lampertheim Milcom from 1960 to 1963, recalls that he was "working a five and a half day week from 0615 [6:15 a.m. to usually 1800 [6:00 PM]" and to "1300 [1:00PM]" on Saturdays. Cyclical training, field exercises, alerts and equipment maintenance accounted for most of his time.[184] Most military personnel had similar duties and responsibilities that required their presence with their unit on their *kasernes*, or in their training areas, away from the German public each day. Sally Hollenbaugh recalls that almost immediately after their arrival in the Erlangen Milcom her husband's armored unit prepared to leave on maneuvers, "The men checked in and began to get the equipment ready to go, and away they went, which turned out to be for a 9 month stay at good old Grafenwoehr on the Czech border! I think about 66 clicks [kilometers] from us." She also recalls that on weekends the wives carpooled the distance to visit their spouses.[185]

This type of segmentation was not uncommon for many military personnel throughout the four decade period of their presence as the high tempo of training and maneuvers repeatedly separated them from families and the German populace. Kevin McEnery also remembers the lengthy deployments as a young lieutenant:

> I really did not have a lot of free time ... we kept an intense training pace and equipment readiness (maintenance) was an imperative. We kept track of time in the field for all personnel on separate rations. During 1983, as the scout platoon leader, I spent 200 days in the field. Graf and Wildflecken gunnery training and Hohenfels exercises, REFORGER, Camp Pitman (Weiden) border duty, and local training areas. Once a part came in we worked around the clock to get the vehicle up. The unit culture was that it was professionally unacceptable to not be ready to roll when the monthly alert was called and not to shoot well on the range.[186]

In a similar context, school age dependent children attended classes in the specially constructed DODDS facilities where authorities certified that instruction met the educational standards of the American public school system. This was important so as to ensure that overseas dependent students did not fall behind their contemporaries in the U.S. It was particularly critical for Milcom high school students who were seeking admittance to colleges

Your Dependents' Schools in Germany

Bringing your children to Europe is an adventure with an element of chance. Naturally you are asking, "What of the schools?" "Will my child keep up with his class back home?" "What kind of teachers will he have?" "What kind of text books and methods are used?" "Will the schools prepare my child for college entrance?" "How can I, a parent, help in the schools?"

These and all of your questions deserve a satisfying answer.

Will my child keep up with his class back home?

Globetrotters of a tender age getting geographic bearings

This question is doubtless uppermost in your thoughts. The answer is "Yes, he will be studying the same things here that his former classmates in the States are covering. He has the same opportunities here for growth and development that he had in the States?"

Why? Because the Dependents School Division staff of specialists sought out the best teachers, texts, courses of study and opportunities for enrichment. And if your child is in high school, it will reassure you to learn that our high schools are accredited by the North Central Association of Colleges and Secondary Schools.

Teachers from the States, whose enthusiasm and ability for developing the best in scholarship and citizenship in our young Americans, have been selected for our Dependents Schools.

Unlike the "average teacher" back home, all of our elementary and high school teachers must have a Bachelor of Arts or Science degree. Many have higher degrees. All have had rich experiences in their profession. Congress has appropriated nearly a million dollars for their pay, and they have to be good to work for Uncle Sam. They have come to Europe with the challenge to provide the best in good basic teaching for your child in the American Way.

Above: DODDS Pamphlet. Extract from a USAREUR pamphlet (c. 1948). Authorities printed the document to familiarize Milcom parents with the details of the Department of Defense Dependents School System in Germany. The text assures parents of the schools' standards of accreditation and comments that the schools will "provide the best in good basic teaching for your child in the American Way." Image source: Norman Kappes with permission. *Below*: DODDS Pamphlet 2. Extract from a USAREUR DODDS pamphlet (c. 1948). The narrative explains that German nationals are present in the schools in various capacities as helpers and encourages goodwill from the students toward them as a way to emphasize the concept of "dignity and worth of the individual, no matter what his nationality or creed." It cautions however, "Wholesome attitudes towards the helpers in the home and the neighborhood are the responsibility of you, the parents," and reveals the existence of some negative behaviors by noting that in "a number of cases" an "attitude on the part of some of the children toward German helpers" had "required the attention of the American teachers." Image source: Norman Kappes with permission.

relationships with other people supplements the work of the school. Our schools teach—and put into practice in daily living—the dignity and worth of the individual, no matter what his nationality or creed. Your own attitudes of respect for others are reflected by your children. They will learn to respect and appreciate the help of the German personnel in the schools. Wholesome attitudes toward the helpers in the home and the neighborhood are the responsibility of you, the parents.

Champions

Germans assist in hot lunch service

The presence of German helpers in the school enables American teachers to give more time to individuals and small groups and so do an all-round better job. But in a number of cases this advantage has been nullified by an attitude on the part of some of the children toward German helpers and required the constant attention of the American teachers. If you will explain to your child the great opportunity open to him to learn a foreign language, and show him that a helpful attitude toward all the German assistants will benefit him personally and will and universities in the U.S. So essential was this consideration that the Frankfurt Milcom high school, which served a wide geographical area encompassing many sub-communities, provided boarding services and dormitories for students who had to travel more than fifty miles to attend. Thus, the existing education system separated older teenage students from their families, German neighbors and friends during the week.[187]

This environment however, was more complicated than it appeared. Although an aspect of segmentation existed there were also some limited opportunities for making new contacts, both American and German. Neil Albaugh, who as a teenager attended Frankfurt American High School (FAHS) from 1955 to 1957, recalls those American dependent students from Milcoms as far away as Sweden, Greece, Libya, and Turkey who attended the school and resided in the dormitories. He also remembers interactions with German youth through sport activities in the German-American Athletic Association as well as exchanges of choral groups. During this time he experienced little if any resentment from the German populace, young or old.[188]

While other family members were occupied American Milcom housewives labored within the bounds of Little America. During the early postwar years, a period of time when the gender-prescribed expectation was for women to remain at home, Milcom wives filled their days with a routine of chores and duties. Housework, shopping, cooking, cleaning, caring for children and maintaining the household budget were some of the time consuming responsibilities.[189] A 1955 *Stars and Stripes* article placed that in perspective by emphasizing that "the average housewife works about 80 hours a week."[190] Whether in the U.S. or overseas that number compared equitably to those of a spouse in the military or children engaged in a mandatory education system. Altogether, the Milcom family mirrored the typical contemporary American family, laboring at the demands of daily routine and having limited spare time to share with others.

A final consideration for the development of segmentation between the German and American Milcom populations, which emerges through first person sources, was the existence of residual animosity leftover from the war. Ed DeLong recalls an unnerving instance during his assignment to Bremerhaven in 1950 when he traveled into the city to explore:

> I sat at a table with a group of elderly Germans. We quickly became conversant and they were eager to help me learn their language and customs. I bought beer all around and we sang drinking songs and swayed with the others as the orchestra played. We were enjoying the day when two young German boys about 17 years old approached the table and asked the oldsters what they were doing, associating with the enemy. They were told that I was just a young man like themselves and they did not consider me an enemy ... the young men left. The people at the table were concerned and told me that I should return to the base at once as these young men were what was left of the Hitler Youth in the area and that their intentions were to harm me when I left. With this ten of the older people surrounded me and escorted me back to the base. The young thugs, who were part of a new organization called the "Frei Deutsche Jugend" or "Free German Youth" watched and scowled, but did not dare attack me while I was guarded by the elderly people.[191]

Assigned to Germany with the U.S. Air Force several years later, Kent Goldsmith carried certain initial impressions with him as he traveled overseas:

> Raised during the 40s, my first thought on learning I would be stationed in Germany was that it would be a bit like being stationed in hell. Wartime propaganda had pretty thoroughly convinced me that the Germans were evil incarnate, and I blithely assumed they were all Nazis or Nazi sympathizers.... I was surprised to find relatively friendly, if somewhat reserved local citizens... the only troubles I recall were always with Brit soldiers when we were out on the town—and local Germans always took our side and even stepped into the fray if we were outnumbered (which was most of the time).[192]

Although his attitude changed over time as he interacted with Germans the impact of wartime propaganda suggests that a number of early Milcom members carried antagonistic attitudes with them overseas and this contributed to a divide between the two cultures. In this vein Hank Johnson who spent time in the Butzbach Milcom as a dependent youth recalls:

> Each time I was in Germany, it was a different "socio-climate." Late '40s-early '50s was VERY tense, w/regard to the Germans. It was the Occupation Years and the Germans had lost WWII. The "psychological wounds" were raw in both directions. They hated us; and we hated them. For our fathers, it was VERY tense—nobody went off post alone (German women were always claiming US officers raped them); and all service members were required to wear their uniforms anytime they left their quarters. Our fathers had very little use for the Germans, and I now realize my father had been in mortal combat with the SS, just 5 short years before.[193]

Though these first person accounts are not representative of the many pleasant interactions between Germans and Milcom members during the postwar years, they do indicate that not all exchanges were friendly and there sometimes existed underlying tensions that disappeared only with the passage of time. Although not addressed in existing histories, barriers like the caloric wedge, fear of contagious illnesses, the demands of daily life and lingering animosities were as equally important in placing both mental and physical barriers between Milcom members and the surrounding German communities during the first two postwar decades as were the construction of isolated dwellings for "Little Americas."

Regardless of the barriers separating the two cultures, within a year of arriving in Europe many Milcom wives were finding ways to become engaged in welfare work and demonstrate good will. For example, they organized into the American Occupation Women's Voluntary Service, which later became the Conference on American Women's Activities in Europe. Individual military units and communities also participated. Many raised funds and gathered clothing for homeless and impoverished Germans, organized Christmas parties for orphanages, and contributed to rebuilding hospitals. *Stars and Stripes* often carried examples of this American beneficence. A full page in the November 23, 1948, European edition showcased a collection of charity events under a banner heading that read "Americans Aid St. Nick in EC Yule Events." Among the Milcom activities to raise funds for German relief were bake sales, raffles, bazaars, and charity balls. The newspaper columns also listed community events such as St. Nicholas Day parties for German students and collections of seasonal garments.[194]

Some groups bridged the gulf between cultures through purposeful design. This was particularly true for those programs involving youth, such as church groups, Boy Scouts, Girl Scouts and sports clubs. Among them, Scout organizations seemed well-situated to affect a grassroots connection between postwar Americans and Germans. President Eisenhower and the military hierarchy in Europe favored the Boy Scouts as young icons of Americanism whose oath charged each individual to "do my duty to God and my country, and to obey the Scout law."[195] Celebrating the anniversary of their founding, Eisenhower extolled their ability to help America "be better able to meet its full responsibility in cooperation with other nations in maintaining peace on earth."[196] In turn, the USAREUR Commander, Lieutenant General Manton S. Eddy, commended the Scouts' "program of character building and citizenship training."[197]

Although historic studies on Scouting during the Cold War are anecdotal at best, archival evidence in hundreds of *Stars and Stripes* articles during the course of the postwar period attest to the importance placed on the American scouting program for its people-to-people connection with Germans.[198] Aside from reports of joint camping events with Boy Scout troops from several countries including England, France, Belgium, and West Germany, there were articles noting the participation of German and American scouts in joint holiday parties.[199] Also highlighted was the involvement of American scouts in charitable work. A November 1954 article, one of many to appear over the years, noted, "Boy Scouts in Giessen recently visited dependent quarters to collect usable items which could be donated to needy German families."[200]

The scouting programs appeared to offer a perfect vehicle for inculcating youngsters in the Milcoms with American ideals while serving at the grassroots level as an example to malleable young Germans. The scouts' unique position along the inter-cultural boundary offered them the opportunity to provide "overseas adventure and border-crossing adolescent friendship" while incorporating "the role of youth in widening America's 'external footprint.'"[201] By May 1950 the Scouting Transatlantic Council came into existence to serve the needs of U.S. citizens and their dependents. Within a decade there were 19,325 American Boy Scouts throughout the network of Milcoms interacting with, and influencing, European scouts.[202]

The most popular and successful youth program however, was the German Youth Activity (GYA), which offered participation in sports, dramatics, handicrafts and discussion groups. As the *Pocket Guide* notes, aside from providing simple recreation it was an opportunity to teach the youth of Germany "the most fertile minds in the country today—just what the American way of life means."[203] *Stars and Stripes* reiterated this in an article of April 25, 1948, which noted that the guide for U.S. Army GYA workers and volunteers emphasized that their job was "to help German agencies rehabilitate and reorient their own youth along democratic lines."[204]

1946	Boys	Girls	Total	Meetings	Military Personnel
August	51,222	58,991	110,213	535	2,870
September	166,541	66,663	233,204	2,326	4,603
October	224,692	105,451	330,143	3,261	10,314
November	257,842	116,932	374,774	3,708	9,340
December	208,317	106,175	314,492	5,105	16,253

Table 1.1. GYA Participation Statistics, 1946. Shows the numbers of German youth participating in the program, the number of meetings and the number of U.S. military personnel involved (instructors, coaches, mentors, administrative support and transportation) August–December 1946. The statistics attest to the increasing popularity of the program during the early occupation period. The slight decrease in total participation numbers during December was a result of problems with transportation and fuel for heating the GYA facilities (Report of Operations of German Youth Activities, 6 January 1947, Headquarters United States Constabulary, Office of German Youth Activities, RG 549, United States Army, Europe, 1942–1991, U.S. Constabulary 1946–1948, Box 3319, National Archives College Park).

But feedback from the German community underscored concerns that "Many Germans fear the Army GYA program is merely an organized attempt to make Americans out of their children—a sort of reverse project to Hitler's prewar attempts" to shape the minds of the young.[205] Ironically, in a survey conducted by the OMGUS, 40 percent of young Germans responded that their only interest in the GYA was "to get candy and food," 26 percent responded that their attraction was "sports and games," only 6 percent were interested in learning about democracy, and 11 percent responded that the GYA "has no value."[206] These types of critiques ruffled the feathers of some American leaders, such as General Clay, who maintained that they were unwarranted and that "the American soldier is [was] the best salesman of democracy in Germany." Clay also observed that many critics "are ignorant of the generous and kindly things he does" such as volunteering time with youth programs such as the GYA.[207] Still, membership in the GYA continued to increase.

Unfortunately, the actions of some young Americans at times undercut General Clay's optimism. Incidents of misbehavior that included displays of rude mocking, vandalism and petty crimes such as shoplifting in German stores, were examples of young Americans' thoughtlessness regarding Germans still struggling to recover and recreate lives from the war's devastation. In some cases American youth residing in the Milcoms ignored the prescribed guidance of good behavior to take advantage of their advantageous economic, political and social positions. In part, many Americans carried certain attitudes and predispositions with them as they arrived in Germany. For example, some social constructs affected the way that certain military members and dependents from regions of the American South thought about race through their experiences with Jim Crow segregation. Other Americans received their cues from materials the U.S. government published and distributed to them before their arrival. This was the case with *A Pocket Guide to Germany* that described Germans as a people more apt to "follow the leader" than act on individual thought.[208]

But just as often, in contrast, unvarnished examples of genuine friendship offset any acts of inappropriateness. This was the case for Tim Gilbert who as a ten-year old dependent of a military family resided in the Frankfurt Milcom from 1952 to 1954. He recalls, "I made friends with a German kid named Wolfgang, and thought his name was really cool. I wanted to change my name to that too." He added, "I would go to his house and pick up lots of pre–World War Two coins that had been thrown in the garden."[209] As Tim Gilbert experienced, not all relationships between young Americans and Germans were born in mistrust and conflict, or existed in an exceptionalist shadow. Norman Kappes, who resided in the Frankfurt Milcom, also has pleasant memories:

> Us kids also spoke German and we became friendly with the German boys in the neighborhood. We played soccer on the street in front of our house. I became good friends with one boy, Hatmut. Sometimes he would come with the family when we went into Frankfurt to a carnival or for sightseeing. From the viewpoint of a young boy, I was 9 thru 12 at the time, the Americans in Neu Isenburg and Frankfurt seemed to get along fine with the population. I do not recall any bad incidents or problems.[210]

Joint religious services, between the American Milcoms and the German community, held regularly, on holidays, or during annual German-American festivities, also served as a bridge between the two cultures. *Stars and Stripes* was rife with examples, such as listings of "joint religious services at Thea-Matthaeus Church and-or Markus Church" as part of the annual Munich Milcom German-American Week celebrations.[211] Regular full-page listings also appeared in the newspaper, on Saturdays, which carried times for a variety of denominational services in both American military and German civilian chapels and synagogues. The "Church Services" listing in the June 26, 1948, issue of *Stars and Stripes* displayed that information for 60 Milcoms and satellite locations.[212] Joint religious worship became a cultural common ground where Americans and Germans both could reach across the gulf separating them to demonstrate fellowship and unity in the face of the atheistic Soviet Bloc.

Still, other bridges existed as thousands of German civilians worked within the Milcom structure filling positions as employees in a variety of occupations. Many served as maids in American households, others maintained buildings and grounds and hundreds of others worked in PX barbershops, bowling alleys and movie theaters. Germans also filled positions in the U.S. government-owned and operated recreation facilities as ski instructors, tour guides, hotel staff and maintenance personnel. By 1953, there were already 15,000 Germans working for the U.S. Army's Ordnance command throughout the country, mostly as vehicle maintenance personnel.[213] Also, by 1957, more than 11,000 German civilians worked in the Kaiserslautern Milcom area within the U.S. Army's logistical base structure.[214] The number of foreign national workers in American facilities and Milcoms continued to grow into the last decade of the Cold War. In addition, Germans filled hundreds of bureaucratic positions on Milcom staffs as community and military liaisons and travel and housing coordinators. This thick presence of local nationals, who easily crossed that boundary between cultures, afforded other opportunities for breaking through the perceived walls of separation.

During the early postwar decades German communities often appreciated Americans' efforts to connect with them through acts of benevolence and friendship, or on common cultural grounds.[215] Unfortunately, the physical realities of separation, occasional acts of misbehavior and the offensive attitudes of some Milcom members, in combination with the sharply-worded text of government publications, created an environment that often threatened efforts at bonding. These instances appeared at odds with the intended projections of superior American values. As a result, the Milcoms functioned within a duality: balancing the expectations of goodwill ambassadorship against existing instances of segmentation. Within a decade, emerging tensions from these internal contradictions and global dynamics would compel Milcom members to understand that the ideals of Americanism were not immutable. This became apparent during the years that followed as the behaviors and attitudes of the Milcom members would mirror changes in American culture and society.

Two

The Footprint of American Culture and Consumerism (1946–1967)

An Image of American Culture

The news media described the International Jazz Club's successful June 1949 concert in the Deutsches Museum's Jubilee Hall as "four solid, thumping hours" of "some of the hottest jazz notes in Europe."[1] The audience included more than 3,000 German and American fans who responded enthusiastically to the performances of bands and singers from both countries. This event was just one of dozens that appeared during the first postwar decade featuring that popular musical venue which consistently attracted large crowds.

Between 1946 and the mid–1960s, American culture left a deep footprint in Europe. The impact was particularly strong in West Germany, which was home to the majority of overseas postwar Milcoms. During this period popular culture and consumerism became recognizable characteristics of the American way of life associated with Americans in general and the Milcoms in particular. Although the intended goals of directive policies and practices were to enhance the lifestyle of Milcom members, an unintended consequence was their penetration of German culture. In this context they often provided convenient examples of American ideals to a still emerging West German identity that were accepted, rejected, or accommodated.[2]

As the network of Milcoms spread after 1946, and people-to-people contacts increased, the Germans became aware of the stark contrast in cultural norms between themselves and the *Amis* [Americans]. American service members and their families became visual signifiers of a separate, unique and dynamic culture that contrasted in many aspects to the traditional ways of Germany. Whether it was intentional or not this was apparent in the Americans' behavior, their dress and the artifacts of their culture such as their music, literature and art.[3] This is consistent with observations of postwar consumption patterns that note the presence of American troops and Milcoms offered unique opportunities for the broadcasting of American ideas and values across the German-American cultural boundary.[4] It was during the innumerable daily interactions at the grass-roots level between Milcom members and German locals that American cultural penetration seemed most influential. That daily exposure to the American consumer culture and popular culture particularly influenced young Germans and encouraged them to invoke their own image of America, as well as imagine a different and better life. This, many of them interpreted as a new sense of cultural freedom. That type of freedom, based on an abundance of wealth, was consistently on display in the Milcoms.[5]

Infected with that mood, younger Germans assigned value to American consumer goods as artifacts of a larger world pregnant with previously absent possibilities, especially after years of fascist restrictions and wartime deprivations. They insisted on smoking Lucky Strikes like the *Amis*, they sought American Levi's jeans to appear stylish and they eagerly drank Coca-Cola, which seemed to flow in an endless stream from American commissaries, PXs, and recreational facilities. As one German readily admitted, "Today, Coca-Cola is a company, in those days it was a *Weltanschauung* [world view]."[6] Coke had maintained its pre-war connection with the German public and continued to be an icon of the West, America, and everything modern and fresh.[7] Another German fondly recalled that "we only had the hots for American clothing ... we felt like kings, when we were at least dressed like them."[8] As one dependent daughter noted, "saddle shoes were all the rage on both sides of the Atlantic."[9] But on a few occasions style was misunderstood. One account notes, "The American teenagers used to wear dungarees and they would roll up the pant-legs half-way up the calf. The Germans would point at them and laugh."[10] Still, German teenagers often made friends with Americans simply to catch a ride in their big Ford or Chevy *Straßenkreuzer* [street cruisers] and so to feel more like them.[11] Of the visual signifiers and cultural bridges that existed, those that were most representative of the Americans in the first postwar decades were the automobile, consumer goods, music and the printed and spoken word.[12]

The American Auto

Standing at the intersection of material consumption and popular culture in the Milcoms were those big American autos, which rumbled over the cobblestones of German villages and towns. They were among the foremost of those artifacts, symbols, and visual signifiers that represented the energy, technology, mobility, and dynamic movement of that new and modern American culture and society.[13] Soon after the establishment of the Milcoms they began to crowd the streets and lanes of West Germany and became a common sight. Having the advantage over the German automotive industry, which was still recovering from a shattered wartime industrial infrastructure, American manufacturers exploited that Milcom market. They understood that Americans' love affair with the car, a manifestation of popular culture, did not end with their deployment overseas.[14] Working closely with the military hierarchy, the larger automotive corporations, such as Ford and Chrysler, were able to offer special deals to Milcom members and help them attain the "four-wheeled answer on how to get around in the zone, and join the parade of American cars in Germany."[15]

In a display of collusion between capitalism, consumerism, and advertising, the EUCOM Exchange System Automotive Activities Center set up shop with "new car sales points," initially located in the Frankfurt and Munich Milcoms. The EES later added a third at the Baumholder Milcom. These served as outlets for new cars sales to Milcom members and they also advertised in *Stars and Stripes*.[16] The newspaper noted the arrival of the first purchase in July 1948, "First 1949 Stateside Car Arrives at BPE."[17] Examples of those ads by the European Exchange System (EES) included one for Plymouths that announced "Every Plymouth Sedan now in stock.... Reduced," and enticed Milcom buyers with choices between the "Standard Model Heater" or the "Deluxe Model Heater."[18] Another EES ad from 1954 noted, "Owning a car in Europe is for many a real necessity as well as a convenience. But driving one of the new 1954 wonders is nothing but pleasure!"[19] It listed several makes and models, Ford, Mercury, De Soto, Pontiac, and Oldsmobile, together with their standard and customized features. For Milcom consumers who were used to scanning their hometown newspaper's classified ads for cars this was like a touch of home.

New Milcom purchasers could apply to make a purchase and the EES Automotive Center placed them on a priority list according to their date of arrival in country and other criteria such as family size, job necessity, and military rank. As their pre-ordered, custom-made auto arrived in port from America, the EES representatives contacted them. EUCOM headquarters made sure that all Milcom members clearly understood the eligibility requirements by issuing statements such as Weekly Directive No. 20, HQ EUCOM December 24, 1947, which outlined the policy for ownership. As early as June 1948, *Stars and Stripes* noted that the "director of the Automotive Activities Center, announced that 810 automobiles were sold during May" of that year.[20] Total sales for 1948 alone were 5,400 cars.[21] The program continued as a great financial success and consumer convenience, until the American presence withered at the end of the Cold War.[22]

Aside from obtaining a car through the EES Milcom, members could also ship their own vehicle overseas at government expense for officers and the three top grades of non-commissioned officers.[23] This process often took weeks to months. It also required owners to maintain a sharp watch of listings in *Stars and Stripes* for the arrival of their vehicle, not unlike watching for the arrival of their dependents. Brief notifications with titles such as "Car Arrivals Listed by BPE," and "155 Private Cars Expected at BPE" were common.[24] Still, the number of American autos arriving in West Germany, either through sales or shipment, was enormous and continued to increase as the population of Milcom members grew.[25] This suggests that the car became an ever more present symbol of dynamic and modern Americanism presiding at the intersection of material consumption and popular culture.

Among the collateral cultural derivatives introduced to the Germans by the infestation of American automobiles was a fixation on safety.[26] As early as March 1948, the commander at the Bremerhaven Port of Entry (BPE) instituted a program that required all Milcom personnel to sign "a safe driving pledge" before they could pick-up their vehicle. Once done, they affixed a sticker that stated "I Drive Safely" to their windshield.[27] Following that, in January 1949, the command required a compulsory safety inspection for newly arrived vehicles. Those with infractions, such as faulty headlights, brakes, or steering, could not depart the BPE holding lot until their owner paid for repairs.[28] By the early 1950s USAREUR Headquarters had issued authorized speed limits for American cars in Germany and had petitioned the Mayor of Stuttgart to erect long absent speed limit signs throughout the city. The latter was in response to the injury of several Milcom pedestrians by speeding Germans.[29] As soon as the opportunity presented itself in September 1953, Milcom members were rushing to German agencies to purchase automobile insurance, something they could not do without back home.[30] Thus the cultural aspect of the car for the Milcom family also became a small economic boon for West German businesses that provided insurance policies, repairs, and fuel.

Evidence of the Americans' emphasis on safety also appeared in Milcom newspapers. The front page of the November 10, 1949, issue of the *Heidelberg Post* featured an article titled "Safety Campaign Keeps Plugging for Safe Driving" that stressed good vehicular maintenance and driving techniques. Accompanying it was a photograph of a service member's wrecked car next to a placard that read "Only Fools Break the Rules: Drive with Care."[31] The front page of the September 15, 1950, issue of the Rhein-Main *Gateway* carried an article under the banner title "Support the Base Safety Campaign." It noted that the rate of traffic accidents in both the U.S. and EUCOM had increased in 1949 and announced a planned crack-down by the military police on Americans who exceeded the posted speed limits on and off post.[32]

Enlisting the interest and support of Germans employed by American Milcoms was another technique to spread safety awareness, and collaterally enforce another cultural bridge. A photograph in the November 1949 issue of the *Heidelberg Post* showed the American community safety director pinning an armband on a German foreman's sleeve that read *Sicherheitsdienst* [Safety Worker]. Next to the photo was a printed eight-point pledge that the Safety Director expected German workers to follow on the job site as well as at home. It emphasized safe practices, awareness, and the need to discuss safety matters with family, friends, and neighbors.[33]

Also detailing the intersection of popular culture, consumerism, and safety was a report from a West German journalist who traveled to the U.S. and witnessed America's fascination with the car first hand. Reporting back to his fellow countrymen he recounted how the automobile offered citizens freedom through mobility and design choice, a sense of community because "almost everyone in America [is] on the road," and safety, which existed through mandated annual checks. He also noted the integrated tenet of capitalism through the presence of toll roads and paid parking, and the consumer convenience of drive-up banking and fast food. His intent was to explain, by association, the automotive behaviors and practices of Milcom members to curious West Germans and to underscore how that one iconic material object exhibited so many "characteristics of the American way of life."[34]

The Milcom Home and Modern Consumption

Increasingly throughout the 1950s, owners of those fantastic American autos could park them in lots convenient to newly constructed government quarters. These were part of the U.S. military construction program that was pressing ahead to keep pace with the rapid expansion of the Milcom network.[35] Although those new "Little America" housing projects sometimes physically segregated the Americans from their German neighbors their interiors served as examples of modern consumerism. Generally laid out in floor plans that mimicked contemporary German construction, they also reflected the efficient rationalism of the Weimar period.[36] They contained all the essential modern appliances necessary for the American family, such as full-sized refrigerators, washing machines, clothes dryers, and new stoves. The intention was that they resemble the ideal American home as closely as possible. When Vice-President Nixon verbally sparred with Soviet Premier Nikita Khrushchev in 1959 during the historic "Kitchen Debates," Milcom wives were already in position to display American superiority through domestic appliances to local women visiting their homes.[37] That consumerist instinct was intrinsic to contemporary Americans' self-identity and was a trait of its cultural profile, as was the condition of relative abundance. In that context, for Americans and members of the Milcoms, consumerism represented a vehicle for demonstrating status and the opportunity for upward mobility as well as individuality and leisure.[38]

That concept of consumer wealth resonated in the Milcoms and in the Big Picture film titled *Operation Friendly Hand*. It depicts a military family, in the Vogelweh Milcom, wel-

American Housing, Bad Nauheim Milcom (c. 1959). These units constructed along *Platenstraße* after the war accommodated Milcom families. The Federal Republic provided most of the funding and labor as a offset to the costs borne by the United States for stationing troops in Germany. Note the great number of late model American cars. Among them sits a lone black VW Beetle. Image source: Frank da Cruz with permission, *Frankfurt American Highschool*, http://www.frankfurthigh.com/history/sub-pages/fahs_housing.htm#Bad %20Nauheim.

coming into their home a young German girl who arrives for a short visit. Coming from a family struggling to make its way through the challenges of the postwar economy, she is grateful for the chance to be a guest in their home. The Americans shower her with kindness and expose her to their largesse. Their Milcom quarters exhibit all the trappings of contemporary consumerism: a television, a refrigerator, games, toys, books, and plenty of food. A new family automobile is just outside in its designated space. During the week-long visit the girl's hosts treat her with new clothing, cosmetics, ice cream, and new shoes. Although it was in reality a staged production, the film attests to the fact that the Milcom is a reflection of the American lifestyle that is a world of convenience, leisure, and consumer wealth, and it suggests these should be the goals of a new Germany.[39]

The print media also reflected the imprint of that consumerist tenet. Every issue of the monthly magazine *U.S. Lady* included advertisements that specifically targeted the Milcom wife and family. The inside front covers frequently carried ads for familiar items such as Kleenex and Alka Seltzer. Located throughout the pages of the magazine were ads for Nabisco, Kellogg, and Colgate products. The issues often carried pages of recipes for the Milcom family "on the go," provided by manufacturers that included Jell-O, Crackerbarrel cheese, Birdseye and Chun King. Among them was a Betty Crocker recipe that quipped it was perfect "whether you're stationed at Fort Dix or Frankfurt." It also noted that these recipes offered "A Touch of Home."[40] American manufacturers were determined to maintain their link with military consumers whether in the States or overseas and Milcom members were glad for that taste of home.

The Sounds of America

But Coke, clothing, cars, and consumerism were only part of the American cultural imprint on display in the Milcom; music also played a large role. That influence was evident with the arrival of Private Elvis Presley at the port of Bremerhaven, Germany on October 1, 1958. As *Stars and Stripes* reported, hundreds of admiring and energetic American and German teenage girls broke through a hastily constructed barrier to mob their idol.[41] After several hectic hours the singer eventually arrived at Ray Barracks, his duty station within the Friedberg Milcom. But Private Presley's arrival in West Germany was not without a hint of coincidental irony. The singer and movie matinee idol, who for many people personified both the good and bad aspects of popular American culture, was now himself a Milcom member. His music, part of the wave of rock and roll that washed onto European shores during the 1950s, represented a fresh, energetic sound associated with an exceptional postwar Americanism, and was complicit in shaping a West German postwar cultural identity.

Rock and roll had followed on the heels of its *avant garde* predecessor, Jazz. Since the 1930s, musical tours from the U.S. had traveled throughout Europe offering its distinctive sound to generally appreciative crowds. By 1945 artists such as Louis Armstrong, Dizzy Gillespie and other Jazz greats were widely known to the German public and like rock and roll that sound was characteristically, and exceptionally, American.[42] Jazz offered an attractive and important outlet because it provided a cultural venue for young Germans to distance themselves from the Nazi association of their elders and other uncomfortable reminders of their past.[43] In that context, after 1945, a flood of American consumer goods and popular culture inundated West Germany causing a cultural reaction. Jazz together with rock and roll arrived on that wave and sounded the clarion call of change. While young American Milcom consumers were flocking to the PX to purchase the latest recordings by Jazz artists like Ella Fitzgerald, or rock and roll icons like Elvis and Bill Haley and the Comets, less affluent, but eager, German youth sought the sounds on their radios via the Armed Forces Network Radio, Radio Luxembourg, Radio in the American Sector (RIAS), or the Voice of America.[44]

During that time, *Stars and Stripes* carried a regular column, by staff writer Johnny Vrotsos, titled "On the Record." It catered to all music lovers but it especially featured news and information about contemporary performers and the release dates of their records. As *Stars and Stripes* reported, European PX record sales for 1955 made it "one of the world's biggest sellers of phonograph records."[45] Consumerism and popular culture in the Milcom seemed to go hand in hand. While some Americans accepted rock and roll, and others criticized it, most tolerated the sound. If there was any concern from Milcom parents, music industry executives allayed their fears by claiming that rock and roll was in fact only a passing fad, and that it "is not developing juvenile delinquents."[46] Meanwhile, Milcom homes, clubs and barracks rooms echoed with the jazz and rock sounds that seemed to resonate with the image of contemporary Americanism. But those tunes could also be the sound of friction at the boundary between German and American cultures.

While American Milcom members identified with the ideas of a popular and consumerist culture in the early 1950s, many West German elites including church leaders, politicians and educators found themselves negotiating ways to accommodate or resist a perceived cultural "Americanization." Often, the tensions and distress this generated for German clergy and conservatives were associated with the perceived dangers posed to the fabric of traditional society. Some German leaders interpreted American consumerism and popular culture as a conflated menace bristling with a variety of threats. They harbored deep-seated concerns regarding the effect of American popular culture on sexual behaviors worrying that it contributed to excessive female sexual expression and male aggression.[47]

It was those pervasive concerns that precipitated a flurry of articles from German weeklies like *Der Spiegel* and *Die Zeit*. A December 1956 cover of *Der Spiegel* featured a photograph of "Elvis the Pelvis" performing on stage. A subtitle to the image read "From Dixieland to Kinseyland" in referring to the sexuality of his gyrating movements. Text of the article served the reader with mental images of swooning, hysterical teens, and like most of the West German press underscored his influence on "the behaviors and worship habits of teenage girls." It also painted the majority of Elvis's fans as delinquents.[48] Still, this perception did not hold true for all Germans. Renate Sabulsky remembers how as a young girl growing up in a small town north of Frankfurt in the 1950s she eagerly tuned in to the Armed Forces radio broadcasts to try to catch the latest popular American music. Her parents were more than indulgent than most, and her mother occasionally enjoyed listening to the music along with her daughter. For Renate's family, the American popular culture, music and movies, were "so wonderful." They "admired the culture" and saw it as a window into another world.[49] In parallel, the marriage of Hollywood and contemporary music had a similar effect on the German public.

The 1956 release of the film *Rock Around the Clock*, starring the music of Bill Haley and the Comets, precipitated a wave of youth riots in both the U.S. and Europe. At first, the European Motion Picture Service, which had the responsibility for advertising and airing films through the Milcom theaters, advertised that "the beat is infectious and old timers as well as hepcats should be pleased with bouncey [sic] tunes such as *See You Later Alligator* and the title song."[50] But within months, the news print began to tell a different, contrasting story. A full page spread in *Stars and Stripes*, which carried photos of both Bill Haley and Elvis included a noted psychiatrist's opinion that rock and roll was a "communicable disease" and that "it appeals to adolescent insecurity … it is cannibalistic and tribalistic [sic]."[51] The article also mentioned a number of youth riots that occurred during the film's showing in Sweden, West Germany, England, France, Japan, and Brazil. A separate *Stars and Stripes* piece also made Milcom members aware of rioting in Norway, "Rock and Roll Riots Jolt Oslo after Film."[52]

Overall, however, Milcom attitudes were not alarmist and appeared to remain more balanced than those of the Germans. The same article that criticized the violent youth reaction also noted an authority who admitted that rock and roll was "one the few permitted forms" of sexual expression and "that's a good thing in a society which allows young people so little self-expression anyway."[53] A different piece in *Stars and Stripes* featured a response by popular bandleader Sammy Kaye, who responded to an earlier criticism that rock and roll was a "communicable disease" by noting that it was "as harmless as the Lindy Hop of the 1930s."[54] Even actor Ronald Reagan, an officer of the Screen Actors Guild, weighed in exclaiming, "The right of the movie industry to express itself is tied in with free speech." He then added that success in films was impossible unless "the audience has an emotional experience."[55] In the same *Stars and Stripes* article a psychiatrist testified he "doubted that movies contributed to a recent increase in sexual crimes among juveniles."[56]

Letters to *Stars and Stripes* editor reflected direct responses by Milcom members. One, penned by a Milcom parent, sought to "point out the high morals and character of the teenagers within the [American] zone," and opined that the juvenile delinquency rate for Milcom teens "compares favorably" with the stateside rate.[57] Another, from a reader in the Kaiserslautern Milcom responded to a criticism of "teen-age music being trash" by doubting that the critic "had the pleasure of listening to all of my generation's music."[58] Still another reader responded that any critic "may not care for popular music but, on the other hand, how many of us go for that long-hair stuff."[59]

Throughout the tempest, AFN radio continued to play Jazz and rock and roll music and included the programming of a "disc show known as *Teentime Tunetime*."[60] As Neil Albaugh, a part-time DJ who worked the show recalls, "the show featured school news, anything of interest that was happening in the local community that would be of interest to Frankfurt High School Students. Things such as the scores of football or basketball games." Most important, "music was a big attraction of *Teentime*. We had a huge choice of music but, of course, we played the latest rock & roll that had come over from the US. *Lost in the Jungle* was a particular favorite because of the line "meanwhile, back in the States." The music was key to attracting a young German audience too."[61] In contrast to Milcom opinions of the effects of popular American culture the German reaction from some quarters appeared harsher.

Through the early 1950s the arrival of "American young rebel movies," such as *The Wild One* (1953) with Marlon Brando, and *Blackboard Jungle* (1955) with Sidney Poitier, served to exacerbate the concerns of German parents and elites about American influences. When the showing of *Rock Around the Clock* [*Ausser Rand und Band*], which was aired in some Milcom theaters, caused widespread rioting in a number of German cities in September 1956, the response by some was to condemn the consumption of American popular culture, especially music and film. After the riots, a distraught West German parliamentarian announced that the teens "modeled their behavior word for word, picture for picture after the American movie *The Wild One*."[62] For the Germans there seemed to be a disconcerting link between "consumption, femininity, lower-class behavior, and African-American culture."[63] The authorities were most concerned however, because rock and roll and American popular culture "seemed to undermine the ideal nuclear families of restrained male breadwinner protectors and asexual female caretakers," roles that they deemed were essential for a postwar West German recovery.[64]

Other types of contemporary American films that aired in European and Milcom theaters received mixed reviews. One public survey describing the early postwar arrival of Hollywood productions in West Germany claimed that, "American films accounted for only 14.7 percent of those on the top-ten list [in Germany] in the 1950s."[65] The first film to rank high, but only at number two, was the blockbuster melodrama *From Here to Eternity* [*Verdammt in alle Ewigkeit*]. According to the survey, Germans preferred European productions within three particular genres: "Heimat films (sentimental stories with regional settings), period films, and musicals based on operettas or filled with pop music."[66] Preferences and survey results aside, opportunities to view American films still attracted many Germans who harbored a curiosity about the nation across the Atlantic and the people who populated the Milcoms.

That attraction was evident. At a time before the Berlin Wall and strictly regulated check points, when the border between East and West Berlin was more porous than outside the city, Western authorities aired American films and provided an open invitation for viewing.[67] In July 1950 alone, more than 8,000 East Germans accepted the offer and crossed over to view them.[68] Again, in February 1953, thousands more crossed over when the HICOG provided an open invitation. The features shown were *Night and Day* (1946) and *Johnny Belinda*

(1948), two dated films that were popular in America.[69] The results of a survey claimed "East Germans like the same kind of movies as Americans."[70] A subsequent article appearing in *Stars and Stripes* quoted a German pastor in Frankfurt enthusiastically exclaiming, "American music and movies are two powerful instruments in promoting understanding between our two peoples."[71] Milcoms also made the most of the attraction and often made a point of showing American films during open houses at military facilities and as part of the schedule for annual German-American week activities.[72] Although the availability of films in theaters and Milcoms attracted many Germans it does not suggest a ready, or wide, acceptance. Rather, it suggests a fascination with a characteristic of popular culture they associated with the American way of life.

Although West Germans were attracted to many American films, which the Milcoms made particularly accessible, interpreting their impact on German culture is complicated.[73] Some German viewers remained critical of American films. Their comments reflected a range of charges. One survey conducted in June 1951, by the American magazine *Ladies' Home Journal*, discovered that German youth felt "Most of your [American] movies are just propaganda to sell your way of life" and that they were "superficial and lacked depth," although they admired the "technical excellence."[74] A HICOG survey conducted in spring 1953 reported that 78 percent of West Germans replied, "They liked German films best," although American films had "a favorable influence on the German population." They also registered an unfavorable impression of Westerns and gangster films.[75] A decade later, *Stars and Stripes* reported that West Germans were still clinging to the feeling that American films "contained too much propaganda," but added that "to judge from the movies all people in the United States are criminals" and that they had gained an "unfavorable impression of the treatment of Negroes in America."[76] This last comment suggests that it also contributed to the lens that Germans used to study and interpret Milcom members' prevalent racial attitudes and behaviors.[77]

Still, American film remained central to the complicated German-American cultural discourse during the first three postwar decades. Milcom theaters continued to reflect American attitudes during the 1950s and early 1960s through films such as *Copper Canyon* and *Fort Osage*, which depicted rugged Western individualism, and *Sound Off* and *My Son, John*, which were looks at the military draft and communism during the time of the Korean War.[78] Other film offerings at the PX theaters included *The Bashful Elephant* and *One, Two, Three*. The former was the desperate story of an escape attempt from behind the Iron Curtain, and the latter was a light-hearted look at American capitalism and commercialism in occupied West Berlin. The second film, which starred James Cagney, was full of quick-witted criticisms of Americans' haughty attitudes and excesses, as well as the comic failures of communism. It stands in evidence however, that Americans could laugh at themselves and possessed at least a vague awareness of how others might see them.[79]

Regardless of attitudes and criticisms of American films, Milcom members continued to pack into the PX theaters during the early postwar years, validating film's central place in America's leisure culture and its role in shaping an American identity. Published figures from the Motion Picture Section of EUCOM Special Services reflected attendance numbers averaging well over 200,000 with a high of 785,040 for the month of August 1949.[80] Influenced by film's popularity with the Americans and its availability through presentations by the HICOG, *Amerika Häuser* and Milcoms, the attraction of Hollywood productions grew among West Germans. They rode the cultural wave in great numbers and began flocking to newly opened theaters. Published figures for 1951 reflect that well over 12 million Germans witnessed showings in Frankfurt's movie houses compared to only 5.4 million before the war in 1935.[81]

These perceptions about film content, criticisms and censorship suggest that although American films collectively opened a window for audiences to interpret their contemporary society, West German viewers applied a guarded judgment that forestalled a rush to full acceptance of this aspect of American popular culture. In that context, the Milcoms, which stood at the boundary between the two cultures, afforded the Germans a convenient and unique opportunity to cross the figurative border, and not rely solely on official events sponsored by the HICOG authorities, to catch a glimpse through the camera's lens of the American character. As a result, West Germans were better able to control the depth of American popular culture's penetration into their own, and recognize those aspects of it they wished to resist or accommodate.

Dates	Attendance
February 5, 1948	205,150
March 17, 1948	228,330
August 20, 1949	785,040
December 6, 1949	204,441
March 2, 1950	206,722
June 1, 1950	217,728
June 6, 1950	206,573

Table 2.1: European Command Movie Attendance. Reflects ticket receipts of Milcom members as well as guests. The higher attendance rate for August 1949 is attributable to the increase in number of showings. For example, the numbers of showings for March 1948 were 1,289 35mm films and 530 16mm films. By comparison, in August 1949 the numbers of showings were 4,197 35mm films and 2,408 16mm films. This increase coincides with greater demands by American personnel for popular films. (Various editons of *Stars and Stripes*, 1948–1950).

Aside from film, another imprint of American culture arrived in the form of the printed word. Prior to, and after the war, the Council on Books in Wartime, under the aegis of the U.S. military's Psychological Warfare Branch, orchestrated the distribution of "overseas editions" of many popular novels. Bound in plain cream-colored covers and bearing an image of the Statue of Liberty emblazoned in red ink on the front, titles included such works as *Men of Science in America* by Bernard Joffe, *Benjamin Franklin* by Carl van Doren, and *GI Joe* by Ernie Pyle.[82] In addition, each edition carried an acerbic notice on the lower front cover that read, "This edition of an American book is made available in various countries only until normal free publishing, interrupted by Axis aggression, can be reestablished."[83]

Occupation authorities made these works available to the German public as well as German POWs. During the early postwar years they issued more than 15 million copies to American soldiers and they found an eager German audience as well. Between 1945 and 1953, a special military unit located in the Bad Nauheim Milcom translated at least 341 titles into German. These included works by authors such as Hemingway, London, Steinbeck, Dos Passos, and Sandberg. The unit focused on books that communicated an impression of the American way of life and eschewed those that, in their estimation, carried communist or leftist messages.[84]

In addition to the Council's Overseas Editions, many other works flowed from commercial publishing houses in the U.S. and found wide distribution in Milcom and German bookstores. These arrived in the form of paperbacks, a wholly new concept in Germany. Accepted in America since before the war, the cultural innovation of the *Taschenbücher* [paperbacks] gained warm acceptance by the West Germans. Publishers and distributors there agreed that "the cheap book series certainly have [made] an important contribution."[85] Paperbacks that were less expensive than hard cover editions were the answer to satisfying the reading needs of an economically depressed populace and "making good literature accessible," especially to the youth.[86] In this one instance both Germans and Americans shared an incontestable cultural thread that was manifest also in every Milcom bookstore.[87]

An effective mode that American officials employed to distribute all these works was another innovation, the bookmobile. They operated both out of the Milcoms and through the system of *Amerika Häuser* [America Houses]. As *Stars and Stripes* noted, in March 1948, at least six mobile library vans were operating out of the Wiesbaden Milcom offering 250,000 volumes, in English and German, to the surrounding communities.[88] By 1953 there were at least 20 bookmobiles in operation, some in remote areas. In one case, during a six month period, the bookmobiles were able to service over 38,000 German customers living in small villages within the British zone near the border of Soviet-occupied Germany.[89]

Aside from the bookmobiles, the libraries within individual *Amerika Häuser* facilities provided another outlet for Germans to obtain access to American works. Each of the 26 libraries contained an average of 20,000 titles including fiction, non-fiction, and technical works.[90] The purpose of these efforts was to open the doors to U.S. culture and deflect the myth that "the U.S. is a mad mélange of lady wrestlers, lecherous Wall Street tycoons and dope-driven jazz fiends."[91] Just as important, there was an ongoing effort within the *Amerika Häuser* to engage speakers from the Milcoms to offer discussions on various aspects of American life and culture to German customers.[92]

By the mid to late 1950s, American literature also found its way into German magazines, which were making a postwar resurgence. They offered the readers a survey of unfamiliar aspects of American society through various authors: views of racial problems (James Baldwin and Ralph Ellison), Jewish voices (Saul Bellow, Philip Roth), the beat generation (Jack Kerouac, Allen Ginsberg), and the American South (William Faulkner, Truman Capote). These stories conveyed an understanding that although America was a model of modernization there remained inherent social problems and consequences. For example, Faulkner's novel, *As I Lay Dying*, exposed the traditional and persistent racial inequities of life in the American South. As a reviewer in *Der Spiegel* noted, Faulkner "relentlessly pushes the American tragedy."[93] In the broader context, German reviewers celebrated "America's contribution to world literature: the short story," and its role in telling the story of American life.[94] The reception of these stories was generally warm. This suggests, that at its best, this exposure offered the West Germans a better understanding of the people living behind the gates and walls of the Milcoms. At its worst, the literature was yet another example of the American cultural hegemony in Europe that took advantage of an early postwar publishing void to condition West German minds to the American way of life.

The collective criticisms of American mass culture, films, literature, music, and consumer goods were echoes of those that began in the early postwar years. German sociologist and philosopher Theodor W. Adorno first registered his agitation in this regard upon his return to his homeland in 1949 from wartime exile in the United States.[95] Disgusted by the apparent effects of commercial American culture on his native society, he and other elites and intellectuals called for a resistance to the prurient tendencies of the German masses. The result was a blossoming of "Goethe Societies," along with the founding of the Cultural League for the Democratic Renewal of Germany, to bring renewed interest to traditional cultural venues. Still, some Germans lamented, "We have lost possession of our *Heimat*."[96] This was a reaction to the perception that traditional social structures were not strong enough to inoculate the populace against the spreading infection of "*Amerikanismus*" [American cultural imperialism], much of which seeped out of the Milcoms. For many Germans that feeling of helplessness completed their "perceptions of the U.S. as the homeland of cultural Philistinism, aesthetic vulgarity, and base popular tastes."[97] This was a popular understanding based on the evaluation that there were two types of culture: *ernste Kultur* [serious culture] and *Unterhaltungskultur* [entertainment culture]. Within that interpretation, German culture represented the first, and all American culture, the second, was little more than a "relentless onslaught of commercialized vulgarity and meretricious mindlessness."[98] In time, as accommodations evolved, many of the feelings of hostility and resistance toward American culture, which lasted at least a decade into the Milcom presence, would melt away.

By the late 1950s and early 1960s, West German attitudes toward the brand of popular culture exhibited by the Milcoms began to soften as it gained wider acceptance. Those changes arrived coincidentally with the period of economic recovery known as the *Wirtschaftswunder* [economic miracle].[99] A key catalyst driving that resuscitation was material consumption. As West Germans began to produce and consume more their acceptance of Western popular culture increased. The result was two-fold: a muting of previous criticisms of the impact of American popular culture, particularly on youthful rebelliousness and the inculcation of consumption as a new German cultural characteristic. This change presented a new bridge across the boundary between the West German and American cultures and would affect how Germans viewed themselves.[100]

Jazz was one example of this new dynamic. Between 1956 and 1962, it continued to join with rock 'n' roll as a powerful influence on postwar German culture, and with the changed political atmosphere both gained in popularity. This revival of the previously eschewed American cultural musical forms gained shape in the Milcom service club system that provided opportunities to perform for both American and German groups. During this period, *Stars and Stripes* frequently carried announcements of scheduled performances, which the U.S. military often included in the list of Milcom open-houses and German-American week activities. These were popular with local Germans who flocked to the Milcoms to watch the VII [7th] Army Jazz Band perform at Frankfurt, the VII Corps Army Band give a Jazz concert at Patch Barracks, or the U.S. Air Force's first Jazz festival in Wiesbaden, which featured several bands.[101] German Jazz clubs, once silenced by Nazi repression and previously criticized by conservatives, soon began reappearing in major cities and would remain as part of the new, modern West Germany.[102]

Another example of the change in attitudes that made Jazz more acceptable was the renewed interest in consumer wealth that followed on the heels of economic revival. By the mid–1950s West Germany began experiencing a strong economic resurgence orchestrated by Ludwig Erhard, then serving as Minister of Economic Affairs under Chancellor Adenauer. Central to that was his promulgation of the ideas of "consumer freedom" and economic enterprise as basic and inalienable rights. For the West German people it heralded an attitude of *Wohlstand für alles* [prosperity for all]. Those who suffered through the deprivations of war now sought the material comforts associated with the Americans and their way of life. Paradoxically, while many West Germans groused that the imprint of American culture and consumerism was corrupting their culture, through material goods and low culture, it was those same things which became the object of their desires.[103]

Still, these types of feelings do not suggest that increased affluence in West Germany during the 1950s and 1960s was a step toward greater "Americanization." The German housewife and homeowner adapted and adopted the consumerist tenet within a framework of consumption patterns that sometimes contrasted with their Milcom neighbors.[104] Germans used cash to make purchases and considered credit an unwanted stigma, unlike Americans. They also demanded durable goods, bought items for performance not prestige, thought that items should be *preiswert* [price worthy] and believed that obtaining goods that were previously unavailable signaled a return to purchasing patterns indicative of a return to a normal life.

If the U.S. typified a modern consumer society in the 1950s, then the Milcoms served as a display window for its goods. The cars, the radios, the televisions, and especially the appliances the Milcom family enjoyed became the standard for the newly affluent West German citizen. As their resources accrued so did their desire for remodeling and modernizing their homes, or installing an "American-style" kitchen with the latest appliances. Special events and associations often reinforced this aim. Groups such as the German-American Club of Heidelberg held a special importance in bringing together hundreds of German and American women who shared in activities and visited one another's homes. It was during these types of visits that the Milcom home was often on display. It was also in that spirit that in 1958 the organizers of the Heidelberg Housewives Fair invited the American Women's Club of Heidelberg to participate by providing a display. Upon completion the exhibit contained a typical American kitchen and living room, each fully equipped with new appliances and furniture. A cooking demonstration, in that American kitchen, by Milcom husbands was part of the event. The Lord Mayor of Heidelberg thanked the Americans for "demonstrating to German housewives the many technical skills employed in the U.S.," particularly in the kitchen. The husbands' culinary proficiency together with the modern kitchen gadgets made a deep impression on West German women.[105]

For many Germans the issue of material wealth was a complicated one during these years of economic recovery. Some, who lived in rural areas, always lacked access to consumer goods. When Americans began occupying their towns and villages exposure to consumer wealth arrived as a welcome contrast to their postwar subsistence level existence and so generated new consumerist desires.[106] Germans living in urban areas during the Weimar interwar period however, were already familiar with the ideas of mass consumption and consumerism, particularly through outlets such as the department store. For them it was a matter of waiting for the revival of their own manufacturing base, which eventually came on the wings of the postwar *Wirtschaftswunder*.[107] Still, most Germans were anxious to embrace the ideas of consumer wealth and mass consumption as vehicles of modernity that would convey them out of the ruins of their postwar economy. This suggests that at times they may have exhibited a range of emotions from jealousy to impatience as they experienced the dawning of a new consumerist society similar to that modeled in the Milcoms.[108]

Another notable impact Milcom consumerism had on West German society was the role it played inspiring a dialogue in the public sphere regarding gender roles. In this interpretation, the increased access and availability of material goods helped inspire a sense of empowerment as German manufacturers structured new consumer groups with women in mind as they increasingly became the objects of market research and advertising in the 1950s. This enabled a majority of middle-class West German housewives to enact a form of political engagement through the exercise of a consumerist rationality that included buying, saving, and discernment of worth.[109] In that regard they became more like the Milcom wife who lived in a world of increasing consumer abundance and for whom engagement with consumption was a form of societal citizenship and participation.[110]

As an example for German wives, when the Henkel Corporation resumed its production of the popular *Persil* detergent line during the early postwar years, it was very sensitive to maintaining the quality of its product. As the chief production officer noted, German housewives "are particularly critical [and will] register any variation in the effectiveness of a detergent with the precision of a seismograph."[111] As a marketing scheme, the corporation also asked over 500 housewife-consumers to provide their hints as how to best clean with the product. This type of episode with *Persil* permitted West German women to enjoy some degree of consumerist leverage. As consumerism was intrinsic to the definition of American economic prowess and abundance, which the Milcoms readily displayed, so it was with the reframing of postwar West German society, which was quick to accommodate it.

By comparison to previous generations, West German teens and young adults had, since the occupation period, already embraced American popular culture and consumerism. In the early postwar years, young Germans had already crossed the border between cultures and found a common ground with their counterparts in the Milcoms. There, the symbols, codes, and currency of consumerism which included music, clothes, cars, comic books, movies, chewing gum, cigarettes, and the ubiquitous Coca-Cola had already shaped their world. As those person-to-person contacts continued there was a blending at the edges of the two cultures born of familiarity and convenience. One such distinct derivative of that blending and cultural interpenetration at the grass-roots level, which gained influence over the years, was the creolization of language.

That hybridization, which took place between German teens and American Milcom members, was however, only one of many contact points where that cultural metamorphosis occurred.[112] By the early 1950s thousands of German civilians worked within the Milcom structure in a variety of occupations. As noted in the previous chapter, many provided service in American households, maintained buildings and grounds, and others worked in PX facilities such as barbershops, bowling alleys and movie theaters. In addition, they filled positions in the U.S. government-owned and operated recreation facilities as ski instructors, tour guides, hotel staff, and maintenance personnel. Thousands of local nationals supported the U.S. military in paid positions as maintenance and logistic technicians as well as security personnel. Still other Germans filled numerous bureaucratic positions on Milcom staffs as community and military liaisons, and travel and housing coordinators. Together with the spread of American popular culture, including consumer goods and movies, AFN radio and later television, and even the spread of print media, this thick presence of local nationals, who easily crossed that permeable boundary between cultures, suggests that the creolization of language was an inevitable and natural occurrence.

From this cultural crucible a new community of language emerged with its own lexicon, which users cobbled together from "pseudo loan words" and direct borrowings.[113] Some examples of those loan words from the 1950s and early 1960s are *"Flutlicht"* for floodlight, *"Schwartzmarket"* for black market, and *"Familienplanung"* for family planning.[114] In the consideration of direct borrowings, using original American words was easier, especially since many American idioms were already in widespread use throughout postwar Europe. In this context, the word "teenager" had already infiltrated the German language by the 1950s, as did "twens," a reference to twenty-year olds. That list also included the following imported words to the contemporary German language: Jazz, weekend, blues, gangster, chewing gum, and supermarket. All these words came into lingual exchange as American popular culture spread with greater acceptance, consumerism gained momentum, and Germans integrated themselves into the structure of the Milcoms.

Moreover, Milcom members often adopted German words and phrases for their own usage and sometimes blended them into English sentences for added color. An example from the contemporary music charts was the song "Danke Schön," which American singer Wayne Newton made popular in 1963. The stylized English lyrics include the repeated verses "Danke Schoen, Darling, Danke Schoen," and "My heart says, Danke Schoen."[115]

The exchange of language could also have unfortunate consequences. Such was the case of one young German mother who "unleashed a stream of invective" toward an American GI she thought was driving recklessly. The occupation authorities considered this a criminal offense and brought her before the local Hesse Military Government summary court. As the judge sentenced her to 30 days' imprisonment "for insulting a member of the U.S. Armed Forces" the young women offered in her defense "she had learned the expressions from conversations overheard on the street and had no idea of their true meaning." The judge suspended the sentence.[116]

In most cases this creolization and fusion of language provided an informal, yet functional, bridge across the cultural boundary between American Milcom members and the Germans. Eventually, many of the words, particularly those of popular culture and in the arena of consumer exchange, gained a globalized status with the spreading of American culture and technology. But central to that community of language was the network of Milcoms that facilitated people-to-people contact and the development of a hybrid language. Still the cultural imprint was deep and since the beginning of its study by German lexicographers in 1945 the collection of words has exploded.[117]

In addition to the evolution of hybrid language, the volume of American dependents having some degree of German language skills also increased during postwar decades. The number of family members who were German, together with DODDS classes, classes at post education centers, and the efforts made by various organizations, such as wives' clubs, to teach the basics of German did contribute to an increased number of Milcom members with some level of language proficiency.[118]

One interesting example was the 4th Infantry Division stationed at Fort Hood, Texas. Prior to their scheduled deployment to Germany in 1957 the soldiers and family members of the entire unit underwent an innovative language training program. The division commander had international traffic signs erected throughout the post and implemented a nine-month-long language instruction program for service-members and their dependents. The intention was "to familiarize personnel with basic German words and phrases and give a background on which to build a better understanding of the German language and people."[119] Peri-

Sprechen Sie Deutsch?

NOTE: Words in brackets [ ] are not expressed in the German. Words in parentheses ( ) help to explain the German but are not necessary in English. Words in single quotation marks ' ' are word-for-word equivalents.

zu Hause (das Haus)	TSUH HAUze (dass HAUS)	at house
Ist Ihre Schwester zu Hause?	ist ihre SHVESter tsuh hauze?	Is your sister at home?
einen	Ainen	one
Vielleicht hat sie einen.	fihlaicht hatt ZIH ainen.	Perhaps she has one.
einige	Ainige	some
Ihrem	IHrem	her
Ja, ich glaube, sie hat einige in ihrem Zimmer.	YAH, ich GLAUbe zih hatt Ainige inn ihrem TSIMMer.	Yes, I think she has some in her room.
Radiergummi (der)	rahDIHR-gummih (dehr)	eraser
Vielleicht gibt sie Ihnen auch einen Radiergummi.	fihlaicht gipt zih ihnen aukh ainen rah-DIHRgummih.	Maybe she'll give you an eraser, too.

EDITOR'S NOTE: *The daily German lessons are taken from the basic course in Spoken German prepared by the editorial staff of U.S. Armed Forces Institute (USAFI).*

German Language Column. This is an example of the column that regularly appeared for years in the *Stars and Stripes*. Source: *Stars and Stripes*, July 11, 1954, 4, with permission.

odically, throughout the duty day, sergeants also quizzed soldiers on words and phrases using language flash cards. Most of the unit was enthusiastic to learn.

Charles Charnquist provides another contemporary example of an initiative to inculcate German language and customs. As a 24 year old draftee and college graduate his commander appointed him "troop information and education specialist for the company" six weeks prior to their deployment to Germany. As he recalls:

> My first and primary duty for nearly two months was to conduct classes for company personnel on a wide variety of topics related to peacetime duty in Germany. To prepare, I attended a whole week of division-sponsored lectures, including history about the area where we would be stationed, cultural mores, travel and travel restrictions, peculiar laws of the land, and most importantly about actions that would foster (or negatively impact) German-American relations. I taught a class a day for two weeks. Amazing how attentive a bunch of GIs could be. It was evident to me then that many of the guys were looking forward to the experience as something far different than a military deployment.[120]

Stars and Stripes also contributed to the language effort by printing a regular short column titled "*Sprechen Sie Deutsch?*" featuring basic German terms and phrases in an attempt to

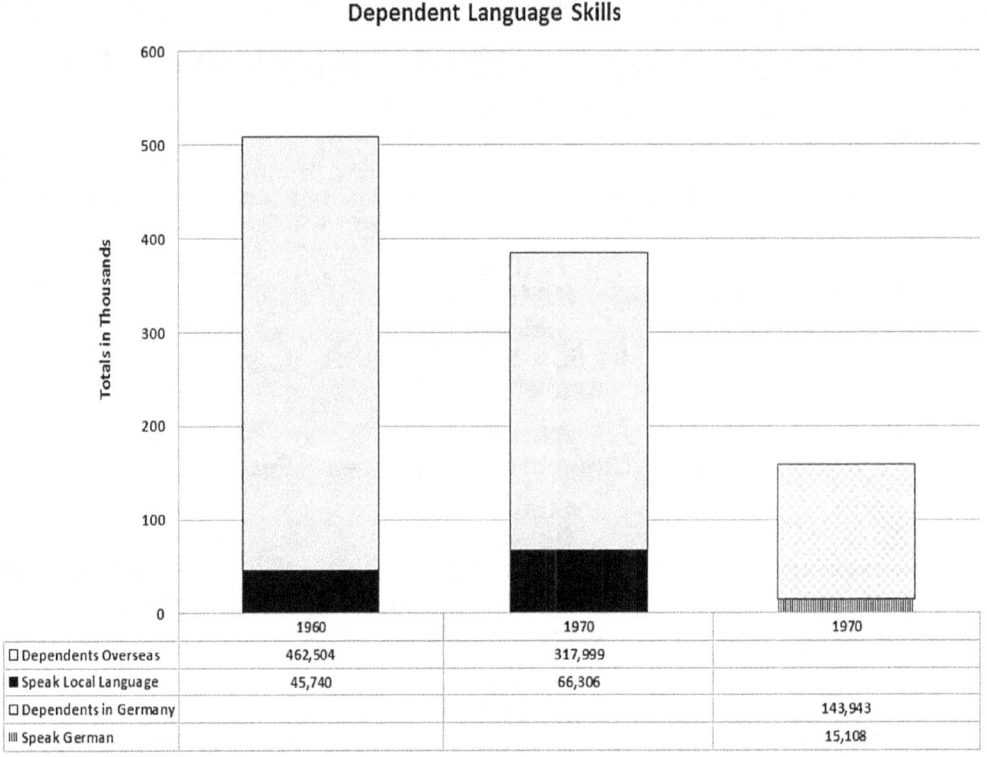

Dependent Language Skills. This chart reveals the small percentages of American dependents in the overseas Milcoms who possessed German and local language skills. Data includes all language skill levels of speakers ages 14 and above. Column three for 1970 represents the only known available data for German speaking dependents. Data source: All data collected from U.S. Census Bureau for years indicated.

inspire interest in learning the language and culture. AFN followed suit and aired a short, 15-minute daily show with the same title and similar content. All these initiatives contributed to the building of cultural bridges through a better understanding of language, as well as customs, although it did vary by individual and community. Some Americans were eager to learn a new language and culture while others were more reticent. Still, few military personnel and family members received any organized language training prior to their arrival in Germany and many neglected opportunities to learn once they arrived in country. This lack of language skills, or effort to acquire them, remained a consistent criticism from the German perspective.

Between 1946 and the mid–1960s, the influences of American culture and consumerism flowed across the boundary between the Milcoms and their German hosts. Although they made an impact, the Germans remained discerning observers and applied the rubrics of *ernste Kultur* and *Unterhaltungskultur* to reject those aspects they felt were too coarse and unappealing. By the late 1960s, and into the following decades, new generations of West Germans continued to trade along the border, making accommodations to accept certain aspects of American culture and consumerism but developing pockets of rejection for other dimensions that were too conspicuously different. As American popular culture changed during that period it also telegraphed shifting ideas about how Americans thought of themselves with the Milcoms serving as barometers of that change.

Three

Religion, Race, Stereotyping and the Media (1946–1967)

The Place of Religion in the Milcom

For President Eisenhower and his conservative evangelist allies, religious belief remained central to traditional American ideals. It was an essential characteristic that separated the West from the communist East. In that context, the President was determined to confirm religion's place among the tenets of Americanism and so focused on the Pledge of Allegiance. Understanding that the flag salute did not contain any reference to God, he supported a congressional action to insert the words "under God" into the pledge. On June 15, 1954, *Stars and Stripes* offered its Milcom readers a front page that proclaimed, "Deity Now Part of Flag Pledge."[1] As Eisenhower observed, "in this way we are reaffirming the transcendence of religious faith in America's heritage and future."[2] Earlier that year, in comments during an American Legion radio-television broadcast, he casually remarked to the audience "there are no atheists in foxholes."[3] But in reality the atheists were already there.

By the time Eisenhower had spoken, some Americans were already in the process of removing God from the classroom and increasing the distance between religion and government. This offered a paradoxical interpretation of America's religious underpinnings and its relationship to the separation of church and state. A series of high profile cases reflected the ongoing debate.[4] Milcom members followed those decisions in articles posted by *Stars and Stripes*. The June 18, 1963, headlines rang out "Court Rules Out School Prayer, Bible Reading" and included Justice Tom C. Clark's majority opinion. His comments read that "The place of religion is an exalted one, achieved through a long tradition of reliance on the home, the church and the inviolable citadel of the individual heart and mind," but he added, "We have come to recognize through bitter experience that it is not within the power of the government to invade that citadel."[5] The decisions had both critics and supporters. Among the critics were some in Congress who during House hearings on religious exercises in public schools exclaimed that prayers in school were as "American and as universal as a taste for apple pie or ice cream or watermelon."[6] Supporters like atheist activist Madalyn Murray claimed, "Christianity has been around for 2,000 years, and we are no more moral now than before. If anything we are more beastly."[7]

When the discontinuance of prayers in DODDS classrooms followed, Milcom members weighed in on the debate. Letters to *Stars and Stripes* editor reveal a split regarding the place of religion in the public realm. One writer from the Schwabisch Gmünd community charged that "By officially allowing school prayers, or setting aside national days of prayer, or publicly broadcasting Bible readings … the government is implying an official advocacy for religion." Another from the Ludwigsburg Milcom asked, "Why is there so much criticism of Madalyn Murray O'Hair who, in a very real sense, is a true defender of freedom and democracy."[8] Contrasting those was a letter from the Amberg community, which noted, "Mrs. O'Hair has only succeeded in momentarily delaying the spread of Christianity while also bringing to a halt the quest for true democratic freedom in our country."[9] A letter from a concerned Knellingen Milcom writer asked, "Should she get her way, will she next have the Pledge of Allegiance to the Flag changed because of the phrase, 'one nation under God?'"[10]

Even among those Americans for whom spirituality was an *axis mundi* there was discord. In a terse *Stars and Stripes* article, Methodist Bishop G. Bromley Oxnam, head of the New York area, claimed, "American liberty is threatened by the Roman Catholic Church as well as by communism."[11] Speaking at an annual Minneapolis Baptist Convention, the head of that denomination declared similar concerns calling Catholics and atheists equal threats to the United States.[12] Although the administration and conservative evangelicals dedicated a great deal of energy and thought to ensure that religion remained central to any definition of Americanism, the conflicting opinions about the influence of faith and its place revealed complicated interpretations suggesting that aspect of the tenet was anything but uniform. In that same context, feelings about race offered yet another contested ground.

By the mid–1950s, many West Germans, particularly those living in the more rural regions such as the Rhineland Palatinate, were studying the American presence through a critical lens. Already exposed to the excesses of consumerism and the extremes of popular culture, its inherent racial inequities also distressed them.[13] This perception came into clearer focus through exposure to contemporary American films, which generally depicted black characters in degrading ways. But it was principally through the behavior of the majority white GIs toward their African-American compatriots, the German women who socialized with them and the Jewish owners of bars and *Gasthauses* that served blacks.[14] Thomas Ward, who served as an African-American soldier in Bamberg, West Germany, relates a confirming anecdote. Searching for a nightclub one evening "he learned firsthand that he was not welcome in the white GI section of town…. He narrowly escaped an ensuing bar fight with the help of a waiter who directed him to … the street where African-American soldiers hung out."[15] As social histories of that time note, all German establishments in the vicinity of American Milcoms, that were exclusive to American GIs, catered to different races. Black and white soldiers socialized in separate locations and avoided contact with one another.[16] As Thomas Ward discovered, the exchanging of expletives between groups as well as physical confrontations were "not the exception but the rule."[17]

By the early 1950s integration on post and in all Federal facilities was well under way and for the most part was an expeditious and efficient process. Lois Chazaud, who worked as a civilian Special Services representative in the Wertheim Milcom in 1953, recalls her impression of the mandated integration of military units:

> Wertheim was an all Negro base and the desegregation of the troops began almost immediately. Troops and equipment moved out, troops and equipment moved in, and by week's end Wertheim was a fully integrated base. The greatest effect this movement of troops and equipment had was on the inhabitants of the town of Wertheim. The local population had lived with the base since the end of World War II, and known only Negro soldiers. Many of the townspeople surmised America must be largely Negro. An interesting observation

was in general the Germans harbored very little racial prejudice. Having not been reared from childhood to view Negroes differently, they were very accepting.[18]

But the physical integration of units did not automatically guarantee acceptance of racial differences. Lois Chazaud also remembers challenges she faced as the Director of the Hammelburg Service Club, when conflicts would quickly arise:

> One night a race riot broke out in the pool room between negro soldiers and white sergeants who didn't belong in the Service Club anyway, because they had their own club just for sergeants. The pool room had four beautiful pool tables fully equipped with balls, racks, and chalk. The pool cues hung neatly on wall brackets. The fight escalated and all I could see were dollar signs flashing in my mind's eye. Horrified by the prospect of having to pay to have even one felt pool table cover replaced, I ran into the middle of the fight with arms out in each direction to separate the brawling soldiers and shouted, "Stop right now. Take it outside!" All were so surprised that the fight stopped dead in its tracks. The sergeants slunk out of the club, and the negro soldiers now subdued, praised me for my bravery.[19]

Still, life away from military units and facilities also remained another matter.[20]

Scenes of animosity between white and black soldiers sometimes played out in the streets of German towns and villages, such as the race riot that occurred in 1955 on New Year's Eve in the town of Baumholder.[21] Other conflicts arose in the vicinity of Milcoms and reflected the trajectory of racial incidents occurring in the U.S. at that time. Although reports of local racial conflict in the pages of *Stars and Stripes* or in official reports were sparse, which may suggest a certain degree of news censorship, there was little effort to hide from Milcom members the ugly realities of racial inequality back home.[22] *Stars and Stripes* did consistently carry reports of the gathering energies of the Civil Rights movement in the U.S. curried from the wire services.[23] For example, it presented the unfolding events surrounding the refusal of the University of Alabama to admit a black female student in 1956, and the crisis surrounding the "Little Rock Nine" in September 1957, to its readership, often as front page news.[24]

Regardless how often the leadership in Washington or the military hierarchy attempted to hammer home to the armed services, or broadcast through propaganda, the traditional American ideal of equality, reality cast their efforts in a bitter light. Many white soldiers from the American South were unwilling to support integration during their off-duty time. They understood racial segregation to be an integral part of the American lifestyle not separate from it. Nor did they consider it as a societal anathema. Aside from the bars and the *Gasthaus*, racial tensions often spilled over into relationships with German women. In particular it was the opportunity of black GIs to associate with local white girls that drove most Southern whites and many Northerners to demonstrations of anger.[25]

The births of "*Negerkinder*" exacerbated those existing tensions.[26] By one estimate, of the 95,000 babies born to American-German relationships during the occupation period, 5,000 were mixed-race.[27] The inability of these children's parents to marry because of discouragement by cultural norms, the military hierarchy, or bureaucratic obstacles placed them on the margin of German society. It also rendered them living reminders of the deep racial divide that haunted both German and American society in the early postwar years.[28]

Initiatives that brought progress and gain in racial equality moved against a strong counter current of regional consensus. *Stars and Stripes* carried articles that announced "Negro General Terms Promotion Significant" and celebrated the 1954 landmark Supreme Court decision to desegregate public classrooms in the *Brown v. Board of Education* decision.[29] But other pieces that proclaimed "4 Governors in South Agree to Protest U.S. Order on Segregation" and "Mississippi Maps Fight on Desegregation" proved contrary to those.[30] Within the DODDS schoolrooms, however, there was no segregation. Aside from the Federal mandate that prescribed integration for Milcom classes, the early lack of facilities and space in war-torn Germany obviated the philosophy of "separate-but-equal" and left little room for Jim Crow on the attendance roster. In evidence, archival photographs and yearbooks reveal the smiling faces of racially mixed classes, clubs and after school sports for students who by all outward appearances were living the American ideal.[31]

Although the administration and the State Department worked to spin the early civil rights efforts in a positive light to show improvement and garner international esteem, the reality of life in the U.S. and the Milcoms belied official images of an exceptional America and its commitment to freedom and equality. African-American GIs and their families stationed overseas during the early postwar decades suffered the cruelty of that duality. Compounding their dilemma were the attitudes of some Germans, who cued on the American model of racism to justify their earlier wartime racial prejudices including their attitudes regarding *Rassenschande* [miscegenation]. Reflecting this unfortunate situation was a 1949 cartoon sketch titled "Jim Crow in Germany."[32] It depicts a goose-stepping American soldier marching past a review stand under the gleeful gaze of a character named "Jim Crow." Among the background ruins is a snickering Joseph Stalin, symbolic of the ever present communist gadfly ready to point out America's social foibles.

But in some ways life for African-American GIs could also be pleasant. Some recent studies describe the exhilarating feeling of many black GIs who experienced "a breath of freedom" while living beyond the shadow of stateside segregation.[33] In this context it is interesting to consider William Gardner Smith's early postwar work of historical fiction, *The Last of the Conquerors*, based on his memories of positive experiences as an African American GI in postwar Germany.[34] More widely accepted in that country than in the U.S., particularly by German women, Smith recalled that many black soldiers in Germany experienced what it was like to be treated with deference and amity, and how they felt a great loss when they had to return home. As a contemporary issue of the black journal *Ebony* noted, "Negroes are finding more friendship, more respect and more equality than they would back home—either in Dixie or on Broadway."[35] An article in the same issue recounted how "*fräuleins* sing a favorite tune, '*Madel, Liebst Du Einen Schwarzen Amerikaner*' [Little Girl, Do You Love a Black American?], which best expresses their warm friendship" with their black boyfriends.[36] Although the harsh dictates of segregation remained constant throughout the early postwar years for African American members of the Milcom, both single and married, *Ebony* noted they tried to maintain a positive outlook:

> Despite anti–Negro propaganda spread by some white Americans in Germany and the undemocratic example set by the U.S. Army in delaying the integration of troops in Germany, the Negro soldier has retained his position in the eyes of the women and children of Germany and is rapidly winning over all but the diehard Nazis among the men.[37]

Still, German attitudes towards African-Americans also remained complicated. Many rural communities often maintained traditional views that abjured inter-racial relationships, yet other areas, particularly cities like Berlin were more welcoming.[38] As former Berliner Peter Schulz remembers, any relationship between a German *Fräulein* and an American soldier, white or black, was a good thing. He opines that perhaps they understood that the connection provided access to much desired consumables, or that the GI was a better choice as paramour than a detestable Red Army Bolshevik, the race of the American did not matter. In the eyes of a Berliner, all Americans, white or black, were "protectors" not occupiers, like the Russians. Schulz did note however, that it was the black GIs who were kindest to the children and who "felt most sorry" for their plight.[39]

The racial tensions between Milcom members in West Germany were often extensions of the attitudes that service members, civilians, and their families carried with them overseas. Many were racist by contemporary standards and these attitudes did not easily disappear even with a Presidential order that directed integration of the services and Milcom housing, or a Supreme Court decision that desegregated public schools in the U.S.[40] Political and military elites understood that this fault in the consensus jeopardized America's image abroad and that it undermined a "soft power" approach in the ideological war with the Soviets. They endeavored therefore to mitigate the damage.[41]

One of the earliest techniques employed was orientation training. At the beginning of the occupation period in 1946, the U.S. government produced a film through the Department of the Army's Office of the Chief Signal Officer titled "Teamwork." It focused on "interracial cooperation in the U.S. Army" and featured "White and Negro" troops participating in various wartime activities.[42] These included operations such as the combat landings at Normandy Beach, transporting supplies, and combat support tasks. The script also incorporated several scenes of well-decorated all-black military units in action.[43] The intention of the orientation film was to establish a foundation of racial harmony among recruits and service members deploying overseas with the thought that their collective efforts toward a higher purpose might overcome the challenges of inherent racial inequities. It would also serve as propaganda to deflect charges of discrimination in the military and society by propagandists in the Soviet East.

Another film, *The Occupation Soldier*, also produced in 1946 by the Department of the Army for the War Department, sought to chastise former Nazis for their past actions and indicated that the Americans had arrived to teach the Germans new ways. Ironically, it charged that the Germans must "learn the meaning of freedom and equality," the meaning of "equality before the law," and commit to the "end of discrimination on the grounds of race, creed, or position," all at a time that the U.S. was struggling with the same issues.[44] Although there is no recorded survey of the effectiveness of either of the two films to allay racial tensions, the fact that the military stopped using these types of productions suggests that the elites in Washington realized the inherent hypocrisy they presented. The military did continue however, to broadcast various positive dimensions of the American exceptionalist consensus to the Milcoms through the Big Picture film series that followed, but it avoided any direct commentary on racial inequalities in America.

Another action the EUCOM military command structure took, as an attempt to polish its image on race, was to employ a staff advisor on Negro affairs.[45] Lieutenant Colonel (LTC) Marcus H. Ray, a black Army officer, filled that position.[46] Prior to filling this position Ray had worked for the Secretary of War as a civilian advisor on efforts to integrate the armed services. During that period of time he travelled extensively to bases in the continental U.S. and overseas. At the time, Ray was of the opinion that efforts at integration of units in Europe were lacking and noted to the Secretary that "to accept the racial prejudices of the German people as a reason for non-utilization of the American soldiers who happen to be non-white is to negate the very ideas we have made part of our re-education program in Germany."[47]

Between 1948 and 1950, Ray returned to Europe to work for the EUCOM commander. Here he travelled all of Europe visiting Milcoms and installations to monitor the pulse of

"Negro affairs." Considering the size of the territory, Ray's task seemed herculean and his efforts token at best. Reports of his travels published in *Stars and Stripes* were sporadic and revealed rhetoric that generally supported the prescribed view that equality and fairness were beginning to take hold. An April 1948 article spoke of LTC Ray's appearance at the German-American Club in Stuttgart. In his presentation he assured the crowd that "less than one percent [of blacks] have shown communist leanings."[48] He also noted that they were encouraged by their future prospects, "The American Negro looks forward with confidence, knowing that education and a growth of understanding will bring a realization of the American ideals of equality and social justice."[49] A year later, speaking before a gathering at the *Amerika Haus* in München, he noted, "slavery is still too fresh in the minds of the Negroes for them [blacks] to choose to return to it" by becoming communists.[50]

One of the last articles reporting LTC Ray's activities, in September 1950, included his comments that there were "substantiated reports" of communist attempts to establish "Red cells" at the segregated Negro training school in the Kitzingen Milcom. Also in the body of the text he noted, "EUCOM chiefs had pushed the Army's Negro equality program a long way during the past three years," admitting that "in some cases there was still some friction between Negroes and whites on a social level" but "it can be removed."[51] LTC Ray departed for his next assignment before the end of that year, and the EUCOM Negro Affairs Office closed with his departure. Whether his activities made an impact in the lives of black soldiers and their dependents in Europe and West Germany is uncertain. But during the years he was active his efforts served the command's interests to appear concerned about race relations and equality and to dispel any fears regarding links between the communists and black service members.

Although Milcom members did receive news of the Civil Rights movement in the States as events and incidents occurred, reports of local occurrences during the 1950s and early 1960s remained harder to find. Some contemporary histories suggest that it was a result of some military leaders who influenced the propagation of racial intolerance and failed to take action against this sort of segregation off base.[52] But that is a treatment that offers too narrow an interpretation and arguments exist on both sides of the issue.

A *Stars and Stripes* article from February 1953 presented one of those occasions when leaders did take action. Located at the bottom of an interior page, it detailed how HICOG administrators had fined two owners of a "swank" night club in Stuttgart for their refusal to admit three "U.S. Army Negro officers." After paying the 50 mark fine the proprietors began "admitting Negro personnel."[53] Although it stands as only an isolated example, it also suggests reluctance by American military leaders to act, not necessarily because of personal prejudice. A *Stars and Stripes* article from December 1964 hints at the possible deeper reasoning with the comment that "German laws prohibit discrimination on a racial basis, but they allow German bar owners to select their clientele and to refuse service to anyone they wish."[54] That placed many local commanders in the uncomfortable position of having to interpret the actions and intentions of local establishment owners, something they were ill-prepared to do. As an Army spokesman noted, that situation confronted military leaders "with a ticklish legal problem and as guests in a host country we cannot violate local laws."[55] It suggests that military leaders understood their positions as goodwill ambassadors and were sensitive not to antagonize local authorities.

Still, as some histories note, "many commanders continued to instruct local proprietors to observe the American model of racial segregation" as a way to "preserve the peace" between the races.⁵⁶ These efforts also extended to the military authorities' support of German landlords who refused to rent to blacks. When black soldiers filed complaints about this type of discrimination the military command structure often failed to take any action. The excuse given was that they did not want to challenge the customs and mores of the local German communities in the vicinity of the Milcom. In that context, commanders from the American South generally ignored these issues of racial discrimination and segregation because their inaction was consistent with their interpretation of race within the structure of American society. In the same context however, commanders understood the importance of eliminating points of conflict among their soldiers, on and off post, in order to maintain unit discipline. High ratings on unit commanders' official performance evaluations often depended on it.

A series of articles *Stars and Stripes* offered between 1963 and 1965 hinted at this proclivity toward reticence by the local military leadership. The first piece, titled "Race Tension Slight in U.S. Europe Forces," reported that although military leaders acknowledged that there were "bars, restaurants and clubs where a kind of voluntary segregation" operated, "there is no discrimination among races practiced or condoned in any aspect of military life of the U.S. Army, Europe."⁵⁷ The article did admit, "There are some intangibles that cannot be legislated out of a man's emotions," an off-hand reference to attitudes of some American Southerners.⁵⁸

A year later, an August 1964 issue of *Stars and Stripes* carried a report, regarding contemporary race issues in the Milcom, titled "Army's Race Trouble in Germany Called Small Problem."⁵⁹ Although the article recognized that there were race problems in the military it tended to down-play their impact, attributing the majority of troubles to the "10 per cent of the men in any Army outfit" who "are troublemakers."⁶⁰ Continuing from a positive perspective it also mentioned that the "number of segregated bars [off base] has decreased sharply" (without statistical reference) and that married soldiers and officers lived in "apartment houses where there is racial integration" and few problems.⁶¹ The final paragraphs presented the story of a soldier who filed a complaint of racial prejudice in his unit. The military hierarchy's inspector general investigated the claim but declared it unsubstantiated. The message in the text was clear: the chain of command is quick to respond to any accusation of racial impropriety, but will likely find that none exists. This suggests an effort to deflect any criticism regardless of the source, politicians, the American public, black soldiers, or investigative journalists.

A follow-on article titled "Gains Made in GI Integration in Germany" appeared in January 1965. It echoed the sentiments of the first two pieces and continued to reflect some positive change, although a rubric of comparison was missing from the narrative. It emphasized that "you can go into bars here [Germany] that used to be exclusive and find mixed groups of white and Negro soldiers," but it also admitted, "There are places in Hanau, Frankfurt and Bad Kreuznach where a member of another race is not welcome."⁶² Staff writers for the newspaper crafted the three pieces and each alluded to the reality of racial difficulties, yet none deemed them profound. This suggests that perhaps there was a conscious effort by military and political elites in Washington and Germany to downplay the effects of racism in the Milcoms, as much as possible, in the context of the struggle with the Soviets to win the hearts and minds of the German people.

Some sources also suggest that such half-measures and half-declarations indicated a resistance based on fear that actions on behalf of black soldiers and their family members overseas "would force the military to intercede in the still segregated communities surrounding military bases in the United States, and especially the American South," an action it was hesitant to take.⁶³ While such interpretations are not incorrect, they do not account for factors that were beyond the military's control. For example, in some cases even the integration of schools on military posts in the U.S. was difficult. As of April 1953, twenty-one of sixty-three schools on military installations remained segregated. This was the result of funding agreements made between federal and state governments, who specified that if the state bore most of the operational costs, then the schools must enforce state and local policies.⁶⁴ This indicates that such conditions may have cultivated sensitivity within the culture of military leadership in the U.S., as well as overseas, to refrain from any aggressive policy that might dictate behaviors contradictory to local customs or statutes. This may have included the forced integration of bars, suggesting that concern for local mores may have carried significant consideration and contributed to hesitancy on the part of the military command structure to resolve off-post racial conflicts and inequities.

State	Installation
Alabama (C)	Maxwell Air Force Base
	Craig Air Force Base
Arkansas (S)	Pine Bluff Arsenal (Army)
Florida (C)	MacDill Air Force Base
	Eglin Air Force Base
	Tyndall Air Force Base
	Naval Air Station, Pensacola
	Patrick Air Force Base
Maryland (S)	Andrews Air Force Base
	Naval Air Station, Patuxent
	Naval Powder Factory, Indianhead
Oklahoma (C)	Fort Sill (Army)
Texas (C)	Fort Bliss (Army)
	Fort Hood (Army)
	Fort Sam Houston (Army)
	Randolph Air Force Base
	Reese Air Force Base
	Shepherd Air Force Base
	Lackland Air Force Base
Virginia (C)	Fort Belvoir (Army)
	Langley Air Force Base

Table 3.1: Segregated Dependent Schools, as of April 1953. (C) indicates segregation prescribed by state constitution. (S) indicates segregation prescribed by state statute. All overseas dependent schools were fully integrated. ("Integration of the Armed Forces, 1940–1965," Defense Studies Series, Center of Military History, U.S. Army, Washington, D.C., 1985.)

The positive experiences that some Milcom members had may have also masked racial problems and complicated authorities' understanding of the wider situation. This could also have forestalled decisions by the military hierarchy to take action. For example, Jane Mulvihill,

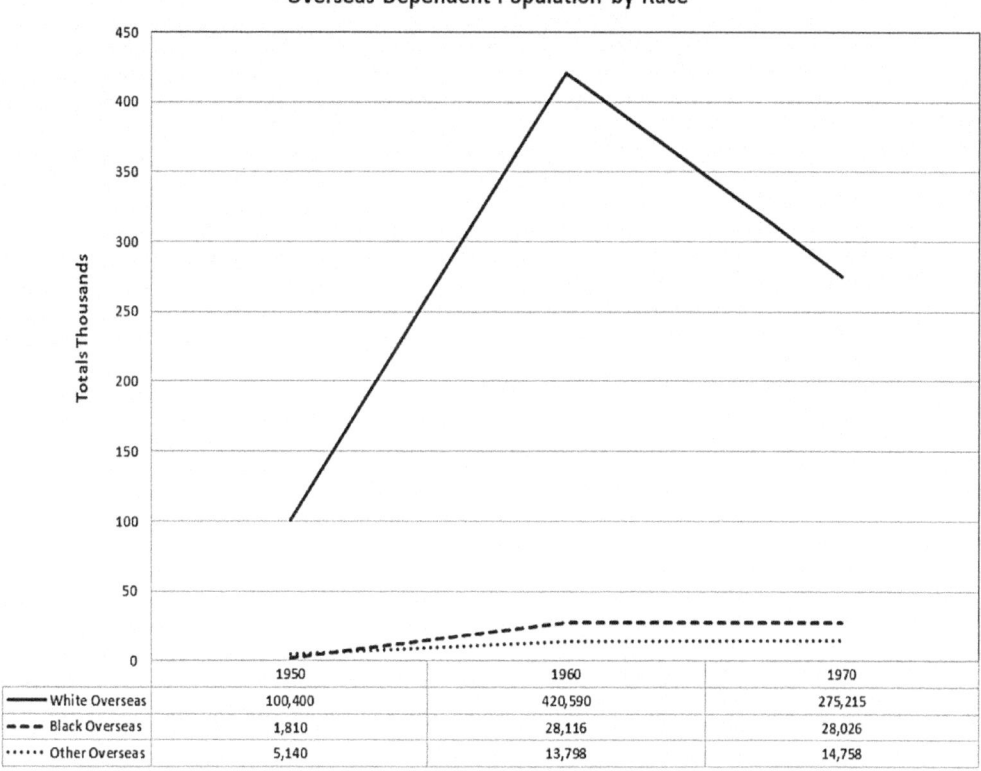

Overseas Dependent Population by Race. For each of the three years measured white dependents comprised the majority. Black dependent numbers consistently measured below the contemporary representative percentage for the U.S. population while the numbers for "others" consistently measured higher. For all years the "Other" category as defined by the U.S. Census Bureau included American Indian, Japanese, Chinese, Filipino and "other races." Data source: U.S. Census Bureau for years shown.

who resided in the Hanau Milcom in 1963, warmly recalls a friendly relationship she had with another American family. Although that family was black, she and the wife "got very close" and "did everything together" including "watching each other's babies."[65] For Jane who grew up in segregated Richmond, Virginia, the new reality was a break from her past experiences. In that situation it seemed natural for all Americans living overseas in the Little Americas to get along and help one another. Perceptions by some white officers serving in the early postwar decades may also have contributed to this impression. Bill Hanne, who served as an Army Lieutenant in the Lampertheim Milcom, from 1960 to 1963, recalls that there were "no racial issues I was aware of, approximately one third to one half of my troop was African-American."[66] Similarly, Winton "Dip" Spiller, Jr., who served as an Army Captain in command of an artillery unit located in the Babenhausen Milcom, from 1964 to 1966, notes, "I do not recall any race relations incidents during my assignment."[67] Although anecdotal, these recollections suggest several interpretations: that not all Milcom members may have been aware of racial tensions, that some Milcom members were able to rise above them, or that conflicts may have been less prevalent than some sources propose.

Still, another possible explanation for the dearth of reporting of racial incidents by the military hierarchy presents itself when examining the demographic composition of Milcom

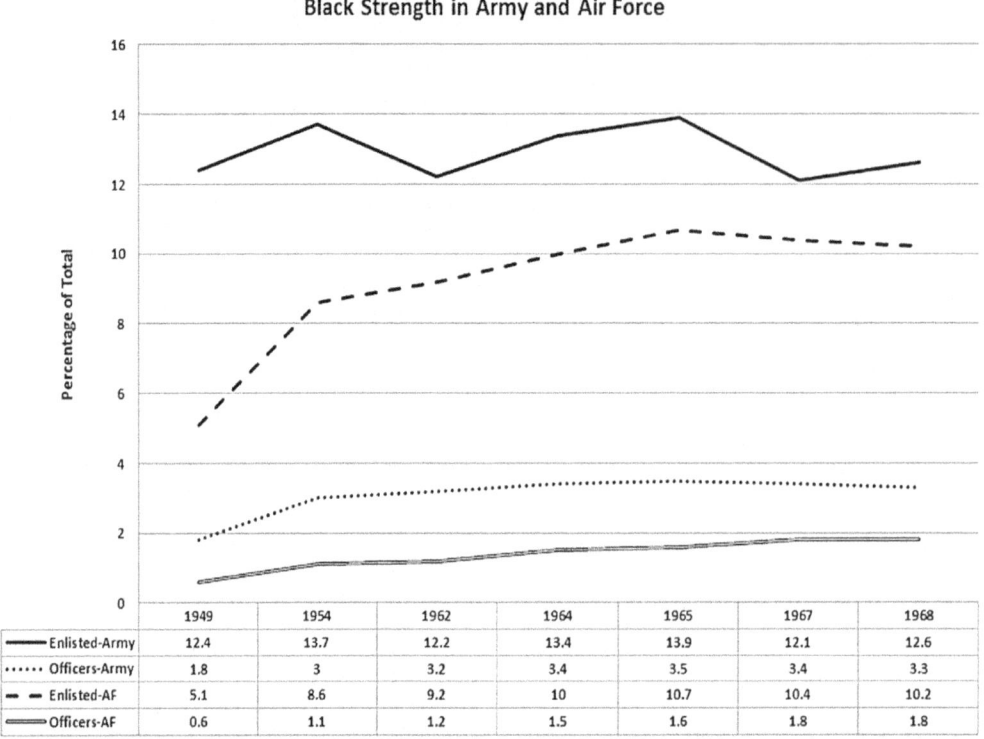

Black Strength in Army and Air Force. The data represents worldwide percentages within each branch for officers and enlisted personnel. As of March 1948 Black Officers represented 1.5 percent of the EUCOM total. Available data for Army personnel in the European Command (EUCOM) for December 1952: Black Enlisted personnel represented 14.4 percent of the total and Black Officers represented 3.0 percent of the total. Available data for Army personnel in the European Command (EUCOM) for June 1955: Black Enlisted personnel represented 11.4 percent of the total and Black Officers represented 3.6 percent of the total. Increases for the period 1950–1954 reflect additional personnel requirements for the Korean War and 1962–1965 for the Vietnam conflict. Data was available from sources only for the selected years. Data sources: "Defense Studies Series: Integration of the Armed Forces, 1940–1965," *Center of Military History*, accessed March 14, 2013, http://www.history.army.mil/books/integration/IAF-22.htm and Statistical Information Analysis Division (SIAD), http://siadapp.dmdc.osc.mil/personnel/MMIDHOME.HTM.

members during the period 1950 through 1970. Although the percentage of black military enlisted service members deployed around the globe initially exceeded the national population average, then decreased to remain relatively constant at 10 percent during that window of time (including Germany), the percentage of black officers and other minority Milcom dependents living overseas was well below that level.[68] During the same period, "White" military and dependent Milcom members overseas remained the majority and the combined percentage of all "Other" minority groups never exceeded 5 percent. A comparison to the contemporary racial composition of the U.S. reveals that blacks and other minority groups comprised a much smaller relative percentage of the overseas Milcom population, including West Germany. That reality may have influenced the behaviors, and attitudes, of both the military and political hierarchy, and added to the impression that even in integrated housing units there were few difficulties.[69]

This interpretation contributes to an understanding, not a justification, of why authorities would have had a lesser regard for concerns of racial inequity, since it affected a much smaller percentage of the black officer and dependent populations. When combined with a reluctance to tarnish the international image of America, the result would have translated into less effort to resolve racial differences or to report them, officially or in the media. Still, this interpretation does not imply that minority Milcom members easily, or rightly, accepted the status quo of skewed equality.

Between 1949 and 1967 letters from Milcom members to the editor of *Stars and Stripes* showed a change in attitudes that did not parallel the consistently guarded approach to racial issues followed by the newspaper or military leaders. A letter from a soldier appearing in a March 1949 issue complimented *Stars and Stripes* for "the manner in which you [sic] treat news which pertains to members of America's minority group, the Negro." In a nearly ingratiating tone it noted that the newspaper's "impartial reporting of this type of news is most ideal and morale boosting." In signing the author identified himself as "an American Negro soldier."[70] But by September 1967 Milcom readers seemed more willing to apply a direct approach to racial issues. In a letter submitted that month a resident of the Wiesbaden Milcom criticized the editorial staff for its depiction of blacks in the news, "I see that most photographs of Negroes [in *Stars and Stripes*] relate to crime and riot.... So the visual image presented to the reader is one of violence."[71] Later, in his narrative, the writer also noted the lack of black characters in the comic section of the newspaper and recommended that the editor find a suitable cartoon strip.

In a similar criticism another letter to the editor from October 1967, from a different member of the Wiesbaden Milcom, chastised the newspaper for appearing to emphasize the race of criminals, especially if they were black. The writer charged that *Stars and Stripes* was attempting to "justify the white American's cause of racial superiority and Negro subjugation; you are cutting America's throat and prestige in the eyes of the entire world," and finally claimed "the biased reporting is not being missed by the German press."[72] Both letters from 1967 arrived on the editor's desk at a time that the percentage of black military overseas dependents had increased considerably. By the latter half of the 1960s the prescribed tenet of equality seemed out of touch with the Milcom's reality as the overseas demographics normalized to reflect the composition of the U.S.

As that demographic composition of the Milcoms changed, the situation for the American military and political leadership in Washington and West Germany became more complicated. Although they made every effort to project an untarnished national image abroad through the 1950s and into the mid–1960s, the realities of racial inequality at home and overseas made that effort increasingly difficult. As President Truman observed, "discrimination damaged U.S. foreign relations" and "our domestic civil rights shortcomings are a serious obstacle."[73]

The German Perception of Race in the Milcoms

West Germans' interest in American racial equality during the postwar years served as a framework for understanding their own struggles and recent history of racial and ethnic discrimination under the Nazi regime. Studying Americans' behavior offered an opportunity to gauge their progress of recovery through *Vergangenheitsbewältigung* [coming to terms with the past] in the laboratory of the Milcom where Americans were playing out the same roles many German did a decade earlier.[74] In this context the Germans did not necessarily see the ill-defined and faulted tenet of racial equality simply as a trait to emulate or reject as much as a shared history that they had already transcended, and hoped that their American allies would also soon resolve. They would later revisit those feelings during the period of America's extended and controversial involvement in Vietnam and the years that followed.

Beginning with the arrival of the first American occupation troops in 1945 however, and the establishment of the Milcom network in 1946, the German public noted the incongruity between the purported tenet of equality and the manner that Americans of different races behaved and interacted with one another. German print media reflected evidence of their interest in, and judgment of, this aspect of American social mores. By the early 1950s German news weeklies such as *Der Spiegel* and *Die Zeit* were tracking the conditions of American blacks and providing critiques.[75]

The January 20, 1954, issue of *Der Spiegel* featured an article titled "School Blues." It noted the "profound upheaval in relations between Negroes and whites since the liberation of slavery" and that the blacks had "not yet overcome their social exclusion" although they were "trying with tough patience to change this world." Perhaps too optimistically it also commented, "The abolition of segregation in the primary and secondary schools would mean the elimination of the racial line."[76] Later that year, in May, *Die Zeit* celebrated the U.S. Supreme Court decision in the *Brown v. Board of Education* case by heralding, "The ruling eliminates deeply rooted social and political views."[77] The articles carried a measured, didactic tone, reporting the facts but also offering criticisms and judgments of American society. This followed through the 1950s and into the early 1960s as the German media kept pace with the unfolding events of the American Civil Rights movement. A December 1955 article in *Der Spiegel* noting conditions in the U.S. and Southern leaders' threat of interposition chastised the "racial pride" and "unwavering dogma" of Southerners who still considered blacks as "second class citizens."[78]

The following years featured print media pieces that maintained their critical scrutiny of America's gradualist policies to resolve its racial issues. At times they seemed incredulous, such as *Die Zeit*'s reflection that only ten percent of Americans considered segregation a "primary concern" to foreign policy, yet 22 percent cited the "rising cost of living."[79] At other times they seemed cautionary, "The Negro emerges as a factor that one day could destroy the American domestic political system."[80] Or, that America's race problems might be "fatal ammunition" for "the anti–American propaganda of Communists."[81] As race tensions in the U.S. worsened, overtones of sympathy crept into narratives. A July 1961 article in *Die Zeit* lamented the failures of the Declaration of Independence, the Constitution, or the Civil War to rectify the dilemma, "the first great historical revolution was the American. Her Americans [sic] betray the spirit of the revolution."[82] In September 1964, *Der Zeit* reviewed America's "long, hot summer" of discontent, which featured riots in Rochester, Chicago and Philadelphia, to pose a question that seemed to thrust at the heart of American ideals, "this America is aware that the Negroes have put the question of the identity of the nation: What is a nation?"[83]

Switching their lens of scrutiny to the Milcoms overseas, the German media found uncomfortable similarities. A July 1964 article in *Der Spiegel* noted, "the strongest discrimination of blacks in Western Germany" was where "racial prejudices were once stirred up by

Hitler," in the "vicinity of US military bases."[84] It observed, "Colored guests [were] not welcome" in many clubs near the "US garrisons of South and South-west Germany" where there was prevalent racial prejudice.[85] To make its case, the magazine cited specific incidents involving black soldiers and the names of off-post clubs. For the Germans, this behavior was nothing more, or less, than an extension of American racialist attitudes.

During the 1950s and early 1960s the German magazines, *Der Spiegel* and *Die Zeit*, as well as *Stars and Stripes*, presented objective and comprehensive coverage of the evolving racial tensions in the U.S. Their coverage differed however in regards to racial tensions involving the Milcoms. While the German media openly revealed problems of discrimination, command-sponsored organs such as *Stars and Stripes* muted its coverage, suggesting instead that race tensions were minimal and easily resolved. During this time also, the German public and its media were studying the U.S.' response to these challenges and evaluating its understanding of equality. Meanwhile, Milcom members were living complicated lives that trapped them between a prescribed consensus of racial equality and bearing witness to the realities around them. This would cause them to reevaluate the tenets of Americanism and struggle to frame a new image of who they were and what they represented to their German neighbors, and the world, as social tensions increased in the coming decades.

Sexual Stereotyping in the Milcoms

As histories of the early postwar period note, American society based the configuration of the home and family on specific gender assignments. The father was the head of the household and the mother was a homemaker.[86] This was the consensual norm of the nuclear family. The earliest treatment of women in the overseas Milcoms, including wives and daughters, civilian workers and military members, was consistent with contemporary societal norms of sexual stereotyping in the U.S. That understanding framed the accepted pattern of behavior for the Milcom family members upon their arrival in Europe, after they first weathered the journey and transition to a life overseas.

Upon arriving in Germany, the Milcom families often faced new challenges. Frequently there was a scarcity of adequate housing, barely adequate food supplies and questionable hygiene conditions including epidemics of communicable diseases. Outside the prescribed behavioral norms provided to some Milcom members in orientation briefings, films and pamphlets, the arduous sea voyage and these obstacles cultivated in many dependents a new and prideful sense of who they were. Often feeling like pioneers in a strange land, surrounded by a foreign culture, they set about building lives in new communities.[87] Unfortunately, for many Milcom spouses, any positive feelings of affirmation existed in tension with the restrictive gender constraints dictated by postwar American society. That tension was evident from the late 1940s through the mid–1960s in a number of ways, but seemed readily apparent in some of the ostensibly innocent, gender-based categorizations that Milcom women endured, such as the labels "military housewife" and "cheesecake" that the print media employed.

From the establishment of the first Milcoms in 1946 to the mid–1960s, *Stars and Stripes* carried articles regularly making reference to the "military housewife" or simply the "housewife." In consonance with widely accepted gender-based behavior assignments, the newspaper connected women to responsibilities that it assumed was in their purview. Often using a demeaning tone, staff writers created a stereotypical character that fit the needs of the Milcom. It was the military housewife who did the family shopping, the household chores, provided child care and who juggled the family budget. She served as the military husband's junior partner in all things, and as the magazine *U.S. Lady* described, her job was to serve as the touchstone of the family in the Milcom. It was the *U.S. Lady's* credo that stated, "No matter how wide the world of a U.S. Lady it centers in the spot where her husband and children are."[88]

A cascade of articles in *Stars and Stripes* during the first two decades of the postwar period helped shape the character of the military wife, at once reflecting the greater American consensus and framing her role. A piece from 1949 linked the cost of sugar to the "Frankfurt housewife," who personally suffered from the increased cost. A number of articles in 1955 mentioned the housewife's long work hours, and in 1958 the "military housewives" were praised as instrumental in making the international Housewives Fair in Heidelberg a success, particularly through their knowledge of cooking and baking. A 1962 article applauded a Pirmasens Milcom housewife's quick action in saving a heart attack victim. *Stars and Stripes* generally directed references about the commissary and shopping to the housewife, noting how problems were "frustrating to any housewife especially when an American housewife shops in Army commissaries."[89] Most telling was a story on the recent marriage of President Lyndon Johnson's daughter. The headline read "Lynda Robb's Eager to be Good Military Wife," and the narrative noted, "Lynda says she has a lot to learn as a housewife for her Marine captain husband."[90] The Milcom housewife was a good partner who understood her prescribed role.

To be sure those Milcom women kept up with the skill set they required to be good housewives, *Stars and Stripes* periodically offered a magazine subscription service. For example, listed among the variety of choices in 1951, under the category "Women and Fashions," were *American Home, Better Homes and Gardens, House and Garden, Ladies Home Journal*, and *Modern Knitting*.[91] The selection varied little through the 1950s but suggests that women's specific interests were in areas that more closely connected them to the home and family.

Visual signifiers contributed to the definition of the Milcom wife as well. U.S. Air Force advertisements in the 1950s issues of *U.S. Lady* depicted the military housewife as the mainstay of the family, always at her husband's side and assuming the dual-parent role in his absence.[92] Pictures accompanying consumer ads in the magazine often showed aproned wives in the kitchen or busy at household chores. Photos carried by *Stars and Stripes* reflected a similar theme, showing wives navigating the aisles of the PX or commissary, or participating in community service projects. The designator "housewife" identified the military wife, described her responsibilities, and set the limits of her powers within a gendered construct. But just as the term "housewife" told the Milcom woman who she was, the term "cheesecake" told the housewife who she wasn't.

From the late 1940s until the mid–1960s, *Stars and Stripes* proudly conducted an annual "Miss Cheesecake" contest. A vestige from the days when the newspaper served all-male combat units during World War II, the practice continued well into the 1960s, without evident concern for the sensibilities of Milcom wives. After selecting Rita Hayworth as Miss Cheesecake of 1947, *Stars and Stripes* noted in a collegial tone, "For those who came in late, let us explain that 'cheesecake' is just an old newspaper term for girl art, pin up stuff in short."[93] With that mild justification, the contest continued every year through 1963, selecting such entertainers as Marilyn Monroe (1950), as well as Italian models and American actresses.[94] *Stars and Stripes* also graciously provided the home address of Miss Cheesecake 1951, Franca Faldini, in answer to a letter to the editor, ensuring all GIs could respond to her friendly offer to receive letters.[95]

When not providing space for the Miss Cheesecake contest, or the winners' addresses, the newspaper casually introduced photographs of scantily clad young women in its pages or dedicated multiple pages to those images, such as photographs of the Miss Universe contestants, or the 1966 two-page photo spread "Say Cheesecake."[96] In response to a number of eager requests it also began introducing photographs of scantily clad females of varied ethnic backgrounds to satisfy a wider male audience.[97] During the first two postwar decades, the images of ladies designated as "Cheesecake" satisfied the prurient interests of male members of the Milcoms without regard to the feelings of female dependents or service members. In that context they provided images of those things that the military housewife was not: unmarried, unfettered by family and household responsibilities, and able to parlay sexuality into power.[98]

Until the mid–1960s, *Stars and Stripes* also carried a weekly feature page titled "Femina." It reported all the information that it considered important to Milcom women. There was a constant parade of articles that addressed, with repetition, the most recent women's club elections, the latest fashions, recipes, wedding announcements, and hobbies of interest to women. The newspaper also dedicated a full page "Femina" spread in June 1967 to Art Linkletter's "Military Wife of the Year" contest.[99] The competition evaluated the Milcom wife's contributions and service to the family, community and host nation, and her positive spirit. The contest continued for several years and noted one winner's comment that, "A happy wife makes a happy husband and a happy home."[100]

Dawning Possibilities and Changing Attitudes

On the periphery of the gendered Milcom arena where the tensions between "housewife" and "cheesecake" played out, there were increasing signs of change for women. Normally relegated to interior pages of *Stars and Stripes*, thin columns of text posted news accounts of events and actions that began to challenge the bounds of prescribed roles and power of the American Milcom wife, although the clarion call for change still remained faint. A 1951 article noted the Senate Judiciary Committee's 7–2 vote calling for a constitutional amendment guaranteeing equal rights for women, and a 1952 piece outlined the United Nations Assembly's approval of a women's rights convention by a 46–0 vote.[101] Two articles in 1957 alerted Milcom readers to actions in the American Congress to move forward on a constitutional amendment guaranteeing women's rights, and a 1963 piece announced the Senate passage of an equal pay bill for women.[102]

Contributing to this awareness of change were occasional pieces that also appeared in *Stars and Stripes*. An October 1951 listing for "Dial Day" AFN radio carried an announcement for the airing of an account of the 1848 Seneca Falls Convention, "the Women's Rights Convention takes you back to the days before the Civil War at 8:30 PM."[103] Although seemingly uncharacteristic for a newspaper that featured "cheesecake" contests, it was a sign of growing awareness, and changing attitudes among Milcom members. Another example from October 1954 was the "Lone Woman Fencer." It was an article that celebrated the accomplishments of "Mrs. Charles D. Smith, a young housewife" in the Munich Milcom who was the "only female member of a new fencing class" organized by a local German club. The text downplayed any feminist advancement however, by noting her comment that "I need the exercise to work off a few *Kartoffel* [potato] calories."[104]

Outside of household chores and family responsibilities many women took advantage of opportunities to participate in women's groups and clubs, and community service projects, particularly in the early postwar decades. Each Milcom had its chapter of an Officers' and Civilians' Wives Club and an Enlisted Wives' Club.[105] Most major communities also had chapters of the European Council of Protestant Women (COPW), the Military Council of Catholic Women (MCCW), and the American Women's Activities in Germany (AWAG). These groups met regularly in large national gatherings at American recreational facilities to discuss charitable initiatives in Germany and ways to strengthen the Atlantic alliance. Noted personalities such as Mrs. Douglas MacArthur II, the FRG President's wife, and retired General Lucius D. Clay often joined them.[106] These types of assemblies, inspired by evangelical groups in the U.S. and framed by religious themes, encouraged the maintenance of religion and family life as essential core values of American exceptionalism.

However, while *Stars and Stripes* printed pages of text noting the groups' activities and photographs of all the newly elected officers, the women generally bore the tag of their husbands' names, including his military rank. Examples of such micro-aggressions included the titles "Mrs. Robert Knowlton, wife of Chaplain (Capt.) Knowlton," and "Mrs. William H. Turley, wife of a Master Sergeant" were common.[107] Still, within this context of socially acceptable gender inequality, the meetings and conventions also contributed to an incipient understanding of gender awareness and the exceptional abilities of women that were to blossom in later years. This was evident in the variety of meeting agendas that included program seminars and classes such as "Operation Know How: Preparation for Leadership Responsibilities," and those that provided instructions on organizing and mobilizing groups, crafting rules and regulations, and making contributions to ongoing service projects.[108] Often, these conventions attracted hundreds of delegates from all the West German Milcoms, who would then return to their home chapters and share the information with other women.

Also within this complicated duality of gendered repression and dawning empowerment women occasionally found space to subtly lampoon the prescribed norm and challenge expectations. One example was a skit performed in 1959 by the Officers' Wives Club of the Mannheim Milcom. Titled "The Weaker Sex," the show celebrated, with tongue-in-cheek humor, women's many accomplishments despite the burden of prescribed gender roles.[109] Another opportunity presented itself when two Milcom wives vacationing on a beach in Turkey saved the life of a male bather by administering CPR after a crowd dragged him from the sea. Although on-looking male bathers were reluctant to let them assist, the women succeeded in saving the man's life. As one wife noted, the crowd realized "that the American woman isn't completely the weaker sex."[110] Although articles such as these occasionally appeared they tended to always emphasize the juxtaposition between expectations and Milcom women's abilities.

Lost, and often neglected, in consideration of the female Milcom population were women in the Women's Army Corps (WACs). Military regulations intentionally kept their percentage small by dictating that female officer, warrant officer, and enlisted strength in the Army could not exceed 2 percent of men's strength in each category.[111] For example, by 1960 there were only 5,034 women in the armed forces overseas, representing .008 percent of the total.[112] Although that percentage grew slightly with increased military operations during the Korean

War, it remained relatively low. Policy barriers also denied WACS the same privileges as their uniformed male counterparts. They could only be married if they had previous military service and could not have any dependents under age 18. Additionally, regulations did not consider a servicewoman's husband and children dependents unless she could prove that she provided them with more than 50 percent of their support.[113] Articles in *Stars and Stripes* kept pace with the changes in regulations and overseas postings concerning the WACs, but like their female civilian counterparts they continued to suffer gender inequalities during the early postwar decades until their full integration into the military in 1978.

Unlike *Stars and Stripes*, which carried a format targeting the entire population of the Milcom, the magazine *U.S. Lady* specifically focused on "service wives, service women, service families."[114] Absent were pictures exhibiting cheesecake and articles with condescending narratives about women. In their place *U.S. Lady* carried pieces highlighting their accomplishments. The magazine presented a regular column titled "U.S. Ladies of the Past." It gave short historical summaries of noteworthy women such as Molly Pitcher, Dorothea Dix, and Liz Custer. It also often exhibited accomplished women on its cover such as the November 1955 issue that featured the picture of Army nurse LT Dolores Soderston. Inside there were several glossy pages of pictures and text that highlighted the accomplishments of LT Soderston and the Army Nurse Corps. The Mid-Winter 1957 issue carried a poem titled "Radiant Regiment" that honored women in the service, and the spring 1957 issue featured the *U.S. Lady* of the month WAF Major Pat Ulrich, who in her free time taught dance to Milcom children and led a Girl Scout troop.[115] If *Stars and Stripes* failed to celebrate and note the contributions of women in uniform, *U.S. Lady* did not. Although the magazine still exhibited many of the traits of prescribed sexual stereotyping, with pages of recipes for Milcom wives and articles on how to make their husbands happy, care for their children and clean their homes, it also stood at the threshold of dawning possibilities for women.[116]

But *U.S. Lady* was not alone in its celebration of women's accomplishments. Some Milcom newspapers such as the *Stuttgart Post News* featured a recurring section titled "Dependents Post News" that carried notes on upcoming social events, favorite recipes, and charitable collections. Within this section it also included a column, "Woman of the Week," that highlighted the life of a noteworthy community woman.[117] The December 20, 1947, issue spotlighted Mrs. M. O. Edwards, wife of a Colonel Edwards, who was active in local charities as well as the German-American Women's Progressive Club. For this she was applauded as "one of the finest possible examples of leadership among the American women in Stuttgart."[118] Other issues featured columns on individuals such as Mrs. A. Dana Hodgdon who "was instrumental starting the first Women's Club," and Doris MacDonald who worked in the office of the Director, Wurttemberg-Baden Land Military Government headquarters.[119] In each case, the details of the story emphasized the contributions the women were making and held them up as examples to others. The case of Doris MacDonald is particularly interesting since it focuses on the life of a successful single woman at a time that societal emphasis was on marriage and family.[120] By noting women's potential, in articles that detailed their leadership and organizational abilities, both the *U.S. Lady* and the *Stuttgart Post News* foreshadowed coming changes within the early postwar consensus.

When examining data that shows the composition of the Milcom dependent population from 1950 to 1970, it is evident that women comprised a large majority. Although their proportion averaged just less than 70 percent for the three census periods (1950, 1960, 1970) it

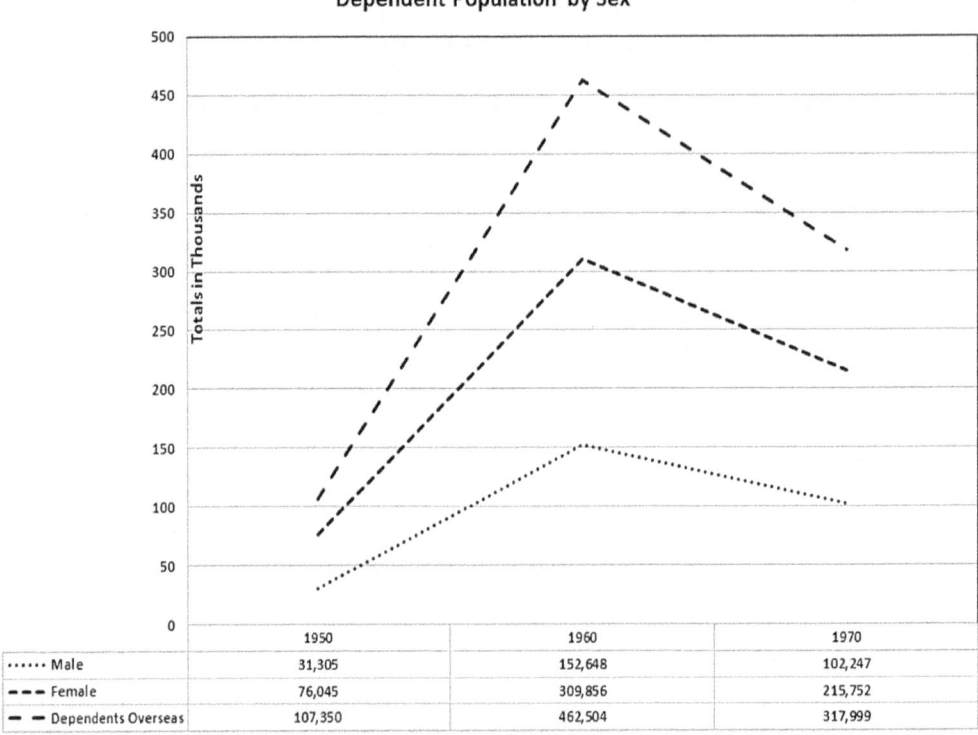

Dependent Population by Sex. (Includes all ages.) These numbers include only dependents (male and female) living overseas in the Milcoms. Of note is that females consistently comprised the majority of dependent population. For 1950, females represented 71 percent of the Dependents Overseas total but were 50.34 percent of the U.S. population total. By 1960, females represented 67 percent of the Dependents Overseas total but were 50.74 percent of the U.S. population total. By 1970, females represented 68 percent of the Dependents Overseas total and were 51.32 percent of the U.S. population total. The average for West Germany for this year alone was 69 percent. It was the only year during this period that the U.S. Census Bureau captured this data. Data source: U.S. Census Bureau for years shown.

is interesting to note that the accepted overseas societal paradigm continued to prescribe patterns of behavior that encouraged preservation of a contemporary American male-centric family and society. Until the national and global women's movement gained momentum in the 1970s, this would remain the character profile that defined the majority of Milcom woman.

There were exceptions, however. *Life* magazine offered a look at groups of single American women migrating to Europe in the postwar years to take jobs with U.S. government agencies, private corporations, newspapers or banks. In a December 1957 issue, *Life* described these women as fiercely, and happily, independent and searching for travel and adventure, showing "people of all lands the American woman is the world's most fascinating creature."[121] Among the legion of secretaries, clerks, and teachers were some shining entrepreneurs such as Marion Rospach. The article described her as "one of Europe's most successful new businesswomen." It was Rospach who established the *Overseas Weekly*, a smaller newspaper popular with enlisted service members. Rospach also served as "president and major stockholder of the International Media Co."[122] Although she would later do battle with the EUCOM military hierarchy over editorial content of her newspaper, Rospach's popularity (she was known as

"Frau Weekly" to the Germans) and her influence seemed to unsettle the exceptional male-centric paradigm. In the context of gender roles and models she appears to us as the antithesis of the Milcom woman. As a representative of an *avant garde* group of female arrivals to postwar Europe she stood closer to the new German woman than the existing American one.

Unlike their American counterparts, equality for German women appeared to be moving forward faster in the early postwar years. With the collapse of the Third Reich and the birth of a sovereign West Germany in May 1949, the opportunity to craft a new federal constitution existed in the early 1950s and it included consideration of women's rights. A December 1953 *Stars and Stripes* article announced "Bonn High Court Rules Women Have Equality" and it noted that Article 3, Paragraph 2 of the Basic Law (constitution) clearly reaffirmed that West German "men and women have equal rights."[123] As simple as that declaration seemed it was not without some controversy. News journals such as *Der Spiegel* carried articles that mirrored the associated tensions in German society. A February 1952 column on marriage and society, written prior to the decision, discussed the difficulties surrounding selection of a surname for the married couple, whether the wife should wear a ring, and communal property rights.[124] Although fraught with inherent challenges, by comparison it was a leap ahead of gender rights for Milcom women who had to find satisfaction in the dilatory efforts of U.S. senators who were still years away from proposing equal pay and equal rights bills.

Another article, which appeared in a 1952 issue of *Die Zeit*, based its argument in favor of equality on the fact that many West German women had already integrated into the national workforce and so needed the protection afforded by the basic law.[125] This was the natural consequence of a situation that assigned great respect to the icon of the *Trümmerfrau* and placed a great burden on the shoulders of West German women who often became the head of a single-parent household in the early postwar years, outnumbering German men by a ratio of 3:2.[126] That reality framed the difference in the evolution of gender rights between West German women and their American counterparts. While the Germans were moving toward greater equality, the constructs of an exceptional contemporary consensus confined Milcom women to roles that were not necessarily beneficial to them.

Looking at their Milcom neighbors, West Germans saw inherent flaws in the American's definition of sexual equality, just as they observed the dissonance of racial equality. Again, their consideration was not acceptance or rejection of an American exceptionalist tenet, but rather its usefulness as a barometer for how far they had progressed.

The Milcom Media

Whether it was information regarding national or global movements for civil or gender rights, politics, economics, sports, or community events, Milcom members received their news and information from select sources during the early postwar decades. Principals among these outlets were the *Stars and Stripes* newspaper and the Armed Forces Radio Service (AFRS).[127] Although other media sources existed such as unit newspapers, community newsletters, home town newspapers, and some international editions of larger news syndicates, such as the *International Herald-Tribune*, only *Stars and Stripes* and the AFRS provided the most consistent and widest coverage focused on a military and dependent audience.[128] *Stars and Stripes* circulation averaged 50 percent coverage for the Milcom population, seven days a week, between

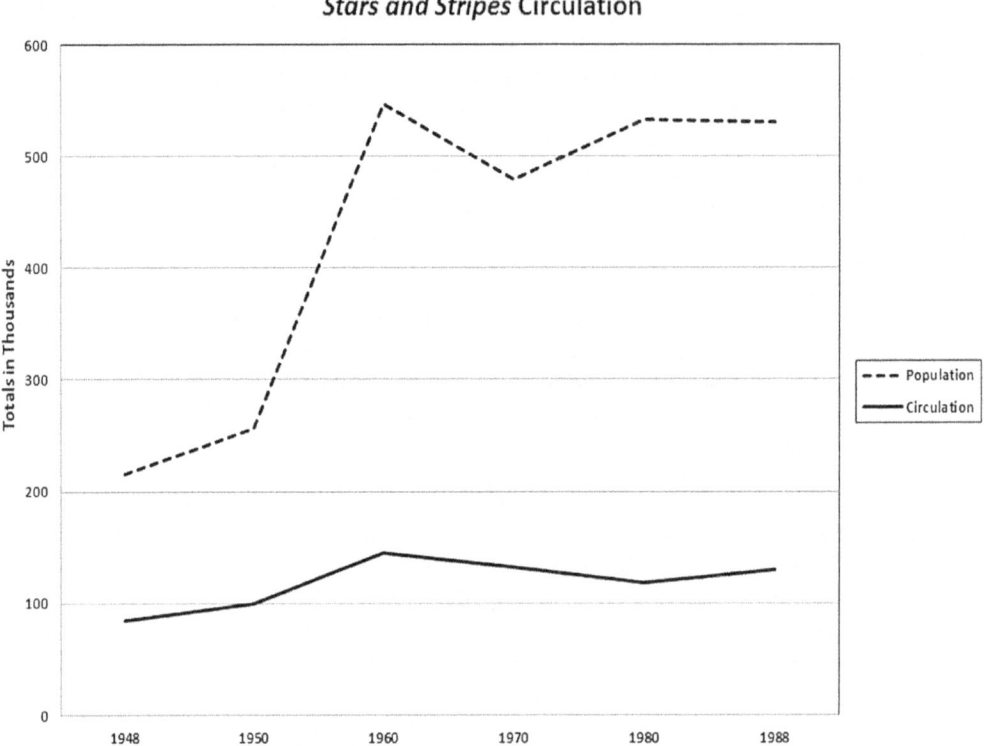

Stars and Stripes Circulation. These figures include total Milcom population, military and dependents, but not German nationals. EUCOM did not circulate the newspaper directly to the West German population. The reasons were two-fold: to avoid influencing Germans domestic affairs and the SOFA that prevented U.S. Forces from acting as a commercial activity. German readership was mostly incidental through the thousands of local nationals who worked on U.S. bases. The figures include all daily published copies, delivered and retail sales. At its highpoint in 1945 *Stars and Stripes* printed 1,500,000 copies daily. That figure dropped as the war in Europe ended. Data sources: *Stars and Stripes* issues 1948–1980 and "The Stars and Stripes-European Edition: History," accessed March 22, 2013, http://www.usarmygermany.com/Units/StarsandStripes/USAREUR_StarsandStripes.htm.

1948 and 1970, leveling off after 1960 as AFRS radio began to increase its area coverage and supplies of paper became controlled.[129]

Readers considered *Stars and Stripes*, which was always proud of its wartime nativity, to be the "GIs' newspaper" during both World War I and World War II. Reaching circulation of 1,500,000 copies daily in 1945, the newspaper consolidated its many staffs and presses immediately after the war to focus on the much smaller occupation army and the arriving dependents. This reduced its circulation to 85,000 copies by 1948.[130] During this period of adjustment the editorial staff became concerned that many readers, including foreign governments, considered the newspaper to be an official organ of the U.S. Army. As a result, they added the word "unofficial" under the title flag on the first page and in the interior masthead shortly after the war. It was also during this time that the newspaper changed its format, which was mainly news from the front and staff cartoons, to news from wire sources (UPI, AP, and INS), syndicated comics, and features to satisfy its wider, mixed Milcom audience. It continued to increase in size from 12 pages to 16 by 1953, and again to 24 pages by 1954 to accommodate these changes.[131]

Station	Channel	Call Sign
Loring AFB, Maine	8	AFL TV
Lajes Field, Azores	8	CSL TV
Wheelus AFB, Tripoli, Libya	8	AJG TV
Keflavik, Iceland	8	TFK TV
Thule AFB, Greenland	8	KOLD TV
Dhahran Airport, Saudi Arabia	8	AJL TV
Kagnew Station, Asmara, Eritrea	8	KANU TV
Kindley AFB, Bermuda	10	ZBK TV
Clarke AFB, Philippine Islands	8	
U.S. Navy Station, Guantanamo Bay	8	WGBY TV
Kadena AFB, Okinawa	8	
Narsarssuak, Greenland		
USF Badoeng Strait	4	
Sonderstrom Air Base, Greenland	8	

Table 3.2: Armed Forces TV Stations (1956). AFB = Air Force Base. USF = United States Forces. ("Current List Armed Forces TV Stations," U.S. Lady 1, no. 8 (Mid-Summer 1956): 31.)

Throughout these early years, *Stars and Stripes* was proud that it functioned as an organ of expression, a voice for the grievances and concerns of service members and families, as well as an unfettered source of information and ideas. In this context it was representative of the American ideal of freedom of expression and was an example to the blossoming number of postwar German newspapers and magazines. A brief column in the March 18, 1945, issue of the *New York Times* celebrated this popular claim by noting that the B-Bag [letters to the editor] column was not only a favorite among soldiers but also their leadership. It noted, "of late, letters from field officers and several generals have made the column."[132] A *Washington Post* article from April 1947 allowed that *Stars and Stripes* "800 inches of news space typify the American way of life, running the gamut from profound reports on atomic matters to police-beat scandals interspersed with photographs of long-legged movie starlets."[133] It added that the newspaper's influence spread beyond the garrison and Milcom to where "German politicians scramble for old copies" and "Moscow radio has commented sharply on an item or two."[134] However, regardless of its intent, the range of its coverage, or its popularity, *Stars and Stripes* often drew criticism, warranted or not, even as American society wrestled with the issue of open expression.

Ironically, some of the earliest criticisms of the newspaper concerned *Stars and Stripes'* too liberal policy of freedom of expression, and came from unexpected sources. One reader, a soldier with combat experience, forwarded a letter in March 1946 complaining, "*Stars and Stripes* has played the role of gadfly in the European theater. It was allowed virtual freedom of comment."[135] In that context, the reader noted, "it published a high proportion of letters critical of officers" and in effect "the paper was constantly the advocate of less discipline for soldiers."[136] The *New York Times* editor, also a veteran, who received the letter added that GI newspapers like *Stars and Stripes* "spread and fostered discontent and poor morale," and that, the "editors failed to realize that they were soldiers first and editors second, that their duty was not merely to reflect the views of their readers but to lead their readers" to the views and opinions of the command hierarchy.¹³⁷ The suggestion ran counter to the efforts of *Stars and Stripes* staff.

Another criticism came from Hans Wallenberg, editor of the U.S. government sponsored postwar German newspaper *Neue Zeitung*.¹³⁸ Wallenberg complained to American authorities in May 1947 that *Stars and Stripes* "is 90 percent cheesecake and the rest is not too hot from the standpoint of news coverage."¹³⁹ He later added that action should be "taken to curb *Stars and Stripes* freedom of news coverage because of its influence on the German press," implying that it made it difficult to manipulate the news with a pro–Western slant.¹⁴⁰ At the time *Neue Zeitung* had a daily circulation of 550,000 in Munich and 140,000 in Berlin.¹⁴¹

Subsequently, on February 26, 1948, McCarthyite Congressman George A. Dondero (R-MI), stood before the U.S. House of Representatives and charged *Stars and Stripes* with "injecting pro–Soviet, pro–Communist, and anti–American material" into the paper.¹⁴² Continuing his attack, Dondero expounded, "Whether this is the result of sheer stupidity or the machinations of a communist clique in the American military government, or both, is for our Department of the Army to find out and act upon."¹⁴³ Taking up the cause of the newspaper General Lucius Clay immediately responded that he "had never seen any anti–American or pro–Communist matter in *Stars and Stripes*." Clay added, "I am very proud of *Stars and Stripes* and I read it every day."¹⁴⁴ Unintentionally, the Soviet-sponsored *Vorwärts* [Forward] also refuted Dondero's charges against the newspaper with its response that "the careful reader must get the impression that *Stars and Stripes* stories are written without kid gloves in Wall Street's new anti-communist campaign."¹⁴⁵ In a short time Dondero's focus shifted elsewhere, but for a few short weeks the newspaper also became a victim of the Red Scare communist witch hunts perpetrated by the House Un-American Activities Committee (HUAC) led by Senator Eugene McCarthy. Paradoxically, in this case, the political elites linked with vociferous anti-communist beliefs worked from within the system to challenge the newspaper and the ideal of freedom of speech.

Three years later, the U.S. State Department also offered criticisms of *Stars and Stripes*. During the Korean War it filed a complaint with the newspaper's editorial staff noting that too many headlines, titles, and descriptions of combat action were gruesome and likely to undermine military morale. It specifically cited terms like "blood baths," "slaughter," "murder" and "Operation Meat Grinder" to make its point. In their defense the editors responded that they received the stories from General Matthew Ridgway's headquarters only after his censors had already cleared them. That seemed to mollify the critics.¹⁴⁶ Still, *Stars and Stripes* did continue to feature stories with captivating titles such as "Heartbreak Ridge was Death Inferno."¹⁴⁷

Sensitive to its charge to remain an organ for freedom of expression, which included being a voice for GI grievances and providing information and news to the Milcoms, *Stars and Stripes* often found itself caught in the cross-fire of conflicting expectations of readers, military and political leadership, and its own staff. Perhaps the most difficult charges however, were not criticisms of print content from its Milcom readership or external sources, but rather accusations of intentional content censorship.

The collective staffs of *Stars and Stripes* offices heard the earliest warning shots of censorship from the Rome bureau of the newspaper in March 1946. Reacting to an attempt by the American theater commander, U.S. Army Lieutenant General C.H. (Court House) Lee, to exercise external editorial control of B-Bag letters staff writers protested, "Do men in uniform give up the rights of citizenship in a democracy?" adding that "an Army newspaper must and can present all the news of the world."[148] The general's initiative died however, quickly and quietly with the inference that he was quashing soldiers' freedom of speech. Although this incident did not directly affect the press in Germany, it did raise the staff's level of awareness and sensitivity toward possible future censorship.

That awareness was piqued again in January 1948 when Secretary of Defense James Forrestal called a conference of national press, radio and motion picture leaders to "discuss the peacetime security problems of the armed forces." Central to the discussion were Washington's suspicions of the press's "unauthorized leaks of the nation's military secrets."[149] For *Stars and Stripes* staff in Germany, this heralded concern over increased external control of the news. That fear materialized with the publication in April 1948 of a EUCOM directive describing the controlled release of information to the public through the press. Placing their fears on the front page, *Stars and Stripes* staff outlined their perceptions that the Army was "attempting to place new curbs on freedom of the press" with worries that it would threaten General Clay's "famed 'goldfish bowl' policy of free and easy access to theater news."[150] Always a champion of the newspaper, Clay waded in and tried to dispel any suspicions by openly denying "there was or would be any censorship of American Military Government activities in Germany."[151] Although *Stars and Stripes* staff interpreted that umbrella statement to include control of the news, it did not remove the suspicion of censorship that hung like a cloud over the newspaper for many years and would occur at least two more times before the end of the 1960s.

The first instance was during the Korean War. The sensitivities of the military hierarchy, both in that theater and in Washington, to the inadvertent release of classified information caused news reporters and staff writers to navigate an increasingly complex set of rules regarding censorship. *Stars and Stripes* in Germany first alerted its readership to the evolving situation in July 1950 in an article titled "Newsmen Bound by Gentlemen's Pact." The text forewarned readers that "while Gen Douglas MacArthur has the power to apply full censorship restrictions any time he wants to, he has not done so as yet. Newsmen have been asked, however, not to disclose certain information."[152] By 1954 controls had tightened, although the Defense Department had "reaffirmed that the only basis for wartime censorship of news dispatches is to prevent vital information from reaching the enemy—not to suppress unfavorable publicity."[153] The concern of newsmen, including *Stars and Stripes* staff, was that this consideration opened the door for censorship at various levels of information distribution and command through contrasting interpretations of the central phrase "vital information."[154]

A decade later another censorship scandal arose when the Defense Department acknowledged, through a *New York Times* account, that the U.S. Army Headquarters in Europe (USAREUR) "had ordered *Stars and Stripes* to drop a dispatch reporting the arrest of the 19-year-old son of the United States Ambassador to West Germany."[155] In its front page report, *Stars and Stripes* noted that the USAREUR commander had ordered the reassignment of the public relations officer who refused to kill the story and that the headquarters "directed that the story be removed from the two later editions" after it had run earlier in the day.[156] In an attempt to mitigate the situation, the editor-in-chief of *Stars and Stripes* claimed "I killed the story," but it was a transparent admission and readers understood that military authorities had exerted undue external pressure to censor the newspaper.[157]

The issue of content censorship exercised either by its' editorial staff or external influences continued to haunt *Stars and Stripes* throughout the Cold War period as it faced conflicting definitions of exceptionalism and freedom of speech. On one hand there were political and military elites who sought to use the newspaper as a vehicle to further the soft-power peddling of American ideals, regardless of how they shaped information, on the other was the newspaper's staff and its efforts to enforce the tenet of freedom of speech regardless of its' palatability. Caught in the middle was *Stars and Stripes*' commitment to provide service as an outlet of news, information, and entertainment, and to serve as a voice for the Milcom members, military, civilian, and dependents, as a unified and identifiable community.[158]

But *Stars and Stripes* was not alone in this quandary. Also fixed in the cross-hairs of censorship during the postwar period was the *Overseas Weekly*. With a circulation that barely crested 40,000 at its peak, the smaller newspaper prided itself on being an outlet for enlisted service members' grievances, and a gadfly to the military leadership and officers. It did not represent itself as an organ for the entire Milcom and carried the soldiers' sobriquet "The Oversexed Weekly," with its "eye-popping pin-up pictures of bosom and thigh."[159] Operating as an adjunct enterprise beginning in 1950, under the direction, ironically, of a female editor, it initially utilized the presses and distribution system of the larger *Stars and Stripes* organization.[160] Although its 28 pages featured "16 pages of full-color comics" it also appealed to Milcom members' consumer instinct by boasting that, unlike *Stars and Stripes*, it contained "advertisements for U.S. products" and so was "your stateside shopwindow."[161] Difficulties for the *Overseas Weekly* began within a few short years after its first issues came off the press.

The weekly newspaper initially fell under scrutiny in the early 1950s, during the time that political and military hierarchies showed concern regarding the inadvertent release of sensitive military information to the public through press organizations. Although the elites did not charge the *Overseas Weekly* in that regard, they took the opportunity to sharply criticize the newspaper for a series of articles that carried "sensational stories of sex and prostitution," which resulted in "numerous protests from commanders in the field."[162] Although USAREUR headquarters did not specify articles in its charges or give the names of the protesting commanders, it was clear that it was revoking the newspaper's contract to publish and distribute through *Stars and Stripes*. Although the editor protested, "this order encroaches on the concept of the freedom of the press," the ban remained in effect, forcing the newspaper to seek an independent German publisher to continue its operation.[163] In response to the editor, a USAREUR spokesman "emphasized that the headquarters did not engage in censorship of publications."[164] Letters of protest, or sympathy, from *Stars and Stripes* readers did not appear in subsequent B-Bag columns, suggesting either Milcom members did not feel that their privileges were threatened or editors intentionally omitted such letters. Still, in that one action, the military leadership had moved to eliminate competition for *Stars and Stripes*, swatted a gadfly that was continually vocal in its criticism of senior officers, and muzzled a press organ it could not control.

But if *Stars and Stripes* failed to challenge the military hierarchy's attempts to gag the *Overseas Weekly*, West German journalists did not. The June 10, 1953, issue of *Der Spiegel* took the Americans to task and castigated U.S. military censors who claimed that the newspaper "triggered a storm of protest of the field commanders and others who seek the moral well-being of military and civilian personnel in our command."[165] In the sardonic estimation of *Der Spiegel*'s staff writer, Marion Rospach and her *Overseas Weekly* fled the oppression of American censorship "to the German freedom of the press."[166] Once again, the societal definitions and cultural expressions of censorship and freedom of expression, between the Milcoms and their hosts, clashed.

The *Overseas Weekly* drew attention again in 1961 with a series of articles that illuminated Major General Edwin Walker's attempts to indoctrinate his troops with materials from the conservative John Birch Society as part of his Pro-Blue anti-communist program. Taking exception to his initiative the *Overseas Weekly's* articles instigated debate in the halls of the U.S. Congress and an investigation of Walker's methods by Secretary of Defense Robert McNamara. He eventually removed Walker from command, which precipitated his retirement from the Army. During the furor Walker fired back at his accusers claiming, "We have Communists and we have the *Overseas Weekly*. Neither one is one of God's blessings to the American people or their soldier sons overseas. Immoral, unscrupulous, corrupt, and destructive are terms that could be applied to either."[167] In sympathy to Walker, USAREUR headquarters directed the removal of the *Overseas Weekly* from Milcom bookstores and newsstands.

Within a year however, the Defense Department permitted the newspaper's return amid accusations of improper censorship practices by a number of groups including the American Civil Liberties Union. A military spokesman contritely noted, "in view of the improvement" in the quality of journalism "there was not sufficient justification for its removal from Army newsstands."[168] The ACLU's white paper published with its 42nd Annual Report for 1961–1962, had called attention to the Defense Department's threat of future action against the *Overseas Weekly*. It declared that, "This plainly subjects the newspaper to all the inhibitions that the threats of censorship present." It also noted that although service members hold a different status than civilians, they did "not believe that this difference justifies the dictation to soldiers of the material they may or may not read."[169]

During the remaining years of the Cold War, both *Stars and Stripes* and the *Overseas Weekly* would again face challenges of criticisms and attempts of censorship. Their Milcom readers understood the vagaries of external control by military and political elites even as the newspapers struggled to safeguard the idea of freedom of the press as an identifying characteristic of the Little Americas. More so, the German public watched with interest. Having recently endured the heavy hand of totalitarian censorship, with Joseph Goebbels's "technique of the big lie," they were satisfied in the early postwar years just to have ink flowing and presses moving even if they only produced editorially managed copy like that found in *Neue Zeitung*.[170]

Other than news, sports, and feature articles, *Stars and Stripes* and the *Overseas Weekly* provided Milcom readers with another essential ingredient to their day, the comics. The Sunday and daily comic strips were a popular feature in most major newspapers in the U.S. since the late nineteenth century. Their appearance in the Milcom newspapers added a familiar touch of home in postwar Germany that was exceptionally American. Together with comic books, which began selling in all PX bookstores immediately after the war, they offered an entertaining diversion for Milcom members. Through their humor and adventure the comics also bore the image of Americans that set them above and apart from other nations.[171]

Comics like Milton Caniff's "Steve Canyon" and George Wunder's "Terry and the Pirates" exhibited the macho militarism of triumphal postwar America. For example, one set of frames from July 1952 depicts the character Terry and his mercenaries reflecting on an upcoming fight with the "Reds," and another shows a character from "Steve Canyon" noting that "There are as many risks in this Alaska Department as in a shooting war in Korea."[172] In both strips the artists represented non–American male characters with distorted features and as either devious or foolish individuals. Non-American females often appeared in the character of *femme fatale*.

Other comics like "Blondie," with her husband Dagwood, humorously portrayed life in the contemporary American family with the prescribed gender roles of a father, who was a slave to his office job, and a mother who worked in and ruled the home. Another featured comic was the "Katzenjammer Kids" with its humorous, but deprecating, depiction of an immigrant family, complete with thick German accents.[173] Collectively these comic strips and their comic books were uniquely and exceptionally part of the culture of America and the Milcoms. However, they also reflected those contemporary characteristics that smacked of an exceptionalist consensus: militarism, imperialistic tendencies, anti-communism, sexual stereotyping, centrality of the family, and an air of triumphal superiority.

As early as 1948 the American comics had drawn fire from critics, women's and church organizations, parents and educators in the U.S., who accused them of "contributing to juvenile delinquency, violating good taste, underlining and making attractive crime and immorality." Regardless of those efforts, comic book publishers recorded an output of 60 million magazines a month as PX bookstore sales to overseas Milcom members continued to increase.[174] By 1950 critics were continuing to claim that "comic strips laden with sex and crime" like the popular "Dick Tracy" were damaging American youth, although they had more than 70 million faithful followers.[175] Artists and publishers chaffed under the thought of any censorship revealing fears of "a tendency in America to shrink from laughing at itself."[176]

Outside the Milcoms, West Germans applied their own cultural lens to the study of comic strips and comic books. As the news journal *Der Spiegel* reported, they agreed with American critics and censors who sought to prohibit scenes of tantalizing sex, the glorification of crime, sadistic behaviors, and glorification of divorce in the cartoons. They also agreed with estimations that comics poisoned the imagination of children and were "the opium of the nursery," but they could not stem the cultural tide that introduced them to Germany through American service members and their families.[177] By 1951 West Germans had their own version of Dick Tracy published in the form of a detective known as "RIP Corby." The other popular German news journal, *Die Zeit*, registered similar concerns about the comics that were "imported from America" and were "halfway between primitive reading and primitive cinema or television."[178] Nevertheless, *Die Zeit* ruefully reported that comic strips had made great inroads to German newspapers and were gaining in popularity with *Blondie und Dankwart* [Blondie and Dagwood] representing the typical American couple and *Li'l Abner's* Daisy Mae no more voluptuously exposed than many actresses in contemporary European movies. The comics represented a uniquely American artifact that Milcoms introduced across the grassroots boundary between the cultures and left an imprint with its complicated considerations of censorship and societal mores.

Between 1946 and 1967, there were contested grounds within American postwar society where Milcom members applied different, and occasionally contradictory, interpretations of American ideals derived from separate social or regional consensuses. The implications were profound and generated fault lines that would challenge the solidity of that consensus. Among the issues that raised the most controversy and produced the most debate within the public sphere were religion, race, sexual stereotyping, and media censorship and its relationship to freedom of speech. Most important, these early postwar societal tensions underscored challenges to the individual and collective freedoms of Americans living within the network of the military communities in Germany. The Germans, susceptible to external influences as they struggled to piece together an economy and society during war's aftermath, became discerning interpreters of social behaviors in the laboratory of the Milcoms. The result was an opportunity for the West Germans to gain some distance from their recent past and judge their own social progress. As they learned more about the Americans through their contact with the Milcoms, they were also better able to make judgments about the characteristics of the American way of life. The Americans in turn continued to discover troubling inconsistencies within the set of ideals that defined their society.

Four

Anti-Communism and Nuclear Concerns (1946–1967)

A Call for American Leadership

The final draft of the manifesto *City of Man*, framed by the Committee on Europe, was a sweeping declaration for the postwar ascendancy of the U.S. Its prelude noted the "awakening of America in 1940" to global events, and its summary proposal addressed its words "to those from Plymouth Rock and to those from Ellis Island, for to both alike, Americans old and new, shines the lamp beside the golden door."[1] Crafted by a mixed group of intellectuals from Central Europe and the U.S., under the titular leadership of German émigré Thomas Mann, the work encouraged America to take the helm in steering the postwar world into the future. It was a call to political action. As the committee observed, "Nothing could be more shocking to America's humility and pride than the necessity to take leadership among the nations," and "yet no necessity is more imperative."[2] Central to those efforts would be democracy and "a new birth of freedom under God."[3]

The overtones of the manifesto: anti-communism, anti-collectivism, celebration of the individual, and spirituality, struck the chords of the American exceptionalist consensus. They also resonated among the founding members of the Committee, particularly intellectuals such as Thomas Mann who carried those attitudes abroad with him when he returned to Europe shortly after the war. Although he eschewed any association with communism during those early postwar years he couldn't escape past associations with left-leaning associates such as Paul Robeson.[4] As a result, there were a number of accusers who despite his previous criticisms of communism, his advocacy of democratic ascendance, and his recent American citizenship, attempted to link Mann with the communist East through charges of "political left-handedness."[5] Mann's struggles to avoid a tarring with the brush of communism and shape his own postwar identity were typical of those that plagued many German and American elites and non-elites alike during those years.

By the late 1940s, the lens of communist suspicion became a tool that Western politicians and policy strategists used to evaluate the postwar world, inform their decision-making and interpret the actions of individuals. For members of the Milcoms in Germany it was an extension of the predominant contemporary political ideology that informed their thinking and influenced how they interpreted the world, their relationships with the host communities, and their mission. As Robert Bierly, a former community member of those early years recalled,

"The perception was that the US Army was there to meet a potential attack of the Soviet Bloc nations. We were deployed to meet that threat. We trained everyday with that thought in mind. We had no doubt that we needed to be there and that the local population was happy to have us there."[6] Although that danger of communist aggression carried great influence in forming identities and attitudes during the Cold War, it was only one of two early postwar engines that drove American politics and policy strategy.

The other driver was a concern about the utilization and deployment of nuclear weapons. As the West's apprehension regarding Soviet mastery of fissionable material increased by the late 1940s, so did its understanding that the atomic bomb would represent a new chess piece on the political game board. It became the keystone for the American defensive strategy in Western Europe and central to negotiations with the Federal Republic regarding troop strength levels and defense costs for both nations. Those considerations sometimes opened contested exchanges between the NATO members as West Germans often fretted over the fear that any failure of military deterrence "would mean the nuclear annihilation of German territory."[7] During these first postwar decades, the German elites often found themselves navigating between political rocks and shoals. On the one hand, negotiating a diminished reliance on nuclear weapons invited the West to station more troops on its soil and increased domestic pressures for a national defense force. This included the possibility of precipitating a conventional Soviet military response. On the other hand, thickening the nuclear shield might forestall Soviet aggression but invite nuclear annihilation in the event of a crisis.[8]

During this period, the House Un-American Activities Committee (HUAC), which discerned links between the Soviets and nuclear secrets through the real and imagined dangers of "Russian spies" and espionage, quickly conflated the fears of spreading communist influence with that of nuclear weapons. This association became apparent through claims by HUAC investigators that Soviet spies "were assigned by Moscow to steal secret information on U.S. wartime atomic and radar developments."[9] In the years that followed, the associative power of communist threats and nuclear war would remain constant. As alarming as all this might seem to the contemporary American public and political elites in Washington, the realities of communist aggression and atomic weapons would become two specters that cast long, abiding shadows over the daily lives of Milcom members often leaving them feeling as if they were pawns in a dangerous game.

The political debates surrounding the stationing of nuclear weapons in West Germany had more than a casual effect on the lives of Milcom members. Unlike Americans back home in the States the impact of a Soviet military attack or a European nuclear conflict on the Milcoms would have been profound. The ever-present shadow of that nuclear cloud, together with fears of a pervasive Communist threat, were concerns they shared with their German hosts that influenced their cross-boundary relationship and informed their beliefs. But just as with the cultural and social issues of race and gender, these challenges generated debate and controversy, and left many Milcom members wondering how to interpret the anti–Communist, pro-nuclear armament line that political and military leaders expected them to follow. Factored into this equation was the continued introduction of officially generated directives, propaganda films and Hollywood productions that influenced the thinking of Milcom members and the American public. By the early 1960s however, it became evident that for the West Germans, the issues of Communism and nuclear armament were not as closely linked. This eventually led to strained relations between the Americans and their hosts.

The Communist Threat: Visual and Printed Prompts

During the early decades of the Cold War the U.S. Army's Signal Corps Pictorial Service played a significant role in instigating and maintaining that heightened sense of awareness of a communist threat among Milcom members.[10] Through the "Big Picture" series the military offered propaganda films that appeared on commercial television networks in the States as well as overseas in theaters and later on armed forces television. Among these productions were several that transmitted a distinct anti–Communist message. One such film, *Challenge of Ideas*, featured several noted contemporary personalities and actors. The lead narrator, newsman Edward R. Murrow, opened his introduction by warning Milcom members, and the wider audience, that the clash of ideologies between the East and West was "a challenge as great as any in our historic past." He went on to caution, "The communist bloc would like to see the entire world under communist domination," and that involvement in the conflict "touches not only the armed forces and their families" but everyone else in the West as well.[11]

Among the speakers who followed Murrow in the film was actor John Wayne who reminded viewers "our heritage of freedom is our most priceless possession" and that the key phrase, which rang throughout the nation's founding documents, was "this nation under God." To emphasize the last point, and provide contrast, Murrow reminded the viewers that in the communist system "man is not a creature of God but of the State."[12] If any doubts remained in the audience's mind, later in the film, Hanson Baldwin, the military editor for the *New York Times*, pointed to a wall map depicting a geopolitically divided world and flatly proclaimed, "The communists initiated the Cold War."[13]

Other Big Picture films that followed a similar anti-communist approach were the *West Berlin Struggle*, and *Germany Today*. The first highlighted both the perceived Soviet duplicity in attempts to manipulate early city elections and the heavy hand of Soviet repression that followed the June 1953 riots by East Berlin workers.[14] Central to the second film was a discussion of West Berlin as a symbol of Western freedom and the U.S. military's role to hold back the tide of communism in Germany and the free world.[15] These films, and others that carried a similar anti-communist theme, appeared on Milcom television listings in *Stars and Stripes* often alongside series such as the "Communist Myth" that aired during the early 1960s.[16]

But there were also a number of other notable films, produced by Hollywood, which offered insights to communism within the context of the public debate. Among these were *The Iron Curtain* (1948), *Big Jim McClain* (1952), *My Son John* (1952), and the *Manchurian Candidate* (1962).[17] Each included marquee stars, such as Dana Andrews, John Wayne, Van Heflin and Frank Sinatra, and each reflected the fears of communist infiltration into various aspects of society. These found their way into theaters throughout EUCOM during the same years that Americans were interpreting the challenges posed by communism to the ideologies of the West. For example, this included scares, real or imagined, such as the dangers of "brainwashing" of American military prisoners by their North Korean captors during that conflict. This fear would encourage President Eisenhower to energize plans to renew ideological training of military personnel in the tenets of Americanism.

Title	Year	Producer	Summary
Face to Face with Communism	1951	Armed Forces Information Film Number 21	A serviceman in town on pass discovers his town taken over by communists.
The Big Lie	1951	U.S. Army	The film is an exposé of Soviet-controlled regimes around the globe.
I Was a Communist for the FBI	1951	Warner Brothers	Stars Frank Lovejoy: FBI infiltrates U.S. Communist Party
Big Jim McClain	1952	Warner Brothers	Stars John Wayne: HUAC agent hunts communists in Hawaii
My Son John	1952	Rainbow Productions	Stars Robert Walker, Van Heflin: A son secretly becomes a communist
Prisoner of War	1954	MGM	Stars Ronald Reagan: An Army officer as a North Korean prisoner of war
Night People	1954	Twentieth Century–Fox	Stars Gregory Peck: A GI is abducted by communists in West Berlin
Trial	1955	MGM	Stars Glenn Ford: Communist influence in a court of law
Communist Blueprint for Conquest	1956	U.S. Government	Hosted by Robert F. Kennedy
The Commies Are Coming, the Commies Are Coming	1957	Warner Brothers	Stars Jack Webb: Communists take over and eliminate civil liberties
Challenge of Ideas	1961	Defense Department and U.S. Army Pictorial Center	Celebrities and media figures discuss maintaining vigilance against communist influences.
Road to the Wall (Big Picture Series)	1962	Directorate for Armed Forces Information and Education	A summary of communism from Marx to the Berlin Wall. Narrated by James Cagney. Nominated for Academy Award Best Short Documentary.
Red Nightmare	1962	Directorate for Armed Forces Information and Education	A man awakens to discover that communists have taken over America and his freedoms are lost.

Table 4.1: Contemporary Anti-Communist Films. This representative sample does not include all available titles of films produced by the U.S. government or Hollywood during this period. (Sources: John E. Haynes, "A Bibliography of Communism, Film, Radio, and Television," *Film History* 16 (2004); "The Red Scare: A Filmography," University of Washington Libraries, accessed June 27, 2013, http://www.lib.washington.edu/exhibits/AllPowers/film.html; and NARA Record Group 111, Office of the Chief Signal Officer.)

In parallel to the exposure Milcom members received via the theaters and AFN radio, the print media also contributed to fueling of anti-communist awareness. During the early postwar decades hundreds of articles appeared in the widely circulated *Stars and Stripes*. For example, as tensions over the 1948 Berlin Blockade crisis mounted so did a plethora of news items intended to capture the attention of Milcom readers. Articles with titles such as "Symington Says Winter Will Not Halt Berlin Lift," as well as "Contact Sought in Spy Inquiry," "Czech Ex-General Tells of Red Purge," and "500 Soviet Soldiers Reported Deserting" were typical of the daily regimen of political print that offered perspectives on communist missteps and duplicity.[18] These stories that compared and contrasted ideologies of the East and the West, and generally provided rhetoric favorable to the West, appeared regularly through the following decades.

During this time, columns that seemed to receive preferential placement in the news featured reports that detailed the exposure of communist agents and secret operations, especially if they smacked of sensationalism. A December 1948 article focused on the actions of "Whittaker Chambers, self-confessed former Communist agent" who provided "proof that information significant to national security was fed out of the State Department." Integral to the narrative were details of how Soviet agents had hidden sensitive microfilms in hollowed-out pumpkins.[19] Chambers linked his revelation to a disclosure that Alger Hiss, a highly-placed official in the State Department, was in fact a Soviet agent. From that first confession to Hiss' public condemnation months later, the American press, including *Stars and Stripes*, followed the dramatic story providing insights to readers about the dangers of communist infiltration to the apparatus of the U.S. government. This type of news continued to provoke Milcom readers' awareness as well as their concerns and opinions.[20]

Grassroots Milcom Perspectives

News releases such as those above, as well as a tense atmosphere contributed to by the Soviets, also fed into the mix of emotions, especially during the 1948 Berlin blockade crisis. A series of letters sent home to the States by the family of Major Sam Kale provides some evidence. In one, he comments with a hint of trepidation, that "Everything is fine here unless the 'Ruskies,' as the Germans call them, decide to come. They can get from Russia to the French Coast in two days as it is now. They have something around 20 divisions to our one. Our equipment is rotten."[21] Writing separately, his dutiful wife noted "Sam did tell me that if the Ruskies do break through unexpectedly to pack the kids in the car and head for Switzerland. Me with my crazy sense of direction would probably land right smack into Russian territory." She also commented on the feelings of their teenage daughter, "Barby says she hopes Italy doesn't turn Communistic before she can get to Rome."[22]

In the American sector of Berlin tensions were just as high. As Brigadier General Frank Howley, Commandant of the sector wrote in his memoir, "Some of our women also were frightened. Mattern, the most rabid of the German Communist leaders, announced in a Soviet-licensed newspaper that when the Russians took over Berlin, American families would be held in concentration camps for further disposition."[23] Still, as Howley noted "The Russians didn't scare us into quitting."[24] As he notes in his work, the West Berliners remained petrified by Russian threats. They feared starvation, a lack of heating fuel, and rumors that "the dreaded Mongolian troops" responsible for the immediate postwar pillaging and rapes would return. American and German residents shared a mixture of fears.[25] In heroic fashion however, Howley announced, "We are not getting out of Berlin. We are going to stay. The American people will not stand by and allow the German people to starve."[26] Struck in the forge of those early postwar tensions was an iron-willed anti-communist link connecting Americans and West Germans.

Important to Stop the Spread of Communism?

1949	West Germans	Yes: 81%	HICOG
1950	West Germans	Yes: 75%	HICOG
1955	West Germans	Yes: 71%	HICOG

Table 4.2. West German Attitudes about Communism.

Unfavorable Opinion of Communism?

1952	West Germans	Yes: 65%	HICOG
	West Berliners	Yes: 69%	HICOG
1953	Americans	Yes: 88.5%	Gallup
1954	Americans	Yes: 91.1%	Gallup
1956	Americans	Yes: 86.4%	Gallup

Table 4.3. Comparison of West German and American Attitudes. (Source for Gallup surveys: Tom W. Smith, "The Polls: American Attitudes toward the Soviet Union and Communism." *The Public Opinion Quarterly* 47, no. 2 [Summer 1983].)

As early as 1949, contemporary polls of West Germans bore evidence of this relationship. Shortly after the successful completion of the West Berlin airlift operation, they understood that the communist East presented a threat to their sovereignty. They voiced a strong opinion (81 percent) in an affirmative response to a survey question asking if it was important to "stop the spread of communism." This began a trend that followed through subsequent surveys, in the early postwar decades, and reflected a consistent, general consensus among West Germans regarding communist hegemonic intentions.[27] Surveys by West German print media during the same period of time reflected attitudes about communism that were generally consistent. In a March 1949 poll the news magazine *Der Spiegel* posed a series of economic and political questions to the West German public. Representative results revealed that 70 percent of the respondents voiced hope that the Western allies would move to stop a potential communist take-over of West Berlin "at any price."[28]

Still, the fevered fear of Soviet aggression that grew with tensions in the isolated city of Berlin and reverberated throughout the network of Milcoms was not always universal. The reminiscences of Gerhardt Thamm, an American intelligence operative, reveal a different reality. Serving as chief of a section that included seven linguists (three Russian, two Polish, one Czech, and one German) he deployed from the U.S. to the East German border on the afternoon the Berlin crisis began. With instructions to situate his section near the Fulda Gap, considered the main avenue of a potential Soviet attack, they sat and monitored all military communications. No Soviet bloc forces menaced the border between East and West and Gerhardt's clandestine section "stayed close to the border for three months" having "a ball" taking "afternoon coffee and cakes in a local café" while living in a hotel. As he recalls, "While the US media got everyone excited about this great Soviet threat, we listened to all the Soviet and East German communications ... and we all knew that there was no threat. In fact, it was 'All Quiet on the Eastern Front.' Not even a threatening peep out of the Soviets or their East

German buddies. Of course, we could not tell our families that this was all government/media hype."²⁹

While the German and American populations of the Allied sectors of Berlin quaked, and Milcom families like the Kales and others prepared for war, the cause for general alarm now seems more complicated and open to suggestion of possible manipulation by political elites to maintain a heightened sense of anti-communism. As Thamm's son Erik notes, "From the home front standpoint, I was 11 when my dad was deployed during the Berlin Crisis. Although he and his colleagues might have been laid back at their Kassel location and sipping coffee, the families were stressed, worried, and wondering if their dads would come back from the potential nuclear conflict."³⁰

These types of events that had an impact on the lives of those in the overseas military communities unfolded against a backdrop of virulent anti-communism back home in the States. Stories just as sensational and worrisome as the reports of the Hiss and Chambers cases followed the diatribes of Senator Joseph McCarthy (R-WI). A central figure on the House Un-American Activities Committee (HUAC), McCarthy quickly developed a reputation for flamboyant oratories and accusations of communist collusion by Washington elites. His political opponents frequently revealed that his charges were misbegotten but they made for good theater with the press, increasing circulation and helping to inflate the specter of a "Red Scare" for the American public and the Milcoms overseas. Coming close on the heels of the Berlin Crisis this stuck a particular chord with Milcom readers when McCarthy claimed to possess evidence of "the presence of Communists and Communist sympathizers holding high positions in our German occupation forces."³¹ Although this bold charge eventually died unfounded it came at a time when anti-communist feelings were already at a high among Germans and Americans.

Still, McCarthy's influence also struck close to home for the Milcoms as he called for the review of books sent overseas claiming that "blatantly pro–Communist, pro–Soviet and anti–American material" was on the shelves of U.S. information libraries in Europe.³² Attempting to balance these charges were politicians and authors who decried McCarthy's actions as nothing more than a contemporary, albeit figurative, version of book-burning practiced by autocratic regimes such as the Nazis, little more than a decade earlier. As one author pleaded, in a too recent historical reference still fresh in Germans minds, it was by such means that "Hitler rode to triumph."³³ These accusations of communist influence, and counter charges of misdirected heavy-handed censorship, offered an opportunity for Milcom members to reinterpret the meaning of freedom of speech. It also suggested that the definition was anything but uniform within American society. Such behaviors inspired consideration by some Milcom members like Robert Weekley who noted that he "had some skepticism about the alleged Soviet subversion of American society. I felt that Senator McCarthy might just be seeking political gain. He seemed unbalanced."³⁴

Contemporary West German feelings paralleled those of many Americans. As early as 1950, the West German media had taken notice of Senator Joseph McCarthy's too virulent anti-communist offensive in America. As American Milcom members learned of his machinations on AFN and in *Stars and Stripes* West Germans read about them in news magazines such as *Der Spiegel*. An April 1950 article ridiculed McCarthy for his bold claims, such as "the US State Department is a Moscow branch of Communists," and described his techniques as little more than "headline hunting" to grab the attention of 150 million Americans.³⁵ Others criticisms followed. A journalist for *Die Zeit* voiced concern that McCarthy was operating "undisturbed from the safe sanctuary of the Senate, which gives him immunity."[36] A subsequent article in *Der Spiegel* observed with greater apprehension, a "sudden, panicked presumption" by the American public that communists were making great gains infiltrating the U.S. government.[37]

By 1952 the tone of many West German journals had taken a more serious turn. In August of that year *Der Spiegel* published a commentary noting McCarthy's use of "explosive slander and unverifiable suspicions" that "contained just enough half-truths" not to negatively affect the public opinion.[38] Through this the writer could see "terror stepped up into hysteria" among political elites and the public. Most alarming however, were accounts of the HUAC-inspired Hollywood black lists and the censorship of printed materials, which in the estimation of the German journalist, were creating an "American Gestapo."[39] In the eyes of many West Germans, these behaviors suggested that Americans were too willing to sacrifice their liberties and freedoms in zealous pursuit of communists.

As the energies of McCarthy's search for communist influence unfolded during the early 1950s, conflict between political ideologies erupted on the Korean peninsula in June 1950. Milcom members read the stunning headlines in *Stars and Stripes*, "Reds Invade South Korea."[40] In the weeks, months and years that followed, newspapers and magazines offered a cascade of related articles that addressed gains and losses during the conflict. When combined with the ongoing trend of columns addressing communist infiltrations, suspicions, accusations and disclosures in various sectors of American life and society, the Red Scare seemed very real to Milcom residents. As they cast their eyes to the east, across the border, toward the opposing Soviet bloc forces the threat of communist aggression seemed more palpable. As former Dachau Milcom resident Robert Weekley recalled, the U.S. troops "were stationed there to defend against invasion by USSR and Warsaw Pact" forces.[41] This was an opinion endorsed by others including Winton "Dip" Spiller former resident in the Babenhausen and Darmstadt Milcoms, who understood that his unit served as a "deterrent to the Soviet threat" and believed that "we were involved in a very worthwhile mission and [he] was proud to be an American."[42]

Do You Support Rearmament as a Means to Stop Communism?
Dec 1951   Yes: 73%   HICOG

Do You Favor Alignment with the West?
Jan 1952   Yes: 55%   HICOG

Should West Germany Resist a Communist Take-over?
Jan 1953   Yes: 53%   HICOG

Are You Sympathetic to the Communist Ideology?
Jan 1953   Yes: 5%   HICOG

Table 4.4. HICOG Poll Results of West German Attitudes. (Anna J. Merritt, and Richard Merritt, eds., *Public Opinion in Semi-Sovereign Germany: The HICOG Surveys, 1949–1955*, Champaign: University of Illinois Press, 1980.)

West German sentiments paralleled those of the Americans. HICOG survey results revealed that they would support ambitious measures to forestall the spread of communism and the threat it might pose to their sovereignty.[43] This suggests that German and American opinions were riding the same wave of fear of communist aggression and subversion that was actively informing and shaping contemporary political decision-making.

By 1954, as the violent energies on the Korean peninsula began to ebb so had Senator McCarthy's celebrity status as a growing number of political elites, members of the media and public began to question his dubious methods. By December of that year Congress censured the senator for his abusive processes and public diatribes. McCarthy's acerbic retort to his critics was "I am being censured because I dared to do the dishonorable thing of exposing Communists in Government."[44] Although the senator quickly passed from the political scene, the momentum of an anti-communist Red hysteria seemed to abate only slightly as there remained troubling periodic reminders to Milcom members of a continuing threat from the communist East. These included incidents that continued to shape political and policy strategies during the 1950s and 1960s and inform Milcom members' thoughts about their purpose for being in Germany.

One of the earliest events to pique fears of communist aggression occurred in November 1956 when Soviet forces rolled into Hungary to crush that nation's incipient bid for independence. As *Stars and Stripes* offered Milcom readers banner headlines that read "Soviets Crush Hungary in Sneak Attack," *Die Zeit* offered its own bleak assessment.[45] The West German news magazine noted the Hungarians' "death-defying" attempt to "break the chains of Soviet and Communist bondage and to shake off the yoke of Moscow." In this account "freedom was thrown to the ground" and the "red banner" again arose.[46] Americans and West Germans alike mourned Hungary's fate and fretted over the potential for future acts of Soviet aggression.

As Hank Johnson recalls of 1956, tensions had increased "because of the Russians. They had just seized Hungary. Talk about justified pucker factor!"[47] As a dependent "brat" he noted, "the Russian problem" was "frightening for a 10 year-old kid. At that time, my dad was commanding a cav [armored cavalry] troop in the 3AD [3rd Armored Division] and the 'Bad Guys' [Soviets] were only 75 miles to the east."[48] To this he adds:

> At least once a month, a frightening ritual was repeated throughout USAREUR (and always in the middle of the night). POVs were kept stocked with water, C rations, and in our case an M-2 carbine (my dad had taken me to the [firing] range with his troop and I qualified). We all had evacuation strip maps and were told to "head for the English Channel—somebody will pick you up on the beach." When the time came each month, it was scary as all get out. An MP jeep would circle the Butzbach housing area, with a siren screaming. Every kid [American dependent] in the neighborhood would gather on the curbs and wait. Soon a rumble could be heard in the fog and all our dads' command vehicles would appear out of the darkness. My dad's M-48 tank would stop and it was always the same. My dad would hug me and say "Hank, I may not be back, and it will be up to you to protect your mother. Be brave!" Then up onto his tank and off to the east and the Fulda Gap. As he departed, he always turned and saluted me.[49]

In comparison to contemporary Stateside Americans Hank observes, "needless to say, today I have a real problem with people my age claiming 'duck and cover' drills in mid–America in the '50s scared them. Give me a break."[50]

Neil Albaugh recalls the Hungarian crisis with a similar intensity. He was attending the Frankfurt American High School at the time and remembers the instructions that family members received. They were to have "prepared a suitcase" with enough clothing and essentials to last several days and be ready to leave on a moment's notice. The military would collect all dependents and truck them to France. From there, somehow, they would then fly out, as was

Hank Johnson as a young dependent. Here he poses atop his father's M26 tank, c. 1949. The image reveals the strong bonds between many Milcom family members and the close association and integration of military units with their dependent populations driven by a segmented environment and perceived dangers during the early postwar decades. Image source: Hank Johnson with permission.

possible, back to the States. This, Neil remembers, generated some concern among the West Germans who feared abandonment to the Soviets. But he also recalls that when the evacuation did not occur the Germans expressed relief that the Americans would remain and share their fate.[51]

Another significant provocative event was the October 1958 demand by Soviet Premier Nikita Khrushchev that the Western powers withdraw from their sectors of Berlin. He charged, "The time has evidently come for the powers which signed the Potsdam Agreement to give up the remnants of the occupation regime in Berlin and thus make it possible to create a normal atmosphere in the capital of the German Democratic Republic (Communist East Germany)." He added that the Western powers had "abolished the legal basis on which their stay in Berlin rested."[52] Milcom service members and their families, particularly those living in the divided city, understood the tone of the message and the potential consequences of the Soviet leader's words. Front page headlines that announced "Russ Halt U.S. Convoy Trying to Leave Berlin" provoked memories of the crisis in 1948, when the Soviets had blockaded the city and brought the world powers to the brink of military conflict.[53] A young Hank Johnson remembers that time also. "By 1959, the Russians started grabbing US convoys going into Berlin. That was probably the closest the US and Russia ever came to World War Three. It was so close, the

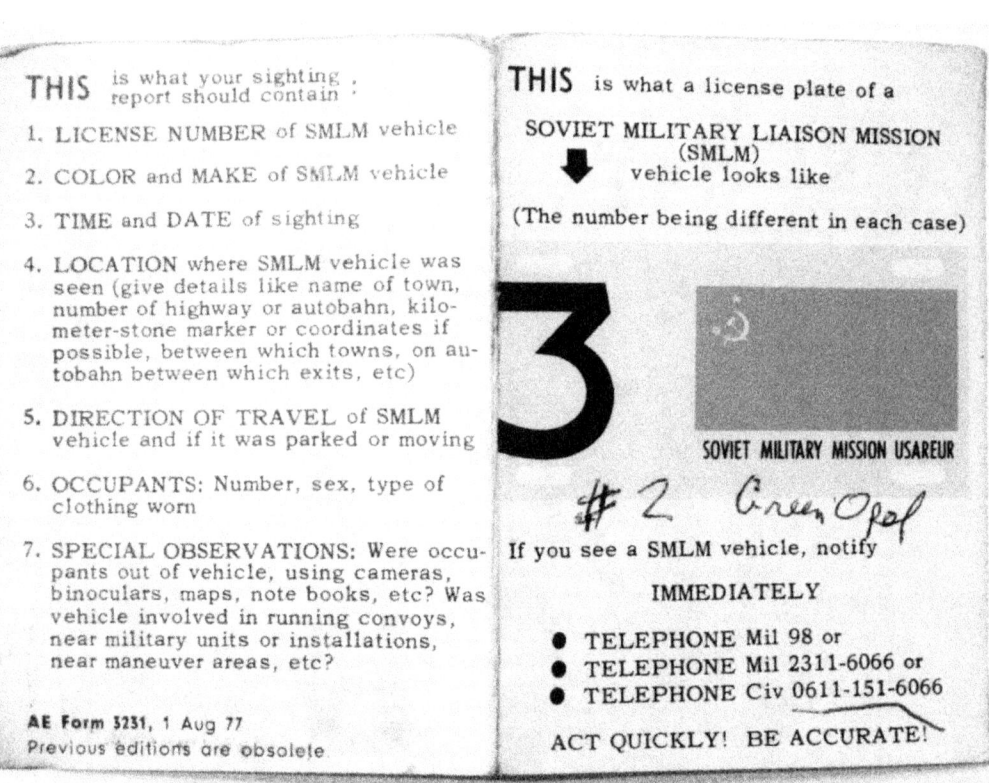

Soviet Military Liaison Mission (SMLM) Card. These cards were issued to Milcoms members for use when sighting a Soviet Military Liaison vehicle in a restricted or sensitive area. It included instructions for reporting the sighting. The cards afforded American and German authorities another tool to monitor Soviet activities in West German sectors. Image source: the author.

Army had Pan Am [airlines] rig cameras on its aircraft so we would have up-to-date aerial photo intelligence."[54]

A lengthy *Der Spiegel* reaction piece outlined West German sentiments. Citing a litany of disastrous results should the Western allies withdraw, the magazine criticized the Soviets for creating a "Central German misery zone" in the east and noted the "horror of West Germans about the sad regime of Ulbricht in Central Germany" that included "forced indoctrination, police state methods" and "forced unions."[55] The fears of losing civil liberties and the undoing of economic gains motivated these powerful anti-communist sentiments. Before the end of the year however, and before the confrontation could intensify, diplomatic talks reduced the escalating tensions within the growing political crisis.[56]

A continued Soviet presence in the American sector also served as a thorn in the side of the military. Jim Ryan, who served in a nuclear-ready missile unit in 1960 remembers, "We were warned and briefed about potential encounters with the Russian observers in West Germany."[57] He notes that at the time:

> The area of the 40th Artillery Group was supposed to be off limits to them ... allegedly they were not supposed to be operating anywhere west of the Rhine River. We were briefed to be on the lookout for the quintessential "big black limousines" in our areas and observing our operations. We were instructed to immediately report our sightings. Special personnel would be summoned to escort them out of the area. It was stressed to us in most emphatic terms that we were never to directly confront and challenge the vehicles or the Russians would shoot to kill us.[58]

The print media noted successive critical flashpoints that again reminded Milcom members of the communist threat in the East and of the susceptibility of their existence in West Germany to the vagaries of international politics. Among the most significant, which captured the news headlines, were the construction of the Berlin Wall in August 1961 and the Cuban Missile Crisis in October 1962. Considered by some histories to be an extension of the crisis that began in 1958, the erection of a wall around West Berlin by the Soviets began with a series of travel restrictions preventing East Germans from traveling into the Western sector. *Stars and Stripes* headlines that read "Vigilantes Cut Refugee Flow" and "1,100 Elude Roadblocks to Reach West" alerted Milcom members to the budding crisis on August 8, 1961.[59] Within weeks, front page news announced high level meetings between the American Vice-President Lyndon Johnson, the Chancellor of West Germany Konrad Adenauer, and the Mayor of West Berlin Willi Brandt.[60] On the heels of these developments President Kennedy called for the mobilization of the American military in Germany and ordered the dispatch of additional troops to reinforce the Allied garrison in West Berlin.[61] Those troops ordered to Berlin came from the Milcoms of the 8th Infantry Division already stationed in the Rhineland Pfalz region.[62] As the full weight of political brinkmanship again fell on the shoulders of the Milcoms in Germany service members prepared for a violent conflict and their families prepared for survival in a war zone or evacuation to France and the United Kingdom under the guidelines for non-combatant evacuation.[63] Amid their greatest fears neither possibility materialized. However, as Milcom member Robert Weekley remembers, "We believed we were on the brink and that war could break out anytime. Soviet actions at that time seemed to validate the concern. Closing off the Eastern European countries from the West led to a perception that the East could more easily mobilize for an invasion without detection."[64]

Jim Ryan also recalls the tensions surrounding the construction of the Wall: "Early in the morning of Sunday, August 13 [1961] we were rudely awakened and ordered to fall out with all our field gear, line up and man our vehicles, and get ready to roll out of the Kaserne on a moment's notice. We were told we were possibly going to war!"[65] When word came down through channels that an American armored column was on its way along the autobahn through East Germany to Berlin tensions ran high. "We loaded all the vehicles and assembled our convoy inside *Des Gouettes* Kaserne [Bad Kreuznach], and then we sat and waited. After several nervous, anxious, and also irritating hours, the word came down. We were to stand down. There was a collective sigh of relief over the news." But in typical soldierly fashion Jim adds, "We were also angry that the better part of a beautiful August Sunday had in our minds been wasted away for naught."[66]

Former nuclear weapons technician Neil Albaugh remembers the same crisis from a different perspective. Assigned to the U.S. Army missile school at Redstone Arsenal, Alabama, he suddenly found himself on orders for a missile unit in West Germany. Sent immediately, he arrived at the Babenhausen Milcom to join the 1st Missile Battalion of the 38th Artillery Regiment. Their mission was to defend the Fulda Gap against Soviet penetration by use of their nuclear-ready missiles. He would remain in Germany until 1963, but remembers the tensions of the time and the endless practice alerts and deployments that filled the following months, often in the cold, and often "in the middle of the night."[67]

Robert E. Green, Jr., assigned to the 4th Armored Division stationed in Ulm recalls that "there was an evacuation plan for dependents if the Russians invaded. I had little confidence in the plan and as Ulm was only 40 miles from the Swiss border, I arranged for my wife and child to drive from Ulm to Switzerland in our car should an emergency arrive."[68]

Many Germans also remember those events of August 1961 with the same intensity. For example, as a young girl Inge Queren, whose family had close associations with a number of Americans, remembers:

> The daily accounts of the events; the masses of people fleeing to western Germany; the sights of crying relatives on either side of the wall; the serious tone of voice by the news commentators; my parents fearful reaction (my mother started stacking rations of canned goods and the like in the basement); the nervous atmosphere that penetrated the daily routine; all of this caused me to live in a daily feeling of fear that never stopped. It was on my subconscious mind day and night, and I was not the only one. This was normal with practically all Germans.[69]

Queren adds, "One news information [sic] was especially horrifying: watching elderly ladies try to jump out of the windows of buildings that belonged to the Soviet Zone into a jumping sheet on the street next to their house which belonged to the American Zone. To watch this as a child was such a penetrating shock that it is unforgettable to me."[70]

Although military and political elites appreciated the potential peril that American Milcom dependents faced, some members of Congress considered their presence almost too provocative. During discussions in 1961 concerning the bolstering of forces in EUCOM Senator John Stennis (D-MS) commented that it was:

> a matter of the deepest concern to me—I do not see how we can impress Mr. Khrushchev with our serious intensions of actually building up our military forces in Europe for the purpose of action, if necessary, if we send additional men there who take their wives and children with them or continue the present practice of taking more dependents to Western Europe.[71]

Representative Frank J. Becker (R-NY) echoed those sentiments:

> We were told that if we did send additional numbers of men we would also send dependents overseas.... I say this is ridiculous. If we are faced with a hot situation, if we are going to make sacrifices today, why not bring home the dependents, and not put ourselves in a position overseas where we can be black-mailed because of the hundreds of thousands of dependents of our servicemen over there.[72]

Although these comments did raise concerns the energies they generated were not enough to cause a reduction in the number of dependents in Germany or curtail their travel overseas.[73]

The atmosphere in the Milcoms continued to remain tense through late 1962 as the U.S. and the Soviet Union sparred diplomatically over the emplacement of nuclear equipped missiles in Cuba.[74] Again, broadcast news on AFN and a continuous series of tense headlines in *Stars and Stripes* kept Milcom readers informed about the unfolding crisis. Banners that read "U.S Calls on U.N. Council to Halt Piecemeal Aggression by Russia" with subtitles announcing "U.S. Prepared to Sink Ships Denying Check" alerted Milcom readers to the severity of the crisis.[75] The physical proximity of the Milcoms to Soviet Bloc military ground forces heightened their awareness of the possibility of violent conflict. When Soviet Foreign Minister Andrei Gromyko visited the Berlin Wall during the crisis and demanded that the Western Allies leave the city the American military members and their families living there again understood the risks and the burden of political brinksmanship.[76]

Inge Queren remembers those tensions as well:

> The Cuban Missile Crisis was just a continuation of the former events, i.e. it meant more fears, not only that the Soviets might take over entire Germany (that fear was always on our minds) but also that in case of a missile launch German would be devastated. So now we lived in a constant fear of death by an atomic war. When the news came that Khrushchev had agreed to withdraw the missile from Cuba, an unimaginable sigh of relief went through Germany; even though we knew the danger was only downgraded but not gone entirely. To me, the Sixties were a decade of constant fear of the Soviets since they seemed unpredictable to us.[77]

To this she adds that it seemed all German politicians "were sort of a nuisance to U.S. politicians for wanting to receive constant reassurances from the Americans to protect West Germany from the Soviets. I think every meeting I saw on TV included the Germans' renewed request for keeping a strong U.S. presence in Germany."[78]

Before the leaders of the U.S. and the Soviet Union had resolved the crisis America's key French, British, and West German allies had pledged their support against the Soviets. Most important, Chancellor Konrad Adenauer announced, "West Germany was ready to share all the risks arising out of the U.S. stand in Cuba."[79] It was a key moment in the relationship between the Americans and West Germans and helped to further cement the connection between the two nations. This trend would continue as West Germany's role as a viable political partner grew and became central to Western policy strategy in the years to come.

In 1963 another event occurred that drew American Milcom members and the West Germans closer. Some had just arrived home from their duty day and others were awaken from their beds, but all were shocked to learn of President John F. Kennedy's assassination. Chaos was the rule on the radio and television. For Sergeant Barry J. Veden it was a singular memory: "Germans flocked to the post, not believing what had happened and wanting more information from us, which of course, we didn't have. Everyone was afraid that the Russians would use the situation in an attempt to force the Allies out of Europe, as you can imagine, we were on a high status of alert for a long time after Kennedy's death."[80] Although the military leaders did not order units to deploy from the Milcoms to counter a possible Soviet threat many remained on alert while Americans and Germans alike mourned the loss of Kennedy's charismatic leadership of the anti-communist West.

Inge Queren also recalls the Germans' high regard for Kennedy: "Most Germans, including myself and my family, started clinging to President Kennedy ... he seemed like a savior to us; in his person we saw the only hope left that could change the course of events. We believed in him; we thought he was strong enough to face the Soviets down." She also confesses that when she was "just about to become a teenager in 1962, I did not have posters of singers or actors on my walls; instead, I had a large poster of John F. Kennedy above my bed."[81] The death of that President drew Germans and Americans together in their grief on that mournful November day.

During the early decades of the postwar period contemporary polls, by groups such as the Gallup organization, captured the meter of American public's feelings regarding political developments between the Eastern and Western powers. Consecutive surveys revealed that by a wide margin Americans held an unfavorable opinion of communism and the Soviet Union in the early and mid–1950s. In 1953, 88.5 percent held a negative view of the Soviets, in 1954 it was 91.1 percent, and in 1956 the figure was 86.4 percent.[82] Still, despite the demonstrations of commitment by Milcom members in Germany, by the end of the decade Americans also expressed a flagging confidence in the capabilities of the U.S. to match the Soviets. Gallup polls for October 1957 registered that 49 percent of Americans believed that "Russia" was "ahead of the U.S.," and for January 1958 recorded that 67 percent of Americans believed that "Russia" was "ahead in the Cold War."[83] In parallel, West Germans collectively remained staunch opponents of communism but their opinions of America's ability to defend them vacillated. Although their relationships with the *Amis* remained strong, and the presence of the Milcoms served as visual signifiers of the America's firm commitment to their defense, HICOG surveys conducted between 1949 and 1955 reveal that Germans remained uncertain of the West's capability to deter aggression from the East.[84]

German Sovereignty

During those early postwar decades, as Milcom members and their German hosts were facing various threats from the Soviet East, major changes were also taking place in the relationship between the U.S., its Western allies, and West Germany. These began on May 24, 1949, when *Stars and Stripes* front page carried a headline announcing, "Charter is Proclaimed at Bonn." Together with that pronouncement it provided text that outlined the details of the new West German constitution.[85] This came on the heels of the approval for the *Grundgesetz* [Basic Law] for the Federal Republic of Germany (FRG), which appeared earlier that month.[86] Together, the pair of acts gave birth to the semi-sovereign West German state and heralded the beginning of the end of the pervasive *Besatzmentalität* [occupation mentality] that had long cast a shadow across the post–1945 German political landscape.[87] They also foreshadowed a loosening of allied political control that would not be complete until May 1955 when the FRG gained full sovereignty from the Western allies. It was a shift in the nature of the political relationship from hegemonic-hierarchical to egalitarian-cooperative, from full American control to an evolving political partnership. That important transformation coincided with a fresh confidence the new Federal Republic demonstrated in its own abilities and the right of self-determination.[88]

Central to that new West German confidence was its continued stand against communism and its continued alliance with the West. This was evident in the actions, and words, of the first West German Chancellor, Konrad Adenauer. Understanding that West German confidence in the abilities of the Western allies to take strong actions against the communists was wavering, he made bold claims that at once verified the FRG's position against communism and assured his nation's place as a valuable and trusted ally of the West. This he hoped would in turn offer leverage for future concessions. Milcom members learned about Adenauer's bold statements through the AFN and in the text of reports in the *Stars and Stripes*. In a February 1951 article titled "Bonn Calls for Voice in Big Four Parley," the Chancellor made a demand that Germans have a voice in proposed four-way talks between the Soviets and the Western allies.[89] Feeling the power that came with blossoming sovereignty, while still under the aegis of the West, Adenauer boldly claimed, "We Germans both from the East and West Germany—are 100 per cent on the side of the West, and not with the East." Employing the same tone he continued, claiming that the communists "only want to neutralize [West] Germany so they can conquer all Germany in a Cold War" and "eventually bring all Europe under their rule."[90] His temerity seemed to persist later that year as he charged, "there is no [such] freedom in the Soviet Zone ... tens of thousands of innocent people are held in prisons and labor camps."[91]

Do You Support Continued Allegiance to the West?

July 1953	Yes: 69% (West Germans)	HICOG
	Yes: 93% (West Berliners)	HICOG

Has American Prestige Remained High?

Dec 1949	Yes: 99% (West Berliners)	HICOG
Jun 1953	Yes: 42%	HICOG
Jan 1954	Yes: 55%	HICOG
Jun 1954	Yes: 48%	HICOG

Do You Still See the U.S. as the Political Leader of the West?

Jun 1954	Yes: 77%	HICOG

Table 4.5. West German Attitudes Toward America and the West. (Source for HICOG surveys: Anna J. Merritt, and Richard Merritt, eds., *Public Opinion in Semi-Sovereign Germany: The HICOG Surveys, 1949–1955*, Champaign: University of Illinois Press, 1980.)

Adenauer's anti-communist rhetoric continued through the 1950s. During discussions surrounding the ratification of a new European Defense Community (EDC) treaty in June 1954, he claimed "only if the entire free world is firmly united in opposing Communist designs for aggression can the world be spared from the cruel fate of a new war." This was consistent with West German anti-communist attitudes reflected in contemporary polls. But at the same time, he offered words of confident support in the abilities of the U.S. In that context, he proclaimed, "What Russia really fears is the overwhelming power of the United States." To this he added that the relationship between the American Milcoms and their West German neighbors was solid and the [West] Germans "regard the Allied troops as defenders and if the troops were to be withdrawn, you may be sure there would be the strongest outcry."[92] Adenauer's projection of growing West German self-confidence as well as its continued reliance on protection of the West was consistent with the trends of public attitudes that ran as high as 93 percent in support of Western allegiance.[93]

An emerging military partnership also arrived with the new sovereignty. It came in the form of the West German *Bundeswehr* [Federal Armed Forces] that began to take shape in

November 1955. Although it grew slowly, by 1956 German officers were participants in the Central Army Group (CENTAG) planning cell coordinating exercises and war games with the American military. Demonstrations of West Germans' commitment to participate in their own defense against the communist East followed. In February1958, the *Bundeswehr* took control of all Rhine River patrol craft. In accepting the responsibility, the new German commander noted "The comrade like aid, the cooperation between Germans and Americans on board the craft and at the bases have demonstrated how much nearer our two peoples have approached each other, and that both nations serve a mutual cause—safeguarding our freedom."[94] By February 1960, German Panzer [tank] units participated in the NATO field exercise WINTERSHIELD for the first time and in January 1965, with the assistance of the Americans, the *Bundeswehr* organized its first missile units, *Flugkörpergeschwander*.[95] Instances of military partnership continued to increase over the ensuing years through joint-training and schools, as well as exchange programs. These provided a myriad of opportunities, especially at the grassroots level, for the West German hosts and the American Milcoms to interact professionally, socially and culturally. Just as important, they offered a platform to exhibit a continued, strong relationship on a common ground of anti-communist political agendas.

The engine of anti-communism was a powerful force that drove American domestic and foreign politics during the early postwar decades. It was a lens that provided Americans at home and in the Milcoms a perspective that defined their actions and evaluated the world. It was also an important catalyst that encouraged a unity between West Germans and Americans, and instigated changes in the relationship between the U.S. and the Federal Republic. But it was also not without complications. In their enthusiasm to forestall the spread of communism Americans exhibited a willingness to sometimes ignore trespasses on their fundamental liberties.

Nuclear Threat

The utilization and deployment of nuclear weapons was the second early postwar engine that drove American politics and policy strategy. Together with the fear of communist aggression it formed a powerfully influential combination that shaped American and West German perceptions of the world. Like the anti-communist dynamic, it was also problematic and fraught with controversy. But as examination of sources reveal, it also existed as a dichotomy within the Milcom-German relationship. Although the possible use of a nuclear deterrent acted as a shared concern between members of both communities, West Germans felt that they would pay a higher price in the event of war. As a result, an "atomic wedge" developed between the two nations that suggested the Germans became less committed to the deployment of America's nuclear arsenal on their soil.

Soon after America's ascent as a nuclear power, political and military elites worked to reassure the populace of their abilities as knowledgeable managers and stewards of its use. They also sought to allay Americans' fears for their safety. Milcom readers bore witness to these attestations through dozens of articles published in *Stars and Stripes*. One example was a July 1949 column, titled "Blandy Asserts A-Bomb Won't Destroy World," in which naval leaders confidently charged that the statement "there is no defense against the atom bomb" was an exaggeration, and that the "atom bomb will not destroy civilization."[96] Polls from the early 1950s appeared to reflect a similar attitude among the American public, with 67 percent agreeing that atomic war would not destroy mankind in 1950. That number declined to 59 percent by 1955.[97]

At the same time however, Milcom readers studied articles that offered evidence of Soviet nuclear tests and forebodings of nuclear doom.[98] This included a warning from the commander of the U.S. Tactical Air Force that Soviet bombers carrying atomic weapons could reach the U.S.[99] It also included concerns over Soviet intentions. A December 1949 poll showed that 45 percent of Americans believed "now that Russia has the atom bomb" another war was "more likely" with 28 percent claiming it was "less likely" and 17 percent saying it made "no difference."[100] Tensions generated by the two contrasting discourses continued to intensify as the specter of nuclear destruction grew with most Americans believing that any future war would certainly include the use of atomic or hydrogen bombs.

In February 1950, the chairman of the Senate Armed Services Committee proclaimed that research and development of nuclear weaponry was gaining momentum and that "with the unfolding years we may look ahead to the possibility of ultimate destruction of the civilization which mankind has been thousands of years creating."[101] That same month former British Prime Minister Winston Churchill acknowledged that the Soviets had "the greatest military force" but the United States had the hydrogen bomb "a thousand-fold more terrible manifestation of this [atomic] awful power." Against these sobering words he added that in the hands of the U.S. it was "the surest guarantee of world peace."[102] But that guarantee was not secure.

On December 1, 1950, *Stars and Stripes* headlines announced to Milcom readers that President Truman was considering the use of the atomic bomb to gain an upper hand in the war in Korea.[103] In that article he associated communist aggression on the peninsula with Soviet imperialist designs underscoring the link between countering communist hegemony and nuclear deterrence. Earlier that year, in September, a poll taken by the American Institute of Public Opinion (AIPO) revealed that 60 percent of the American public had already voiced opposition to the use of nuclear weapons in that conflict against 28 percent favoring their employment.[104]

For Milcom members living in West Germany, within easy striking distance of Soviet tactical missiles, the specter of nuclear destruction loomed larger than life, especially if the Eastern bloc military forces chose to reciprocate for the use of nuclear weapons by U.S. forces in Korea. That potentiality also added urgency to the periodic Non-Combatant Evacuation Operation (NEO) exercises for Milcom dependents and other non-combatants. The reality of that danger became evident for Frank Hubp who arrived at his new duty station with a 280mm Field Artillery (Atomic Canon) battalion in the Heilbronn Milcom in 1956. As he notes:

> I bought a used car after Jan [wife] joined me in Germany, and was surprised to be handed a pack of papers when I picked up the license plates. When I opened the envelop I found some maps and instructions for Jan—in case the Russians invaded, she was to take our newborn son and another wife with her—and drive the car to the coast for evacuation. With the amount of atomic weapons targeting that area, most of Germany, including my unit, probably would not have survived if the Russians had attacked—and we'd actually have to use those big guns.[105]

Adding to this consternation were periodic news stories such as an August 1954 article that appeared in the *New York Times* that revealed the Soviets had been mining nuclear grade ore in the East German zone. Providing alarming details, the article noted that the "Russians have produced enough uranium in East Germany since World War II to make forty-four atomic bombs." Employing thousands of workers, the "Soviet secret police" were actively securing the site located not more than 25 miles from West Germany and American troops positioned along the border.[106]

Throughout the 1950s and early 1960s, nuclear-capable units continued to deploy from the U.S. to West Germany in waves, becoming part of the existing troop structure of USAREUR and finding homes in the network of Milcoms. The weaponry included the 280-mm atomic cannon, the Corporal and Honest John Missile systems, the nuclear-capable Davy Crockett firing device and eventually the Sergeant Missile system.[107] The arsenal also included an array of Atomic Demolition Munitions (ADMs).[108] The first unit equipped with "atomic artillery" arrived in late 1953 and on October 23rd of that year appeared in a demonstration at the Mainz Ordnance Depot for American, British, and French newsmen.[109] *Stars and Stripes* heralded this event as front page news just as it did other exercises and deployments involving nuclear capable units such as exercises crossing the Rhine River with the large Atomic Cannon, field testing of the Davy Crockett, or the tactics of Honest John-equipped units.[110] The American military leadership in Germany never hid the existence of these weapons from the American public, the Soviets, or the German public as their vehicles filled the cobbled-stoned motor pools of kasernes and plied the narrow streets of town and villages, their soldiers moved into the barracks and their families occupied housing areas of Milcoms. This occurred throughout the period in cities and towns as widespread as Mainz, Crailsheim, Augsburg, Bad Kreuznach, Pirmasens, and Heilbronn, in both the V Corps and VII Corps areas.[111] In a scene that often repeated, *Stars and Stripes* captured the arrival of the 216th Field Artillery Battalion on March 26, 1955. The 500-man unit disembarked from the U.S. Navy Transport *General Patch* at the port of Bremerhaven complete with 280-mm cannons, 54 wives, and 102 children. Tired, but excited, military transport soon whisked them all to housing awaiting them in the vicinity of *Cambrai Kaserne* in the Darmstadt Milcom.[112]

Vehicles and equipment of nuclear-ready units were often on display for viewing by Milcom families, German neighbors and the media during periodic "open-house" events and all accepted their universal presence. Soldiers showed pride in their individual and crew achievements during periodic competitions and in their mission in USAREUR, often competing for bragging rights. So thick was the presence of nuclear-ready units in some locations that like the Ansbach Milcom they earned the nickname "Atomic City."

Although caught in the web of tensions surrounding the specter of nuclear war Milcom members understood the role their physical presence played as a deterrent to Soviet aggression and the importance of nuclear weapons as a key game piece on the political chessboard. As retired Army officer Larry Applebaum remembers, "After the formation of NATO and the Warsaw Pact, it was absolutely necessary that the Americans remained a dominant force to lead NATO in light of the perceived threats from the East." The U.S. forces in West Germany, "with their tactical nuclear weapons, to include those assigned to the nuclear-capable non–US forces provided a good and credible deterrent."[113] That sentiment carried into the 1960s and 1970s as evidenced in news articles that voiced the West's resolve in the face of nuclear threats from the Soviets. As the Kremlin announced intentions to test a 50-megaton bomb in November 1961, the alliance of Western European nations and the U.S. exhibited a "stiffening and indeed a bristling against the Soviets."[114] This environment generated a duality of both fear and resolve that overshadowed life in the Milcoms.

That grim resolution displayed by Milcom members resonated through the 1960s and on into later years as well. Ron Chiste arrived at his assignment with a nuclear-ready artillery unit in the Hanau Milcom and remembers a tense briefing that accompanied a rapid deployment exercise:

> I was in awe attending my first briefing and listened intently as the general described the little amount of time the battalion would have to get to its position from the time it got the alert. In the time he gave us it would have been impossible to load all TO&E equipment and get to the position within or adjacent the Fulda Gap. At the end of the briefing the general asked if there were any questions. I raised my hand, to the utter disbelief of all the more senior officers in the room. I was a bit naive about the protocol at this point in my career. I was acknowledged and asked the question about the time he was allowing us. His response was amazing to us all, "You will not be taking tents, field kitchens, or anything like that with you. C and B Batteries will be racing across the Fulda River and A Battery will be held in reserve. And even more sobering was the general's next comment, which probably no one at that briefing has ever forgotten, "We don't expect C and B to come back."[115]

Often the seriousness exhibited by military units and personnel in training, carried over to their families. Robert Weekley, commander of a battery of nuclear capable artillery cannon, recalls, "We definitely felt that nuclear war was a realistic possibility" and that "our families in Germany shared our concerns and feelings." So serious were they that ample attention was dedicated to the "preparation of packing our NEO kits—emergency food, medicine, and fuel—to enable our families to evacuate." To emphasize his concern Weekley also confided that "I arranged a secret rendezvous place in the Colorado Mountains where my wife and I would try to reunite someday if a world nuclear war broke out."[116] The existence of that serious attitude resonates also in the memories of Winton "Dip" Spiller, assigned to an artillery unit in the Babenhausen Milcom. He recalls that "we trained constantly on the proper procedures to take in the event of nuclear attack" and unit commanders "took actions to insure that their units were as well prepared as possible" to sustain themselves in such an event.[117]

All American military units in EUCOM trained for the eventuality of nuclear war and integrated associated tasks and drills with scheduled exercises. Units also produced their own policies and procedural guidelines for individual service members and units of various sizes. While training for nuclear capable artillery and missile units generally focused on the offense, all other units prepared for defensive maneuvers and decontamination. Most units provided soldiers with simplified pocket guides to augment published guidance. All nuclear-associated training was subject to evaluation and grading and was a key component of a unit's Mission Essential Task List.

Although most American units conducted their training seriously within the context of nuclear warfare attitudes among individuals did vary. Bill Hanne, a lieutenant in a mechanized cavalry squadron acknowledged that "tactical nuclear war was a given and we trained accordingly—we were outmanned and we knew it and the only equalizer was the nuclear warhead, regardless of its delivery method." But he also admitted, "Nuke warfare never cost me any sleepless nights or concerns."[118] Variances in attitudes such as this may have been a function of individual perceptions, rank and access to information, proximity to Soviet forces, or command emphasis. Each could account for the use of a different lens through which to interpret the political atmosphere. Contemporary opinion polls, media releases, and most oral histories, however, suggest that during the late 1950s and early 1960s there was a general consensus of fear concerning nuclear war.

Contributing to the tensions felt by Milcom members were propaganda films produced by the government and the private sector. The Federal Civil Defense Administration, working in conjunction with the National Education Association (NEA), generated a cautionary 10-

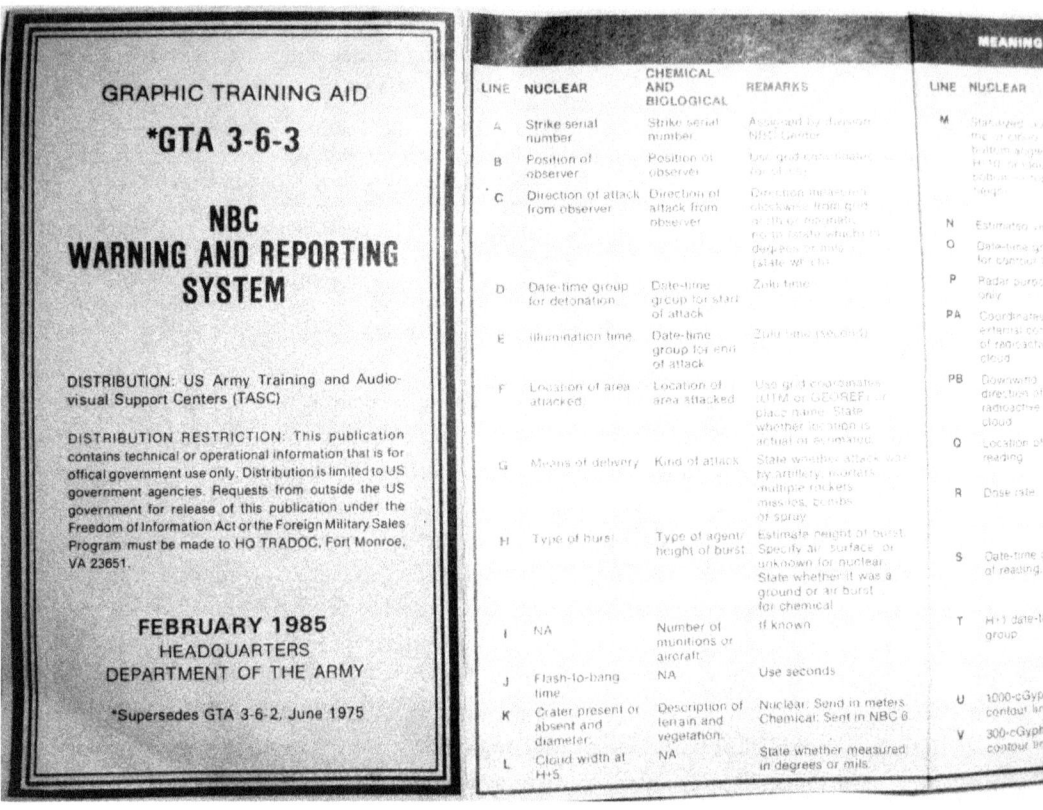

Nuclear Biological and Chemical (NBC) Warning and Reporting System Card (1985). Issued by the U.S. Army. After the appropriate training an individual leader or soldier would be able to use this card to report a nuclear detonation, to determine the size of the blast and to determine residual radiation levels on objects such as vehicles, buildings, and trees. Image source: the author.

minute cartoon in 1951 that gave instructions to American school children on how to best protect themselves in the event of a nuclear attack. The U.S. government titled the film "Duck and Cover" and ensured that the production had the widest distribution to school systems in the U.S. as well as overseas in the DODDS.[119]

Newsreels, shown in public theaters stateside as well as in EUCOM, followed the theme of atoms for war and peace. One, released in June 1952, heralded the laying of the keel of the first submarine driven by nuclear power and coolly noted that it was "a deadly weapon for war or peace."[120] Another, filmed in November 1961, focused on "Project Plowshares," an initiative to explode an atomic weapon underground in order to drive an electric turbine. The narrator noted that it, too, was "a major step in peaceful atomic use."[121] The production studios of Walt Disney lost no time in contributing to the atomic propaganda apparatus with its 1956 film, *Our Friend the Atom*. Although the narrator warned the audience of the dangers of uncontrolled use of atomic power, the 60-minute movie emphasized its peaceful applications for the military, science, and in medicine.

Altogether, films produced by the government and commercial studios piqued Americans' awareness of the benefits and dangers of atomic power and assured that they understood the important role nuclear weapons played in the high stakes game of global politics. For Milcom members, these films provided a backdrop to the myriad of daily reminders they were already receiving through news articles, radio reports, military training and field maneuvers, practice alerts, and NEO exercises.

By 1964, nuclear weapons continued to figure as a prominent theme in both domestic and foreign politics. It was central to debates concerning executive control during the U.S. Presidential campaign as Republicans and Democrats challenged one another over release authority in the event of war. Senator Barry Goldwater, the Republican candidate, advocated that control of nuclear weapons should remain with American military leaders in Europe and incumbent President Lyndon Johnson advocated keeping control in the White House.[122] Also, by December of that year the U.S. was insisting on having "a veto over use of any nuclear force created by the Atlantic Alliance [United States, Britain, France, and West Germany]." This included an understanding that "there would be no nuclear assault from this force [Atlantic Alliance] without the decision of the [U.S.] President."[123] Although in this context there was some room for debate among the Western allies, the U.S. was insisting on a very exceptional political and military leadership role.

Development of an Atomic Wedge

For West Germans the issue of nuclear weapons was as complicated and problematic as it was for the Americans. This was evident in the dichotomy of attitudes between West German political elites and the general public. While leaders, such as Chancellor Adenauer and other conservatives, were quick to voice their support of the Western Allies and project themselves as staunch anti-communists, they also tried to downplay the fears and concerns that came with the deployment of nuclear weapons on their soil. Concomitantly, Adenauer and other political elites walked a fine line between accepting America's European defense strategy, which included a strong nuclear deterrent, and mitigating West Germans' feelings of helplessness. An April 1954 HICOG public survey of Germans confirmed those fears, as 41 percent of West Germans voiced their concern that their country was the "most likely target for atomic weapons" during a future war.[124] These were feelings that Americans in the Milcoms shared as they prepared to evacuate their homes every time the Soviet saber rattled as it did in 1953, 1956, 1961 and 1962.

These concerns contributed to public debate on West Germany's rearmament and a bolstering of NATO forces as ways to lessen the West's heavy reliance on nuclear weapons to counterbalance the Soviet bloc's numerical superiority in ground forces. In that context Adenauer and other political leaders carefully navigated between support for a dominant nuclear American military and leveraging greater sovereignty through some degree of rearmament. If he came too close to the first he would risk losing domestic political power, too close to the second and he would risk animosity from allies such as France and Britain.[125] This was evident as Adenauer worried that "latent terror inspired by the atom bomb and even more by the hydrogen bomb could be worked up into a decisive opposition to his pro–Western policy."[126]

Editorials in news magazines such as *Die Zeit* also reflected West German concerns that America would not consider Europeans' concerns in the political equation. *Die Zeit's* editors suggested that as American resolve against the Soviets grew during the 1950s, so too did a strengthening of "American nationalism." Combined with its "material prosperity" and "scientific genius" the U.S. might feel as if it could act unilaterally in Europe. This "emergence of national arrogance" the editorial explained, manifested itself in manipulation of policy strategy in the West and ignored the interests of European allies.[127] The inherent concern was over a perceived exclusive decision-making by Washington regarding the employment of nuclear weapons.

The results of HICOG polls, during the 1950s, revealed these trepidations among the West Germans as well as the development of an "atomic wedge" that would exist between them and the Americans. In the first years after the war, both Americans and West Germans felt that the U.S. had the right to progress scientifically and develop weapons technology and conduct testing beyond the atomic bomb. Both sets of surveys, collected by the Gallup organization and the HICOG, reflected this trend. While 70 percent of Americans supported this course in October 1947 a similar question regarding manufacture of the hydrogen bomb drew 63 percent approval from West Germans.[128] As subsequent interpretation reveals however, early in the 1950s this parallel began to diverge.

In early February 1950 *Stars and Stripes* provided Milcom members with a review of the details of President Truman's decision to move forward with development and testing of the hydrogen bomb. The banner headline for February 2, 1950, announced the "1st Hydrogen Bomb Test Predicted within Year" and accompanying text predicted that the weapon would be "two to ten times" as powerful as the existing atomic bomb.[129] Subsequent articles outlined and amplified the estimated power and destructive capability of the hydrogen bomb noting that theoretically it could be "1,000 times more powerful" than the atomic bomb, and its blast radius ten times greater.[130] Despite these dire predictions Americans continued to support development and testing of the H-bomb.[131]

By this time however, it was evident that West Germans were harboring a different attitude than their American allies and neighbors in the Milcoms. When asked in a July 1951 HICOG survey if the U.S. would use the atomic bomb at the outset of a new war, 23 percent of the West Germans responded that the American military would probably use it immediately. Of that same group, 49 percent predicted that the American military would wait.[132] In comparison, 77 percent of Americans polled remarked that their nation would use the bomb immediately in the event of an attack.[133] When asked about the Soviets, 37 percent of West Germans predicted that they would use it immediately, and only 33 percent thought the communists would wait.[134]

That divergence in opinions and attitudes between the Germans and Milcom members continued to develop. This becomes evident by examining other survey questions crafted by the HICOG Reactions Analysis Staff, for the West Germans, which purposely required more nuanced answers on these issues. The results from those questions, posed between July 1951 and April/May 1954, revealed broader considerations than those exhibited by the Americans.[135] When queried about a possible cross-border attack by Soviet forces onto their soil, only 35 percent of West Germans favored using a nuclear deterrent immediately, while 36 percent considered using it only after the Soviets did. The remainder of the survey population offered no opinion.[136] This was in contrast to the Milcom military members for whom it was a foregone conclusion and who were ready to execute that mission. Other HICOG survey results revealed that 14 percent of West Germans unconditionally opposed any use of nuclear weapons, 26 percent supported their use if the "other side" [Soviets] used them first, and 32 percent supported using them only in "special circumstances." More than a quarter (28 percent) was uncertain and provided no response.[137]

West Germans' fears of figuring among the first casualties of the next war, and having their nation serve as a "target for atomic weapons" suggests a reason for this reluctance to support a too heavy reliance on a nuclear defense. Soviet rhetoric fed those growing concerns by frequently charging that the U.S. was "converting West Germany into an atomic base" adding a warning that the Germans were "playing with fire."[138] Challenges such as this would also threaten West Germany's fuller integration with the West, a priority item on Adenauer's political agenda.[139] Consequently, the debate over the placement of nuclear weapons on West German soil would not disappear. It remained central to other important political discourses of the time such membership in a European Defense Community (EDC), rearmament and remilitarization, and considerations of future reunification.[140]

The polemics surrounding the stationing of nuclear weapons on German soil occurred against a backdrop of other associated fears. By the mid–1960s worry emerged concerning the safety and security of nuclear weapons during their handling and transportation. Although a number of mishaps had already occurred in the U.S., those that transpired in Europe quickly captured the attention of the Germans. One of the worst examples was a mid-air collision of a B-52 bomber with a tanker aircraft during a refueling operation over the Mediterranean near the coast of Spain in January 1966. As the bomber crashed it jettisoned three hydrogen bombs onto farmers' fields and one into the ocean.[141]

During the ensuing weeks and months articles in *Stars and Stripes* and other American dailies, such as the *New York Times* and the *Washington Post* as well as in the German press outlined for their audiences the massive recovery operations. Most disconcerting to both American and German readers however, were reports of faint traces of radioactive contamination of soil and on some Spanish police who were first on the scene.[142] Although the American press reports tended to be factual and avoided discussing danger of contamination the German press was critical of American recovery efforts and focused on potential hazards. A February 1966 column in *Der Spiegel* likened the ocean recovery of the nuclear weapon to a scene from the James Bond movie "Thunderball," for all its complex technological gadgetry, and reported a cost of 4.5 million DM per day.[143] It also noted sardonically, that tomatoes from that Spanish town "are delivered primarily in the Federal Republic" implying that radioactive particles might ultimately reach Germany one way or another.[144] Other West German articles continued to emphasize the problems of "leaked radioactivity" and the fact that it took the U.S. Navy 81 days to locate the submerged bomb.[145] The knowledge that the press had been reporting similar accidents since 1958, and that the U.S. government acted behind a veil of security and was less than forthcoming with information, added to Germans' flagging confidence about the safety of atomic weapons on their soil.[146]

The fact that American military nuclear-ready units and storage facilities existed in close proximity to German populations was a reason for exacerbating those feelings. A survey of a number of those American artillery and missile units from the 1950s and 1960s reveals that with few exceptions their distance from clusters of German populations was less than 5 miles. This reality presented German locals with constant daily visual reminders of the physical presence of nuclear weapons and the haunting concerns of accidental contamination or targeting by enemy forces or terrorist groups. When combined with the evidence of accidents it provided a powerful inducement of worry and questioning of the need for a nuclear shield.

Training accidents and concerns over potential mishaps were not uncommon. As William Terry, assigned to a 280mm artillery unit, recalls:

> For the annual exercises and training we went either to Baumholder or Grafenwoehr [training areas] and convoyed there. At Graf we had to fire from off-base positions, either near Vilseck or Pegnitz. At one training trip, when firing from near Pegnitz, we were using a new batch of proximity fuses, when one was set off by a rain cloud. I understand it sprinkled shrapnel over three towns. For those not familiar with the 280mm round, it weighed 600 pounds and was about 5 feet long.[147]

Other mishaps, which occasionally inspired local consternation, occurred when these large pieces of equipment attempted to navigate the narrow roadways of villages and towns. Buildings were sometimes damaged, road signs and stonewalls ruined, or traffic blocked. The M65, 280mm Atomic Cannon, often referred to as "Atomic Annie," was 84' long, 16' wide and weighed 84 tons. One misadventure captured in an August 1954 *Stars and Stripes* photo shows recovery crews struggling to retrieve a cannon carrier from a roadside ditch along a winding Bavarian road.[148] These units were not training with nuclear rounds at the time these accidents occurred. The mishaps would have been more disastrous had they been.

As the West German public equivocated on the issue of a nuclear presence within their borders, American military units continued to park their nuclear weapon carriers behind guarded gates in German communities and deploy them out of the Milcom garrisons on periodic training exercises. As missile launchers and atomic cannons rumbled through West German cities, towns and villages the inhabitants continued to wonder over their fate should a full military confrontation between the West and the East occur or if some accident happened.

Nuclear-Capable Artillery Unit and Location	Nearest Populated Areas	Distance
42nd Field Artillery (FA) Brigade (1957)		
59th FA Battalion 280mm		
Pirmasens	French Border	4.6 miles
264th FA Battalion 280mm		
Bad Kreuznach	Bad Kreuznach	0.0 miles
	Bad Munster	1.5 miles
	Rüdesheim	1.8 miles
265th FA Battalion 280 mm		
Baumholder	Ruschberg	1.5 miles
868th FA Battalion 280 mm		
Baumholder	Ruschberg	1.5 miles
530th FA Missile Battalion (Corporal)		
Mainz-Gonzenheim	Schierstein	2.6 miles
	Wiesbaden	3.6 miles
559th FA Missile Battalion (CPL)		
Mainz-Gonzenheim	Schierstein	2.6 miles
	Wiesbaden	3.6 miles
601st FA Missile Battalion (CPL)		
Zweibrücken	Contwig	2 miles

Table 4.6. Proximity of U.S. Military nuclear-capable units to the nearest populated areas (c. 1957). This representative sample reflects only units of the 42nd Field Artillery Group. There were other nuclear-capable units in the U.S. V Corps and in the U.S. VII Corps, as well as U.S. Air Force weapons located at airbases in Germany. The first U.S. Army nuclear-capable units began arriving in 1953 and were all in position in West Germany by 1957, although the locations of these units sometimes shifted

from the original locations. These weapons—the 280mm artillery cannon (M65 Atomic Cannon) and the Corporal missile (MGM-5 Corporal)—were tactical nuclear weapons for use only within the theater of operations and did not have the capability to reach the Soviet Union. ("42nd Field Artillery Brigade," U.S. Army in Germany, accessed June 14, 2013, http://www.usarmygermany.com/Sont.htm?http&&&www.usarmygermany.com/Units/FieldArtillery/USAREUR_42nd%20Arty%20Group.htm)

West Germans realized that if the American non-combatants should ever leave the Milcoms for the rear areas, in a coordinated or headlong retreat, the German population would remain in place. This precipitated grievances over the lagging efforts of the Federal Republic to allocate adequate funding for civil defense programs. Contemporary editorials noted that "adequate protection of the population with the previous methods can no longer be guaranteed" and questioned vague policies for ensuring the protection of food stocks from "radioactive contamination."[149] Continuing into the 1960s, West Germans complained of lack of sufficient funding for contingency plans to include items such as "radioactive and debris-safe shelters."[150] Over time, concerns for the placement of nuclear-ready weapons on their soil, fears of nuclear holocaust, and a national policy that required them to remain in place as American non-combatants evacuated in the event of war, generated antipathy among West Germans.[151]

During the early postwar decades, concerns for a perceived communist threat and reliance on a nuclear arsenal to thwart aggression from the East were two sides of a political coin. On one, a joint German-American distrust for the Soviets forged a strong alliance that strengthened political, military and even economic ties between the two nations. On the other, American dependence on nuclear weapons generated deep fears from a West German public that worried that their country could face annihilation should it become an atomic battleground. The first dynamic endorsed a contemporary consensus of anti-communism, the second formed a wedge between partners that generated political tensions that would last through the end of the Cold War.

Five

Challenge to American Economic Dominance (1946–1967)

With 7,000 export orders at the end of 1948, the diminutive Volkswagen Beetle had become the "best-selling imported car in the USA."[1] In December 1962, VW again held that position with sales approaching 230,000 vehicles, and by May 1963 the company reported a 22 percent sales increase over the previous two year period.[2] That uniquely shaped automobile, emblematic of pre-war German industrial capability, had become an icon of West Germany's phenomenal postwar economic recovery. That revival, which occurred between 1947 and the mid–1950s, resulted from a combination of programs and policies by the U.S. and the strong work ethic of the German people. It formed an essential link that bound the two nations through connections that were both economic and political for most of the Cold War period.

For nearly two years after the war the German economy languished under the strictures of JCS 1067.[3] The document outlined severe conditions that sought to ensure that Germany could never again mobilize its resources, economic and industrial, to conduct war. By 1947, however, conditions in the AMZON had become dire. With a shortage of housing, coal for heating or industrial use, and reduced food supplies, the German economy appeared paralyzed and the people were suffering excessively.[4] Eventually gaining appreciation of these conditions, and their humanitarian and political impact, the U.S. government moved to provide relief and economic stabilization. By the mid-point of that year America focused on bringing Europe, and in particular West Germany, back from the brink of starvation and desperation. This included programs to improve caloric intake, provide employment, improve existing infrastructure, and ignite a spark for reindustrialization and reconstruction.[5] The eventual result was a vibrant economy that by the mid–1950s began to rival that of the U.S. and other Western European nations.

This economic miracle, or *Wirtschaftswunder*, proved an essential ingredient in shaping a strong, new anti-communist partner for the West, although at first the German public and private sectors did not always understand or welcome the intentions behind the initiatives. But that unique trajectory of economic success, which continued through the following decades, had several points of contact with the American Milcoms that affected their relationship with the host nation: employment of the local populace, a changing Deutsche Mark rate, the black market, and taxes.

Setting the Stage for Economic Recovery

The starting signal of the economic resurgence sounded when Secretary of State George Marshall introduced the European Recovery Plan (ERP) on June 5, 1947, during a speech at Harvard University. Following closely on the heels of President Truman's introduction of the "Truman Doctrine" to the U.S. Congress three months earlier, the ERP was the culmination of numerous policy and strategy decisions by the Administration to solve the dilemma of continuing economic difficulties in Europe. Both programs were initiatives by the U.S. to step forward into a leadership role in the postwar world.[6] Noting the "dislocation of the entire fabric of [the] European economy" by the war's end, Marshall reasoned to his audience at Harvard that the U.S. "should do whatever it is able to do to assist in the return of normal economic health in the world." The ERP he further explained "is not directed against any country or doctrine but against hunger, poverty, desperation, and chaos."[7]

Regardless of Marshall's words about doctrines, however, Washington political elites saw this as an opportunity to revitalize Europe, in particular Germany, and fill a void before communist adversaries could act.[8] This attitude suggests a mindset that sprang from the context of an American anti-communist predisposition and out of an extant advantage of surplus and wealth, which contributed to feelings of superiority and translated into a postwar posture of power and triumphalism. For example, by 1949, the U.S. with 7 percent of the world's population was enjoying 42 percent of the world's income, and the average American was consuming 3,186 calories daily, compared to drastically lower levels among Western allies.[9] For the U.S. the challenge in Europe appeared twofold: first to facilitate a wide acceptance of the ERP, then to shape and enable the recovering economies along an "American way."[10]

A survey of contemporary polls reveals various levels of acceptance and understanding of the ERP among West Germans. One sampling conducted of West Berliners by the HICOG in December 1949 recorded that only 23 percent of the 63 percent who had heard of the plan thought it would bring improvement.[11] In contrast, that same month, a larger population of West Germans (60 percent) responding to a set of questions voiced approval of the Marshall Plan with 68 percent adding that U.S. aid was "furthering reconstruction" of their nation.[12] By August of the following year the trend continued with 65 percent of survey respondents noting they felt that the distribution of Marshall Plan aid helped "all Germans not just certain groups." The same sample population in the AMZON reflected strong confidence (70 percent) that the ERP was making "a real contribution to reconstruction," while those in West Berlin were more confident (91 percent), showing a strong improvement over December 1949.[13]

By comparison, during the same relative timeframe, most Americans were subscribing to the highest ideals associated with the ERP. In August 1947, 59 percent of those polled by the Gallup organization knew of the plan, and of those 50 percent approved of it. By February 1948, a Roper poll showed that 86 percent of Americans surveyed knew of the plan and of those 77 percent agreed with the statement "We ought to do our best to help out people who are hungry and sick, and the Marshall Plan does that."[14] Articles in *Stars and Stripes* assured American Milcom members that the ERP was achieving success. Norman H. Collisson, representative of the Economic Cooperation Administration (ECA) and the ERP in West Germany, confidently noted to readers "In the first 18 months of its existence the Marshall Plan accomplished its first major objective ... reestablishment of the European economy on something approaching a normal basis." He also encouraged them to look about the communities where they lived and compare "the Germany of today as against the Germany of a year ago." While also assuring Milcom readers that they could feel good about their nation and themselves, Collisson noted that the plan "was devised as an instrument for economic recovery" and that it was not "charged with responsibilities in the political field."[15]

To encourage those feelings within military communities, the government also produced a propaganda film through the Big Picture series for airing on television in the U.S. and at theaters overseas. Titled "The Changed Face of Europe," it focused on the Marshall Plan and began by describing the early postwar European environment of "economic chaos" populated by a "peoples exhausted by war" whose main "preoccupation was with essentials." The film then described the Americans who, with great compassion and "Christian intent," "gave from a wealth—the greatest in the world" to provide succor to the European masses. The initiative, noted the narrator, was the "Marshall Plan" and was "the greatest humanitarian step in all of history." He also added, a bit duplicitously, that it "took no regard of politics, only human need." The film finally noted, with triumphal overtones, that it was "truly the power of the New World come to redress the imbalance of the Old."[16]

A survey by the Institut für Demoskopie at Allensbach, conducted in November 1950, queried Germans regarding the purpose of the ERP.[17] Proposing the statement that "One hears very different views as to why the Americans introduced the Marshall Plan" it asked respondents to select from a listing of nine reasons. Most (58 percent) supposed that it was because "America wants to prevent Western Europe from becoming Communist." The next highest group (32 percent) chose that it was because "America wants to win allies in case there should be a war with Russia." Further down the list, 29 percent selected "America is using the Marshall Plan as a means of getting rid of its surpluses" and only 19 percent chose the reason that "America is genuinely anxious to help hungry and needy persons." Other options that hinted at more sinister motives, such as America's use of the plan to control "the whole of Western Europe" or to dominate the European market "by force," received lesser percentages.[18] Against these last types of contrary charges President Truman emphatically argued that the U.S. was not fostering any imperialistic designs, foreswearing "any thought of territorial aggrandizement or economic domination through the Marshall Plan."[19]

This survey suggests that the majority of West Germans perceived that the intentions or influence of the ERP might extend beyond the boundaries of pure humanitarian efforts or economic revival and that they understood there was a political connection. If not already apparent to American Milcom members this connection became evident in early 1950 when the plan administrator W. Averell Harriman admitted in a radio broadcast from Paris that the Marshall Plan would "enable the Western world to become a united bulwark for freedom." He then added with emphasis, "Aggressive communism is on the defensive in Western Europe" intimating that the ERP was key to maintaining a strong united front.[20] With the outbreak of hostilities on the Korean Peninsula in June of 1950, a rapidly cascading succession of events occurred that subsequently drew West Germany closer into the circle of Western alliance. These included its membership in the Council of Europe in July 1950, the revision of the Occupation Statute in March 1951, and its membership as a founding state of the European Coal and Steel Community (ECSC) in April 1951.[21] All of these actions signaled an appreciation for West Germany's phenomenal postwar economic recovery and an increasing recognition by the U.S. of that nation as a viable ally.

By November 1951, economic aid to Germany through the ERP and other plans had totaled $3.5 billion dollars. Of the $1.3 from the Marshall Plan just more than half went to German industry for "machinery, tools, and critical raw materials."[22] By 1952, the total amount from the plan that West Germany received was $1.6 B. At the end of the first postwar decade this influx of aid stabilized the economy, lowered the level of unemployment, opened the economy to global trade, generated a moderate level of prosperity for the average West German, and introduced consumerism on a broad scale.[23]

Perhaps one of the best indicators of the economy come full circle was the ubiquitous Volkswagen. In June of 1948, German manufacturers were lamenting that their "automotive industry is fighting for its life."[24] By 1954, however, the cover of *Time* magazine featured an image of the triumphant General Director of VW, Heinrich Nordhoff, under the title "The Volkswagen Miracle." Within three years they were crowing with pride, "Dulles is driving his second Volkswagen already."[25]

The VW had always been a favorite of many service members and families stationed overseas. Some remembered the model's durability from wartime encounters, and others appreciated the price.[26] When compared with the larger, more modern and more costly American automobiles available through the PX system, the smaller VW was a better fit for the family budget. As Norman McCracken recalls, "In late 1955 I bought a new VW Beetle, the first legally made for the U.S. market, for about $1,200 in Marks. The car sold for around $1,800 stateside."[27] Jon Wolfe fondly remembers, "In June 1960, I bought a brand new VW from a car dealer in Mannheim with money I had saved from paper routes and pumping gas as a kid in Austin, Minnesota, plus money I had saved in the Army. I drove my VW all throughout Europe on leave and eventually shipped it back home at the end of my Army service. A great little car. I wish I still had it today."[28]

Although the VW was a hit with Milcom members, and was well-received in the U.S., its reception was not always the warmest. During a 1949 German Industrial Exhibition held at the Rockefeller Center in New York City the Committee to Combat Anti-Semitism staged a demonstration. Jewish protestors gathered and held placards reading "Nazis Keep Your Bloody Goods" and "Today Volkswagen, Tomorrow the Death Wagon."[29] Regardless, the Volkswagen was a popular choice for many former GIs and Americans and benefited from American economic assistance.

When the U.S. terminated the ERP in the summer of 1952 West German political leaders quickly voiced their gratitude by thanking America for raising their nation to "a position of full equality ... with other nations of the world." In addition, leaders noted that American aid had an "extraordinary political and moral effect on the German people."[30] Later in that decade the momentum of those good feelings continued as reflected in a poll of West Germans in the AMZON who overwhelmingly (58 percent) claimed that America's intentions in Europe were to "safeguard peace and democracy." This was opposed to the 28 percent who suggested that America was only interested in selling products on world markets."[31]

The conclusion of the Marshall Plan marked a milestone on West Germany's path to full recovery as a global economic entity, signaled its movement toward greater sovereignty, which would come in 1955, and indicated its readiness to shoulder a portion of the responsibility for the defense of Western Europe. Most important, it created an environment of greater economic integration of the Milcoms and the German host nation.

One of the keys to greater German-American integration was labor. Even before the American occupation authorities had established the first military communities in April 1946,

U.S. military forces in West Germany were utilizing German civilian labor for various tasks. Sources reveal that they served in positions ranging from the mundane such as tailoring and laundry, to the labor intensive such as facilities and housing construction, to the more technical such as vehicular maintenance. This employment trend continued as American military and civilian families began to pour into the garrison towns and Milcoms throughout West Germany. Even as employment opportunities were scarce during the occupation period prior to the infusion of economy-boosting capital through aid programs and the ERP, the Milcoms were employing hundreds of West Germans.

An early example was the hiring of qualified Germans for air-traffic controller jobs at airports in the AMZON in 1947.[32] Within months U.S. military officials continued to make available other essential jobs at those facilities such as freight handlers, repair and maintenance of aircraft, installation maintenance, and communications.[33] Another example was the hiring of Germans to act in liaison and semi-supervisory capacities for the GYA in each of the *Landkreise* [states].[34] But central to the core of German workers were those serving in the military government. A March of 1948 tally reveals that there were at least 2,571 serving in various staff and liaison positions.[35] U.S. authorities within the Military Government however, followed specific criteria for hiring based on the Allies' postwar program of denazification, demilitarization and disarmament. Regulations outlined those Germans who were not eligible for hiring based on previous membership in the Nazi party and certain skills and professions that were not open to Germans. For example, in the case of aeronautics, Germans could not apply for pilot's licenses or engage in the manufacturing of aircraft. This continued until the program gradually lost momentum by the mid-1950s when the Western Allies saw a need for German partnership in defense against the Soviets.[36]

EUCOM also employed large numbers of German nationals by forming them into Labor Service Guard Units and Labor Service (Quartermaster Labor) Units. Among the first were 500 German men hired in August 1948 to support loading and transportation of supplies used in the Berlin Airlift. By June 1949 the military government had created eight companies of workers. Undergoing several reorganizations during its history it eventually developed into the Civilian Support Agency by 1981 and employed approximately 75,000 German nationals in a variety of maintenance and logistics positions. Similarly, in 1947, USAREUR began hiring individuals to form Labor Service Guard units. The number of Labor Service Guards grew to approximately 7,000 by 1949. These numbers increased to 17,457 by 1952 and reached a high of 19,573 by 1953, decreasing during the following years as American military police gradually replaced them. Their primary duties were to guard American military facilities and depots to prevent pilfering and incidents of sabotage.[37] A preponderance of displaced persons (DPs) residing in Germany at the close of the war, including Poles, Czechs, Balkans, and Eastern Europeans, originally filled the ranks of both the Labor Service and Labor Service Guard units. By 1948 however, the Americans formed many new units from the increasing number of newly returned German POWs. Within several years almost 95 percent of some units were German.[38]

By the early 1950s, even as the national rate of unemployment exceeded 10 percent, German workers continued to become essential employees within the infrastructure of the Milcoms. Evidence of an increased integration included the evolution of the German Employees Council that gave them a representative voice to file labor grievances, conduct arbitration, and recognize work-place achievements.[39] Evidence of the importance of these workers' groups was the attention they received in the Milcom press. A December 1949 issues of *The Heidelberg Post* carried a front page article regarding the meeting of the Milcom commander with the Heidelberg Military Post (HMP) German Employees Council. The text of his comments included recognition that the "foundation of this council was a milestone in good labor relations with Heidelberg" and that it would provide a "two way channel between the Post Commander and his employees."[40] Present at that meeting were representatives of the 7,000 German workers in the Heidelberg Milcom.[41] They included areas such as the military run hotels, PX and commissary operations, vehicular maintenance, dependent schools, the service club system, and the security guards.

Also important for German employees was a decision negotiated between the German government and EUCOM headquarters to shift the responsibility for workers' wages to the individual Milcoms. This move permitted the U.S. forces to "become the direct employer of their German help" giving the Americans full responsibility for their pay as well as hiring and firing.[42] It was in this context that various German Employees' Councils sent letters of intent

German Labor Service member. Unknown worker stands on the road to the camp at Eschborn near Frankfurt, c. August 1949. There were originally two companies at this location, each with 300 men. They wore American military uniforms dyed black with a distinctive shoulder patch. Members received lodging, meals, toiletries and a small stipend in return for the labor they provided. Many considered themselves lucky to have such positions at a time when the war-ravaged economy had little to offer in the way of employment. Image source: "Labor Service Division," *U.S. Army Germany*, accessed November 11, 2013, http://usarmygermany.com/Sont.htm?http&&&usarmygermany.com/Units/HqUSAREUR/USAREUR_LaborSvc.htm with permission.

to strike when there was a delay in payment of wages in June 1948.⁴³ Although it never materialized, it was indicative of both the still unsettled economic environment in West Germany and the growing relationship between the Milcoms and their civilian labor force.

By 1953, there were already more than 15,000 Germans working for the U.S. Army's Ordnance command throughout the country, mostly as vehicle maintenance and refurbishment personnel.⁴⁴ This included 1,200 at the maintenance facility at the Boeblingen Milcom.⁴⁵ The Ordnance Automotive Center, headquartered in Stuttgart, employed an additional 14,000 skilled workers.⁴⁶ Dozens more worked at the USAREUR communications center in Heidelberg as dial control and wire technicians.⁴⁷ In addition, by 1957, more than 11,000 German civilians worked in the Kaiserslautern Milcom area within the U.S. Army's logistical base structure at more than 300 types of jobs. As the Big Picture film *Foreign Nationals* noted, this made available to the U.S. military the "use of a large reservoir of locally available workers" and did "much to strengthen the economy."⁴⁸

The impact of hiring and employment within the official Milcom structure as well as on its periphery was noteworthy, although it was logically strongest in areas where there were concentrations of American military facilities and communities. Other than working in official capacities for the Americans, enterprising Germans exploited opportunities to establish jobs

West German Unemployment Rate, 1948–1967. Data sources: Deutsche Bundesbank, *Trading Economics*, http://www.tradingeconomics.com/germany/unemployment-rate. Accessed: August 10, 2013 and *Institut für Arbeitsmarkt und Berufsforschung, Bundesandstalt für Arbeit* [Institute for the Labor Market and Occupational Research, Federal Office of Labor], accessed August 10, 2013, http://doku.iab.de/zfibel/03_06_02.pdf and *Der Spiegel On-Line, Wirtschaft, Arbeitslosigkeit in Deutschland*, accessed August 10, 2013, http://www.spiegel.de/flash/flash-26018.html.

in the service and entertainment sectors. German taxi drivers, food vendors, bars, restaurants and souvenir shops profited from the Milcoms' presence. German landlords also profited by making rooms available to let for American families, at prices that often exceeded normal ceilings. On the darker side, prostitution, gambling establishments and crime also blossomed in the vicinity of U.S. military garrisons. Frequently, German towns suffered the dichotomy of economic boom and moral decay, as depicted in films such as the *Golden Plague*, a contradiction that often found its way into the public debate.[49]

One example of a garrison town that faced this type of economic boom was Baumholder in the Rhineland-Palatinate. Construction programs for military facilities, including family housing and barracks, provided jobs and lowered the local unemployment from 22.4 percent prior to March 1950, to 1.4 percent afterward. By one estimate, in 1954, the American military employed 17 percent of the Birkenfeld County workforce, which included the town of Baumholder.[50] Other cities, towns, and villages that benefited in a similar way were Heidelberg, Frankfurt, Mainz, Stuttgart and Grafenwoehr. These opportunities contributed to the overall national trend of decreasing unemployment rates that lasted through the mid–1960s when the average stood at less than 1 percent. The American military presence provided a needed boost to the West German economy through increased employment opportunities as well as increased spending in the vicinity of the Milcoms. This condition began prior to the advent of the *Wirtschaftswunder* and continued well into the 1960s. Along with economic benefits both nations realized a closer integration and dependency on one another that fostered their postwar alliance. Still, another dimension of the economic resurgence that influenced the relationship between West Germans and the American Milcoms was the currency reform of 1948.

Stars and Stripes banner headline that broadcast "Mark Changes Tomorrow Western Allies Announce Reform" heralded the most important spark to ignite the *Wirtschaftswunder*.[51] The media, both German and Allied in the Western zones, had carried stories of the consideration for currency reform for months. Upon making the decision to introduce a new tender during the London Conference of 1948, the Western allied governments released a joint statement that the action would "eliminate the consequences of the destruction of the currency caused by National Socialism [Nazism]."[52] In truth, the Allies saw it as a necessary step to affect economic stability, an act they hoped would subsequently precipitate a unified German nation. Intentions aside, that initiative contained an element of disruptive political resonance and served as a catalyst for Soviet counter-reactions, which included a withdrawal from the Allied Control Council (ACC) and involved the blockade of Berlin.[53] Nevertheless, for West Germany it would solve the problem of a swollen money supply, eliminate restrictive price controls, undercut the value of the black market and provide incentive to wage earners.[54]

Prior to June 1948, Milcom members had enjoyed an exchange rate of one U.S. dollar to ten Reichsmarks (RMs), the existing currency. That ratio provided favorable economic leverage for the Americans when purchasing goods or services from West Germans during the occupation period. Also, in a West German society where empty store shelves were the norm, Americans' wealth of consumer goods, food, and sundry items such as cigarettes, placed them at an advantage. That surfeit of goods, hard to find within the West German economy, often fed into the black marketplace encouraging criminal activity and preventing a normalization of the economy. Evidence of this widespread gangster-land type of activity was available almost daily to Milcom readers on the pages of *Stars and Stripes*. For example, one article featured the sensational discovery and break-up of a large ring operating in Germany that included 140 arrests.⁵⁵ Another account told of the seizure of 3,800 pounds of black market coffee.⁵⁶

Some reports claimed that black market activities affected all levels of the military in Germany, with officers, enlisted personnel and civilians attracted to "the lure of getting rich quickly with little risk or worry."⁵⁷ One American officer noted that "nobody who sold a few cartons [cigarettes] was considered a criminal. It was the big wheeler-dealers who dealt in cars, diamonds and tens of thousands of dollars" who the investigators were after.⁵⁸ Consequently, the black market remained an active alternative to the incipient German economic system from the 1940s and through the 1950s. Wolf W. Schmoekel remembers that time, "Circumstances in Germany were all but chaotic, mass starvation threatened, and a black market flourished which was doubtlessly unprecedented in history."⁵⁹ Subsequently:

> The Second's [2nd Armored Cavalry Regiment] new duties consisted mainly of police work, raids on black market centers, and an occasional show of force to discourage any would-be conspirators. A nation-wide black market ring was broken up in the fall of 1946. A platoon of C Troop–42, stationed at Ingolstadt, tracked down some men who had broken into the local food office and stolen a large number of ration stamps. It was discovered that they belonged to a well-organized ring of black marketers, who were subsequently arrested by American and British officials.⁶⁰

Morton C. Mumma III arrived at his assignment just outside Munich in August 1950 and had similar experiences:

> Many Americans soon learned that the black market, normally in coffee, tea and cigarettes was an easy way to buy those pictures, cameras, and projectors so desired by many of those in the Occupation Force. The Germans selling those items roamed through the housing areas which were off-base and they did a good business. Many of the Germans parlayed their on-site sale into legitimate business establishments, in Munich and other cities. The German police and American authorities did their best to squelch black marketing but it was a lost cause, basically ineffective until the later currency reform.⁶¹

In a related incident, the offices of AFN Nüremberg, which was often short of necessary repair parts and supplies, also resorted to the black market as an expedient alternative: "[T]he station's first birth was January 28, 1950, when studios were opened in the prestigious Grand Hotel. When the local Commanding General threw the switch, he didn't know the switch had been purchased on the black market for two pounds of coffee."⁶²

Seen through an economic lens, an advantageous exchange rate, consumer largess and dabbling in the black market suggest reasons that Milcom members may have felt confident and secure within the context of their relationship with the struggling Germans. The currency reform of June 20, 1948, however, changed some of that. Almost overnight, the introduction of the Deutsche Mark (DM) had a profound effect on the lives of West Germans and their Milcom neighbors. For individual Germans, who dubbed this *"der Tag X"* [X Day], the initial impact seemed daunting.⁶³ Directed to exchange their old Reichsmarks for the new Deutsche Marks, at disadvantageous rates, many saw their hard-earned savings disappear. The prescribed rate of exchange was one DM for one RM up to the first 600 RM. After that, the rate was one DM for ten RM.⁶⁴ Specific groups suffered as well. Many German university students saw their chances to stay in school evaporate as the change in currency suddenly made an education unaffordable. Sixty percent of those students attending university at Munich dropped their studies for the fall semester of 1948.⁶⁵ Elderly pensioners suffered as their limited income lost value, and in the immediate aftermath of the currency reform unemployment among men rose 42.5 percent and women by 70 percent.⁶⁶ Although these adjustments and sacrifices appeared unfair they quickly solved the economically crippling problem of inflation caused by excessive currency in circulation. Changes in the marketplace followed as well.

Some common items took more from West Germans' purses than did others after the conversion. One contemporary survey showed that the price of a briefcase jumped from RM 40 to DM 48, a bicycle increased from RM 110 to DM 155, a man's suit from RM 90 to DM 105, and a gas stove from RM 130 to DM 186.[67] On the positive side, fuel and consumable items appeared more affordable. On the average, a liter of gasoline dropped from RM 10 to DM .75, a chocolate bar from RM 20 to DM 2, one pound of butter from RM 250 to DM 18, one pound of coffee from RM 360 to DM 15, and most important, the price of American cigarettes declined from RM 100 per pack to DM 8.[68] This last change had a substantial impact on disrupting black market operations. Before the June reform cigarettes had constituted a universal currency in that realm and afterward their substantial devaluation undercut their value. By June 23rd, military and civil authorities celebrated the fact that with the change in currency the "busy black market had folded most of its tents today and quietly stolen away."[69] Although black market operations would continue for years their influence and power to shape the postwar economy and their stranglehold on the daily existence of West Germans began to wane.

The civilian work force suffered another important consequence of the currency change. Although there was a 50 percent across-the-board increase in prices for goods and services beginning in June 1948, West Germans found only a 15 percent increase in their pay envelopes.[70] That situation continued to fester with resentment until the autumn. On October 28th "dissatisfied trade unionists" organized demonstrations in Stuttgart against existing economic policies that fostered the pay inequity. In short order rioting broke out and the West German police were unable to handle the crowd. The military governor quickly called out the "highly mobile troops" of the U.S. Constabulary force who were armed with machineguns and tanks, and used tear gas to restore peace.[71] It was the only instance since the end of the war that American military forces acted to quell a public disturbance in the AMZON. West German labor historians have dubbed this significant event the *Stuttgarter Vorfälle* [Stuttgart incident].[72]

On November 12, a second general strike followed, numbering between 8 and 9 million workers in the major cities of the British and American zones. Against fears that General Clay would again use military force, the demonstrations and rallies remained peaceful. Only German workers in factories, coal mines and steel mills participated, while employees of the U.S. military government were not involved.[73] Both sets of incidents forced the hand of Chancellor Adenauer who directed Ludwig Erhard, the architect of Germany's economic recovery, to again implement a series of price controls. But for West German free-market economists like Erhard, who were following an American capitalist model, it was a victory over the power of organized labor and unions.[74] HICOG survey results of contemporary public trends reveal that immediately after the introduction of the reform 54 percent of West Germans complained, "Their living conditions were worse than they had been one year earlier." By January of 1949, however, 52 percent of the survey population admitted, "they were better off than during the previous year."[75] Another survey revealed that most West Germans (52 percent) thought trade unions were useful in protecting workers' rights, but only 29 percent approved of strike actions.[76] After initial difficulties most Germans began to realize the benefits of the conversion plan.

The currency reform affected American Milcom members in different ways. Besides readjusting the currency exchange rate, which changed immediately from one dollar = RM

10 to one dollar=DM 3.33, PX prices rose. Four days after the conversion to the DM, Milcom members awoke to front page news in *Stars and Stripes* that the European Exchange System (EES) was increasing prices in merchandise and services as a result of the reform. In some instances the increase was as much as 50 percent. That was the case with cigarettes, which rose from 80 cents per carton to $1.25, and laundry soap, which increased from 10 cents to 15 cents a cake. The justification used by the EES management was a need to increase revenues by 10 percent monthly to cover raises in salaries for German EES workers, added freight costs and increased costs to German merchants.[77] News of changes to PX prices, resulting from the currency reform, held Milcom readers' interest for months.

To placate any grumbling from Milcom consumers, the EES was quick to show evidence that, despite the recent price increases, the European PX was still a good place to shop. In a survey that compared prices between PX systems in the U.S. and in Europe authorities showed that most items in overseas Milcom PXs were cheaper. This, they emphasized, was particularly true for tobacco products. All "popular brands" of cigarettes in EUCOM were 9 cents a pack, 14 cents in U.S. PXs, and 15–20 cents in a civilian store. The survey also listed as cheaper other items such as razors, toothpaste, and film.[78] Still, Milcom members complained. One letter in the B-Bag column from a concerned reader outlined the higher costs of fruit and vegetables in the EES than in the U.S. The reasons, explained the Chief of EUCOM Special Services, were the costs of preservation and overseas shipping and handling, which in turn had increased with the currency reform.[79] These changes continued through the next year with price increases periodically announced in *Stars and Stripes* for various items on the PX shelves.

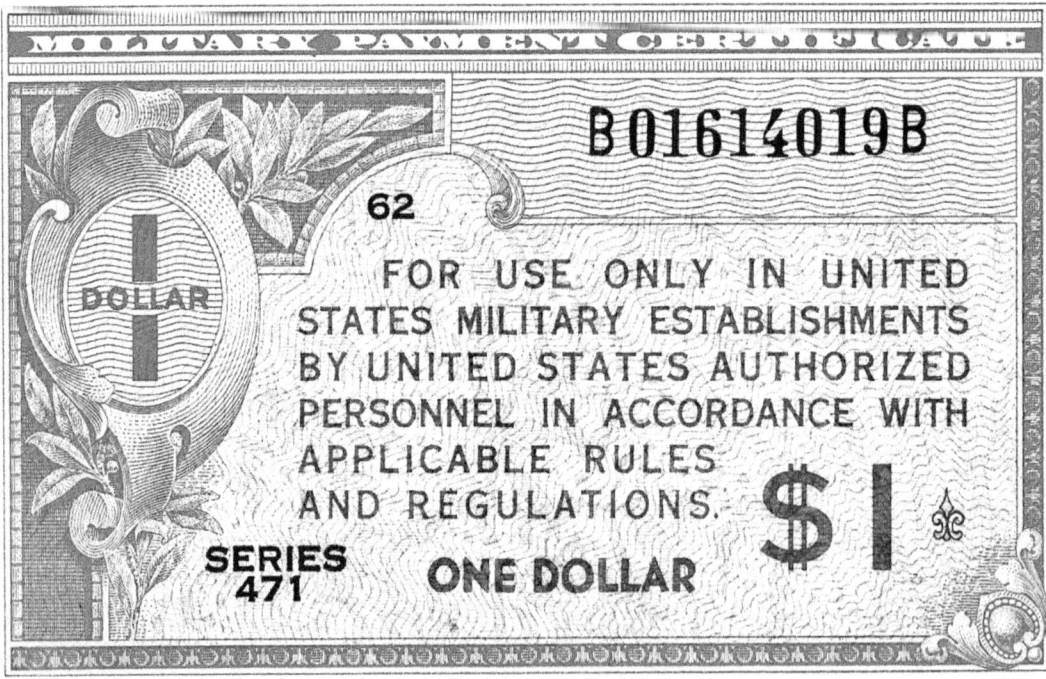

Military Payment Certificate (MPC) Series 471 (c. 1947). Also known as "scrip" these certificates were issued in occupied Europe by American authorities as a method to control inflation and black marketing activities. Image source: Jeremy Steinberg, *World Paper Money*, accessed July 29, 2014, http://www.banknotes-steinberg.com/usmpcs with permission.

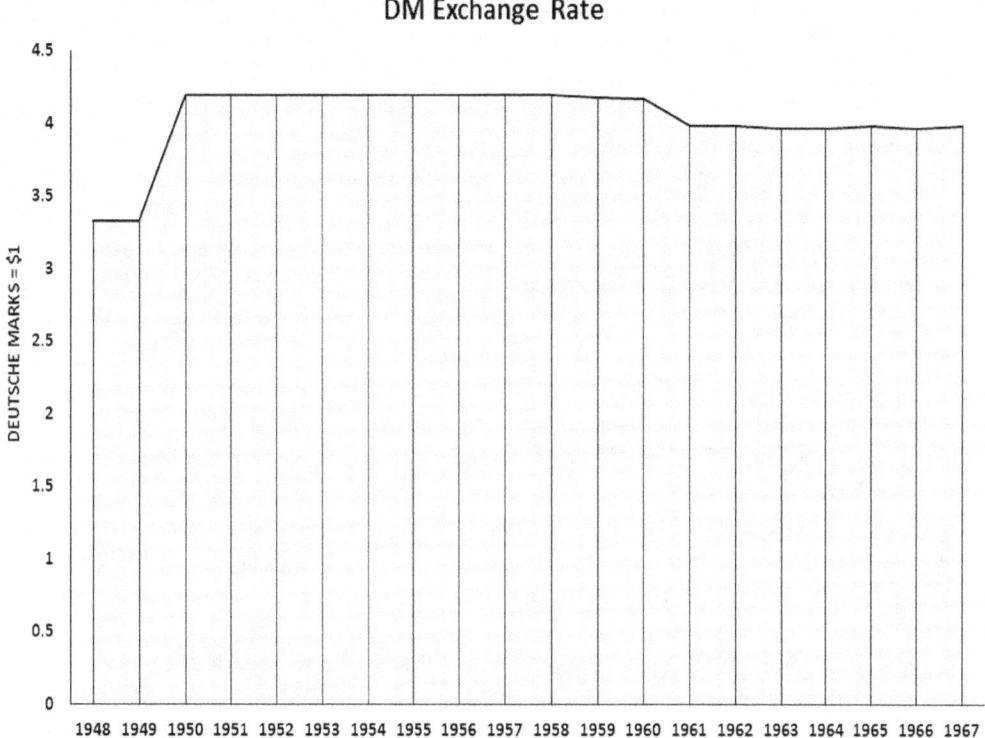

Deutsche Mark to Dollar Exchange Rate, 1948–1967. From April 1945 to June 1948 the German unit of currency was the Reichmark (RM). That exchange rate was $1= RM 10. During the June 20, 1948 currency conversion the military government replaced the RM with the DM. The initial exchange rate became $1=DM 3.33. Data source: *Historical Dollar-to-Marks Currency Conversion Page*, accessed August 10, 2013, http://www.history.ucsb.edu/faculty/marcuse/projects/currency.htm#tables.

It was not until 1950 that the EES was able to reduce a number of prices. These actions coincided with an adjustment in the dollar to DM rate from $1=DM 3.3 to $1=DM 4.2. By May of that year Milcom shoppers were able to read a column in *Stars and Stripes* titled "PX Prices Cut on 50 Items," which carried the good news that "economies in operating expenses have enabled EES to reduce prices on approximately 50 items." The savings were in Wildroot Cream Oil, Vitalis Hair Tonic and other popular hair care products, as well as clothing and nylons.[80] A two-page spread appeared in *Stars and Stripes* in July titled "Operating Economy: Savings Days" that proclaimed, "EES expense cuts bring you new low PX prices." This article also listed reduced items that included menswear, German-made cameras, watches, household items, and food.[81] Until the early–1960s the EES managed to hold the line on prices. An exchange rate with the dollar that remained above DM 4 made that possible.

As Milcoms members gradually came to terms with the currency reform, and the effects it had on their lives, they also had to negotiate the use of Military Payment Certificates (MPC). Also known as "scrip" the MPC program was a parallel initiative to curtail the destabilization of the German economy by preventing an overabundance of U.S. dollars in circulation that could cause uncontrolled inflation. Instead, Milcom members throughout the AMZON exchanged their dollars for an equivalent amount of MPCs that they then used to make purchases at locations such as the PX and commissary as well as at post theaters, clubs, and recreation facilities. They could also exchange scrip for an equivalent amount of DMs for use on the German economy or if traveling abroad. This was important because not all European nations accepted the American scrip.[82]

German black marketers constantly tried to corrupt the program by illegally buying or exchanging MPCs from Milcom members at rates below the official exchange rate. To foil these attempts American governing authorities periodically staged unannounced, but mandatory, scrip exchanges for the entire AMZON. At this time old scrip was replaced one-for-one for new scrip usually of different design and color to prevent local black marketers from printing counterfeit certificates. The operation was so controlled and secretive that the new certificates often arrived at night under heavy guard to distribution centers.[83] Unfortunately, all Milcom members, military and civilian, often had to endure long lines to make the exchange when offices opened, although a grace period of several days usually followed the announcements. A survey of sources reveals that during the postwar decades, when scrip was in use, American military governing authorities conducted very effective campaigns to control the illegal production and exchange of MPCs.[84] Together, the use of MPCs and the currency conversion sometimes made financial transactions challenging for Milcom members especially when conducting the routine of daily life such as shopping or paying bills. The use of MPCs finally ended on May 27, 1958, with the announcement of the conversion of all circulating scrip to dollars.[85]

From 1950 through the late–1960s American Milcom members lived in an economic Golden Age. The dollar remained strong in relation to the new DM and they took full advantage of opportunities that this affluence presented. It was not until the late 1960s that a precipitous downward trend in the DM to dollar exchange rate began. But those Americans not living in government quarters were already facing challenges. Often neglected by contemporary histories these American Milcom families, military and civilian, were "living on the economy" in German-owned properties. Their lives followed a different economic trajectory. As the German economy strengthened and costs drifted upward, so did rent and utilities, such as heating fuel and the associated taxes. Still, like other Milcom members, American families living on the economy did not have to pay German taxes on other types of goods or services. However, by the mid–1950s more than 6,000 U.S. service personnel and their dependents were participating in the economy, their numbers outpacing construction of new housing as troop strength in Germany increased into the early 1960s.[86] Wives of these families often bonded into groups such as the Stuttgart Economy Wives Club to discuss solutions and vent frustrations about "costly utilities, lack of bathtubs, and landlord trouble."[87] Very often, these Milcom members discovered that their family budgets were lacking, as the "exorbitant rent" charged by German owners exceeded "by far" the housing allowances permitted by the U.S. government.[88] This initially caused some difficulties when AMZON officials introduced the new currency in June 1948, and then again as the DM gained strength against the dollar beginning in the mid–1960s.

Sluggish increases to the military rate of pay, particularly housing allowances, exacerbated those problems for Americans living in Germany. From October 1949 to October 1963 there were few adjustments to the Basic Allowance for Quarters (BAQ). Modest increases of 14 percent in 1952, and 7 percent in October 1963, preceded a relatively stable period for the exchange rate between the dollar and the DM, inspiring little adjustment by the Department of Defense, although groups such as the Stuttgart Wives Economy Club continued to voice their grievances.[89] However, as the dollar's value slipped after 1967, Milcom members again endured greater financial hardship through the latter half of the decade and into the 1970s.

American service members, civilians, and their families who were assigned and sponsored by one of the hundreds of Milcoms received a number of protections under the Status of Forces Agreements (SOFA) that were negotiated between the U.S. and West Germany beginning with the end of the occupation period. Principal among these was the understanding that all Milcom members were exempt from prosecution under German law for crimes committed while living in a Milcom. Instead, they were all subject to the Uniform Code of Military Justice (UCMJ). For Milcom consumers however, the greatest benefit of the SOFA was exemption from the West German value added tax (VAT) levied on the purchase of goods or services.[90]

The VAT for Germans, known as the *Mehrwertsteuer* (MwSt), averaged over 10 percent for most goods. But in accordance with contemporary U.S. military policies, Americans were "exempt from German taxes that are based on residence or domicile in Germany." Furthermore, Milcom members were also "exempt from German taxes that are imposed upon movable property intended, for personal or domestic use and upon income from official activities."[91] This included automobiles bearing license plates registered with the U.S. forces. Periodically, over the years, *Stars and Stripes* would feature articles that provided updates to American Milcom members on the SOFA with West Germany. One constant that did not change was the exemption from paying the MwSt. Germans employees of the Americans Milcoms however, also received some exemption from tax, although it was a single, unique case. The West German government agreed to waive taxation for any worker who received a monetary prize under the American awards program for employees who provided a good idea.[92] Regardless of the DM fluctuations over time, the Americans were able to realize a comparative financial benefit not enjoyed by their German hosts.

By the late–1960s the halcyon days of unchallenged economic advantage for Milcom members were slowly slipping away. Billions of dollars of aid through programs such as George Marshall's ERP together with Ludwig Erhard's policies and planning, and the much needed currency reform, had created the necessary environment for the popularly dubbed *Wirtschaftswunder*. West German employment was on the rise, production lines began humming, the agricultural sector was again reaping much needed caloric bounties, coveted consumer goods were appearing on store shelves and the black market's muscle was atrophying. But, these conditions also described an economic miracle that existed as a dichotomy. On one hand, the U.S. had willingly traded off its economic advantage by nurturing and tutoring its West German protégé in the ways of American capitalism until it grew into a free-market competitor. In this context it had sacrificed some of its postwar triumphal swagger and to a degree negated attitudes of unique exceptional material wealth and bounty. In contrast, the U.S. had created a strong ally that was ready to serve as a keystone in the West's anti-communist bulwark for decades to come. Changes also transpired at the grassroots level between the Milcoms and the West Germans. The Americans provided some of the first welcome employment opportunities for West Germans and like their German neighbors Milcom members had to endure financial adjustments when the new Deutsche Mark arrived in circulation. This sometimes included loss of buying power and frustrations that involved negotiating rent and costs of living for those Americans in German housing. These were some of the challenges of life for Milcom members in West Germany, which often went unappreciated by their stateside contemporaries.

Six

Fast Food, Violence, Crime and Drugs (1967–1990)

A Taste of America

Billy Wilder's film, *One, Two, Three* (1961), and Wolfgang Becker's *Good Bye Lenin!* (2003) bookend the building and razing of the iconic Berlin Wall.[1] Both serve as contemporary social and cultural critiques wrapped in satire—the former during the Wall's construction, the latter at its demise. Common to each, however, is a thread of American consumerism, woven through both narratives, connecting them and serving as a catalyst that shapes the characters' lives and inspires their actions. The emblematic reagent in both cases is Coca-Cola, which is central to the first film and omnipresent in the second.[2] But within that consumerist context a new cultural artifact makes its appearance in Becker's movie with the introduction of *fast food*. That new arrival takes shape in the form of Burger King and plays the role of a welcome alternative to, but corrupting force of, traditional German culture. As the storyline unfolds in a newly unified Berlin, the fast food franchise is a modern siren that lures a previously dutiful daughter away from her university studies with the promise of a new life through work at the drive-thru window. Together with the ubiquitous Coca-Cola, Burger King's fast food represented the smothering, and often narcotic, artificiality of American culture arriving on the whispered promises of consumerist wealth that began in the early postwar years and gained momentum through the following decades.

By the mid–1960s, cars, fashions, films, and music, the widely recognized markers of postwar popular American culture in Europe, found general acceptance into West German culture.[3] Their omnipresence eventually painted them with the brush of expectant normalcy that blurred their integration at the boundary between the two worlds and completed their absorption.[4] An alternate interpretation is that the popularity of European music eventually eclipsed that of the Americans.[5] Regardless of the causality, just as that first wave of "cultural imperialism" seemed to crest and begin to lose momentum a second arrived. Riding that next wave to hit Europe's shores was the popular American cultural concept of fast food.

Among the first franchises to establish beachheads were A&W and Kentucky Fried Chicken (KFC). The first A&W, which opened in 1962, and the first KFC, which followed in 1969, were both located in Frankfurt.[6] Each sought to penetrate the West German restaurant market by initially locating near areas saturated with an American presence to take advantage of consumers' familiarity with the menu choices.[7] Other than businessmen and tourists who frequented the area, and exchange students who studied there, the greater Frankfurt metropolitan region was also home to numerous American Milcoms with thousands of military members, civilian employees, and their families.[8] These initial ventures however, were still slow to gain popularity with Germans who eschewed the idea of non-traditional dining on mass-produced food served across a counter in paper or plastic containers.[9]

Hoping to find success in the German market, McDonalds opened its first restaurant in München in late 1971 to take advantage of the influx of visitors for the 1972 Olympic Games. From that start the corporation employed a different strategy that avoided populated American areas and instead pandered to German cultural tastes. In place of a typical modern, sleek, interior design its décor was subdued and featured dark wooden partitions to create an environment that was intimate and *gemütlich* [comfortable and informal]. In addition, it served beer. But as a replicator of German epicurean desires, McDonalds was a failure.[10] At the time, the German media slighted all American fast food initiatives, claiming that the "idea of quick feeding in technically standardized food outlets with a limited, single menu" was not appealing. Further criticism disclosed that the concept of business franchising had not yet caught on in Germany.[11] But within a short period of time those attitudes would change.

Between 1971 and 1976 the number of McDonald's franchises grew to 31 and their interiors reverted to the familiar, minimalist, modern décor. More important, the corporation began to construct its newer restaurants closer to areas populated by Americans. As the number of its franchises swelled to nearly 900 by 1990 approximately 31 percent were either co-located within a Milcom or within a short travel distance.[12] There is also an associated correlation between the growth in the size of the total American military population in West Germany between 1970 and 1980 and the increase in the number of franchises.[13] This suggests that McDonalds recognized the advantage of increasing profits by selling to an American clientele who were already familiar with its standard menu and were hungry for its product line.[14] It also suggests an understanding of the influence Milcoms could continue to have as agents of American consumerist culture. Just as they had served as a conduit for Western consumer goods, music, and fashion during earlier decades, Milcom members did familiarize West Germany with the concept of fast food through their frequent patronage and association with Germans both on-duty and off-duty. Any consideration that fast food did not catch on in Germany until German culture and society changed to adopt the faster pace of modern life is not complete without considering the influence of already existing pockets of thousands of Americans in the Milcoms.[15] That impact becomes more evident when examining print source documents such as *Stars and Stripes* and German weekly journals. These publications reveal an increasing engagement of German culture with fast food that followed close on the heels of its integration with the Milcoms.

The fact that the average American Milcom member and their family enjoyed fast food was no secret. As the availability of McDonalds increased, so did the number of references to fast food, especially hamburgers, in *Stars and Stripes*. A February 1977 column, "Consumer Watch," revealed that the "all-American hamburger is a real winner" at the post exchange (PX) snack bars and that "AAFES managed to wrap up $5,071,686 in hamburger sales during fiscal year 1977." It also confided that it was a healthier alternative to a German wurst "with its high fat content."[16] A feature article from later that year highlighted the inroads that American fast food franchises were beginning to make to the West German restaurant scene and their gradual acceptance. Besides the popularity of McDonalds and Kentucky Fried Chicken, it also mentioned a newcomer to the scene, Burger King.

Beginning with a single restaurant in West Berlin in 1976, Burger King capitalized on the early mistakes of its predecessors by quickly establishing itself near American populations. Within a year of its first franchise, Burger King had opened a total of three in West Berlin and seven in the Frankfurt area.[17] Realizing the benefits of co-locating in the vicinity of Milcoms, the fast food corporations sought to sign deals with the military. By the early 1980s Burger King, McDonalds and Wendy's began opening on military bases in the U.S. when military and political elites determined that "military personnel and their families wanted name-brand fast-food products, not an AAFES burger."[18] Those initiatives precipitated a landmark deal between Burger King and the Army and Air Force Exchange System (AAFES) to establish franchises in West Germany located within the bounds of military facilities and overseen by military authorities.[19] The first of these was in the Ansbach Milcom in 1984. As corporate authorities noted "we feel we are providing a little bit of home to the personnel on base while providing significant additional revenue to the Morale, Welfare and Recreation fund."[20] *Stars and Stripes* first alerted Milcom readers to this agreement with a front page announcement that "Burger King, AAFES OK Fast Food Outlets."[21] By 1990 Burger King had 21 restaurants operating in Milcom facilities in West Germany and many others located nearby.[22]

To reach those American sub-communities at distances from larger Milcoms, and to service military units deployed out to field training areas, Burger King began to employ mobile restaurant vans. By December 1986 the company had three in operation and a total of nine planned for use.[23] The strategy of placement in and near the Milcoms was profitable for both Burger King and AAFES with two-thirds of total country-wide profits coming from the restaurants in Frankfurt and the Ansbach Milcom.[24] In addition to providing food the franchises offered employment. An AAFES spokesman noted that of the 1,800 Burger King employees on the "AAFES payroll" almost 1,700 were Milcom family members or "military members working part time."[25] Other than strengthening its relationship with Americans through employment Burger King also supported some local sports teams such as the Mann-

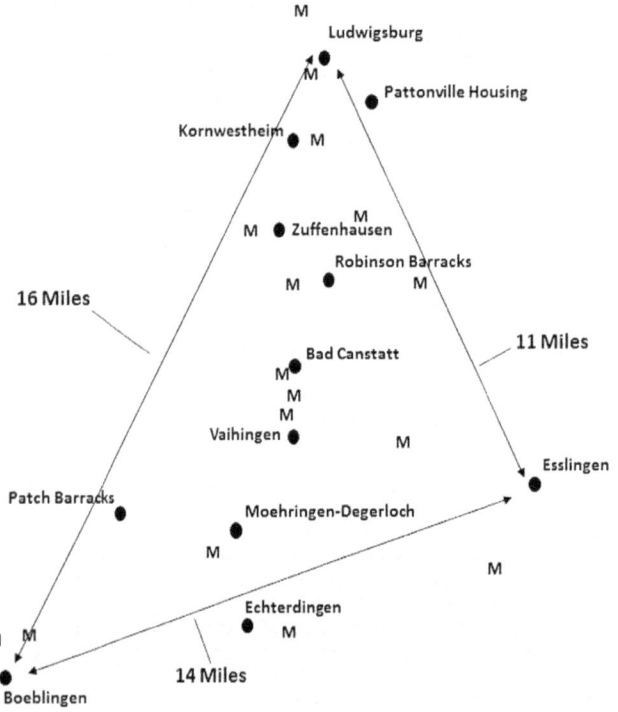

McDonald's locations. Map of the Greater Stuttgart Military Community (c. 1989) showing the correlation between military *Kasernes*, facilities and housing areas (represented by dots) and the McDonald's franchises (represented by the letter M). The dispersal of the restaurants suggests an intentional co-location to take advantage of the American population. There were 17 McDonald's locations within a 77 square mile area. Illustration source: the author. Data source: *Restaurants in Germany*, accessed May 25, 2013, http://www.gps-data-team.com/poi/germany/restaurants/.

heim Burger King Tornadoes, a Milcom baseball team, which often played in German-American invitational events.²⁶ Fast food franchises also served as an occasional venue to exhibit beneficence as American military units sponsored parties for local orphanages in the restaurants.²⁷

Because of its business relationship with AAFES Burger King was also able to advertise in *Stars and Stripes*. This was one of the very few instances when the EUCOM command structure granted permission for a corporation to utilize its print media, an earlier example was for the sale of automobiles.²⁸ In a series of full page ads that ran during the latter half of 1985 Burger King invited Milcom members to "Try a Homeburger," and encouraged them to "Take your family back home for a meal."²⁹ The ads also notified readers of future openings and current locations of the franchises. As *Stars and Stripes* reported, the "yearning of displaced Americans in Europe for a taste of home" made the franchise a "whopper of a success."³⁰

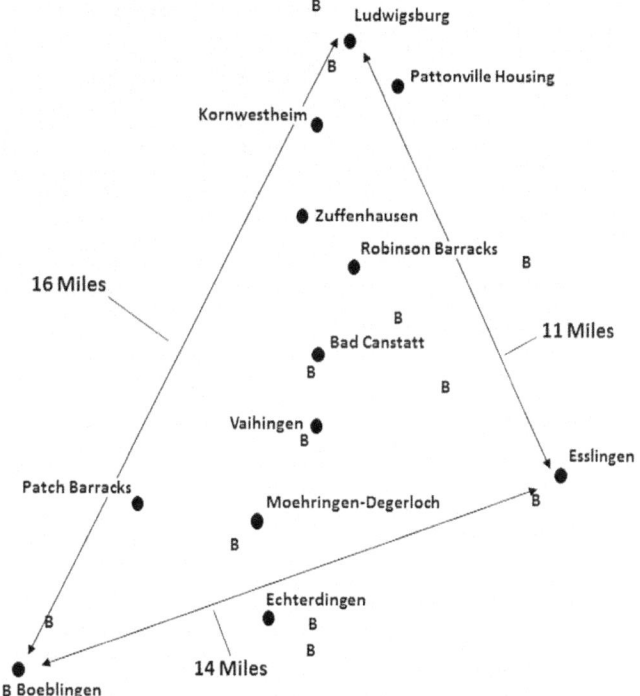

Burger King Locations. Map of the Greater Stuttgart Military Community (c. 1989) showing the correlation between military *Kasernes*, facilities and housing areas (represented by dots) and the Burger King franchises (represented by the letter B). Like other franchises the dispersal of the restaurants suggests an intentional co-location to take advantage of the American population. There were 13 Burger King locations within a 77 square mile area. Illustration source: the author. Data source: *Restaurants in Germany*, accessed May 25, 2013, http://www.gps-data-team.com/poi/germany/restaurants/.

The remembrances of many former Milcom members echoed those feelings. One former officer recalls, "American fast food was a piece of home in Germany. We loved to go to McDonalds or Burger King." But he also noted, "Judging by the business these fast food places did, I think the Germans liked them too."³¹ When they weren't accessible Milcom residents also made their feelings known. In a letter to the editor of *Stars and Stripes* a reader lamented, "Up here in the fog at Hahn we have been forgotten (gasp!). All we have is a mobile unit Burger King, but alas no McDonald's, Pizza Hut, etc. So when do we get ours?"³²

But not all former Milcom members recall fully embracing the fast food fad. Douglas Gaskell recalls: "I viewed them with ambivalence. I was amused by the [Americans' complaints] because there were always more Germans in the store than Americans. For many of the younger soldiers I do think it provided a strong link with American culture."³³ Similarly, former Neu Ulm Milcom member Thomas Rehm notes, "I guess fast food joints were nice— especially for families with kids—but they were not my cup of tea. I didn't hear any Germans talk badly about McDonald's—or talk at all about them. When I went by, they tended to have plenty of customers."³⁴

The exposure to fast food that the Germans gained through employment at newly established franchise restaurants, observing Americans' preference for the fare, spotting the occasional mobile unit as it rolled through their town, and by associating with Americans in the Milcoms, began to change their attitudes towards fast food. A survey of contemporary news magazines corroborates that transformation over time. After the concept failed to gain acceptance in the early 1970s the West German media finally deemed the establishment of fast food enterprises a success by mid-decade. In April 1976 *Der Spiegel* published an article that satirically contrasted the United States' dismal contemporary foreign policy record in Asia, Africa, and Eastern Europe with its exceptionally successful exportation of fast food to Europe by exclaiming, "McDonald's conquered Germany." It went on to observe that "with the same missionary zeal the Americans once dedicated to exporting democratic ideals, Ray Kroc and his emissaries spread their message by fast food." A West German corporate representative noted a more subtle cultural change with his comment that "we educate people to a whole new way of life—to eat with the fingers rather than a knife a fork," which was a decided departure from traditional German manners.[35]

Der Spiegel continued to track the cultural penetration of fast food. In June 1978 it commented that the "Americans of the counter" had swept aside the traditional use of "eating utensils" and replaced them with food served in cardboard. But it also noted the realization of positive benefits from fast food, such as the ability to feed an entire family "for less than 20 marks" and its ability to quickly satisfy workers on a hurried lunch break.[36] Those types of comments continued to resonate into the 1980s together with two other particular aspects of the fast food imprint: West German corporate chains began to mimic the techniques and strategies of corporations such as McDonald's and Burger King, and Germans began to appreciate the rationalized processes that led to efficient and profitable operations. The familiar Kaufhof department store group entered the lucrative fast food market in 1980 by opening in-store stands that sold hamburgers, fries, and Coke, and the popular North Sea seafood chain began selling hamburgers.[37] But the Germans also admired the "lightning success" of the streamlined, "clinically sterile" American fast food process with its "standardized" dining room and its formulaic mode of operation.[38]

The West German McDonald's and Burger King franchises did however retain certain cultural characteristics. As former military Milcom member Tom Tracy remembers, "Off post, McDonald's had [its] particular oddities for Americans but seemed popular for the younger German generation."[39] In those restaurants not located on Milcom property beer found its way onto the fast food menu. In addition, male employees wore ties and metal cutlery and ceramic dinnerware were an available option for diners' pleasure. As condiments went ketchup was available, but only for purchase, and powdered "whitener," not cream, was the only choice for coffee.

By 1987 the American cultural artifact *fast food* seemed to have become a permanent fixture in West Germany. From the mid–1960s when franchising was an unacceptable mode of business operation for German restaurateurs, and customers disdained eating without utensils, fast food had become the industry standard bearer with its "limited product range," "new forms of self-service," and "rationalized catering."[40] Just as the Milcoms of the early postwar decades had served as a useful and available conduit for the American popular culture artifacts of music, fashion and film, after the late–1960s they served the same purpose for the introduction of fast food. Their population functioned both as a ready and reliable customer base for the franchises and as agents to facilitate intercultural penetration and absorption at the grass roots level.

Any suggestion, however, that this intrusion of fast food was a consumerist phenomenon singularly associated with the spread of American culture is incomplete. By widening the scope of interpretation it becomes apparent that the introduction of fast food, which benefitted greatly from the presence of the Milcoms, was at once a trait of contemporary American popular culture and emerging postwar globalism. Prior to 1940, American corporations such as Coca-Cola had been conducting trans–Atlantic operations, but by the postwar decades Coke, together with newer corporations such as McDonalds, Burger King, and Kentucky Fried Chicken, were establishing global networks. Many of these franchises also strove to cast off a purely American image by advertising a global unity and by appealing to unique national desires, such as the sale of beer in Germany. This created an interesting dichotomy for the Milcoms, as fast food franchises such as Burger King stressed "a touch of home" to the Americans but emphasized a broader, global appeal to the Germans. Nevertheless, the American population in West Germany was instrumental in facilitating the spread of fast food as an artifact of both popular culture and globalism.[41]

America through a Dark Violent Lens

Although fast food was able to migrate across the permeable German-American cultural boundary there were other aspects of contemporary American culture that did not achieve absorption in Europe. These became magnets of great criticism and points of resistance and included the characteristics of increased violence, crime and drug usage. This toxic combination emerged as a set of dominant defining traits of popular culture in the U.S. beginning in the mid–1960s and continuing through the mid–1980s. Their effects resonated in the Milcoms and had an impact on the interactions Americans had with one another as well as with the surrounding West German communities. They represented the precipitates of a cultural alchemy that spilled from a crucible of change effected by global societal, political and economic tensions.[42]

Of the three, however, violence possessed the longest cultural legacy that Germans and Americans sometimes identified as being a true defining tenet of Americanism. Each culture appreciated how historians had previously scripted the narrative of America's past in the context of violent warfare. That approach provided a set of milestones in national development from revolution, to frontier, to civil war and conquests overseas.[43] In particular, Americans and Germans idealized and romanticized the rough and tumble American West of the nineteenth century. Prior to 1945, the novels of author Karl May, whose literary heroes and villains were characters of the "Old West," were vastly popular with Germans.[44] He often laced his tales with thrills and violence, which to his readers became familiar American themes. That concept of rugged frontier individualism personified the American in novels and on the movie screen where violence emerged as the most convenient tool in conflict resolution.[45] Among those contemporary actors who best portrayed that ideal was John Wayne whose characters were often ready for action, used rough language, applied gross generalities and often resorted to brute force.[46]

Hollywood productions of the 1960s through the 1980s at once reflected this attitude and fueled it. The studios distributed a steady diet of films about war, the Wild West, and crime to theaters in the U.S. and overseas. These led Germans to understand that violence and crime was symptomatic of American culture and an integral part of Americans' identity that shaped their ideas about themselves. Aside from *The Godfather*, very few of these contemporary films appealed to Germans.[47] Other than possessing a common theme of violence, the premise of war movies such as *The Dirty Dozen* (1967), *A Bridge Too Far* (1977) and *The Big Red One* (1980) featured American and allied forces repeatedly drubbing the German *Wehrmacht*. This suggests another possible reason for their lack of popularity with local audiences. Regardless of German sensitivities however, the October 1980 European premier of *The Big Red One* was in an AAFES theater located at Cooke Barracks in the Göppingen Milcom, home of the First Infantry Division ("The Big Red One").[48] Americans appeared equally unabashed about crime. During the international premier in Hamburg of the movie *Dollars*, a German reporter challenged the film's American writer-director, Richard Brooks, about the immorality of crime. Brooks boldly responded, "That's crap! You know it, and I know it! Crime does pay!"[49]

Year of Release	Film Title	Theme
1967	The Dirty Dozen	World War II
1967	In Cold Blood	Contemporary Crime/Violence
1968	Once Upon a Time in the West	Western Violence
1968	The Green Berets	Vietnam War
1969	Easy Rider	Contemporary Crime/Violence
1969	True Grit	Western Violence
1969	Butch Cassidy and the Sundance Kid	Romanticized Western Crime/Violence
1969	The Wild Bunch	Western Crime/Violence
1972	The Godfather	Contemporary Crime/Violence
1976	The Missouri Breaks	Western Violence
1976	Rocky	Contemporary Violence
1977	A Bridge Too Far	World War II
1977	Star Wars	Futuristic Violence
1978	The Deer Hunter	Vietnam War
1978	Superman	Contemporary Violence
1979	Rocky II	Contemporary Violence
1979	Apocalypse Now	Vietnam Violence
1980	The Big Red One	World War II
1982	First Blood	Contemporary Violence
1982	Rocky III	Contemporary Violence
1984	Rocky IV	Contemporary Violence

Table 6.1. Violent Hollywood Films. A representative listing of Hollywood productions, from 1967 to 1984, that featured themes of violence. Many of these films appeared in EUCOM and West German theaters. (*Stars and Stripes* and the Internet Movie Database [IMDb] website.)

American television shows available on AFN-TV or on local German channels offered little variation from these attitudes. Violent World War II serial dramas such as *Combat!* as well as "shoot-'em-up" westerns such as *Bonanza* and *Gunsmoke* entertained viewers who did not attend the theaters. Other shows, such as *Miami Vice* and *Dallas*, offered Germans an introspection of American culture and society emphasizing problems of "greed, violence, lawlessness, and moral decay."[50]

The culture of violence eventually led to a general disillusionment within American society at home and abroad in the Milcoms as the U.S. endured a prolonged engagement in Vietnam, race riots at home and political assassinations. Among the American leaders who spoke candidly was the Reverend Dr. Martin Luther King, Jr., who proclaimed, "the greatest purveyor of violence in the world today [is] my own government."[51] The West German media echoed that sentiment. A lengthy editorial in *Der Spiegel* titled "United States/Kennedy Murder: What a Country" spoke in disparaging terms of Germans' disappointment with Americans' violent behavior. Written as a follow-on commentary to the assassination of Robert F. Kennedy (June 1968) it recounted the deaths of John F. Kennedy (November 1963) and Martin Luther King, Jr. (April 1968) claiming, "Shame came again over the largest and most violent nation in the Western world." It went on to charge that "America [is] unmasked again as a country in which the power of the Colt [revolver] is still not fully broken and still determines the curriculum vitae of the nation." It suggested that the rise in the total number of violent crimes in America by 47 percent between 1960 and 1965 was indicative of its "love of violence."[52]

That perception continued through into the 1970s with the atrocity at My Lai, South Vietnam. Another editorial piece claimed to summarize the feelings of outrage most Germans felt with the "act of inhumanity" committed by the American forces in South Vietnam. It was a violent act that could only be associated "with the worst days of Hitler, Stalin and other cruel despots," and it was representative of a people and culture inured with a predilection to violence and crime.[53]

During these post–1967 years Germans re-evaluated their relationship with the Americans through this new lens, wondering what had become of the triumphal nation that in the early postwar decades had offered so much to the world. It seemed that "the American way of life, which seemed a safe path to freedom, peace and prosperity after the Second World War" had instead become "more like a dead end."[54] In the estimation of many Germans, the U.S. had undergone a significant transformation. It had changed from a nation that once "offered countless oppressed and tormented [people] refuge for a hundred years," and couched its finest ideas of freedoms in Woodrow Wilson's "idealistic 14 points," to become one of "intolerance, moral perversion and spiritual desolation."[55] The words and ideas of an exceptional America that once defined a victorious people striding abroad in a new postwar world were ringing hollow.

Americans in the Milcoms interpreted these events in the same way as they digested their regimen of news from AFN radio, AFN-TV, *Stars and Stripes* and other outlets. By the early 1970s, the atmosphere in the West German Milcoms appeared dismal. In September 1971, the *Washington Post* published a series of articles titled "Army in Anguish." It featured a journalistic examination of conditions in the U.S. military with a particular focus on West Germany. There it claimed military units, as well as their associated Milcoms, had devolved into an environment of "crime, drugs, racial conflict, rebellion against officers, boredom and attitudes that always have been anathema to armies." It also underscored a perceived "breakdown in spirit, in ethics and in discipline."[56] The series continued in print for several days, describing violence and crime in the barracks, rampant drug dealing, and leaders' frustration over the influx of criminals coming into the military "some of them sent there by judges as the alternative to going to jail."[57] Much of this was a reflection of the realities of life back in the U.S. and as many Milcom members watched much of it spilled out of the barracks and into the surrounding community.

Crime in the Milcoms

President Richard Nixon attempted to address this darker dimensions of contemporary American culture and society through his administration's emphasis on combating the rise in crime and violence in the U.S. Implementing programs and framing legislation for his "law and order" initiative he called for a national crackdown on crime that turned also into a political football in time for the 1970 congressional elections. Nevertheless, it produced some important legislation such as the Organized Crime Control Act, which seemed timely as the mayor of Detroit, Roman Gribbs noted, "Crime is now—and has been for the past few years—the No. 1 problem in urban areas." Contemporary crime statistics from the Federal Bureau of Investigation (FBI) confirmed these observations with a somber report that concluded, "The existence of crime, the reports of crime and the fear of crime have eroded the basic quality of life of many Americans." Its statistics showed that the rate of violent crime in the U.S. for 1969 was 2.4 per 1,000 individuals.[58] For Fiscal year 1970–1971 that rate was slightly less for the U.S. Army as a whole at 2.04. In USAREUR, the rate was 2.9 among black service members and 0.74 for whites.[59]

During the 1970s, the rate of crimes against property in the USAREUR Milcoms spiked at a high of 30.38 per 1,000 reported incidents in 1972, and reached a high of 2.21 per 1,000 for violent crimes in 1974.[60] Crimes against property, which soldiers generally committed against other soldiers in the barracks, decreased sharply by 1973, then continued to settle to just under 20 incidents per 1,000 in 1979. By the mid-1980s it was at 15 incidents per 1,000. Violent crimes decreased only slightly during the 1970s from 2.4 incidents per 1,000 in 1971 to 1.61 in 1979, then declined slightly to 1.0 in 1984. If there was a bright spot to find, it was in the Milcom school system. There, authorities reported, "DODDSEUR has a lower [crime] incident rate than comparable systems in the U.S.," including violence and drug abuse.[61]

Milcom members kept abreast of the crime trends back in the U.S. and in Europe by tuning into the AFN radio or AFNTV daily news broadcasts, and by reading *Stars and Stripes*. The newspaper provided readers with a constant feed of crime reports in articles and features that wittingly, or unwittingly, fed into their anxiety about their own safety within the military community and the state of affairs back home. A parade of articles with titles such as "First of 9 GIs Charged with Robbery Sentenced," "Violent Crime in Barracks is on Rise," and "Soldier is Sentenced to 18 Years for Rape," kept their concerns piqued through the 1970s and 1980s.[62] Other than postings about military members, readers also found stories that told of dependents charged with crimes whether they were violent or against property, including family members involved in robbery.[63] When Milcom members read of misdeeds by those within the command structure these anxieties became more exacerbated. Such was the case when the commanding officer of the Armed Forces Recreation Center (AFRC) in the Garmisch Milcom fell under investigation for his misuse of property and funds.[64] In addition

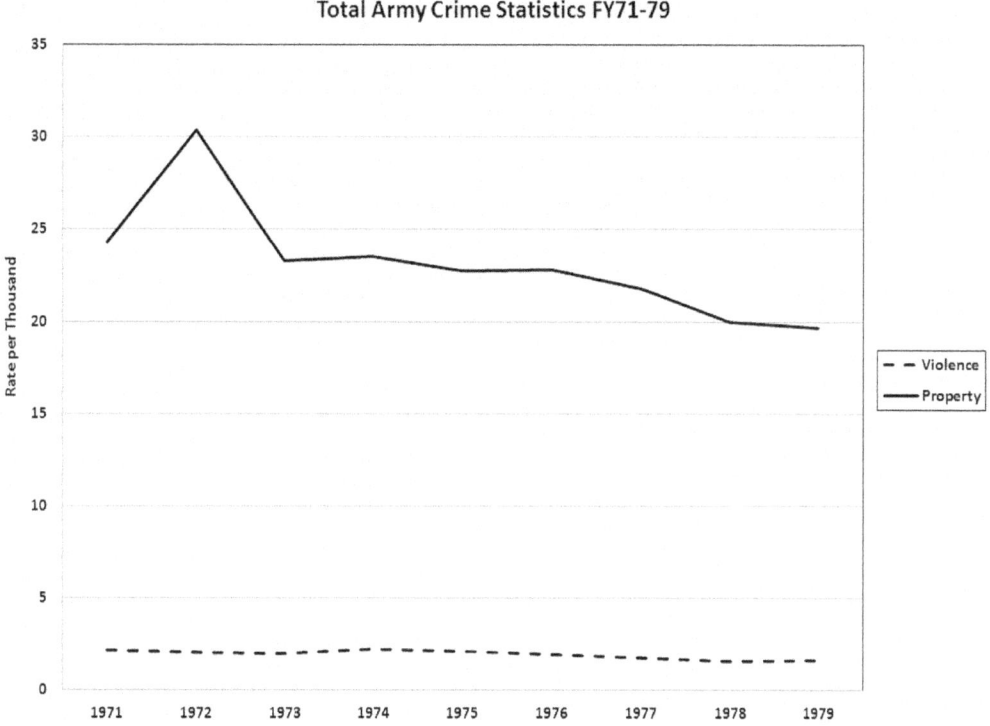

Total Army Crime Statistics, Fiscal Year 1971–1979. Data includes convictions for violent crimes committed against U.S. personnel or foreign nationals (assault, wounding, murder, and rape) and crimes against property (private or public). Data source: Department of the Army Historical Summary (DAHSUM) FY 1971 through FY 1979, *Center of Military History*, http://www.history.army.mil/html/bookshelves/collect/dahsum.html.

to these reports other articles about life in the U.S. that told stories of the spread of crime in America, Detroit's "Murder Tag," and the lives of the underworld crime bosses, contributed to Americans' concerns.[65]

Milcom members often gave voice to their fears and worries through letters to the editor of *Stars and Stripes*. One writer, a teacher in DODDS, challenged the rights of individual criminals. In his perception "we argue fallaciously that unless we go overboard protecting the rights of the criminal we will surely become a Fascist police state. We are asking for trouble, and crime statistics indicate that we are getting it."[66] Another writer commented, "Crime in the USA is indeed an unmitigated disgrace." He went on to share his thoughts that "The cause of crime and the social tendency for violence is multi-factorial," but emphasized "Its roots lie in our cultural heritage and national history which are rife with examples of violence and violent heroes."[67] Still another writer, from the Augsburg Milcom, lamented a perceived lack of funding for law enforcement. He recommended that a budgetary increase would make it possible to "eliminate all of the illegal drug trafficking, have police forces that are more efficient at solving violent crimes, provide more billeting space for more prisoners, and have longer prison sentences for criminals convicted of violent crimes."[68] In response to the statistical increases in the crime rates and the outcry from Milcom members, American authorities eventually began to take action.

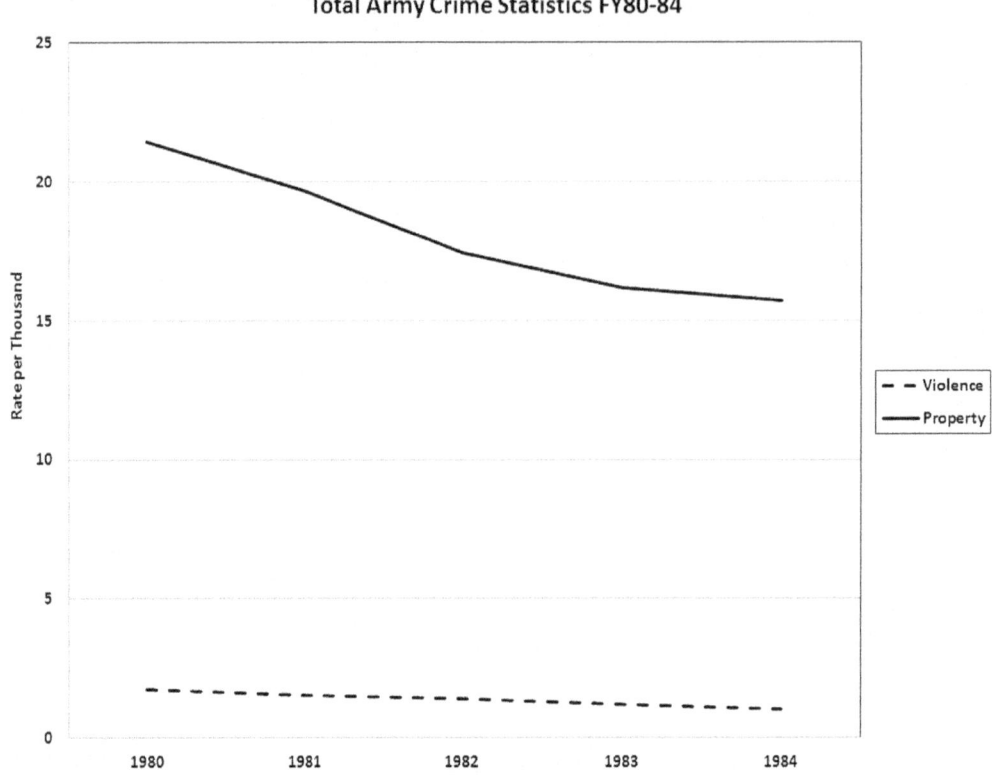

Total Army Crime Statistics, Fiscal Year 1980–1984. Data includes convictions for violent crimes committed against U.S. personnel or foreign nationals (assault, wounding, murder, and rape) and crimes against property (private or public). Data source: Department of the Army Historical Summary (DAHSUM) FY 1980 through FY 1984, Center of Military History, http://www.history.army.mil/html/bookshelves/collect/dahsum.html.

By the late 1970s the EUCOM command structure implemented comprehensive crime prevention programs within the Milcoms. At the grass roots level they consisted of special councils for dependent families that developed strategies for keeping housing areas safe. Authorities also aired crime prevention tips on AFN radio and television and offered them in lectures to military members living in the barracks. Many of these included ideas such as marking pilferable property with owners' names, securing property properly, traveling in groups and avoiding dangerous areas at night. Military police also presented programs to Boy and Girl Scout groups and at Parent Teacher Association (PTA) meetings. One of the more active aspects of the command-wide crime prevention program was an on-the-ground presence. It included increased Milcom neighborhood patrols by Military Police (MP) teams and liaisons interacting with DODDS students. At the schools the police presented safety and security classes, monitored the playgrounds, and assisted at crosswalks. Their strategy was "if we can reach the kids we can reach the parents."[69]

Another important dimension of the anti-crime initiative was the rape prevention program. As the number of female Milcom residents grew, the relevance of this initiative also increased. By 1970, female Milcom dependents represented 69 percent of the total for West Germany and the number of female military personnel in EUCOM grew from 473 in 1972, to 13,671 by 1978.[70] A major month-long campaign took shape in 1980 to address the issue as the number of rapes in USAREUR reached 219 in 1979 and 220 in 1980. Most disconcerting for the surrounding local communities was that 70 percent of those crimes were against German women. The program of lectures, seminars, classes and awareness training for females as well as male Milcom members continued cyclically through the 1980s.[71] In 1987 the USAREUR command structure announced another major prevention campaign using previously successful techniques of classes and lectures. Although the rates remained high they had decreased to levels below those at the beginning of the decade with 155 reported incidents in 1984, 120 in 1985, and 157 in 1986. Still, authorities understood that these numbers indicated their program was not completely effective and the violent crime of rape, committed by American Milcom members was still too rampant.[72]

During the 1970s and early 1980s, the crime and violence that did spread from the Milcoms to the surrounding communities continued to have a profound impact on the lives of German neighbors. Other than rape, this often involved instances of robbery, assault and murder. Examples include the sentencing of two soldiers from the Nüremberg Milcom with the armed robbery and murder of a German taxi driver in November 1972, the conviction of four soldiers from the Würzburg Milcom for the July 1974 armed robbery of a German autobahn restaurant and the conviction of a soldier from the Kirchgoens Milcom for the June 1984 stabbing death of a German taxi driver.[73]

The German reaction to these heinous crimes was strong. In the Bamberg Milcom one German labor union was so upset with the crime U.S. soldiers were committing "outside the gates" that they wrote an open letter, which they published in a local German newspaper, asking the American military leadership to "send in either Russian, British or French officers to teach GIs discipline."[74] To placate and protect their populace the German court system also began to exercise jurisdiction in an increasing number of cases that involved American Milcom members. That increase for 1973 was 30 percent over the previous year. As a USAREUR spokesman noted, the Germans were "exercising their right to try servicemen accused of crimes against Germans and third-country nationals because they feel the [American] military [was] being too lenient in its treatment of offenders."[75] An April 1975 public opinion poll queried West Germans asking if they "had the impression that the crime rate in Germany is generally increasing." The response was an overwhelming 75 percent in the affirmative.[76]

In an interesting parallel, the German outcry over crimes committed by Milcom members did elicit some isolated instances of backlash. When the *Erlanger Tagblatt* featured an article that reported an "alarming increase of crimes on the part of U.S. soldiers" in the city of Erlangen the Milcom commander was quick to respond that it was unfounded. First, he sardonically commented, "There is no increase in crime. But there certainly is an increase in the amount of crimes being reported and charged to Americans." Then he followed by noting, "30 percent of the local crimes blamed on U.S. soldiers were committed by offenders unknown to German police," intimating that the Germans were too quick to blame any crime not committed by one of their own on the Americans as opposed to other groups such as guest workers.[77] The tone of the article revealed the tensions that were developing between the Milcoms and the surrounding communities within the context of crime. Germans maintained a heightened awareness of the Americans' complicity in the rising crime rate and were becoming quicker to point out GIs' infractions. In contrast, Milcom members began exhibiting an acute sensitivity to accusations suggesting an embarrassment over their inability to curb the trend and

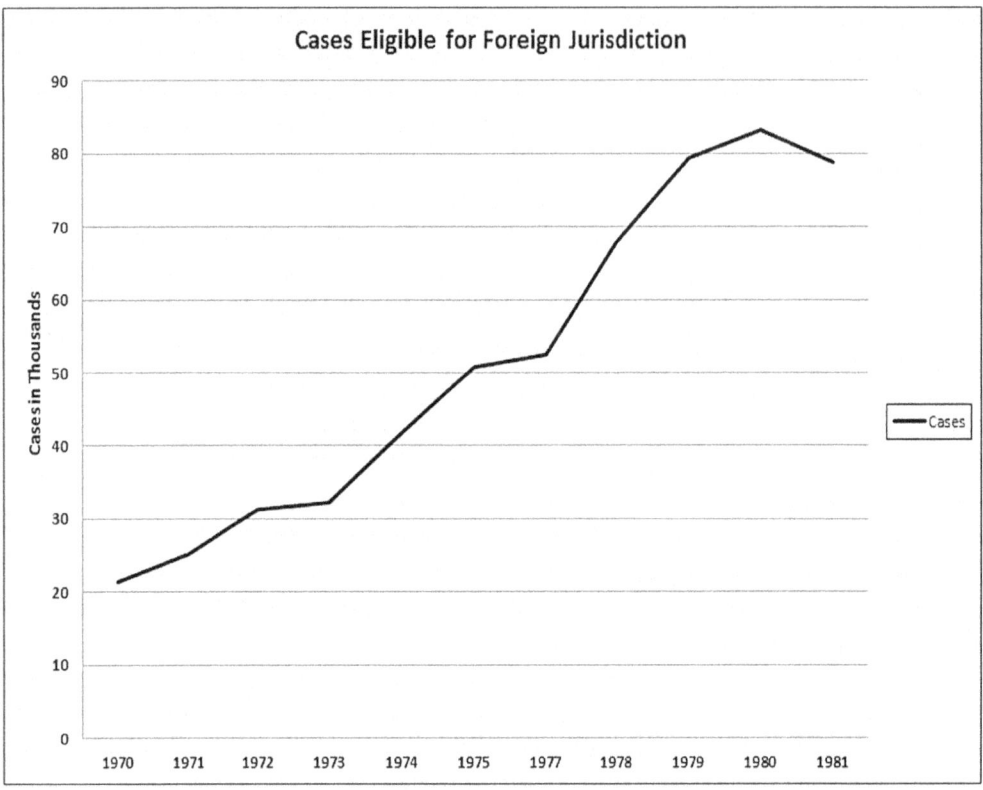

Cases Eligible for Foreign Jurisdiction, Fiscal Year 1970–1981. Information not available for FY76. Data source: Department of the Army Historical Summary (DAHSUM) FY 1970 through FY 1981, Center of Military History, http://www.history.army.mil/html/bookshelves/collect/dahsum.html.

an understanding that it was eroding the image of Americans as an exceptional, law-abiding people.

One concession made by the U.S., to alleviate these tensions, was to allow an increasing number of cases involving Americans to fall within the jurisdiction of a foreign court. From 1970 to 1980 that number increased steadily from 21,278 cases to 83,196 cases. It included military personnel and civilians as well as their dependents for violent crimes as well as robbery and theft. Eventually, by 1981, the trend began to reverse with the number of cases declining to 78,751.[78] Although the U.S. offered that concession, with an increase in the potential for Americans to suffer the punishment of foreign judicial systems, the Germans rarely selected that option. Statistics reveal instead that for the same period of time, 1970 to 1981, foreign courts waived their right an average of 94.04 percent of the time.[79] Whether the reticence was due to overt pressures exerted by the U.S., mutual agreement, or was the result of a residual "occupation mentality" as one journalist implied, the result was that most guilty Milcom members remained subject to the Uniform Code of Military Justice (UCMJ).[80]

Instead of being pleased when the U.S. acted forcefully and deliberately to punish capital crime infractions, West Germans sometimes balked. This happened in a number of cases that resulted in the awarding of the death penalty to American service personnel. A series of three particular cases during the 1980s captured the Germans' attention. The first involved the brutal beating and murder of a German woman in 1982, the second was the armed robbery and murder of a German taxi driver in 1984 and the last was the murder by a sergeant of his dependent wife and two step-sons.[81] Although the Germans and many Americans found the crimes heinous and shocking, the Germans found the decision to apply the death penalty abhorrent.

Tracking the German public's opinion regarding the death penalty over time, the *Institut für Demoskopie Allensbach* revealed a sharp drop-off of support after the mid–1960s. Favorable opinion of the punishment as a viable option fell from 50 percent in 1967 to 26 percent in 1980, although the West German Basic Law of 1949 had already eliminated the death penalty.[82] The greatest decrease however, occurred between 1967 and 1973 as support declined from 50 percent to 30 percent.[83]

During the same period of time, the death penalty, which still remained an option for capital crimes in the U.S., continued as a contested issue in the realm of public debate.[84] This was also the case within the military as Milcom readers followed exposés that discussed the constitutionality of the issue and drew parallels between the German system, which eliminated capital punishment, and their own.[85] By coincidence, or design, these commentary pieces appeared during the time surrounding the two high profile murders of Germans by American soldiers in 1982 and 1984. Letters to the editor of *Stars and Stripes* also reveal the evolving controversy within the Milcoms. As early as 1973 a letter submitted to the editor supported the death penalty noting "In the New Testament we are warned that we shall reap what we have sown."[86] Another, from 1974, criticized the judicial system for allowing a GI, convicted for murdering a German, to serve a life sentence in a German prison in lieu of facing the death penalty in an American court.[87] That trend continued into the early 1980s even as Milcom letter writers argued against the privileges given to convicted criminals.[88] By the latter years of that decade letter writers reflected changing attitudes. Citing studies that showed "the use of capital punishment results in the increase of homicides," and that the death penalty "costs more than keeping a prisoner in jail for life," a member of the USAREUR Criminal Investigation Division sharply criticized its use.[89] In 1989, another Milcom letter writer simply claimed, "I think the death penalty completely disregards the basic right to life."[90]

Still, the Germans saw in American culture and society violent currents and spoke and acted against them. As one journalist for *Der Spiegel* wrote, during the 1980s the Germans viewed the U.S. through a Rambo-esque lens. It was a time of renewed patriotism when Americans were again flexing their muscles and it reflected in Hollywood productions such as *Rambo: First Blood* (1982) and *Rocky IV* (1985). But also disconcerting to many Germans were the brash slogans on some Americans' fashionable T-shirts such as one that read, "Join the Army, travel to distant countries, meet interesting people, and kill them." This seemed to go hand in glove with the prevalent culture of violence that included the death penalty for capital crimes.[91] This last point inspired West German Justice Minister Peter Caesar to reestablish jurisdiction in a case involving two American soldiers charged with the rape and murder of a German woman in August 1989. Citing the right afforded the Federal Republic under the NATO SOFA agreement, Caesar acted to prevent the handing down of a death sentence by U.S. military authorities on West German soil.[92] A related German editorial supported the decision and encouraged the "Federal Government" to negotiate with the Americans to win final jurisdiction over any such future cases especially since the death penalty "has been abolished in the Federal Republic."[93] Although the Germans pushed for greater control and discipline within the Milcoms to curtail increasing crime trends, they refused to endorse the death penalty seeing it as feeding into the currents of violence that already existed in American culture and society. This dichotomy placed additional torque on the already-frayed relationship between the Americans and their German neighbors.

Drugs in the Milcoms

Drug abuse was the other emergent dimension of Western culture that the Germans struggled against. An attribute of a broader "counter-cultural" renaissance— which was creating an atmosphere of permissiveness within Western societies that younger generations perceived as too authoritarian—drugs offered a vehicle of escape and rebellion.[94] That behavior made its way into the armed forces of the U.S. through the induction of younger Americans into its lower enlisted ranks. Combined with the experimental use of drugs by many Vietnam veterans, the situation was exacerbated.[95] When these military personnel made their way to their assignments in West Germany they often carried those habits and attitudes with them. By one estimate, 78 percent of the soldiers using drugs "first started before coming to Germany; and 65 percent began before entering the Army."[96] Jeff White who lived in the Bad Kreuznach Milcom recalls of that time, "The majority of people [in the barracks] were heads." In his estimation "90 percent of those living in the barracks did get high."[97] Still, another former Milcom member recalls, "Drug usage was something that was fairly prevalent. I was surprised at the amount of hash that was smoked, since I grew up in a military family and knew that the drug culture was something that was not tolerated (or at least wasn't supposed to be)." He went on to add, "Often times, walking down the barracks hallway (usually on the weekends), I could see towels along the bottom of a room door, which would be indicative of smoking in the room (not to mention the smell since it would still get past the towel)."[98] But drug abuse was not limited to use by just the lower ranking enlisted men. One former non-commissioned officer admits, "I did smoke some hash in France and Germany, maybe a handful of times but never with my men. A few other young sergeants and Spec–5s would get together for poker or bridge games and a hash cigarette would be passed around."[99]

Although remembrances such as these do not suggest that every unit or every Milcom had prevalent drug-related problems it does suggest that occurrences of drug abuse were widespread enough to raise concerns among military leaders. It also suggests that from the late 1960s through the 1980s the Milcoms continued to remain a microcosm of American society reflecting the negative cultural attributes of violence, crime, and drug abuse.

In this context it also became clear to military authorities, outside agencies and the interested media that crime and drug abuse in USAREUR, as in the U.S., were often bedfellows. The fact that drugs were "a key factor in barracks crime," particularly theft and break-ins, was well known. As one soldier noted, "the Army doesn't pay very much and people get broke and they steal things to sell. You know, for dope and stuff."[100] One investigative report noted, "Some soldiers are earning from $500 to $600 a week dealing in drugs." Users who were supporting a $3,000 a month heroin habit would "steal anything from shoes to t-shirts" and stereos to finance it.[101] According to Jeff White, it was also possible to procure drugs on an installment plan by promising a percentage of the next payday check to the supplier. This, he notes, soldiers referred to as "copping on pay-day stakes."[102] Other examples of drug-related crime were barracks room robberies at knifepoint to obtain drugs and violence between "rival hashish dealers attacking each other in the style of bootleggers during prohibition."[103] This type of crime also spread through the Milcoms and spilled out into the surrounding German communities as drug users often resorted to robbery and theft outside the barracks to be able to afford their habits. Unsuspecting individuals, such as German taxi drivers, often were prey for these criminals.

German opinion polls probed the public's concern with questions such as, "Do you think that drugs pose more of a threat to young people in Germany than they did a year ago, or is it the same, or has it increased?" In 1972, 49 percent of respondents replied that the danger had increased, 35 percent that it was the same, and 15 percent that there was less danger. In contrast, by 1978, 51 percent replied that the danger had increased, 33 percent that it was the same, and only 6 percent felt that there was less danger.[104] The German print media fueled this anxiety. An April 1972 commentary noted, "Every second American soldier stationed in the Federal Republic" had tried marijuana, and that "the crime numbers have almost doubled since 1969." It went on to claim that 46 percent of GIs had used hashish, 16 percent smoked marijuana at least three times a week, and every unit had at least one "LSD addict."[105] Painting a bleak picture, it stated that "drug addicts who have no money for this stuff, steal from their comrades" and "the GIs in Europe take almost as much drugs as GIs in Vietnam," a charge that was unfounded.[106] The Germans continued their avid interest in drug abuse in the Mil-

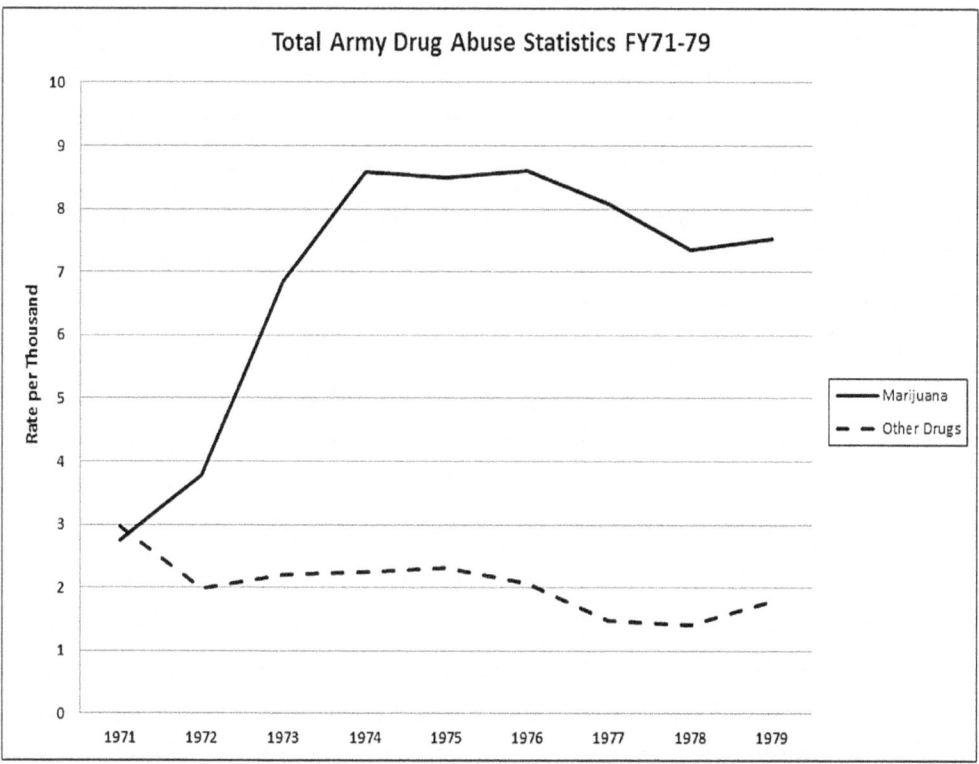

Army Drug Abuse Statistics, Fiscal Year 1971–1979. Data includes convictions for illegal use of marijuana and other drugs (LSD, cocaine, heroin, and hashish). Data source: Department of the Army Historical Summary (DAHSUM) FY 1971 through FY 1979, Center of Military History, http://www.history.army.mil/html/bookshelves/collect/dahsum.html.

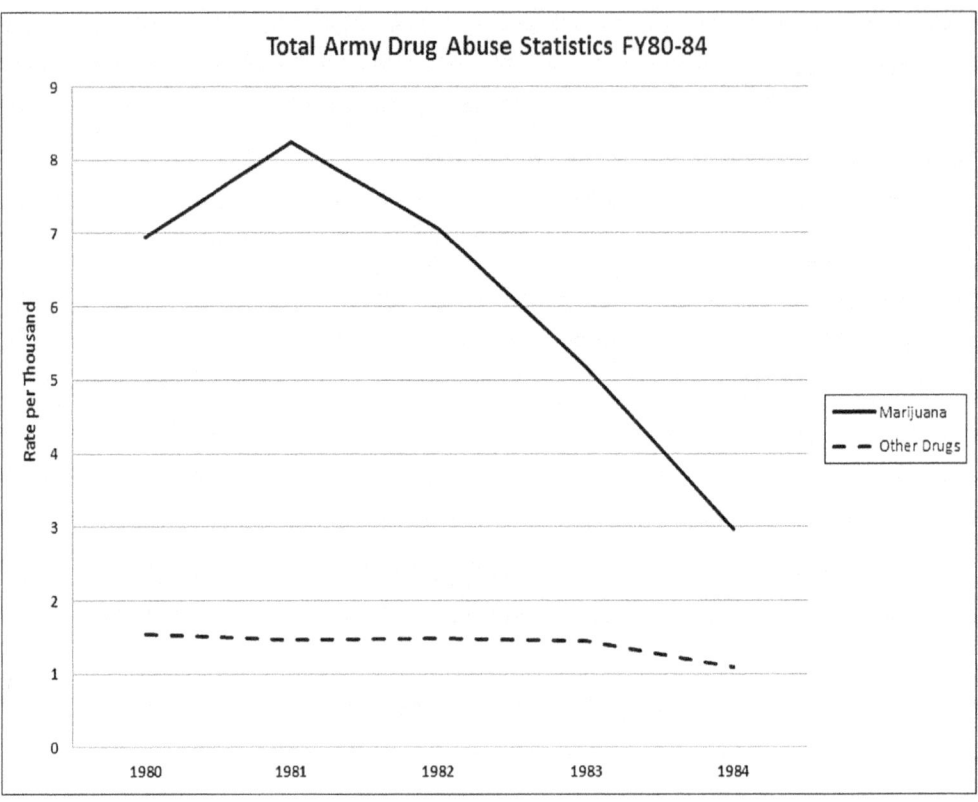

Army Drug Abuse Statistics, Fiscal Year 1980–1984. Data includes convictions for illegal use of marijuana and other drugs (LSD, cocaine, heroin, and hashish). Data source: Department of the Army Historical Summary (DAHSUM) FY 1980 through FY 1984, Center of Military History, http://www.history.army.mil/html/bookshelves/collect/dahsum.html.

coms through that decade and into the 1980s. A September 1973 article recounted the finding of "40 clinical cases of heavy drug abuse" among GIs attending an outdoor rock concert in Frankfurt.[107] Other articles continued to maintain a lens of scrutiny on the U.S. military's seeming inability to come to terms with widespread drug abuse in its ranks. For example, a January 1974 column highlighted a high court's challenge to the constitutionality of the U.S. Army's urinalysis testing.[108]

By 1979 the German print media was heralding the end of the American Volunteer Army (VOLAR) and predicting a return to conscription by assigning failure to "lack of motivation, alcohol, drugs and disciplinary misconduct."[109] Seen through a separate lens however, the situation bore both differences and similarities. In contrast, American military leaders commented that the VOLAR of the late 1970s contained better disciplined soldiers and that the absent-without-leave (AWOL) rate had decreased "more than 50 percent" since the end of conscription in 1974. They also noted that "barracks crime, rampant just a few years ago, is no longer a big problem," and "race relations have improved a lot." In agreement with the media however, they did admit that "drugs—especially heroin and hashish—remain a lingering Army problem" and that "usage is on the rise again after a dip in recent years."[110] Statistics maintained by the U.S. Army bore this out.

Military law enforcement authorities in USAREUR separated the trend lines for drug abuse, which they described as a driving force for much of the reported crime, into two categories: "marijuana" and "other drugs."[111] Of the two, the trend line representing incidents involving "other drugs" generally behaved as did those for crime, decreasing from a high in 1971 of 3.0 reported incidents per 1,000, to approximately 2.0 in 1979, 1.6 in 1980 and 1.0 by 1984. The trend for marijuana was different. Reported incidents for its use climbed from 3.0 per 1,000 in 1971 to approximately 9.0 in 1974, and then generally remained above 7.0 until 1981 when it began to decrease to 3.0 again by 1984.[112] That sharp upward trend in 1974 was coincidental with the introduction of the VOLAR, although hard evidence making a direct correlation between the two is absent.[113]

The memories of individual Milcom members correspond to these trend lines and the near absence of drug related problems prior to the 1970s. Robert Weekley stationed in the Dachau Milcom recalls, "At that time (1960–1963) drug problems were almost nonexistent in my unit and *Kaserne*."[114] Robert Bierly, Jr., remembers a similar situation, "The primary drug problem was too much German *Bier* [beer] and schnapps in the local gasthauses. Occasionally, there would be a drug case but it was not rampant. Generally, it would be brought back from leave in Holland where drugs were freely available."[115]

By the end of the Vietnam War the environment in the Milcoms had changed. Tom Tracy remembers that as a dependent teen in the Frankfurt Milcom from 1977–1979, "drugs and alcohol seemed rampant. I visited a friend, as a teen, who was a soldier in the barracks and his soldier room-mate was smoking weed with no repercussions. Frankfurt was terrible."[116] In some locations, such as the Bamberg Milcom, the situation seemed dire. "Drugs were a big problem when I first got to 2/78 FA," Thomas Rehm recalls, "I still recall the picture the Battery Commander kept under the glass on his desk of about 10 troops [soldiers] partying with obvious drug pipes. He crossed one off each time that he chaptered them out of the Army. He and the First Sergeant got each and every one."[117] By the latter half of the 1980s conditions had improved, and Thomas Rehm noted the difference, "By my second tour [1989–1991] drugs were not a significant problem." The experiences of Aschaffenburg Milcom member Bruce Harding corroborate this, "Drugs were still a problem, but as with race relations I think things were improving. Having said that, drug busts and drug related disciplinary actions were not unusual, but I didn't know of a unit that was incapacitated or unable to perform its mission because of drugs."[118]

The military command structure in EUCOM invested a great deal effort in identifying and apprehending drug abusers in the Milcoms. Perhaps the most representative initiative was the mandatory random urinalysis program that the military instituted in Europe in September 1971.[119] It paralleled similar programs that began in the U.S. and Vietnam earlier that year and by the end of its first month was processing up to 22,000 samples a week. The program, which service members dubbed "Operation Golden Flow," was initially costly and drew criticism from the media who charged the U.S. government with creating "a sort of mini-military industrial complex" that incorporated a vast network of shipping and testing facilities.[120] Regardless of such comments, the program remained in use and within a few years military authorities such as those in the Kaiserslautern Milcom reported, "Our drug abuse detection rate has increased since 1973. We identified 33 drug abusers in 1973, 101 in 1974 and 100 in 1975."[121] Still, they had to admit that the overall use of illegal drugs had not declined and service members had developed ways to beat the urinalysis system, such as switching to (then) non-detectable drugs like hashish and marijuana.[122]

Charles Sheeley, who worked at the 97th General Hospital in Frankfurt during that time recalls:

> Until the spring of 1976 the Army in Europe was still trying to rehab [rehabilitate] drug users. Heroin was a major problem. It came from Afghanistan to Germany via Amsterdam. It was snorted—as most G.I.s did not have the "fix-works" of a needle and syringe. Nevertheless, the users could become quite addicted. These were the days that preceded the affordable widespread drug testing as we have had since the 1980s. Subsequently one of the associated problems was the spread of Hepatitis B, even among snorters.... We had a single Hepatitis ward at the 97th General Hospital with about 40 to 50 beds. Other problem drugs were hashish and over-the-counter German dietary suppressants.[123]

Occasionally, military authorities orchestrated sweeping raids using a combination of unannounced urinalysis tests, drug dogs, and searches of vehicles and billets. *Operation Snow White*, conducted in the Hanau Milcom in 1978, uncovered $1.2 million in drugs and included 103 arrests between October and December of that year.[124] *Snow White II* conducted between April and June of 1980 in the same Milcom area uncovered $2 million in drugs and included 89 U.S. service members as well as 13 Germans and "third country nationals."[125] During the latter decades of the Cold War Milcom readers could follow the results of continued drug suppression efforts in *Stars and Stripes*, other print media and on the AFN daily news broadcasts. The scope and dedication of resources for many of these actions appeared to parallel the ongoing covert intelligence programs between the U.S. and the Soviets and included close cooperation with the German police. For example, a December 1978 article announced the arrest of 101 GIs and 17 civilians in the Hanau Milcom.[126] A later column informed readers of the arrest of 24 GIs as well as three West German women and a Turkish man in the Oppenheim Milcom.[127] An article from August 1979 reported the arrests of 49 GIs in the Stuttgart Milcom and another reported the arrests of 50 GIs in the Nüremberg Milcom that also netted $343,000 in hashish, marijuana, and LSD.[128]

One result of these operations, which soon became apparent, was that the arrests also netted persons other than American service members. These often included German civilians as well as third-country nationals. But, occasionally, they did include American dependents. An example was the apprehension of a teen-age female family member during a vehicle check in the Bremerhaven Milcom in April 1979.[129] More sobering however, was news of the apprehension of a large group of students at the Nüremberg American high school during the Christmas season of 1984. As a result of the "crackdown" military police and civilian investigators detained 40 teenage male students "from families of civilians and soldiers from many levels of the rank structure." Of those, the military command sent 15 back to the U.S. under EUCOM's civilian misconduct policy. Many of those who remained in Germany participated in mandatory rehabilitation programs.[130]

Although the American military in Germany did invest a great deal of time and effort in strategies to curtail drug abuse through discovery and apprehension during the 1970s and 1980s it also dedicated efforts toward recovery and rehabilitation. The principal program established in the early 1970s was the Army Alcohol and Drug Abuse Prevention and Control Program (ADAPCP). It utilized a combination of education, counseling and medical support to execute its mission to "offer rehabilitative services to substance abusers and restore them to duty." Failing that, it was a means of "identifying individuals who [cannot] be rehabilitated and [were] considered unfit for the service."[131] By December 1976, more than 15,000 soldiers world-wide were in the program.[132] Another aspect of the program for recovering addicts in some Milcoms was mandatory participation in Moral Support Activities as part of their rehabilitation. This included team sports, arts and crafts, music, choir, and drama.[133] Although these types of programs focused on helping individuals deemed recoverable, and discharging from the service those who were not, they were indicative of the military's reaction to the wider cultural and societal problem of substance abuse.

Date	Population in Rehabilitation Programs
1972	28,789
1975	17,569
1976	31,322
1977	22,543
1978	22,647
1979	24,226
1980	24,008
1981	26,385
1983	51,858
1984	65,198

Table 6.2. Population Numbers of Rehab Programs. Numbers include military personnel, civilians, and dependents enrolled in a substance abuse rehabilitation program, by year. Data is not available for FY 1973 and 1974. During this time, a pending court case challenged the military's right to conduct urinalysis testing. As a result, identification of abusers was difficult. The military began drug testing Reserve Component personnel activated-for-training in FY 1983. The increase in participation for FY83 and FY84 reflects that change. After FY 1984, the military shifted its focus from drug abuse to other areas of special interest such as the fuller integration of women into the armed services. (Department of the Army Historical Summaries, Center of Military History, http://www.history.army.mil/html/bookshelves/collect/dahsum.html.)

Throughout the 1970s and 1980s, Milcom members made their anxieties and associated concerns about the drug problem in Germany known through letters to the editor of *Stars and Stripes*. A survey of these letters reveals that they generally fell into three categories: those sympathetic to the abusers, those that criticized the military's recovery programs and those that addressed reasons for abuse. Typically, those that were sympathetic to the substance abuser frequently made comments such as, "Is it not human to have frailties?" They also often suggested, "Drug abuse is a sickness" and recommended abusers should not be "turned away without help."[134] Some also recommended a measure of understanding for abusers and their problems equal to that of an "understanding of race relations."[135] Among those letters that criticized programs such as ADAPCP there were comments that it was "a big flop" based on observations of the "complete lack of change" in many participants.[136] Another criticism came from a staff member of one of the detoxification wards who claimed a glaring shortcoming was that mandatory urinalyses only applied to military patients under the age of 25. He felt this prejudiced the program against lower enlisted personnel.[137] Finally, those letters that sought to address the reason for drug abuse in the Milcoms often focused on problems external to the abuser. These often included failures of the military command structure to effectively utilize soldiers' time through meaningful training or a lack of adequate billeting and recreation activities, which generally led to boredom and lack of purpose resulting in drug abuse.[138]

Just as Americans in the Milcoms struggled with substance abuse, so did the wider German community. One news report noted that there were 600 recorded heroin deaths in West Germany for 1979, and 50,000 heroin addicts. The report also revealed that 22.5 percent of the users were less than 21 years of age. This profile also exhibited certain characteristics that were consistent with the young American Milcom drug abuser—they were bored, felt peer pressure, lacked motivation, felt a limitation to their creativity, and were uncertain about their futures.[139]

This parallel perspective, coming late in the 1970s, represented a shift in attitudes by Germans who in the aftermath of the Vietnam War were quick to point the finger of blame solely on the Milcom for introducing the blight of drug abuse. In the late 1960s and early 1970s many West Germans focused on how the problems of American society and culture such as drugs, violence, and crime had "spilled over into German society ... especially in areas contiguous to military facilities." They remarked, "There was an increase in crimes perpetrated by American soldiers against German civilians" including the spread of a "drug culture" into the surrounding population.[140] While a great deal of evidence shows that the Milcoms did introduce an element of violence and crime into German society, and Americans did arrive in the Milcoms bearing the burden of substance abuse, closer examination reveals that by the late 1970s and early 1980s the challenge of drug abuse was a common concern shared across the boundary between the two cultures.

During the 1970s, numerous reports and articles in the Milcom media were already recording the involvement of both German and non–German nationals in drug trafficking in the Milcoms. The German media was reporting the growth of drug addiction in the Federal Republic that trafficking with the Milcoms alone could not have inspired and an increasing number of American service members and civilians were procuring drugs from sources outside the Milcom. As one American wrote in a *Stars and Stripes* letter to editor, "As I walked through Grueneberg Park in Frankfurt.... I was approached three times in less than 45 minutes by three non–American males asking if I wanted to buy hashish. It's common knowledge that lots of drugs are bought and sold there."[141] The editor replied that the park was not the only known location where drug trafficking was occurring. Many younger service members knew where to go outside their barracks and the Milcoms and the watchful eyes of the American and German police, to purchase drugs. Among the less clandestine locations, was the local German *Drogerie* [pharmacy] where "amphetamine-like products and some sedatives [were] available without prescription."[142]

More sobering than casual encounters in parks were reports of heavy influxes of drugs from sources outside the Federal Republic. An August 1978 report based on United Nations intelligence sources projected a "30 percent increase in the availability of heroin in West Germany" by that fall. It noted, "7,000 pounds of heroin moved from East Germany into West Germany" the year prior. The targets of these drugs were the NATO forces with the hopes that their use would undermine "combat readiness."[143] Drug users and sellers, and sources of supply, were a combination of Americans, Germans, and third-country nationals. This understanding was central to some of the earliest Congressional investigations into the extent of drug abuse among the Milcoms. As the record noted "Germany is of increasing importance because of the numbers of our servicemen stationed there, and because of itinerant workers from Turkey and the Middle East who often smuggle drugs in and because of Germany's importance as a transportation center for Europe."[144]

Dependents and Drugs

Although concerns over drug abuse focused first on military personnel and unit readiness, it soon became apparent that the problem was also spreading out of the barracks and into the housing areas and schools in the Milcoms. Reports of drug abuse problems among dependents began appearing in *Stars and Stripes* as early as 1969 when a local investigation by the military police in the Heidelberg Milcom identified 20 teen abusers. Military authorities immediately returned three of that group to the U.S. and placed 17 on indefinite suspension while requiring their parents to maintain close supervision of their activities.[145]

The scope of the drug problems among dependents became evident through the 1970s as reports began appearing with greater frequency in *Stars and Stripes*. One investigative reporter working for the newspaper surveyed several hundred American high school students. His findings revealed that the drug of choice for dependents was not marijuana, which was difficult to obtain in Europe, but rather hashish. The "hash" he noted arrived in Germany via smugglers from Turkey, Morocco, Lebanon "And other Mideast lands."[146] Other problems *Stars and Stripes*' reporter noted in his study were the ability of dependents to purchase drugs in the local Germany community, the lack of parental education about drug abuse in teens and the reluctance of the German police to enforce drugs laws. This last discovery seemed most frustrating to the American authorities because German police were "quite lax concerning American teenage drug violators," and most chose to ignore the problem with the knowledge that "If they arrested U.S. teens, it would mean additional expense to the German taxpayers."[147] All these problems were challenges that continued to confront Milcom parents through the decade.

Other media stories corroborated this emerging crisis. A March 1970 feature article about the situation facing USAFE dependents touched on many of the same points. In particular, it addressed the same concern regarding German drug laws. A *Stars and Stripes* staff writer highlighted that fact that "in Germany, the laws governing drug violators are more lenient than they are in America" and first time offenders normally received very light punishment.[148] More sobering were the charges leveled by the German District Attorney from Wiesbaden who claimed "that many German youths who are caught with either hashish ... or speed or LSD in their possession were introduced to the drug by either an American serviceman or an American dependent." Although he also admitted it was an ongoing exchange: "We have found that most Americans buy hashish and other illegal drugs from a German pusher. The American in turn, will introduce it to a German friend."[149] The October 8, 1970, front page of *Stars and Stripes* announced, "Sixty-seven per cent of American dependent 18-year-old high school boys interviewed in a survey admitted having used drugs at least once." The contents of the associated article also noted that 45 percent of 18-year-old dependent high school girls admitted the same.[150]

The drug problem among service members that had demanded the attention of military and political elites in the early 1970s also existed among overseas dependents. As programs to identify and deal with military abusers developed, those for dependents lagged behind. One rare example was the opening of a Frankfurt Youth health center that offered medical aid and counseling to dependent youth on a voluntary basis.[151] There was, however, no mention of the drug challenges facing dependent family members in the Department of the Army Historical Summaries (DAHSUM) prior to 1975, and then it simply noted, without elaboration or breakdown by location, that the military had provided assistance for alcohol and drug abuse to 9,000 civilians and dependents.[152] The next drug reference in the DAHSUM was in 1976 and the Army merely provided a blanket statement that "The Army continued its efforts to prevent the abuse of alcohol and other drugs by soldiers on active duty, reservists, retirees, their families, and civilian employees."[153] It provided no details.

The absence of official reporting of dependent drug data remained until the FY 1980 DAHSUM. The subparagraph on *Alcohol and Drug Abuse* noted that 38,104 dependents had received instruction on alcohol and drug abuse avoidance through classes, orientations, and briefings.[154] Although this aggregate, for the entire Army, appears to be a large number it was actually negligible when considered against the worldwide total of 488,726 overseas dependents of which 169,000 were in West Germany. Nevertheless, it suggests a dawning awareness among the military leadership in Washington and USAREUR that more proactive programs were necessary. Milcom members could read about these unfolding initiatives in *Stars and Stripes* beginning in the 1980s.

A July 1984 article explained one of the pilot programs to introduce anti-drug abuse materials including booklets, pamphlets, and films to the overseas schools systems through the DODDS.[155] The intention was to provide a uniform program among the schools and fill in the gaps where one was absent. This eventually led to the incorporation of the Drug Abuse Resistance Education (DARE) program into the curriculum of the Milcom schools system in Germany by 1986.[156] The program arrived at a time when Milcom dependents' deaths were still occurring from the abuse of stimulants.[157] The positive impact of the drug education initiative was encouraging. Subsequent articles carried the details of favorable comparisons between Milcom teens and their counterparts in the U.S. In February 1988, 28 percent of Milcom youth reported trying marijuana against 36 percent in the U.S., 3 percent reported using hallucinogens against 6.4 percent in the U.S., and 4.1 percent reported the use of amphetamines compared to 12.2 percent in the U.S.[158] This trend continued through to 1990 as a DODDS survey revealed that only 7 percent of Milcom parents in Germany thought the use of drugs by teens was still a problem against 36 percent in the U.S.[159]

As effective as these programs were there were some missteps along the way. One example was an attempt to require certain non-military Milcom members to also participate in a mandatory urinalysis program. The recommendation first came in 1972 from Brigadier General John K. Singlaub, the Deputy Assistant Secretary of Defense for Drug and Alcohol Abuse. His reasoning was that it was effective as a tool to control drug abuse by service members and therefore would suffice as a control for dependents as well.[160] At the time the military did not implement the idea outside the requirement for civilians working in positions that required the handling of secret or sensitive materials. Authorities in the Pentagon quashed Singlaub's proposal and offered it only on a voluntary basis. The idea did briefly resurface in October 1986 as a possible requirement for DODDS teachers in Europe, but protests from teachers' unions forestalled it.[161]

The use of drugs by dependents in Germany during the late 1960s through the 1980s followed a trajectory that was parallel to that of American service members and was just as problematic. The difference however was in the attention political and military elites in Washington and EUCOM applied to solving the problems of service members, particularly when they tied the threat of drug abuse to unit combat readiness. This was further complicated when the impact of drug abuse was conflated with the challenges of crime and race. Nevertheless, the increasing concern of Milcom parents over time suggested that another dimension, stability of the home, could also factor into soldier morale and contribute to the undermining of readiness. This eventually brought the necessary attention to the incipient crisis of drug abuse among dependents by the 1980s. This became easier as the destabilizing energies of racial conflict, crime, and rampant drug abuse by service members seemed to have run their course by that time.

Like crime and violence the growing drug problem in the U.S. and many Western nations was a reflection of the prevalent cultural and social *Zeitgeist* that existed from the mid–1960s to the 1990s. The intersection of all three troubles at the Milcom placed a strain on contemporary German-American relations. Although the West Germans were eager to embrace certain American cultural artifacts such as fast food they continued to resist and deflect any infusion of violence, crime and drugs. It became apparent over time however, that the drug problem was a wider phenomenon that passed both ways across the cultural boundary. In that context, it evolved as a mutual concern that left neither nation feeling exceptional.

Seven

Race, Feminism and Media Manipulation (1967–1990)

Racial Challenges in the Milcom

Glancing through the black and white photographs of DODDS yearbooks from the late 1940s and early 1950s, a reader could find images of racially-mixed student bodies sharing classrooms, engaging in team sports, attending prom and riding buses together.[1] This might suggest that the dependent schools in West Germany had been integrated by design in advance of the 1954 landmark Supreme Court decision.[2] But any such understanding is misleading if one assumes any uniform existence of racial harmony. As this study has revealed, the degree of racial disharmony within the Milcoms prior to the early 1960s reflected that of the greater American society. In many cases it mirrored regional attitudes often carried over by service members and their dependents from those areas of the U.S. where Jim Crowism was prevalent. Examination of source materials also reveals that early efforts by the military command structure to engage existing problems between the races was frequently superficial at best and anecdotes of violence often failed to make the daily news. As evidence has suggested, various dynamics such as personal bias, reticence of military leaders to admit any manner of disciplinary problems and a weak, if non-existent, reporting system complicated the relations between the races in the early Milcoms. The result was a consistent, but pyrrhic, projection of racial equality. But problems associated with race, left to fester and influenced by cultural dynamics, would eventually begin to erupt by the late–1960s as the societal atmosphere of the U.S., and the reality within the Milcoms, began to change. As one white Army officer lamented to a reporter during the worst of the tempest, "race is our most serious internal problem." He then sardonically added, it takes "all my time—now and then I get around to running a company."[3]

By the late 1960s, the demographics of the Milcoms were in transition. The percentage of black enlisted service personnel in EUCOM was increasing again to match the pre–Vietnam average of 13.5 percent and would rise to 17 percent by 1972.[4] Just as important, as the percentage of white dependents living overseas was decreasing, from 91 percent of the total to 87 percent, the number of black dependents was increasing from 6.1 percent of the total to 8.8 percent.[5] Although this change appeared modest, evidence suggests that it was enough to begin to raise the awareness of the military leadership in Europe in light of the tempestuous events unfolding in the U.S. These included the bloody suppression by the police of civil rights marchers on their way to Selma in March 1965, the Watts riots of that same year, the Detroit riots of 1967 and the assassination of Dr. Martin Luther King, Jr., in April 1968. Milcom members, both black and white, became sensitive to the issues when they received that type of news via broadcasts on the AFN radio network, on the front page of *Stars and Stripes* newspaper, or other magazines and print materials they received from the States.[6]

Still, some blind spots to the emerging race reality existed. There were some political and military elites who simply reported that race problems in Europe were almost non-existent. For example, after a three-week tour of EUCOM facilities in 1968, two Defense Department officials reported that they were "satisfied that the armed forces have done an excellent job of [racial] integration in Europe." Although their investigation involved interviewing a number of soldiers and airmen they found that only "isolated complaints of discrimination continue to be made by Negro servicemen."[7]

Regardless of the report's findings, incidents of violence between the races continued, such as the knifing deaths of three black soldiers by a white. Paradoxically, in that instance, a decision by a military court permitted the white soldier to escape a murder charge by arguing self-defense.[8] In addition, news reports of the emergence of white supremist Ku Klux Klan (KKK) elements in EUCOM also contributed to the increasing strain on race relations. Although Army investigations originally found no basis for the claim, further queries prompted by the Secretary of the Army discovered some basis to the assertion. The findings ultimately revealed, "Negro and Puerto Rican troops" in the Fulda Milcom, "were the victims of organized racial hostility" perpetrated and tolerated by both white non-commissioned and commissioned officers.[9] The situation in the Milcoms appeared dire.

A series of investigations by the Department of Defense eventually began to make important discoveries regarding the depth of racial inequity among the armed forces in Europe. A 1970 report based on a study by representatives from the Pentagon revealed, "A communications gap was developing" in USAREUR between "minority group enlisted men and their white company grade officers and non-commissioned officers." It also noted that black soldiers believed a "dual standard of punishment was being imposed." The investigative team found that although blacks accounted for only 13 percent of the troop strength they received approximately 25 percent of the non-judicial punishments and comprised 50 percent of the stockade population.[10] This was a principal complaint voiced by both black troops and officers.[11]

Some communities took matters into their own hands. The Mannheim Milcom organized a Race Relations Council to bring together soldiers of different races and provide avenues of communication between them. Some of the issues they discovered during their open sessions were as simple as a need for policy guidance concerning the length of Afro-style hairdos and as troubling as the feigned ignorance of officers and sergeants who "never hear of fights or areas where problems exist between blacks and whites."[12] The council also addressed concerns that there was an absence of lectures on "the black man's background and history" and that many problems between black and white soldiers stemmed from "Negroes going out with white girls."[13]

Some grassroots leaders took the initiative and acted to confront the issue of racial disharmony head-on. Leon Ceniceros recalls:

> In Germany, for whatever reason, there was a huge black versus white anger. Especially in the armor and infantry units. There were always articles in the *Overseas Weekly* newspaper ... while nothing was ever mentioned in the *Stars and Stripes* newspaper. When I was assigned to the 98th and took over as barracks sergeant,

> I noticed that there were all black areas and all white areas in the barracks. I put a stop to that by assigning the bunks by blood groups that might be necessary in an emergency for blood collection. There were a couple of small fights on the weekends for the first couple of months but then things quieted down as the men got used to each other. Another benefit was that being bunk mates, the men started going to the movies, the snack bar, the EM Club and the Gasthaus together. The white EM [Enlisted Men] would tease the black EM that they would have to "cover their asses" at the Gasthaus because the local German young men hated black soldiers with a passion. While black EM's could date white German women in the major cities, it was never tolerated in the smaller towns.[14]

The first major coordinated effort to come to terms with the scope of racial issues in EUCOM came through a late 1970 initiative conducted by the Deputy Assistant Secretary of the Defense, Frank W. Render II.[15] The effort included two teams, one from the Department of the Army and a second from USAREUR, and both were composed of civilians, officers, and enlisted personnel. They came together for an inspection tour of units and Milcoms in Italy, Great Britain, and West Germany.[16] As its stated purpose, the group formed to assess the "effectiveness of the present policies and programs of the Department of Defense and Military Departments related to Equal Opportunity and Race Relations."[17] Included in the surveyed groups were dependents as well as service members. Of the total number interviewed (5,650) there were 3,350 from the Army, 950 from the Navy and 1,350 Air Force personnel. The assessment team conducted all the Army interviews at West German Milcoms.[18]

Brewing racial tensions appeared during the month-long course of the investigation as Render's group discovered "a higher level of frustration and anger among blacks than was anticipated." They also encountered "small cores of alienated blacks" who explained to him "they had no reason to be fighting in a white man's Army." Although Render was a black man they also accused him and the team of trying to "brainwash" the disquieted blacks and often interrupted question and answer sessions with "verbally inflammatory language rank with profanities and obscenities."[19]

A summary of the Render Report's findings revealed several principal concerns: the failure of military leaders to act in a timely manner on grievances and points of conflict between the races, the perception that white leadership too often referred to "any black who asserts himself in any way as militant," the perception by many blacks that commanders discriminated against them in the meting out of punishment and inconsistencies in the ability of existing grievance systems to effectively communicate problems to higher authorities.[20] Added to these complaints there were "enumerations of problems" that included "fear [among whites] of the rise of black awareness and the thrust for black identity," lack of uniformity in policies and directives concerning racial equality and a critical lack of black officers and non-commissioned officers (NCOs).[21] The U.S. government published the full 19 page Render Report, under the title "U.S. Military Race Relations in Europe—September 1970," on November 2, 1970.

Reaction to the investigation began even prior to its completion and continued close on the heels of the publication of the report. Some field commanders in Europe quickly pledged resolution to problems. The commanding general of the 20,000-man U.S. 4th Armored Division, stationed in the Göppingen Milcom, made "harmonious race relations the first priority." He also urged all members of his unit and the Milcom to "do what they can at every turn to insure [sic] that any discrimination cease immediately."[22] General Polk, the USAREUR commander-in-chief, announced the creation of "flying squads" of Army investigators who would descend unannounced on lower level units to "insure that there is no discrimination in this command."[23] In a related action the Nuremberg Milcom, within Polk's area of responsibility, quickly opened an Equal Opportunity Office with the goal of assisting "the military man and his dependents" and serving as an outlet to "air their problems."[24] Later that year, the Fuerth Milcom opened a second Equal Opportunity Office to meet the growing need in that community. Part of its mission was to "instruct and counsel junior officers and NCOs in communication, sensitivity, and leadership techniques."[25] Still, it was too early to tell whether these initiatives and words were simply a means to placate elites in Washington, or merely stop-gap measures until the establishment of foundations for effective and responsive organizations.

Close on the heels of the Render investigation was another initiative conducted in January 1971, by a three-member team representing the NAACP. Led by General Counsel Nathaniel R. Jones, the group traveled to West Germany to conduct interviews with approximately 500 black service personnel as a follow-up to Secretary Render's government-sponsored trip. For three weeks Jones and his team traveled to a number of Milcoms including Berlin, Frankfurt, Mannheim, Heidelberg and Stuttgart. They listened to black soldiers' grievances about promotion rates, punishments, acts of overt discrimination and conferred with white commanders and leaders. Findings from Jones' team generally echoed those from Render's and emphasized the need for "prompt and sincere action on its recommendations for change and warned of possible catastrophic results if existing conditions are allowed to continue."[26]

Among the team's recommendations was a need to increase black legal representation in Germany, creation of a system to monitor the equitability of punishments by race, establishment of offices to prevent discrimination in housing, the expansion of recreational opportunities for blacks and the hiring of additional black faculty for the DODDS schools. There was also a recommendation for the NAACP to establish an office in West Germany "to serve the needs of the upwards of 25,000 Negro servicemen and civilians" stationed there.[27] Eventually, by 1980, the NAACP had a chapter office in Frankfurt, its president a serviceman. It also considered establishing ten more throughout Europe.[28] The team's complete findings and recommendations are contained in the 26-page published booklet *The Search for Military Justice: Report of an NAACP Inquiry into the Problems of the Negro Serviceman in West Germany* (1971).

The realities of these race problems in the European area of operations continued to attract the increasing attention of the military hierarchy in USAREUR and reflected in the narratives of the Department of the Army Historical Summaries (DAHSUM) beginning with the Fiscal Year 1970 report released in October 1971.[29] The Personnel section of that summary emphasized that the Continental Army Command in the U.S. had inaugurated intensive "equal opportunity and racial tension seminars" and at the direction of the Secretary of the Army had begun to develop courses of instruction on race relations "for presentation at training centers and service schools."[30] Though these efforts were longer term, and did affect soldiers destined for postings in Germany, other measures were of more immediate impact to black soldiers in USAREUR. These included introducing greater "variety of merchandise stocked in post exchanges" and expanding the literature "carried in libraries and on newsstands ... to encompass the needs and tastes of members of minority groups." Just as important, attention fell on the need to increase the recruitment of minority group junior officers.[31]

If the initiatives outlined in the FY 70 DAHSUM seemed too cursory those taken in FY 71 and FY 72 appeared more direct and focused. In October 1971 the Department of Defense established the Defense Race Relations Institute (DRRI) at Patrick Air Force Base in Florida to train equal opportunity and race relations instructors for the armed forces. Its other purpose was to provide instruction to senior level commanders such as generals and admirals.[32] In addition, that same year, the Department of the Army introduced mandatory instruction at service schools for officers and NCOs "designed to develop ... an understanding of the basic factors in race relations, the causes of racial tension, and measures to foster racial harmony."[33] Many of these leaders deployed directly to their assignment with units in USAREUR.

The race relations initiatives for FY 72 focused on affirmative action. In June of that year, the Chief of Staff of the Army (CSA) directed the development of Affirmative Action Plans (AAP) at every installation, Milcom, and unit of brigade-size or larger.[34] His guidance encouraged tailoring the plans to the specific needs of the unit and community. The DAH-SUM also included statistics that displayed the success of the minority recruitment program, which reached historic levels for enlisted personnel and senior officer advancement programs initiated two years earlier. This was one of the concerns minority soldiers had voiced to the Render investigative team during their USAREUR tour in 1970. Included in officer accession were increases in enrollment of blacks to the U.S. Military Academy at West Point, from 9 in 1968 to 53 in 1971, and attendance at the Officer Candidate School from 2 percent in 1971 to 5 percent in 1972. Both sets of numbers were overly optimistic.[35] Despite these stated improvements, the overall strength of black junior officers (lieutenants and captains) continued to lag behind the representative demographic of 13 percent for the U.S. population.

Academy	Class of 1969	Class of 1970	Class of 1971	Class of 1972	Total Negro	Total Attendance
Army	10	7	5	9	31	3,285
Navy	2	8	8	15	33	4,091
Air Force	6	10	13	23	52	3,028
Totals	18	25	26	47	116	

Table 7.1. Black Attendance at Military Academies. These numbers reflect the efforts of the military services to increase minority accessions for officers. After 1969, the Navy and Air Force increased noticeably, while the Army's accession rate flat-lined. (Defense Studies Series: Integration of the Armed Forces, 1940–1965, Center of Military History, accessed March 14, 2013, http://www.history.army.mil/books/integration/IAF-22.htm).

As the DAHSUM records show, however, two of the most significant race-related initiatives the Army attempted were in 1974. The first was the revision of several important Army regulations. These underwent changes to accommodate the new focus on race relations and equal opportunity, and expanded requirements and support for execution of policies and training. They included AR 600–18, *Equal Opportunity in Off-Post Housing*, AR 600–21, *Race Relations and Equal Opportunity*, and AR 600–42, *Race Relations Education for the Army*. The importance of this action was that once published they required the creation of a corresponding cascade of regulations and policies at each successively lower echelon of command thus ensuring dissemination of race relations and equal opportunity policies uniformly throughout the military.

The second important initiative was an extensive minority recruiting program for the Army's Judge Advocate General's Corps (JAG). Working with the National Association to the Black American Law Students Association, the National Association for the Advancement of Colored People (NAACP), the National Urban League, and the National Conference of Black Lawyers, the number of minority JAG officers increased. By the end of the year there were 32 blacks, 19 women, 8 Mexican-Americans, 5 Puerto Ricans, and 6 Orientals [sic] serving as lawyers in the Army.[36] This, the military leadership hoped, would serve to alleviate any perceived or actual discrimination in the meting out of justice or sentences in the military court system that the Render Report disclosed. This was particularly important in Germany where black soldiers felt an undue proportion of punishment levied against them in comparison to whites.[37] As one *New York Times* reporter noted about USAREUR, "Black soldiers account for three times as many reported cases of rape, robbery, and aggravated assault as do the whites."[38] At the time only two of the 46 judges assigned to EUCOM were black, but none of the defense attorneys were black.[39] One solution to this shortfall, proposed by the NAACP's General Counsel Nathaniel R. Jones, was for the military to enlist the aid of black civilian lawyers. These advocates, flown to Germany at the military's expense, could then fill the need of defense attorneys for black soldiers on trial.[40] This proposal was not accepted.

These efforts and energies to come to terms with race challenges continued to resonate in USAREUR during this period. Among the earliest initiatives was an effort to put an end to discrimination in housing. Policies directed by the Secretary of the Army, Stanley R. Resor, established Milcom housing offices to assist black GIs with families, "especially in Germany," obtain quarters where local "landlords often go unchallenged in their refusal to rent to Negroes."[41] At the same time, the military leadership in USAREUR continued to voice concern about racial matters. The new commander, General Arthur S. Collins, admitted during a command-wide conference on equal opportunity, in May 1971, that "Though there's been considerable progress made, we still have a long way to go" and promised the audience support for existing and evolving programs.[42] In a similar vein, the commanding general of the VII Corps Artillery endorsed ongoing efforts within his command, offered praise for their achievements and declared "Discrimination will not be tolerated and equal opportunity will be given every man, woman and child in the VII Corps Arty family."[43] Aside from examples of positive rhetoric, on-the-ground programs also reported progress. In December 1971, a race relations instructor in the Hahn Milcom equal opportunity office commented, "Americans have begun healing their nation's racial wounds in recent years." This he credited to "a new attitude in the form of mutual understanding and respect."[44]

The voices of Milcom members, heard in letters to the editor of *Stars and Stripes*, echoed the encouraging attitudes but also endorsed the need for continued vigilance. A senior NCO from the Heidelberg Milcom commented that "I have met good men and bad men of both races" and that it was "a step in the right direction to eliminate out and out bigotry and discrimination" through existing programs.[45] Another, from the Sembach Milcom wrote, "I believe that if we all live by what we know is right, EO and HR [Equal Opportunity and Human Relations] are only going to help us."[46] A writer from the Wiesbaden Milcom commented, "We are trying to correct a very lopsided social structure" adding "meaningful social balance demands understanding and accepting black cultural traits as part of our national character."[47] A letter from a Hanau Milcom member read, "As a member of my unit's human relations council, I have witnessed the beauty of race relations in the Army." But she also noted, "Racism still exists in this organization and it's not going to be solved by shoving this communication under the rug."[48]

Other letters followed that reflected the encouraging attitudes about the level of progress made toward racial equality in USAREUR during the early 1970s. But they also revealed a level of concern about how some Milcom members interpreted it. In January 1973, a group of letters arrived on the desk of *Stars and Stripes* editor from black service members and dependents that challenged opinions that the equal opportunity programs were encouraging "favoritism" toward blacks. They did this by recounting the high percentage of incarcerated minority service members, and noting, "In day to day dealings with black officers, NCOs, and EM [Enlisted Members], I find that very few want any kind of favoritism."[49] A letter writer from the Kaiserslautern Milcom observed, "The thrust of the Army programs ... focuses on dialogue and the fostering of understanding among the races." He added, "In my short three-year Army career, I have seen what I consider to be progress."[50]

Among those letters that voiced continued frustration, one charged, "If white America views the token programs that have benefitted a relatively few blacks since the last decade as 'much favoritism,' then [it] is obviously not prepared to take those necessary steps to guarantee real equality and opportunity."[51] Another writer, responding to an opinion that the government had dedicated too much time to concerns of racial equality simply noted, "There will never be 'too much time' placed in any of the problem areas of race relations, equal opportunity, civil rights, and human rights."[52]

Taken together all these letters suggest that the feelings of Milcom members toward the Army's equal opportunity and race relations programs during the first half of the 1970s were complex. Evidence reveals that many service members, government civilians, and dependents in USAREUR welcomed the open acknowledgment of existing problems and recognition that remedial systems and policies were necessary, and that the civilian and military elites were taking the correct steps. But it is also evident from their words that for every step taken they recognized others were still necessary to reach the goal of "civil and equal rights."[53] Regardless of the positive gains these programs and initiatives made in the early 1970s it was still progress attained under very trying circumstances.

Radicalization of the Race Struggle in the Milcoms

The radicalization of certain elements of the civil rights struggle in the U.S., during the late 1960s and early 1970s, had resonance in the West German Milcoms. Taking their cue from American radicals, some black service members assumed militant roles in voicing their dissatisfaction with existing conditions. A number of times this resulted in incidents of ill-discipline and violence. Such was the case in September 1970, when a full blown race riot exploded at McNair Barracks in West Berlin. Only the arrival of another Army unit wearing full battle gear and wielding fixed bayonets quelled the brawl, which involved hundreds of black and white soldiers. The underlying cause was racial name calling amid accusations of discrimination in promotions, punishments and housing, and perceptions of uncaring leadership.[54] Ironically, the commanding general of the Berlin unit declared, "there is no discrimination in housing, schooling, job assignments, food or anything else that affects a soldier's daily life."[55]

Just as sobering, though less violent, were actions that mirrored the protests and demonstrations in the U.S. A rally to condemn "American racism" attracted over 700 black, white, Mexican, and Puerto Rican soldiers in the Kaiserslautern Milcom in October 1970.[56] Earlier that year, on July 4th, more than 700 black soldiers, together with a contingent of German students, filled an auditorium at Heidelberg University to initiate a "Call for Justice Day." It was to serve as a "counter-celebration" to American Independence Day and bring attention to racial inequities in the U.S.[57] Subsequently, in June 1971 approximately 1,000 mostly black soldiers demonstrated in front of the headquarters of the West Berlin military garrison pumping the black power fist salute in the air and carrying cloth banners proclaiming "stop racism, discrimination, and end the Viet Nam war—now."[58]

Out of these active and passive protests grew a network of non-sanctioned organizations and underground newspapers that supported black American activism in the West German Milcoms. Among the militant blacks were a litany of groups such as the Black Panthers, the Third World, the Black Baptists, the Moorish Church, the United Black Soldiers, the Black Action Group, the Blacks in Action and the Black Defense Group. The large number of these groups suggests the determination of a core of black soldiers in Germany to respond to the perception of racial discrimination in the military by imitating the effective techniques of the civil rights movement in the U.S., which included public protest and the threat of associated violence. It also reflected their understanding of empowerment by organizing into groups and networks. In addition, it served as a response to efforts by the military hierarchy to quell the activities of troublesome activists by transferring them to other units or Milcoms since the various groups did maintain effective networks of communication. In the words of one sergeant, who was the founder of the Unsatisfied Black Soldier group, these organizations sprang out of frustrations "over attempts to end racism" and signaled a move from a "position of conciliation to revolutionary, defensive and violent stands" by black service members in Germany.[59]

The demonstrated effectiveness and impact of these radical GI groups was apparent through media reports of their activities. For example, as the Render team was conducting its investigation of race conditions in USAREUR it encountered various black groups that threatened to boycott question and answer sessions. Black activists claimed the team was "a direct insult to us and a waste of time and taxpayers' money," because it was set-up as a "whitewash of the racial problems in Germany."[60] When they did later speak with Render's team their words carried more gravity, especially with declarations such as "I've bled for my country way off in the Nam. Now, if need be, I'll bleed for myself—for my people."[61] In another example, the group Unsatisfied Black Soldier was responsible for organizing the July 4th protest rally that attracted 1,000 black GIs to the University of Heidelberg.[62]

Several of these groups also generated a collection of underground newspapers and circulars, "some published with the help of radical German student groups," as mouthpieces for their opinions and beliefs.[63] Among the publications circulating in Germany was *The Voice of the Lumpen*: "Speaking to All GIs in USAREUR." It advertised itself as the organ of the Revolutionary People's Communications Network and exhibited on its figurehead images of Che Guevara and Huey Newton.[64] These publications tended to be radical in their views, often associating themselves with international consortiums of revolutionary groups and advocating violent means to their ends. Although the size of their circulation is difficult to determine the presence of these broadsheets suggests an opportunity for the more militant voices among black service members to vent their frustrations and so draw attention to their cause.

In that context, they also filled a necessary void for providing information and perspectives about activities and events that the official press or media, such as *Stars and Stripes*, or the *New York Times* and the *Washington Post*, did not offer, such as the dates and times of protests. It is apparent however, that these radical publications also served as an irritant to military officials who must have attempted to confiscate copies whenever possible. This is evident by the disclaimer on the front page of the *Lumpen* that stated "This paper is legal, but the PIGS will probably bust anyone caught reading it. So be cool!!! Check out AR 381–135 (D) [*Control of Subversive Publications Disseminated at Army Installations*] in case they do happen to vamp on you." That particular Army regulation guaranteed the rights of an individual to read and retain commercial publications for their personal use.

Also disconcerting to the military hierarchy was the interest that many black soldiers maintained in the activities of the radicalized Black Panther Party in the U.S. Often voicing solidarity with that group many black American military activists stylized their behaviors and dress after the Panthers. Some saluted using the unauthorized Black Power fist and wore black leather jackets and berets when off duty or during protests. Both black and white Milcom members followed the activities of radical activists such as Angela Davis and Kathleen Cleaver in the press and on AFN-TV. Newspapers such as *Stars and Stripes*, *New York Times*, and the *Washington Post*, as well as the popular black presses such as the *Daily Defender* and the *Chicago Defender* kept readers apprised of their actions. The August 24, 1970, issue of the *Daily Defender* announced that the FBI had "carried its search to West Germany for Black Panther member Angela Yvonne Davis." They were seeking her in connection with the murder of a judge in California.[65] By 1972 they were also tracking her travels during a speaking tour of the Soviet Bloc.[66]

The majority of the Black Panthers' actions depicted in *Stars and Stripes* followed themes of violent confrontations with the police, militant protests and relationships with international terrorist organizations and anti–American governments. Many dozens of articles published in the newspaper between the late 1960s and mid–1970s reveal the military hierarchy's reticence to paint the Black Panthers in anything other than a negative light. A number of editorials, by conservative commentators such as Victor Lasky, Ernest Cuneo and William F. Buckley mocked the group's attempt to depict itself as a victim of political oppression and underscored their connection with anti–American governments.[67] Numerous other articles with titles such as "Panthers Charged in Detroit Slaying," "Al Fatah Trains Panthers, But Denies Terror Drills" and "Militant Groups Hold Gun Drills in Calif. Desert," continually emphasized the Panthers' predisposition toward militancy and violence.[68]

Few if any published pieces, editorials or articles, provided sympathetic views of the Black Panthers. On occasion however, the editors of *Stars and Stripes* did publish letters from Milcom readers that sought to defend the group. In January 1970 one enlisted soldier wrote to say that the Black Panthers were being unfairly "hounded because their actions are open and public knowledge." He then asked, "Who hounds the Ku Klux Klan?"[69] That same month, another writer from the Vaihingen Milcom commented that the "Panthers are not as violent as the Ku Klux Klan. For many years the Klan has been killing black people and the white people accepted it." It appeared as if the military hierarchy was providing a context for the rejection of the Black Panthers by Milcom members by offering predominantly negative stories about them. At the same time, the newspaper afforded only a small window of opportunity to voice views that were radical and contrary to the hierarchy's. This may have only been to portray an appearance of freedom of expression since the weight of evidence supported the opposite. Still, as student activists in the U.S. and Germany worked toward the politicization of the race issue in both countries, through groups such as the Black Panthers, it appeared as if military commanders in EUCOM worked toward distancing the race issue in the Milcoms from that political effort. Had they not, there was the possibility it would have contributed to the further undermining of morale and discipline in the military units by moving it outside their control. As one reporter for the *New York Times* commented, "Reporters for *Stars and Stripes*, the principal soldier publication in Germany, say they have been told to avoid racial stories."[70]

Just as blacks had begun to organize in the early 1970s so too did some reactionary whites. As contemporary American and German media reports reveal, there was a burgeoning presence of the Ku Klux Klan (KKK) in the vicinity of many Milcoms. Stories of burning crosses in the Crailsheim Milcom, soldiers wearing KKK regalia during the commission of violent attacks against blacks and open confessions of membership in the Klan by some whites struck fear into many black GIs, civilians and dependents. The belief that blacks were unfairly benefitting from equal opportunity programs inspired a number of white soldiers "to rebel against the blacks" by joining the KKK.[71] The momentum of that white reaction continued through the 1970s and into the 1980s in EUCOM as officials continued to charge individuals with the unauthorized, and racially provocative, burning of crosses and attempts to recruit new members. In the sobering words of one local American KKK "commander" the Klan "has expanded from the bases at Bitburg, Hahn and Spangdahlem into other parts of Germany."[72] Although difficult to prove, this type of continued racial backlash was not encouraging to military and civilian leaders.

There were also occasional letters to the editor of *Stars and Stripes* that displayed white attitudes contrary to racial harmony. One letter penned in November 1973 declared that time spent in an equal opportunity seminar was misspent, "the race relations class presented twenty hours of making the white feel guilty of crimes against the black." This appeared to irritate the sensitivities of the writer who felt the class made blacks seem superior to whites.[73] Another letter also criticized the equal opportunity program by asking a series of challenging questions: "Have you ever noticed that you never hear white soldiers being praised by the Army media for contributions to the U.S. Army? Have you ever wondered what the basis is for this exclusion? Have you ever wondered why there are no culture programs for whites in the Army?"[74] The writer directed his complaint against command-directed policies for training in race relations but he also offered a sobering admonition "Whites do not speak with one voice. But, believe me, the time is near when, if you don't speak with one voice, you won't be able to speak at all."[75] A letter submitted to the editor in February 1981, from the Zweibrücken Milcom, protested the removal of a group of military policemen from their duties because of their membership in the KKK. The writer asked, "Why are whites in the military reclassified for being with the KKK and blacks aren't for being with the NAACP?"[76] These types of attitudes did not surface very often, either because they were not that prevalent, or because the editorial staff of *Stars and Stripes* suppressed them in the hopes of reducing antagonisms. Regardless, they represented only one voice heard among the many during this period of racial introspection in the Milcoms.

Broadening Minority Awareness in the Milcoms

As sensitivities regarding racial equality in EUCOM grew between the late 1960s and the 1980s, so did opportunities for other groups to establish their ethnic identities. Among them were the Hispanic American Milcom members. With increasing frequency during the 1970s articles and letters to the editor appeared that spoke of their demands for identity similar to black service members. An auxiliary bishop of the Roman Catholic Church visiting installations in Germany charged, "Race relations in the military must involve more than blacks and whites." To this he added, "There is a man in the middle—the Spanish-speaking serviceman—who needs to be recognized."[77] Letters to the editor of *Stars and Stripes* confirmed these feelings among Milcom members.

A letter writer from the Stuttgart Milcom described feelings of "otherness" by Spanish speaking service members by stating, "People will act like Americans when treated like Americans." He also challenged those who were critical of ethnic pride by adding that it was "ridiculous ... to state that a reason for clinging to our Mexican culture is because we do not wish to fully Americanize. We pay our taxes and serve our country."[78] Another letter writer concurred, "The implications that identifying oneself as a Chicano is disloyal is absurd!" He added, "Our [American] society is very much pluralistic and therefore a Chicano can contribute greatly to our democracy and still retain his ethnic culture."[79] A continuing series of letters offered other feelings of frustration. A soldier from the Bamberg Milcom lashed out, "We are tired of being put down, no matter where we are or where we go. We *La Raza* are proud of our heritage and we will stand up to defend it." He also lamented, "We *La Raza* try to get along but it doesn't do any good. There is always some fool opening his mouth calling us wet backs or spics."[80]

Just as it had acted to correct inequalities for blacks the military hierarchy listened to the protests of Hispanic Milcom members and moved to make corrections. One of the most important, as recorded in the DAHSUM for FY 1974, was consideration of the demographics of the Judge Advocate General (JAG) Corps. Taking a proactive stance, the Department of the Army (DA) ensured a more varied ethnic and gender mix. For that year there were 32 blacks, 19 women, 8 Mexican-Americans, 5 Puerto Ricans, and 6 Orientals [sic] serving as lawyers in the JAG.[81] By September 1977 those numbers had increased to 57 blacks, 11 Mexican-Americans, 7 Puerto Ricans, and 10 Orientals [sic].[82] In FY 1978 the Army also began tracking the composition of personnel in the law enforcement specialties. As of June 1978, it recorded that blacks comprised 13.2 percent of military police and Hispanics 1.7 percent. Because that did not match favorably with the actual percentages of blacks and Hispanics among enlisted personnel (it was 28.9 percent and 3.8 percent respectively), the DA initiated a special recruiting initiative for the MP specialty.[83] Also important was the military's adoption of the Department of Commerce standard classifications of *White, Black, Hispanic, Asian*, and *Native American*. This permitted the military to begin to track the effectiveness and equity of programs such as promotion, punishment, and equal opportunity by race as well as ethnicity, a capability that was not previously present for neglected groups.[84]

The successes of the equal opportunity and race relations efforts in the Milcoms during the 1970s and 1980s reflect in letters to the editor of *Stars and Stripes*. Two from 1978 noted the gains made, but also cautioned against contentment. The first letter, from a soldier in the Bamberg Milcom observed, "We are in a period of calm in the area of race relations" but warned against cutting the budget in these programs because of perceived gains.[85] The second letter from an "opportunity specialist" agreed with the first but encouraged ongoing efforts and cautioned, "Let's not become too complacent."[86]

The equal opportunity and race relations programs of the late 1960s through the late

1980s recorded successes and gains through a variety of affirmative action and awareness initiatives. These solved many of the existing problems of discrimination that threatened to undermine the morale and discipline of military units in Germany. Still, these programs made advances across a cratered landscape fraught with misunderstandings, sharp racial divides and innate prejudices. At times, the presence of a vibrant drug culture magnified this degree of difficulty.

A *Washington Post* exposé titled "The U.S. Army: A Battle for Survival," published in September 1971, highlighted a connection between crime, drugs and racial conflict in the military.[87] As one commander in the Nüremberg Milcom confessed, gang assaults over drugs clearly broke down "along racial lines." This inter-twining of the problems of drugs, crimes, and race made it more difficult for the military hierarchy to find effective solutions. Soldiers living in the barracks acknowledged this reality. A report from the Bamberg Milcom noted a barracks room robbery at knifepoint of four white soldiers by a gang of blacks who demanded, "Give us your dope."[88] The "predominant viewpoint" according to one reporter was that there were no longer "safe firebreaks between black militancy, violence and drugs. They are all mixed together in an explosive combination."[89] Conflicts between the races sometimes centered on turf wars between rival gangs of black and white GI hashish dealers. The influx of "gangsters" arriving in the Army, particularly USAREUR, "sent there by judges as the alternative" to jail time, exacerbated the situation. The dealers often found the environment in Europe lucrative.[90]

The Subcommittee on Drug Abuse in the Military addressed that intersection of race and drugs in its February 1972 report to the Senate Armed Services Committee. The narrative noted that drug dependency was much more debilitating to black service members. It noted that many of them came to the service from environments where there was an existing drug culture and that some brought that behavior with them into the military. More important, the report noted that many black service members left the service full of distrust for the system because of inherent racial discrimination and so were not likely to take advantage of recovery programs available through the Veteran's Administration.[91] In addition, the "Findings from the 1971 Survey of Drug Use," which was part of the subcommittee report, provided information about military-wide drug usage by general race categories. It revealed that 8.9 percent of black service members reported using "narcotics" on a daily basis, as compared to 4.0 percent for whites, and 75.0 percent of blacks reported never using drugs as compared to 82.7 percent for whites.[92] The summary of the report provided a profile of frequent daily users in the Army that revealed they were less educated, less than 21 years of age, and "nonwhite."[93] While these findings did not condemn any one group they did suggest yet another interpretation of the intertwining of race and drugs in the military and in the USAREUR Milcoms.

There were also skewed perspectives occasionally voiced by soldiers who found comfort in the vibrant drug culture. One letter to the editor of the *Stars and Stripes* from a young soldier offered a solution to racial conflict. He wrote, "Drugs make the race problems better. One reason blacks and whites have so many problems is because they have no chance to relate. When they take drugs together, this makes for a stronger relationship."[94] This was a point of view endorsed by Jeff White, who recalls the sharp racial divide in the barracks and how it seemed to melt away when "they got together to get high," then they were all just "part of the crowd."[95] The American military hierarchy however, never endorsed this concept.

German Interaction with the Milcoms through Race Relations

As in the years prior to the war in Vietnam, the German populace continued to exhibit mixed reactions to the presence of black Americans in the Milcoms from the late 1960s to the 1980s. Although there is ample evidence from existing source materials that underscore the Germans' greater openness toward mixing of the races than contemporary Americans, there is also evidence that points to the existence of pockets of Jim Crow style racism.[96] In the case of the latter, some sources indicate it was borne by some Germans who harbored "their own 'unfinished business' when it came to race relations."[97] Other sources indicate that these instances of racial prejudice by Germans were attributable to the effects of regionalism where rural communities were less open and welcoming of outsiders of any race, or to pervading attitudes imported by American service members, civilians and their families. In the last instance there is an interpretation that Germans often "channeled" their own racism "by drawing on the American model of segregation."[98]

During the 1970s, contemporary German media sources sometimes supported these perceptions through their interactions with black Milcom members. A June 1971 exposé published by *Der Spiegel* interviewed two disgruntled black soldiers who claimed that there was "a great conspiracy" by the white military hierarchy to keep their promotions slow and assign them only the most menial tasks. They also disclosed the existence of KKK activity in military units. The article also prompted the soldiers by inquiring if the "U.S. Army imported American racism to Europe" and if as a result the Germans responded in an increasingly unfriendly way to black GIs. The soldiers responded in the affirmative, alluding to the spread of racism into housing and restaurants, although there was no corroborating evidence in the text to support that linkage.[99]

Subsequent articles that the German media published during the 1970s vacillated between condemnation and praise of American race relations in the Milcoms. An October 1972 article celebrated the recent selection of Major General Frederic E. Davison as the first "colored" division commander in the history of the U.S. Army at a time of great racial tension in the military.[100] It also commented, "After years of inaction" the "Pentagon finally seems to have decided to proceed effectively" by advancing Davison as well as eight other black generals.[101] An article published in August 1973 dealt with the existence of "white racism" in Germany via an active "American Nazi Party" in Frankfurt alluding to a membership exclusively of white servicemen.[102] Another, printed in January 1976, noted the continuing existence of racism in the U.S. that kept many black families from reaping the benefits of an American middle-class lifestyle although it admitted some progress, particularly in housing and employment.[103] In addition, a short column that appeared in February 1978 contributed the perspective of ongoing racial problems in the soldiers' barracks by surveying the types of graffiti on the stall doors in the latrines. It revealed that prejudices still existed but also that the authors had distributed their vitriol evenly against blacks, other sexes, Hispanics and the Germans.[104]

Available sources also make it apparent that throughout the late 1960s and 1970s German generational perceptions influenced attitudes regarding racism in the Milcoms as much as regional behaviors, lingering wartime feelings, or influences from American Jim Crowism. A 1975 poll conducted by a research group asked German respondents to select from a listing of the types of persons with whom they would not tolerate associating. Of those who claimed they would not tolerate blacks the largest percentage (36 percent) was in the age 60 and over category. The most tolerant were the 16–29 year-olds who registered only 14 percent intolerance.[105] An associated query from the same poll however, noted that across the age groups 78 percent of German men would "probably not" marry a black woman, and 82 percent of German women would "probably not" marry a black man.[106] This suggests that overall German attitudes about racial mixing may not have been as different from contemporary American attitudes as some sources indicate. Nevertheless, it is apparent that when Germans crossed the intercultural boundary to become involved in the racial arena of the Milcoms it was the younger generation who took the first determined step.

As sources also indicate, German university students took active roles in engaging black activism in the Milcoms.[107] They encouraged black soldiers to gather at places such as Heidelberg University to air their joint grievances and supported the establishment of Black Panther chapters in Germany to demonstrate their solidarity with American blacks against racism. German student radicals also coordinated protests and rallies such as one staged in Zweibrücken on March 6, 1971, to demand the release of two black ex–GI prisoners involved in shooting of a gate guard at a U.S. military kaserne. The students had organized the demonstration in league with the German Black Panther Solidarity Committee and attracted over 1,200 German and American protestors who paraded through the town chanting "Revolution in America and West Germany!"[108] Their involvement also extended to inviting representatives from the American Black Panther Party to speak to groups that included black Milcom members. This led to the appearances of party representatives Albert Howard at the University of Heidelberg in January 1970 and Kathleen Cleaver at the University of Frankfurt in July 1971.[109] Both of these were cities had extensive American military communities.

But as the Black Panther Party's power contracted beginning in 1972, and the radical energies of black service members lost momentum because of progress attained in race relations, German student involvement began to dissipate as public debate surrounding the centrality of violence in activism became more intense.[110] Still, these changes did not telegraph an end to the struggle against racism in the EUCOM. Although a number of existing sources tend to portray German discrimination against black and minority Milcom members primarily as a derivative of contemporary American racism, or as a collection of isolated incidents, other evidence instead suggests some persistent and widespread discrimination by Germans.

By 1967 the black press in the U.S. was providing insight to the race bias that existed in Germany. An article in the *Daily Defender* noted, "Negro Americans in Germany are bearing the brunt of German resentment" towards Americans stationed there. It went on to comment that the black troops "are the current scapegoats being persecuted by both the Army and the German people." Although the writer emphasized the inequities of the American military structure, it also emphasized German reticence at welcoming blacks into "restaurants and other places."[111] The primary source for the article was a black American mother who had lived for a period of time in the Bad Kreuznach Milcom. The article also did not intimate any coupling of American and German racist behaviors. Sometimes, tensions between blacks and Germans erupted into physical confrontations. Such was the case outlined in an October 1970 *Daily Defender* article when several black soldiers in the Frankfurt Milcom lashed out and assaulted a number of German men on the street out of pent up frustrations regarding discrimination. Included in the text were perceptions of "clandestine attempts to poison the minds of the German Fraulein against blacks."[112]

Housing however, was the most central issue among the various ways black American service members and their families felt the sting of German discrimination. Throughout the 1970s and into the early 1980s black Milcom members registered a litany of grievances to the American authorities and the media. A February 1971 incident involved six black American officers who charged a German housing agent [realtor] with discrimination. When the military hierarchy was slow to intercede on their behalf, they filed a complaint against EUCOM with the Secretary of the Army. Included in the grievance was the observation that 90 percent of the [German] landlords listed with the Hessen Support District's Family Housing Office "indulge in discrimination," and as one plaintiff added "I'm sure this situation isn't limited to just this area of Germany either."[113] Another officer commented that these practices had "not abated despite regulations against it." He also warned, "Unless something is done fast more racial explosions will follow."[114]

Other than bringing continued awareness to Milcom readers of the existence of discriminatory practices by German housing agents and landlords the case also precipitated a number of important reactions. One was the creation of an administrative form by American military authorities that required a signed pledge by each German landlord that they agree, "rentals will be open to all military personnel without regard to race, sex, creed, or national origin."[115] Another initiative was the granting of authority to local commanders "to place off-limits the property of any German landlord who refused to rent to blacks."[116] This would prevent all military personnel, black or white, from renting that property thereby threatening the property owner with loss of income for non-compliance.

The 1971 NAACP report, *The Search for Military Justice*, echoed the concerns of black service members in Germany and used strong language to communicate the need for remediation. It observed that:

> Without question the most pervasive problem confronting Negro soldiers in West Germany is that of housing. Regardless of rank or age of the servicemen, there were strong feelings expressed about the discrimination being practiced by Germans against the black soldiers. It, more than any other problem, caused blacks to regard Germany as an unfriendly country and to wonder aloud why they should be stationed there.[117]

By the end of that year the American military in Germany had taken strides toward resolving the housing issue for all its soldiers through the establishment of 55 Housing Referral Offices (HRO) located among the Milcoms. The staffs included American military and civilian personnel as well as German nationals to ensure there were no communication difficulties.[118]

Thanks to focused efforts by American military authorities discrimination in housing began to abate by 1972. Still, instances remained as evidenced by the publication of lists of German landlords whose properties the HROs had placed off-limits. One such list appeared in a December 1972 issue of *Stars and Stripes*.[119] It included the county, the city or town, the address and the name of the landlord. The Chancellor of West Germany, Willi Brandt, also weighed in when he referred to discrimination's lingering presence. During a Brotherhood Week celebration he "chastised" fellow Germans "who were guilty of arrogance and a misplaced feeling of superiority" toward foreign guest workers [*Gastarbeiter*] and black American soldiers.[120] The black press also continued to monitor the situation reminding readers that "two kinds of racism" still existed in USAREUR. The first was "the home-grown brand imported from America." The other was "from the Germans themselves."[121] Despite the awakened sensitivities of Germans and Americans to episodes of racism it continued in West Germany through the 1970s into the 1980s.

In August 1982 a full page article in *Stars and Stripes* revealed that it took minorities longer to find housing in German-owned properties than it did white Milcom members. The contents of the piece included statistics from several Milcoms that showed waiting times for minorities to be longer in each case but one (the Heidelberg Milcom). Although the differences were only a few days, for example in Frankfurt 29 days for minorities and 25 days for non-minorities, and in Hanau 53 days and 46 respectively, suspicions were that discrimination might be the root cause. As one American housing authority noted "It can well be that a house owner has given the [real estate] agent instructions about how many and which foreigners he wants in his houses. So it's discrimination almost impossible for us to discover."[122]

Despite charges by German student activists that racism in their country was anecdotal, or primarily a derivative of imported American attitudes, the perspective from within the Milcoms shows that its existence was more complicated and pervasive than believed. From the late 1960s through the end of the 1980s, racial discrimination ebbed and flowed across the permeable boundary between the two cultures and societies with both Germans and Americans acting equally as villains of prejudice and champions of progressive race relations. Still, neither society could lay claim to the moral high ground. Evidence suggests that for the Americans the synergy of the efforts improved the lives of Milcom members by redefining the meaning of equality and widening the scope of inclusion. For the Germans, involvement with the American racial dilemma served as both an opportunity for a cathartic coming to terms with their past as well as a chance to inform and shape American postwar society.

Feminism and the Milcom

After the mid-point of the 1960s the energies of the evolving feminist movement also shaped life in the Milcoms. In that context, three particular dynamics had an impact on contemporary Milcom members: a developing divide between traditional and non-traditional roles of women, the increasing empowerment of women and the reaction of the military infrastructure to the precipitate changes.

Although the seeds of the feminist movement in the U.S. preceded World War II, a succession of political actions and social changes after that time had provided momentum to actions that resonated in the nation and the Milcoms.[123] These included initiatives such as President Kennedy's establishment of a Commission on the Status of Women in 1961, Helen Gurley Brown's publication of *Sex and the Single Girl* in 1962, the passage of the Civil Rights Act including Title VII in 1964 and the establishment of the National Organization of Women (NOW) in 1966. Although none of these actions specifically targeted the military or families in the overseas Milcoms they did have an impact on the lives of women whether they were military or civilian, in the U.S., or living abroad. In particular, they provided challenges to the contemporary paradigm of traditional thinking about the roles of women.[124] In that context, they raised the level of consciousness regarding identity and brought attention to that evolving conflict in the Milcoms, effecting a split in attitudes by the late–1960s.[125]

That divergence was evident to Milcom members through the media. For example, those who picked up a copy of the June 15, 1970, issue of *Stars and Stripes* found a juxtaposition of printed pieces that epitomized that tension between opposing views. One was an article that described the grousing of female delegates at the 50th anniversary convention of the Women's Bureau of the Labor Department when they discovered that President Nixon had declined their invitation to attend. Although First Lady Pat Nixon was present they charged the President with a "lack of concern for women" and commented, "We don't want coffee. We want equal rights."[126] Tucked just below that report, on the same page, was the second printed piece, a provocative photograph of a scantily clad female receptionist from Tampa, Florida. The caption below the image noted her love for the sun, beaches, and palms. It would be difficult for any reader to miss the contrasting irony between the article and photograph or the important difference in their projection of women's images.[127]

Still, the media kept Milcom members continually aware of that struggle between traditionalists and feminists as it continued to unfold on the national stage through the 1970s and 1980s. For example, other columns and articles that appeared in *Stars and Stripes* highlighted the activities of Phyllis Schlafly, a devout advocate of traditional values who located the responsibilities of home and family at the center of women's lives. In October 1970, Milcoms readers could follow her attempts to upset a liberal Democratic rival for a congressional seat in Illinois as she campaigned on a conservative Republican ticket that supported traditional roles for women.[128] In the years that followed, the newsprint captured the arc of Schlafly's enduring efforts as a principal representative of that position for Milcom readers. By 1976, the media tagged her as "The Woman Who is trying to Torpedo the ERA" and a December 1977 series of *Doonesbury* cartoon strips in *Stars and Stripes* lampooned her as an annoying gadfly of both liberals and feminists.[129] The momentum of Schlafly's energies as the standard bearer for women opposed to feminist initiatives continued into the 1980s, even as she delivered a letter to the editor of *Stars and Stripes* criticizing comments by editorialist Carl Rowan with the rebuke "Doesn't he understand how offensive it is to refer to full time homemakers as women who don't work? Or as breeders of babies?"[130]

By comparison, moderate feminist positions and initiatives received an equitable amount of ink and exposure.[131] Milcom readers received information about the activities of the National Organization of Women (NOW) including an article in June 1970 that offered an introduction to Betty Friedan, "NOW Movement's Leading Lady," who claimed, "the enemy of women's liberation is not men but the inhuman way women are treated by society."[132] *Stars and Stripes* continued to offer articles to its readers about the organization as it gained momentum and increased its membership and voice through the 1970s. This included a several page spread in January 1971 that again focused on its first president Betty Friedan, "The Mother Superior of Women's Lib," as well as the efforts of NOW to secure expanded rights for women.[133] The newspaper also printed articles and made frequent reference to Friedan's seminal work, *The Feminine Mystique*, thus keeping its readers abreast of relevant published works on feminist themes.[134] In addition to these efforts, the newspaper followed up with pieces by staff writers, such as Kay Scanlon, who criticized both *Playboy* and *Penthouse* magazines with her comment that "Women are rebelling against such degradation and stereotyping."[135] Her column also offered insights to the writings of other feminist authors such as Germaine Greer who penned *The Female Eunuch*, which suggested, "Women's passive sexual role ordained by society condemns her to a repressed life."[136]

From the 1970s through the 1990s *Stars and Stripes*, the principal printed media for the Milcom, provided its readers with a reasonable balance between opposing viewpoints and opinions regarding emerging women's rights issues and their traditional roles. For example, a survey conducted within the scope of this work reveals that the European edition of the newspaper published more than 600 separate articles that followed progress on the Equal Rights Amendment (ERA) and over 300 that addressed the controversies surrounding the 1973 landmark Supreme Court decision in *Roe v. Wade*.[137] These reports and think-pieces offered an opportunity for Milcom readers to study the issues, refine their opinions and make informed decisions regarding the issues surrounding the women's rights movement. *Stars and Stripes* also lent voice to readers' attitudes and sentiments as they struggled to come to terms with the consequences of the increased empowerment of women and redefined gender roles after the mid-point of the 1960s.

Among the earliest contemporary debates that engaged readers was *Stars and Stripes'* continued publication of "cheesecake" photos. A letter to the editor in November 1968 by a Milcom wife, who protested the newspaper's use of a provocative female image, drew a cascade of criticisms. In almost every case the replies to the editor came from male service members who provided denunciations of her opinion. One comment accused her of being "jealous," another suggested she "should clean up her mind" and one observed that she had "attained the epitome of prudery."[138] The letters lacked sympathy for her suggestion that those types of photographs were not suitable for children or families, or might carry a hint of denigration of women. Only one letter, of the group of eighteen, from a sergeant in the Hahn Milcom provided support with the comment "If I want to be enticed by the female form, I will buy the Oversexed Weekly."[139]

The polemics concerning cheesecake in *Stars and Stripes* carried on to at least mid–1970, when one of the last associated flurries of letters to the editor addressed the debate. Once again, a husband and wife criticized the newspaper's "insistence upon regularly printing of scantily clad young women," and suggested they "seek professional help."[140] But they also did receive the support of another female Milcom member who commented, "We simply don't need this type of garbage in our newspaper."[141] Whether the newspaper became sensitive to its readers' comments or bowed to the growing energies of the feminist cause is not evident, but its publication of cheesecake photos all but ceased after the mid–1970s.[142]

If the battle over provocative photographs of women resulted in a minor victory for Milcom feminists, the debate associated with the Equal Rights Amendment (ERA) was longer-lived and more heated. Milcom members began making their voices heard almost as soon as both houses of the Congress passed the proposal and forwarded it to the states for ratification in 1972. One of the first letters to the editor of the *Star and Stripes* from a female Milcom member in Berlin proclaimed "this amendment would deny [women] of their most basic right— the right to be a women." It went on in alarming tones to claim among other things "women would be subject to the draft" and would lose custody of their children in the case of divorce.[143] It concluded by encouraging other female Milcom members to write their state legislator to argue against ratification and to discover the real dangers of the ERA by sending "15 cents for a copy of The Phyllis Schlafly Report," she included an address.[144]

Numerous other letters flowed into the crucible of debate concerning the ERA from both sides of the argument. A two-page feature in the April 16, 1973, issue of *Stars and Stripes*, written by a female staff member, served as a platform for those who favored it. The article offered a collection of comments from female Milcom readers' letters that rebutted criticisms of the amendment. One of the arguments claimed the "ERA will take the chains off women" by "challenging underpayment [of women] and other forms of discrimination," and another claimed it would lift the limit of number of hours a day a woman could work.[145] The controversy surrounding the ERA continued into the early 1980s with letters to the editor from both sides of the debate continuing to fill pages of the newspaper. There were those who cried out against the "outright sexism, prejudice and prehistoric politics played by those states" that refused to ratify it and others who continued to encourage readers to "send $10, $50, or as much as you can to: Stop ERA, Phyllis Schlafly, Box 618, Alton, Ill. 62002."[146]

Regardless of the arguments and debates between Milcom members over the developing women's rights issues, changes in the nation's attitudes took place and resonated in the military communities. Among them was the passage of Title IX of the 1972 Education Act which prohibited discrimination in any university or school program. This afforded numerous opportunities for women's athletics in the U.S., including the offering of scholarships for female athletes. This also resonated in the Milcoms overseas as the DODDS system began expanding its offerings of competitive teams for girls. Eventually, by January 1980, Milcom members could turn to the sports section of *Stars and Stripes* and read of the accomplishments of female student athletes in competitions that were previously open only to boys, such as volleyball, golf, and basketball.[147]

Another indicator of the changing environment in EUCOM was the appointment of Colonel Ruby R. Stauber as the new editor-in-chief of *Stars and Stripes*, European Edition, in March 1979. Colonel Stauber was the first female to serve in that position in the history of the newspaper, following a succession of males who steered the content of the publication since the end of World War II.[148] She had previously worked in public relations for the military and possessed a degree in journalism.[149] Her accession to that position coincidentally came at the same time that a number of women's groups in the U.S., such as the National Organization of Women Judges, were pressing for another first, the appointment of a woman to the Supreme Court.[150] Stauber's appearance as editor-in-chief was also coincidental with the disappearance of cheesecake photos from the newspaper.

These were years when previously closed doors, in the nation and the Milcom, were beginning to open for women. It represented a shift in paradigms from the restrictive roles and expectations that kept women within the safe container of the home during the 1950s and early 1960s, to attitudes that allowed greater inclusion and provided more opportunities.[151] The changes in the overseas Milcoms paralleled those occurring in the U.S. More important, many Milcom members were beginning to accept that reality.

Evidence of that increasing recognition of opportunities for women was the changing of opinions about women in the military, a subject that was central to the preparedness of the American forces in EUCOM.[152] A series of letters to the editor of *Stars and Stripes* from Milcom members revealed their feelings. A female dependent from the Pirmasens Milcom described the feelings of empowerment she felt during the 1979 Federal Women's Week that inspired her to go "out into the world and make something of myself." Encouraged by her military husband she sought to enlist in the Army in Germany.[153] Other letters argued for allowing women in combat. One letter from a Milcom wife noted that the "bravery of women in wartime has been illustrated in this century by the female resistance fighters throughout Europe during World War II." She also observed that in the event of war "it must be fought by both men and women" or else "the argument for equality for women becomes a specious one."[154] In that same context, a letter from a female non-commissioned officer in the Nuremburg Milcom assured readers that military "females are trained to fight," and that she "personally would defend my area of operation if the situation arose." She also noted that there was no non-combatant evacuation order (NEO plan) "for female soldiers in Europe," intimating that non-combatant females and males would be ordered to leave.[155] A 1987 article penned by Janet Howells-

Tierney, a staff writer for *Stars and Stripes*, quoted retired Brigade General Evelyn P. Foote, "It's a great time [for women] to be a soldier because men are more accepting of our leadership."[156] It was recognition of the changing times in the military and in the Milcom.

Other articles and letters also recognized the changing environment in EUCOM and official initiatives to support women's efforts in the Milcoms to press against, and break through, the social bounds established for earlier generations. During the mid and late 1970s various local chapters of NOW, such as the one in the Wiesbaden Milcom, periodically sponsored luncheons with speakers and discussions regarding the ramification of the ERA.[157] During that same decade, most major military commands in Europe offered a full schedule of events each year that paralleled the celebration of Federal Women's Week in the U.S. For example, activities listed by EUCOM in August 1979 included the broadcasting of interviews and seminars on women's issues on AFN-TV and AFN radio, as well as a variety of local events. Some of these activities, sponsored by various Milcoms, included prayer breakfasts for women, luncheons on "How to Get and Use Power," lectures on job searching, and seminars on trauma, sexual harassment and marital abuse.[158]

In addition to these events, major commands such as the VII Corps also periodically sponsored symposiums to provide Milcom women with an opportunity to air their grievances and work on solutions. One of the first gatherings attracted women who represented female service members, civilians, and family members from 15 military communities. Among their complaints were an inadequate supply of uniforms and accessories for female enlisted personnel and a lack of training "and promotion paths to leadership for women in civilian and military work structures." Female spouses also requested the removal of the term "dependent" from all official references noting, "It gives them the status of second class citizens."[159] Although the symposium did not solve all the problems it did represent a new openness and recognition of the needs of women in the Milcoms that was absent during previous decades.

But Milcom women were not content to let military and political elites alone dictate the pace of change. They also acted on their own behalf to establish grassroots groups and take actions to consolidate gains and open new opportunities. A series of letters to the editor of *Stars and Stripes* revealed some of the steps taken. One wife protested on behalf of others because the military bureaucracy in her community would not permit them to use the term "Ms." before their last names.[160] Another wife wrote of the establishment of a group known as WIN (Women Involved Now) in her community and its actions to enforce women's rights. These included the formation of a consciousness raising sub-group for women, protests against the unofficial barriers preventing girls from joining the community football team and an organized boycott against merchants and advertisers who "feature stereotyped women or who degrade women's intelligence."[161]

The debate over women's rights in the Milcom continued through the 1970s and into the 1980s. It included polemics regarding equal opportunities for advancement in civilian and military positions, the challenges of sexual harassment on the job, closing the earnings gap between the sexes and the arguments surrounding the pro-choice campaign. Still, by comparison, these were issues that did not appear in letters to the editor or through specially organized symposiums during the first postwar decades. The best Milcom women could hope for during the early years were annual conventions organized by religious groups, such as the PWOC and the MCCW, that offered periodic seminars on grassroots leadership and organizing for community service.[162] The same agenda existed for white-gloved social gatherings in officer and enlisted wives' clubs. Changes in EUCOM however, kept pace with changes in American society beginning in the 1970s and were responsible for redefining the roles, responsibilities and rights of women in the Milcoms in West Germany during the latter decades of the Cold War.

Women's Rights as a Bridge Between Societies

Much like race, the women's rights movement also served as a bridge between the German and American societies. Together, women of both nations discovered that beside a commonality of needs and desires there was also a parallel development of organizations and advocacy groups and a sharing of information and experiences through literature and personal contacts.

During the early postwar years there was initially some divergence between the expected behaviors and roles of Milcom wives and their West German counterparts. While societal expectations established walls that kept American women within the bounds of home and marriage, the majority of German women were shouldering the unexpected burdens of carrying their nation out of the rumble of war as single-parent *Trümmerfrau* [literally, "women of the rubble"].[163] German political elites eventually recognized that new reality and granted women equal rights under the law with the passage of Article 3, Paragraph 2 of the Basic Law (constitution) in 1949. But with the eventual repatriation of male German POWS and their integration into the workforce and society, German women again found that the reach of their power and authority, like that of American women, seldom extended beyond the boundaries of their homes. By the late 1950s, as contemporary histories note, women in both countries had suffered a common fate as the temporary "emancipation" of the war years gradually evaporated and they found themselves "being subjected to roles that no longer corresponded to the requirements of modern society."[164]

As conditions began to change with the renewed energies of the postwar feminist movement, American women in the Milcoms and their female German hosts acted in parallel to organize and advocate for their rights. While the Americans were joining organizations such as local chapters of NOW or creating smaller community groups such as the WIN initiative, German women were organizing into the Frankfurt Women's Council and the Berlin Action Council for Women's Liberation.[165] Women from both nations also separately participated in popular consciousness-raising groups.[166] The commonality of need drove those parallel actions in both societies and often precipitated similar examples of "provocative events." In the case of the German women it was a nation-wide rejection by thousands of women of Paragraph 218 of the Basic Law that outlawed abortions.[167] They created a public spectacle by claiming, "My womb belongs to me" and admitted they had violated that policy, risking prosecution under the law.[168] They followed their verbal defiance with battling police in the streets of Berlin and Frankfurt.[169] For the American women it was the feminist rejection of society's definition of women by demonstrating through Guerilla Theater tactics at the 1968 Miss America Pageant.[170]

Still there was a community of understanding between the two movements regarding abortion rights. With the initial passage of the *Roe v. Wade* decision in 1973, women living in the Milcoms were able to seek abortions in military facilities overseas, provided they were eligible for medical benefits. Within two years, policy changed preventing abortion at federal expense and women had to return to the U.S. for procedures.[171] By 1977 overseas facilities again opened to permit abortions, on a private pay basis, if other alternatives were not available.[172] This continued through the 1980s with the understanding that they could only occur if there was an issue of the health of the mother.[173] In a parallel, the easing of restrictions on abortions for German women in the early 1980s made possible the availability of limited abortions for Milcom women. As German society opened and became more accepting of abortions Milcom women still had limited options. The German organization *Pro-Familia* provided an alternative. It offered counseling and advice about contraceptives and abortion to all women including those in the Milcoms.[174] In this regard it also offered an abortion referral service. A number of American women sought abortions in clinics located in places such as Holland. Working through German organization such as *Pro Familia*, which formed a bridge across societies and cultures, Milcom women were able to navigate through the limitations placed in their way by contemporary military policy.

Although commonalities existed between the women's movements in the German communities and the American Milcoms, certain variances in conditions existed that complicate any simple comparison of organizations and actions between the two. While the German women were reasonably free to organize and protest as they wished within the bounds of their laws, the ability to organize from among the scattered Milcoms and within the policies of the military command limited American women. Although large groups of American women did not organize to stage protests or demonstrations, as German women, most military commands did schedule a number of events in recognition of women's weeks, such as symposiums, seminars and lectures, which gave Milcom women an opportunity to gather and air their grievances. In this context, women of both societies continued to find vehicles to air their concerns.

German and American women also shared information and experiences associated with the women's rights movement through popular literature. Betty Friedan's seminal work, the *Feminine Mystique* [translated into German as *"Weiblichkeitswahn"*] (1963) found wide acceptance in both countries and in the Milcom, as did the works of other Americans, Shulamith Firestone, Gloria Steinem, Marilyn French, Germaine Greer, and Shere Hite.[175] Hite's work, the *Hite Report on Female Sexuality*, reached number six for 1978 among bestselling non-fiction works in West Germany.[176] As part of the book's release, Hite made appearances at book fairs in Frankfurt where she shared her experiences with international audiences about gathering data for her work as well as her thoughts about challenging common "beliefs about women and sex."[177]

Although there is a possibility that American women in the Milcoms and their counterparts in the German host communities did occasionally participate in joint demonstrations of solidarity over women's rights, each group did follow its own parallel path toward equality of the sexes. They did come together however, through the commonality of mirrored needs and instances of shared experiences reflected in the popular writings of women's rights advocates such as Friedan, Firestone, and Hite, and through grass roots agencies such as *Pro-Familia*. If the energies between the societies were not synergistic they were at least sympathetic and the experiences afforded German and American women an opportunity to gauge the progress they were making in their own societies through proximate comparison.

The Milcom Media

The principal media outlets that kept the Milcoms informed about global events and changes within American society also remained under public scrutiny from the mid–1960s through the end of the 1980s. As members of the overseas military communities became aware of the unfolding challenges and opportunities surrounding the civil rights movement and women's rights initiatives they also became conscious of the presence of a threat to freedom of speech. This became apparent through information management and censorship of the media, in particular *Stars and Stripes* and the American Forces Radio and Television Service (AFRTS).

An existing Cold War environment that encouraged the manipulation of information within the arena of propaganda between the East and West had already sharpened Americans' sensitivities to the reality of its use.[178] At the same time, a continual parade of articles and letters in *Stars and Stripes* kept Milcom members' awareness piqued regarding the use of manipulation and censorship around the globe and its infiltration of American society. One example was a January 1969 article titled "Press Freedoms Suffered More Setbacks in 1968" that focused on various restrictive government regimes around the world. The narrative identified nations within the communist sphere emphasizing the harsh controls placed on information flow and reporting by the Soviets, the Communist Chinese and the Cubans. It also noted the 1968 invasion of Czechoslovakia whose "reform regime's attempt to free its information media was crushed by Soviet arms."[179] By the end of that decade, however, Milcom readers also came to the conclusion that information management was not only happening in those nations behind the Iron Curtain but also in their own. Other articles and letters revealed its imprint on American society and the military together with the resulting polemics.

The news reports that offered insight to ongoing censorship and information manipulation practices in society addressed arguments for and against making certain types of information available to the public. An opinion piece published in April 1971 lamented that in regards to the publication of pornography, "In the United States and other democracies, censorship has to all intents and purposes, ceased to exist."[180] A later editorial in *Stars and Stripes*, by conservative newsman James Kilpatrick, celebrated a practice by certain library staff members in the U.S. of denying students and children access to certain books that they deemed "salacious." He considered this simple "common sense."[181] A subsequent opinion piece on censorship noted the banning of certain textbooks in schools. As the writer noted, "Censorship, many people believe, is something that happens in faraway, undemocratic countries." A pervading concern of civil liberties groups, he also observed, was that censorship advocates "want to eliminate books dealing with civil rights and liberties, women's rights and the evils of slavery."[182] But if these pieces provided Milcom readers with a sensing for the issues surrounding the manipulation and censorship of information in American society their reactions suggest that it was the reports and stories concerning their own media that most directly informed their opinions.

Several examples illustrate the depth of censorship and manipulation of the print and broadcast media that inspired concern among contemporary Milcom members. The first appeared in European edition of *Stars and Stripes* in April 1970, with an article that alerted Milcom members in Germany to the brazen censorship practices of the newspaper's Pacific edition's editorial staff in Vietnam. A former enlisted reporter disclosed a media culture there that was "so controlled by the military that little objective reporting" reached the soldiers in country, adding that for them "there is no escape from the military's hand on the news."[183] He included accounts of stories that omitted facts or manipulated information so as to lessen the number of friendly losses or to obscure defeats and failures. The reporter also noted that appeals to politicians in Washington brought no relief but instead elicited comments that reports of censorship were little more than "cases of editorial judgment."[184] For readers who remembered the arguments surrounding information censorship during the Korean War years this must have seemed both familiar and troubling as they considered the depth of editorial control of the newspaper.

A second example of media manipulation involved the AFRTS. In a story that began in January 1970 and ran until October of that year the radio and television service received criticism for censoring information and reports. Although the management staff had denied any manipulation or censorship for years, sources from the AP and UPI broke the story that John C. Broger, the director of AFRTS, admitted that "overseas military broadcasts are edited to avoid offending local governments" or to "aid an enemy."[185] By October the criticisms mounted and included charges from former military reporters that news programs were subject to censorship. Examples provided were the quashing of a report about 6,000 sheep accidentally killed by the military with a dose of lethal nerve gas, and the deletion of a story about contraception. Critics also charged that the AFRTS was "dominated in its approach to news by military thinking rather than detached professional news judgment."[186]

A few years later another incident occurred that offered Milcom members an added significant example of command-directed censorship. In January 1984 the NATO Commander, American General Bernard Rogers, placed a gag order on a report that the West German Defense Minister had forced West German General Günter Kiessling to retire on the grounds he was a security risk based on speculations of his homosexuality. When asked why the command authorities had enforced such censorship the Deputy Commander of EUCOM explained that the story was "highly speculative and sensationalistic." He added that the report might be "detrimental to the good order and discipline of a readership that includes many U.S. military personnel who work and train closely with their German allies."[187] Although the story appeared in other news outlets such as the *New York Times* on January 24 and 31, 1984, its first appearance in *Stars and Stripes* was not until February 2, 1984.[188]

The lapse in time over the reporting of the Kiessling incident caused consternation for many Milcom readers. A number of them responded with letters to the editor of *Stars and Stripes*. Claiming that it was "insulting to have our leaders censor our reading material under the guise that it might hurt discipline among U.S. servicemember," one writer asked, "Have we taken a step backwards as Americans?"[189] Another commented that he found the "intervention of Hq USEUCOM heavy-handed and unwarranted."[190] Still another Milcom reader observed that the "*Stars and Stripes* has a responsibility to print the whole story and let the readers decide what's important."[191] Feeling the need to respond to the letters, the USEUCOM Deputy Commander-in-Chief, General Richard L. Lawson, attempted to mitigate the military hierarchy's actions. Noting that the military command, "Rarely finds it necessary to intercede in *Stripes* editorial operations" he went on to explain that in "unusual circumstances" it would naturally "exercise its responsibility for editorial content." Less as an effort to placate readers than to clarify the extent of his powers, the Deputy Commander finally explained that "I decided that highly speculative and sensational news reports" such as that regarding General Kiessling, "would serve no useful information purpose and could be inimical to good relations with our host nation."[192] His reply suggests that the command structure did not care to deny the charge of censorship; it merely wished to explain its application. Some readers of *Stars and Stripes* failed to accept the reasoning.

One reader was former Managing Editor of the newspaper, Ken Zumwalt, who began to exchange letters with Senator William Proxmire (D-WI) regarding the issue of censorship. Investigating the allegations the senator was not impressed with the response he received from the military that stated speculative reports and news "could possibly result in undisciplined behavior in the form of innocent but ill-chosen and uninformed remarks or actions." To this Senator Proxmire commented, "Imagine that. The general [Lawson] decided that the military personnel are so weak of character that they must be protected from news stories so they don't say something wrong. What nonsense!"[193] Concern for censorship and manipulation of the news continued for several years longer and resulted in a May 1987 Congressional investigation of *Stars and Stripes* inspired by Senator Proxmire.[194]

The Government Accounting Office (GAO) eventually published the results of the investigation in a December 1988 report titled *Stars and Stripes: Inherent Conflicts Lead to Allegations of Military Censorship*. Although the report noted that censorship of the Pacific edition of the newspaper was endemic, it found that "by DOD's standards, the European paper has been censored a few times. Military commanders and their representatives in both theaters have repeatedly attempted to influence the reporting of news."[195] Focusing on external pressures, the report also commented in its executive summary that "as an agent of the government, the editor in chief has a formal responsibility to uphold the principles of a free press because the DOD policy states that he is specifically forbidden to engage in censorship or news management."[196] To correct these perceptions and instances of information manipulation the report included among its recommendations that the newspaper should have a civilian editor-in-chief who would serve for no more than 5 years, and that "military officers shall not interfere with or attempt to influence news content."[197] The newspaper later adopted these corrections.

Although the Proxmire-inspired investigation is a prime example of external oversight and the application of remediation to correct instances of manipulation and censorship, Milcom members had for decades been sensitive to any perception of infringement of their right to freedom of speech through inappropriate management of information and entertainment. This is evident through an examination of other letters to the editor from the late 1960s through the 1980s that reveal a consistently high level of concern regarding any censorship or editorial management of information or entertainment. For example, in May 1968, a reader from the Herzogenaurach Milcom voiced strong concern that a proposed administrative consolidation of the AFN global network signaled the "inevitability that news broadcasts would be managed, controlled, and censored," a charge vehemently denied by AFN directors.[198]

Milcom readers and listeners continued to interpret the simplest intimation of any change to the status quo as an infringement of their rights. Other letters included charges of "sound censorship" when AFN station managers prevented popular songs, such as the Beatles'"Ballad of John and Yoko" and Simon and Garfunkel's "Mrs. Robinson" from airing because they considered them too controversial.[199] In rebuttal, the Officer-in-Charge of AFN replied "We do not censor records here at AFRTS...we don't include plain dirty records in our program package."[200] A flurry of charges of censorship occurred again with the removal of a popular program "Underground" in December 1970. The AFN managers felt that the DJ had not afforded them an opportunity to edit its content for offensive materials prior to airing. The response by Milcom listeners was consistent with protests that asked, "Is not the fight for freedom of speech (hearing) somehow included in the overall goal of USAREUR?"[201] As the collection of letters reveals these challenges to control of information and content by AFN continued for years.

Just as Milcom members criticized *Stars and Stripes* and AFRTS for censoring information and entertainment during these decades, they also occasionally came to their defense when someone requested the editing of specific content. This was the case in August 1987, when a Milcom viewer criticized the television service for not censoring an episode of the show *Saturday Night Live* for its content that lampooned the military. Responses immediately took the critic to task and a number argued that they were all in the military to defend the Constitution and First Amendment rights. As two writers noted, "Your request that AFN practice prior censorship of political satire strikes me as both unconstitutional and un–American," and "We are fighting for freedom. And freedom of information is integral to the American way of life."[202]

Milcom members' responses to either perceived or real infringement of their right to freedom of speech during this time were often immediate and vigorous. This sensitivity suggests that they assigned that right a special significance, which offers several interpretations. The first is that they saw the right to freedom of speech as a characteristic that especially denoted their separation and difference from the Soviet Bloc forces and the strictures of communism, an important distinction in the philosophical sparring between the Cold War superpowers. Another interpretation is that Milcom members understood that right as an immutable foundational tenet of an exceptional and open American society that should remain protected and unchanged during the years of cultural upheaval and social change. A third possibility is that almost any cry of "censorship" quickly placed military elites on the defensive, a situation that normally powerless lower enlisted personnel would enjoy creating. Regardless of whether these motivations had individual or collective importance, Milcom members stood strongly against censorship and media manipulation, and were ready to make their voices heard.

By the late 1960s, the fault lines precipitated by Americans' varied interpretations of societal ideals, which stretched from the early postwar decades, had finally generated tensions that shook the exceptional American consensus. Among the issues that were central to the emerging controversy and debate were racial equity, women's rights and media manipulation. Americans living in the overseas Milcoms experienced the changes that introduced a new definition of equality and inclusion for racial and ethnic minorities, opportunities and empowerment for women, and a strong resolve to safeguard freedom of speech. Gone were some of the troubling inconsistencies within the early postwar paradigm of an exceptional American society, replaced with an understanding that their usefulness was limited and their value reduced. But that process also demonstrated to Americans that the resiliency of their society lay in its continued openness, its ability to meet societal challenges head-on and a willingness to work together to find solutions.

Eight

Testing German-American Bonds (1967–1990)

Vietnam—The First of Three Tests

By 1967 the Vietnam conflict emerged as a common denominator among protest groups in the U.S. and overseas. Although various histories debate its centrality and causal effects on shaping student movements, the public debate that emerged did provide a framework for dissent and protest within the military communities in Germany during the late 1960s and early 1970s.[1] This became manifest through the activities of both military and civilian Milcom members and included participation in passive and active, organized and impromptu, anti-war demonstrations of opposition and protest. At one end of the spectrum they exercised their rights of free speech while remaining within the bounds permitted by law and military policy, in the extreme they employed measures such as an underground press or resorted to desertion. In all cases many American Milcom members felt that participation in the public debate concerning the Vietnam conflict was their obligation and right within the ideals of Americanism.

As the war unfolded through the 1960s, members of the military communities in Germany were able to follow the events through articles carried in *Stars and Stripes* and other print media sources as well as on daily news broadcasts by AFN radio. In addition, repeated rotations of many military members from assignments in West Germany to tours of duty in Vietnam, and back, also sensitized them to the contentious contemporary issues associated with America's presence in Southeast Asia.[2] Still, as the number of student protests grew on college campuses in the U.S. and in major European cities, Milcom members also began to voice their opinions about the war. Numerous letters to the editor of *Stars and Stripes* offer testament to the varied spectrum of feelings within the Milcoms.[3]

Initial expressions of opinion, just prior to and after the Tet offensive of 1968, generally supported America's actions in Vietnam.[4] A letter from May 1967 stressed the importance of free speech for military members by defending a Navy pilot guilty of insubordination for advocating "all-out war in Vietnam." While the author endorsed the pilot's point of view he also defended the flier's "constitutional right of free speech without facing the threat of a court-martial."[5] Another letter from a Bitburg Milcom member in October 1968 railed against a cessation of offensive military air action. Noting that it was with "bitter regret" he read of the "President's decision to halt the bombing of North Vietnam" during peace negotiations, the writer then drew a parallel between American military involvement in Vietnam and Korea, where "we did not win either." The writer also offered support of the "Domino Theory," which he considered was completely "valid" in its warning of communist hegemony.[6]

A collection of letters dated December 15, 1969, also gave voice to perceptions that strongly supported the American presence in Vietnam. One writer suggested, "Those so-called [antiwar] protestors really are traitors; or what would you call a person who carries the banner of a country which we are fighting to the grave?"[7] Another letter from a sergeant in the Herzo Milcom challenged the fairness of the American press asking, "Why hasn't equal billing or rating been given to the supporters of the U.S. involvement in the Vietnam war?" He went on to ask, "Has any war been won by peace marches, demonstrations or the like?"[8] A third letter, from a Milcom spouse in Munich, expressed exasperation, "I am getting perturbed over all the dissatisfied people who are milling about day and night protesting everything under the sun from the war in Vietnam to the U.S. government." Ultimately, she recommended they "go to the nearest Russian embassy and ask for a visa to Russia."[9] Other letters to the editor continued to follow a similar line through the early 1970s. One from October 1972 criticized American "bleeding hearts" that only care about "the terrible acts of war the U.S. is committing over North Vietnam" without having "compassion for the "women and children of South Vietnam who are killed or maimed" by the North Vietnamese.[10] Another letter taking a pro–American stance asked, "Where are the mock trials, mass world condemnation" of the jailers of American POWs who were "cruel, cynical violators of Geneva Convention rules?"[11] This was in reaction to a feature article that focused on the suffering of captive American fliers.

But as the archives of *Stars and Stripes* reveal, while the war edged on the volume of letters from Milcom members who offered dissenting opinions of American involvement in Vietnam increased rapidly after 1968. A letter from May 1969 suggested America's withdrawal from "our limited and unsuccessful conduct of the war" as a solution to the nation's preeminent concern for its international "image." "In this way," the author noted, "the U.S. might save face, preserve its image and perhaps bring a solution to the foremost problem of Southeast Asia."[12] This letter suggests that some Milcom members were already sensitive to the tarnished American image and corrosion of residual exceptionalist ideals. This is consistent with contemporary histories that describe the change in American and global attitudes after the Tet offensive as an end to the "grand American illusion" as an evangelist of democratic freedoms.[13] This affected American domestic political opinion and resonated abroad including the network of overseas Milcoms.

Other letters reflect that emerging current of attitudes among Milcom members in opposition to the war. Several that arrived on *Stars and Stripes* editor's desk in November 1969 spoke of the right to dissent against the war. One from the Baumholder Milcom commented, "Since I was young enough to understand the word freedom, it has always been my sincere belief that the primary right of an American citizen has been his right to dissent."[14] A second from the Frankfurt Milcom echoed that feeling, "To brand as traitors those who voice on [sic] intelligent opposition to the war is a callous statement indeed. Such a statement is directly contrary to many fundamental constitutional guarantees, not the least of which are the rights to free speech and assembly."[15] These letters of opposition eventually reached numbers that were comparable to those that supported the war effort and reflected the growing dissent among the ranks in Germany.

Although this does not suggest that dissenting attitudes existed uniformly in every unit and Milcom they do suggest that they were increasingly present and often arrived with soldiers newly assigned to Germany, or developed once they were there.

This trend of vocal opposition continued well into the 1970s. One letter writer chastised both the U.S. and South Vietnam for violating the 1954 Geneva accord agreements by choosing to "violate the proposed election plan when it became apparent, as President Eisenhower said that Ho Chi Minh would get about 80 percent of the vote." The result would have united the divided halves of Vietnam under a communist regime, something the U.S. would not tolerate.[16] Another letter emphasized the folly of wasted resources on a questionable war, "the question of the actual morality of war aside, we have admitted our participation in this war to be an error yet we refuse to cease, offensive combat; we have squandered vast sums of money and human lives, seemingly only to the benefit of the war industries and assorted profiteers in and around the military establishment."[17]

Criticisms of President Nixon's bombing campaign of North Vietnam also appeared. One writer commented, "I wish to extend my congratulations to the American people for their part in continuing this fiasco." He then went on to lament that "Americans would rather throw away more tax dollars in Vietnam than give it to the American poor living on welfare, for the rehabilitation of the men and women inhabiting our prisons, or for more medical research."[18] In the same context, another writer was critical of the President's action to veto several domestic bills that would have protected the environment and supported school funding and instead supported aid for Vietnam. The letter chided, "The administration is boosting efforts to aid in the rehabilitation of Vietnam. The money proposed will go toward rebuilding schools, in training the people for jobs, and in the construction of new hospitals" at a time that needs in America were just as great.[19] By 1973 the tone of many letters was one of war weariness mixed with concern over squandering of national treasure and a questioning of national morals.

But this exceptional freedom of expression, voiced through letters to the editor as opposition to the war, was just one dimension of protest the Milcom members exhibited. There were also physical aspects to their dissent that included demonstrations, participation in discussion groups, publication of anti-war materials and desertion. These other manifestations found both tolerance and censure within the military structure yet drew increasing participation by Milcom members as the war progressed.

One example of actions taken by American DODDS students was participation in the National Vietnam Moratorium Day on October 15, 1969, across campuses in the U.S. Although numbers varied by school, dozens of Milcom high school students wore black armbands in support of the anti-war movement. As various principals reported, approximately 100 of the 1,400 students at Frankfurt American High School participated, as did 150 at the Kaiserslautern American High School. In response to a reporter's question, one student at FAHS commented, "The armband means I am in mourning for the people who have been killed in the war." Another student added, "The armband simply means that I don't like war and killing, any war and any killing."[20] Although the tone of the article was that of indulgence and toleration it could not obscure the fact that by participating in the anti-war demonstration Milcom students were openly expressing their opposition to American policy in league with thousands of fellow students stateside and at American college campuses overseas. A letter to the editor of *Stars and Stripes*, published a week after the moratorium, challenged the article's condescending attitude by boasting, "The Moratorium was not ignored at the University of Maryland Münich campus."[21] It noted that there was broad support by both the student body and faculty although many felt harassed by constantly "being photographed by CID agents from roving cars on McGraw Caserne."[22]

Another aspect of physical demonstration was service members' attendance at coffee houses that featured anti-war discussion groups, reading materials, music, dancing, and advice on how to avoid deployment to Vietnam. As one exposé noted, it was here that they were "surrounded by posters including portraits of Ho Chi Minh" and "sometimes guitar-plunking folk singers lament a Vietnamese baby killed by napalm."[23] This was a popular venue in the U.S. with a network of establishments opening their doors near military posts during the late 1960s and early 1970s. Examples were the *Oleo Strut* in Killeen, Texas near Fort Hood, the *UFO* outside Fort Jackson, South Carolina, and *Mad Anthony Wayne's* outside Fort Leonard Wood, Missouri. These often gained notice when military authorities moved to have their doors closed, sometimes after prompting by local authorities, or when notable personalities such as Jane Fonda and Donald Sutherland made appearances there.[24]

In contrast to the States, there were two types of coffee houses available to Milcom residents in West Germany. One set was located on military compounds and had sponsors such as the United Service Organization (USO), women's clubs, or religious groups.[25] These, the military authorities sanctioned and were the only type referenced in official publications such as *Stars and Stripes*. The other set, cafes comparable to the anti-war venues of *Oleo Strut* and the *UFO*, did exist overseas although their locations were more difficult to find. Information on their whereabouts was available by word of mouth or via unofficial flyers and newsletters. American service members operated some and others existed in local establishments. Many of them were the haunts of German student activists who offered a safe haven away from American military authorities where open anti-war discussions took place. One *Stars and Stripes* staff writer noted condescendingly that it was in old university towns like Heidelberg that female students "in low cut peasant blouses tried to entice the GIs into their coffee houses for meaningful debate. But "when it became apparent the guys had something more meaningful in mind, both sides lost interest."[26] As research of source materials reveal however, this is a skewed generalization of German-American relations between students and service members and does not account for the existence of more meaningful social and political bridges between the two groups. As this study has noted, those connections that evolved between German students and black GI activists provided vehicles for social protests against racial inequities within American society and the military structure.[27] Within the context of the Vietnam War, these connections provided impetus for more active modes of political protest by Milcom members, specifically through underground newspapers and desertion.

The Underground GI Press

By a conservative estimate, there were approximately 200 newspapers, newsletters, circulars, and broadsides that comprised the global underground GI press between 1967 and 1977.[28] A survey of the publications reveals that these numbers varied during that period because some of them lasted for only one issue, others for several, and still others for longer, so that such media outlets were always available, though not always in the same volume or with regular frequency. Sometimes the papers would appear when like-minded individuals in a Milcom got together, only to disappear when they were transferred to other locations or left the service. In West Germany alone, approximately 20 known papers appeared in print; of those, at least nine also served double duty as organs for the voice of anti-war dissidents, as well as black Milcom members protesting racial inequities in the service.[29] Among those available for anti-war dissidents were "*We Got the Brass*" from the Frankfurt Milcom, "*Call Up!*" and "*FTA with Pride*" from the Heidelberg Milcom, "*Up Against the Wall*" and "*Forward*" from the Berlin Milcom, and "*The New Testament*" from the Schweinfurt Milcom.

City/Milcom	Title	Dates
Berlin	*Where It's At*	1968–1969
Berlin	*Up Against the Wall*	1970
Berlin	*Forward*	1971
Bitburg	*Write On*	1973
Blumenscheinweg	*The Word*	1973
Butzbach	*The Bridge*	1972–1976
Frankfurt	*We Got the Brass*	1969
Frankfurt	*Voice of the Lumpen*	1971
Heidelberg	*The Graffiti*	1969
Heidelberg	*Lamboy Times*	1970
Heidelberg	*FTA with Pride*	1971–1973
Heidelberg	*The Wiley Word*	1972
Heidelberg	*FighT bAck*	1972–1976
Heidelberg	*Squadron Scandal*	1975
Heidelberg	*OB4 Notes*	1976
Mainz	*Dig It*	1971
Paris, France	*The Baumholder Gig Sheet*	1971
Schweinfurt	*The New Testament*	1972

Table 8.1. Listing of Underground Newspapers. These were available to Milcom members in West Germany between 1968 and 1976. The publications lasted from several issues to several years. Some organizations printed theirs outside the country and distributed them either by mail or by hand. One example was *The Baumholder Gig Sheet*, published in France. (Independent Voices, "GI Underground Press," accessed March 2, 2014, http://www.revealdigital.com/page/titlelist-GIUP/title-list-gi-underground-press; G.I. Publications, "African-American Involvement in the Vietnam War," accessed February 1, 2014, http://www.aavw.org/served/gipubs_voice_lumpen_abstract01.html.)

Often these publications were associated with particular ad hoc groups, such as the Unsatisfied Black Soldiers, the Heidelberg Liberation Front, the America Soldiers' Union or the Second Front International; but in all cases they served as organs for service members in EUCOM to voice their dissenting political opinions about the war in Vietnam, to gripe about life in the ranks and to critique the military structure, which they frequently considered oppressive. An example was *We Got the Brass*, published in Frankfurt, which broadcast those sentiments on its first cover in the spring of 1969:

THIS IS THE FIRST ISSUE OF WE GOT THE BRASS—PUT OUT BY G.I.'S, EX-G.I.'S, AND RESISTORS IN EUROPE UNITED BY OUR OPPOSITION TO THE MINDLESS WAR IN VIETNAM AND THE PAWN OF THAT WAR, THE U.S. ARMY.

WHAT UNITES US IS SIMPLE—the unwillingness to kill and be killed in a war that makes others rich, that our parents pay for, and that neither the Vietnamese or the majority of the American people want. And the daily oppression of life in the army, taking orders from stupid lifers, learning the robot discipline that gets us prepared for life (?) on the outside.[30]

Service member dissidents understood these publications to be within their right to freedom of speech and to represent only their opinions. Statements to this effect often appeared on the front pages. The December 1972 issue of *FTA with Pride* carried this disclaimer on its cover:

> We hope the people reading this paper are not wondering if it reflects official government policy or views, it does not! We are not now, nor have we ever been, associated with, the FBI, the CIA, DAR or KKK. The MI, although seen frequently close behind us, have no effect on our editorial policy, and unfortunately, we have none on theirs.[31]

Many publications also reminded their readers that it was within their rights to possess a copy should military authorities make any attempt to confiscate it. The front page of the March 1971 issue of *Forward*, published in West Berlin, made this clear:

> THIS IS YOUR PROPERTY! IT CANNOT BE TAKEN FROM YOU! AR 381–135 (D): Unit commanders shall further ensure that there is no interference with the U.S. Mail and that every individual under his command has the right to read and retain commercial publications for his own personal use.[32]

As a source, these assorted newspapers, circulars and newsletters add value to an investigation of life in the Milcoms by providing information that was not available in sanctioned sources such as *Stars and Stripes* or official summaries such as the DAHSUM series.[33] As a result, they reveal a dimension of agency achieved by Milcom members not often reflected in extant histories. These were actions and initiatives taken by American service members, civilians and dependents, beyond the parameters outlined by policy, but within their own interpretation of their exceptional right as citizens to voice opposition to the war. One instance, reported in the Schweinfurt Milcom's *The New Testament*, was an early June 1972 Memorial Day march staged by "60 to 100, and at times more" service members and dependents. As the writer noted they "walked in protest against the war in Viet-Nam and their unwilling participation in the WAR MACHINE."[34] The event included the handing out of anti-war leaflets and cigarettes to German nationals and a discussion of "GI rights."[35] A brief reciprocal article in *Stars and Stripes* did note the event but only offered a few contradictory details that "most of the demonstrators were German" while only a "half dozen were soldiers."[36]

Also indicative of the type of information carried by these publications, in contrast to *Stars and Stripes*, was the report printed in the July 19th issue of *The New Testament* of a soldier accused by the Army of being a "leader-organizer for the day's activities" during the previous June anti-war march.[37] He appeared before a court-martial and received charges of being AWOL, failure to obey orders and a breach of peace for shouting anti-war slogans in a Milcom housing area. A successful defense by a legal team, which included a military lawyer and a counsel from the American Civil Liberties Union, resulted in the dismissal of most charges and awarding of a minor punishment. The article noted, "We consider this a victory" in that it was "another attempt by the Army to suppress G.I. rights. The Army's defeat on this point proves we do have the rights that are guaranteed under the First Amendment."[38] There was no reciprocal article on the trial or outcome in *Stars and Stripes*.

Aside from announcing the locations for GI coffee houses, underground papers also carried information on gathering times and places such as the November 1969 issue of *The Graffiti* that advertised weekly meetings, discussions and gatherings held "Every Saturday at 7PM" at the Republican Club in Mannheim.[39] Another example was the November 1972 issue of *FightT bAck* [sic] that featured a proposed "GI Meeting" to "work out a common plan of action" to fight back against cases of perceived harassment by military authorities.[40] The

March 1973 issue of *FightT bAck* featured an article announcing a conference on GI rights, organized by the Lawyers Military Defense Committee (LMDC) to occur at the Collegium Academicum at the University of Heidelberg.[41] The purpose was to educate service members on becoming legal counselors to others living in the barracks.

On occasion, the underground press also carried articles that seemed more of a public service, with cautions about drug abuse and information about counseling programs and rights during searches and testing.[42] Realizing the value of this type of publication as a vehicle to fight drug abuse, the USAREUR Special Action Office for Drug Abuse (SAODA) sought to maximize the opportunity. The physician in charge of the program noted with a touch of irony, "The most effective propaganda instrument in drug abuse is the underground press. [It is] A service that talks about which drugs are worth buying and which are not saves a lot of people from [becoming] buying casualties." He went on to comment "USAREUR has no choice but to rely on informative, drug-culture-oriented, publications to educate our numerous isolated troops."[43] Although there is no evidence that reflects the number of users reached or effectiveness of this method the military hierarchy paradoxically realized the potential of the underground press to make a difference in the lives of service members and respected its credibility among its readership.

A survey of the material printed in these periodicals however, reflects anti-war rhetoric similar to that of contemporary publications found in the American mainstream media or on college campuses in the U.S. It is apparent that in many cases those who staffed the publications simply cut and pasted articles or copied them word for word into their own pages. GI editors also dedicated a great deal of space to repetitive reminders of service members' rights under the UCMJ and information on how to contact non-military affiliated legal associations such as the LMDC.[44] In many cases the underground GI press also dedicated numerous pages to lampooning the local military leadership through short articles and stories that directed accusations laced with hyperbole at the hierarchy or posted derisive, crudely-drawn cartoons of officers and sergeants. While these newspapers did serve a purpose as a venue to express political opinions, or provide information on gathering or organizing, some individuals exploited their existence as an opportune vehicle to list personal grievances or spout popular anti-authoritarian rhetoric. This did little more than offer a challenge to good order and discipline within the military, such as repetitive references to both officers and non-commissioned offers as "pigs."

Some underground publications expressed a more radical edge, such as the West Berlin *Forward* that endorsed unionization of the military with: "election of officers by the rank and file," an "end to saluting and sir-ing of officers," a declaration that no troops be "used against workers on strike," and petitions for the "right of collective bargaining."[45] Still another example was the Heidelberg community's *FighT bAck*, which offered critiques of the "capitalist class" that "hopes to isolate the war resisters from the growing struggles they face at home. The capitalists hope to keep militant GIs from joining and leading working people in the fight against the attacks on our living and working conditions in the States."[46] Some of these publications also had affiliations with radical political student groups such as the Students for a Democratic Society (SDS) in West Berlin. It wrote, edited and organized the printing of *Where It's At* in Berlin with a staff composed of American and German students as well as a number of "unnamed" service members. The *Voice of the Lumpen* was another example. Sponsored by the Revolutionary People's Communication Network it was a strong advocate for racial equality and "anti-imperialist liberation struggles" combined with protesting the war in Vietnam. It advertised itself as a replacement for the former Ministry of Information of the Black Panther Party.⁴⁷

By late 1969, the military elite began to react to the increased volume of world-wide dissidence among service members. As part of this campaign they directed a portion of their deliberate actions against the large number of underground GI publications overseas and in the U.S. The combination of the invective nature of the newspapers' articles, their politically subversive editorializing, their railings and defamatory criticisms of the leadership structure, and their association with certain radical groups suggested a threat to the good order and discipline of the military that could not go unchallenged. One of the first salvos fired by the military hierarchy was the bringing of charges against an editor and "organizer of an anti-war coffeehouse for GIs" in the vicinity of Fort Dix, New Jersey. A court-martial board sentenced the serviceman to six months hard labor and a reduction in rank for "unauthorized distribution of an underground newspaper critical of America's role in the Vietnam War."⁴⁸ Two months later, *The Graffiti*, from the Heidelberg Milcom, reacted with a commentary that lamented the fact that it was a chaplain who had reported the accused soldier to military authorities. The newspaper also remarked that the military's action was "part of a frenzied effort" to control the distribution of these materials worldwide noting other cases against military editors and publications.⁴⁹

As part of the effort to manage the impact of the underground press the military also issued Department of Defense Directive 1325.6, *Handling Dissident and Protest Activities among Members of the Armed Forces*, in September 1969.⁵⁰ The directive outlined the responsibilities of the military leadership in curtailing dissident activities. This included the distribution of unofficial anti-war print media and clarifying the rights of service members to possess these materials. Most important, for the editors of the underground newspapers the directive encouraged military leaders to "impose only such minimum restraints as are necessary to enable the Army to perform its mission." It directed that "a commander not prevent a publication simply because he does not like its contents ... a commander must have cogent reasons for any denial of distribution privileges."⁵¹ It also noted that membership in service men's unions could not be restricted, nor attendance at coffeehouses or the possession of an unauthorized publication. The intent was to "safeguard the service member's right of expression to the maximum extent possible," a very exceptional consideration.⁵²

Still, DOD Directive 1325.6 also provided military leaders with some leverage of control by permitting them to use their best judgment regarding unofficial publications. In this context the directive offered leaders sufficient latitude of consideration by stating:

> A commander may require prior approval of publications to be distributed on a military installation through other than official outlets to determine if the publication would: create a clear danger to the loyalty, discipline, or morale of military personnel; or materially interfere with the accomplishment of the military mission. Distribution of any publication determined to be a danger in any of the areas [in the previous paragraphs] of this enclosure shall be prohibited.⁵³

A survey of sources of underground newspapers, as well as *Stars and Stripes*, reveals that not many editors received punishment nor did the military leadership confiscate papers as a result of official policy guidance, although the presence of the publications continued to remain an irritant to the military hierarchy.

This unofficial press did however provide an important vehicle for the broadcasting of anti-war political views while offering a sense of a right of free speech to those service members, civilians and students involved with publishing or reading its contents. By the mid–1970s, the underground GI press in Europe appeared to die a natural death closely linked to the end of the conflict in Vietnam, the diminishing of global anti-war protests and the conversion of the military from conscription to a voluntary force between 1973 and 1975.[54]

Desertion

While many Milcom service members in Germany demonstrated their opposition to American foreign policy decisions by participating in local protest events, gatherings and meetings, or voicing their opinions in newsprint, a small percentage chose to desert. Extant histories reveal an entrenched, well-orchestrated network of German students who figured into the calculus of protest by facilitating the escape of dissident American service members.[55] This was through the efforts of a well-conceived and executed campaign to target the Milcoms and entice military members to leave their places of assignment in Germany and flee via an underground network of safe houses and routes. These led westward into France and Great Britain, or northward to Sweden. The students' propaganda generally focused on the war but also included critiques on the ills of American society and racial tensions. One technique often used by German activists was to "rely heavily on the charm of the fairer sex to get the message home." In these cases female members of activist groups, nicknamed "Brides of the Revolution," visited bars frequented by American servicemen and worked to entice them through drinks and dancing to desert.[56] As revealed by a number of sources, however, the overall net effect was small.

By January 1968, *Stars and Stripes* began maintaining a casual tally of defections from units in EUCOM. One of the first articles to record desertions reported that the number of service members seeking asylum in Sweden had reached nine.[57] It also noted that the Swedish Vietnam Committee "promised it would see that the figure grew bigger by the day," a forecast that would not materialize. By May 1968, *Stars and Stripes* reported that the total of American service members seeking asylum in Sweden had risen to 49, although it also noted that during the previous two months 12 had already returned to the their units in Europe or the U.S.[58] By April 1969 the newspaper was reporting that another 58 were in processing by the Swedish Alien Commission to leave that country and return to their units. Of that total, 43 came from "bases in Germany."[59]

But trying to track a verifiable number of deserters during the late 1960s and early 1970s is difficult as various sources reveal a tangle of interpretations and correlations. For example, in January 1970 *Stars and Stripes* reported that since July 1966 over 1,400 military personnel had deserted from their units of assignment. But authorities in the Pentagon noted that in only 107 of those cases "was there any clear-cut evidence the desertion was a protest against the Vietnam War." They also noted that 371 deserters of the original number had already returned to their units.[60] Other sources such as the Department of the Army Historical Summaries (DAHSUMs) for 1968 through 1972 show a variance of numbers for desertion rates that are generally difficult to correlate with those shown in print media but do reveal downward trends. They show a high of 185 total desertions for the entire U.S. Army in 1970, dropping to a low of 97 by 1972. After that date the Army no longer recorded a number for desertions in subsequent DAHSUMs. One suggestion is that the military considered the figure beyond concern.[61] A comment accompanying the figure of 140 desertions for 1969 noted that the desertion rate for that year was "in line with those of 1952 at the peak of the Korean War."[62] The world-wide rate for soldiers charged as Absent Without Leave (AWOL) however did remain elevated until it began to decline in 1972.[63]

Evidence of the questionable effectiveness of the German activists' campaign to entice GIs to desert is also present in reports from the civilian organizations that worked to pass information to Americans in the Milcoms.[64] As the chairman of the Frankfurt War Objectors Branch lamented in January 1968, "It's been very discouraging and we may not go on with the distributions. Most soldiers ... tear up the leaflets and throw them away." The deputy chairman added, "The barracks in Hanau was the worst. The GIs spit on us and threw cans of Coca-Cola and beers on our heads from the barracks windows—full cans. That's dangerous, you know."[65]

Fiscal Year	AWOL	Desertion
1968	1,100	139
1969	1,158	140
1970	1,349	185
1971	1,586	114
1972	1,491	97

Table 8.2. AWOL/Desertion Rate. These figures reflect the unauthorized absentee rate in the U.S. Army, 1968–1972. (Department of the Army Historical Summaries for FY 1968, 1969, 1970, 1971, 1972, Center of Military History, http://www.history.army.mil/html/bookshelves/collect/dahsum.html.)

With the exception of the few underground newsletters in Sweden, there was also a lack of support for desertion in the underground press in Germany. Although these papers saw great service as a voice of grievance and anti-war sentiments they did not include articles that encouraged desertions from assigned units. A survey of archival sources reveals that desertion appeared infrequently in articles and then it was only in terms of reporting isolated cases of individual service members charged with the crime under the UCMJ.[66] The newspapers in Sweden generally offered sharp leftist critiques of the U.S. or practical information necessary for deserters' to maintain residency there.[67] This suggests that even among disaffected Milcom members desertion was not a first or second choice as a means of protest.

This interpretation, based on evidence gathered from several sources, is in contrast to assertions made in some histories that claim "in many cases, personnel acted on their disapproval of the military by simply leaving their units, going AWOL (absent without leave) or deserting" and that "throughout 1967 and 1968 thousands of GIs deserted their units, often causing severe personnel shortages" in USAREUR.[68] Recent evidence also stands to refute conclusions that "desertion did become a serious problem in the early 1970s."[69] As contradictory evidence suggests, anti-war protestors in the Milcoms chose to demonstrate or write about their dissatisfaction rather than desert.

Missile Protests—The Second Test

By the early 1980s new protests and concerns replaced the anti–Vietnam War political tempests that had resonated across the German countryside and through the Milcoms more than a decade earlier. These newer tensions drew their impetus from a German populace that was reacting to the deployment of additional nuclear-ready missiles on their soil. The proposed placement of a new generation of the intermediate range Pershing II and the Tomahawk cruise missiles in West Germany precipitated the crisis as the U.S. acted to counter a perceived threat from the Soviet deployment of SS-20 intermediate range missiles in western Russia.[70] The fear was that "Soviet superiority in theatre nuclear systems could undermine the stability achieved in inter-continental systems and cast doubts on the credibility of the Alliance's [NATO] deterrent strategy."[71] Once again, as in the 1950s and 1960s, the West Germans were greatly concerned that their territory would turn into a nuclear battleground between the superpowers, and again that particular fear would stand between them and their American allies.[72]

The American administration, however, underestimated the German reaction. As early as October 1981 then Secretary of Defense Caspar Weinberger commented that although the spreading anti-nuclear protests in Europe were "obvious expressions of concern by a free people, they do not represent a widespread view of West European citizens."[73] This perspective was in contrast to the results of a public opinion poll taken earlier in November 1979 that reflected only a slim percentage (38 percent) of West Germans in favor of the deployment of "medium-range" missiles to counter the deployment of "Russian medium-range missiles."[74] Weinberger's prognosis also failed in light of the protest marches organized by groups such as the European Nuclear Disarmament committee that coaxed more than 1.8 million people into the streets of West Germany, Belgium, Italy, the Netherlands and Finland in the fall of 1981.[75]

Serving in a variety of key leadership positions during that period, Lieutenant General (Ret) R.L. "Sam" Wetzel recounts the events as they unfolded:

> From June '78 to June '79 I was General Al Haig's executive to the SACEUR at SHAPE. In August 1978 the Soviets were deploying the SS-22's, which could reach all the way to Spain. We only had the short range Pershing I. So we took a map and drew a line on it from Germany to the edge of Moscow, then wrote a secret message to the U.S. telling them to develop the Pershing II ASAP with the 1800 km range. The U.S. did and now fast forward to December 1983. The German Bundestag was debating whether or not to permit [Pershing] II's to come to Germany. At 10 p.m. they said OK. I was now the DCINC USAREUR with responsibility for all nuclear weapons. We called Cape Canaveral and they launched the C-5's with Pershing II's, which arrived the next morning. I met the first one down the ramp at Ramstein AFB. We then had a secret convoy at night to get them to Schwabisch Gmund, where lots of protestors camped out in the snow and rain and mud. That deployment got the Soviet attention that they could not compete with us, and is one of the reasons the Wall came down later in my opinion. I was involved from inception to deployment—just by accident. Many nuclear protestors marched in Heidelberg outside my quarters during that period as well as elsewhere all over Germany.[76]

Deployment of the missiles began in late 1983, but between late 1981 and 1984 a rash of demonstrations against the arrival of the Pershings and the Tomahawks erupted throughout West Germany capturing the attention of Americans living there.[77] As early as April 9, 1982, the announcement that various anti-war, anti-nuke and religious groups were planning a series of nation-wide demonstrations made a splash in *Stars and Stripes*, "Germans Plan Easter Marches."[78] The German police projected this to be "the biggest peace protest revival since the late 1960s" and estimated crowds numbering "between 300,000 and 500,000 campaigners."[79] The demonstrations did take place and participation did reach the numbers authorities projected with events occurring in locations as widespread as Frankfurt, Munich, and Stuttgart.[80] They continued through the following year and featured a 60-mile long human chain of protesters linking arms. The chain stretched from EUCOM headquarters in Stuttgart to Wiley Barracks in the Neu-Ulm Milcom, one of the destinations for the Pershing II missiles.[81] These activities also appeared in the American press with the *New York Times* reporting on the demonstrations in October 1983.[82] Different groups would continue to stage missile protests of varying size and duration in the cities, towns and villages of Germany, and at the gates of American military *Kasernes* through the latter years of the 1980s.[83]

As media reports reveal, attitudes of the demonstrators towards the Americans varied. Some exhibited a less aggressive nature than others. For example, a protest against the arrival of the missiles outside the Americans' Carl Schurz Barracks in the port city of Bremerhaven resulted in the arrests of 255 demonstrators but there was an absence of violence directed toward the families in the Milcom housing area located just a short distance away.[84] In the same context, *Stars and Stripes* reported that the anti-missile protestors who formed the miles-long human chain in Neu-Ulm also carried placards that read, "We like Americans but not Pershings and poison gas."[85] Reports note that during the event, "the demonstration was peaceful," the "atmosphere was festive" and some groups "handed bread and wine to U.S. soldiers to symbolize German-American friendship."[86] If there was an existing gap between American and German politics at this time it still seemed narrow enough to support social and cultural bridges.

But other media reports carried more ominous messages that provided contrast to the other projected images of *Gemütlichkeit* [bonhomie] between Germans and Americans. During the same period of time as the peaceful human chain demonstration in October 1983, "rebel anti-nuclear groups" had planned "widespread violence and blockades" of missile sites and munitions storage areas. As the German magazine *Der Spiegel* noted, their protest was "directed against missile deployment, which they want to stop by using every kind of violence possible."[87] These threats manifested themselves through occasionally violent action such as a rock-pelting attack on the car of American Vice-President George Bush during a state visit that year.[88] Another instance resulted in the arrest of 188 German protesters who harassed American soldiers training in the area of the Wildflecken Milcom by throwing rocks at them and spray-painting anti-war slogans on vehicles and missiles.[89]

These reports, which appeared in *Stars and Stripes*, as well as other print media such as the *New York Times*, elicited responses from Milcom members that reveal a range of feelings from strong support for missile deployment to sympathy for the demonstrators. Such was the case with Thomas Rehm who served in Germany as an artillery officer. He notes:

> In my opinion, the protests were more about general anti–Americanism and the feeling that anything the U.S. wanted to do was likely wrong. Note that participants were in the age groups with the greatest anti–American sentiment—and I recall only a few were aggressive about it when you met them socially. [I] saw Easter marches in 1989–1991. In particular, I recall one Easter march while doing nuke duty at a PSG site. The folks in the front of the groups were loud and obnoxious. Most of the folks were just hanging out with friends on a nice day. *Polizei* [German police] had things under control at all times so far as I could see.[90]

Still, Rehm feels that the Germans' attitudes were not justified:

> Justified about being a nuclear battleground? Certainly there was a possibility of nuclear war depending how a potential conflict unfolded. However, feeling badly about something does not justify the marches versus Americans. To my mind, it was a political question—Germans should have been lobbying their political representatives or Soviet embassies.[91]

Some Americans like Douglas Gaskell experienced the full brunt of the anti-missile protest movement including a tension-filled demonstration at the gates of his *Kaserne* on Easter weekend in 1983. Assigned to Wiley Barracks, a Pershing missile site in Neu Ulm, he witnessed events at one anchor point of the human chain that later that year would stretch from EUCOM headquarters in Stuttgart to his location. Although the latter event would prove to be peaceful his afternoon in April was not. As he recalls:

> I remember Easter of 83 well. We were assigned responsibility for the front gate and the adjoining fence line. In addition to our platoon [of artillerymen] there were a large number of Federal Border Police, Bavarian State Police, U.S. Army Military Police, and C Company, 2d Battalion, 4th Infantry all within the confines of the kaserne. There were dogs, water cannons; a couple of armored cars ... the only thing missing was a Navy destroyer.
> Easter Sunday the press reported 1.3 million protestors in the area. I know that outside the front gate, there were more people than I could count. The overall plan was to let the Bavarian and Federal police deal with the protesters. Sometime after lunch, the authorities decided that they wanted an additional show of force. The protesters were shaking the fence and gate and there seemed to be concern that they might breach the fence. The Bavarian and Federal police sent the dog handlers outside the gate and it was not very pretty. The dogs got hold of several of the protesters and the photographers had a field day.[92]

After a period of 30 minutes, military authorities summoned Gaskell's platoon to place concertina wire 20 feet behind the fence line for additional security:

> We left the M16s [rifles] and came out with ax handles, formed up and marched the 100 meters to the gate, deployed on line facing the gate to cover the wire team behind us. When we got up within twenty or so feet of the gate, the crowd got ugly. But then, the most amazing thing happened. The protesters quit climbing the gate and backed off a foot or so. I gave a command to advance two steps and the protesters backed up two feet or so. We advanced again and the protesters backed up two feet or so. By that time the wire team had laid down the concertina and we came back through the wire. That was one of the few times that I felt scared. I wish I could tell you it was no worry, but I was scared. Forty of us and thousands of them shouting and screaming is more than a little frightful. But I was fascinated by the command and control of the protesters. I remember seeing two guys in the crowd with radios and wondered if they were directing the protesters. It was obviously not spontaneous.[93]

The *Stars and Stripes* report of that event recorded that "some 300 people" had blockaded the gate at Wiley Barracks causing the Bavarian police to use "tear gas and dogs" to maintain control.[94] The Pacific edition of *Stars and Stripes* noted the number as "500 anti-nuclear protesters."[95] In contrast, the *New York Times* reported, "some 6,000 demonstrators linked arms to form a human chain around Wiley Barracks."[96] Gaskell's 40 man platoon had likely faced the 6,000.

Still another potentially dangerous situation unfolded during a demonstration at a Pershing II missile site at Mutlangen when a U.S. military guard fired three warning shots into the air after several demonstrators breached an outer perimeter fence and began to cut through a second. German police eventually subdued the small group. The event occurred during one of many nationwide anti-missile demonstrations that day in April 1984. A member of Germany's conservative Christian Democrat party called the protesters "useful idiots for the Soviet Union."[97] But the incident continued to underscore the extreme lengths some groups would go to in demonstrating their opposition to the joint German-American decision to deploy the missiles.

Many Americans resented the German attitudes and registered their annoyance in letters to the editor of *Stars and Stripes*. One writer commented, "Comparing U.S. missiles in Europe to Soviet missiles in Cuba is like comparing apples to oranges." He went on to observe, "Whether the German people even want it or not, what effective deterrent do they have to counter Soviet medium-range missiles?"[98] This type of reaction remained consistent through the mid–1980s. In May 1983 a frustrated service member from the Nüremberg Milcom wrote, "I often wonder what we're doing here. The people of this land are genuinely warm and friendly people, especially to American GIs, yet they protest our government for deploying nuclear missiles (to counter those) which are already pointing at them."[99] In September of that year another reader aired his grievances with an exceptionalist strain, "I want to get back to the way of life I love—the American way of life. I am here to protect that way of life—not just for me, but for all Americans. We are a unique people in that we are free to choose the life we want to lead."[100] Lashing out at both American and German protesters he continued, "Don't these people realize in order for us to be able to have the freedoms we love, we must also be ready to defend ourselves against those that might take that freedom away from us?... We all want to be able to live in peace. But we must have the capability to be able to preserve the peace. In strength one can achieve it."[101] A letter writer from the Moeringen Milcom added, "If these missiles are deployed in Europe it just might even the balance of nuclear power between the Soviet Union and Europe."[102]

Aside from these Americans, there were some Germans who supported deployment of the missiles and showed unity with the *Amis*. One letter writer to *Stars and Stripes* who had a special connection to the U.S. military appeared incredulous. After reading a series of articles in *Stars and Stripes* and German journals about the anti-missile protests she commented:

> I am a German, married to a member of the U.S. Army and lately I worry a lot about the safety of my husband. I do not understand the German people anymore. I am only 25 years old, but I know what the Americans have done for Germany. Without them the people in Berlin would have starved to death after World War II. America was, and not only then, always there to help the Germans. Now, I guess, everybody has forgotten about it.[103]

Another letter from an official in the German Ministry of Defense reiterated the strong connections between Germans and Americans. Colonel Horst Prayon observed:

> The protests and blockades staged by a small, yet vociferous group, in front of our barracks and yours do not reflect a true picture of our population. Also, their disproportionately great representation in the media is no true gauge of the actual mood ... by far the greater majority of the population is behind you. In August 1983, for instance, it was found that 78 percent of the population of the Federal Republic of Germany feel that peace is made rather more secure by the presence of U.S. forces in this country.... The German people also know that they can depend on their American allies. You and your ethical, moral and humanitarian values have the same roots. The German-American tri-centennial celebrations have once again given evidence of the deep friendship between the United States of America and the Federal Republic of Germany. This U.S.-German friendship, this standing up for common values and basic convictions, has not been decreed from "above" but has grown from "below." I may be permitted to mention the great number of friendships between U.S. servicemen and soldiers of the *Bundeswehr*.[104]

But others offered contrasting views. A member from the Katterbach Milcom wrote to the editor of *Stars and Stripes*:

> There is a lot of deep hurt here in Germany felt by the German people. I can understand, as my grandparents came from here. We cannot expect them to want a nuclear war; I don't either. These people are tired of war and having their country torn apart, their family and countrymen killed. It is too soon for the wounds to be healed and forgiven; to think of another war, above all in Germany again.[105]

A service member from the Augsburg Milcom also wrote to the newspaper:

> The world already has enough nuclear weapons to destroy itself so many times over and I appeal to "rational thinking" people: Why on earth do we need anymore? Would Americans accept multitudes of German nuclear weapons being strategically placed all over the U.S. and the Germans having control and the U.S. population having nothing to say about it?! I doubt it very seriously.[106]

Through the end of 1983 and into early 1984, the issues surrounding the missile deployment continued to remain complicated and tense. As evidence reveals, part of this was the complex German-American relationship and the cooperative involvement of political activists from both nations. In December 1983 a group of three Germans and an American priest broke into an American military *Kaserne* in Schwäbisch Gmund and "smashed windows and headlights on a truck they believed was a nuclear missile transporter." The German police arrested them immediately and identified them all as members of an international anti-missile peace group calling itself Plowshares.[107] That same month a writer to the editor of *Stars and Stripes* also noted the existence of joint German-American initiatives. He commented, "Many Americans have even joined the demonstrators both here in Germany and at home in the United States."[108] He went on to say, "During the 'human chain' demonstration on Oct. 22, many Americans joined with our German friends and took part in the demonstration. There was, for example, a group of about 30 Americans representing the Munich-American Peace Committee."[109] Although American participation was infrequent, it did continue to at least 1986 when German police arrested seven with a group "attempting to block access to the U.S. Army's Pershing II nuclear missile storage depot at Mutlangen."[110] A police spokesman commented, "It was not the first time Americans had been arrested for protests around the tiny Mutlangen base."[111]

By late 1984 the political tempest concerning the missiles was calming but American attitudes remained resolute. A *Stars and Stripes* front page article published in October of that year reported that tens of thousands—instead of an expected hundreds of thousands—of protesters had turned out for scheduled weekend nation-wide demonstrations. Although various peace groups had staged rallies in a number of cities, "So few showed up that an attempt to form a 130-mile human chain between the Ruhr industrial city of Duisberg and a planned U.S. Army installation at Hasselbach ... failed. There were mile-wide gaps in many places."[112] A *New York Times* article from that year reflected the same trend noting the "lost campaign against the deployment of medium-range missiles in Europe" and that the "biggest anti-missile coalition" in West Germany had "started to fall apart."[113] This development continued into 1985 and later. As a report in a March issue of the news journal *Die Zeit* reflected, outside the American missile depot at Mutlangen "the Village of Peace is leaving" and with it a feeling of "resistance" against them.[114] It also acknowledged the dwindling volume of protesters at other sites such as Schwäbisch Gmund and Heilbronn and the return to near normalcy for the Americans, which includes "wrenching music" and "lots and lots of beer flowing."[115] But as the German reporter noted, the perspective of many Americans' seemed exceptionally determined. One American sergeant commented "During the Vietnam War we gave you a reason to protest against us. But now everything is different. We are here as a defensive army, and most demonstrators, shouting at us, simply do not understand this." Another soldier concurred, "The historical mission of the U.S. Army in Germany was to protect Germany against the Red Army. This is still true. We counter the threat from the East."[116]

Like the Vietnam War before it, events surrounding the deployment of upgraded nuclear-ready missiles to West Germany in the 1980s revealed the complexity of German-American political relations. As during the previous period, Germans and Americans each offered divided opinions on the issue. Unlike that earlier time, however, American Milcom members played a less active role in political protests. They appeared less vehement in their opposition and invested less time in finding venues to express their feelings, such as through the underground press. The transition from a conscription force to an all-volunteer army by the 1980s suggests one reason that Milcom members voiced less opposition; another is that the global anti-war energies that were present during the Vietnam era had dissipated. Regardless of the reasons, sources reveal that Milcom members generally felt stronger about their mission in Germany than in earlier decades, and the political tensions that evolved from the missile deployments were not strong enough to rend the existing amicable German-American relations.

Terrorism—A Third Test

A witness to the explosion remembered that he "felt it more than heard it. The first sensations were the air in the room slapping me, stinging my face, and the impact tremor beneath my feet." Outside the morning air was "raining large metal fragments" and "a large, mushrooming cloud on the other side of the building began to darken the sky." The bomb that detonated in a nearby parking lot, on that day in August 1981, left cars "obliterated, twisted and piled atop each other, burning, as was the front of the headquarters building." It also left bodies "strewn everywhere." Former airman Robert Gelinas recalled "life changed for me that day."[117] Although German authorities in Bonn eventually assigned blame for the attack that left 15 people injured on a terrorist group known as the Red Army Faction (RAF), it was not the first, nor would it be the last, such incident.[118] Between 1971 and 1993, the RAF was responsible for killing at least 34 people.[119]

During the latter decades of the Cold War, the contemporary German-American political relationship that had already endured the strain of anti-war and anti-missile protests was tested a third time as it fell under the shadow of terrorist threats. A litany of violent acts that began in the early 1970s and lasted through to the late 1980s hammered at the network of Milcoms in Germany generating a pervasive atmosphere of fear and worry. Claiming responsibility for millions of dollars of property damage, personal injury and death were a collection of radical and disaffected groups operating in Europe whose goal was to make a political statement by striking at emblems of American imperialism. These included military facilities and any government perceived to be in collusion with the U.S.[120] Most important, they sought to further strain the existing German-American political bonds. In reality however, unlike the divisive political debates over Vietnam and Pershing missiles, terrorism offered a bridge for Americans to connect with their German hosts as both groups drew closer when confronting the common threat.

This specter of terrorism placed in jeopardy all members of the Milcoms and those Germans in close association with them through professional and social relationships. The cost of the threat paid by the Milcoms, in personnel casualties, mental anguish, and property damage was however far greater than histories and archived sources appraise. Collectively, these incidents informed American service members' and civilians' thinking about their mission in Germany and shaped their concerns about safety for themselves as well as that of their families. It was also a threat of long duration that occurred in three separate waves.

The first wave of attacks against the Milcoms began with two separate events, on May 11 and May 24, 1972, when terrorists detonated hidden explosive devices at the V [5th] Corps headquarters in Frankfurt and the USAREUR headquarters in Heidelberg. One American serviceman died and 13 others received injuries in the first incident, and three American service members died and five others received injuries in the second.[121] The Baader-Meinhof Gang, composed of leftist German political radicals claimed responsibility for both incidents dubbing this their "May offensive."[122] This was the beginning of the terrorists' anti-capitalist and anti-imperialist campaign directed against the Americans that sources show would ebb and flow for the next two decades.

Immediately after the May 1972 incidents the USAREUR command authority mobilized American Military Police (MP) assets for participation in counter-terrorist operations. As part of this the 709th MP Battalion "committed 100 percent" of its resources "for an extended period of time" to bolster security at the Creighton Abrams Complex, site of the V Corps headquarters.[123] At the same time, assets from the 15th MP Brigade received notification to assist local police authorities in providing roadblocks to prevent the infiltration of bombers into military facilities and housing areas in the greater Stuttgart Milcom region.[124] Press releases over the following days reveal the military hierarchy's heightened state of sensitivity to the vulnerability of attacks directed at the widespread network of Milcoms. Press releases reveal the military's elevated levels of anxiety and concern, "We expected things like this in Saigon, not here in Germany," noted one officer, and another lamented "it would be damn easy for anyone to plant a bomb" in the Officer's Club or the V Corps headquarters.[125] Concerns remained high as the German police headquarters in Augsburg was bombed the day following the attack on the American military headquarters. Responsibility for the assault, which resulted in extensive property damage and included some number of injuries, also fell to the Baader-Meinhof Gang.[126]

Reports of the arrest of Andreas Baader, leader of the gang and a small group of followers in a German police raid on a garage near the Frankfurt PX on June 1, 1972, bore mixed feelings.[127] While news of his arrest brought some relief it also generated fears of reprisal attacks. News sources reveal that military police and "a host of new security guards were checking ID cards, vehicle registrations, drivers licenses and other identification papers" at all American military facilities.[128] In addition, other precautions to protect dependent family members included the temporary closing of a number of DODDS schools, recreation facilities such as theaters and bowling alleys, and some PXs.[129] Aside from increasing physical security measures with increased guards, use of checkpoints and vehicle searches, local American military command authorities made some efforts to inform soldiers and their families and provide guidance about personal security awareness. Jeff White recalls that in November 1972 he and other new arrivals at the Rhein-Main Air Base in-processing point received a briefing that warned them "not to dress like Americans" when they traveled during off-duty time, "not to travel alone" and to constantly "look over your shoulder" for signs of danger. Once he reached his unit in Bad Kreuznach he received another series of warnings "to be on guard for drive-by shootings" by unknown assailants and "not to stand too close" to street-side windows in the barracks so as not to present a visible target.[130] Also during this time there was a joint American-German effort to raise awareness through the distribution of wanted posters for terrorist gang members still at large. These appeared in public places and in the Milcoms, especially in communal living and gathering spaces. American service members would see them on bulletin boards in the barracks, in recreation rooms, and often behind latrine doors.[131]

Sources suggest, however, that by late summer of 1972 heightened concerns over terrorist attacks on the Milcoms began to wane when reprisal attacks failed to materialize after the June capture of Baader. Reports of threats to military facilities dissipated and were quickly replaced by other front page news coverage that included the signing of a new Berlin accord

Opposite: German wanted poster for the Red Army Faction. Both the German civil and American military authorities distributed millions of these posters, in German and English, during the 1970s and 1980s to provide easier identification of gang members who were still at large. Image source: the author.

POLICE request  **BKA** your assistance.

Total of DM 4 million in rewards

Members of the terrorist association "Red Army Faction (RAF)" have committed these offenses:

- December 18, 1984 – attempted explosives attack on the NATO school in Oberammergau
- February 1, 1985 – murder of MTU executive Dr. Ernst ZIMMERMANN in Gauting
- August 8, 1985 – explosives attack on the U.S. air base in Frankfurt/Main and murder of U.S. serviceman Edward F. PIMENTAL in Wiesbaden
- July 9, 1986 – murder of SIEMENS director Prof. Dr. Karl Heinz BECKURTS and of his driver Eckhard GROPPLER near Strasslach
- October 10, 1986 – murder of ministry official Dr. Gerold von BRAUNMÜHL in Bonn-Ippendorf.

The following persons are among those wanted by police in connection with the offenses perpetrated by the "Red Army Faction":

Henning BEER
28 years old, approx. 180 cm (5'11") tall, large protruding ears, sometimes wears spectacles, presumably writes with left hand

Sabine Elke CALLSEN
25 years old, approx. 175 cm (5'9") tall, dimpled chin, V-shaped incision in middle of upper lip, 2 parallel horizontal neck wrinkles

Wolfgang Werner GRAMS
33 years old, approx. 180 cm (5'11") tall, skin blemish by left side of the nose

Birgit Elisabeth HOGEFELD
30 years old, approx. 170 cm (5'7") tall, sometimes wears glasses

Andrea Martina KLUMP
29 years old, approx. 170 cm (5'7") tall, skin blemish on left cheek

Barbara MEYER
30 years old, approx. 160 cm (5'3") tall, vertical postoperative scar on abdomen

Horst Ludwig MEYER
30 years old, approx. 175 cm (5'9") tall, approx. 1 cm long horizontal scar on forehead

Christoph Eduard SEIDLER
28 years old, approx. 180 cm (5'11") tall, right earlobe pierced, wears earring, approx. 1 cm long scar above right eye, skin blemish on left side of neck, sometimes wears glasses

Thomas SIMON
33 years old, approx. 180 cm (5'11") tall, wart on right temple

Sigrid STERNEBECK
37 years old, approx. 170 cm (5'7") tall, large protruding ears, earlobes attached to cheeks, sometimes wears glasses

Inge VIETT
42 years old, approx. 165 cm (5'5") tall, scar on right forefinger (1 cm long, on lower side of the third finger joint), sometimes wears glasses

The individual rewards offered are as follows:

- DM 1 million by the Bavarian Ministry of the Interior for information leading to the apprehension of the offenders involved in the attempted explosives attack on the NATO school in Oberammergau and the murder of Dr. Ernst Zimmermann;
- DM 3 million by private parties for information leading to the arrest of the "RAF" members involved in the murder of Prof. Dr. Karl Heinz Beckurts and his driver Eckhard Groppler;
- up to DM 50,000 for information leading to the apprehension of "RAF" members.

The rewards will be conferred and distributed with no recourse to courts of law. The offer of rewards does not apply to anyone whose professional duties include the prosecution of punishable acts. Every informant is free to use a person enjoying his/her confidence to supply information or to receive the reward so as to remain completely anonymous toward the authorities. Informants, or persons enjoying their confidence, providing information to criminal justice authorities can be given an assurance that the information they provide will be treated confidentially; this also applies to persons from the terrorist scene.

Current as of December '86

Terrorists
Caution – Firearms!

To offer information, contact any police service.

by the "Big Four" that would ease "East-West tensions which have simmered for more than 25 years" by permitting easier travel for Germans between the two halves of the divided city.[132] Even *Stars and Stripes* headline news of Angela Davis' acquittal in a sensational murder trial seemed to overshadow cares of terrorist threats to the Milcoms.[133] Although the remnants of the Baader-Meinhof Gang continued attacks against German targets during this time, hoping to leverage release of their leader, for the next four years they directed none of their vitriol against American targets in Germany.[134]

A lack of counter-terror activities during this respite suggests that instead of the American military and political elites awakening to a long-term threat, an atmosphere of complacency gradually descended upon the Milcoms. Although many of the increased security checks remained in place, the absence of other substantive steps makes this clear. For example, the publication of directive policy guidance and training procedures on how to prepare and react to potential terrorist threats was still years away. Even with the tragic September 1972 terrorist attack at the Münich Olympic Village, which left 11 Israeli athletes and coaches dead, the reaction of American leaders in Germany appeared tepid.[135] Although Milcom military police units provided support to German authorities during the Olympic incident military and political elites appeared to do little else to react to any threat.[136] In addition, the fact that a plethora of terrorist attacks against Americans occurred in other overseas countries between 1972 and 1976 suggests that a shift in the focus of attention to those locations may have contributed to the sense of complacency and false security among the Milcoms in the Federal Republic.[137]

On May 8, 1976, the suicide death of gang co-leader Ulrike Meinhof while incarcerated in a German prison triggered a second short wave of attacks on American Milcom targets. These lasted from June 1976 to January 1977. A series of explosions at the V Corps Headquarters and the nearby Officers' Club on June 1, 1976, was the signal event. During this incident the blasts injured 16 people including six service members, seven dependent wives, one American teenager, one American civilian, and one German civilian.[138] The next day, firebombs destroyed two trucks at the Air Force base in Wiesbaden. Claiming responsibility, the Revolutionary Cells released a message that proclaimed, "We see in our action a continuation of the armed anti-imperialist struggle."[139] The end of the year witnessed the next attack with a blast that destroyed the Officers' Club at Rhein-Main Air Base, near Frankfurt. Only eight people in the lunch-time crowd received injuries but officials estimated the property damage at nearly $1 million.[140] The Revolutionary Cells again claimed responsibility. The final event of this second, short terror wave occurred with the bombing of a fuel storage tank at a depot in the Giessen Milcom near Frankfurt. The Revolutionary Cells also bragged about this attack recorded in a short *Stars and Stripes* article buried on page 27, just above the daily stock report.[141] Once again, the thunderheads of terrorist threat seemed to pass quickly from over the Milcoms while authorities did little more than continue to maintain earlier security precautions.

A State Department historical summary of attacks against Americans for 1976–1977 reflects only the bombing in December at the Officers' Club; there was no mention of the June injuries at the V Corps Headquarters.[142] During these years the Department of the Army Historical Summaries (DAHSUM) also failed to mention the assaults against the Milcoms in Germany. The focus of terrorist concerns for the 1975 DAHSUM was for strengthening of security around nuclear storage sites, long considered potential terrorist targets.[143] There was also no mention of terrorism in the 1976 DAHSUM and in the 1977 summary the concern was only for a general determining of "the proper role for law enforcement agencies in countering terrorism on military installations and in assisting other federal agencies to counter the terrorist threat."[144] Hard guidance from political and military elites was still absent. By this time the total of casualties among the Milcoms in Germany was four Americans killed and 43 injured.

But if popular attention outside Germany failed to register concern over the attacks of this second wave, the atmosphere within the Milcoms throughout EUCOM was different. A litany of articles in *Stars and Stripes* through late 1977 reflected both the American's and Germans' struggle to come to terms with the terrorist threat and to understand its logic. There were some articles that simply sought to provide information such as one that offered "thumbnail sketches" of the various terror organizations. Titled "Terror Groups," it simply described "the terrorist groups of Western Europe" as a "varied collection of separatists, dedicated ideologues, and anarchists with deadly fervor but fuzzy goals."[145] Among the groups briefly described were the Red Army Faction, the Red Brigade, the Irish Republican Army and Red Aid. But carrying more gravity among contemporary print media pieces were those that cast a light on the questions of fundamental liberties that caused consternation for the Germans.

Suffering many more terrorist attacks, which resulted in greater casualties and more property damage than the American Milcoms during this time, the Germans found the challenge of balancing security with personal freedoms to be perplexing.[146] Articles in *Stars and Stripes* as well as other newspapers such as the *New York Times* outlined the fundamental issue facing the Germans. It was "how to sustain broad civic freedoms, tolerance, protection of the right to dissent and differ," while defending themselves "against an obsessive minority determined to destroy them."[147] As Americans in the Milcoms watched, "popular cells" in the German government called for tougher laws "even at the cost of due process and the erosion of some constitutional guarantees." As an example, by October 1977 the German government had forbidden defense lawyers "suspected of active collusion with the Red Army Faction" access to their incarcerated clients.[148]

These news articles also described confusion among the German people who began to see "violence from the left [as] all the more incomprehensible because it [did] not seem to be based on glaring social ills or injustices" especially at a time when West Germany was enjoying an economic resurgence.[149] Concerns for the violent strain in society were also present as one student activist remarked, "There is growing awareness that from a leftist position one can no longer condone such crimes. They hurt our cause."[150] The German populace was growing weary of the constant violence and threats. As one columnist observed, "the terrorist onslaught has led to demands for stiff law and order legislation in West Germany."[151] In parallel, a journalist for the *New York Times* noted that the continued global campaign of terrorism was "as much a *leitmotiv* in our time as Indian raids or burning heretics" in an earlier age.[152] Even Rudi Dutschke, political activist and organizer of many student-led anti-war protests in Germany, distanced himself from the violent energies noting, "We know only too well what the despotism of capitalism is. We do not want to replace it with a despotism [sic] of terror."[153]

Inge Queren, a German citizen, recalls with dismay returning home to Germany at this time after having lived in the U.S. with her husband for several years. As she remembers:

> Shortly after my return, the RAF murdered several high-ranking men like the president of the German Federal bank, and others. I remember my feelings of horror for having returned to a country that was now in the hands of the RAF it seemed. The news was full of reports about the RAF. At that time, having lived

in the US, and now living in Germany in the town of Kiel with no Americans anywhere near, I would call my state of mind as feeling out of place, struck by disbelief that something like the RAF was possible in Germany, and a deep regret for having returned to Germany. Again, to me there was this strong fear of uncertainty and insecurity, now not only from an enemy outside but also from the enemy (RAF) within. I felt much safer when we lived closer to American installations and we returned to Bavaria in 1983, and lived not too far away from the Grafenwoehr/Vilseck US military communities.[154]

Some Americans in the Milcoms voiced their frustrations as well. A letter to the editor of *Stars and Stripes* lashed out at terrorists and those that supported them. Commenting on the tenuous state of the contemporary Middle East peace process a writer from the Gelnhausen Milcom chastised those in that region who showed "support for the so-called Red Army Faction, a group that has no political affiliation and is in fact nothing more than a collection of assassins."[155]

As the previous collection of commentaries and remembrances suggest, the tense atmosphere in the Federal Republic provided an opportunity for the Americans to observe the German struggle with its complex demands of liberal democracy just as they had for decades faced the same issue through the challenges of the Civil Rights Movement and protests over involvement in Vietnam. It also afforded the Germans an opportunity to better appreciate the challenges that the Americans had faced during those years. In this they could both realize a reflection of themselves in one another and so the two societies could draw closer together across a bridge formed by that common challenge and experience.

During the four year hiatus in terror attacks against American targets that followed the January 1977 bombing in Giessen, the Department of Defense at last began to issue policy guidance.[156] An early document was DOD Directive 2000.12, "Protection of Department of Defense Personnel Abroad Against Terrorist Acts" issued in the form of a handbook. An attached cover letter from the Assistant Secretary of Defense noted that the document was not "formal DOD guidance" but it encouraged each component of the military services and local commanders to take necessary action to warn their personnel of existing terrorist threats and to provide for their proper training and protection.[157] Most important for the Milcoms, it stated as its purpose "to provide information and suggestions for reducing the risk and vulnerability of DOD personnel, their dependents, facilities, and material to acts of terrorism."[158] This general guidance inspired the publication of long-needed documents such as Army Regulation (AR) 190–52, *Countering Terrorism and Other Major Disruptions on Military Installations* (1978), and Department of the Army (DA) Pamphlet 190–52, *Personnel Security Precautions Against Acts of Terrorism* (June 1978) that provided more specific guidance to unit commanders and individuals. Examples of personal protective measures recommended to "members and their families" were practices to "minimize the likelihood of terrorist success" by avoiding daily routines, notifying co-workers and family of travel or work schedules and remaining aware of ones' surroundings.[159]

By early 1981, the RAF resumed its attacks on the Milcoms. For the next five years the German police together with their American military counter-parts and civilian investigators followed a trail of destruction in their attempts to thwart the threat against the German public and the American Milcoms. For the military communities the third wave of terrorist assault began in the early morning hours of March 29, 1981, when a bomb caused heavy damage to a building used by a U.S. Military Intelligence detachment in the town of Giessen. Although there were no injuries, the explosion caused approximately $100,000 in damages.[160] Close on the heels of this attack, terrorists fire-bombed the Frankfurt Milcom civilian personnel office.[161]

Again there were no injuries, but there was $10,000 in damages. These incidents received no notice in the U.S., overshadowed perhaps by concurrent headline news of the assassination attempt on President Reagan. Associated reports lasted for several days commanding most of the front page space of *Stars and Stripes*.[162] But within EUCOM the terrorist attacks did serve as a clarion call for the Milcoms to heighten their awareness and prepare for an extended siege that would last for the next few years.

The spring of 1981 witnessed subsequent attacks in April on the military duty train traveling between Bremerhaven and Berlin and a May firebombing of a new Army dining facility (mess hall) that caused $10,000 in damages.[163] During late August of that year terrorists staged a sensational bombing of the USAFE Headquarters at Ramstein Air Base within the greater Frankfurt Milcom. Fifteen individuals, civilian and military, received injuries and of those, two were German nationals.[164] That news stayed in the headlines for days joined by the report of a fire-bombing of service members' personal vehicles in a housing area in Wiesbaden during the small hours of the morning. In that incident the destruction totaled only four cars and a motorcycle.[165] If Milcom members felt unsafe at work, these other attacks would make them feel vulnerable at home as well. As David Kaylor recalls:

> U.S. military vehicles were easy to spot because of the license plates. Some of these home-grown German terrorists began targeting those vehicles with improvised car bombs. Eye witnesses said the car explosions began with a bright flash of light then the bomb detonated. We were given security briefings suggesting we start our vehicles with driver's door still open and one leg outside the vehicle. I know of at least one Army member who saved his own life by this method to start his car, which gave him time to dive from the vehicle when the light flashed before bomb detonation. The powers that be decided to change all U.S. military personal vehicle license plates from green to white—the color of normal German plates—and reduce the size. Our plates were still larger and more square than the rectangular German plates, and we still had "U.S.A." stamped on the plates, but it was a definite improvement.[166]

Date	Event	Casualties/Damage	Group Responsible
May 11, 1972	Bomb at V Corps HQs Frankfurt	1 killed, 12 injured	Baader-Meinhof Gang
May 25, 1972	Bomb at USAREUR HQs Heidelberg	3 killed, 5 injured	Baader-Meinhof Gang
Terrorist Attacks Disrupted by Arrest of Leaders, May 1972–June 1976			
June 1, 1976	Bombs at V Corps HQs Frankfurt	15 injured	Red Army Faction
June 2, 1976	Fire bombs Destroy 2 Air Force Trucks	Damage only	Revolutionary Cells
Dec 1, 1976	Bomb at Rhein-Main AFB Officers' Club	8 injured	Revolutionary Cells
Jan 7, 1977	Bomb Blast Destroys Gas Storage Tank	Damage only	Revolutionary Cells
Terrorist Attacks Against American Targets in Germany Abate, January 1977–March 1981			
Mar 29, 1981	Bomb destroys Frankfurt CPO office	Damage only	Red Army Faction
Mar 30, 1981	Bomb Destroys MI Building	Damage only	Red Army Faction

Date	Event	Casualties/Damage	Group Responsible
Aug 31, 1981	Cars Burned in Housing Area	Damage only	Red Army Faction
Aug 31, 1981	Bomb at USAFE HQs Ramstein	13 injured	Red Army Faction
Sep 15, 1981	Attack on GEN Kroesen's car	Damage to vehicle	Red Army Faction
Dec 7, 1981	Bomb Destroys Army Office in Kassel	2 injured	Red Army Faction
Jun 1, 1982	Bombs at Officer Clubs: Hanau, Bamberg, Frankfurt, Gelnhausen	Damage to buildings	Revolutionary Cells
Aug 3, 1982	Bombs Destroy 2 Jeeps	Damage to vehicles	Unclear
Aug 7, 1982	Bomb at Karlsruhe Officers Club	Damage to building	Red Army Faction
Aug 13, 1982	Bomb Damages American Car	Damage to vehicle	Red Army Action
Oct 9, 1982	Bomb Destroys Cars in Housing Area	Damage to vehicles	Red Army Faction
Oct 31, 1982	Bomb Destroys Cars in Housing Area	Damage to vehicles	Unclear
Dec 12, 1982	Bomb Destroys Cars in Housing Area	1 injured	Red Army Faction
Aug 8, 1983	Bombs Damage Hahn Officers Club	Damage to building	Red Army Faction
Aug 7, 1985	Attack on individual soldier	1 soldier killed	Red Army Faction
Aug 8, 1985	Bomb at USAFE HQs	2 killed, 10 injured	Red Army Faction
Nov 24, 1985	Car bomb at Frankfurt PX	33 injured	Red Army Faction
Apr 6, 1986	Bomb blast destroys Berlin nightclub	1 killed, 60 injured	Libya
	Totals	8 killed; 159 injured	

Table 8.3. Terrorist attacks against American targets. This consolidated listing shows attacks against American targets, casualties and damage in West Germany, 1972–1986. It only reflects the numbers of dead and injured Americans. (*Stars and Stripes*, *New York Times*, the *Washington Post* and the pamphlets "Lethal Terrorist Actions Against Americans, 1973–1985," Threat Analysis Division, Diplomatic Security Service, Bureau of Diplomatic Security, U.S. Department of State, undated; and "Terrorism Chronology: 1981–1986, Incidents Involving U.S. Citizens or Property," Report No. 86–531 F, Congressional Research Service, Library of Congress, January 29, 1986.)

September 1981 continued as one of the most violent months the Americans would endure in Germany. On Sunday, September 13th, terrorists assaulted the Frankfurt home of the U.S. Consul with three fire-bombs. There were no injuries and only minor damage.[167] But, only two days later, the Red Army Faction brazenly attempted to assassinate the USAREUR Commander-in-Chief, Frederick J. Kroesen, as he and his wife were riding in his chauffeured limousine just outside Heidelberg. The weapons used by the assailants included rocket-propelled grenades. They were unable to penetrate the armored car, but did surprise investigators with their sophistication. The shock effect of the ambush was widely felt. Front page news underscored the fact that, "the attack was the fourth on Americans in 16 days."[168] The West German government rushed to issue assurances that it would "do everything to guarantee the safety of U.S. troops, who are stationed in the Federal Republic for the protection of Western Europe."[169] The German press voiced concerns over Germany's image in the American media as a nation fraught with violence and ready to succumb to terrorist pressures. As one journalist in *Die Zeit* lamented, it was because of "the chain of attacks on American soldiers" and the "ugly images from Berlin" that the U.S. saw them as "defeatist" and that "European pacifism" was little more than a euphemism for a "Better Red than Dead" attitude. This was but one perspective in balance with those who also saw that the Federal Republic and the U.S. also had "a large reservoir of political, strategic and cultural similarities" to draw on to maintain their bond and withstand the blasts of terrorist bombs.[170]

December 1981 witnessed another attack with the bombing of an office used by a detachment of the U.S. Army 5th Artillery in the city of Kassel. Two servicemen received slight injuries and there was only minimal damage to the building. The article did however note, "There have been at least 15 attacks this year on U.S. installations in West Germany," but corroboration of that statistic is not possible through existing sources such as newspapers, official reports, or oral histories.[171] A survey of these sources for purposes of this study reveals the number to be only six. This suggests that the count reported by the journalist is either ambitious, erroneous, or that military and political authorities were controlling the news reports for other reasons, perhaps to allay general feelings of panic or worry among the Milcom populations.

The resurgence of a terror campaign in 1981 coincided with the beginnings of a nationwide peace and anti-nuke movement in Germany that followed the announcements to deploy the Pershing II missiles. As well-intended political groups gathered to protest the plans for NATO's upgraded missile shield some pundits in Germany noted the efforts of the RAF to integrate its aims with those of the peace movement and use the wave of anti–Americanism to create more havoc. However, a commentary in the news journal *Die Zeit* noted the failure of that plan. As the journalist observed, neither group was willing to compromise its principles. The RAF interpreted the "pacifism of the peace movement for weakness" and the Green Party, leaders in anti-nuke activism, "quickly distanced itself" from the RAF claiming that "by no means, individual or collective, was terror a suitable means to stop the nuclear movement in Europe."[172] Had the two combined, understanding where to draw the lines between peace and terror, and civil liberties and security, would have been less distinct making it more difficult for German and American authorities to react appropriately.

Still, the string of violent terrorist attacks by the Red Army Faction and the Revolutionary Cells continued periodically after 1982 and on through the following four years. There were seven separate incidents in 1982 beginning with a series of four nearly simultaneous bombings in June. In this, the largest attack of the year, three bombs detonated in the Frankfurt Milcom, one again at the V Corps Headquarters and two at a nearby Officers' Clubs. At the same time, there was an explosion at the Bamberg Milcom Officers' Club south of Stuttgart. There were no injuries although military investigators estimated the total damage to the buildings at $130,000.[173] The Revolutionary Cells claimed responsibility and noted in a communique "they hoped the bombings would be a prelude to what President Reagan" would experience during his visit to Germany the following week.[174] For the remainder of that year there were bombings in housing areas, a military motor pool, and an additional Officers' Club. The tally of damage included several jeeps, approximately a dozen personal vehicles belonging to Milcom members, and the Karlsruhe Officers' Club front door. Altogether, there was only one minor injury.[175] The only reported terror attack during 1983 was against the Hahn Air Base Officers' Club resulting in limited property damage with no recorded injuries.[176]

Through the early years of the 1980s military installations and local commanders were taking steps to increase their level of protection for their facilities and personnel even in the absence of specific directives from higher military commands. Some of these included "comprehensive ID card checks" and the "moving of parked cars away from possible terrorist targets" at major installations such as air bases.[177] Military authorities generally advised units and communities to "increase vigilance and take appropriate security measures."[178] Still, reaction to the string of attacks was not uniform throughout the Milcoms. For example, a spokesman for the V Corps Headquarters announced that aside from thorough identification checks "no other additional security measures were being taken as a result of Monday's bombing," even after repeated assaults on that facility.[179]

In reaction to the flush of terror assaults in 1981, including the ambush of General Kroesen, USAREUR headquarters in Heidelberg established an Anti-Terrorism Operations Center in 1981. The purpose was to coordinate information gathering from intelligence services regarding possible attacks, issue warnings when possible, and suggest improvements to counter-terrorist security measures.[180] But in 1983 an official from the center "warned against overreaction" by members of the Milcoms, commenting that "there are more people killed on the Autobahn or training accidents than in terrorist attacks."[181] He also advised, "It's really important that people don't develop a siege mentality."[182] In contrast however, an official from the same headquarters admitted, "Most of the attacks were aimed at soft targets like housing areas, motor pools, officers' clubs—facilities that are relatively vulnerable and much more difficult to secure."[183] It is difficult to understand how the purpose of these comments could assuage the concerns of Milcoms members in light of the previous attacks and attempts to increase local security measures.

With a brief lull in terror activity during 1984, authorities at USAREUR headquarters once again appeared quick to downplay terrorist concerns. Intelligence operatives opined "the threat from European terrorist groups is under control" and that "some of the most obvious security measures may disappear if the terrorist situation remains quiet."[184] A military police representative did add that both the Army and Air Force had "taken extra steps to protect generals and VIPs, the symbolic targets of terrorism."[185] In evidence of this, General R.L. "Sam" Wetzel recalls:

> In June 1984 after I took command of the U.S. V [5th] Corps in Frankfurt, the Germans arrested two terrorists in an apartment in Frankfurt. They found my picture and a sketch of the exact way to get in the Abrams building, go up the steps to the second floor, go down the hall to Room 120 to General Wetzel's office. That obviously got my attention. As a result we drove our Mercedes 500 armored car 5 different ways to get from my quarters in government housing in Bad Vibel to the Abrams building. Entrance to the government quarter's area was guarded, my house had closed circuit TV watching, and we had a safe room

upstairs. Traveling we had a chase car with men in civilian clothes and automatic weapons following us. By the way, my POV [privately-owned vehicle] had German license plates, changed every week. The CIA gave me a bulletproof metal briefcase for protection, and it was always in the back seat of the Mercedes 500.[186]

Another front page report crafted by *Stars and Stripes* staff journalists commented "police say there is no indication the [earlier] attacks have been aimed at American servicemembers [sic] and their families." It also noted, "There is no evidence the average GI or his family is a target."[187] This seems contradictory since sources reveal that up to this time the preponderance of attacks occurred against "soft targets," housing areas and officers' clubs, those places where Milcom members congregated.

During this period, Milcom members reacted in a variety of ways to the myriad of complicated tensions generated by the threat of terrorist activity. Sometimes they revealed frustration and at other times voiced attitudes contradictory to those officially prescribed by the hierarchy in news releases. One letter writer to the editor of *Stars and Stripes* from the Pirmasens Milcom declared her annoyance that newly emplaced security measures prevented the civilian taxi that regularly brought her to the PX from entering the military installation. By way of an explanation the deputy community commander commented, "There is no easy solution to the dilemma posed by the threat of terrorism on the one hand and inconvenience on the other hand."[188] Another letter writer from the Stuttgart Milcom chastised community members who flaunted security measures because of their inconvenience, especially senior officers. He suggested that "Anti-terrorism is a 'game' in which a life can easily be at stake, and it is about time that individuals with more rank than brains realized that the rules must be followed by everyone."[189] A number of Milcom members still showed concern for the level of security judging it to be insufficient, regardless of observations from higher levels of command. One service member offered his critique that:

> We claim to have good security at our bases, yet something like this (Ramstein) happens. If we don't make our military bases airtight, this type of thing is going to happen again. We can't afford to be lax. We need to concentrate on a strategy that can deal with these clowns. Just the other day, I was driving through the front gate in civilian clothes, flashed a green credit card at the guard and he waved me right through. For all he knew, I could have been Mr. Khadafy himself. Again, I say, we need to formulate a security system that is airtight.[190]

Another Milcom member's comments were in agreement. She noted, "I fail to see any evidence of repetitive security provisions in any of the places I visit. The measures taken are as individualized as the guards performing the duties." Commenting that guards "with baseball bats and empty weapons only leave me with feelings of doubt regarding combat readiness" she added, "realistically, all our lives are in danger, we just do not realize it yet."[191]

During this same time some Germans continued to voice their support for their American partners who were suffering these assaults. An officer of the *Bundeswehr* [German Army] commented in a letter that during unit meetings:

> We have often discussed the terrorist crimes of the Red Army Faction against installations of American armed forces. The crimes are a sign of ingratitude towards that power which saved us from a communist occupation after WWII and which made it possible the building of a democratic state by its military as well as a political shield. All terrorist actions are executed by an anarchistic minority which in no way can be seen as representing all the German people. I want to thank all American soldiers for their service to peace. They can be sure of the loyalty of the Germans.[192]

In the midst of the tension a separate letter sent to the editor of *Stars and Stripes* from an 18 year-old German student offered an apology:

> I want to apologize for everything some people of my country have been doing to the American soldiers during the past few years. I'm really ashamed of the way some show their gratitude toward people who are spending their time here in Germany, serving the U.S. armed forces to protect us, our freedom and our country. The people who throw bombs in American buildings, destroy American property and kill Americans who are here to help us do not deserve to be protected by you.[193]

By the summer of 1985 Milcom members' concerns regarding security proved to be well-founded as their estimate of the situation was closer to the truth than those of USAREUR authorities. In August of that year American and German investigators linked the murder of a young soldier near Wiesbaden to the bombing of the USAFE Headquarters just outside Frankfurt. As they discovered, terrorists had used identification documents taken from the soldier's body to gain access to the installation.[194] The blast of that attack at Rhein-Main Air Base on August 8th killed two Americans, a service member and a dependent wife, and injured 20 other service members and civilians. Property damage to personally-owned vehicles and military structures was extensive.[195] Investigators noted that it was no coincidence that the bomb exploded in the morning hours when the greatest number of service members would be arriving for work. As a base representative noted, "it was done very smartly to inflict very serious damage."[196] A week later Red Army Faction terrorists also claimed responsibility for the bombing of an AFN radio tower in Mönchengladbach that silenced transmissions for a short period.[197]

The November 24, 1985, terror bombing of the crowded Sunday afternoon Frankfurt PX contributed to removing any lingering doubts about Milcom members being primary targets. The car-bomb explosion injured 35 shoppers including 19 service members, 2 Department of Defense civilians, 11 American dependents, a German national and a Filipina. The American ambassador to Germany, Richard Burt, declared the bombing a "cowardly attack against men, women and children."[198] He later added, "The act was not only an attack on the United States, but also was an attack on German-American relations, on German freedom and democracy and on the rule of law."[199] Still, it wasn't until April 1986 when a terrorist's bombed ripped through a Berlin nightclub full of American service members and civilians that military and political authorities were finally ready to concede that U.S. personnel, facilities, and equipment in Germany were the primary targets.[200] Taking into consideration the previous incidents as well as current information received from intelligence sources German Interior Minister Friedrich Zimmermann announced that it was apparent "The U.S. military is the No. 1 target for Germany's terrorist Red Army Faction."[201] As a young dependent student attending a DODDS school Kyle Winward recalls the tense atmosphere of that time:

> The tensest days I recall were following the air strike in Libya by U.S. forces on April 14, 1986 (in response to the Berlin disco bombing, determined to be sponsored by Libya). Whether American students lived in post housing or on the Germany economy, normally we rode a U.S. Army olive drab bus to school. However, the week of the airstrikes we were bused in German public transportation buses. Portions of the post housing and exchange were barricaded. It was a very tense time—the closest that I personally felt to my life being in danger.[202]

The bombing of the *La Belle* disco in Berlin however was the last attack that specifically targeted Americans prior to the end of that decade and the conclusion of the third wave of violence. By that time a total of 8 Americans died and 159 sustained injuries at the hands of the Baader-Meinhof Gang, the Red Army Faction and the Revolutionary Cells. Today a memorial plaque is set on a wall near the original location. It reads simply, "In this building, on the 5th of April 1986, young people were killed by a criminal bombing." There is no reference to a terrorist attack."[203]

The total cost in Milcom human casualties and property damage through this third phase of terrorist threats however remains obscured in official summaries and histories. A report from the Congressional Research Service of the Library of Congress compiled in January 1986 titled "Terrorism Chronology: 1981–1986, Incidents Involving U.S. Citizens or Property" neglects a number of incidents that directly affected the lives of Milcom members in Germany.[204] Those missing were a string of attacks on vehicles in open housing areas, the bombing of the Hahn Officers' Club in August 1983, and the murder of Specialist 4 Edward F. Pimental by the Red Army Faction who robbed him of his identification.[205]

The Department of the Army Historical Summaries are less inclusive. The 1981 DAHSUM only references the assassination attempt on General Kroesen without mentioning other incidents or the attack on USAFE Headquarters. The 1982 DAHSUM mentions only the development of a threat analysis template without reference to a series of bombing in Milcom housing areas or the damage rendered to several officers' clubs by terrorist bombs. The 1983 DAHSUM simply states, "In West Germany the Revolutionary Cells terrorist group took credit for the bombing of two U.S. military bases," although there were many more attacks that year. It did however discuss the re-issuance of a number of previously released counter-terrorist training circulars, pamphlets, and regulations written to provide some guidance at the large unit or installation level.[206]

It was not until the 1989 DAHSUM that the terrorist threat overseas again received attention. A paragraph titled "International Terrorism and Espionage" noted:

> Although it did not seriously threaten the United States or American military capabilities, terrorism was a significant national security issue. Members of the Army and their dependents stationed abroad, because of their high visibility and symbolic representation of American policy or involvement in assisting local government to combat terrorism were among the terrorists' favored targets.[207]

That had been the case since 1972.

Congress also seemed to react slowly in alleviating the tense atmosphere in the American Milcoms in Germany. During the period lasting from the earliest attacks in the 1970s to the mid–1980s at least six legislative efforts failed to reach fruition until the passage of the 1984 Act to Combat International Terrorism became law on October 19, 1984.[208] Although its contents dealt primarily with establishing international cooperative initiatives to deal with terrorist activities it did acknowledge the existence of the tense atmosphere in which Americans overseas lived. In this regard it discussed the politically destabilizing efforts of groups such as the Baader-Meinhof Gang and West Germany's response by altering its penal code that limited certain individual liberties.[209] Most important, it referenced the existence of a "semi-permanent terrorist subculture" that spawned the appearance in West Germany of "second and even third generation terrorists," this suggested a reason behind the long duration of the terrorist threat against the German populace and the Americans in the Milcoms.[210] Still, this Congressional effort did not provide specifics to guide the armed forces or offer detailed guidance for force protection and security. The handful of DOD publications that eventually made their way down to the unit levels in EUCOM contained those.

As a third test of the German-American political bonds the terrorist threat revealed that a pervasive worry for violence was not a wedge that could drive the two partners apart. Instead, it provided a bridge over any chasm of differences that allowed them to draw closer in their concern, understanding and support for one another. In that context it served as a lens through which the Germans and Americans could study one another's reactions to the

ANNEX C

AUTOMOBILE SECURITY SUGGESTIONS

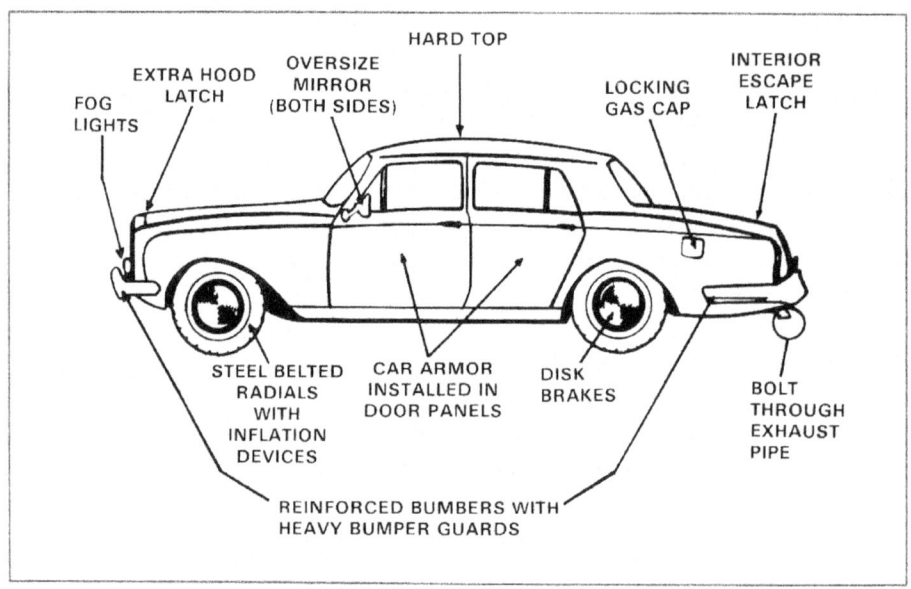

The following is a list of basic safety equipment you should always carry:

- Extra set of keys.
- Two spare tires and jack.
- Flashlight and high power lantern.
- Safety reflectors.
- Fire extinguishers.
- First aid kit.
- Sand or gravel for ice and snow.
- Knife, tools, shovel, and extra car parts.

The following are some additional suggestions for increasing your car's protection and safety:

- Intrusion alarm system.
- Automatic car starter.
- Additional car armor.
- Bullet-proof glass.
- Two-way radio.
- Roll bar construction.
- Extra battery.
- Reinforced gas tank, radiator, and battery.

G-10

Automobile Security Suggestions, TC 19–16. Annex C, "Automobile Security Suggestions." This figure from Appendix G, "Self-Protection Guide" of TC 19–16, printed at the height of attacks against American targets in Germany, provides individual service members, government civilians and dependents with tips to avoid becoming a terrorist casualty. Image source: the author. Publication source: TC 19–16, *Countering Terrorism on U.S. Army Installations*, April 1983. Permission granted by Public Domain.

challenges of maintaining the civil liberties of a democratic society in a crucible of terror. In the end, eight Americans died and 157 received injuries.

During the latter decades of the Cold War there were three sheering forces acting on the political bonds between Germany and America. Tensions generated by America's prosecution of a war in Vietnam generated the first test. The second developed from differences regarding deployment of upgraded nuclear missile systems on German soil. The third arrived with the flash and bang of a terrorist's bomb. In the first case American Milcom members discovered a need to test their exceptional civil rights by expressing themselves through free speech and demonstration. In the second Americans discovered that even occasional sharp differences could not rend a bond of friendship plaited from many essentially strong political, cultural, social, and economic fibers. In the last case Germans and Americans drew closer when each eschewed violence as a viable political option and saw in one another a partner struggling to preserve the delicate rights of a democracy.

Nine

Economic Challenges (1967–1990)

From "Rich Cousins" to "Poor Devils"

On August 1, 1973, *Stars and Stripes* ran a short article that reported the good fortune of a single American soldier living in the small community of Oberammergau. This was the result of his German landlady lowering his rent by 40 Marks. Commenting, "I didn't know the dollar devaluation had hit soldiers so hard," she readjusted it to a level comparable to February of that year, before the dollar's value had again suffered a decrease.[1] Although buried on page nine of the newspaper the story is significant for the insight it offers to the economic challenges American Milcom members faced during the latter decades of the Cold War. At the same time that one soldier gained a financial reprieve, others in the Milcoms were not as fortunate. Many individuals and families faced difficult financial decisions about purchasing food, paying rent and utility bills, foregoing entertainment or travel and whether to send family members back to the U.S. where life might be less expensive.[2]

These realities stood in stark contrast to the environment of vibrant growing economies that both the U.S. and West Germany enjoyed through the 1950s and the 1960s.[3] At that time the dollar generally maintained a commanding relationship with the Deutsche Mark (DM) and Americans in the Milcoms suffered few depravations caused by financial shortfalls. By the start of the 1970s however, emerging global dynamics resonated within the economic atmosphere in EUCOM. Central to these energies were the decoupling of the dollar from the gold standard on August 15, 1971, with the closing of the "gold window" by President Richard Nixon and the embargo of crude oil by the Organization of Petroleum Exporting Countries (OPEC) in October 1973.[4] The first action was a response to lax American economic policies that permitted a troubling trade imbalance and an excessive outflow of gold reserves.[5] A consequence of this was a 13.57 percent revaluation of the Deutsche Mark (DM) against the dollar in December 1971.[6] Eventually, the dollar would lose up to 60 percent of its value against the Mark by August 1996.[7] The second action by OPEC was a punitive response by Middle Eastern powers to the West's continued support of Israel during that period.[8] But both actions provided impetus to bring down the final curtain on an "economic golden age" that was "engendered in the United States" and signaled the start of an economic tempest for the Milcoms to weather.[9]

The economic *Wirtschaftswunder* of the 1950s and 1960s had revived West Germany's economy and set her on a course to become a powerful economic and political partner for the U.S. in latter decades. As American economic fortunes took a downturn with the devaluation of the dollar and the oil embargo, the economic juxtaposition between the nations changed. Within a short period of time many Germans noticed that the "rich cousins [Americans] have become the poor devils."[10] As in earlier postwar years the economics of the Milcoms again intersected those of the host communities at key points of contact such as a changing Deutsche Mark rate, fuel prices, taxes and hiring of local nationals. But unlike previous times, emerging economic realities presented different and often troubling crises for American service members, civilians, dependents and retirees living overseas.

Effects of the Changing Mark—The First Crisis

Within a week of President Nixon's decision to decouple the dollar from the gold standard monetary exchange centers through Europe reflected devaluations averaging of "about one percent."[11] West Germany however, had already begun the devaluation process and just prior to Nixon's announcement had lowered the dollar's value by 6.4 percent pegging the exchange rate at DM 3.425 to $1.[12] This followed a slight downward trend that had started two years earlier, but it was also the herald of a more precipitous drop off that would witness the decline of the dollar's value continuously through 1980. At that time it would eventually

Deutsche Mark to Dollar Exchange Rate, 1967–1990. The $ to DM ratio reached a low of $1= DM 1.82 by 1980, then eventually dipped to $1=DM 1.62 by 1990. Data sources: Historical Dollar-to-Marks Currency Conversion Page http://www.history.ucsb.edu/faculty/marcuse/projects/currency.htm#tables and Federal Reserve Bank of St. Louis http://research.stlouisfed.org/fred2/data/EXGEUS.txt.

reach a low of DM 1.74 to $1.[13] Many Milcom members wasted little time voicing their concerns.

By January of 1972, when the DM to dollar exchange rate registered DM 3.23 to $1, worries existed that pay and benefits were insufficient to meet basic and sundry needs. One senior enlisted service member from the Heidelberg Milcom recorded his apprehension in a letter to *Stars and Stripes* editor that a recent 7.21 percent pay increase could not keep pace with cost increases. He cited recent increases in fuel and EES prices as his main concerns particularly referring to an announcement that claimed, "Increased [operating] costs plus currency revaluation" were the primary reasons.[14] His letter also listed increases in other areas such as "laundry and dry cleaning services and bakery and ice-cream specialty products" as well as automotive items such as tires, batteries and repair parts.[15] A reply from an EES representative claimed that organization was "fully aware of the economic stress that American servicemen are under in Europe" and planned to "hold the line on prices to the extent that such action is economically feasible."[16] Meant to serve as a palliative, it could hardly have sufficed in the face of economic developments to come. One month after this letter the West German Bundesbank announced the official exchange rate at DM 3.185 to $1. Through the remainder of that year the dollar continued to slowly lose ground against the Mark so that twelve months later, in February 1973, it rested at DM 3.005 to $1.

As the Mark rate continued to sink, Milcom members remained vocal. A precipitous one-month drop of 7 percent in March 1973 inspired a letter from a Hanau Milcom spouse. Writing to the editor of *Stars and Stripes* she claimed that the existing economic situation was cheating "loyal Americans" like she and her husband. Observing "throughout history, countries that have won wars always came out better than the ones that have lost" she opined that "the Japanese and Germans have come out further ahead in the long run."[17] She went on to note that her husband's $12 pay raise "can't even compare with the rise in commissary [prices] and cost of Marks." As evidence she cited the increase of Enfamil baby formula from 24 cents to 32 cents a can, and sugar from 55 cents to 66 cents per five-pound bag.[18] The day after this spouse's diatribe appeared in print, *Stars and Stripes* officially announced the new rate of DM 2.81 to $1.[19] Letters such as these were representative of the emotions running high in most military communities as evidenced by contemporary press releases, and they insinuated the possible emergence of grassroots tensions between Americans and their host nation communities. But difficulties of that nature never truly materialized although living in close proximity to the Milcoms the Germans did witness the changes in their Milcom neighbors' lifestyles.

A feature article in the news magazine *Die Zeit* reported that of 200,000 service members stationed in the Federal Republic "16,000 are poor."[20] It also observed that the "invisible fences around the garrisons between Frankfurt and Heidelberg, Kaiserslautern and Ansbach have become even higher," shutting out German vendors who had peddled cheap artwork and carpets to the Americans, and shutting in those who could not venture far into the surrounding community because of the crippled dollar.[21] Noting the condition of their lives, *Die Zeit* added that many Milcom members could not then afford telephones or cars so that many either walked or rode the tram to work and that "a smart GI was sometimes spotted on a skateboard on the way back to the barracks."[22]

The devaluation of the dollar and the associated economic hardships soon became recurring front page material for *Stars and Stripes*. A headline article titled "Devaluation Hits GIs Hard," highlighted the difficulties most Milcom members commonly faced, although it provided few unexpected revelations to readers. The article featured the struggles of a junior non-commissioned officer (sergeant) who was working part-time at a movie theater to supplement his military pay because he could no longer afford to provide his children with "school paper or lunches."[23] The sergeant also noted, "We don't have a car. We can't afford it. To take the baby to the hospital, we have to take a taxi."[24] He was also considering sending his wife and children back to the States where they could "get along better on his pay than they do in Germany."[25] Most of these challenges, the article noted, were the result of the recent steep devaluation of the dollar by as much as 10 percent in February of that year and a German inflation rate of 8 to 10 percent per year.[26] The latter made shopping on the German economy more difficult for Milcom consumers, who sought deals to deflect rising PX and commissary prices.

Articles in *Stars and Stripes* were representative of the troubling economic trend in the Milcoms. Until late 1980, when the DM to dollar ratio changed again in the favor of the Americans, stories such as "Pfennig-Pinching GIs are Hurting" were common. It explained how the commanding general of the 8th Infantry Division confessed, "100 of his men had to send their wives home" because of economic difficulties, and how some soldiers in West Berlin were "crossing the Wall into Communist East Berlin for cheaper steak-and-wine meals."[27] A year later, an article titled "But when you can't Afford Things..." continued the theme of hardship. It described a common shortfall in soldiers' pay caused by the devalued dollar that precipitated challenges in managing rent, as they had to pay more than their wallets could offer. One example described how a military family in the Frankfurt Milcom received a monthly housing allowance of $128.10 but was paying DM 600 ($244.90) for a two-bedroom apartment. They made the difference up from an already taxed paycheck. Another soldier explained how his family's rental cost was normally $176 but "because of the dollar drop ran us about $184 last month."[28] These types of complaints and concerns echoed in articles and letters to the editor through to the early 1980s. For Joseph Weber, who arrived in the Amberg Milcom as a single soldier in 1975, expectations clashed with realities:

> At medic school in Fort Sam Houston, San Antonio, Texas, all the old timers, when they heard we were going to Germany, regaled us with stories of how well we would do for money over there. They all remembered 4 DM to the dollar. Told us all about how well we would do eating out, drinking up a storm, all the frauleins, etc. Well, it was about 2.5 DM to the dollar when I got there (1975) and headed down to 2 DM by the time (1978) I left.[29]

Although the declining exchange rate affected all Milcom members the hardest hit during these years were the families of the newest enlisted military personnel who had served in uniform less than two years. Policy forced them to live in German housing because they were not "command-sponsored" and therefore not permitted to reside in U.S. government quarters or rent-subsidized housing.[30] The expectation was that they would arrive in Germany without their families, but as many newspaper and journal articles reveal, a number of them made the personal decision to pay from their own pockets to bring over their spouses and children. Although they could not live in government housing in most cases their limited privileges did permit them to at least shop in the Milcom PX and commissary. Unfortunately, the military pay of a lower enlisted person was often not sufficient enough to weather the vagaries of fluctuating exchange rates or increases in PX prices, thus many of them lived on a financial edge often precariously balanced between just getting by and making hard choices. A perplexing policy web developed earlier in 1970 to govern the assignment of quarters in USAREUR only

Table 1
Point Scale for Grade

A Officer	B Warrant	C Enlisted	D Points
O-5		E-8	30
O-4	W-4	E-7	22
O-3	W-3	E-6	15
O-2	W-2	E-5	9
O-1	W-1	E-4	4

NOTES:
a. During a sponsor's initial housing processing, or when acting upon request for concurrent travel, points will be determined for grade. For example, an O3, W3 or E6 is awarded 15 points for rank.
b. When a sponsor is promoted, points will be recomputed for the new grade and the new DOR and added to those for DDCONUS.
c. Civilian employees' points will be determined the same as for military sponsors.

Table 2
Point Scale for Date of Rank (DOR)

A Months in Grade	B Points
1	.08
2	.17
3	.25
4	.33
5	.42
6	.50
7	.58
8	.67
9	.75
10	.83
11	.92
12	1.00

NOTES:
a. During a sponsor's initial housing processing or when acting upon a request for concurrent travel, determine points for DOR.
b. The initial computation will assign points through the end of the current calendar year. For example, a sponsor arriving 1 July with 2 years and 6 months in grade would be given 3.00 points (2.50 points for 2½ years in grade and .50 points projected to end December). On 1 January 1 additional point will be awarded for the coming calendar year.
c. The points given for DOR cannot exceed the point spread between grades, as shown in Table 1. For example, an E6 with 9 years in grade can only be given 7 points for DOR. (The difference between 15 points for E6 grade and 22 points for E7 grade).

Table 3
Point Scale for Date Departed CONUS (DDCONUS)
Month Departed CONUS and Creditable Points

Day Deptd CONUS	Jan	Feb Leap Year	Mar	Apr	May	Jun	Jul	Aug	Sep	Oct	Nov	Dec
1	12.00	11.00	11.00	10.00	9.00	8.00	7.00	6.00	5.00	4.00	3.00	2.00	1.00
2	11.97	10.96	10.97	9.97	8.97	7.97	6.97	5.97	4.97	3.97	2.97	1.97	.97
3	11.94	10.93	10.93	9.94	8.93	7.94	6.93	5.94	4.94	3.93	2.94	1.93	.94
4	11.90	10.89	10.90	9.90	8.90	7.90	6.90	5.90	4.90	3.90	2.90	1.90	.90
5	11.87	10.86	10.86	9.87	8.87	7.87	6.87	5.87	4.87	3.87	2.87	1.87	.87
6	11.84	10.82	10.83	9.84	8.83	7.84	6.83	5.84	4.84	3.83	2.84	1.83	.84
7	11.81	10.79	10.79	9.81	8.80	7.81	6.80	5.81	4.81	3.80	2.81	1.80	.81
8	11.77	10.75	10.76	9.77	8.77	7.77	6.77	5.77	4.77	3.77	2.77	1.77	.77
9	11.74	10.71	10.72	9.74	8.73	7.74	6.73	5.74	4.74	3.73	2.74	1.73	.74
10	11.71	10.68	10.69	9.71	8.70	7.71	6.70	5.71	4.71	3.70	2.71	1.70	.71
11	11.68	10.64	10.66	9.68	8.67	7.68	6.67	5.68	4.68	3.67	2.68	1.67	.68
12	11.65	10.61	10.62	9.65	8.63	7.65	6.63	5.65	4.65	3.63	2.65	1.63	.65
13	11.61	10.57	10.59	9.61	8.60	7.61	6.60	5.61	4.61	3.60	2.61	1.60	.61
14	11.58	10.54	10.55	9.58	8.57	7.58	6.57	5.58	4.58	3.57	2.58	1.57	.58
15	11.55	10.50	10.52	9.55	8.53	7.55	6.53	5.55	4.55	3.53	2.55	1.53	.55
16	11.52	10.46	10.48	9.52	8.50	7.52	6.50	5.52	4.52	3.50	2.52	1.50	.52
17	11.48	10.43	10.45	9.48	8.47	7.48	6.47	5.48	4.48	3.47	2.48	1.47	.48
18	11.45	10.39	10.41	9.45	8.43	7.45	6.43	5.45	4.45	3.43	2.45	1.43	.45
19	11.42	10.36	10.38	9.42	8.40	7.42	6.40	5.42	4.42	3.40	2.42	1.40	.42
20	11.39	10.32	10.34	9.39	8.37	7.39	6.37	5.39	4.39	3.37	2.39	1.37	.39
21	11.35	10.29	10.31	9.35	8.33	7.35	6.33	5.35	4.35	3.33	2.35	1.33	.35
22	11.32	10.25	10.28	9.32	8.30	7.32	6.30	5.32	4.32	3.30	2.32	1.30	.32
23	11.29	10.21	10.24	9.29	8.27	7.29	6.27	5.29	4.29	3.27	2.29	1.27	.29
24	11.26	10.18	10.21	9.26	8.23	7.26	6.23	5.26	4.26	3.23	2.26	1.23	.26
25	11.23	10.14	10.17	9.23	8.20	7.23	6.20	5.23	4.23	3.20	2.23	1.20	.23
26	11.19	10.11	10.14	9.19	8.17	7.19	6.17	5.19	4.19	3.17	2.19	1.17	.19
27	11.16	10.07	10.10	9.16	8.13	7.16	6.13	5.16	4.16	3.13	2.16	1.13	.16
28	11.13	10.04	10.07	9.13	8.10	7.13	6.10	5.13	4.13	3.10	2.13	1.10	.13
29	11.10		10.03	9.10	8.07	7.10	6.07	5.10	4.10	3.07	2.10	1.07	.10
30	11.06			9.06	8.03	7.06	6.03	5.06	4.06	3.03	2.06	1.03	.06
31	11.03			9.03		7.03		5.03	4.03		2.03		.03

NOTES:
a. During a sponsor's initial housing processing, or when acting upon a request for concurrent travel, points will be determined for DDCONUS.
b. For example, a sponsor departing CONUS on 19 July. Enter the table on day departed CONUS and across to the month of July and awarded 5.42 points for the current calendar year. Note that the table projects the points through the end of the current calendar year (.42 points for July and one point each for months August, September, October, November, and December.)
c. On 1 January for each succeeding year 12 points will be awarded to all sponsors for the coming calendar year.
d. The DDCONUS will be determined in accordance with Annex H.

Tables for Housing Eligibility. Tables 1–3 of the 1970 USAREUR policy for determining housing eligibility. They governed officer grades O-1 to O-5, warrant officer grades W-1 to W-4 and enlisted grades E-4 and above. Source: *Stars and Stripes*, December 3, 1970, 8, with permission.

seemed to entangle and confuse them more when balanced against the availability and cost of housing that varied by each Milcom.[31]

As a result of the difficult policy rubric, lower enlisted Milcom members often registered their frustration through letters to *Stars and Stripes* editor. Although there is no data to support such a suggestion, the possibility exists also that negative attitudes regarding conscription contributed to these feelings by compounding the anger surrounding housing problems.[32] Still, some examples of this consternation came from a collection of pleas that included comments such as:

> Why are Americans stationed in Europe being sacrificed? Why do we have to carry the burden of the dollar devaluation? Many men in Europe are E-4 [sergeant pay grade] and below. They have their families here. It will soon be impossible for them to keep their families here. That means wives and children go home and Dad goes back to the Drug Den (the barracks). What kind of a morale [sic] will the Army have with this type of a situation?[33]

A similar complaint joined the first on the same page:

> If we live on the economy we pay double for housing with practically no protection from the American or German governments. This taking advantage of Americans as a group is apparent in other areas also. We have watched our young soldiers send their wives and children home because the value of the American dollar has plummeted drastically.[34]

Joseph Weber also recalls the plight of the non-command sponsored family well:

> Housing for the unaccompanied family [non-command sponsored].... Well, you had to do the best you could, what you could afford. You got your extra money for having a dependent, but not the extra money for having a dependent in Germany...[your] spouse did not really exist in Germany as far as the Army was concerned. So, yes, it was tough. It had to be tough. Glad I did not have to deal with it. The unaccompanied family got the "American penthouse" housing out in town. You know, that European top floor just under the roof, with the sloping ceiling. Many a man has hit his head on the ceiling using the toilet tucked under the sloping roof. Sometimes the apartment would not even have access to hot water. People (the wives) would heat water on [the] stove and take bird baths from the sink for a year ... seriously. The male soldier could just go and use the barracks' showers.[35]

The military hierarchy in USAREUR was, however, not blind to the plight of Milcom families caused by the devalued dollar and attempted to provide some financial relief. In August 1973, a new series of Cost-of-Living Allowance (COLA) indices appeared on the front page of *Stars and Stripes*. The indices determined the authorized COLA based on geographical region (Index 104, 120, or 130) and grade (rank) and number of dependents within each index. It included non-command-sponsored dependents of both officers and enlisted personnel.[36] The need for clarification of both housing eligibility and COLA allocations was apparent as the cries for financial relief increased and Milcom commanders began assessing the housing costs and requirements for their communities. This was accomplished in part by the use of a Housing Cost Data Survey (DD Form 376) conducted annually among Milcoms. As well-intended as these initiatives were, they were not a complete palliative for the existing economic malaise.[37]

Although exact historical data is not available for each Milcom during the 1970s, it is still possible to understand the difficulties communities faced through periodic references highlighted in news stories. The Bamberg Milcom offers a historical snapshot of one community's struggle to balance needs against availability and affordability of housing. In December 1977 there were 6,000 service members plus 3,300 dependents residing in the German town of 75,000. For that population the military provided 722 sets of government quarters for command-sponsored families. Another 1,300 families were living in a circle of German communities around the military *Kaserne*, Warner Barracks. Of the second group, 550 families were non-command- sponsored.[38] That equated to 27 percent of the Milcom families at Bamberg living in non-sanctioned housing, with reduced privileges, on a meager pay check that was losing ground against the DM. Their circumstances were dire and the community sergeant major lamented as he fretted over the challenge facing young enlisted soldiers, "Somebody has got to tell people back in the States what the situation is here."[39] It was not with a note of irony that this feature article shared front page space with another titled "Dollar Plunge Continues," that announced "for the second day in a row the dollar fell to new lows against

Cost-of-living Index 104

Grade	none	1	2	3	4	5
O8-10	$0.80	$0.95	$1.00	$1.05	$1.10	$1.15
O7	.75	.95	1.00	1.05	1.10	1.15
O6	.75	.90	.95	1.00	1.05	1.10
O5	.75	.90	.95	1.00	1.05	1.10
O4	.70	.90	.90	.95	1.00	1.05
O3	.65	.80	.85	.90	.95	1.00
O2	.60	.75	.75	.80	.85	.90
O1	.55	.65	.65	.70	.75	.80
W4	.70	.85	.90	.94	1.00	1.05
W3	.65	.80	.85	.90	.95	1.00
W2	.60	.75	.80	.85	.90	.95
W1	.60	.70	.75	.80	.85	.90
E9	.70	.80	.85	.90	.95	1.00
E8	.65	.80	.80	.85	.90	.95
E7	.60	.75	.75	.80	.85	.90
E6	.55	.65	.70	.75	.80	.85
E5	.50	.60	.65	.70	.70	.75
E4	.45	.55	.60	.60	.65	.70
E3	.45					
E2	.45					
E1	.40					

Cost-of-living Index 120

Grade	none	1	2	3	4	5
O8-10	$3.90	$4.80	$5.00	$5.25	$5.50	$5.75
O7	3.80	4.70	4.90	5.15	5.40	5.65
O6	3.75	4.60	4.85	5.05	5.30	5.55
O5	3.65	4.50	4.70	4.95	5.20	5.45
O4	3.55	4.40	4.60	4.85	5.10	5.35
O3	3.35	4.10	4.30	4.50	4.75	5.00
O2	3.05	3.65	3.85	4.05	4.30	4.55
O1	2.70	3.20	3.35	3.55	3.80	4.00
W4	3.45	4.25	4.45	4.70	4.95	5.20
W3	3.35	4.05	4.25	4.50	4.70	4.95
W2	3.10	3.75	3.95	4.15	4.40	4.65
W1	2.95	3.50	3.70	3.95	4.15	4.40
E9	3.40	4.10	4.35	4.55	4.80	5.05
E8	3.20	3.90	4.10	4.30	4.55	4.80
E7	3.05	3.65	3.85	4.05	4.25	4.50
E6	2.85	3.35	3.55	3.75	3.95	4.20
E5	2.55	3.00	3.20	3.40	3.60	3.80
E4	2.30	2.75	2.90	3.10	3.25	3.40
E3	2.20					
E2	2.15					
E1	2.05					

Cost-of-living Index 130

Grade	none	1	2	3	4	5
O8-10	$5.85	$7.20	$7.50	$7.85	$8.25	$8.60
O7	5.70	7.05	7.40	7.75	8.10	8.50
O6	5.60	6.95	7.25	7.60	7.95	8.35
O5	5.45	6.75	7.10	7.40	7.75	8.15
O4	5.35	6.60	6.95	7.25	7.60	8.00
O3	5.05	6.10	6.45	6.80	7.15	7.50
O2	4.55	5.45	5.75	6.10	6.45	6.80
O1	4.00	4.75	5.05	5.35	5.65	6.00
W4	5.20	6.40	6.70	7.05	7.40	7.75
W3	5.00	6.05	6.40	6.70	7.05	7.45
W2	4.70	5.60	5.95	6.25	6.60	6.95
W1	4.40	5.25	5.60	5.90	6.20	6.65
E9	5.05	6.15	6.50	6.85	7.20	7.55
E8	4.85	5.85	6.15	6.45	6.80	7.20
E7	4.55	5.45	5.75	6.05	6.40	6.75
E6	4.25	5.05	5.35	5.65	5.95	6.30
E5	3.80	4.50	4.80	5.05	5.35	5.70
E4	3.50	4.10	4.35	4.60	4.90	5.10
E3	3.30					
E2	3.25					
E1	3.05					

USAREUR *per diem* Cost-of-Living Allowance (COLA). The indices reflect grade (rank) and number of dependents. Source: *Stars and Stripes*, August 15, 1973, 9, with permission.

the West German Mark," reaching a rate of DM 2.13 to the dollar. The news also recorded the sarcastic observation of a Swiss banker who noted, "There is only one thing that is certain. The dollar is the new downhill world champion."[40]

Command-sponsored or not, living on the economy in German housing during times of economic duress presented a daunting set of challenges for most married Milcom members and often caused elevated emotions. One incensed spouse wrote to the editor of *Stars and Stripes* to claim that soldiers living on the economy would have to send their families home because they "are not getting any help from the President." She went on to observe that if "any man" wants to be in the armed forces "to keep his country free" then "at least the President should help keep his family with him."[41] Another letter writer highlighted a common frustration that Milcom members could not exchange their dollars into DMs at a fixed rate but were instead subject to the vagaries of one that fluctuated on a daily basis. This made it more difficult to pay their German landlords a consistent amount. The lengthy official reply from an officer in the Finance and Accounting Division of USAREUR Headquarters provided cold comfort by essentially noting that it was the result of an established operating system agreed upon between the U.S. Treasury Department and the German State Bank, and was not going to change.[42]

By December 1977 the difficult circumstances of Milcom families living on the economy still dominated the front page of *Stars and Stripes*. The banner headline for December 3rd read "Dollar Debacle Leaves GI Families on Economy Eking out a Bare Living."[43] An annotation by the editor just beneath the headline noted that the "U.S. Dollar had dropped to an all-time low last week in West Germany when a single greenback would buy 2.14 Deutsche Marks."[44] The text of the two-page article offered recurring scenarios that had appeared in print consistently during that decade: wives who had to take jobs to make ends meet, bills that could not be paid, families that might be sent home and individual frustrations. One soldier lamented, in a less than exceptional tone, "If they're (the military services) supposed to be taking care of their people, they're not. If they'd give me an honorable discharge right now, I'd take it."[45]

As Randy Tucker recalls, living on the economy, even when authorized because of a lack of government quarters, did hold its own unique set of challenges:

> There was a marked change in GI economic situation from June 1971 to May 1974. In my specific case, with 3–4 of us in a [German] house and the 4–1 exchange rate we did well. Hohenpeißenberg had a tiny PX at the station but in 1971 [it] wasn't used much, with the person in charge mostly stocking baby food and diapers for his girlfriend's family. I ran the PX from 1972 to 1974 and as the exchange rate dropped it was used more and more. Frozen pizza, canned food, and even beer could be purchased. Instead of making the run to the Münich PX to restock once a month, we were going twice. As the exchange rate went down, the two of us that had cars started saving the gas ration coupons, instead of driving the cars to Münich we drove one of the site 3/4–ton trucks. I don't remember early on but by 1972 all our married troops lived in military housing. Although not allowed, we also might use liquor and cigarettes for payment at the bar we visited most often.[46]

Regardless of the hue and cry that appeared in print from disgruntled Milcom members, the military command structure was not insensitive to the burdens facing Milcom members living on the economy. It showed concern by bringing available resources to bear. One example was a "Concern Conference" hosted by the Army's V Corps headquarters in June 1971. The focus was the "forgotten men of the military community" and included enlisted soldiers in the grade of E-5 and below and their spouses. The purpose was to acquaint those living on the economy with facilities and services available to them through the Army Community Services office (ACS) as well as the engineer and personnel offices.[47] These types of gatherings continued periodically, at the major unit level, during subsequent years.

Others examples of organized initiatives exist. As commanding general of the 1st Infantry Division (Forward) in Göppingen from 1977–1978, GEN R. L. "Sam" Wetzel recalls:

I formed a Woman's Advisory Council that included reps from young wives on the economy. Members included the PX and Commissary Managers, the Transportation Manager, the Post Engineer and wives of Commanders including my wife. I chaired the once a month meeting. We worked on subjects like economy housing managers gouging our troops. We had inspections of their conditions, etc. We set up a bus system for the economy wives. One wife said, for example, why can't the buses stop first at the child care building and last at the commissary so the ice cream does not melt? We changed the routing the next day! Many other facility hours were changed for those living on the economy. The other thing we did in Göppingen was to beef up the sports program for the troops with commissioners for each of many sports to keep the troops and their families off the streets and away from the drugs, and the bad discos dealing drugs and charging high fees.[48]

Another effort to bolster the economic welfare of families living on the economy was the awarding of Station Housing Allowance (SHA) pay. This varied by region and community according to the average rent by type of available housing. An annual USAREUR-wide Housing Cost Data Survey, which targeted all community members living on the economy, captured the input used in determining the SHA allocations made to Milcom members' pay to offset periodic increases in rent. Though well-intended this initiative often fell short of its goal. As a USAREUR representative noted in response to a soldier's query "shortcomings in the survey were evident."[49] Foremost was the fact that the previous year's survey was the basis for the current year's SHA. This meant allocations never matched needs as the dollar continued a monthly slide against the DM. The data survey also fell short because some respondents "did not report all housing costs" such as heating fuel or electricity and others did not respond because they "considered it an invasion of their privacy."[50] Still, each year authorities added an increasing number of communities to the list of those eligible to receive the SHA.

Efforts such as COLA adjustments, SHA, and the Housing Cost Data Survey were necessary at the time considering the numbers of Milcom members residing on the economy. By the spring of 1973 the chief of the USAREUR Housing Office announced that there were approximately 50,000 Army, Air Force, and Navy families living in non-government sponsored housing.[51] Of that number 35,000 were Army families in Germany but only 16,000 of those were eligible for government housing. The military however did not "have the quarters to give them."[52] The remaining 18,000 families were "not authorized government quarters under any circumstances under the current criteria."[53] By comparison, the Air Force listed 6,100 families on the economy with 4,600 eligible for government housing.[54] By late summer of that year the Army was reporting that the more than 17,000 non-command-sponsored families in Germany had experienced a 40 percent increase in "what they must pay for rent, utilities, telephone, transportation, and other services." This increased hardship was a result of the devalued dollar and the high rate of inflation in Germany.[55] In this context, the U.S. government began to act to alleviate the housing crisis yet another way in light of the dollar's chronically weakened state. A report carried in *Stars and Stripes* outlined the Defense Department's plan to "double the number of leased and rental –guarantee family housing units" by 1974.[56] The majority of those would be in Germany in Milcoms with the heaviest troop concentrations such as Aschaffenburg, Baumholder, Kitzingen, Landstuhl, and Mannheim. Although it would take years for the impact of such actions to come to realization initiatives such as the COLA adjustments, SHA, the Housing Cost Data survey and increases in leased housing were necessary efforts to alleviate financial hardship and maintain core morale among the Milcom members not living in government quarters tucked behind the walls of the Little Americas. By April 1979 the situation was critical as the dollar was worth only DM 1.88.[57]

It wasn't until almost 1979 that the plight of EUCOM's lowest ranking enlisted service-

Families on the Economy Cartoon. The dollar devaluation during the 1970s forced many lower-enlisted families to make hard financial decisions. Image source: *Stars and Stripes*, December 15, 1977, 8, with permission.

members finally resonated in Congress. The House Military Compensation Committee held hearings to investigate the "financial problems" experienced by the junior enlisted personnel overseas in May and December of 1978. As the chairman noted, the reasons for the hearings was that the "plight of our junior personnel has received a considerable amount of media coverage and has been the source of numerous complaints by concerned citizens, government officials, and parents, and by service members themselves."[58] These concerns were however, several years late. Still, as a result of the hearings the military suggested adjustments in compensation for lower enlisted personnel that included increases in weight allowances for shipment of household goods overseas, a refundable tax credit, and a $30 monthly family separation allowance.[59] It also gained leverage for increased funding to support the construction of much needed housing units in Germany. As the hearings also revealed, by 1979 there were 293,000 service members of all grades in Europe (90 percent Army) and of those, approximately one third were lower-enlisted personnel with less than 2 years in service.[60] For them the burden was the greatest.

American Retirees Abroad

Another Milcom sub-group living on the economy, which grew in size during the immediate postwar decades, was the community of military and civilian retirees. It was a population within EUCOM that reached nearly 24,000 by May 1973 and, like other Milcom groups, was competing for limited resources.[61] As the economic downturn began for Americans overseas, many retirees felt as if they "were indeed the forgotten man of the Armed Forces."[62] Summarizing their challenges, one retiree lamented that they did not have access to the PX and commissary, could not vote in U.S. elections without permanent residency in the U.S., did not enjoy equal opportunity for employment at U.S. overseas facilities, could not cash checks at military banking facilities, could not use tax-free gasoline coupons at EES stations and had limited access to Army Post Offices (APO).[63] This placed them at a disadvantage for conducting most personal business and shopping on the German economy where the dollars from their retirement pay often drew rates less advantageous than the greater Milcom population. As one retiree recalls of that time, they "monitored the exchange rate on a daily basis hoping to convert their dollars when the situation was most favorable. This was not an easy task. It was more like shooting dice than a scientific statistical analysis."[64]

Over time the chorus of disgruntled retirees continued to grow. Another letter writer offered a protest that for retirees "Equal Opportunity is nothing but a slogan but in reality not a practice!" His claim was that both USAREUR and USAFE had "put out the word to civilian personnel officers that dependent personnel have priority for jobs over retirees."[65] A retired sergeant major living in Germany concurred in a separate correspondence adding, "I thoroughly disagree with some of the policies that state it's cheaper and better to hire a dependent. Why, look at the rate of turnover of dependents."[66] A retired master sergeant noted the years of experience that retirees could contribute if hired by the U.S government to fill overseas positions and added, "The [U.S.] government says 'Stop the gold flow!' I say, okay, hire us, and we'll stop spending so much money on the German economy. We pay taxes on the German economy, not to Uncle Sam."[67] The military hierarchy was not unsympathetic to the woes of these retired Americans. Attempting to deflect the litany of charges and accumulated complaints the editor of *Stars and Stripes* used a lengthy response to outline the official policy found in the Status of Forces Agreement (SOFA) that governed access to privileges for Americans living in the Milcoms:

> The Status of Forces Agreements with many countries precludes exchange, commissary and other tax-free privileges for retirees. The Defense Department does not encourage overseas residence of retirees because it throws an added burden on the existing medical facilities, etc. While any purchases retirees make tend to increase logistics requirements for the various posts and bases abroad. The residence of retirees abroad contributes to the dollar drain or U.S. balance of payments deficit. Any privileges that retirees lose in living abroad tend to diminish the purchasing power of their retirement income. For example, U.S. military retirees residing or visiting in West Germany who wish to patronize exchange and commissary stores are required to obtain a status document through MP customs units and to pay 19 per cent duty to a German customs office on all of their monthly purchases at U.S.-controlled facilities.[68]

Believing they were suffering neglect, and in some cases worse economic challenges than lower enlisted families living on the economy, retirees attempted to organize. One frustrated member of that group exclaimed, "As single individuals, we are without voice enough to impress anyone and very few people are tuned to our wavelength." He added, "Banding together into a strong group will make our situation change for the better."[69] Shortly afterward, the Voice of the European Retirees (VOTERS) had formed with 300 members.

Unfortunately, the VOTERS' well-intentioned efforts to maintain a presence and voice for the retirees during the economic trials of the 1970s eventually came to naught. Although the group held periodic meetings such as the one scheduled for October 13, 1973, at the Bavarian American Hotel in Nuremberg, an absence of subsequent references to VOTERS in available sources suggests that the initiative lost momentum and members abandoned it at some point.[70] The one gain may have been in its raising an awareness of the retirees' presence for the USAREUR command structure. But this did not appear until October 1979 with the creation of an Army Retirement Service Office (ARSO) within the USAREUR Personnel Office. An announcement in *Stars and Stripes* noted, "The council's purpose will be to represent the interests of retirees in Europe by directing their concerns to policymakers."[71] It listed hotlines to call and encouraged interested retirees to request membership through the ARSO.

Still, it is not clear that the retiree council did little more than serve to placate some disgruntled individuals. A meeting of the council a year later focused on "getting retirees involved with voluntary work in USAREUR" and did not include in its planned agenda any discussion of obtaining improved privileges for retirees or easing economic burdens.[72] Notable however, was the drop in population numbers of retirees in EUCOM. The council referenced its efforts to assist "some 4,000 retired soldiers living in Europe."[73] This was a significant decrease from the 24,000 reported just six years earlier in May 1973. That drop was not a surprise to some. As retired officer Larry Applebaum notes:

> The retirees who were no longer employed had to face the challenge of making ends meet, because they were essentially on a fixed income without any cost of living adjustments.... When the exchange rate became unfavorable, many retirees who had residence in Germany opted to return to the States. Similarly, future retirees who were considering retiring in Germany changed their plans and went back to the States.[74]

Still, evidence of USAREUR's inability to resolve core issues of employment and increased privileges for retirees remained into the 1980s. A letter to the editor of *Stars and Stripes* in July 1982 echoed the same concerns presented a decade earlier. Its writer reiterated how "U.S. and German authorities have ignored job discrimination against U.S. military retirees in Germany" noting "this has been going on for many years."[75] The blame again fell on the standing SOFA that "not only denies employment to a certain group of people, it denies employment to QUALIFIED personnel."[76] A reply from a representative of USAREUR's civilian employment office offered little resolution and only cited a confusing amalgam of German and American policies that stated "U.S. residents of NATO countries" could only gain employment in non-appropriated fund positions "under local national employment conditions."[77] There is a dearth of evidence that shows whether retirees' difficult economic situation ever received full attention from USAREUR or EUCOM authorities or gained any degree of resolution prior to 1990. Instead, military and civilian retirees, peripheral members of the Milcoms, continued to suffer the same vagaries of uncertain economic conditions tied to the fluctuating DM rate that affected all Americans living on the economy.

Fuel Embargo – The Second Crisis

Exacerbating the problems of a devaluated dollar was a second crisis in early 1974. On February 22nd of that year a banner headline in *Stars and Stripes* announced a 50 percent increase in gas prices.[78] Coming at a time when Milcom members' dollars were already stretched thin, the price of gasoline increased by 15 cents a gallon for premium, 17 cents for regular.[79] According to the EES Commander, Brigadier General Arthur Gregg, the increase was attributable to the existing "energy crisis."[80] Understanding the wider consequences the general admitted, "We are very unhappy about the increase because the impact on service personnel and their families will be significant."[81] This increase followed a 36 percent increase in EES gasoline prices enacted the summer prior, in July 1973. The responsibility for that action Gregg also assigned to "devaluation of the dollar plus higher costs for bulk gasoline."[82] Out of necessity, USAREUR authorities also decreed a parallel rationing of 200 liters of gasoline per month, per registered vehicle. For all Milcom members it was an inconvenience but for those living on the economy any distance from where they worked or shopped it was an added burden. One Milcom member from Schwäbisch Gmünd wrote to the editor of *Stars and Stripes* suggesting an exception to the policy for "persons living further than 15 kilometers from work or persons working part-time jobs."[83] Authorities never issued any such exception. But like the devaluation of the dollar the subsequent "energy crisis" would also plague Milcom members during the 1970s and contribute to their financial woes.

Although the OPEC nations lifted the oil embargo by March 1974 the price of fuel would never revert to the pre-embargo levels either in the U.S. or overseas. By July 1974 EES again announced the necessity for an increase in fuel prices, this time it was for 3 cents. Simultaneously however, ESSO officials in Germany announced, "The price of automobile fuels in the Federal Republic of Germany is either stable or decreasing."[84] When queried by journalists about that increase an EES representative once again noted that vagaries of the dollar to DM rate made it impossible to accurately project prices of fuel which came from German suppliers, "The decline in the value of the dollar coupled with a slight increase in the cost of gasoline from our suppliers made the price increase necessary."[85] As the cost of fuel continued to drift upward over the following years without hope of relief Americans living overseas learned to accept the additional financial hardship. This was evident even in the leisure section of *Stars and Stripes* that periodically featured articles such as "Fueling Around with Your Vacation" that explained how to best plan vacations so as to get the most out of limited and costly fuel resources.[86] The article included mileage charts to major European cities and vacation spots, the price of gasoline in each NATO country and tips about tuning up your car for fuel efficiency.

Still, the issue of fuel prices continued to weigh on Milcom members' nerves and wallets. Aggravated more at the report of another increase than at the comparative price of fuel for Germans which in 1976 was more than double that for Americans at $1.29 per gallon of regular, some exasperated Milcom members lashed out. In a letter to the editor of *Stars and Stripes*, an anonymous writer known only as "Unhappy AAFES User," charged the exchange system hierarchy of price-gouging at the expense of its beleaguered customers.[87] He accused AAFES of "pushing through" a "new pricing policy" in 1974 based on a decision that "the market would bear prices equal to civilian Stateside prices" all under the guise of "the oil problems and turmoil of that time."[88] Among the indictments was the charge that "in the fall of

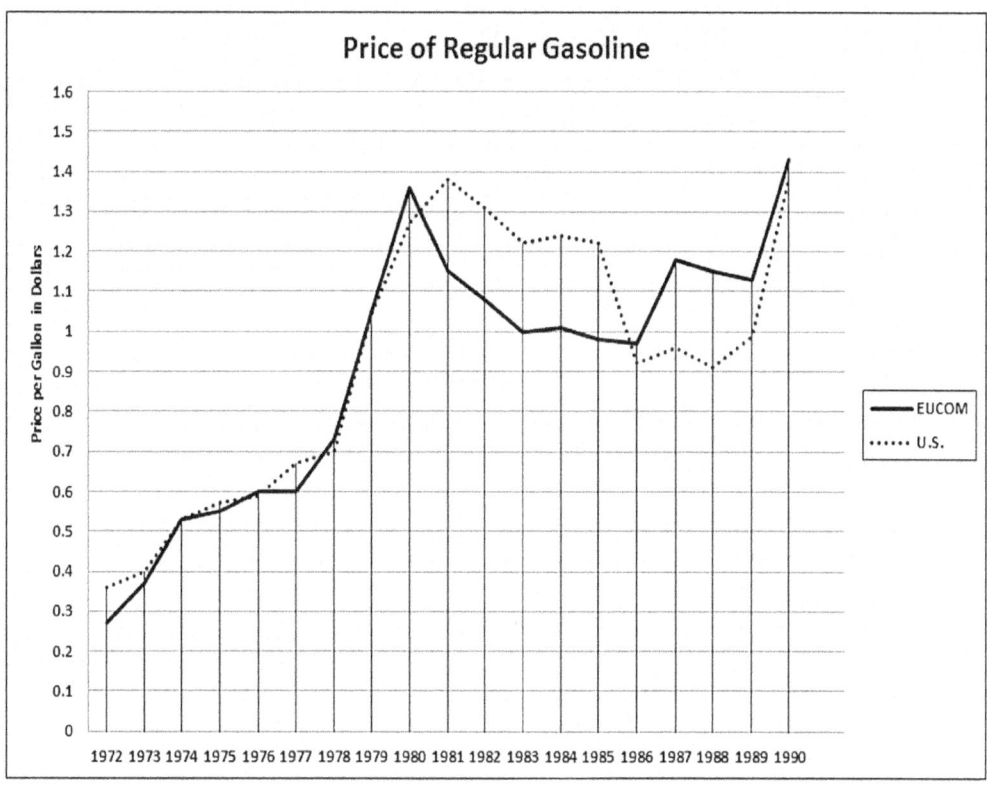

Comparison of Gasoline Prices. The chart shows a comparison of prices for a gallon of regular gasoline for customers in EUCOM Milcoms and in the United States. The cost of fuel for AAFES customers declined significantly with the resurgence of the dollar's strength for several years during the 1980s then climbed again as the dollar weakened. Prices shown do not include diesel fuel. U.S. prices are the average for the entire United States. Source for AAFES fuel prices various *Stars and Stripes*, 1972–1990. AAFES prices are only for Germany. Sources for U.S. fuel prices Bureau of Labor Statistics (BLS), http://data.bls.gov/cgi-bin/surveymost?ap and Department of Energy (DOE), http://www.eia.gov/totalenergy/data/annual/showtext.cfm?t=ptb0524.

'74, AAFES was reaping unprecedented profits" on the sale of fuel, which assisted in covering overall net losses in other mismanaged and antiquated areas of operation."[89]   An exchange system official offered a measured response to that accusation claiming, "AAFES Europe did not use the oil embargo as a tool to increase the selling price of gasoline. We have only passed on the prices increases of gasoline (which have amounted to 145 percent since April 1972) as well as operating costs, to our customers."[90] He went on to reveal, "At present, our profit objective on gasoline sales is 5 cents per gallon. We have sometimes exceeded that profit figure when the dollar/Deutsche mark conversion rate was favorable."[91] There is no evidence to show whether the official answer placated the letter writer but the existence of these periodic challenges and rebuttals suggests that frustrated Milcom members were seeking answers not only to the problem of higher fuel costs but to the wider conundrum of economic difficulties they were facing.

In May 1977, *Stars and Stripes* featured a front-page announcement for the start of a "new flexible pricing system" that would adjust the price of fuel monthly "based on product costs and the exchange rate between the Deutsche mark [sic] and the dollar." The difference in the pricing between the old and new methods was an opportunity for the Milcom customer to "take advantage of currency fluctuations" to purchase fuel at lower prices instead of being slaved to a fixed bulk rate price.[92] Adding to the relief that announcement may have offered to AAFES' customers there was another welcome front page notification that appeared two months later. It noted that "for the second month in a row" the exchange system was lowering its gas prices.[93] AAFES lowered the cost for a gallon of regular gas, purchased through coupons, from 59 cents to 58 cents. The price of premium gas fell also from 65 cents to 64 cents.[94] Although the changes seem minimal in hard economic times these AAFES initiatives must have appeared welcome.

By August 1977, however, the prices of gasoline again rose and would continue an upward trend, easily traced by successive reports in *Stars and Stripes*, through to the summer of 1980. At that time they would peak at $1.36 a gallon for regular and $1.45 for a gallon of premium.[95] The price of gas in the U.S. was little better and averaged $1.27 for all grades at that time. There was little difference between AAFES prices and those in the U.S. for all grades of gasoline during the 1970s. Most important, during this time the fuel crisis offered a common ground of suffering between the Milcoms and the Germans even as it increased the burden of Americans dealing with the disadvantage of currency exchange rates. In that context, for the Americans it may also have been some small measure of comfort that although they paid a larger percentage of their paychecks to their German landlords for rent, they were at least paying less at the gas pump.[96]

The Value Added Tax

Another economic challenge for Milcoms—coming before the dollar devaluation and the fuel crisis but enduring through both—was the German national value added tax (VAT). Commonly known as the *Mehrwertsteuer* (MWST), the tax was introduced by the German government on January 1, 1968, as a replacement for the older "turn-over tax," the *Umsatzsteuer*.[97] Intended to increase revenues, it served as a consumption tax on goods and services levied on the German public. But American Milcom consumers did not escape its reach. As an announcement in *Stars and Stripes* made clear, the VAT would affect "U.S. servicemen, civilians and dependents who spend any money on the German economy."[98] Most important, it would impact Milcom members living on the economy and would mean "higher utility bills at the end of the month" for things such as gas, water and electricity, "but not necessarily higher rents."[99] It would also be "very noticeable" on *Gasthaus* and restaurant tabs by a 6 percent increase on the total. When first introduced, the dollar to DM ratio was 4.0 to 1 and the VAT seemed little more than an inconvenience. During the following years however, as the dollar began to suffer increasing devaluation, the German value added tax became yet another factor in the equation that determined Milcom members' financial wellness.

Among the first groups to suffer from the new tax were Milcom retirees who, like service members, civilians and their families residing off post, had to endure the increase in utility costs. However, unlike others in that group the German government required American retirees to pay a tax on any purchases they made through AAFES and the commissary system. Under the older *Umsatzsteuer* that amounted to a 4 percent levy on goods and services. With the coming of the *Mehrwertsteuer* that varied from 15 to 19 percent.[100] Retirees already living on a military pension sometimes worked in non-appropriated funds positions within the European exchange or commissary systems, or found jobs in the German economy to make ends meet. The increased VAT quickly erased any economic advantage retirees possessed and rendered them some of the first Milcom casualties of the emerging economic downturn. By June 1971 the VAT was at 11 percent for most goods and services but at the same time news sources were reporting that the German Bundestag was already considering an increase to 12 percent.[101]

During the early 1970s, Milcom members continued to encounter the presence of the MWST in various ways. They had to account for the extra cost of the 11 percent value added tax in most items purchased on the German economy from clothing to cuckoo clocks and beer steins, and in their favorite gasthaus. For many of them perhaps a greater disappointment was to discover that suddenly they also had to pay the VAT when purchasing new foreign-made automobiles whether through a German dealer or the AAFES system. An exception to this, if the buyer wanted to circumvent the tax, was to make the purchase through the Canadian forces exchange system where there was no VAT on automobiles. But that exercise often involved traveling to Canadian facilities and navigating additional paperwork. Still, the manager of that system noted that by 1974 they were selling approximately 1,000 cars per year to Americans stationed in Germany.[102] The VAT also had an unexpected impact on Milcom recreational hunters. It appeared as an increase in trophy fees particularly in the purchase of venison from animals taken. When the announcement appeared in *Stars and Stripes* "Outdoors" section in the winter of 1973 it declared, "If the hunter wants to purchase an animal he has shot, he must pay the local wholesale price, plus the added value tax (*Mehrwertsteuer*)."[103] Whether through large or small purchases, or in recreational pursuits, the VAT had become an economic presence that Milcom members could not ignore, especially as the dollar lost its value.

By late 1974, as the dollar continued its downward spiral, USAREUR authorities acted to lift some of the burden by devising a way to relieve some of the value added tax. In December of that year the Assistant Deputy Chief of Staff for Personnel at USAREUR headquarters announced a plan "whereby USAREUR troops could gain tax exemption when shopping on the economy."[104] This, USAREUR accomplished by reinterpreting the SOFA agreement between the NATO forces and Germany so that purchases made on the economy for the sole use of Milcom members and their families could be made through offices of the military hierarchy, which would act as "official procurement agencies."[105] The process was not very complex, but was time consuming. It required the Milcom member to obtain an invoice from a German merchant for the item desired, make payment minus the VAT to a military funds custodian, and receive back both a check issued in the equivalent amount of DM and an official form stating that the Milcom consumer was tax exempt (*Abwicklungschein*). The Milcom member then made payment to the merchant with the check and the VAT relief stamped document.[106] In the first year after its inception military authorities estimated that Army and Air Force personnel had "saved millions of dollars on purchases on the economy." Approximate figures were $53,000 in savings for Air Force consumers and $4 million for those in the Army.[107] The procedure changed slightly over the next few years to streamline the purchasing of DM checks through any American Express or German Bank. Although it remained simple it was still time consuming, but that was an inconvenience Milcom members were bound to accept as they tightened their economic belts and the MWST increased to 12 percent.[108]

Very few complaints regarding the VAT arrived at USAREUR or USAFE headquarters or appeared in letters to *Stars and Stripes* editor through the 1970s and 1980s. Those that did generally revealed misunderstandings of the proper procedures to gain relief. Comments such as "the system is so complicated and cumbersome that it's not worth the effort" were the exception.[109] Even as the MWST edged up to 13 percent by 1980 military authorities continued to make adjustments through negotiations with the German government to benefit Milcom members. Through new agreements Americans were finally able to purchase foreign-made automobiles without the VAT and the minimum amount for goods and services eligible for tax relief changed from DM 225 to DM 50. According to a USAFE Financial Management Division representative his office was then processing more than 11,000 applications for relief annually.[110] By 1983 the Army's tax relief offices had processed 132,000 transactions in one year "worth a total of $82 million" even as the VAT climbed again to 14 percent.[111]

Although efforts by authorities lessened the impact of the tax through the remainder of that decade the VAT process together with complex requirements for computing the COLA and SHA, plus increasing prices at the gas pumps and the uncertain dollar–DM exchange rate all continued to factor into the confusing and burdensome financial formula that confronted Milcom members as they attempted to figure their way through uncertain economic times. Sometimes partial solutions appeared that brought some small measure of relief but then sometimes the reality of their situation seemed overwhelming and Milcom members stepped outside legal bounds to find an answer.

Alternative Solutions–Learning to Make Do

One small legal measure adopted by some military units in Germany to alleviate the financial crisis was to permit the families of lower enlisted personnel living on the economy to eat in the dining facility (mess hall). The program began on April 1, 1978, and lasted in trial for only 9 months, though it did attract some numbers. According to one report from a facility in Würzburg, "we get about four or five dependents eating here on weekdays. It's usually around 20, 25 on the weekend."[112] The meals offered good nutrition at acceptable prices, less than a meal at a German restaurant at $1.45 for lunch and $1.65 for brunch with dependents under the age of 12 paying half price.[113] Although records do not show the total number of participants the program's intent was to "boost the morale of soldiers hit by the dollar decline" targeting those who did not "qualify for free military housing."[114] Still, some dependents did benefit from the less expensive meals and the initiative does suggest that the plight of junior soldiers and their families did not go unnoticed, especially at the unit level.

The kindness of neighbors also provided some succor, if only symbolic. Untold numbers of care packages sometimes appeared on Milcom members' doorsteps from concerned German neighbors. In one instance, 13 American families living on the economy in the small village of Zellhausen received gifts just prior to Christmas. The baskets included items such as "baby dolls, sweaters, pants, boots, slippers, handkerchiefs, candy, cookies, a beer stein, wine and a host of other items."[115] Attached to one basket was a note:

> Beloved American citizens: In 1946, when the German people were very hungry, I received from the American people, CARE packages that helped me a lot. I was seven years old at the time. I want to give today while my situation is very good, some small gifts for you and your children, to say thank you for the help I received so long ago.[116]

Although moments such as these might serve to dissuade any residual feelings of economic superiority among American Milcom members, they also provided assurance that the wider German community was sympathetic to their plight. But gestures such as these were few and far between and some Americans instead took matters into their own hands.

The difference in prices between American and German goods during most of the 1970s offered a provocative temptation to some Milcom members interested in bettering their economic situation through the black market. As one German customs investigator noted, "The reason for trading is obvious—the enormous difference between the German and American prices. A carton of American cigarettes costs about $1.70 in a military commissary in Frankfurt. A few blocks away at a local tobacco shop a German must pay nearly $10 for a similar carton."[117] An undercover American counterpart added, "Just walk down to *Kaiserstrasse* (in Frankfurt) on payday and see the GIs hurrying down to sell their cigarettes, it's a comedy."[118] With the help of a good middleman an individual could realize a sizeable profit. One servicemember active in Berlin's black market remarked, "A person in the market who knows enough people can make 2,000 marks (about $800) a month."[119]

Sources reveal this type of behavior was not uncommon. As one feature article noted, in the words of a German customs agent, "At the military level it is the soldiers but not only them. The civilians (U.S. Forces) also carry on the business. And also the dependents of Americans are there. The housewife might want to put a little extra money in her pocketbook."[120] A separate article echoed the first reiterating that the illicit activity stretched across the spectrum of Milcom members, "they come in all shapes and sizes" and included "U.S. military personnel, wives of servicemen, civilian employees of the U.S. military and children of Americans."[121] Aside from providing needed additional income sources note that many black marketers felt little remorse, they simply "did not see anyone getting hurt by the business."[122] One dependent who participated in the illicit activity commented, "It's not criminal. It's just a simple case of taking money away from the German government. And anyway you're stimulating the economy and helping the gold flow. You're not hurting the little person."[123]

According to one investigative report, Americans generally participated in the illegal activities in one of two ways: direct exchange of goods to satisfy a debt such as monthly rent or a bill, and exchange of goods through a middleman solely for monetary gain.[124] Understanding that feelings of *bonhomie* might induce some Milcom members to offer gifts to German friends or neighbors, USAREUR established a policy that provided limits.[125] An October 1976 issue of *Stars and Stripes* carried a reprint of those rules for the benefit of its readers. The guidelines reminded Milcom members "giving as gifts any rationed items in quantities greater than the following without clearing them through German customs is in violation of regulations."[126]

25 cigarettes or 10 cigars or 60 grams (2.1 ounces) of smoking tobacco
500 grams (17.6 ounces) of coffee or 124 grams (4.4 ounces) of coffee extracts
One bottle of spirits, not to exceed 1.2 liters (approximately one imperial Quart)[127]

Still, policies and the fear of punitive punishment did little to dampen their participation.[128]

It is difficult to determine the actual scope of the trade during the 1970s and 1980s by simply estimating the numbers of Milcom members involved. Many avoided arrest, some participated infrequently, some constantly, some only during payday and others only when there was a need. Also complicating a proper accounting are inconsistencies in collecting and categorizing data. Source materials reveal that various headquarters and agencies displayed information in different ways. For example, the USAFE headquarters customs violations unit listed 227 Air Force personnel involved in black market investigations for 1974. In addition, it listed "107 foreign nationals, 25 dependents, and 15 persons not identified."[129] For 1975 it listed 347 Air Force personnel as well as "70 foreign nationals, 25 dependents, and 10 individuals not identified."[130] For that same year German customs officials reported that of 25,500 cases of black marketing in Germany with 13 percent involving "foreign troops" of all military branches, with more than 90 percent of those being Americans.[131] Breaking it down further for 1975, the data revealed that in Frankfurt 29 percent of all German cases involved U.S. service members, in Kaiserslautern that figure was 37 percent and in Nüremberg it was 46 percent.[132] Consistent through all the data however, regardless of the method of collecting and categorizing the information, is the understanding that large numbers of Milcom members, service personnel, civilians and dependents were participating in black market activities during the two decades that economic hardship had the greatest impact.

Seen differently through the lens of financial loss, the impact of black marketing was just as profound. Reports from the 42nd MP Group (Customs) indicated that in 1974 the "U.S. tax free value" of all stereo equipment "turned up" in black market deals was $91,626. By 1975 the figures had risen to $232,394.[133] For the first three months of 1975 the customs unit reported handling cases that involved $1.3 million in U.S. tax free items of all types.[134] Those figures translated into monies lost to the German tax system through illicit dealings. But, like the numbers of personnel involved it was difficult for authorities to determine an accurate breakdown of black market dealings. At the time, investigators for the customs unit merely noted, "It is not possible to say how much goes undetected" and that probably "less than 20 percent of the black marketing cases are ever uncovered."[135]

A German journalist's report offered a similar perspective of the scope of participation and its impact. Noting the "regular small custom's offenses between members of the [U.S.] army and their German neighbors and apartment landlords" in the proximity of military bases he cited the prevalence and wide acceptance of black market activities in the conduct of daily business whether it was paying rent or taxi fares.[136] An estimate of the total amount of taxes lost to the German government by such activity was "between five and fifty million marks." So extensive was the exchange in some areas that it seemed as if "almost everyone dealt with the Yanks. Standing in Lautzenhausen are hundreds of neat cottages, which were built with American money," profited from the black market.[137] According to the article it was also not unheard of for service members to pay part of their rent in "liquid currency [whiskey] or blue haze [cigarettes]," or to satisfy loans and bribe judges with "almost mint condition stereos."[138] The complicity of many Germans made black market activity mutually rewarding for both Americans and their neighbors, and contributed to frustrating the best efforts of each nations' customs investigators. Throughout the 1970s and 1980s black market activity continued to thrive as an alternative source of income for American Milcom members seeking relief from economic pressures. Not everyone participated and authorities caught some but let slip more. Still, the numbers suggest that many believed the risks of capture and punishment were worth the financial gain.

Hiring of Local Nationals—A Point of Friction

During these years of economic depression, there was one particular area where friction did develop between Germans and Americans. That was in the hiring of local nationals (LN).

Although they were a part of the workforce supporting the U.S. military structure in Germany since the end of World War II aspects of their hiring and pay caused rancor among some Milcom members especially when Americans began clamoring for jobs.[139]

Complaints registered in letters to *Stars and Stripes* editor noted the perception of preference in selecting LNs over American civilians and dependents for employment. As early as March 1972 a pair of writers offered challenges to their understanding of the standing policy. One complained, "I hear and read constantly that various departments and agencies are very short staffed, but U.S. citizens cannot fill these positions, and by law they must be filled by local nationals."[140] The second letter, submitted the same day, echoed the first "There is a great shortage of jobs available to American dependents. However, there are hundreds of jobs available to German nationals (or anyone who doesn't carry an American passport)."[141]

The belief of inequities in hiring practices continued through that decade and into the 1980s. A letter writer from July 1980 was more expansive, submitting a series of challenging questions about the length of time it took to hire American dependents, why LNs received higher wages and more benefits than dependents for similar work, and why LNs seemed to staff all the positions at some facilities.[142] By 1986 these concerns had changed very little. In January of that year a frustrated spouse looking for employment at an AAFES outlet in the Grafenwöhr Milcom observed, "90 percent of these workers were German nationals."[143]

The answers provided by USAREUR civilian manpower management representatives offered some conciliatory responses paired with explanations of mandated constraints, not necessarily to assuage ill feelings toward the Germans but rather to clear the air. Understanding the urgent need for Milcom members to supplement their paychecks as the dollar lost ground against the Mark, military officials gave preference to "dependents for commissary, food service and ward attendant appropriated funds positions throughout Germany."[144] In addition, in 1972, USAREUR began giving dependents "first priority for appointment to NAF [Non-appropriated Fund] jobs normally given local nationals, who are now considered only when no dependents apply for openings."[145] As one personnel manager noted, the purpose of the dependent hire program was to "provide an opportunity for military families to supplement their total income because of economic difficulties experienced in overseas areas where the cost of living is exceedingly high."[146] By 1986 the number of dependents employed by USAREUR had increased to 27,000 from approximately 5,000 in 1971.[147] But USAREUR representatives also explained, "because of the Army's mission in Europe, a civilian manpower mix of U.S. citizens and LNs is required."[148]

U.S. Department of Defense (DOD) mission requirements dictated requirements to hire a certain number of local nationals to fill job positions in Germany, not the NATO-SOFA agreement as some Americans assumed.[149] As a spokesman from the USAREUR Personnel Office explained to curious Milcom members, "Since many more people are seeking employment than there are jobs available, a fair and balanced U.S. citizen and German workforce consistent with mission needs and financial prudence is our goal."[150] As to concerns regarding unequal pay and benefits, a representative from the USAREUR Civilian Personnel Division acknowledged that a dual system existed. In the first, a collective tariff agreement between the U.S. and Germany set the rules and standards for LNs employed by the U.S. forces. In the second, American employees "work and are paid under laws and practices applicable to federal service workers enacted by the U.S. Congress."[151] So, to the consternation of some Milcom members, American authorities remained powerless to rectify inequities in pay

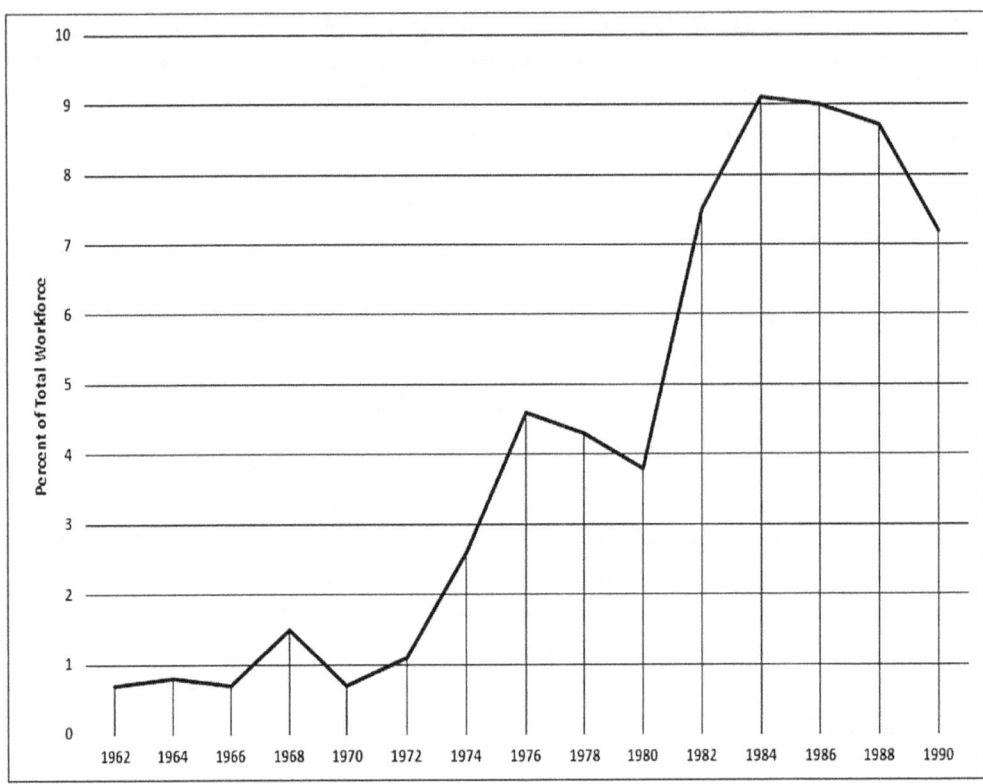

German Unemployment Rate, 1962–1990. Unemployment in West Germany remained relatively low, averaging below 5.0 percent during the worst period of economic hardship for the Milcoms from 1975 to 1980. As the dollar began to recover against the DM in 1980 unemployment again grew and remained high through 1990. A large percentage of those unemployed however, were "guest workers" not German citizens. Sources: Judt, *Postwar*, Kindle electronic edition: Chapter XIV, *Diminished Expectations*, Location 10602 and *Institut für Arbeitsmarkt und Berufsforschung, Bundesandstalt für Arbeit* [Institute for the Labor Market and Occupational Research, Federal Office of Labor], accessed: August 10, 2013, http://doku.iab.de/zfibel/03_06_02.pdf .

and benefits between them and German workers and "under no circumstances" could LNs "be separated to make positions available for the employment of dependents."[152] Just as some Americans remained less than mollified with the explanations surrounding the LN-American workforce relationship during the economic downturn so too was the German government.

Banner headlines such as the one printed in *Stars and Stripes* on February 17, 1978, registered Bonn's backlash against the practice of hiring increasing numbers of American dependents. The article noted the German government's petition to reduce "the number of Americans holding jobs" with the military forces in the Federal Republic.[153] A representative of the finance ministry claimed that at the time more than 10,000 American civilians were filling positions "originally reserved" for German workers. With a 5.4 percent unemployment rate the Germans were eager to claim those positions.[154] Negotiations between the two sides followed. Working hard to maintain a solid relationship with its political and economic partner, and to satisfy the needs of Milcom members American authorities found themselves walking a fine line. At best they could only promise, "No Germans will be fired to make more jobs available for Americans."[155] Fortunately for German-American relations, these tensions over hiring practices

A Brief Economic Resurgence, 1980–1985

Between 1980 and 1985 the dollar again gained ground against the Deutschmark. In January 1980, it stood at $1=DM 1.724 and by January of the following year it had reached $1=DM 2.010. It continued its ascent until February of 1985 when it achieved its zenith at $1=DM 3.302.[156] The engine driving the economic turnaround for the Milcoms was a rejuvenated American economy. During his inaugural speech on January 20, 1981, newly elected President Ronald Reagan announced his intentions to "reawaken this industrial giant, to get government back within its means, and to lighten our punitive tax burden."[157] The pillars of his economic strategy were the reduction of government spending, the federal income tax, government regulation and inflation.[158] By late 1982 the plan began to show effect and as the nation began to recover economically so too did the Milcoms.

In November 1982, a front page *Stars and Stripes* headline trumpeted "Election Boosts Dollar in Europe."[159] The news story connected the mid-term elections in the U.S. with boosting the "dollar to its best level in years in Europe."[160] The text noted that it was a victory for the Reagan administration and a vote of confidence for its economic policies but more meaningful for Milcom members was the comment that "in Frankfurt the dollar closed at its best level since 1976–2.5737."[161] For them it was a sign of long-awaited economic relief that would continue for the next few years, and they took advantage of it. The German community also enjoyed the resurgent dollar particularly as it began to lead Milcom members back into local shops and restaurants. Although it was not a boon at a national macro-level for the Federal Republic where German economists moaned, "America, the America of Ronald Reagan, is again at the top," at the grass roots micro-level the robust exchange of goods and currency between Milcom members and German merchants was again welcome.[162]

Milcom members were quick to exploit the dollar's strength against the Mark during the early 1980s. According to one journalist's report some used the financial leverage to pay off bills or shop, others to travel, and others to increase their savings. For example, one service member purchased a new BMW automobile that had previously been out of reach. He determined that the "strong dollar saved him about $1,000 on the price of his new car."[163] A single soldier living in the Schwabach Milcom noted that the resurgent dollar meant more entertainment, "I have more marks to spend in gasthauses," and another claimed it meant "better meals" at local restaurants. A Milcom spouse admitted that she intended to "buy bedroom furniture for her children because the [dollar] rate is so high." She also added, "Just after Reagan came into office, the rate went over two to the dollar. I cried."[164]

Also central to the administration's economic strategy at this time was a significant increase in military spending. It included money for infrastructure improvements in each military branch and contracts for new weapons systems, but more important, it also meant significant pay raises for service members of all grades.[165] A comparison of existing pay charts reveals that in 1979 an E-3 with less than 2 years in the service (usually living on the economy with his non-command sponsored family) earned a base pay of $519.60. By 1981, that had increased to $642.60 and by 1985 was $723. In addition, the associated basic allowance for quarters (BAQ) for families at that rank increased from $160.80 in 1979, to $205 in 1981, and to $238.50 in 1985.[166] That equated to an increase of 40 percent in earnings. When partnered with the strengthening dollar rate the lower enlisted personnel who had suffered the most through the difficult economic times of the 1970s could at last afford to pay their rent and bills. They might also have enough money remaining at the end of the month for discretionary purchases, such as going to the movies, eating fast food, or buying an inexpensive vehicle.

The economic upswing for the Milcoms drove consumerist instincts through the next few years. Of all the types of purchases, automobiles appeared to be one of the most sought after commodities. Separate car dealers located near Milcoms in Frankfurt and Wiesbaden observed, "The strong dollar makes people feel good. It gives them confidence. It makes them buy," and "When the dollar hit 3.14 marks, buyers were lined up outside the door for hours. I never saw anything like it."[167] For 1984 alone, AAFES Military car sales programs sold 30,000 new American and foreign models making it a record year.[168] One estimate was that "millions of dollars have been saved by buyers as result of the strong dollar."[169] Although Milcom members enjoyed the many benefits, drawbacks existed in other areas.

An AAFES' representative noted that the strong dollar "may have cost" them "more than $30 million in sales in Europe" in 1984.[170] This was the result of Milcom members spending their earnings "off base and into stores and restaurants on the local economy."[171] The one advantage to AAFES was that with a strong exchange rate against the Mark the exchange system would save on the salaries paid to its "more than 7,000" German wage-scale employees.[172] Unfortunately, AAFES also contributed 50 percent of its earnings to the Morale, Welfare, and Recreation (MWR) accounts that supported all Milcom members. But service members probably did not notice any reduction to MWR programs as more of them then had the ability to access recreation and entertainment on the economy and were less restricted the barracks by lack of funds.[173]

Eventually, the economic resurgence of the early 1980s lost its momentum. By February 1986 *Stars and Stripes* recorded the change noting how "in just one year the dollar lost 70 percent of the gains it racked up against the German mark in the previous five years."[174] The dollar had tumbled from DM 3.47 to DM 2.29 during that time. This occurred in part because of actions taken by the U.S. government that argued, "A weaker dollar will reduce America's lagging trade imbalance." It also happened as a result of a "concerted plan" between the U.S. and other world powers to bring "the dollar's value into line with world economic conditions."[175] Regardless of the reasons, Milcom members again felt the financial sting of earlier years.

Once again, those living on the economy suffered to a greater degree than those in government housing. For many of them rent, goods and services increased in cost. As one service member watched, his rent and telephone bills, both payable in Marks, increased significantly. His lament was "if the dollar continues to fall, more and more people living on the economy will be requesting government housing."[176] By late 1987, the halcyon days of the early 1980s were all but gone. At the time, *Stars and Stripes* staff began to again write about service members who were sending family members home and how even those living in government quarters were having "trouble escaping financial woes."[177] One spouse observed, "We cannot shop on the economy because we can't afford to buy things there."[178] Once again the PX and commissary were attracting Milcom shoppers with commissary sales gaining 12 percent over the previous year.[179]

News about the dollar continued to get worse over the next few years. Special columns in the business section of *Stars and Stripes* kept watch for Milcom readers, but offered little encouraging news. An October 1988 piece titled "Experts Predict Dollar's Drop to 1.75 Marks" announced how "The embattled dollar continued its retreat on the foreign exchange markets last week, and some currency traders are now talking in terms of the buck falling [further] in value."[180] By November of 1989 the dollar's bleak prospects had not changed. The business column in *Stars and Stripes* announced, "Dollar Drops to lowest Mark Rate in Months," observing how "the West German Mark continued to attract investors away from the dollar over the past week, driving the U.S. currency to its lowest level in more than 10 months."[181] The conclusion was familiar, "U.S. servicemembers in West Germany are taking it on the chin."[182] From February 1985 to February 1990 the dollar had fallen from DM 3.30 to DM 1.67, a decline of DM 1.63.[183]

Complicating financial matters for Milcom members was another round of increases at the gas pump beginning in 1986.[184] A cascading effect was a surge to purchase the cost-saving AAFES coupons. So great was the demand that supplies ran out and the exchange system resorted to handing out rain checks for Milcom customers who were too late. An AAFES representative announced the unwelcome news, "Fuel prices in Germany and the Netherlands will increase by an average of 20 cents a gallon when the new prices take effect," adding that it would equate to "a jump of more than $10 for a 200-liter book of super gas coupons."[185] Fuel prices were also increasing in the States but not at the same rate as for Americans living in Europe. When the price for a gallon of unleaded gasoline was nearing $1 in the U.S. it was $1.20 for AAFES customers.[186] That disparity continued until late 1990 when the gap eventually narrowed. For many Milcom members the higher fuel costs added to an already stretched budget especially for those living on the economy and driving their cars to work and shopping.

Aside from a brief period of time during the early 1980s when they enjoyed increased prosperity, Milcom members endured long years of economic challenges during the 1970s and 1980s. As in the decades prior to 1970 the economics of the Milcoms intersected those of the German communities at key points of contact such as a changing Deutsche Mark rate, fuel prices, taxes and hiring of local nationals. But unlike those times, new economic realities presented very different and troubling crises and consequences for American service members, civilians, dependents and retirees living overseas. American economic superiority had again evaporated.

Conclusion

America for Me
'Tis fine to see the Old World, and travel up and down
Among the famous palaces and cities of renown,
To admire the crumbly castles and the statues of the kings,—
But now I think I've had enough of antiquated things.
Oh, it's home again, and home again, America for me!
I want a ship that's westward bound to plough the rolling sea,
In the land of youth and freedom beyond the ocean bars,
Where the air is full of sunlight and the flag is full of stars.

I know that Europe's wonderful, yet something seems to lack!
The Past is too much with her, and the people looking back.
But the glory of the Present is to make the Future free—
We love our land for what she is and what she is to be.
Oh, it's home again, and home again, America for me!
I want a ship that's westward bound to plough the rolling sea,
In the land of youth and freedom beyond the ocean bars,
Where the air is full of sunlight and the flag is full of stars.
—Henry Van Dyke (1852–1933)[1]

James Alling recalls that as a young dependent living in the early postwar Heidelberg military community his DODDS teacher required that his class memorize this poem.[2] It seemed fitting for a time when a triumphal America was planting its flag abroad amid the ruins of Europe. Yet the words also ring with post–Cold War irony, as emerging realities did send thousands of Americans "home again, and home again."

But if the text of Van Dyke's poem offers a prelude to establish a starting point for an American presence in Heidelberg and Germany, then a *Sonderbeilage* [special supplement] to the May 11, 2013, issue of the Heidelberg *Rhein-Neckar-Zeitung* (RNZ) titled "Bye, bye Heidelberg," provides a suitable epilogue and brings closure to the American presence there. A collection of articles within the enclosure offer headings such as "Occupiers then Friends…," "Return of Facilities to Germans," "The Beginning of the End" and "Thank You and Welcome Back!"[3] They provide a chronology of Cold War events that affected that city as well as a litany of remembrances along a spectrum of German-American cultural, social, political and economic interactions. They mention joint wives' clubs activities, *Volksfests*, the shared anxiety of terrorist attacks and German-American marriages —"The Best of Two Nations."[4]

Aside from wistful dedications to lasting friendships between the city and its' departing Milcom members there is also a discernable current that courses through all the text within the news supplement. It suggests new beginnings and opportunities for Germany with the

Former American Housing Area, July 2013. One of several former American housing areas closed during the American withdrawal from Heidelberg. Image source: the author.

departure of the Americans and a resurrecting "Heidelberg Spring" that comes with the ending of an era.[5] In all cases however, the authors assign credit to the *Amis* for the many changes they introduced and inspired by their presence: democracy, civil liberties, a vibrant economy and especially a "guarantee for peace and a guarantee that the ending of the war would bring a better lot."[6] The result by one German scholar's estimate is an "exceptional heritage" for the two nations.[7]

Still, between the words of Van Dyke's poem and the text of the RNZ supplement stretches a trajectory of change that resonates in both the host nation and the military communities. That change describes the falling away of an American exceptionalist façade from pressures generated by emerging challenges in the prevailing cultural, social, political and economic discourses in the U.S. and around the globe during the four postwar decades. The derivative tensions informed and shaped that narrative of Americanism in the military communities while also testing the very identity of the Milcoms that the ideals had framed. As a result, Milcom members, as individuals and as members of a community, faced choices to either endorse existing attitudes and ideals broadcast by the U.S government and society or accept a rescripting of an exceptional narrative that had succumbed to the influences of changing global cultural, social, political and economic dynamics. These decisions affected how the Americans presented themselves to the German community, how the host nation interacted

Former American Hospital Area, July 2013. American authorities shuttered the Healthcare Center in Heidelberg during the drawdown. General George S. Patton died at this facility while receiving medical care for injuries suffered during a motor vehicle accident in December 1945. Image source: the author.

with them and how members of the Milcom reconceptualized and articulated what it meant to be an American.

Understanding the energies that these changes manifested and the importance of the coincidental construction of trans-cultural, social, political and economic bridges, as well as cross-boundary social and cultural inter-penetrations between the Milcoms and host communities becomes apparent. First, from the outset of the American occupation of Germany and the establishment of the Milcom network, the impact of consumer wealth and popular culture was evident. Cars, Coca-Cola, cigarettes and blue jeans offered insight to the American culture by introducing Germans to a foreign system that placed great value on material possessions. At the same time, the Milcoms exposed them to new sounds of music and a film industry that served as a window to a different, alluring way of life. Most important, this first wave of cultural penetration provided an opportunity to cast a new postwar identity for a younger generation of Germans anxious to break free from the limitations of a recent authoritarian past and establish themselves as a separate entity from their cousins in the East. After 1967 the second wave of American cultural penetration arrived bringing the concept of fast food and introducing the dark shadows of violence and drugs. But this second cultural coming was also important because it revealed the inherent paradoxes of a modern Western culture replete with rationalized food preparation but suffering ills that were symptomatic of its dynamism. In this the Germans were able to act as sophisticated agents accepting some aspects for inculcation and rejecting others. But intrinsic to those actions was the eventual acknowledgement of fatal flaws in the exceptional culture by both the Milcoms and their host communities.

An examination of America's society through the Milcoms produces similar revelations. Although racial equality existed as an American tenet, it quickly fell to scrutiny by Germans who began forming their own opinions of African-Americans from their interactions during the war and from early postwar inter-racial behaviors. It became evident that American declarations of racial equity were hollow and the reality of inequity existed from the earliest occupation years. The trace of that imbalance continued through the 1960s and to the end of the Cold War exhibiting desperate aggressive tendencies that resonated in American society in the States as well as in the Milcoms. Significantly however, the Germans' critiques of American society served as a yardstick to measure their recuperation from a fascist disease that assayed great weight in racial taxonomy.

Other societal considerations included gender and feminism as well as scrutiny of the media as an organ of free speech. In the first case early postwar understandings of the exceptional American household, that prescribed restrictive gender relationships and roles, mired the evolution of women's rights, a predicament that carried over to the Milcoms in Germany. It was not until after the social upheavals and challenges that came on the wings of broader global movements, that women in the Milcoms, as in the States, could face a future with greater possibilities. In this context, the Milcom served as a window of change displaying those gains of female spouses, civilian employees, students and military members as they sought and achieved greater empowerment. The women's rights struggle, akin to that of race, presents itself as both an obvious flaw in the exceptional consensus as well as a process of societal maturation bringing an open admittance of existing faults while charting a course of remediation. A parallel development was a similar situation for German women, who after some promising initial advancement suffered a degree of reversal during Germany's period of reconstruction, losing their hard-won postwar gains to the droves of men returning from Allied prisoner of war camps. Most significant in the longer run were the bridges of understanding German and American women constructed during their struggles and the corresponding barometer that each group provided for the other to measure gains.

A societal concern over free speech, an iconic tenet of American freedoms, existed in the Milcoms throughout the entire Cold War period. Whether it was over the type of music played by AFN radio or stories that appeared in print in *Stars and Stripes*, Milcom members were sensitive to any hint of manipulation or editorial control by military or civilian hierarchy. In the context of the struggle between East and West, freedom of the press emerged as an essential identifying characteristic of Americanism. The German public, who had recently suffered the heavy hand of totalitarian censorship, watched with special interest as Milcom members were vocal in their efforts to safeguard that American ideal.

As with societal issues, German-American political relationships reveal a complexity of bonds and divisions. For example, common ground existed in the strong anti-communist sentiments of both partners. For the Americans anti-communism was an essential tenet of exceptionalism formed of a rejection of that ideology's denunciation of religion and individualism as well as its reliance on socialist schemes and planned economies. For the Germans it was also the immediate fear of a Soviet hegemon that cast a long shadow across the plains of Western Europe. In this opposition the Germans and Americans came together to establish a solid bond that lasted from the end of the war to the fall of the Berlin Wall. In that context the Milcoms served a purpose as a physical manifestation of a commitment by the U.S. to foil any Soviet aggressive designs.

Another strong bond emerged with the eruption of terrorist attacks coordinated by groups such as the Baader-Meinhof Gang in the latter decades of the Cold War. Both the Milcoms and the Germans exhibited fear and anxiety over the violent anti–American and anti–Western political expressions which targeted each. Unfortunately, during that period Washington's anti-terrorist focus was not on the Milcoms in Germany. Instead, it lay primarily on activities in South America and the Middle East. As a result, American casualties mounted in West Germany before military and political elites in Washington released late protective guidance. Although the West German public and American Milcom members continued to share a joint rejection of terrorist extremism during these years there was a greater depth to that feeling for the Germans who had just a decade earlier freely criticized the violent strain in American culture. It was with a mixed mood of humility and determination that they committed themselves to ensuring the safety of Milcom members and senior military personnel after repeated attacks on housing and shopping areas and the sensational ambush of General Kroesen.

Still, it was the United States' image as a purveyor of global violence through its involvement in the Vietnam War in particular that contributed the earlier negative critiques of American politics and drew protestors into the streets of Germany during the 1960s and 1970s. That was the first of two notable political divides between the Germans and Americans. As Milcom members struggled to make sense of their nation's participation in the war, German activists organized protests, gatherings and anti-war coffee houses, supported the publication of underground newspapers and encouraged the desertion of American service members. Although the numbers of Milcom service members choosing to desert was superficial at best, it was symbolic of American dissatisfaction with participation in the war.

A second political divide was the German-American rift concerning the use of nuclear weapons in Europe. From the earliest postwar decades German public attitudes had been less enthusiastic for their potential employment than that of the American public or Milcoms. Driving the wedge of opinion was an understanding that the central German landscape would serve as the battleground for a nuclear war. While American military members focused on their missions Germans worried over the loss of their lives and property. Evidence from polls reveal the depth of this divide as did the throngs of protesters pressing the gates at U.S. missile installations like Wiley Barracks or linking arms to form human protest chains across the countryside. Still, that political nuclear wedge was not strong enough to sever the bonds of cultural *Gemütlichkeit* that evolved over the postwar decades. As one placard noted, "We like Americans but not Pershings and poison gas."[8]

Another early bond between Germans and Americans was economic. This was born of the European Recovery Plan (ERP) of 1947, which launched the West German *Wirtschaftswunder* [economic wonder] of the 1950s and had a profound impact. It established West Germany as a solid political ally integrated into the defense of Western Europe and as a strong economic trading partner. Within this arena there were important grass-roots contact-points between the Germans and Americans. These included adjusting to the impact of the DM conversion, host nation taxation, employment of local nationals by the Milcoms and black market interactions. Most important, and of the greatest consequence to members of the military community, were the effects of economic vagaries such as the devaluation of the dollar during the latter decades of the Cold War that challenged them as they struggled to balance the maintenance of homes and families with their military mission. Regardless, the economic connection between the two nations was just as strong as were their cultural, social and political links.

In a broader sense, the course of this study of life in the Milcoms also reveals areas that have received superficial, if any, attention in earlier studies. These include ideas about segmentation and marginalized Milcom members. Although extant historical works describe the separation of the two populations as functions of the physical sequestering of Milcom members behind the walls of "Little Americas" and a general, but ill-defined, reticence to engage with their local German neighbors, the reality was more complex. Unpacking the question of segmentation reveals other salient issues that included differences in levels of sustenance, here described as a "caloric wedge," separation to prevent the spread of disease, lingering wartime aggressions and the varied requirements of daily existence. As unfortunate as these realities were, none carried a malevolent intent but did function to keep the Germans and Americans at a distance and provide obstacles to the building of bridges. The lives of American military retirees existing overseas along the margins of the Milcoms also comes to light as the challenges they continue to face and the contributions they made became clear. Their presence in surrounding host communities served as a bridge of understanding across and inter-cultural boundary, yet it was apparent that hierarchies in Washington as well as in EUCOM undervalued and neglected that presence. Instead of a fuller participation in the life of the Milcom, elites marginalized the retirees and considered them a liability.

The postwar initiative to establish American military communities in Germany fulfilled a number of purposes. It brought discipline back to disquieted occupation troops, calmed the anxious worries of the host nation, and reunited families separated by distance and military requirements. It also made a bold statement about America's commitment to stand firm against aggression from the East. Most important, the Milcoms served as a conduit of soft power to sell the ideals of an American way of life. But as this work shows, the ideals associated with that were not immutable and changed with the times causing members of the military communities to reinterpret their meaning and renegotiate their interactions with one another and the host nation.

By one estimate, from 1946 to 1990 between 15 and 20 million American service personnel, civilian employees and family members lived and worked in West Germany.[9] During those postwar decades they braved a myriad of challenges on a daily basis that their counterparts back home in the States never faced. These included surviving difficult financial circumstances, navigating a foreign culture, language and economy, fear of terrorist attacks and executing their military mission while living in the shadow of a hostile military force that threatened nuclear annihilation. Understanding that existence assigns greater agency to that network of overseas Milcoms and the millions of Americans who lived there, removes them from the periphery of Cold War history, and re-situates them along its front lines.

Chapter Notes

Preface

1. American military authorities and German representatives of the city of Heidelberg participated in an official closing ceremony for Campbell Barracks in September 2013. See "Storied U.S. Barracks Closes with Little Fanfare," *New York Times*, Europe, on-line version, accessed July 2, 2014, http://www.nytimes.com/2013/09/08/world/europe/storied-us-barracks-closes-with-little-fanfare.html?pagewanted=all&_r=0.

Introduction

1. Some early examples include Alexis de Tocqueville, *Democracy in America* (New York: Penguin, 2003), John Hector St. John de Crevecoeur, *Letters from and American Farmer* (Mineola: Dover Books, 2005), Frederick Jackson Turner, *The Frontier in American History*, accessed: June 24, 2014, http://xroads.virginia.edu/~HYPER/TURNER/. On Bancroft's contribution see James W. Creaser, "The Origins and Character of American Exceptionalism," *American Political Thought* 1 (Spring 2012), accessed June 24, 2014, http://www.polisci.wisc.edu/Uploads/Documents/Ceaser.pdf.

2. See also Seymour Lipset, *American Exceptionalism: A Double-Edged Sword* (New York: Norton, 1997) and George Schulman, "American Exceptionalism Revisited: Taking Exception to Exceptionalism." *American Literary History* 23, no.1 (December 2010).

3. See Elaine Tyler May's description of the centrality of the family in American Cold War society and culture in *Homeward Bound* (New York: Basic Books, 2008) and Douglas Field, ed., *American Cold War Culture* (Edinburgh: Edinburgh University Press, 2005) on thoughts about race, gender, sexuality and politics during this period.

4. Peter Bergmann, "American Exceptionalism and German 'Sonderweg' in Tandem." *The International History Review* 23, no. 3 (September 2001), 527. Bergmann observes that in general postwar consensus historians such as Richard Hofstadter "agreed that Europe had nothing to teach America." See also Arnon Gutfeld, *American Exceptionalism: The Effects of Plenty on the American Experience* (Portland: Sussex Academic Press, 2002).

5. Bergmann, 527.

6. Frances Stonor Saunders, *The Cultural Cold War: The CIA and the World of Arts and Letters* (New York: Free Press, 1999), 158.

7. See Lori Bogle, *The Pentagon's Battle for the American Mind: The Early Cold War* (College Station: Texas A&M Press, 2004).

8. West Germany achieved semi-sovereign status on May 23, 1949. For a fuller explanation see Henry Ashby Turner, *Germany from Partition to Reunification* (New Haven: Yale University Press, 1992).

9. This study presupposes the existence of the network of military communities as a single unified entity although large distances did separate individual locations and there were certain regional differences in host community cultural and social attitudes. Uniting the Milcoms were unique communal characteristics such as a single language, a single currency and economic system, a uniform set of governing laws and print and broadcast media. See Benedict Anderson, *Imagined Communities* (New York: Verso, 2006) and Charlotte Wolf, *Garrison Community: A Study of an Overseas American Military Community* (Westport, CT: Greenwood, 1969). It is Wolf who also declares, "If overseas military people and their actions were to be understood, they would have to be viewed as embedded in a community context." *Ibid.*, xi.

10. This youth movement in Germany found impetus in rejection of its nation's historical past and sought redemption through protest that was anti-authoritarian, anti-war, anti-nuclear armament and ecologically minded. It criticized Germany's political and economic alliance with the United States as an imperialist collusion. See "40 Years 1968: The Discreet Charm of the Rebellion," *Der Spiegel*, February 1, 2008, accessed: August 27, 2014, http://www.spiegel.de/kultur/gesellschaft/40-jahre-68er-der-diskrete-charme-der-rebellion-a-531864.html.

11. Correspondence, notes and audio recordings are in the author's personal files. In general, oral and written histories may be biased or dimmed by the passage of time so the author worked to analyze input by comparing it with similar shared experiences in primary and secondary sources. This ensured that the first person perspectives informed the narrative by complementing information gathered from all levels of the approach.

12. These newspaper sources contribute to an understanding of the Americans' grassroots perspective but were evaluated and interpreted in the context of

sources that were subject to editorial management and censorship. Chapter 3 of this project includes a fuller discussion of media manipulation in the Milcoms.

13. See Mark W. Falzini, *Letters Home: The Story of an American Military Family in Occupied Germany, 1946–1949* (New York: iUniverse, 2004) the collected letters and memories of a military family who resided in the city of Würzburg after the war and Richard Reeves, *Daring Young Men: The Heroism and Triumph of the Berlin Airlift, June 1948-May 1949* (New York: Simon and Schuster, 2010) an account of the Berlin Airlift that includes personal impressions of the pilots who flew the relief missions to West Berlin.

14. Maria Höhn, "The American Soldier Dances, the German Soldier Marches: The Transformation of German Views on GIs, Masculinity, and Militarism," in *Over There: Living with the U.S. Military Empire from World War Two to the Present*, Maria Höhn, and Seungsook Moon, eds. (Durham: Duke University Press, 2010), 269.

Chapter One

1. At the time General Clay was the Deputy Military Governor of Germany and General Clark was the U.S. High Commissioner of Austria.

2. For some accounts see "379 Dependent 'Pilgrims' Landed 9 Years ago," *Stars and Stripes*, May 3, 1955, 4 and "40 Years Ago, the First GI Families Arrived," *Stars and Stripes*, April 28, 1986, 8.

3. Original plans called for 10,000 dependents a month to pass through Bremerhaven. John P. Hawkins, *Army of Hope, Army of Alienation: Culture and Contradiction in the American Army Communities of Cold War Germany* (Birmingham: University of Alabama Press, 2005), 6.

4. The first notice appeared on June 1, 1946. See "More Dependents to Dock in Germany Tomorrow," *Stars and Stripes*, June 1, 1946, 4. See also other examples such as "Dependent Ship Buckner Due at Bremerhaven Today," *Stars and Stripes*, March 13, 1948, 5, "224 Scheduled to Arrive on Gibbons Today," *Stars and Stripes*, August 12, 1949, 5 and "Barry Due Tomorrow with 269 Dependents," *Stars and Stripes*, November 4, 1949, 2. Military members and dependent families continued to travel to and from Europe by ship until the early 1960s, thereafter by scheduled commercial airliner. The European Command assigned priority to those service members with the longest time in theater. See "Families of Men Here Longest to Get Transportation Priority," *Stars and Stripes*, May 29, 1946, 1.

5. Jane Mulvihill (military dependent spouse in the Hanau Milcom, Life Long Learning Institute, Chesterfield County) in conversation with the author, November 2012.

6. Terry Dean (former dependent who resided in the Mainz Milcom, 1959–1962) in correspondence with the author, June 5, 2014.

7. Tim Gilbert (military dependent child in the Frankfurt Milcom) in conversation with the author, March 2013.

8. Lamar Holt, "MSTS Puts the 'Sea' in Travel," *U.S. Lady* 4, no. 6 (November 1959): 10 and 41.

9. Venereal disease (VD) reached a peak in August 1945 with an average infection rate of 19 percent among American troops. Some regiments reported rates as high as 89 percent. See Petra Goedde, "From Villains to Victims: Fraternization and the Feminization of Germany, 1945–1947, *Diplomatic History* 23, no.1 (Winter 1999): 1. Overall, VD rates rose 235 percent from VE Day to the end of 1945. See John Willoughby, "The Sexual Behavior of American GIs during the Early Years of the Occupation of Germany," *The Journal of Military History* 62, no. 1 (January 1998): 157.

10. Anni P. Baker, *American Soldiers Overseas: The Global Military Presence* (Westport: Praeger, 2004), 45.

11. John Gimbel, *A German Community under American Occupation, Marburg, 1945–52* (Palo Alto: Stanford University Press, 1961), 3 and 202, Eugene Davidson, *The Death and Life of Germany: an Account of the American Occupation* (Columbia: University of Missouri, 1999) and (retired Major General) Franklin Davis, Jr. *Come as A Conqueror: The United States Army's Occupation of Germany, 1945–1949* (New York: Macmillan, 1967). All attest to the dire living conditions in early postwar Germany and the tenuous relationships between the Germans and the American occupying forces.

12. The wives identified themselves as representatives of the Servicemen's Wives and Children's Association. Donna Alvah, *Unofficial Ambassadors: American Military Families Overseas and the Cold War, 1946–1965* (New York: New York University Press, 2007), Alvah, 21.

13. Alvah, 24. Margaret Chase Smith (R-ME) was the first woman to serve in both the U.S. House and Senate. She served on numerous panels and committees during her 33 year political career including the House Armed Services Committee, House Naval Affairs Committee, the Senate Armed Services Committee, and the Senate Aeronautical and Space Committee. Smith also sponsored the 1948 Women's Armed Services Integration Act.

14. Martha Gravois, "Military Families in Germany, 1946–1986: Why They Came and Why They Stay," *Parameters* XVI, no. 4 (Winter 1986): 58. Regimental-sized units at this time were between 3,000 and 5,000 personnel.

15. Gravois, 58.

16. *Ibid*.

17. "VD–Less Units Cited," *Stars and Stripes*, February 11, 1948, 5.

18. Anna J. Merritt, and Robert L. Merritt, eds., *Public Opinion in Semisoveriegn Germany, The HICOG Surveys, 1949–1955*, Report No. 6 (6 March 1950), 58.

19. There were 99 American military bases in West Germany in 1947 and 278 in 1967. By one account 44,337 American dependents resided in West Germany by 1950, and 183,896 by 1960. Alvah, 46, 139.

20. As an example of the continued increases during the Cold War period the number of family members grew from 58,000 in 1953 to approximately 170,000 by 1959. See Mary Ellen Condon-Rall's "NATO and the Army Family in Europe," Center for Military History, accessed March 3, 2012, http://www.history.army.mil/html/.

21. Davidson, 189.

22. "Dependents" is an officially recognized term for all military family members living overseas who are legally sponsored by a service member.

23. U.S. Census Bureau, Vol. III Selected Area Reports, 1c. Americans Overseas, Table 1 Age of the US Civilian Population Abroad by Type, by Color, Gender and Sex: 1960, 1–5. This population also included foreign born dependents. 1950: Whites 93.5 percent of the Dependents Overseas Total. Blacks: 1.7 percent of the Dependents Overseas Total. National average was 9.99 percent. Others: 4.7 percent of the Dependents Overseas Total. National average was 0.5 percent. 1960: Whites: 90.0 percent of the Dependents Overseas Total. Blacks: 6.1 percent of the Dependents Overseas Total. National average was 10.5 percent. Others: 2.9 percent of the Dependents Overseas Total. National average was 0.9 percent. 1970: Whites: 86.2 percent of the Dependents Overseas Total. Blacks: 8.8 percent of the Dependents Overseas Total. National average was 11.1 percent. Others: 4.7 percent of the Dependents Overseas Total. National average was 1.4 percent.

24. See Heritage Foundation report "Global U.S. Troop Deployment, 1950–2003" *Center for Data Analysis Report* 04–11, accessed March 7, 2012, http://www.heritage.org/research/reports/2004/10/global-us-troop-deployment-1950-2003.

25. See Martin Klimke and Maria Höhn's "The Civil Rights Struggle, African American GIs, and Germany—A Digital Archive," German Historical Institute, accessed July 20, 2011, http://www.aacvr-germany.org.

26. For example, in 1963 West Germany hosted 180,049 dependents and Japan 50,025. These numbers correspond in close ratios with the numbers of military personnel stationed in those countries, 70 percent for Germany and 56 percent for Japan. The number of dependents in each country was a function of evolving military missions and availability of satisfactory housing. Racial, ethnic, or cultural differences were not considerations. See David W. Tarr, "The Military Abroad," *Annals of the American Academy of Political and Social Science* 36 (November 1966): Table 4, 36. Also see "Global U.S. Troop Deployment, 1950–2003," The Heritage Foundation, accessed July 20, 2012, http://www.heritage.org/research/reports/2004/10/global-us-troop-deployment-1950-2003.

27. Christian Seaford in Richard Reeves's *Daring Young Men*, 26. See also Lucius D. Clay, *Decision in Germany* (Garden City: Doubleday, 1950), Gail S. Halvorsen, *The Berlin Candy Bomber* (Springville, UT: Horizon, 1997), Daniel F. Harrington, *Berlin on the Brink: The Blockade, the Airlift, and the Early Cold War* (Lexington: University Press of Kentucky, 2012), and Arthur Pearcy, *Berlin Airlift* (Shrewsbury: Swan Hill Press, 1998).

28. Quoted in Reeves, 27.

29. Quoted in Reeves, 30. This was a particularly trying time for Truman, who was also making political decisions that would position him to capture the Democratic Presidential nomination in advance of the November 1948 election. See also Truman's comments regarding the decision to stay at the Harry S Truman Library and Museum site, *Oral Histories*, accessed February 7, 2012, http://www.trumanlibrary.org/whistlestop/study_collections/berlin_airlift/large/index.php?action=other

30. See Reeves, 45 for a detailed description of "Operation Vittles," and John Lemza, "The Berlin Airlift: Relief for a City Held Hostage," http://mason.gmu.edu/~jlemza/Final&20Assignment%20Home.html.

31. Lucius Clay, *Decision in Germany*, 386.

32. Clay, 386.

33. Diethelm Prowe, "Berlin: Catalyst and Fault Line of German-American Relations in the Cold War," in *The United States and Germany in the Era of the Cold War, 1945–1990: A Handbook, Volume 1: 1945–1968*, Detlef Junker, ed. (Washington, D.C.: German Historical Institute and New York: Cambridge: University Press, 2004), 166.

34. The OMGUS all but lifted the wartime fraternization ban by October 1, 1945. The new ban only prohibited marriages and co-habitation. Occupation authorities eventually removed the marriage ban between American servicemen and German at the end 1945. By June 1950 American servicemen had returned to the U.S. with 14,175 German brides. See Petra Goedde, "From Villains to Victims," 11. Political theorist Joseph S. Nye coined the term "soft power" which referred to the indirect, non-confrontational manner that nations could exert their influence on one another. See Joseph S. Nye, *Soft Power: The Means to Success in World Politics* (New York: Public Affairs, 2004), 5 and Alvah, *Unofficial Ambassadors*, 50.

35. See Kenneth Osgood, *Total Cold War: Eisenhower's Secret Propaganda Battle at Home and Abroad* (Lawrence: University Press of Kansas, 2008), 48 for a fuller description of the change in postwar strategy by the United States.

36. These included NSC 4 in December 1947, NSC 20/4 in November 1948 and NSC 68 in April 1950.

37. The Psychological Strategy Board, Operations Coordinating Board, Office of Policy Coordination, United States Information Services and United States Information Agency respectively. The People-to-People program also produced films through the Department of Defense such as "Morning Coffee with Dorothy Thompson" a 27 minute video interview with a veteran journalist and radio broadcaster who informed service wives living overseas how their behavior related to support of U.S. foreign policy. Contemporary journalists referred to Thompson as the "First Lady of Journalism."

38. This included Eisenhower's People-to-People Program. See Osgood, *Total Cold War*, 233.

39. "Expert Asserts 1/3 PWs Yielded to Brainwashing," *Stars and Stripes*, February 24, 1956, 7.

40. "Report: GIs in Korea Too Soft," *The Chicago Defender*, January 10, 1959, 9.

41. Ibid.

42. The military issued the Code under executive Order 10631 on August 17, 1955. See details at "Code of the United States Fighting Force," accessed September 4, 2012, http://en.wikipedia.org/wiki/Code_of_the_United_States_Fighting_Force.

43. "Army Adopts New Education Program to Back Up New Conduct Code," *Stars and Stripes*, September 5, 1955, 24. There was also some mild interest among

some Washington elites for expanding the precepts of the Code to include American civilians. Among them was Admiral Arthur Radford, the Chairman of the Joint Chiefs of Staff (CJCS). In October 1955 he observed that "all Americans should live by the Armed Forces' code of conduct" and that "every American should be dedicated to his country and understand thoroughly the meaning of its way of life." "Service Code Called Guide for Americans," *Stars and Stripes*, October 27, 1955, 23.

44. Former news correspondent John B. Adams and his wife Alvalee Adams were the independent owners and publishers of *U.S. Lady*. The first issue was in 1955 and the last in April 1968.

45. "U.S. Lady's World," *U.S. Lady* 1, no. 6, May 1956, 8.

46. "Soldier! Why are you Here?" *Stuttgart Post News*, December 2, 1950, 8, RG 549, Records of the U.S. Army Europe, 1942–1990, Box 3355, National Archives College Park.

47. Ibid.

48. From text of speech by Joseph McCarthy at Wheeling, West Virginia, February 9, 1950. See *History Matters*, GMU, accessed May 2, 2013, http://historymatters.gmu.edu/d/6456/. See also John E. Haynes, *Red Scare or Red Menace: American Communism and Anticommunism in the Cold War Era* (Chicago: Ivan R. Dee, 1996) for a full understanding of Christian anticommunist initiatives and the link with McCarthyism.

49. For a fuller description of the Freedom Foundation's principles and their strong links with President Eisenhower see Bogle, *The Pentagon's Battle for the American Mind*, 77–80.

50. After retirement, numerous military leaders went to work on the staff of the foundation. They included Major General Harlan N. Hartness former director of the Armed Forces Information and Education Program, Admiral Felix Stump former commander of U.S. Naval forces in the Pacific and Admiral Arthur Radford former Chairman of the Joint Chiefs of Staff, see "Retired General Joins Freedoms Foundation," *New York Times*, February 12, 1956, 85 and "Freedoms Foundation Names Admiral as Aide," *New York Times*, October 14, 1958, 6.

51. "Freedom—My Heritage, My Responsibility," *Stars and Stripes*, February 11, 1968, 8 and "My Hopes for America's Future," *Stars and Stripes*, May 22, 1969, 9.

52. "Yanks Sponsor Essay Contest for Germans," *Stars and Stripes*, February 24, 1951, 5.

53. "USAFE Stations Cited," *Stars and Stripes*, May 5, 1967, 8.

54. John C. Broger of the Christian-based Far East Broadcasting Company developed the concept. He later became head of the Directorate for Armed Forces Information and Education.

55. See Lori Bogle's description of the program in *The Pentagon's Battle for the American Mind*, 127 and Kenneth Osgood in *Total Cold War*, 314.

56. "Yank Classes on 'Militant Liberty' Set," *Stars and Stripes*, November 24, 1955, 24.

57. "Pentagon Tests 'Liberty' Plan," *Stars and Stripes*, January 1957, 9.

58. The program had a number of advocates in the U.S. Congress. Among them were Senators Thomas E. Martin (R-IA) and Strom Thurmond (R-SC). But it was infighting between the State Department, the CIA and the military that killed it. See "Militant Liberty: Antidote for Communism," *Congressional Record*, January 5, 1956, A25 and Congressional Hearings: Military Cold War Education and Speech Review Policies, Part 3, 1035.

59. Walker named the program 'Pro-Blue' to contrast 'Communist Red.' He was a decorated combat veteran of both World War Two and the Korean War. Walker was a staunch conservative who often expressed segregationist views. Later investigative reports revealed that he survived an assassination attempt by Lee Harvey Oswald days before the killing of President Kennedy. See "Gen. Edwin Walker Dies; Controversial Warrior," Richard Pearson, *Washington Post*, November 2, 1993, B6 and "Gen. Edwin Walker, 83, is Dead; Promoted Rightist Causes in 60's," Eric Pace, *New York Times*, November 2, 1993, B10.

60. Hargis was a member of the John Birch Society and was a known segregationist. More than 500 radio stations and 250 television stations broadcast his conservative *Christian Crusade* ministry in the 1950s and 1960s. See "Billy James Hargis," *The Economist*, December 16, 2004, accessed September 5, 2012, http://www.economist.com/node/3499528?story_id=3499528.

61. "Walker Cites Threat of Communism," *Stars and Stripes*, April 16, 1961, 1.

62. Ibid.

63. Ibid.

64. The Hatch Act of 1939 made it a violation of federal law for employees, including the military, while in official capacity to participate in partisan political activity.

65. "Walker Tried to Sway Votes: McNamara," *Stars and Stripes*, September 7, 1961, 1.

66. "Sen. Bridges Has Praise for Walker," *Stars and Stripes*, May 19, 1961, 24.

67. For a fuller discussion of this religious penetration see Bogle, *The Pentagon's Battle for the American Mind*, 58.

68. "4 Freedoms Cited at Dedication of Neckarsulm Chapel," *Stars and Stripes*, December 29, 1952, 5.

69. A common religious-military image in many military chapels is the scene of George Washington praying at Valley Forge.

70. The window, dedicated in October 1950, commemorated the successful Berlin Air Lift of 1948–1949.

71. CONUS was the military acronym for 'Continental United States.'

72. See Big Picture film "Of Soldiers and Altars" US Army Chaplaincy, Office of the Chief of Information, Army Pictorial Center, accessed July 2, 2014, https://www.youtube.com/watch?v=Ez9pw0PMTvg.

73. Bogle, 80. See also "Eisenhower Declares Free Government Is Based on Deeply Felt Religious Faith," *Washington Post*, February 6, 1953, 1.

74. Bogle, 100.

75. Anne C. Loveland, *American Evangelicals and the U.S. Military: 1942–1993* (Baton Rouge: Louisiana State University Press, 1996), 37.

76. The Vogelweh Milcom near Kaiserslautern was the largest military community outside the continental United States. "Vogelweh to Hear Graham," *Stars and Stripes*, May 26, 1955, 1.

77. "Changing Attitudes Toward Billy Graham Crusades," *Stars and Stripes*, July 17, 1960, 11 and "Billy Graham: 14 Years Odyssey of an Evangelist," *Stars and Stripes*, August 26, 1963, 11.

78. Ken Zumwalt, *Stars and Stripes: World War II and the Early Years* (Austin: Eakin Press, 1989), 139.

79. "Dial Day: Your Guide to Good Listening in Europe," *Stars and Stripes*, December 29, 1952, 5.

80. Schuller's "Hour of Power" program appeared in Sunday television listings for AFNTV-Germany in the *Stars and Stripes*. See "Sunday Television," *Stars and Stripes*, February 2, 1981, 22 and "Sunday Television," *Stars and Stripes*, April 25, 1982, 21. Also see "Hour of Power Trimmed to 30 Minutes," *Stars and Stripes*, November 23, 1989, 39.

81. Patrick Allitt, *Religion in America Since 1945: A History* (New York: Columbia Univrsity Press, 2003), 22. Allitt describes how American religious groups were "terrified of Russian aggression and horrified by the Communists' militant atheism" and used their political and financial leverage to influence military culture. See also Jonathan P. Herzog, *The Spiritual-Industrial Complex* (New York: Oxford University Press, 2011) for an understanding of how individuals such as Francis Cardinal Spellman "became a fierce advocate for religious awakening in the name of national security." Herzog, 62.

82. "Women in World Leadership," *Stars and Stripes*, September 10, 1966, 16.

83. "MCCW Opens Berchtesgaden Meeting," *Stars and Stripes*, September 27, 1958, 8.

84. The reference is to John Winthrop's comment in 1630 regarding the spiritual founding of the colony in Massachusetts. Consensus historians such as Daniel Boorstin frequently cited this event to describe the strong feeling of American destiny. See Daniel Boorstin, *The Americans: The Colonial Experience*, 3.

85. One example of these types of films is "Your Job in Germany," War Department Orientation Film, U.S. Army Information and Education Division, *Der Spiegel On-line*, accessed February 10, 2012, http://www.spiegel.de/video/video-26590.html. See also Osgood, *Total Cold War*, 244.

86. US Forces European Theater, Information and Education Service, *Orientation Program for Dependents* (1946), 18.

87. The Headquarters United States Forces European Command (EC) and the Office of the Secretary of Defense, Armed Forces Information and Education Division (AFIED) published these two pamphlets respectively.

88. *A Pocket Guide to Germany*, Office of the Secretary of Defense, Armed Forces Information and Education Division (Wash, DC: US GPO, 1950), 8.

89. *An Introduction to Germany*, Office of the Secretary of Defense, Armed Forces Information and Education Division (Headquarters, US Forces European Theater, G-1, 1947), 19. The Joint Chiefs of Staff, *Directive to the Commander in Chief of U.S. Forces of Occupation Regarding the Military Government of Germany* (JCS 1067) published in April 1945 stated as its purpose to "make certain Germany would never again become a threat to the peace of the world." See S.G. Wennberg, "Some Economic Problems of Allied Occupation Policy in Germany," *American Journal of Economics and Sociology* 5, no. 4 (July 1946): 426.

90. *An Introduction to Germany*, 19.

91. *A Pocket Guide to Germany*, 9, 12.

92. *A Pocket Guide to Germany*, 26.

93. "Your Job in Germany," War Department Orientation Film, U.S. Army Information and Education Division, RG 111, ARC ID 4529712, Local ID 11-OF-8, *Der Spiegel On-line*, accessed February 10, 2012, http://www.spiegel.de/video/video-26590.html.

94. See Big Picture film *Defense against Enemy Propaganda*, Arc Identifier 2569629/Local ID 111-TV-360. Notable actors and journalists narrated the film series. Among them were Edwin R. Murrow, John Wayne, Helen Hayes, Alexander Scourby, Walter Cronkite, Lorne Greene, Raymond Massey and Ronald Reagan. See also Big Picture film "The Code of the Fighting Man," Arc Identifier 2569693/Local ID 111-TV-428.

95. "Film by Pentagon Depicts U.S. Ideal," *New York Times*, July 16, 1961, 42.

96. See Big Picture film *Challenge of Ideas*. By the film's release date in 1961Murrow was serving as the Director of the U.S. Information Agency.

97. The Big Picture series ran from 1950 to 1970.

98. ABC television and its network of affiliates aired the series from 1951 to 1964 to the American public.

99. See Big Picture film "Army Newsreel Number One," ARC Identifier 2569658/Local ID 111-TV-390.

100. The size of the Milcom viewing audiences grew between the late 1950s and the 1990s as AFN television coverage spread to include smaller Milcoms and satellite residential locations.

101. See Big Picture film *Information and Education Overseas*, ARC Identifier 2569468/Local ID 111-TV-198. Access to education was central to how Americans viewed themselves as an exceptional people.

102. See Big Picture film *People-to-People*, ARC Identifier 2569695/Local ID 111-TV-430.

103. See Big Picture film *Operation Friendly Hand*, NARA ARC ID 2569605, Local ID 111-TV-336.

104. See the Big Picture film *Germany Today*, NARA ARC ID 2569714, Local ID 111-TV-455.

105. See Big Picture film *Ottumwa, U.S.A.*, ARC Identifier 2569655/Local ID 111-TV-387.

106. See aslo Big Picture film *Eisenhower the Soldier*, ARC Identifier 2569699/Local ID 111-TV-435. Freedoms Foundation awarded the series three consecutive annual presentations of its George Washington Honor Medal for patriotic achievement.

107. See Robert P. Grathwol and Donita Moorhus, *Berlin and the American Military: A Cold War Chronicle* (New York: New York University Press, 1999), John P. Hawkins, *Army of Hope, Army of Alienation* and Richard Pells, *Not Like Us: How Europeans Have Loved, Hated, And Transformed American Culture Since World War II* (New York: Basic Books, 1998).

108. Hawkins, 6.

109. Gravois, 62. This reference is to "Shipment of Dependents," *Stars and Stripes*, April 14 and 18, 1946, 88. The more fundamental reference is to exceptionalist imagery proposed by historians such as Daniel Boorstin who noted that American innovation and independence of spirit was born of challenges that came early in national development. See Boorstin's *The Americans: The Colonial Experience* (New York: Random House, 1958).

110. Scott Hambric (former Sergeant assigned to the 11th Armored Cavalry Regiment in the Fulda Milcom, 1975–1978) in correspondence with the author, July 2014.

111. This episode comes from a collection of letters addressing the Kale family's experiences during the early occupation years in Germany. See Mark W. Falzini, *Letters Home*, 55.

112. During the next few years the US government had alleviated most food shortages for the Milcoms through increased shipments of consumable items and the opening of relatively well-stocked commissaries.

113. Falzini, 132.

114. Falzini, 30.

115. Military policy directed that the first properties seized should be those that belonged to former Nazi party members or supporters. The priority for housing was initially to U.S. military personnel, then displaced persons (DPs). After that, authorities made housing available to German communities for their use. By mid–1946 military policies directed that American dependents and civilians receive housing "in a manner comparable to that on U.S. posts in 1937." See *The U.S. Army in the Occupation of Germany, 1944–1946*, Center of Military History, U.S. Army (Washington, DC: GPO, 1975) note 76, 442.

116. Franklin M. Davis, Jr., *Come as a Conqueror*, 189.

117. *Ibid.*, 188. Davis notes that the exact number was 30,143 properties that included 24,502 private houses, 1,458 apartment houses, 780 hostels, 569 schools, 333 office buildings, 263 factory buildings, 222 warehouses and depots, 103 retail stores, 179 barracks, 457 pieces of land, and 1,279 other properties. These were available for use by military as well as dependent personnel.

118. This was the case in Marburg where the American military forced the relocation of German residents from an entire section of the town. John Gimbel, *A German Community under American Occupation*, 55.

119. *An Introduction to Germany*, 43. In some isolated instances, such as for the Bad Kissingen Milcom, authorities housed families in area hotels. See also *Introduction to Germany*, 44.

120. Falzini, 9.

121. The term "brat" is a colloquialism for a military dependent youth or child.

122. A 'Gauleiter' was a regional Nazi political boss.

123. Hank Johnson (former dependent youth living in the Nuremberg Milcom 1949–1953), in correspondence with the author, February 2014.

124. Norman Kappes (former dependent youth living in the Frankfurt Milcom 1946–1950), in correspondence with the author, February 2014.

125. Terry Dean (former dependent who resided in the Mainz Milcom, 1959–1962) in correspondence with the author, June 5, 2014.

126. American license plates which bore the initials 'USA' were the same size and shape as those in the United States; German plates were longer. American plates were light green during the early postwar years and German plates were white. Milcom members were able to ship their privately owned vehicles (POVs) to Germany at government expense. Their arrival was as anxiously anticipated as was the arrival of family members and they were also listed in the *Stars and Stripes*. See "58 Vehicles Wait at Port," *Stars and Stripes*, February 13, 1948, 5.

127. As part of the occupation requirements and reparations West Germany had to finance the construction of American facilities. See Grathwol, caption, 62.

128. Prisoners of War (POW). See Eugene Davidson, *The Death and Life of Germany*, 139. The United States also took control of some housing from the French forces after their departure from West Germany upon France's withdrawal from NATO in 1966.

129. Commissaries provide subsistence items similar to a food market and post exchanges (PX) serve as small department stores. The system of Department of Defense Dependent Schools (DODDS) also developed an extensive network to accommodate the Milcom families. The first facilities opened in Germany in October 1946.

130. This was a commonly used term. See: Gravois, 62, Alvah, 30 and Baker, 56.

131. Charlotte Wolf, *Garrison Community*, 2. Wolf's comment reflects the opinion of local nationals who yearned for the higher standard of life that appeared available to American Milcom members residing in the segregated and sometimes restricted living areas.

132. Wellington Long, "The American Presence," *American-German Review* 32, no. 6 (1966): 3.

133. Wellington Long, 4.

134. Joe Kiely (Former Air Force officer stationed at Ramstein air base, 1952–1955) in correspondence with the author, June 2014.

135. See Adam Seipp's study of the U.S. military's struggle to navigate between its needs and limiting the disruption to contemporary German lives in the early 1950s. *Strangers in the Wild Place* (Bloomington: Indiana University Press, 2013).

136. See Martha Gravois description of privileges available to Milcom members in the AMZON during the early occupation years. Gravois, 64.

137. The Status of Forces Agreement (SOFA) negotiated legal rights and privileges for the American forces (including dependents) in West Germany. The two nations clarified and renegotiated the agreement several times in later years. They completed this first, as part of a mutual security pact in 1951, then when West Germany joined NATO in 1955. See *An Introduction to Germany* for additional details of life in the American Zone. There were some exceptions to the legal SOFA protections particularly in the case of capital crimes.

138. AFN would later become Armed Forces Radio and Television Service (AFRTS) with the introduction

of television in the 1950s. The German government assigned specific bandwidths to AFN and AFRTS which in turn directed their broadcasts to target only Milcom areas although there was some bleed-over to German communities.

139. The *Stars and Stripes* newspaper originally published for servicemen during the war but gradually began refocusing its content to accommodate a broader spectrum of Milcom members after 1946.

140. This quote requires context. During the early postwar years many German publishing houses were just restarting their presses under American licensure. It is not realistic to expect that a greater percentage of American civilian employees would speak German or that a greater percentage of books in American libraries would be in German. See Eugene Davidson's work, *The Death and Life of Germany*, 354.

141. *U.S. Lady*, January 1967, 3. Members of the selection committee included Mrs. Cyrus Vance wife of the Deputy Secretary of Defense, and the wives of the secretaries of each branch of the armed forces, as well as the wife of the ambassador to Vietnam.

142. *U.S. Lady*, April 1967, 14.

143. Alvah, Unofficial Ambassadors, 106.

144. The reference is to a bag used by the military for mail. The editorial staff changed the *B-Bag* column title in 1968 to the more familiar *Letters to the Editor*.

145. "Saw Freedom on the March," *Stars and Stripes*, May 14, 1948, 2.

146. "Hitchhiker Criticism," *Stars and Stripes*, December 27, 1950, 4.

147. "Veterans' Day Program," *Stars and Stripes*, November 28, 1956, 14.

148. "U.S. Opposes State Force, Russian Newsmen Told," *Stars and Stripes*, January 25, 1968, 16.

149. "Forces Outline Personnel Policy," *Stars and Stripes*, March 7, 1950, 4.

150. "Business Booms for Democracy's Salesmen," *Stars and Stripes*, April 1, 1951, 4.

151. "Army Decorates Two Ex-PWs for Defying Captors," *Stars and Stripes*, August 25, 1954, 7.

152. Chapter 3 of this study discusses media management and its relation to free speech during the early postwar decades.

153. The 1953 event in the former capital drew "more than 500,000 Berliners." "Armed Forces Day Events Set by Units in USAREUR," *Stars and Stripes*, May 14, 1954, 8.

154. Between 1948 and 1990 the *Stars and Stripes* routinely carried extensive listings of annual Armed Forces Day events. "Forces Plan Mightiest Display Since War Today," *Stars and Stripes*, May 16, 1953, 4.

155. *Ibid*.

156. Jack Cipolla (former corporal in the 8th Infantry Regiment stationed in Berlin, Life Long Learning Institute, Chesterfield, Virginia), in discussion with the author, November 2012.

157. Pells, 38.

158. Hawkins, 7; and *An Introduction to Germany*, 51.

159. Charles Millstein (a former military dependent he and his family resided in the Kaiserslautern Milcom, 1952–1954) in correspondence with the author, June 2014.

160. Falzini, 97.

161. Alvah, 8, 136.

162. See Charlotte Wolf, *Garrison Community*, 2, for a fuller explanation of the overseas military community. Although the focus of Wolf's study was a small military community of Air Force personnel in Turkey her findings and conclusions apply uniformly across the broader spectrum of most contemporary Milcoms in Europe. Wolf does acknowledge that the behaviors of Milcom members contributed to "the enhancement or tarnishing of the United States' 'image' by reflections from such interpersonal contacts."

163. Other than the loss of manpower to work fields and land gone fallow, Allied mandates divested Germany of approximately 25 percent of its arable lands by assigning them to Poland with the postwar Oder-Neisse Line boundary shift in the east. See Henry Ashby Turner, Jr. *Germany from Partition to Reunification* (New Haven: Yale University Press, 1992).

164. The population total was 49 million. Henry Ashby Turner, *Germany from Partition to Reunification*, 6, 30.

165. OMGUS was the Office of Military Government, United States. The occupational control of West Germany passed from the OMGUS to the High Commissioner of Germany, HICOG, in December 1949.

166. By 1947 approximately 25 percent of all Displaced Persons (DPs) in Germany were Jewish. Food distribution authorities avoided a crisis in early 1947 when 10 million pounds of kosher beef arrived from the Irish Republic. See Mark Wyman, *DP: Europe's Displaced Persons, 1945–1951* (Philadelphia: Balch Institute, 1989).

167. By July 1946 the U.S. Department of the Army had opened a special budget line for food supplies for Germany: Government Aid and Relief in Occupied Areas (GARIOA). It remained in effect until March 1950. Wilfried Mausbach, "Restructuring and Support: Beginnings of American Economic Policy in Occupied Germany," in Detlef Junker, *The United States and Germany in the Era of the Cold War*, Vol. 1, 282.

168. Most stock items arrive at overseas commissaries through a special direct supply pipeline from the United States.

169. *An Introduction to Germany*, 52. By May 1946 imports from the United States accounted for 50 percent of the German bread ration. "Zone Receives 50 percent of Bread from U.S.," *Stars and Stripes*, May 31, 1946, 2.

170. See "Text of the Hoover Missions' Findings on the Food Requirements of Germany," *New York Times*, February 28, 1947, 13, and "Hunger Strikes in Germany," *New York Times*, February 5, 1948, 22. German workers walked off their jobs to protest distribution problems that reduced their caloric allocation to levels "which often approach those of the Nazi concentration camps."

171. See "West Europeans Eat Almost as Well as in '39, Survey Says," *Stars and Stripes*, November 27, 1949, 2.

172. "Tuberculosis Rises Sharply in U.S. Zone," *New York Times*, May 29, 1946, 15 and "Tuberculosis Called Rampant in Germany," *New York Times*, December 13, 1946, 13.

173. "Tuberculosis Rises in Germany," *New York Times*, July 14, 1947, 8.
174. "Tuberculosis Now Epidemic in Europe," *Washington Post*, February 12, 1949, 11.
175. "Danish TB Teams Fighting Warborn Spread of Scourge," *Stars and Stripes*, March 24, 1949, 2.
176. "Decreasing TB Mortality Rate Leads to Hope Disease May Become Rare," *Stars and Stripes*, January 24, 1951, 4.
177. "World's No.1 Enemy: Drive to End Tuberculosis Urged," *Stars and Stripes*, October 2, 1954, 10, and "VA Speeding Recovery of TB Patients," *Stars and Stripes*, March 2, 1957, 9.
178. "Yanks Warned on Diphtheria," *Stars and Stripes*, February 4, 1950, 2.
179. See "Measles Takes Hold," *Stars and Stripes*, June 11, 1949, 2, "6th Inf Regt Treating 6,612 at Berlin Festivities," *Stars and Stripes*, December 22, 1952, 5, and "Measles Outbreak Eases," *Stars and Stripes*, December 27, 1954, 4.
180. "174 Polio Cases in Bavaria," *Stars and Stripes*, August 2, 1948, 5.
181. "Frankfurt Area Has Vaccine for Measles," *Stars and Stripes*, July 6, 1964, 9.
182. See "Author Oks German Guests for Berlin's 'Night Must Fall,'" *Stars and Stripes*, January 25, 1948, 10 and "Yule Spirit Overcomes Measles Quarantine," *Stars and Stripes*, December 24, 1962, 9.
183. See Elaine Tyler Mays' explanation of gender roles and expectations in the postwar period in *Homeward Bound*, 5–6, 8.
184. Bill Hanne (former Army officer in the 3rd Squadron, 8th Cavalry Regiment), in discussion with the author, March 2013.
185. Sally Hollenbaugh (former Army spouse lived in the Erlangen Milcom with her husband assigned to the 4th Armored Division in 1956) in correspondence with the author, June 25, 2014.
186. Kevin McEnery (former Army officer, 1st Battalion, 37th Regiment, 1st Armored Division, Katterbach Milcom, 1982–1985) in correspondence with the author, June 13, 2014.
187. See Frankfurt American High School website, http://www.frankfurthigh.com/history/subpages/fahs_history.htm. FAHS was one of five high schools the DODDS operated from 1946 to the late 1990s. See the American Overseas Schools Historical Society website, http://www.aoshs.org/LinksOverseasSchools.html.
188. Neil Albaugh (former military dependent, resided in the Mannheim Milcom, 1954–1955, and the Heidelberg Milcom, 1955–1956, also attended Frankfurt American High School, 1956–1957) in phone conversation with the author, February 2014.
189. See Susan Douglas, *Where the Girls Are: Growing Up Female with the Mass Media* (New York: Three Rivers Press, 1995), for a full discussion of postwar gender expectations and roles.
190. "Survey Shows Wives Work 80-Hr Week," *Stars and Stripes*, September 3, 1955, 5.
191. Ed DeLong (former enlisted member of the U.S. Navy assigned to the Port of Bremerhaven, 1950–1952) in correspondence with the author, June 2014.

192. Kent Goldsmith (former enlisted member of the U.S. Air Force assigned to the 6th Shoran Beacon Squadron in the Landstuhl Milcom, 1954–1956) in correspondence with the author, May 2014.
193. Hank Johnson (former Army dependent whose father commanded a cavalry troop in the 3rd Armored Division lived in the Butzbach Milcom during the late 1950s) in correspondence with the author, February 2014.
194. "Americans Aid St. Nick in EC Yule Event," *Stars and Stripes*, November 23, 1948, 11.
195. "Boy Scouts Hailed by Ike," *Stars and Stripes*, February 9, 1953, 3. For a better understanding of the strong link between the Army and Scouting see the 1961 Big Picture film "The US Army and the Boy Scouts," ARC Identifier 2569758/Local ID 111-TV-520.
196. *Ibid*. See also Dwight D. Eisenhower: "Message to the Boy Scouts of America on Their 43d Anniversary," February 7, 1953. Online by Gerhard Peters and John T. Woolley, *The American Presidency Project*, accessed April 27, 2013, http://www.presidency.ucsb.edu/ws/?pid=9862.
197. "Eddy Extends Greetings to Boy Scouts," *Stars and Stripes*, February 8, 1953, 2. USAREUR is an acronym for the United States Army in Europe.
198. There are some ongoing projects that promise to shed light on early postwar Scouting activities. See Mischa Honeck's "Young Patriot's Abroad: A Global History of the Boy Scouts of America, 1910–1960," *GHI Bulletin Supplement* 8 (2012): 43–44, accessed November 4, 2012, http://www.ghi-dc.org/files/publications/bu_supp/supp008/043.pdf.
199. "U.S., German Troops Join in Yule Party," *Stars and Stripes*, December 24, 1954, 10.
200. "NACOM Units at Work on Christmas Plans," *Stars and Stripes*, November 23, 1954, 10.
201. Honeck, 43.
202. "BSA Roster Tops 19,325 in Europe," *Stars and Stripes*, February 7, 1962, 8.
203. *Pocket Guide to Germany*, 30.
204. "GYA: Army's EC Youth Program Completes Second Year," *Stars and Stripes*, April 25, 1948, 11.
205. "GYA: Army's EC Youth Program Completes Second Year," *Stars and Stripes*, April 25, 1948, 8.
206. Richard L. Merritt, *Democracy Imposed: US Occupation Policy and the German Public, 1945–1949* (New Haven: Yale University Press, 1995), OMG Survey #56, 278. Both the OMGUS and the HICOG generated hundreds of surveys in the early postwar years to keep their finger on the pulse of German public opinion in the AMZON.
207. "GYA: Army's EC Youth Program Completes Second Year," *Stars and Stripes*, April 25, 1948, 8.
208. A Pocket Guide to Germany, 26.
209. Tim Gilbert (former Frankfurt Milcom dependent child), in discussion with the author, March 2013.
210. Norman Kappes (former dependent youth living in the Frankfurt Milcom 1946–1950), in correspondence with the author, February 2014. Norman Kappes' parents were both immigrants to the United States in 1929 and 1930. His extended family of aunts, uncles, and cousins all remained in Germany during the war.

His father worked as a civilian for American Airlines during the war and the company transferred him to Frankfurt afterward.

211. "Music, Sports, parties to Highlight G-A Week," *Stars and Stripes*, May 4, 1967, 8.

212. "Church Services," *Stars and Stripes*, June 26, 1948, 11.

213. "German Workers to Take Ordnance Safety Course," *Stars and Stripes*, December 11, 1953, 9.

214. See the Big Picture film "Foreign Nationals," ARC Identifier 2569584/Local ID 111-TV-387 for a fuller description of Milcom employment of local nationals.

215. For examples of both casual contacts and organized events and examples of American beneficence that were useful in bridging the gap between the cultures see Maria Höhn and Martin Klimke, *A Breath of Freedom* (New York: Palgrave, 2010), Maria Höhn, *GIs and Frauleins* (Chapel Hill: University of North Carolina Press, 2002) and Höhn and Seungsook Moon, *Over There*. Richard Reeves provides an iconic example of an entire city showing appreciation in his history of the Berlin airlift, *Daring Young Men*.

Chapter Two

1. "Jazz Grips Germany," *Stars and Stripes*, July 16, 1949, 7.

2. The ideas of America's role as a cultural hegemon, which used its culture as an imperative to leverage influence in West Germany are similar to the perceptions presented by Clifford Geertz in *The Interpretation of Cultures* (New York: Basic Books, 1973) and Richard Pells in *Not Like Us*.

3. This is consistent with the image of the American as a new Adam, separated from the European past, "its history and habits" and "poised to start a new history." RWG Lewis, *The American Adam* (Chicago: University of Chicago Press, 1955) 1 and 4. Boorstin offers a similar perspective with his understanding that Americans had a sharper vision toward the future because Europe had accumulated a rich but cumbersome cultural baggage." Boorstin, 145 and 149.

4. See Pekka Hamalainen and Samuel Truett, "On Borderlands," for a fuller discussion of cross boundary exchanges, *The Journal of American History* 98, no. 2 (September 2011): 338–361. Also see Reinhold Wagnleitner, "Propagating the American Dream: Cultural Policies as Means of Integration," *American Studies International* 24, no. 1 (April 1986): 67 and Maria Höhn, *GIs and Frauleins: The German-American Encounter in 1950s West Germany*. Chapel Hill: University of North Carolina Press, 2002.

5. For a fuller understanding of how the economy and culture of abundance shaped ideas of and exceptional America and contributed to a sense of freedom see David M. Potter's *People of Plenty: Economic Abundance and the American Character* (Chicago: University of Chicago Press, 1954).

6. As quoted in Höhn, *GIs and Fräuleins*, 79. By 1954 the Coca-Cola Corporation had 96 bottling plants in West Germany, more than in any other European country. See Richard Pells, *Not Like Us*, 199.

7. The Coca-Cola Corporation introduced its products into Germany in 1929. The Nazis selected it as one of three official drinks of the 1938 Olympics. After 1945 it regained its prominence as a drink of preference. The Billy Wilder directed film "One, Two, Three" starring James Cagney is a comic postwar look at capitalism in general and the penetration of Coca-Cola into German culture in particular. See "Coca-Cola History: A 'Refreshing' Look at German-American Relations," by Jeff R. Schutts, GHI Bulletin no. 40 (Spring 2007): 127–142, accessed May 3, 2013, http://www.ghi-dc.org/files/publications/bulletin/bu040/127.pdf.

8. As quoted in Höhn, *GIs and Fräuleins*, 81.

9. Falzini, 129.

10. *Ibid.*, 19.

11. Literally, "ocean liners of the road," referring to the large American automobile. The automobile emerged as a central figure and artifact of American popular culture and consumerism. The reference is from Höhn, *GIs and Fräuleins*.

12. There were similar experiences of this American cultural penetration in other countries in Europe and Asia, such as Japan. See "America as Desire and Violence," Shunya Yoshimi, Inter-Asia Cultural Studies 4, no. 3, 2003, accessed January 31, 2014, http://web.mit.edu/condry/Public/cooljapan/Mar23-2006/YoshimiShunya03AmViolDesire.pdf.

13. Dina Smith's discussion of mobility, machine aesthetics and kinetic architecture is easily understood as a lens to view the American automobile, see "Movable Containers: Cold War Trailers and Trailer Parks," in Douglas Field, ed., *American Cold War Culture* (Edinburgh: Edinburgh University Press: 2005), 69–87.

14. For a fuller understanding of that social and cultural connection, see Karal Ann Marling, "America's Love Affair with the Automobile in the Television Age," *Design Quarterly*, no. 146 (1989): 5–20.

15. "New Cars Roll Fast on EC Arrival," *Stars and Stripes*, May 24, 1949, 5.

16. This was one of the infrequent instances when the *Stars and Stripes* permitted advertising for commercial purposes. It was possible because it was an offer made through the European Exchange System, a government-affiliated department that supported the morale and welfare of military members. Although there was a degree of readership among Germans, especially those who worked on American installations, information on exact circulation numbers among the German public is not available. The *Stars and Stripes* geared its articles and advertisements toward American readers.

17. "First Stateside Car Arrives at BPE," *Stars and Stripes*, July 2, 1948, 4.

18. Plymouth ad, *Stars and Stripes*, November 2, 1952, 9.

19. Automotive ad, *Stars and Stripes*, March 14, 1954, 41.

20. "810 Cars Sold by EES in May," *Stars and Stripes*, June 18, 1948, 5.

21. "New Cars Roll Fast on EC Arrival," *Stars and Stripes*, May 24, 1949, 5.

22. Automobile sales offices were a common fixture

just outside the main gate of larger American kasernes throughout the Cold War period.

23. Lower ranks could ship a vehicle only if approved by their commander. There was also a nominal charge of $300 for Department of Defense civilians and Red Cross workers. See "Jam Broken, Ships Ferry Cars to BPE," *Stars and Stripes*, April 17, 1954, 3.

24. BPE was the Bremerhaven Port of Entry, the same location where dependents arrived.

25. Although exact numbers are difficult to determine it is possible to understand the large volume of automobiles arriving in EUCOM through port records for BPE. As examples, for the early postwar decades they indicate that 229 arrived during the first two weeks of May 1948, and 1,500 were arriving in the country by April 1954. These totals combine with other numbers such as EES car sales that totaled 810 for May 1948. "BPE Car Record Looms for May," *Stars and Stripes*, May 25, 1948, 5, "Jam Broken, Ships Ferry Cars to BPE," *Stars and Stripes*, April 17, 1954, 3, and "810 Cars Sold by EES in May," *Stars and Stripes*, June 18, 1948, 5.

26. Concerns over automotive safety began in 1941when the U.S. government recorded 39,969 traffic-related deaths. After the war it established the House Sub-Committee on Traffic Safety to investigate ways to keep the public safe. This included testing new devices such as the safety belt and pressuring manufacturers to make cars safer for the driver. The Federal Aid Highway Act of 1956 also outlined a more active role for the Federal government to take in overseeing traffic safety. See *Federal Highway Administration: Highway History, Chapter 4, The Federal Role in Highway Safety*, accessed November 3, 2013, https://www.fhwa.dot.gov/infrastructure/safety04.cfm. Also see "Firms Pressed on Safer Car," *Stars and Stripes*, May 2, 1954, 7.

27. "BPE Drivers Wearing 'No Accident' Braid," *Stars and Stripes*, March 4, 1948, 4.

28. "One in 10 Private Cars Found Unsafe at BPE," *Stars and Stripes*, January 21, 1949, 5.

29. "Authorized Speed Limits for American Cars in Germany," B-Bag, *Stars and Stripes*, June 25, 1953, 13 and "Army Officials Urge Stuttgart to Curb Traffic," *Stars and Stripes*, September 21, 1954, 4.

30. "Yanks Rush to Get German Insurance," *Stars and Stripes*," September 28, 1953, 5.

31. "Safety Campaign Keeps Plugging for Safe Driving," *Heidelberg Post*, November 10, 1949, 1.

32. "Support the Base Safety Campaign," *Gateway*, September 15, 1950, 1.

33. "Safety Director Introduces Plans to Cut Accidents," *Heidelberg Post*, November 3, 1949, 1.

34. "We Live Correctly Say the Americans," *Die Zeit*, December 11, 1952, accessed March 28, 2013, http://www.zeit.de/1952/50/wir-leben-richtig-sagen-die-amerikaner.

35. Concurrently, American and German authorities were working to alleviate the housing shortage for West Germans and Displaced Persons (DPs) in the AMZON. These efforts suggest four parallel initiatives: construction of housing for Americans to relieve demands on German housing, return of requisitioned properties to German control, construction of new housing for Germans and resettlement of DPs to areas outside West Germany. See "U.S. Taxpayers Build 33,000 German Homes," *Stars and Stripes*, February 3, 1952, 17, "U.S. Derequisitions 80 percent of EC Properties," *Stars and Stripes*, January 31, 1951, 1, "Housing Ok'd by Bundestag," *Stars and Stripes*, February 26, 1950 2.

36. See Eric D. Weitz's discussion of new architecture and modern interior design in *Weimar Germany: Promise and Tragedy* (Princeton: Princeton University Press, 2007), 175–183.

37. The verbal exchange between Nixon and Khrushchev took place on July 24, 1959 at the American National Exhibition at Sokolniki Park in Moscow. During the debate Nixon emphasized how the peaceful application of American technology provided affordable furnishings and equipment for the contemporary American home. Examples he pointed out included washing machines and full-sized refrigerators, appliances already present in most kitchens of newly constructed Milcom kitchens. As Donna Alvah notes, "for many years" military wives stationed overseas had been enacting the type of "competition" to which Nixon alluded. See Alvah, *Unofficial Ambassadors*, 116. See "The Cold War's Hot Kitchen," *New York Times*, July 23, 2009, accessed August 23, 2013, http://www.nytimes.com/2009/07/24/opinion/24safire.html?_r=0.

38. See Elaine May's discussion of consumerism and status, *Homeward Bound*, 19–21. Also see David Potter's *People of Plenty* and his explanation that "relative abundance is, by general consent, a basic condition of American life" as was the "availability of a generous quota of goods ready for use." Potter, 84.

39. See the Big Picture film "The Friendly Hand." As an example of soft-power duplicity and propaganda Army Signal Corps Captain Joseph Boyle directed the production and posed as the main character, an Army sergeant. Boyle's real family played the other characters but under assumed names. See "The Friendly Hand," *U.S. Lady* 1, no. 8 (Mid-Summer 1956): 51.

40. "Recipes," *U.S. Lady*, January 1967, 10.

41. Elvis, inducted into the U.S. Army months earlier, arrived on the *USS General George M. Randall* with a thousand other soldiers. The military assigned him to Company D, of the 1st Battalion, 32nd Regiment, of the 3rd Armored Division. He remained with that unit during his two year tour of duty. See "Hundreds Greet Singer on Arrival in Germany," *Stars and Stripes*, October 2, 1958, 2.

42. Jazz is a unique music form that is widely recognized as distinctly American. Its roots are in a mixture of African and European sounds. Jazz developed in African-American communities in the American South at the beginning of the twentieth century.

43. In many cases German youth, as opposed to older generations, quickly associated with many aspects of American culture such as Jazz, movies, clothing, and behaviors as ways to distinguish themselves from guilty associations with Nazism that their parents were suffering. See Ralph Willet, *The Americanization of Germany: Postwar Culture, 1945–1949* (London: Routledge, 1992), 114.

44. See Uta Poiger, *Jazz, Rock, and Rebels: Cold War Politics and American Culture in Divided Germany*

(Berkeley: University of California Press, 2000), and Erica Carter, "Alice in Consumer Wonderland: West German Case Studies in Gender and Consumer Culture," in *West Germany under Construction: Politics, Society, and Culture, in the Adenauer Era*, Robert G. Moeller, ed. (Ann Arbor: University of Michigan Press, 1997) and Alexander Stephan, ed., *Americanization and Anti-Americanism: The German Encounter with American Culture after 1945* (New York: Berghahn, 2008).

45. "Booming Record Business," *Stars and Stripes*, February 4, 1955, 13.

46. "Rock and Roll Called Short Fad," *Stars and Stripes*, April 4, 1956, 5.

47. These fears were deep-seated among conservative elites and affected the early acceptance of American culture. Many German officials and parents feared racial blending through music that might detract from a traditional view of sexual roles. See Uta Poiger, "Rock and Roll, Female Sexuality, and the Cold War Battle over German Identities," in Moeller, *West Germany under Construction* and Uta Poiger, *Jazz, Rock, and Rebels*, 114, 168, and 206.

48. See "Elvis, the Pelvis," *Der Spiegel*, accessed February 15, 2012, http://www.spiegel.de/spiegel/print/d-43064913.html. The reference "Kinseyland" in the subtitle is to Alfred Kinsey, the American biologist whose studies of human sexuality in the 1940s and 1950s provoked great controversy and public debate.

49. Renate Sabulsky (resided in the West German town of *Ziegenhain* until the mid–1960s, Life Long Learning Institute, Chesterfield, Virginia), in discussion with the author, February 2013.

50. "Current Films: Rock Around the Clock," *Stars and Stripes*, June 24, 1956, 15.

51. "Rock, Rock, Rock," *Stars and Stripes*, October 17, 1956, 12.

52. "Rock and Roll Riots Jolt Oslo after Film," *Stars and Stripes*, September 22, 1956, 3.

53. "Rock, Rock, Rock," *Stars and Stripes*, October 17, 1956, 12.

54. "Bandleader Blasts Psychiatrist over Rock-Roll Disease Claim," *Stars and Stripes*, April 1, 1956, 5.

55. "Sex, Brutality Hit as Movie Probe Begins," *Stars and Stripes*, June 18, 1955, 3.

56. "Sex, Brutality Hit as Movie Probe Begins," *Stars and Stripes*, June 18, 1955, 3.

57. "Sgt Lauds Zone Teenagers," *Stars and Stripes*, June 27, 1954, 4.

58. "Couth Cha-Cha-Cha," *Stars and Stripes*, B-Bag, July 11, 1965, 10.

59. B-Bag Letter, *Stars and Stripes*, July 11, 1965, 10.

60. "AFN Stuttgart Airs 2 Teen-Age Shows," *Stars and Stripes*, August 14, 1953, 9.

61. Neil Albaugh (former military dependent, resided in the Mannheim Milcom, 1954–1955, and the Heidelberg Milcom, 1955–1956, also attended Frankfurt American High School, 1956–1957) in phone conversation with the author, February 2014.

62. As quoted in Uta Poiger, *Jazz, Rock, and Rebels*, 71.

63. Ibid., 72.

64. As quoted in Uta Poiger, "Cold War Politics and American Popular Culture in Germany," Detlef Junker, *The United States and Germany in the Era of the Cold War*, Vol. 1, 442. Some contemporary histories argue that younger Germans adopted that unsettling American culture as a "resource in their battle against old-guard and class-bound culture codes." Victoria de Grazia makes the case for cultural Americanization as a tool to leverage gain against the "old-guard" and cites Uta Poiger's work *Jazz, Rock, and Rebels* in that same context. See de Grazia, *Irresistible Empire: America's Advance through Twentieth-Century Europe* (Cambridge: Belknap Press, 2005), 555. See also Kaspar Maase, "Establishing Cultural Democracy: Youth, Americanization, and the Irresistible Rise of Popular Culture," in *The Miracle Years: A Cultural History of West Germany, 1949–1968*, Hanna Schissler, ed. (Princeton: Princeton University Press, 2001): 428–450.

65. Thomas Koebner, "Hollywood in Germany," in Detlef Junker, *The United States and Germany in the Era of the Cold War*, Vol. 2, 350.

66. Ibid, 350.

67. In April 1952 Soviet authorities instituted a tightly controlled pass system that curtailed easy movement from East to West Germany. But there was no control requirement within the city of Berlin until 1956. East Germany began construction of the Berlin Wall on August 13, 1961. See Mary Fulbrook, *The Divided Nation: A History of Germany, 1918–1990* (Oxford: Oxford University Press, 1992).

68. "8,727 from East See U.S. Movies in Berlin," *Stars and Stripes*, July 31, 1950, 2.

69. *Night and Day* was a biopic of the songwriter Cole Porter. It featured several of Porter's popular songs. *Johnny Belinda* was a melodrama involving difficult social issues of rape, unwanted pregnancy and homicide.

70. "East Germans Flock to See U.S. Movies," *Stars and Stripes*, February 4, 1953, 7.

71. "Forces 4 Keys to Amity Hailed by German Cleric," *Stars and Stripes*, May 8, 1956, 9.

72. For example, the Frankfurt Milcom listed plans to show American movies "to the city's residents, including children." "Frankfurt Plans Big Week of G-A Friendship Events," *Stars and Stripes*, April 9, 1956, 10. Also see "G-A Week Free Movies for Germans," *Stars and Stripes*, April 25, 1962, 9.

73. See Frank Stern, "Film in the 1950s: Passing Images of Guilt and Responsibility," in Hanna Schissler, ed., *The Miracle Years*, 266–279. See also Pól Ó Dochartaigh and Christaine Schönfeld, eds. *Representing the "Good German" in Literature and Culture after 1945: Altruism and Ambiguity* (Rochester: Camden House, 2013).

74. "Magazine Reports Young Germans Both Admire, Criticize Americans," *Stars and Stripes*, June 13, 1951, 4.

75. "The Impact of American Commercial Films in West Germany," Report No. 197, Anna J. Merritt, ed., *Public Opinion in Semi-Sovereign Germany: The HICOG Surveys, 1949–1955* (Champaign: University of Illinois Press, 1980), 237.

76. "W. Europeans Enjoy U.S. Films But—," *Stars and Stripes*, April 1, 1964, 3.

77. Contemporary West German attitudes towards

American blacks were ambivalent. Contingency and established regional attitudes were more important drivers than generational perceptions. Maria Höhn's study of the postwar Rhineland-Palatinate region, *GIs and Fräuleins*, makes it clear that many Germans' opinions of black GIs improved over time with exposure to them during the occupation period.

78. EC film listings in *Stars and Stripes* for December 3, 1950, May 4, 1952, and June 22, 1952.

79. Coincidentally, Bavaria Film and the Mirisch Corporation filmed the movie on site in Berlin and West Germany during the construction of the Berlin Wall. They released the film in December 1961.

80. "785,048 Saw June Movies," *Stars and Stripes*, August 20, 1949, 15.

81. "Movie Attendance Up," *Stars and Stripes*, February 25, 1952, 11.

82. Sitting on the Council were representatives from W.W. Norton, Random House, and Doubleday publishers. See William Leary, Jr., "Books, Soldiers and Censorship during the Second World War," *American Quarterly* 20, no.2, Part 1 (Summer 1968): 237–245, and Paul Fussell, *Wartime: Understanding Behavior in the Second World War* (New York: Oxford University Press, 1990): 228–251.

83. For examples of associated artwork, cover notices, and overseas editions see "The Council on Books in Wartime, 1941–1946," *Books for Victory*, accessed March 28, 2013, http://www.booksforvictory.com/2013/03/the-council-on-books-in-wartime-194146.html.

84. Martin Meyer, "American Literature in Germany and its Reception in the Political Context of the Nachkriegs (Postwar) Years," in Detlef Junker, *The United States and Germany in the Era of the Cold War*, Vol. 1, 462. Reinhold Wagnleitner notes that by "October 1946 about 170,000 German volumes of the Overseas Editions and 10,000 books in English had been distributed in the American zone in Germany alone." Wagnleitner, "Propagating the American Dream," 73.

85. "The Answer: Paperbacks," *Die Zeit*, October 23, 1952, accessed March 28, 2013, http://www.zeit.de/1952/43/des-raetsels-loesung-taschenbuecher.

86. Ibid.

87. See "Success Story: Dixie Cup Literature," *Stars and Stripes*, December 19, 1959, 11.

88. "Mobile Libraries Lend Books to Germans," *Stars and Stripes*, March 27, 1948, 11.

89. "British Zone Town Lifts U.S. Book Ban after Explanation," *Stars and Stripes*, March 3, 1953, 5. Local German authorities permitted the bookmobiles to enter the area after American officials made it clear that they were lending books not selling them.

90. "Opening the Doors to U.S. Culture," *Stars and Stripes*, November 19, 1950, 18.

91. Ibid., 17.

92. Ibid., 18.

93. "Writer/Faulkner: Intruder in the Dust," *Der Spiegel*, November 18, 1953, accessed August 25, 2013, http://www.spiegel.de/spiegel/print/d-25657983.html. That tragedy was the failure of American society and culture to escape the "disgust of Europe" with its own set of inherent class and social inequities. In this context it also revealed the fallacy of the American exceptional consensus that claimed freedom from the traditional and restrictive baggage of a European past. See RWs Lewis' *The American Adam*.

94. "America's Most Important Contribution to World Literature," *Die Zeit*, June 12, 1958, accessed August 25, 2013, http://www.zeit.de/1958/24/amerikas-wichtigster-beitrag-zur-weltliteratur.

95. Theodore Adorno was a member of the noted Frankfurt School of critical theory where along with other intellectuals such as Walter Benjamin, Ernst Bloch, Max Horkheimer and Herbert Marcuse he wrote critiques of modern society and culture. He immigrated with the others to the United States as war clouds gathered in the 1930s.

96. Quoted in Höhn, *GIs and Fräuleins*, 86. *Heimat* is a reference to more than just the literal translation 'homeland.' It also connotes attachment to a familiar cultural framework and is an integral part of an individual's identity.

97. As quoted in S. Jonathan Wiesen, *West German Industry and the Challenge of the Nazi Past, 1945–1955* (Chapel Hill: University of North Carolina Press, 2001), 163.

98. See Michael Ermath, "The Influence of American Popular Culture on the Federal Republic," in Detlef Junker, *The United States and Germany in the Era of the Cold War, 1945–1968*, Vol. 2 (Washington, DC: German Historical Institute and New York: Cambridge University Press, 2004), 334.

99. After the mid–1950s West German elites began to change their ideas about material consumption. This followed a general trend of Cold War liberalization that began with the political ascendancy of Ludwig Erhard and a liberal collection of intellectual and political elites and economists. See Uta G. Poiger, "Cold War Politics and American Popular Culture in Germany," in Detlef Junker *The United States and Germany in the Era of the Cold War*, Vol. 1, 442–443.

100. See Uta Poiger, "Cold War Politics and American Popular Culture in Germany," in Detlef Junker *The United States and Germany in the Era of the Cold War, 1945–1968*, Vol. 1 (Washington, DC: German Historical Institute and New York: Cambridge University Press, 2004), Eric D. Weitz, "The Ever Present Other: Communism in the Making of West Germany" and Arnold Sywottek, "From Starvation to Excess? Trends in the Consumer Society from the 1940s to the 1970s," in Hanna Schissler, ed., *The Miracle Years: A Cultural History of West Germany, 1949–1968* (Princeton: Princeton University Press, 2001): 341–358.

101. "Varied Activities Mark NACOM Observance," *Stars and Stripes*, May 6, 1956, 9, "U.S. Forces in Germany Slate Friendship Week Events," *Stars and Stripes*, May 3, 1958, 9, and "Events Crowding Calendar for G-A Friendship Week," *Stars and Stripes*, May 3, 1961, 9.

102. Jazz, a unique American musical form, became a key to defining a new postwar cultural identity for West Germans. The Milcoms played a role by offering numerous opportunities for performances, providing exposure to the German public and encouraging Jazz's cultural penetration. See Edward Lackey, "Popular

Music in Germany: The Genesis of a New Filed of Discourse," in Detlef Junker, *The United States and Germany in the Era of the Cold War*, Vol. 2, 445.

103. That important economic metamorphosis and a changed political environment were the catalysts that permitted a greater inter-cultural penetration between the Americans and the Germans. See Erica Carter, "Alice in Consumer Wonderland," in Moeller, Wagnleitner, "Propagating the American Dream," and Pells, *Not Like Us*.

104. The West Germans were not strangers to consumerism having experienced it during the inter-war years. They did however negotiate an acceptance of the American brand of consumerism, displayed in the Milcoms, tailoring it to fit their needs and preferences. See Ingrid Schenk, "Producing to Consume Becomes Consuming to Produce," in Detlef Junker, *The United States and Germany in the Era of the Cold War*, Vol. 1, 584.

105. "Mayor of Heidelberg, Hodes Laud G-A Amity," *Stars and Stripes*, April 30, 1958, 8 and "Males Cook Up a Surprise," *Stars and Stripes*, May 6, 1958, 8.

106. See Maria Höhn's *GIs and Fräuleins* description of postwar life in the rural Rhineland Palatinate region for a broader understanding of this effect.

107. See Eric D. Weitz, *Weimar Germany: Promise and Tragedy* for an explanation of culture and mass society during the inter-war years in Germany.

108. See Arnold Sywottek, "From Starvation to Excess?" in Schissler.

109. See Richard Pells, *Not Like Us*, 198, and Erica Carter, "Alice in Consumer Wonderland," in Moeller, 349.

110. American wives' engagement with consumerism helped shape their early postwar role in society. The Milcom wife's role with consumerism may however been more ambiguous as it was governed by the limitations of her role as a military dependent and the goods and services available at the local PX. However, there was greater latitude to act within this context when she would return to the United States and engage the economy with other citizen consumers.

111. "The Full Circle," *Der Spiegel*, August 31, 1950, accessed February 14, 2013, http://www.spiegel.de/spiegel/print/d-44449569.html

112. Language, and its hybrids, served as a bridge between Germans and Americans as a key acculturated artifact during the postwar years. Heidrun Kämper, "The Americanization of the German Language," in Detlef Junker, *The United States and Germany in the Era of the Cold War*, Vol. 2, 326.

113. Kämper, "The Americanization of the German Language," 327. See also Benedict Anderson's discussion of language and community identity, *Imagined Communities* (New York: Verso, 2003), 67.

114. *Ibid*.

115. West German bandleader Bert Kaempfert first recorded the song in 1962.

116. "Girl Gets 30 Days for Insulting GI in Sidewalk Terms," *Stars and Stripes*, July 14, 1948, 5.

117. One estimate is that the exchange could fill a three-volume dictionary. Kämper, "The Americanization of the German Language," 327.

118. Many Milcoms required newly arrived soldiers to attend "Head Start" language and customs classes sponsored by the local U.S. military education center. For examples see "Constab [ulary] Unit Attends German Language Class," *Stars and Stripes*, March 5, 1948, 7, and "Language Class," *Stars and Stripes*, September 8, 1955, 10.

119. "Preparing for Duty in Germany," *Stars and Stripes*, September 18, 1957, 18.

120. Chuck Charnquist (former medic assigned to the 13th Medical Company Bad Kreuznach Milcom, 1956–1958) in correspondence with the author, June 2014.

Chapter Three

1. "Deity Now Part of Flag Pledge," *Stars and Stripes*, June 6, 1954, 1.

2. *Ibid*.

3. "Ike Praises Legion's 'Back to God' Program," *Stars and Stripes*, February 2, 1954, 7.

4. They included *McCollum v. Board of Education* (1948), *School District of Abingdon Township v. Schempp* (1963) and *Murray v. Curlett* (1963). For a comprehensive description of the contemporary court cases see Patrick Allitt, *Religion in America Since 1945*.

5. "Court Rules Out School Prayer, Bible Reading," *Stars and Stripes*, June 18, 1963, 4.

6. Rep. Frank J. Becker (R-NY) proponent of a bill to reinstate prayer in public schools made the comment. See "Prayers in School—American as Apple Pie," *Stars and Stripes*, April 24, 1964, 7.

7. "I'll Never Forget the Shock of It," *Stars and Stripes*, October 12, 1966, 4.

8. Madalyn Murray remarried after the famous court cases in 1963 and joined her new husband's name to her own. See "Madalyn O'Hair," *Stars and Stripes*, Letters to the Editor, February 6, 1969, 8.

9. "Madalyn O'Hair, *Stars and Stripes*, Letters to the Editor, January 24, 1969, 8.

10. "None of Madalyn's Business," *Stars and Stripes*, Letters to the Editor, March 29, 1973, 12.

11. "Catholic Church Threatens Liberty, Oxnam Charges," *Stars and Stripes*, December 13, 1949, 11.

12. "Baptist Unit Call Catholics, Atheists, Equal Perils to U.S.," *Stars and Stripes*, August 31, 1960, 6.

13. Many Germans still retained in their recent memories the many beneficent black GIs of the occupation period who showed great kindness toward them in the immediate aftermath of the war. This in turn provided an opportunity for "many Germans to rethink their racial worldview." Höhn, *GIs and Fräuleins*, 90.

14. Maria Höhn, *GIs and Fräuleins*, 192–96.

15. For details of this oral interview and about the experiences of African-Americans in the postwar period see Maria Höhn and Martin Klimke, "The Civil Rights Struggle, African-American GIs, and Germany," *Oral Histories*, GHI, accessed October 28, 2012, http://www.aacvr-germany.org/AACVR.ORG.

16. For a fuller understanding of the segmented socialization processes of American GIs in the early postwar years see Maria Höhn, *GIs and Frauleins*, 97.

17. Höhn, *GIs and Frauleins*, 97.

18. Lois Chazaud (former Special Services civilian

assigned to the Wertheim Milcom 1953–1955) in correspondence with the author, July 7, 2014. Although her comment that the local populace "surmised America must be largely Negro" is speculation the easy acceptance of African-Americans by many Germans is consistent with extant histories.

19. Lois Chazaud, *ibid.*

20. Of the approximately 97,000 soldiers in West Germany in 1948 "some 10,000" were black. See Höhn and Klimke, *Breath of Freedom*, 40.

21. Information about the incident comes only from local police reports and personal interviews. According to findings there were "hundreds of soldiers involved." There is an absence of information regarding the riot in the *Stars and Stripes* and U.S. military officials issued no statements. One possible reason that authorities muted publicity was the scheduled visit of Cardinal Francis Spellman to the Milcom on January 9, 1956 and their desire to play down disciplinary problems. See Höhn, *GIs and Fräuleins*, 98 and note 72, 262 and "Spellman Arrives Today; To Meet with Adenauer," *Stars and Stripes*, January 8, 1956, 23.

22. As research for this study later reveals there was a certain degree of media censorship that brought both public and official scrutiny to the *Stars and Stripes*.

23. Other than its own staff writers the *Stars and Stripes* often included news from wire services such as the Associated Press and the United Press.

24. See "U.S. Speeds Showdown at Little Rock," *Stars and Stripes*, September 6, 1957, 1.

25. For additional understanding of American regionalism and attitudes towards racial integration see Maria Höhn in Hanna Schissler, *The Miracle Years*, 152.

26. *Negerkinder* literally means 'Negro children' and refers to the mixed-race offspring of a black GI and white German woman. Other terms were "occupation babies" and "*Negermischlinge*" [Negro-mixed]. Also see Maria Höhn, *GIs and Fräuleins*, 259 (n. 36).

27. See "German Brown Babies" at the website "*Mocha Jüden*" [Brown Jews] for information concerning the postwar lives of these individuals, accessed October 29, 2012, http://mochajuden.com.

28. In August 1945 the Office of the EUCOM Chief of Staff discouraged marriage between a Negro GI and a white German female because it was "considered against the best interest of the service" since it "would create a social problem upon return to the United States." See "Germany's Brown Babies Must be Helped! Will You? U.S. Adoption Plans for Afro-German Children, 1950–1955," Yara-Colette Lemke Muniz de Faria, *Callalo* 26, no. 2 (Spring, 2003): 345.

29. The references are to then–Brigadier General Benjamin O. Davis, Jr. only the second black in the history of the U.S. Armed Forces to rise to that rank, "Negro General Terms Promotion Significant," *Stars and Stripes*, November 2, 1954, 3 and the case of *Brown v. Board of Education, Topeka, Kansas*, "High Court Bans School Segregation," *Stars and Stripes*, May 18, 1954, 1.

30. "4 Governors in South Agree to Protest U.S. Order on Segregation," *Stars and Stripes*, January 26, 1956, 2 and "Mississippi Maps Fight on Desegregation," *Stars and Stripes*, July 15, 1954, 7.

31. For additional anecdotal evidence, ephemera and photographs see the website "Where FAHS Families Lived," accessed October 28, 2012, http://www.frankfurthigh.com/history/subpages/fahs_housing.htm.

32. The cartoon is from a pamphlet published by the Committee against Jim Crow in Military and Training. See Martin Klimke, "The African American Civil Rights Struggle and Germany, 1945–1989," *GHI Bulletin* No. 43 (Fall 2008), 97.

33. Höhn and Klimke, *A Breath of Freedom*, 41.

34. See William Gardner Smith, *Last of the Conquerors* (New York: Signet, 1949).

35. "Germany Meets the Negro Soldier," *Ebony*, October 1, 1946, Volume 1, Issue 11, 5.

36. "Song of Girls and GI's," *Ebony*, October 1, 1946, Volume 1, Issue 11, 10.

37. "The New Germany and Negro Soldiers," *Ebony*, January 1, 1952, Volume 7, Issue 3, 55.

38. See Höhn, *GIs and Frauleins*, Chapter 3, "When Jim Crow Came to the German *Heimat*," 84, for an understanding of how the arrival of African-American GIs affected small communities' ideas about race.

39. Peter Schulz (former Berliner and member of the US Air Force, Life Long Learning Institute, Chesterfield, Virginia), in discussion with the author, November 2012.

40. Truman's Executive Order 9981 issued on July 26, 1948 directed the gradual integration of the armed forces. *Brown V. Board of Education of Topeka Kansas*, May 17, 1954, declared that separate public schools for black and white students were unconstitutional. See John Lemza, "Brown v. Board of Education of Topeka, Kansas (1954)," in *The Public Debate over Controversial Supreme Court Decisions*, edited by Melvin I. Urofsky (Washington, DC: CQ Press, 2006), 197–205.

41. See Mary L. Dudziak's *Cold War Civil Rights: Race and the Image of American Democracy* (Princeton: Princeton University Press, 2000).

42. See War Department Orientation Film, O.F. 14 "Teamwork," RG 111, ARC Identifier 36078/Local ID 11-OF-14, accessed: April 4, 2013, http://www.youtube.com/watch?v=IxVqC9r1McI.

43. These included the 332nd Fighter Squadron, the 769th Field Artillery, and the 761st Tank Battalions.

44. See War Department film, O.F. 22, "The Occupation Soldier," 1946, RG 111, ARC ID 36083/Local ID 111-OF-22, accessed April 4, 2013, http://www.youtube.com/watch?v=6X5PPHCka04.

45. EUCOM is the United States' military European Command.

46. LTC Marcus H. Ray was a field artillery officer. He commanded a unit in Italy during the Second World War. Ray served as a civilian aide to Secretary of War Robert P. Patterson from 1945–1947. In late 1947 the Army recalled him to service as special advisor on Negro affairs to the EUCOM commander.

47. Phillip McGuire, ed., *Taps for a Jim Crow Army: Letters from Black Soldiers in World War II* (Lexington: University Press of Kentucky, 1993), 246. Although Ray was aware of racial inequities in the armed services he endorsed policy driven quotas that capped black

service personnel at 10 percent of the total and plans to draw down the numbers in excess of that ceiling.

48. "Negro Population Cold to Communists, Ray Says in Talk," *Stars and Stripes*, April 29, 1948, 4.

49. Ibid.

50. "Ray Calls Negro Foe of Red Slavery," *Stars and Stripes*, February 13, 1949, 2. Ray's presentations always struck a balance between discussing equal rights in the military services and denying links between the Communist Party and American blacks. This was at a time of heightened concern by many politicians over communist infiltration of the U.S. government and the armed forces.

51. "Racial Integration Gaining, Ray Says," *Stars and Stripes*, September 6, 1950, 7.

52. Höhn and Klimke, *A Breath of Freedom*, 25.

53. "Two Fined for Discrimination," *Stars and Stripes*, February 8, 1953, 6.

54. "Army Reports Progress in Europe on Anti-Bias," *Stars and Stripes*, December 29, 1964, 23.

55. Ibid.

56. Höhn and Klimke, *Breath of Freedom*, 86.

57. "Race Tension Slight in U.S. Europe Forces," *Stars and Stripes*, September 15, 1963, 4.

58. Ibid.

59. See "Army's Race Trouble in Germany Called Small Problem," *Stars and Stripes*, August 9, 1964, 4.

60. Ibid.

61. Ibid.

62. "Gains Made in GI Integration in Germany," *Stars and Stripes*, January 1, 1965, 23.

63. Höhn and Klimke, *Breath of Freedom*, 86.

64. Morris J. MacGregor, Jr. *Defense Studies Series: Integration of the Armed Forces, 1940–1965*, Center of Military History, accessed March 14, 2013, http://www.history.army.mil/books/integration/IAF-22.htm.

65. Jane Mulvihill (former Hanau Milcom family member, Life Long Learning Institute, Chesterfield, Virginia), in discussion with the author, November 2012.

66. Bill Hanne (former military officer in the 3rd Squadron, 8th Cavalry Regiment) in conversation with the author, March 2013.

67. Winton "Dip" Spiller (former military officer in the 3rd Battalion, 80th Field Artillery Regiment and the 2nd Battalion, 5th Field Artillery Regiment, April 1964-June 1966) in conversation with the author, March 2013.

68. Recommendations in the Gillem Board report capped the number of black troops at no more than 10 percent of the total for integrated units in EUCOM. President Truman charged the board, chaired by General Alvan C. Gillem, Jr., to investigate the degree of integration of the U.S. armed forces and make recommendations to speed its progress. See War Department Circular No. 124, "Utilization of Negro Manpower in the Postwar Army Policy," 27 April 1946, accessed February 2, 2014, http://www.trumanlibrary.org/whistlestop/study_collections/desegregation/large/documents/index.php?documentdate=1946-04-27&documentid=10-4&studycollectionid=mp&pagenumber=1. Also see EUCOM Directive AG 300.2 GPA-AGO dated 1 April 1952 that directed "the Negro element of integrated combat units will approximate 10 per cent of the unit's strength." Accessed February 2, 2014, http://www.trumanlibrary.org/whistlestop/study_collections/desegregation/large/documents/index.php?pagenumber=2&documentid=15-7&documentdate=1952-04-01&studycollectionid=coldwar&groupid=.

69. See "Race Tension Slight in U.S. Europe Forces," *Stars and Stripes*, September 15, 1963, 4. A contributing factor to the small percentage of minorities in the Milcom population during this period of time may also have been a standing military policy that required the annotating of travel orders with racial designations. These may have influenced the processing in ways that delayed families' departures or shaped the composition of the population in certain Milcoms. See Morris J. MacGregor, Jr. *Defense Studies Series: Integration of the Armed Forces, 1940–1965*, Center of Military History, Chapter 8, "Segregation's Consequences."

70. "S&S is Appreciated," B-Bag Column, *Stars and Stripes*, March 23, 1949, 2.

71. "Negro Comic Strip," B-Bag Column, *Stars and Stripes*, September 19, 1967, 14.

72. "Objective Reporting," B-Bag Column, *Stars and Stripes*, October 24, 1967, 14.

73. Dudziak, 80. See Dudziak's description of efforts the U.S. government made to "Fight the Cold War with Civil Rights Reform," Chapter 3.

74. See Wilfred Mansbach, "America's Vietnam in Germany-Germany in America's Vietnam: on the Relocation of Spaces and the Appropriation of History," in *Changing the World, Changing Oneself: Political Protest and Collective Identities in West Germany and the U.S. in the 1960s and 1970s*, Belinda Davis, ed. (New York: Berghahn Books, 2010), 42.

75. *Der Spiegel* and *Die Zeit* offer representative voices and attitudes of the West German populace. *Der Spiegel*, "The Mirror," founded in 1947, is a weekly news magazine that has a circulation of over one million. It is known for quality investigative journalism and uncovering political scandals. In 2010 it supported the publishing of Wiki-leak documents form the U.S. State Department. Jeffrey Herf notes that by 1980 the magazine enjoyed a 10 percent readership among the German population over 14 years of age and that it "is West Germany's leading weekly newsmagazine and has been so since it was founded." Jeffrey Herf, *War by Other Means: Soviet Power, West German Resistance, and the Battle of the Euromissiles* (New York: Free Press, 1991), 69–70. *Die Zeit*, "The Time," founded in 1946, is a weekly newspaper that has a print circulation of over 500,000 and an on-line readership of two million. Its political direction is centrist or occasionally to the right.

76. "School Blues," *Der Spiegel*, January 20, 1954, accessed February 19, 2013, http://www.spiegel.de/spiegel/print/d-28955004.html.

77. "Black and White in Class," *Die Zeit*, May 27, 1954, accessed February 19, 2013, http://www.zeit.de/1954/21/schwarz-und-weiss-in-einer-klasse

78. Interposition was a movement by many white Southern political leaders to take a position between Federal mandates to integrate public schools and their interpretations of the Constitution as grounds to main-

tain segregation. "The Whites Disappear," *Der Spiegel*, December 14, 1955, accessed February 19, 2013, http://www.spiegel.de/spiegel/print/d-31971732.html

79. The article refers to a Gallup Institute poll. "Time Mirror: Complaint of the Week," *Die Zeit*, September 26, 1957, accessed February 19, 2012, http://www.zeit.de/1957/39/zeitspiegel.

80. "The Seeds of Violence," *Der Spiegel*, May 2, 1956, accessed February 19, 2013, http://www.spiegel.de/spiegel/print/d-43062114.htm.

81. "Civil War in United States," *Die Zeit*, October 5, 1962, accessed February 19, 2013, http://www.zeit.de/1962/40/burgerkrieg-in-usa.

82. "US Birthday 1961," *Die Zeit*, July 7, 1961, accessed February 19, 2013, http://www.zeit.de/1961/28/us-geburststag-1961.

83. "America's Long Hot Summer," *Die Zeit*, September 18, 1964, accessed February 19, 2013, http://www.zeit.de/1964/38/amerikas-lange-heisser-sommer.

84. "Black Handel," *Der Spiegel*, July 15, 1964, accessed February 19, 2013, http://www.spiegel.de/spiegel/print/d-46174768.htm.

85. *Ibid*.

86. See Elaine Tyler May, *Homeward Bound: American Families in the Cold War Era*, Susan Douglas, *Where the Girls Are: Growing Up Female with the Mass Media* and Joanne Meyerowitz, *Not June Cleaver: Women and Gender in Postwar America, 1945–1960* (Philadelphia: Temple University Press, 1994).

87. See Martha Gravois's description of the conditions facing Milcom members in the first two postwar decades and their attitudes in "Military Families in Germany, 1946–1986: Why They Came and Why They Stay," 57–67. The broader reference is to Daniel Boorstin's re-interpretation of FJ Turner's frontier thesis and the birth of an independent, innovative American. See Boorstin's *The Americans: The Colonial Experience*.

88. "A U.S. Lady's World," *U.S. Lady* 1, no.6 (May 1956): 8.

89. "Meat Cutter Shows Skill at Giessen," *Stars and Stripes*, February 10, 1965, 9.

90. "Lynda Robb's Eager to be Good Military Wife," *Stars and Stripes*, December 25, 1967, 15.

91. "The Stars and Stripes Magazine Subscription Service," *Stars and Stripes*, December 27, 1950, 7.

92. See *U.S. Lady* 1, no. 3 (November 1955): 3.

93. "Stars and Stripes Picks Rita Hayworth as Miss Cheesecake of 1947," *Stars and Stripes*, January 1, 1948, 1.

94. For examples see "Miss Cheesecake Collins Thrilled at S&S Title," *Stars and Stripes*, January 6, 1950, 6, "S&S Selects Venus as Miss Cheesecake," *Stars and Stripes*, January 1, 1952, 12 and "Don't Knock Cheesecake, Ann Warns," *Stars and Stripes*, March 29, 1956, 14.

95. "Miss Cheesecake Enjoys Letters," *Stars and Stripes*, Letters to the Editor, February 26, 1952, 4.

96. "Sweet Thirteen," (photo caption) *Stars and Stripes*, July 1, 1963, 3, and "Say Cheesecake," *Stars and Stripes*, September 10, 1966, 14. For July 1963 alone the newspaper featured seven articles with images of swimsuit clad Miss Universe contestants.

97. "Soul Sister for Soul Brother," *Stars and Stripes*, Letters to the Editor, April 2, 1968, 13.

98. See Ruth Rosen, *The World Split Open: How the Modern Women's Movement Changed America* (New York: Penguin, 2006), 159–164, for a discussion of women's struggle against definition by appearance.

99. "Military Wife Finalists List Interests, Goals," *Stars and Stripes*, June 17, 1967, 15. Hollywood celebrity Art Linkletter and Wilson Harrell chairman of the Board of Harrell International Incorporated launched the program in 1967. Harrell was a fighter pilot during World War Two and a postwar business entrepreneur.

100. "USAREUR Wife Tops in the World," *Stars and Stripes*, May 28, 1970, 1.

101. "Resolution Voted on Women's Rights," *Stars and Stripes*, May 26, 1951, 6 and "UN Assembly Asks Austria Treaty," *Stars and Stripes*, December 22, 1952, 3.

102. "Senate Gets Amendment Plan Guaranteeing Women's Rights," *Stars and Stripes*, April 6, 1957, 5, "Women's Rights," *Stars and Stripes*, September 1, 1957, 7, and "Senators OK Equal Pay Bill for Women," *Stars and Stripes*, May 3, 1963, 3.

103. "Dial Day Listing," *Stars and Stripes*, October 15, 1951, 11.

104. "Lone Woman Fencer Parries Swords of Dozen Men in Club," *Stars and Stripes*, October 28, 1954, 10.

105. These clubs were similar to those that existed on almost every military post and installation in the United States.

106. See "Mrs. Luebke to Address AWAG Delegates," *Stars and Stripes*, March 9, 1963, page 16, and "6th Annual Conference American Women's Activities in Germany (AWAG)," *Stars and Stripes*, March 24, 1962, 14. At the March 1962 meeting GEN Clay gave the keynote address "The World of Free Choice."

107. "Protestant Women to Hold Training Meet May 27–31," *Stars and Stripes*, May 4, 1963, 16. Micro-aggressions and micro-insults refer to those negative assumptions and comments made about individuals or groups that limit their agency and value.

108. "Protestant Women to Hold Training Meet May 27–31," *Stars and Stripes*, May 4, 1963, 16.

109. "Notes from American Communities Overseas: Clubs Embark on Fall Programs," *Stars and Stripes*, October 4, 1959, 15.

110. "U.S. Women Save Life of Turkish Man," Femina Section, *Stars and Stripes*, August 23, 1958, 14.

111. See Bettie J. Morden, *The Women's Army Corps, 1945–1978*, Center of Military History, US Army, Washington, DC, 2000, Chapter 2, 41, accessed March 14, 2013, http://www.history.army.mil/html/books/030/30-14-1/cmhPub_30-14.pdf.

112. See US Census Bureau for 1960, Volume III, Selected Area Reports, 1c. *Americans Overseas*.

113. Bettie Morden, 42.

114. See the cover of *U.S. Lady* 1, no. 1 (September 1955). These words appeared on every issue just below the magazine title.

115. "Radiant Regiment" appeared in *U.S. Lady* 2, no. 1 (Mid-Winter, 1957): 31 and "Our Fair Lady" appeared in *U.S. Lady* 2, no. 2 (Spring, 1957): 14.

116. The best examples of women's potential were the articles on the *U.S. Lady* of the Month and Year.

They featured confident women such as LT Soderston and Major Pat Ulrich, as well as Aurelia Richards who the magazine selected as U.S. Lady of the Year (1957) for her charitable works and interaction with host communities.

117. This is particularly noteworthy because the *Stuttgart Post News*' initiative preceded that of the *U.S. Lady* by several years.

118. "Woman of the Week," *Stuttgart Post News*, December 20, 1947, 4, RG 549, United States Army Europe, 1942–1991, Box 3355, National Archives College Park. Interestingly the article never reveals what Mrs. Edward's name is, only referring to her by initials or as the Colonel's wife, despite her accomplishments.

119. "Woman of the Week," *Stuttgart Post News*, December 13, 1947, 4 and "Woman of the Week," *Stuttgart Post News*, November 20, 1948, 6, RG 549, United States Army Europe, 1942–1991, Box 3355, National Archives College Park.

120. Nine women composed the staff of the Dependents Section of the newspaper.

121. See William Brinkley, "They All Say: Look at the American Signora!" *Life Magazine* 43, no. 26 (December 23, 1957): 66.

122. Ibid., 70.

123. "Bonn High Court Rules Women Have Equality," *Stars and Stripes*, December 21, 1953, 5.

124. See "Begging to the Quandary," *Der Spiegel*, February 1, 1952, accessed February 24, 2013, http://www.spiegel.de/spiegel/print/d-21048453.html.

125. See "Marriage is Common Destiny Between Two People," *Die Zeit*, July 24, 1952, accessed 21 March 2013, http://www.zeit.de/1952/30/ehe-ist-schicksalsgemeinschaft-zweier-menschen.

126. *Trümmerfrau* translates to 'women of the rubble' and refers to the platoons of women who diligently worked to clear away the rubble from the devastated German cities. Jessica Gienow-Hecht, *Transmission Impossible: American Journalism as Cultural Diplomacy in Postwar Germany, 1945–1955* (Baton Rouge: Louisiana State University), 70.

127. The Armed Forces Radio Service (AFRS) became the Armed Forces Radio and Television Service (AFRTS) in 1954 with the introduction of television broadcasts and then the American Forces Radio and Television Service on July 1, 1969.

128. The *International Herald Tribune* however, was not available until May 1967. As of October 2013 its owners have retitled it the *International New York Times*. Other periodicals such as *Time*, *Newsweek* and *Army Times* were also available by individual subscription or through the PX book stores. AFRS was also the only in-country English language radio station, other than the Voice of America, available to Milcoms in Germany. For histories of the establishment of AFN and *Stars and Stripes* see Ken Zumwalt, *The Stars and Stripes: World War Two and the Early Years*, "The Stars and Stripes: European Edition," *U.S. Army Germany* accessed March 22, 2013, http://www.usarmygermany.com/Units/StarsandStripes/USAREUR_StarsandStripes.htm, and "Armed Forces Network: Europe," *U.S. Army Germany*, accessed March 22, 2013, http://www.usarmygermany.com/Sont.htm?http&&&www.usarmygermany.com/units/afneurope/usareur_afneurope.htm, and *AFN Europe*, accessed March 22, 2013, http://www.afneurope.net/AboutUs/tabid/85/Default.aspx.

129. By the mid–1950s competition with German newspapers for available paper from mills in Germany and the United States placed a governor on the *Stars and Stripes'* ability to increase its circulation numbers. The newspaper also faced limited competition from the *Daily American* (Rome only), the *American Daily* (5 days a week) and the *Overseas Weekly* (limited circulation). Zumwalt, 151.

130. The newspaper had presses in London, Paris, Rome, Liege, Nice and several locations in Germany by the end of the war. "The *Stars and Stripes*: European Edition," *U.S. Army Germany*, accessed March 22, 2013, http://www.usarmygermany.com/Units/StarsandStripes/USAREUR_StarsandStripes.htm.

131. Zumwalt, 77, 116, 151, 155, and 224.

132. "The B-Bag for Gripes," *New York Times*, March 18, 1945, 13. Of 200 letters received weekly the newspaper only printed 20. "GI Paper is Paying its Way-Plus," *Washington Post*, April 13, 1947, B2.

133. "GI Paper is Paying its Way-Plus," *Washington Post*, April 13, 1947, B2.

134. Ibid.

135. "Soldier Press Abuses," *New York Times*, March 10, 1946, 12.

136. Ibid.

137. Ibid.

138. The US State Department funded the *Neue Zeitung* beginning October 17, 1945 to print pro–American and pro–Western views in the American and British zones and so serve as a foil to pro–Soviet propaganda. Ironically, the same presses that produced Joseph Goebbels's Nazi newspaper the *Völkischer Beobachter* printed the first issues of *Neue Zeitung*. Gienow-Hecht, 12.

139. Zumwalt, 206.

140. Ibid.

141. Ibid., 207.

142. 80 Cong. Rec. H1812 (daily ed., February 26, 1948) (statement of Rep. Dondero).

143. Zumwalt, 201.

144. "Clay Defends Stars and Stripes," *Stars and Stripes*, March 3, 1948, 1.

145. "S&S Hit by Red Paper," *Stars and Stripes*, March 5, 1948, 1. The *Vorwärts* was the official Socialist Unity Party (SED) organ.

146. Ibid., 208. After General Douglas MacArthur's ouster Ridgway took command of all United Nations forces in Korea for the duration of the war.

147. "Heart Break Ridge was Death Inferno," *Stars and Stripes*, October 11, 1951, 7.

148. "Protest Censoring Stars and Stripes," *New York Times*, March 7, 1946, 13.

149. "Forrestal Calls Security Parley of Press, Radio, Film Leaders," *Stars and Stripes*, January 22, 1948, 6.

150. "Army Denies Curbing Press; Clay Reaffirms Open Policy," *Stars and Stripes*, April 26, 1948, 1.

151. Ibid.

152. "Newsmen Bound by Gentlemen's Pact," *Stars and Stripes*, July 4, 1950, 6.

153. "Forces Limit Censor Role," *Stars and Stripes*, September 24, 1954, 7.

154. For a further description of the censorship process during the Korean War see Steven Casey, *Selling the Korean War: Propaganda, Politics, and Public Opinion, 1950–1953* (New York: Oxford University Press, 2008).

155. "Pentagon Confirms Curb on G.I. Paper," *New York Times*, March 4, 1967, 53.

156. "Pentagon Says Story Killed by USAREUR," *Stars and Stripes*, March 5, 1967, 1.

157. Ibid.

158. See Benedict Anderson's explanation of language and newspapers as identifiable characteristics of a community. Benedict Anderson, *Imagined Communities*, Chapter 5, Old Languages, New Models, 67–82.

159. "The G.I.'s Friend," *Time Magazine*, June 9 1961, 48.

160. "Overseas Weekly, New EC Paper, Appears Today," *Stars and Stripes*, May 12, 1950, 12. Marion von Rospach was editor and publisher of the newspaper. See William Brinkley, "They All Say: Look at the American Signora!" Life Magazine 43, no. 26 (December 23, 1957): 66–74.

161. Ibid. The newspaper also claimed that 50 percent of its print space was dedicated to ads. See "The G.I.'s Friend," *Time Magazine*, June 9, 1961, 48.

162. "Army Cancels License of Overseas Weekly," *Stars and Stripes*, May 22, 1953, 2. The articles included a serialization of former GI George Jorgensen's sex change process and operation, and the details of a call girl's journey into prostitution. See "The G.I.'s Friend," *Time Magazine*, June 9, 48.

163. Ibid. A Frankfurt publisher began printing and circulating the newspaper shortly after this episode.

164. Ibid.

165. "Open Word is Murder," *Der Spiegel*, June 10, 1953, accessed April 5, 2013, http://www.spiegel.de/spiegel/print/d-25656850.html.

166. Ibid.

167. "Walker Attacks Service Weekly," *New York Times*, April 17, 1961, 15.

168. "Overseas Weekly to Continue Sales," *New York Times*, March 22, 1962, 35.

169. "Freedom through Dissent," *American Civil Liberties Union*, 42nd Annual Report, July 1, 1961 to June 30, 1962, 5.

170. By 1952 readership reached 7 percent nationally and 29 percent in West Berlin. A majority, 55 percent reported that they liked the newspaper a great deal. Only 13 percent objected to pro–Western slanting and propaganda in the text but 58 percent "accepted the idea of having an American-sponsored newspaper." See *Public Opinion in Semi-Sovereign Germany: The HICOG Surveys, 1949–1955*, 37, 38 and 193. By the time the *Neue Zeitung* ceased publication in January 1955 German politicians and journalists considered that "the German-American relations are now normal," which made the newspaper "superfluous." The US Information Agency sold off the operation piecemeal. See "Who's Interested?" *Der Spiegel*, January 26, 1955, accessed April 6, 2013, http://www.spiegel.de/spiegel/print/d-31969035.html.

171. See Matthew J. Costello, *Secret Identity Crisis: Comic Books and the Unmasking of Cold War America* (New York: Continuum, 2009).

172. "Terry and the Pirates," cartoon, *Stars and Stripes*, July 27, 1952, 27 and "Steve Canyon," cartoon, *Stars and Stripes*, July 27, 1952, 13.

173. "*Katzenjammer*" literally means 'hangover' in German.

174. "Comic Magazines Set Up Hays Office," *Stars and Stripes*, September 1, 1948, 2. During the early 1950s the *Stars and Stripes* also advertised a magazine subscription service that offered a variety of comic books including Crime Detective Comics and Dick Tracy. "Magazine Subscription Service," *Stars and Stripes*, July 3, 1952, 7.

175. "Editor Debate Possibility of Harm to Youth from Sexy Crime Comics," *Stars and Stripes*, May 3, 1950, 4.

176. Al Capp, creator of Li'l Abner, made the comment. "Comic Magazines Set Up Hays Office," *Stars and Stripes*, September 1, 1948, 2.

177. "Opium of the Nursery," *Der Spiegel*, March 21, 1951, accessed April 5, 2013, http://www.spiegel.de/spiegel/print/d-29193570.html.

178. "Comics without Comedy," *Die Zeit*, December 27, 1951, accessed March 28, 2013, http://www.zeit.de/1951/52/comics-ohne-komik.

Chapter Four

1. The *City of Man* was a treatise composed by a mixed body of European and American intellectuals just as the nation was preparing for war in 1940. They originally called themselves the 'Committee of Fifteen' but later changed the name to the 'Committee on Europe' as new members joined. Noted members included Thomas Mann, Reinhold Niebuhr, Oscar Jászi, G.A. Borgese, and Lewis Mumford. The Committee saw Americanism as the guiding light for a global future. See *The City of Man* (New York: Viking Press, 1940), 15, 72.

2. Ibid., 61.

3. Ibid., 81. The concept of spirituality as a basis for morality was central to contemporary American ideals. See Lori Bogle's *The Pentagon's Battle for the American Mind*. America stood as a leader among the "covenant" nations against the "demonic" Soviets in the early Cold War. See also Jonathan P. Herzog's *The Spiritual Industrial Complex* (New York: Oxford University Press, 2011).

4. The entertainer Paul Robeson was an avowed communist and Thomas Mann was not but because he appeared with Robeson and other known communists on a 1951 Peace Crusade the HUAC tried to tar him with the same brush. See Jeffrey Myers, "Thomas Mann in America," *Michigan Quarterly Review* 51, no. 4 (Fall 2012): 578–594, accessed August 19, 2013, http://hdl.handle.net/2027/spo.act2080.0051.419. Mann had also become an American citizen and attracted the ire of left-leaning German émigrés such as Berthold Brecht. "Peace Crusaders Lose Sponsorship of Thomas Mann," *Stars and Stripes*, February 15, 1951, 7. See also Mann Distinguishes Between Nazism, Pure Communism," *Stars and Stripes*, July 26, 1949, 12.

5. Although Mann was a member of Friends of Democracy, an organization that worked to identify American Nazis during the late 1930s, early probes by the House Un-American Activities Committee were quick to associate him with a certain "Communist-created and controlled front organization" for peace as early as 1949. See "Petitioners Ask Congress to End House Committee," *Stars and Stripes*, January 4, 1949, 6, and "East Germans Claim Mann," *Stars and Stripes*, June 12, 1950, 2. Also, John E. Haynes, *Red Scare or Red Menace?* (Chicago: Ivan R. Dee, 1996), 25.

6. Robert Bierly, Jr. (former military officer with the 93rd Engineer Company and 168th Engineer Battalion, Stuttgart Milcom, 1960–1963) in correspondence with the author, March 2013.

7. Detlef Junker, "Politics, Security, Economics, Culture, and Society," in Detlef Junker, ed., *The United States and Germany in the Era of the Cold War*, Vol. 1, 10. For a fuller description of the employment of the nuclear shield in Germany see David Clay Large, "Partners in Defense: America, West Germany, and the Security of Europe, 1950–1968, in Detlef Junker, ed., *The United States and Germany in the Era of the Cold War*, Vol. 1, 209–216.

8. To the disadvantage of the Germans both the United States and the Soviet practiced a "dangerous atomic diplomacy" at this time. See Mary Nolan, *The Transatlantic Century: Europe and America, 1890–2010* (New York: Cambridge University Press, 2012), 215.

9. "House Probers Launch Hunt for Mysterious Atomic Spy," *Stars and Stripes*, September 15, 1948, 7.

10. The U.S. Army's Signal Corps Pictorial Service worked closely with the Armed Force Information Service (AFIS) during this period. John C. Broger became director of the service and was responsible for developing an anti-communist ideological framework for the military.

11. Murrow clashed with Senator Joseph McCarthy during the latter's broad campaign to identify communist personalities in the 1950s. At one point during HUAC hearings Murrow had to refute McCarthy's charge that "he was a member of the old International Workers of the World." "McCarthy: U.S. Stalled H-Bomb; Ike: Never Heard of Any Delay," *Stars and Stripes*, April 8, 1954, 1. See also the Big Picture film "Challenge of Ideas." ARC Identifier 2569750/Local ID 111-TV-512.

12. *Ibid.*, The Big Picture film "Challenge of Ideas." Contemporary audiences also knew Wayne from his appearance as Big Jim McClain in the eponymous film from 1952 about HUAC agents hunting communists in postwar Hawaii.

13. *Ibid.*, The Big Picture film "Challenge of Ideas." These types of narrative treatments resonated with contemporary beliefs that placed spirituality and individual freedoms central to the American identity and staked the nation's position to the moral high ground. Daniel J. Boorstin notes that spiritual anchor that fixed the Massachusetts Bay colony with John Winthrop's words, "Wee [sic] shall be as a Citty [sic] upon a Hill." Boorstin, *The Americans*, 3.

14. See the Big Picture film *The West Berlin Struggle*, NARA ARC ID 2569836/Local ID 111-TV-628.

15. See the Big Picture film "Germany Today," NARA ARC ID 2569714/Local ID 111-TV-455.

16. The "Communist Myth" was a short series of video commentaries that worked to explode propaganda from the East such as the idea that racism was a tool used by the upper classes to repress the lower classes and that the Soviet military was invincible.

17. Some film historians consider *The Iron Curtain* to be Hollywood's first true effort to come to terms with Cold War political issues. See "The Iron Curtain (1948): Hollywood's First Cold War Movie," *Historical Journal of Film, Radio and Television* (U.K.) 18, no.1 (1998).

18. *Stars and Stripes*, August 12, 1948, 3.

19. "Chambers Bares Secret Data," *Stars and Stripes*, December 5, 1948, 6. Whittaker Chambers was an American writer and editor, and member of the CPUSA until 1938. He discussed his defection from the Party and made disclosures about its operations in the United States in his personal memoir, *Witness* (New York: Random House, 1952). Chambers attributes his change of heart to a spiritual awakening and a newfound belief in God.

20. Alger Hiss was an American lawyer and official in the U.S. State Department who was also involved in the establishment of the United Nations. During a HUAC investigation Whittaker Chambers accused Hiss of conducting espionage for the Soviets a charge Hiss denied under oath. Later proven guilty, Hiss went to prison for perjury. Chambers claimed that the "No. 1 source [spy] in the State Department was Alger Hiss." *Witness*, 28.

21. Falzini, 98.

22. *Ibid.*, 142.

23. Frank Howley, *Berlin Command* (New York: Putnam's Sons, 1950), 199. Brigadier Frank Howley served as commandant of the American sector during the Berlin blockade crisis.

24. *Ibid.*

25. *Ibid.*, 198.

26. *Ibid.*, 200.

27. Those strong feelings decreased only slightly over time falling from 81 percent in 1949 to 71 percent by 1955. That trend remained consistent in comparison to a second survey question that asked if respondents had an overall "unfavorable opinion" about communism. In 1952, 65 percent of West Germans queried responded that they carried an unfavorable opinion and 69 percent of West Berliners responded in a similar manner. West Berliners consistently responded more strongly against communism in response to all survey questions.

28. Spirituality and Christianity were central exceptionalist themes and fundamental statements against communist atheism. "Survey: Your Opinion," *Der Spiegel*, March 5, 1949, accessed June 10, 2013, http://www.spiegel.de/spiegel/print/d-44436013.html.

29. Gerhardt Thamm (former German soldier, U.S. military interrogator, and intelligence operative with the Army Security Agency, resided in the Frankfurt Milcom and Berlin during the periods 1953–1956 and 1965–1968) in correspondence with the author, February 2014.

30. Erik Thamm (former military dependent) in correspondence with the author, February 2014.

31. "Sen. McCarthy Hurls Charge In Hiss Case," *Stars and Stripes*, October 23, 1950, 2. McCarthy established his reputation and rose to national prominence behind claims that he had acquired a list of 205 names of communist agents working in the U.S. State Department in February 1950. For a fuller understanding of anti-communist initiatives during this period see Haynes, *Red Scare or Red Menace?*

32. "McCarthy Raps Criticism of Book-Burning," *Stars and Stripes*, January 11, 1954, 3.

33. "Author Burke Hits Ban on His Work as Book Burning," *Stars and Stripes*, January 15, 1955, 2.

34. Robert Weekley (retired artillery Colonel who commanded Battery B, 3rd Gun Battalion, 39th Artillery Regiment while stationed at Dachau Kaserne, during the period May 1960 to May 1963) in correspondence with the author, September 2013.

35. "State Department: Communists in the Family," *Der Spiegel*, April 20, 1950, accessed June 7, 2013, http://www.spiegel.de/spiegel/print/d-44448078.html.

36. "McCarthy and Post-WWII," *Die Zeit*, September 6, 1951, accessed June 7, 2013, http://www.zeit.de/1951/36/mccarthy-und-der-mccarthyismus.

37. "United States: What a Phenomenon," *Der Spiegel*, September 19, 1951, accessed June 7, 2013, http://www.spiegel.de/spiegel/print/d-29194792.html.

38. "United States: Fifth Column of the Patriots," *Der Spiegel*, August 13, 1952, accessed June 7, 2013, http://www.spiegel.de/spiegel/print/d-21977497.html.

39. *Ibid.*

40. "Reds Invade South Korea," *Stars and Stripes*, June 26, 1950, 1.

41. Robert Weekley (former military officer with the 3rd Battalion, 39th Field Artillery Regiment, Dachau Milcom, 1960–1963) in correspondence with the author, March 2013.

42. Winton "Dip" Spiller (former military officer in the 3rd Battalion, 80th Field Artillery Regiment and the 2nd Battalion, 5th Field Artillery Regiment, April 1964-June 1966) in conversation with the author, March 2013.

43. In December 1951, 73 percent responded that they would support rearmament to "stop communism." By January 1952, 55 percent favored remaining aligned with the West for the duration of the Cold War, and a year later 53 percent responded that they would actively resist a "communist take-over" of their country. By January 1953, only 5 percent of West Germans responded that they were "sympathetic" in any way to the communist ideology. See the HICOG surveys: Merritt and Merritt, eds. *Public Opinion in Semi-Sovereign Germany*.

44. "Senate Votes Censure of McCarthy Twice," *Stars and Stripes*, December 3, 1954, 1. It was McCarthy's brash methodology and his readiness to use the specter of communism as a weapon against his political rivals that undid him and affixed the sobriquet "McCarthyism" to crude, manipulative techniques. Credit for first coining the term goes to political cartoonist Herblock. See *Herblock's History*, Library of Congress, accessed June 19, 2013, http://www.loc.gov/rr/print/swann/herblock/fire.html.

45. "Soviets Crush Hungary in Sneak Attack," *Stars and Stripes*, November 5, 1956, 1.

46. "Smothered in Blood and Flame," *Die Zeit*, November 8, 1956, accessed July 1, 2013, http://www.zeit.de/1956/45/erstickt-in-blut-und-flammen.

47. Hank Johnson (former dependent in the Nüremberg Milcom, 1949–1959) in correspondence with the author, February 2014.

48. *Ibid.*

49. *Ibid.* POVs were privately owned vehicles and C-rations were boxed military meals normally issued to service personnel during deployments and field exercises.

50. *Ibid.*

51. Neil Albaugh (former dependent in the Mannheim and Frankfurt Milcoms, 1954–1957) in phone conversation with the author, February 2014.

52. "Khrushchev Fanned Crisis on Berlin, But West Deflated Threat," *Stars and Stripes*, November 16, 1958, 4.

53. "Russ Halt U.S. Convoy Trying to Leave Berlin," *Stars and Stripes*, November 16, 1958, 1.

54. *Ibid.*, Hank Johnson.

55. "Berlin/Soviet Notes: The Match," *Der Spiegel*, December 10, 1958, accessed June 10, 2013, http://www.spiegel.de/spiegel/print/d-42620898.html.

56. For a fuller understanding of the motivations of the Soviets and the associated diplomatic maneuverings see Henry Ashby Turner, Jr., *Germany from Partition to Reunification* and Mary Fulbrook's *The Divided Nation*.

57. Jim Ryan (former military missile specialist assigned to Battery A, 333rd Artillery, 40th Artillery Group (Redstone), Bad Kreuznach Milcom, August 1960-February 1962) in correspondence with the author, February 2014 and extracted with permission from his website *My Army Redstone Days*, page 6, accessed February 8, 2014, http://www.myarmyredstonedays.com.

58. *Ibid.* At the time the unit was located in the vicinity of Bad Kreuznach and east of the town at Wackernheim.

59. *Stars and Stripes*, August 3, 1961, 1.

60. "Johnson Flying to Berlin: Will Meet with Adenauer and Brandt," and "Adenauer Vows Hike in Military," *Stars and Stripes*, August 19, 1961, 1.

61. "1,500 U.S. Troops Sent to Bolster Berlin Force," *Stars and Stripes*, August 20, 1961, 1.

62. "Battle Group of 8th Div. on Move," *Stars and Stripes*, August 20, 1961, 1.

63. Most military units in the EUCOM had Non-Combatant Evacuation Operation (NEO) plans. The details included timelines for evacuation of family members and non-combatants in the event of pending hostilities, plans for transportation to evacuation sites, and recommended lists of items to bring. Many of the plans included evacuation to the United Kingdom, or stop-overs there enroute to the United States as a final destination. Periodically, during the Cold War, units conducted drills and exercises, with representative population samples of non-combatants, to determine the effectiveness of the plans. As a contemporary example see Joint Publication 3–68, *Noncombatant Evacuation Operations*, 22 January 2007.

64. Robert Weekley (retired artillery Colonel who commanded Battery B, 3rd Gun Battalion, 39th

Artillery Regiment while stationed at Dachau Kaserne, during the period May 1960 to May 1963) in correspondence with the author, September 2013.

65. Jim Ryan (former military missile specialist assigned to Battery A, 333rd Artillery, 40th Artillery Group (Redstone), Bad Kreuznach Milcom, August 1960-February 1962) in correspondence with the author, February 2014 and extracted with permission from his website *My Army Redstone Days*, page 10, accessed February 8, 2014, http://www.myarmyredstonedays.com.

66. *Ibid.*

67. Neil Albaugh (former Army missile technician assigned to the 1st Missile Battalion, 38th Artillery, in the Babenhausen Milcom, 1961–1963) in phone conversation with the author, February 2014.

68. Robert E. Green, Jr. (former armor officer assigned to the 4th Armored Division in the Ulm Milcom, 1960–1962) in correspondence with the author, May 2014.

69. Inge Queren (German resident of Neuhaus, Germany who resided in the vicinity of a number of Milcoms and had numerous interactions with Americans throughout her life), in correspondence with the author, February 2014.

70. *Ibid.*

71. John Stennis (MI). "Foreign Aid—Financing of Development Loan Fund." *Congressional Record* 0728 (1961) p. 13919. (*Text from Congressional Record Permanent Digital Collection*); accessed: June 15, 2014.

72. Frank J. Becker (NY). "Authorizing the President to Order Units and Members in the Ready Reserve to Active Duty." *Congressional Record* 0731 (1961) p. 14054. (*Text from Congressional Record Permanent Digital Collection*); accessed: June 15, 2014.

73. This type of discussion did however raise concerns from dependents who feared the U.S. government would prevent them from joining their sponsors overseas during the political crises. The magazine *U.S. Lady* reflected these worries in a series of commentaries in the column 'Capitol Command Post' that ran from September through November 1961. Titles such as "Could Dependents in Europe Help Cause War?" and "Overseas Dependents are to be Reduced" included narratives such as "With these dependents where they are, we might lose a war almost before it got started. Hundreds of thousands of wives and children might be held for ransom." These fears never reduced the size of the dependent population. See "Could Dependents in Europe Help Cause War?" *U.S. Lady* 6, no.4 (September 1961): 5, 34, "Overseas Dependents are to be Reduced," *U.S. Lady* 6, no.5 (October 1961): 29, 46 and "Nuclear Policy Endangers Dependents Abroad," *U.S. Lady* 6, no. 6 (November 1961): 16.

74. Although the focus of the crisis was the island nation of Cuba, the world's military forces were on alert for a potential global conflict. The United States feared that a move against Cuba might trigger a reciprocal action against Berlin. For fuller details of the crisis timeline and decision making see Robert F. Kennedy, *Thirteen Days: A Memoir of the Cuban Missile Crisis* (New York: W.W. Norton, 1999).

75. *Stars and Stripes*, October 24, 1962, 1.

76. "Gromyko Visits Wall, Demands Allies Leave," *Stars and Stripes*, October 25, 1962, 5.

77. Inge Queren (German resident of Neuhaus, Germany who resided in the vicinity of a number of Milcoms and had numerous interactions with Americans throughout her life), in correspondence with the author, February 2014.

78. *Ibid.*

79. "Action Supported," *Stars and Stripes*, October 28, 1962, 7.

80. Barry J. Veden (former sergeant with the 4th Armored Division, Fuerth Milcom, 1961–1964), in correspondence with the author, July 2015.

81. Inge Queren (German resident of Neuhaus, Germany who resided in the vicinity of a number of Milcoms and had numerous interactions with Americans throughout her life), in correspondence with the author, February 2014.

82. See Tom W. Smith, "The Polls: American Attitudes toward the Soviet Union and Communism," *The Public Opinion Quarterly* 47, no. 2 (Summer 1983): 280.

83. Contemporary polls often interchanged the terms 'Russia' and the 'Soviet Union' or 'Soviets.' These two polls particularly reflect Americans' concerns over perceived Soviet technological advancement after the successful launch of the *Sputnik* satellite on October 4, 1957. See Smith, "The Polls: American Attitudes toward the Soviet Union and Communism," and Joseph T. Thompson, "The Cuban Missile Crisis in Context," Rivier Academic Journal 6, no. 1 (Spring 2010), accessed June 23, 2013, http://www.rivier.edu/journal/ROAJ-Spring-2010/J389-Thompson.pdf.

84. The data source is a collection of 213 reports made by the Reactions Analysis Staff of the Office of the High Commissioner of Germany. See Merritt and Merritt, *Public Opinion in Semi-Sovereign Germany: The HICOG Surveys, 1949–1955*. In August 1950, 70 percent of the populace felt confident that the Americans would come to their defense, but by December 1950 that figure fell to 55 percent. Still, during that same month a poll revealed that 75 percent of West Germans would reject a reunification of East and West Germany under a communist regime.

85. "Charter is Proclaimed at Bonn," *Stars and Stripes*, May 24, 1949, 1.

86. The German Basic Law established the Federal Republic of Germany as a parliamentary democracy. The terms 'West Germany' and the 'Federal Republic of Germany' (FRG) are synonymous and refer to western Germany prior to the reunification process in 1990.

87. The term 'occupation mentality' describes pervasive feelings and attitudes of America as a hegemonic suzerain and Germany as a submissive dependent.

88. This perspective is consistent with conclusions draw by Anna and Robert Merritt in their edited collection of HICOG surveys, *Public Opinion in Semisovereign Germany*, as well as with Turner in *Germany from Partition to Reunification* and Fulbrook in *The Divided Nation*.

89. Article by the same title in *Stars and Stripes*, February 12, 1951, 2.

90. *Ibid.*

91. "Adenauer Dares East to Let UN Run All-

Germany Vote," *Stars and Stripes*, September 28, 1951, 1.

92. "Adenauer Receives American Newsmen," *Stars and Stripes*, June 11, 1954, 2. Over the objections of France both the United States and Britain campaigned for West Germany to become a "full partner and equal partner" in the EDC. See "Truman, Churchill Back Bonn Equality in Defense," *Stars and Stripes*, January 11, 1952, 1.

93. Adenauer's prestige with the West German populace continued to remain high through the 1950s. A 1954 HICOG poll gave him a 59 percent approval rating. Merritt and Merritt, *Public Opinion in Semisovereign Germany*, 18.

94. "Germany Takes Helm of Rhine Patrol Craft," *Stars and Stripes*, February 2, 1958, 8.

95. See also "CENTAG and 3rd Armored Division," *U.S Army Germany*, accessed February 12, 2014, http://www.usarmygermany.com.

96. "Blandy Asserts A-Bomb Won't Destroy World," *Stars and Stripes*, July 20, 1949, 3.

97. Hazel Gaudet Erskine, "The Polls: Atomic Weapons and Nuclear Energy," *The Public Opinion Quarterly* 27, no. 2 (Summer 1963): 185.

98. See "Soviet Explosion Listed as 9th Atomic Blast," *Stars and Stripes*, September 27, 1949, 6 and "Hiroshima Chief Fears A-War," *Stars and Stripes*, September 27, 1949, 3.

99. "Russ A-Bombers Could Hit States, Weyland Warns," *Stars and Stripes*, June 12, 1954, 9.

100. Erskine, "The Polls: Atomic Weapons and Nuclear Energy," 185.

101. "Tydings Forecasts X-Bomb," *Stars and Stripes*, February 18, 1950, 3.

102. "Churchill Urges Highest Level East-West Peace Talks," *Stars and Stripes*, February 15, 1950, 12.

103. "Truman Says U.S. Considers Use of Atom Bomb in Korea," *Stars and Stripes*, December 1, 1950, 1.

104. Erskine, "The Polls," 157.

105. Reminiscences of Frank Hubp (former LT with B Battery, 867th Field Artillery Battalion, Heilbronn Milcom, 1956–1958) "210th Field Artillery Group," *U.S Army Germany*, accessed February 13, 2014, http://www.usarmygermany.com.

106. "East Zone's Yield of Uranium Cited," *New York Times*, August 27, 1954, 3.

107. The M65, 280mm Atomic Cannon arrived in USAREUR in 1953, the MGR-1, Honest John Missile system in 1954, the MGM-5, Corporal Missile system in 1955, the M28/29, Davey Crockett tactical nuclear recoilless gun in 1961, and the MGM-29, Sergeant Missile system in 1964.

108. Military engineer units had the mission of emplacing ADMs to obstruct enemy movement by destroying bridges, roadways and other structures an invading force might use. The ADM could also be useful in channelizing an approaching enemy into a preplanned kill zone. The main ADM was the W54 with a yield equaling between 10 Tons and 1 Kiloton of TNT.

109. "280-MM Guns Unveiled," *Stars and Stripes*, October 24, 1953, 1. See also *Annual History*, USAREUR, 1 July 1953–30 June 1954, HQ USAREUR.

110. See "280-MM Guns Ferried Across Rhine in Test," *Stars and Stripes*, May 12, 1954, 1, "Honest John Missilemen Hit and Run," *Stars and Stripes*, February 17, 1958, 8, and "Army Testing Hand-Carried Mortar," *Stars and Stripes*, January 13, 1959, 7.

111. For a complete listing see units and locations at "USAREUR Field Artillery in the European Theater," *U.S Army Germany*, accessed February 12, 2014, http://www.usarmygermany.com.

112. "By Ship, Rail, 'Little Gyroscopers' Arrive at new Home," *Stars and Stripes*, March 27, 1955, 1.

113. Larry Applebaum (former Lieutenant in the 1st Battalion, 13th Artillery Regiment stationed in Augsburg) in correspondence with the author, April 2013. NATO was established in April 1949, the Warsaw Pact in May 1950.

114. "Big Bomb Stiffens West, Scares Far East," *Stars and Stripes*, November 1, 1961, 4.

115. Ron Chiste (former artillery officer in the 6th Battalion, 40th Field Artillery Regiment, Hanau Milcom, 1970–1972) excerpt from "The EDP Briefing," *Vets Speak Out*, 3rd Armored Division website, accessed July 15, 2014, http://www.3ad.com/, with permission. TO&E was the Table of Organization and Equipment and listed all equipment issued to a unit, from weapons and vehicles to items as mundane as furniture.

116. Robert Weekley (retired artillery Colonel who commanded Battery B, 3rd Gun Battalion, 39th Artillery Regiment while stationed at Dachau Kaserne, during the period May 1960 to May 1963) in correspondence with the author, September 2013. His battery was composed of 280mm artillery pieces.

117. Winton "Dip" Spiller (former military officer in the 3rd Battalion, 80th Field Artillery Regiment and the 2nd Battalion, 5th Field Artillery Regiment, April 1964–June 1966) in correspondence with the author, September 2013.

118. Bill Hanne (Former Lieutenant in the 3rd Squadron, 8th Cavalry Regiment, stationed in the Lampertheim Milcom, during the period December 1960 to June 1963) in correspondence with the author, September 2013).

119. "Duck and Cover," Federal Civil Defense Administration, 1951, accessed July 25, 2013, http://archive.org/details/gov.ntis.ava11109vnb1.

120. "Newsreels: Laying of Keel for Nautilus," Universal International, June 16, 1952, accessed July 25, 2013, http://archive.org/details/1952-06-16_Atom_Sub.

121. "News in Brief: New Mexico," Universal International, November 30, 1961, accessed July 25, 2013, http://archive.org/details/1961-11-30_New_Mexico.

122. See "Declaration Vary on Bomb Use Authority: Pentagon Mum on Nuclear Role," *Stars and Stripes*, September 25, 1964, 2.

123. "U.S. Would Study Europe Control of Alliance A-Force," *Stars and Stripes*, December 15, 1964, 2.

124. Merritt and Merritt, *Public Opinion in Semisovereign Germany*, Report #199, 240.

125. France and Britain, both former enemies of Germany, were initially suspicious of any initiative to rearm, even if it meant bolstering NATO forces. For an overview of the political options and alternatives fac-

ing Adenauer during the early 1950s see Turner's *Germany from Partition to Reunification*, 121–125.

126. "Abroad: Europe's Defense is at Issue in West Germany's Election," *New York Times*, August 29, 1953, 16.

127. See "American Nationalism," *Die Zeit*, April 15, 1954, accessed June 7, 2013, http://www.zeit.de/1954/15/der-amerikanische-nationalismus.

128. Respective sources are Merritt and Merritt, *Public Opinion in Semisovereign Germany*, Report #13, 62 and Erskine, *The Polls*, 63.

129. "1st Hydrogen Bomb Test Predicted Within Year," *Stars and Stripes*, February 2, 1950, 1.

130. "Hydrogen Bomb Gets Energy Like Sun," *Stars and Stripes*, February 3, 1950, 4 and "Power of H-Bomb Cited," *Stars and Stripes*, February 4, 1950, 6.

131. An April 1954 poll recorded 71 percent in favor of proceeding and three years later a May 1957 poll recorded 63 percent in favor even if other nations curtailed their efforts. Respective sources are "Gallup Poll Finds: Public Approves Future H-Bomb Tests," *Spartanburg Herald*, April 24, 1954, 6, and Erskine, *The Polls*, 184.

132. Merritt and Merritt, *Public Opinion in Semisovereign Germany*, Report #91, 127.

133. Erskine, *The Polls*, 181.

134. Merritt and Merritt, *Public Opinion in Semisovereign Germany*, Report #91, 127.

135. Merritt and Merritt, xxiii.

136. Merritt and Merritt, Report #91, 127.

137. Merritt and Merritt, Report #199, 240.

138. "Moscow Sees Bonn as U.S. atom Base," *New York Times*, April 9, 1957, 4.

139. Adenauer and West German conservatives had worked diligently after the war to take steps toward increased sovereignty while aligning themselves as full supporters of the West. For a fuller understanding see Mary Fulbrook's *The Divided Nation*.

140. These were key political issues of the Adenauer years and required a careful navigation between the expectations of Western partners and the desires of the German people. See a fuller description of missed opportunities and the demands of foreign relations in Mary Fulbrook's *The Divided Nation*.

141. "Spain/H-Bombs Crash: Terrible Mystery," *Der Spiegel*, February 14, 1966, accessed November 20, 2013, http://www.spiegel.de/spiegel/print/d-46265687.html.

142. "Spanish Police at A-Crash Site Show Traces of Radioactivity," *Washington Post*, January 22, 1966, A1.

143. "Spain/H-Bombs Crash: Terrible Mystery," *Der Spiegel*, February 14, 1966, accessed November 20, 2013, http://www.spiegel.de/spiegel/print/d-46265687.html. In the film *Thunderball* (1965) James Bond must recover two nuclear warheads stolen by a master criminal.

144. Ibid.

145. "As the Bombs were Falling," *Die Zeit*, February 16, 1968, accessed November 20, 2013, http://www.zeit.de/1968/07/als-die-bomben-fielen and "H-Bomb in the Tomato Fields?" *Die Zeit*, February 25, 1966, accessed November 20, 2013 http://www.zeit.de/1966/09/h-bombe-im-tomatenacker.

146. Between February 1958 and January 1966 there had been no fewer than 12 reported incidents of military handlers accidentally dropping, burning, damaging, or temporarily losing nuclear weapons in the United States or during transportation overseas. There is speculation that there were several additional unreported incidents. See "Chances of Nuclear Mishap Viewed as Infinitesimal," *New York Times*, March 27, 1966, 80.

147. William Terry (former 280mm Atomic Cannon crewman in the 264th Field Artillery Battalion, 42nd Field Artillery Brigade, stationed in the Bad Kreuznach Milcom, during the period October 1953 to February 1957) "42nd FA BDE," *U.S. Army Germany*, accessed February 12, 2014, http://www.usarmygermany.com. Because of the greater range of the weapon it required the relocation of the cannon to off-base positions to accommodate the impact of the round within the limits of the designated on-base impact area.

148. "Army's 280-MM Cannon Retrieved from Ditch," *Stars and Stripes* (photograph), August 22, 1954, 24.

149. "Air-Raid Shelter in the Nuclear War," *Die Zeit*, February 7, 1957, accessed August 3, 2013, http://www.zeit.de/1957/06/Fluftschutz-im-atomkrieg.

150. "How Much is the Civil Defense?" Die Zeit, October 14, 1960, accessed August 3, 2013, http://www.zeit.de/1960/42/was-kostet-die-zivile-verteidigung/seite-1.

151. The Residence Regulation Law was one of the emergency laws that permitted authorities of the Federal Republic to stop a mass exodus or to order a mass evacuation in the event of war or natural disaster.

Chapter Five

1. Ralph Willet, *The Americanization of Germany*, 114.

2. "VW Best-Selling '62 Import With 230,000 Cars," *Stars and Stripes*, December 31, 1962, 3, and "VW Sales Up 22 percent in 1962," *Stars and Stripes*, May 7, 1963, 23.

3. U.S. Joint Chiefs of Staff Directive 1067 was the occupation directive for postwar Germany. The U.S. government issued it in March 1945. It contained restrictions on economic recovery.

4. 10 months after the war Germany's economy was at a standstill with industrial production at zero, and a rate of output at 10–12 percent in the AMZON. Trade was non-existent and exchange on the black market was rampant. For a complete understanding of these conditions see Wennberg, "Some Economic Problems of Allied Occupation Policy in Germany," 425–447.

5. For a comprehensive overview of the impetus behind early postwar economic programs in West Germany see Mary Fulbrook, *The Divided Nation*, 130–154.

6. The 'Marshall Plan' was the popular eponymous title for the ERP. Melvyn Leffler notes the importance of both humanitarian considerations as well as political reasoning in the framing of the ERP. See his work *For the Soul of Mankind* (New York: Hill and Wang, 2007), 57–70.

7. Jussi M. Hanhimäki and Odd Arne Westad, eds., *The Cold War: A History in Documents and Eyewitness Accounts* (New York: Oxford University Press, 2003), 121. A.A. Berle, Jr. provides an early evaluation of the economic and political goals and objectives of the plan, including Soviet objections in "The Marshall Plan in the European Struggle," *Social Research* 15, no.1 (March 1948): 1–21.

8. President Truman petitioned in December 1947 to have Congress expand the program to include Germany against protests by many politicians and leaders in other countries, such as France, who argued to the contrary. "Germany to Share in Marshall Plan," *New York Times*, December 9, 1947, 1. Diane Kunz provides insight to the full set of motivations behind the plan including diplomat George Kennan's estimation that "economic maladjustment ... makes European society vulnerable to exploitation by any and all totalitarian movements." See Kunz's "The Marshall Plan Reconsidered: A Complex of Motives," *Foreign Affairs* 76.3 (May/June 1997): 162–170.

9. Potter, People of Plenty, 83.

10. The 'American way' would introduce a revamping of European economies along lines followed in the United States. This included planning, resourcing, labor-management relations, capital infusion, and development of industrial infrastructure and integration of free market strategies. The intent was to lure European economists and industrialists away from the planned economic strategies of the East. See Manuela Aguilar, *Cultural Diplomacy and Foreign Policy* (New York: Peter Lang, 1996) and Harald Hagemann, "The Influence of the United States on German Economic Thought," in Detlef Junker, *The United States and Germany in the Era of the Cold War*, Vol. 1, 362–369.

11. A HICOG survey team asked the question just months after the relief of the Berlin Blockade that ended in May 1949. It is possible that existing conditions in the city influenced the responses. Merritt and Merritt, *Public Opinion in Semisovereign Germany*, Report #5, 65.

12. This second sampling was from the larger AMZON population and did not include the much smaller Berlin sector population. Merritt and Merritt, *Public Opinion in Semisovereign Germany*, Report #17-S, 67.

13. Merritt and Merritt, *Public Opinion in Semisovereign Germany*, Report #39, 85.

14. Nicolaus Mills, *Winning the Peace: The Marshall Plan and America's Coming of Age as a Superpower* (Hoboken: John Wiley, 2008), 10.

15. "The Marshall Reaches Its First Objective," *Stars and Stripes*, December 3, 1949, 5.

16. Keeping within the context of a postwar exceptionalist consensus the film touched on several important core tenets such as the bounty of America's resources and wealth, the centrality of Christianity, and essential differences between the New World and Europe. See the Big Picture film *The Changed Face of Europe*.

17. The Institut für Demoskopie, Allensbach, founded in 1947, collects opinion and marketing data. The "Allensbach Institute" is its more popular name.

18. For this particular set of survey questions respondents could choose two answers. Elisabeth Noelle and Erich Peter Neumann, eds., *The Germans: Public Opinion Polls, 1947–1966* (Bonn: Verlag Fur Demoskopie, 1967), 548.

19. These types of charges were challenges that came from contemporary Soviet propaganda. "President Denies U.S. Imperialism in Marshall Plan," *New York Times*, October 10, 1947, 1.

20. "Harriman Says Marshall Aid Will Create West Bulwark," *Stars and Stripes*, February 21, 1950, 2.

21. West Germany's integration with the Western allies and gradual drift toward greater sovereignty resulted from its increasing economic power and the realization by the United States of its importance as an ally against the Soviets. See Frank Schumacher, "From Occupation to Alliance," in Detlef Junker, *The United States and Germany in the Era of the Cold War*, Vol. 1, 90–96.

22. Those funds not received through the ERP came from Government and Relief in Occupied Areas (GARIOA) programs which had their own line entries in the Congressional budget. "Germany's Economic Revival Due to $3.5 Billion in Direct U.S. Aid," *Stars and Stripes*, November 20, 1951, 4.

23. For a fuller understanding of the effects and benefits of the Marshall Plan see Gerd Hardach, "The Marshall Plan," in Detlef Junker, *The United States and Germany in the Era of the Cold War*, Vol. 1, 301- 309. For an understanding of the birth of postwar consumerism in West Germany see Sywottek, "From Starvation to Excess?" in Schissler, *The Miracle Years: A Cultural History of West Germany, 1949–1968*, 341–358.

24. "Unproductive Message," *Der Spiegel*, June 19, 1948, accessed April 10, 2013, http://www.spiegel.de/spiegel/print/d-44417231.html.

25. The reference is to Secretary of State John F. Dulles who purchased a VW for his personal use. The story of the VW's rebounding success was a symbol of "West German postwar recovery at home and abroad" made possible through the *Wirtschaftswunder* inspired by the ERP. See Bernhard Rieger's "From People's Car to New Beetle: The Transatlantic Journeys of the Volkswagen Beetle," *Journal of American History* 97, no. 1 (2010): 91–115.

26. Those GI remembrances helped the VW "become a popular import in the early fifties." See "VW Kübelwagen and Schwimmwagen: Germany's WW2 Jeeps," *The Truth about Cars*, accessed February 18, 2014, http://www.thetruthaboutcars.com/2010/04/vw-kubelwagen-and-schwimmwagen-germanys-ww2-jeeps/.

27. Norman McCracken (former clerk-typist assigned to Headquarters, 7888th AU, Special Troops, Heidelberg Milcom, 1955–1956), "26th Support Group," *U.S. Army Germany*, accessed February 18, 2014, http://www.usarmygermany.com. Depending on customization and special ordering a Ford could cost between $1,600 and $3,000.

28. Jon Wolfe (assigned to the 656th Engineer Battalion (Topography), Engineering Intelligence Center, Tompkins Barracks, Heidelberg Milcom, c. 1960), "656th Engineer Battalion," *U.S Army Germany*, accessed February 18, 2014, http://www.usarmygermany.com.

29. Petra Goedde, *GIs and Germans: Culture, Gen-*

der, and Foreign Relations, 1945–1949 (New Haven: Yale University Press, 2003) 200.

30. The U.S. Congress terminated the ERP in June 1952. "Bonn Leader Voices Thanks for U.S. Aid," *Stars and Stripes*, July 6, 1952, 4.

31. Noelle and Neumann, 549.

32. "40 Germans Selected for Air-Traffic Jobs," *Stars and Stripes*, December 2, 1947, 2.

33. "Ban Continued on Air Activity by Germans," *Stars and Stripes*, September 18, 1950, 15.

34. "GYA to Hire Germans," *Stars and Stripes*, January 17, 1948, 5.

35. "239 MG Jobs for Civilians to Open in June," *Stars and Stripes*, March 7, 1948, 6.

36. Authorities in the Military Government did not always apply the Denazification program uniformly for individuals and critics often considered its application to be lax. See Cornelia Rauh-Kühne, "Life Rewarded the Latecomers: Denazification during the Cold War," in Detlef Junker, *The United States and Germany in the Era of the Cold War*, Vol. 1, 65–72.

37. These types of organizations employed thousands of Germans from the early years of the occupation through the following decades. See "Labor Service Division," *U.S. Army in Germany*, accessed November 9, 2013, http://usarmygermany.com/Sont.htm?http&&&usarmygermany.com/Units/HqUSAREUR/USAREUR_LaborSvc.htm.

38. See "10,000 Leave DP Centers in EC Monthly," *Stars and Stripes*, May 31, 1949, 4 and "For Some, Miesau Depot is Labor of Love," *Stars and Stripes*, October 12, 1987, 1 and 3. USAREUR Regulation 660-400, later Army in Europe (AE) Regulation 690-40, provided guidelines for employment of a local national workforce, including the Labor Service and Security Units. The Brentano-Trimble Agreement of 1957, signed by the U.S. Minister to Germany, William C. Trimble and the West German Foreign Minister, Heinrich von Brentano, was the basis of understanding for use of this workforce and delineated their responsibilities as non-combatants in wartime.

39. "German Employees' Council," *Stars and Stripes*, October 27, 1951, 2, and "Riesel Applauds German Workers for Labor Record," *Stars and Stripes*, July 26, 1958, 8.

40. "Post Commander Addresses Meeting of German Council," *Heidelberg Post*, December 22, 1949, 1, RG 549, United States Army, Europe, Heidelberg Military Post, *Heidelberg Post*, 1949–1950, Box 3337, National Archives College Park.

41. Ibid.

42. "Military Posts to Handle Pay of Germans," *Stars and Stripes*, September 17, 1948, 4.

43. "Delay in Pay for Germans Stirs Protests," *Stars and Stripes*, June 15, 1949, 10.

44. "German Workers to Take Ordnance Safety Course," *Stars and Stripes*, December 11, 1953, 9.

45. "Boeblingen Ordnance Depot Rebuilds 24,000th Vehicle," *Stars and Stripes*, August 12, 1954, 10.

46. "Ord Auto Center Marks Fourth Anniversary," *Stars and Stripes*, April 3, 1950, 5.

47. "USAREUR's Modern Communications Network," *Stars and Stripes*, August 3, 1956, 12–13.

48. This film from the Big Picture series, also told the story of the hiring of local nationals by the U.S. government in both Japan and West Germany to support the American military presence and assist the economies.

49. Maria Höhn offers a description of this uncomfortable contradiction in her postwar study of the Rhineland-Palatinate region, *GIs and Fräuleins*. Another source of examples is Anni P. Baker's *American Soldiers Overseas*.

50. Maria Höhn, *GIs and Frauleins*, 40–41.

51. "Mark Changes Tomorrow Western Allies Announce Reform," *Stars and Stripes*, June 19, 1948, 1. The Western Allies and the Soviets met during the London Conference, February to March and April to June 1948, to discuss economic conditions in Europe. This included a decision to finally extend Marshall Plan aid to the western zones of Germany. At that time, discussions concerning currency reform were central to other plans to form a West German government. See Henry Ashby Turner, Jr. *Germany from Partition to Reunification*, 23–24. "Mark Changes Tomorrow Western Allies Announce Reform," *Stars and Stripes*, June 19, 1948, 1.

52. Ibid.

53. For the strategy behind the currency reform and the results see Werner Plumpe, "Opting for the Structural Break: The West German Currency Reform and its Consequences," in Detlef Junker, *The United States and Germany in the Era of the Cold War*, Vol. 1, 293–300.

54. The Western Allies delayed the introduction of the Deutsche Mark in their Berlin sectors while they awaited a reaction from the Soviets. By the end of the year, and in the midst of the Soviet blockade, the residents of West Berlin were using the DM thus strengthening their economic ties with West Germany. Those DMs introduced into the city bore a stamped letter 'B.' Berliners dubbed them either 'B-Marks' or 'Clay-Marks' after the American military governor. "Before Currency Reform … and After," *Stars and Stripes*, December 18, 1948, 6.

55. The black market operated throughout postwar Europe during this time and prospered most in countries receiving large, hard-to-control volumes of external aid. "140 Face Trial in Top Black Market Case," *Stars and Stripes*, May 8, 1948, 11.

56. "Black Mart Raid Nets Huge Stocks," *Stars and Stripes*, April 16, 1948, 1.

57. Kevin C. Ruffner, "The Black market in Postwar Berlin, Colonel Miller and an Army Scandal, Part 1," *Prologue Magazine* 34, no. 3 (Fall 2002), National Archives, accessed March 2014, http://www.archives.gov/publications/prologue/2002/fall/berlin-black-market-1.html#f23.

58. Ibid. FN 22.

59. Wolf W. Schmoekel, *The Dragoon Story: A History of the 2nd Armored Cavalry Regiment* (Greensboro: Randall Printing, 1958), 161.

60. Ibid., 163.

61. Morton C. Mumma III (former fighter pilot assigned to the 527th Fighter Bomber Squadron, 86th Fighter Bomber Wing, Neubiberg Airbase, 1950 to 1951) in correspondence with the author, June 2014.

62. "AFN Nürnberg: Armed Forces Network, Europe," *U.S Army Germany*, accessed February 18, 2014, http://www.usarmygermany.com.

63. Ingrid Schenk, "Producing to Consume Becomes Consuming to Produce," in Detlef Junker, *The United States and Germany in the Era of the Cold War*, Vol. 1, 581.

64. The West German government mandated that citizens turn in all old RMs by June 26. After that date "all money not registered ... will be worthless." "Mark Changes Tomorrow Western Allies Announce Reform," *Stars and Stripes*, June 19, 1948, 1.

65. "Currency Reform May Force Students to Quit University," *Stars and Stripes*, July 13, 1948, 6.

66. Elizabeth Heineman, "The Hour of the Woman: Memories of Germany's 'Crisis Years' and West German National Identity," in Hanna Schissler, *The Miracle Years: A Cultural History of West Germany*, 37.

67. "Cracks in the Price Building: Emergency Measure," *Der Spiegel*, July 31, 1948, accessed August 12, 2013, http://www.spiegel.de/spiegel/print/d-44418579.html.

68. "The New Deutsche Mark Pays its Way," *Stars and Stripes*, December 18, 1948, 6, and "Hesse Survey Shows Fall in Black Market," *Stars and Stripes*, August 25, 1948, 5.

69. "Currency Reform Puts Serious Crimp in Black Market," *Stars and Stripes*, June 23, 1948, 1.

70. "Before Currency Reform ... and After," *Stars and Stripes*, December 12, 1948, 6.

71. "U.S. Forces Quell Stuttgart Riot," *Stars and Stripes*, October 29, 1948, 1.

72. This little heralded event is gaining in importance in studies of the early postwar economy. See Jörg Roesler, "Two Tanks against Protestors," *Ossietzky*, accessed November 9, 2013, http://www.sopos.org/aufsaetze/51bf24b10373e/1.phtml.

73. Bizonia was comprised of the American and British zones. "8 Million Workers in Bizonia Strike Against Prices Today," *Stars and Stripes*, November 12, 1948, 1.

74. German labor history tends to see the series of strikes as a campaign against economic inequities and a struggle for control of the economy. See "A General Strike, Which Could Be None," *Der Freitag*, November 7, 2003, accessed August 15, 2013, http://www.freitag.de/autoren/der-freitag/ein-generalstreik-der-keiner-sein-durfte.

75. Merritt and Merritt, *Public Opinion in Semisovereign Germany*, Report #17-S, 67.

76. Merritt and Merritt, Report #148, 180.

77. Ironically, this announcement shared the front page with news of the start of relief flights by the U.S. Air Force to the blockaded city of Berlin. "Mark Increase Forces Rise in PX Prices," *Stars and Stripes*, June 23, 1948, 1.

78. "Survey Shows PXs Sell Far Below U.S.," *Stars and Stripes*, June 30, 1948, 4.

79. "Commissary Complaint on Prices," B-Bag, *Stars and Stripes*, September 2, 1948, 2.

80. "PX Prices Cut on 50 Items," *Stars and Stripes*, May 27, 1950, 5.

81. "Operating Economy: Savings Days," *Stars and Stripes*, July 25, 1950, 8.

82. Germany, France, Britain and Greece were among the nations where scrip was in use during the early postwar years. Scrip came in denominations of 10, 25 and 50 cents, one dollar, and five dollars.

83. "Army Converts All Scrip to Foil Black Marketers," *Stars and Stripes*, June 21, 1954, 2.

84. See "News for Living," *Stars and Stripes*, June 3, 1951 for an example of a contemporary explanation of the use of MPC. See also "Huge Turn-in Slows FMP Scrip Change," *Stars and Stripes*, June 21, 1954, 2, for a description of the effectiveness of periodic scrip exchanges in foiling black marketeers, as the American military police "estimated that upward of $100,000 was lost by Munich area black-market operators in this morning's scrip conversion." The use of MPC by American forces in Europe began on September 16, 1946 and ended on May 27, 1958.

85. "Forces in 3 Nations Get Greenbacks," *Stars and Stripes*, May 28, 1958, 1. Concerns over the cost of the program by certain members of Congress forced the program to end.

86. "Life on the Economy: Budgets and Burdens," *Stars and Stripes*, March 26, 1957, 11. Also see Figure 1.1 of this study.

87. "Mainly, They Like It," *Stars and Stripes*, August 22, 1959, 12.

88. "Five-Year Limit on Government Quarters," B-Bag Letter, *Stars and Stripes*, March 14, 1964, 13.

89. "Don't Query Allotments, Army Asks Dependents," *Stars and Stripes*, May 23, 1952, 2 and "New BAQ Law Becomes Effective Jan 1," *Stars and Stripes*, November 7, 1962, 8. Although the Secretary of Defense Robert S. McNamara requested an 18.5 percent increase for BAQ in March 1962 Congress agreed to only a 7 percent increase. It arrived in military paychecks in October of that year only for those families living on the economy. Persons living in government sponsored quarters automatically forfeited their BAQ.

90. Article X of the NATO SOFA signed on June 19, 1951 provided specific exemption from taxation for all NATO service personnel, civilians, and their families.

91. "Bonn Conventions: This is the Way it Will Be," *Stars and Stripes*, May 6, 1955, 14.

92. "Ruling Frees Germans of Tax on Ideas Prizes," *Stars and Stripes*, April 26, 1957, 8.

Chapter Six

1. Wolfgang Becker and his production studio released the award winning film "Good Bye Lenin!" in 2003. It is the story of the extreme measures the children of a former East Berlin citizen take to protect her from the new realities of Western consumerism that invade her socialist homeland after the fall of the Wall. The theme of both films is the pervasive influence of consumerism that transcends politics and society to unite people and eventually break down traditional cultural barriers to modernity.

2. In "One, Two, Three" the main character works for Coca-Cola trying to improve sales in 1961 Germany. In the storyline Coke represents everything that is modern and free, a metaphor for Americanism as a direct

contrast to the communist oppressed societies of the East. In several scenes communist operatives sneak drinks of Coke while listening to forbidden modern music. In the second film, Coca-Cola serves the same purpose, arriving in East Germany with new freedoms and modern behaviors. In one scene a large banner bearing the emblem of Coke replaces one heralding socialist achievement.

3. Although the process was long and often controversial these aspects of popular American culture, often introduced through the Milcoms, eventually found traction in Europe and West Germany particularly with younger generations. Older Germans also came to accept, if not accommodate, these intrusions of American culture. For additional discussion of the associated intercultural penetration see Richard Pells, *Not Like Us*.

4. That absorption generally occurred first with younger generations but eventually achieved status as an indigenous cultural artifact. See Sabrina P. Ramet and Gordana P. Crnkovic, eds. *Kazaaam! Splat! Ploof! The American Impact on European Popular Culture since 1945* (New York: Rowman & Littlefield, 2003), 5.

5. Mary Nolan suggests that British rock music, particularly by the Beatles and the Rolling Stones, replaced American popular music as the dominant popular sound by the mid–1960s. See Nolan, *The Transatlantic Century: Europe and America*, 244.

6. At its height A&W had three restaurants in Germany but by 1990 all three had closed their doors. By the end of 1969 KFC had two restaurants in Frankfurt.

7. "Blitzing Deutschland with Yankee Fast –Food," *Stars and Stripes*, December 2, 1977, 14.

8. Through the late 1980s the city of Frankfurt and the immediate surrounding area was home to at least 17 American military facilities, kasernes, and housing areas. These included the Abrams Complex, Headquarters of the U.S. Army V Corps and the 97th General Hospital. In addition, nearby, there were the well-populated satellite sub-communities of Hanau, Darmstadt, Bad-Nauheim, and the U.S. Air Force Rhein-Main Air Base.

9. Traditional European restaurant dining included at least a wait staff, metal cutlery, ceramic dinnerware and table cloths.

10. Bee Wilson, "Burger Off," *New Statesman* 135, October 2, 2000, 48.

11. "The Unloved Hamburger," *Die Zeit*, August 25, 1972, accessed September 1, 2013, http://www.zeit.de/1972/34/die-ungeliebten-hamburger.

12. For purposes of this study a "short travel distance" is 10 miles or less. A similar correlation of locations also applies to the Burger King franchises. The term 'co-location' for the time period refers to locations only in the same town or village as the Milcom not specifically within the confines of a military facility or housing area. By 1990 Burger King had 143 locations of 250 (57.70 percent) in the FRG located in or near a Milcom and McDonalds had 276 locations of approximately 900 (30.66 percent). Data collated from a variety of sources including *Stars and Stripes*, *Der Spiegel*, *Die Zeit*, *New York Times* and the websites *Restaurants in Germany* and *List of U.S. Army Installations in Germany*.

13. Between 1970 and 1980 the total Milcom population in West Germany increased from 346,867 to 414,020. See Chapter 1, *Military and Dependent Populations*, this study.

14. In evidence, the West German town of Bamberg had approximately 80,000 residents including 10,000 Milcom members, but by 1990 had 2 McDonalds and 2 Burger Kings. "Command War: Crimes of Violence in USAREUR Dip Drastically Following Drive," *Stars and Stripes*, December 27, 1974, 9.

15. For one understanding of the acceptance of fast food into a society see Victoria de Grazia, *Irresistible Empire*, 469.

16. "Consumer Watch," *Stars and Stripes*, February 4, 1977, 19.

17. Ibid.

18. *Hearing before the Morale, Welfare and Recreation (MWR) Panel*, 101st Congress 1 (1987) (statement of Dan Daniel Representative of Virginia). http://congressional.proquest.com.mutex.gmu.edu/congressional/result/pqpresultpage.gispdfhitspanel.pdflink/http percent3A$2f$2fprod.cosmos.dc4.bowker-dmz.com$2fapp-bin$2fgis-hearing$2f8$2f1$2ff$2f5$2fhrg–1987-ash–0023_from_1_to_157.pdf/entitlementkeys=1234|app-gis|hearing|hrg–1987-ash–0023

19. McDonald's had a similar deal with the Department of the Navy.

20. A share of the profits went to support programs for military and civilian Milcom members and their families. See "Military, Chains Join Forces: Fast Food Boosts Troop Morale," *Nation's Restaurant News*, December 1987, accessed June 12, 2011, http://findarticles.com/p/articles/mi_m3190/is_n51_v21/ai_6213509/, and "Burger King Clinches Landmark Military Deal; Signs Agreement to Build 185 Units over Next 5 Years," *Nation's Restaurant News*, June 1984, accessed February 12, 2012, http://findarticles.com/p/articles/mi_m3190/is_v18/ai_3313012/.

21. "Burger King, AAFES OK Fast Food Outlets," *Stars and Stripes*, May 23, 1984, 1.

22. "AAFES-Burger King Contract Explained," letter to the editor, *Stars and Stripes*, December 31, 1986, 11.

23. These mobile vans were reminiscent of the successful book mobiles that plied the byways of remote areas two decade earlier. See "Burger King to Hit the Road for Military," *Stars and Stripes*, September 12, 1985, 1.

24. AAFES and Burger King split the profits 50/50. "AAFES' Burger King Franchise Proving to be Sizzling Success," *Stars and Stripes*, April 23, 1986, 8.

25. Ibid.

26. "Comets, Tornadoes, Rangers, Amigos Win," *Stars and Stripes*, April 18, 1982, 21.

27. "U.S. Military Promoting Holiday Bliss," *Stars and Stripes*, December 23, 1986, 1.

28. But there was an important difference between the two. The sale of automobiles through the *Stars and Stripes* was for a shorter duration lasting only several years. The benefit was solely to the Milcom families who had few options for purchasing a car in the early

postwar years in Germany. Neither the military, nor the newspaper, realized any financial gain from those advertisements. In contrast, by contractual agreement, the military did receive a share of fast food profits to support morale and welfare funds. Advertising Burger King and McDonald's supported this initiative.

29. Paid Advertisement, *Stars and Stripes*, November 20, 1985, I, and Paid Advertisement, *Stars and Stripes*, December 9, 1985, I.

30. "AAFES' Burger King Franchise Proving to be Sizzling Success," *Stars and Stripes*, April 23, 1986, 8.

31. Name withheld by request (former military officer in the 32nd Signal Battalion, V Corps, Frankfurt Milcom, 1977–1981) in correspondence with the author, September 2013.

32. The reference was to the Hahn Airbase Milcom. A Burger King did open there in October 1989. "Hahn Soon to Get 'Taste of America,'" letter to the editor, *Stars and Stripes*, February 16, 1989, 11.

33. Douglas Gaskell (former military officer in the 1st Battalion, 81st Field Artillery Regiment, Neu Ulm Milcom, 1981–1983 and the 56th Field Artillery Brigade, Schwäbisch Gmünd Milcom, 1983–1985) in correspondence with the author, September 2013.

34. Thomas Rehm (former military officer in the 2nd Battalion, 78th Field Artillery Regiment, Bamberg Milcom, 1981–1984 and the 1st Battalion, 9th Field Artillery Regiment, Neu Ulm Milcom, 1989–1991) in correspondence with the author), March 2013.

35. Ray Kroc was the founder of the McDonald's fast food corporation. "Gastronomy: Biscuit in Mull," *Der Spiegel*, April 12, 1976, accessed September 1, 2013, http://www.spiegel.de/spiegel/print/d-41238258.html.

36. "Gastronomy: War on the Sausages," *Der Spiegel*, June 12, 1978, accessed September 1, 2013, http://www.spiegel.de/spiegel/print/d-40615565.html.

37. "Department Stores: Fast Bucks," *Der Spiegel*, August 24, 1980, accessed September 1, 2013, http://www.spiegel.de/spiegel/print/d-14323927.html.

38. *Ibid*. George Ritzer makes mention of the German predilection toward rationalization by describing an association between the calculated effectiveness of mass-produced death during the Holocaust of World War Two and Germans' admiration for the streamlined fast food operations. See George Ritzer, *The McDonaldization of Society* (Washington, DC: Sage, 2013), 32.

39. Tommy Tracy (former military dependent 1971–1975, Heidelberg Milcom, and 1977–1979 Frankfurt Milcom, and retired military officer 1st Battalion, 22nd Field Artillery Regiment, Zirndorf Milcom, 1986–1989) in correspondence with the author, September 2013.

40. "Modern Life: Fast Food in Advance," *Der Spiegel*, August 17, 1987, accessed September 2, 2013, http://www.spiegel.de/spiegel/print/d-13525345.html.

41. For a fuller discussion of the spread of American cultural imperialism within the context of globalism and Americanization see Steinar Bryn, "The Coca-Cola Co. and the Olympic Movement: Global or American?" and Marianne Debouzy, "Does Mickey Mouse Threaten French Culture?" in Sabrina P. Ramet, and Gordana P. Crnkovic, eds., *Kazaaam! Splat! Ploof!*

42. Histories variously attribute these tensions to a reaction against the authoritarianism of the early Cold War period, the ongoing public debate over America's involvement in Vietnam, rejection of a consumerist society and a struggle for inclusion and civil liberties by previously disenfranchised social and ethnic groups. See Maurice Isserman and Michael Kazin, eds., *America Divided: The Civil War of the 1960s* (New York: Oxford University Press, 2008) and Bruce J. Schulman, *The Seventies: The Great Shift in American Culture, Society, and Politics* (Cambridge: DeCapo Press, 2002).

43. One example is the military lens provided by Russell F. Weigley's *The American Way of War: A History of United States Military Strategy and Policy* (Bloomington: Indiana University Press: 1973).

44. Karl May was a popular prewar German author of Wild West stories. Greg Langley, "A Fist Full of Dreams: Taming the Wild West in the Old World," the Karl May Historical Society, accessed April 1, 2013, http://www.karl-may-gesellschaft.de/kmg/sprachen/englisch/seklit/langley/index.htm.

45. Thomas Koebner provides an excellent interpretation of violence in American in his essay "Hollywood in Germany," in Detlef Junker, *The United States and Germany in the Era of the Cold War*, Vol. 2, 349–354.

46. *Ibid.*, 352.

47. *Ibid.*, 350.

48. The "Big Red One" is a Hollywood production that portrays that American infantry division's World War Two combat role against the Germans.

49. *Dollars* was a popular international crime film, released in 1972. "Dollars Film Pay Off on International Market," *Stars and Stripes*, February 22, 1972, 4.

50. Michael Geisler, "Transatlantic Reflections: German and American Television," in Detlef Junker, *The United States and Germany in the Era of the Cold War*, Vol. 2, 369.

51. King made this statement during a speech titled "Beyond Vietnam" to the group Clergy and Laymen Concerned About Vietnam at the Riverside Church, New York City, on April 4, 1967.

52. "United States/Kennedy Murder: What a Country," *Der Spiegel*, June 10, 1968, accessed September 19, 2013, http://www.spiegel.de/spiegel/print/d-46020982.html.

53. "United States/My Lai: Only One Finger," *Der Spiegel*, November 16, 1970, accessed September 19, 2013, http://www.spiegel.de/spiegel/print/d-44906692.html.

54. "Mirror Report on the American Forces in the Federal Republic," *Der Spiegel*, April 17, 1972, accessed September 19, 2013, http://www.spiegel.de/spiegel/print/d-42953738.html.

55. The reference is to President Woodrow Wilson's Fourteen Point manifesto intended to provide the world with a peaceful course after the devastation of World War One. "Observations of the German-American Relationship," *Die Zeit*, September 23, 1983, accessed September 19, 2013, http://www.zeit.de/1983/39/haben-wir-uns-auseinandergelebt/seite-1.

56. "The U.S. Army: A Battle for Survival: Army in Anguish," *The Washington Post*, September 12, 1971, A1.
57. Ibid.
58. "America's Crime Epidemic," *Stars and Stripes*, August 17, 1970, 11. The President signed this act into law on October 15, 1970. It focused on organized gambling and witness protection. See "Nixon's New Look at the Justice Department," *Stars and Stripes*, February 24, 1970, 11. The 'law and order' theme was central to the conservatives' political platform of the 1960s and 1970s. Between 1968 and 1970 Nixon proposed 13 pieces of legislation to bolster police departments and the judicial system. See Schulman and Zelizer, eds., *Rightward Bound* and Dan T. Carter, *The Politics of Rage* (Baton Rouge: Louisiana State University Press, 2008).
59. Although these statistics validate an elevated violent crime rate in USAREUR for that period of time they became central to a larger controversy involving prejudicial racial reporting and a biased judicial system. "Conference Receives USAREUR Report on Black GI Crime Rate," *Stars and Stripes*, November 13, 1971, 2.
60. Violent crimes included homicide, assault, rape, murder, and child or spouse abuse. Crimes against property included theft, larceny, destruction or damage to public or private property.
61. DODDSEUR was the Department of Defense Dependents Schools, Europe. "School Violence," *Stars and Stripes*, August 11, 1976, 9.
62. "First of 9 GIs Charged with Robbery Sentenced," *Stars and Stripes*, December 17, 1980, 27, "Violent Crime in Barracks on Rise," *Stars and Stripes*, November 17, 1981, 1, and "Soldier is Sentenced to 18 Years for Rape," *Stars and Stripes*, March 7, 1982, 2.
63. "Military Family Member Accused in Robbery," *Stars and Stripes*, August 7, 1986, 2.
64. "Commander of AFRC Sent Back to U.S.," *Stars and Stripes*, March 7, 1982, 2.
65. "Crime in America: It's Moving West, South," *Stars and Stripes*, May 25, 1979, 13, "Ridding Detroit of its Murder City Tag," *Stars and Stripes*, February 22, 1983, 13, and "Underworld's 'Honest Brokers,'" *Stars and Stripes*, August 24, 1984, 14.
66. "Rights of Individual, Society," letter to the editor, *Stars and Stripes*, September 6, 1976, 12.
67. "Crime: An Unmitigated Disgrace," letter to the editor, *Stars and Stripes*, October 26, 1981, 11.
68. "Criminals' Rights Could Destroy America," letter to the editor, *Stars and Stripes*, September 25, 1986, 11.
69. "MP Has a Busy Beat as 'Officer Friendly,'" *Stars and Stripes*, May 9, 1981, 2 and "Officer Friendly Helps Heidelberg Kids," *Stars and Stripes*, January 22, 1982, 9.
70. See also Bettie J. Morden, *The Women's Army Corps, 1945–1978*.
71. "Rape Prevention Program in Effect," *Stars and Stripes*, March 8, 1981, 1.
72. "Campaign Seeks to Prevent Date Rape," *Stars and Stripes*, October 18, 1987, 1.
73. "Two GIs Sentenced for Murder," *Stars and Stripes*, November 11, 1972, 26, "Four GIs Convicted in Robbery of German Inn," *Stars and Stripes*, July 17, 1974, 10, and "GI Gets Death Penalty for Murder of Taxi Driver," *Stars and Stripes*, November 21, 1984, 28.
74. "Command War," *Stars and Stripes*, December 27, 1974, 9.
75. The SOFA provided some latitude of interpretation regarding which nation should reserve the right for trying certain violent crimes committed against Germans. Until the early 1970s the German judicial system usually gave precedence to the Americans. After the increase in the crime rate they decided to reserve the right in more cases. "Germans Take Jurisdiction in More GI Cases," *Stars and Stripes*, December 7, 1973, 4.
76. Elisabeth Noelle and Erich Neumann, eds., *The Germans: Public Opinion Polls, 1947–1966* (Bonn: Verlag für Demoskopie, 1967), 156. This statistic is comprehensive and includes crime by Americans against Germans as well as Germans against Germans. It suggests that the crimes Americans committed fed into, and exacerbated, the German public's feelings of anxiety.
77. "GIs Defended," *Stars and Stripes*, May 15, 1979, 9.
78. See Department of the Army Historical Summaries (DAHSUM) for the Fiscal Years 1970 thru 1981. The DAHSUM did not reflect the data for 1976, or years after 1981. The series is available through the U.S. Army Center for Military History. http://www.history.army.mil/html/bookshelves/collect/dahsum.html.
79. See DAHSUM series for the Fiscal Years 1970 thru 1981.
80. "Germans Take Jurisdiction in More GI Cases," *Stars and Stripes*, December 7, 1973, 4.
81. "Soldier Gets Death In Woman's Murder," *Stars and Stripes*, March 6, 1982, 26, "GI Gets Death Penalty for Murder of Taxi Driver," *Stars and Stripes*, November 21, 1984, 28, and "Army NCOs Death Sentence First in USAREUR Since 1984," *Stars and Stripes*, December 19, 1987, 2.
82. Article 102 GC, of the German Basic Law of 23 May 1949, forbade capital punishment as being too cruel and violating the sanctity of life.
83. Noelle and Neumann, *The Germans: Public Opinion Polls*, 171.
84. See "Is the Death Penalty Dying Out in U.S.?" *Stars and Stripes*, October 5, 1967, 11 and "Is the Death Penalty Making a Comeback?" *Stars and Stripes*, April 12, 1973, 14.
85. Examples from that time include "The Military's Troubled Death Penalty," *Stars and Stripes*, June 8, 1983, 14 and "Death Penalty for Rape Clarified," *Stars and Stripes*, December 14, 1984, 2.
86. "Capital Punishment," letter to the editor, *Stars and Stripes*, May 22, 1973, 11.
87. "Prison Life," letter to the editor, *Stars and Stripes*, February 23, 1974, 12.
88. "Children Should Come First," letter to the editor, *Stars and Stripes*, February 1, 1983, 11.
89. "Writer Opposes America's Death Penalty," letter to the editor, *Stars and Stripes*, October 8, 1989, 11.
90. "Arguments Made Against Death Penalty," letter to the editor, *Stars and Stripes*, November 5, 1989, 11.
91. "Rambo, America's Hero, We Want You," *Der*

Spiegel, July 15, 1985, accessed September 24, 2013, http://www.spiegel.de/spiegel/print/d-13515002.html.

92. "Germans to Try Two GIs in Murder Case," *Stars and Stripes*, August 18, 1989, 28.

93. "Death Penalty: Silly Setup," Der Spiegel, July 17, 1989, accessed September 2013, http://www.spiegel.de/spiegel/print/d-13494485.html.

94. For a more comprehensive contemporary understanding of how the drug culture grew in American society see Schulman, *The Seventies*, 14–17, and Isserman and Kazin, *America Divided*, 159–164.

95. Drug abuse among Vietnam veterans was high, particularly the use of marijuana. For an understanding of the actions military authorities took to curtail the use of drugs and deal with abusers in Vietnam see Meredith Lair, *Armed with Abundance: Consumerism & Soldiering in the Vietnam War* (Chapel Hill: University of North Carolina Press, 2011), 137–138.

96. "Our Strung-Out Troops and the Big O," *The Washington Post*, September 14, 1971, A1.

97. Jeff White (formerly assigned to the 8th Supply and Transportation Battalion, in the Bad Kreuznach Milcom, 1972–1973) in phone interview with author, February 16, 2014.

98. A former enlisted serviceman, name and unit withheld by request (assigned to the Mannheim Milcom, 1986–1988) in correspondence with the author, March 2014.

99. A non-commissioned officer, name withheld (assigned to the Verdun Milcom in France then the Neubrucke Milcom in Germany, 1967–1968) in correspondence with the author, March 2014. A 'Spec–5' was a Specialist 5th Class a rank equal to an E-5. It was a rank assigned to those military personnel who generally specialized in a service support skill area such as clerical, supply, maintenance, or medical.

100. "The U.S. Army: A Battle for Survival," *The Washington Post*, September 12, 1971, A1.

101. "Our Strung-Out Troops and the Big O," *The Washington Post*, September 14, 1971, A1.

102. Jeff White (formerly assigned to the 8th Supply and Transportation Battalion, in the Bad Kreuznach Milcom, 1972–1973) in phone interview with author, February 16, 2014.

103. "GI Crime, Violence Climb Overseas," *The Washington Post*, September 13, 1971, A1.

104. Noelle and Neumann, *The Germans: Public Opinion Polls, 1967–1980*, 97.

105. "Mirror Report on the American Forces in the Federal Republic," *Der Spiegel*, April 17, 1972, accessed September 19, 2013, http://www.spiegel.de/spiegel/print/d-42953738.html.

106. Ibid.

107. "Entertainment for the Katz," *Der Spiegel*, September 17, 1973, accessed September 12, 2013, http://www.spiegel.de/spiegel/print/d-41898018.html.

108. "U.S. Army Lost Case," *Der Spiegel*, January 21, 1974, accessed September 12, 2013, http://www.spiegel.de/spiegel/print/d-41810877.html.

109. "United States Quick to End," *Der Spiegel*, February 5, 1979, accessed September 12, 2013, http://www.spiegel.de/spiegel/print/d-40351818.html.

110. "Army in Europe: New Set of Problems," *The Washington Post*, November 19, 1978, A1.

111. The other hard drugs included heroin, LSD, hashish, and cocaine. Authorities noted that barracks room theft and robbery went to finance purchase of drugs and violence often transpired between dealers.

112. See Department of the Army Historical Summaries (DAHSUM) for the Fiscal Years 1971 thru 1984.

113. A similar sharp decline in crimes involving property also exists.

114. Robert Weekley (former military officer with the 3rd Battalion, 39th Field Artillery Regiment, Dachau Milcom, 1960–1963) in correspondence with the author, March 2013.

115. Robert Bierly, Jr. (former military officer with the 93rd Engineer Company and 168th Engineer Battalion, Stuttgart Milcom, 1960–1963) in correspondence with the author, March 2013.

116. Tommy Tracy (former military dependent 1971–1975, Heidelberg Milcom, and 1977–1979 Frankfurt Milcom, and retired military officer 1st Battalion, 22nd Field Artillery Regiment, Zirndorf Milcom, 1986–1989) in correspondence with the author, September 2013.

117. Thomas Rehm (former military officer in the 2nd Battalion, 78th Field Artillery Regiment, Bamberg Milcom, 1981–1984 and the 1st Battalion, 9th Field Artillery Regiment, Neu Ulm Milcom, 1989–1991) in correspondence with the author, March 2013.

118. Bruce Harding (former military officer in the 1st Battalion, 4th Infantry Regiment, 3rd Infantry Division, Aschaffenburg Milcom, 1977–1980) in correspondence with the author, March 2013.

119. USAREUR Supplement 1 to Army Regulation 600–85, *The Army Substance Abuse Program*, provided military commanders with the power to direct their personnel to "provide urine specimens when, in the judgment of commanders, individuals may be abusing drugs."

120. "GIs Urine Tests Produce Lab Boom," *The Washington Post*, September 13, 1971, A2. The initial testing facilities were at Wiesbaden Air Base for the Air Force and the Bioscientia Laboratories at Ingelheim Am Rhein for the Army.

121. "Drug Abuse," *Stars and Stripes*, March 24, 1976, 5.

122. The Secretary of Defense ordered urinalysis testing suspended on 18 July 1974 as a result of a court case that challenged its constitutionality (*Committee for GI Rights v. Froehlke*). After a successful appeal by the Army the SECDEF reinstituted the testing on 7 January 1975 implementing different, but legal, parameters for discharges under policies for substance abuse. Central to the plaintiffs' concerns was the annotating of discharge papers with the marking 'SPN 384.' This indicated a discharge for drug abuse and might lessen chances for future employment.

123. Charles Sheeley (former Army non-commissioned officer assigned to the Out-Patient Mental Health Clinic in the 97th General Hospital in the Frankfurt Milcom, June 1976 to July 1977), in correspondence with the author, July 2014.

124. "Drugnet Payoff," *Stars and Stripes*, June 14, 1980, 28.
125. Ibid.
126. "101 GIs Arrested in Drug Crackdown," *The Washington Post*, December 14, 1978, B12.
127. "24 U.S. Soldiers Arrested in Drug Ring in Germany," *The New York Times*, August 27, 1979, A4.
128. "49 GIs are Arrested in W. German Raids," *The Washington Post*, A5, and "50 G.I.'s Seized in Drug Case," *New York Times*, October 26, 1982, A3.
129. "24 GIs, 1 Teen Grabbed in Drug Bust," *Stars and Stripes*, April 6, 1979, 2.
130. "17 Students Set for Drug Rehabilitation," *Stars and Stripes*, February 22, 1985, 8.
131. "Crossroads: Dilemma of Substance Abuse," *Stars and Stripes*, May 24, 1983, 12.
132. "Drug, Alcohol," *Stars and Stripes*, December 9, 1976, 8.
133. "Recreation Prescribed for GIs with Drug Problems," *Stars and Stripes*, January 27, 1984, 9.
134. "Not the Solution," letter to the editor, *Stars and Stripes*, February 2, 1972, 12.
135. "Crackdown on Drug Abuse," letter to the editor, *Stars and Stripes*, March 12, 1973, 13.
136. "Purpose of Drug Program," letter to the editor, *Stars and Stripes*, August 6, 1974, 12.
137. "Farces of the Drug Program," letter to the editor, *Stars and Stripes*, March 24, 1976, 12.
138. "Drug Problem," letter to the editor, *Stars and Stripes*, July 15, 1974, 12, and "Lack of Meaningful Training," letter to the editor, *Stars and Stripes*, March 19, 1979, 11.
139. "Lifelong Task for the Addict," *Der Spiegel*, December 3, 1979, accessed September 12, 2013, http://www.spiegel.de/spiegel/print/d-39867564.html.
140. Some earlier contemporary essays on the postwar relationship between the United States and West Germany are not incorrect, but incomplete, and neglect to account for shared responsibilities at the boundary between the cultures. See T. Michael Ruddy, "A Limit to Solidarity: Germany, the United States, and the Vietnam War," in Detlef Junker, *The United States and Germany in the Era of the Cold War*, Vol. 2, 126–134.
141. "Drug Traffic in Grueneberg Park," letter to the editor, *Stars and Stripes*, July 16, 1982, 11.
142. *Drug Abuse in the Military: Hearings on S. 2139, S. 2999, S. 1189, Before the Subcommittee on Drug Abuse in the Military*, 92d Cong. 270 (1972) (Statement of John E. Ingersoll, Director, Bureau of Narcotics and Dangerous Drugs, U.S. Department of Justice).
143. "Heroin Rise Feared in Germany," *Stars and Stripes*, August 18, 1978, 5.
144. *Drug Abuse in the Military: Hearings on S. 2139, S. 2999, S. 1189, Before the Subcommittee on Drug Abuse in the Military*, 92d Cong. 251 (1972) (Statement of John E. Ingersoll, Director, Bureau of Narcotics and Dangerous Drugs, U.S. Department of Justice).
145. USAREUR Supplement 1 to Army Regulation 55–46, *Early Return of Dependents*, provided for the return of dependents to the United States for "the convenience of the government," for conduct that was "embarrassing" to the government, or was "prejudicial to good order and discipline" of the US forces. See "20 Dependents Disciplined for Drugs," *Stars and Stripes*, May 26, 1969, 27.
146. 'Drug Abuse: A Growing Dilemma," *Stars and Stripes*, February 23, 1970, 19.
147. Ibid.
148. "The Illegal Drug Situation in USAFE," *Stars and Stripes*, March 25, 1970, 19.
149. Ibid.
150. "Dependents, GIs…Drugs, Drinking," *Stars and Stripes*, October 8, 1970, 1.
151. "Frankfurt Drug Center Aids Youths," *Stars and Stripes*, April 19, 1973, 9.
152. DAHSUM for FY 1975, Chapter V: *Personnel, Alcohol and Drug Abuse*, 47.
153. DAHSUM for FY 1976, Chapter V: *Personnel, Alcohol and Drug Abuse*, 49.
154. DAHSUM for FY 1980, Chapter 6: Human Resources Development, *Alcohol and Drug Abuse*, 49.
155. "Schools Get Drug Warning Package," *Stars and Stripes*, July 29, 1984, 28.
156. "Kaiserslautern Sixth-Graders take DARE and Learn to Say No," *Stars and Stripes*, March 26, 1990, 8.
157. One example was the death by aerosol inhalant of two high school students, which was cause for alarm in the Milcoms during the winter of 1988. "Survey," *Stars and Stripes*, February 11, 1988, 24.
158. Ibid.
159. "DODDS Earns Good Marks in Poll of 70,000 Households," *Stars and Stripes*, October 17, 1989, 2.
160. "Drug Tests," *Stars and Stripes*, May 3, 1972, 8.
161. "Drug Tests Being Considered for DODDS Teachers," *Stars and Stripes*, October 24, 1986, 1.

Chapter Seven

1. For examples of class year books from that period see the *Frankfurt American High School* (FAHS) website with archived yearbooks, 1947 through 1995, http://www.frankfurthigh.com/history/subpages/fahs_yearbooks.htm.
2. The reference is to *Brown v. Board of Education*, May 1954.
3. "G.I.'s in Germany: Black is Bitter," *New York Times*, November 23, 1970, 26.
4. Department of the Army Historical Summary (DAHSUM) for FY 1972, Chapter 6: *Personnel*, 83. Accessed: October 12, 2013, http://www.history.army.mil/books/DAHSUM/1972/index.htm.
5. See strength charts in Chapter 3 of this study. Population figures are composites from US Census Bureau surveys for the years indicated.
6. An example was the banner headline "Dr. King Slain," *Stars and Stripes*, April 6, 1968, 1. Milcom members received other print media such as hometown newspapers, larger syndicated press publications such as the *International Herald Tribune* or magazines they ordered on an individual basis. Exact circulation numbers are difficult to determine but the prevalent news source was AFN radio and television and the *Stars and Stripes*.
7. "Europe GI Integration is Praised," *Stars and Stripes*, July 12, 1968, 1.

8. "Justice for Black GIs Poses Query," *Chicago Defender*, November 9, 1968, 5.

9. "Army Finds no Proof of GI Klan in Germany," *Stars and Stripes*, June 2, 1970, 2 and "Army Again Probing GI 'Klaven' Charge," *Stars and Stripes*, June 12, 1970, 2.

10. Unit commanders levy non-judicial punishment under the Uniform Code of Military Justice (UCMJ) and include fines, reduction in pay or rank and extra duty or training. It does not require the convening of a court. "Panel Reports Discrimination in USAREUR," *Stars and Stripes*, January 31, 1970, 8 and "G.I.'s in Germany: Black is Bitter," *New York Times*, November 23, 1970, 1.

11. This evidence is consistent with findings by NAACP legal counsel Thurgood Marshall that of 68 courts-martial charges for 'misbehavior before the enemy' brought against soldiers during the Korean conflict 60 were against blacks and 8 against whites. Convictions followed the same pattern: 32 black and 2 white. Richard Lentz and Karla K. Gower, *The Opinions of Mankind: Racial Issues, Press, and Propaganda in the Cold War* (Columbia: University of Missouri Press, 2010), 68–69.

12. "Council Meets Race Problems Head-On," *Stars and Stripes*, May 2, 1970, 10.

13. Ibid.

14. Leon Ceniceros (a sergeant assigned to the 98th General Hospital in the Neubrucke Milcom, 1967–1968) in correspondence with the author, March 2014.

15. President Nixon provided the impetus behind the probe. See "Nixon Orders GI Race Probe in Europe," *Stars and Stripes*, September 1, 1970, 2.

16. The areas visited in Germany included USAREUR Headquarters in Heidelberg and the Milcoms in Mannheim, Karlsruhe, Berlin, Nuremberg and Stuttgart.

17. *The Render Report*, Department of Defense, Manpower and Reserve Affairs, Memorandum for the Secretary of Defense, "U.S. Military Race Relations in Europe—September, 1970," 1.

18. Ibid., 6.

19. Ibid., 7–8.

20. Ibid., 9–10.

21. Ibid., 12–13.

22. "Race Relations First Priority, Gen. Cobb Says," *Stars and Stripes*, November 7, 1970, 8.

23. "Polk Sets Up Racial Flying Squads," *Stars and Stripes*, October 14, 1970, 1.

24. "Equal Opportunity Office Established to Serve Nuernberg Community," *Stars and Stripes*, November 28, 1970, 10.

25. "Fuerth Gets 2nd Opportunity Office," *Stars and Stripes*, December 19, 1970, 9.

26. Jones traveled with Julius E. Williams, Head of the NAACP Department of Armed Services and Veterans Affairs, and Melvin Bolden from the NAACP Legal Department. See "Discrimination Charged in Germany," *Stars and Stripes*, April 24, 1971, 1.

27. The Search for Military Justice: Report of an NAACP Inquiry into the Problems of the Negro Serviceman in West Germany (New York: NAACP Special Contribution Fund, 1971), 26.

28. "NAACP is Hoping to Open 10 More Europe Chapters," *Stars and Stripes*, February 11, 1980, 8.

29. The Department of the Army (DA) published the DAHSUM annually beginning with FY 1969. The DA fiscal years ran from October to October of each year.

30. DAHSUM for FY 1970, Chapter V, *Personnel: Military Personnel*, 58–59.

31. The presence of hair care products and cosmetics specifically for blacks, and magazines such as *Ebony* and *Jet* began appearing with regularly on PX and bookstore shelves; ibid.

32. "High Officers Will Attend Race Classes," *Stars and Stripes*, November 1, 1972, 6.

33. DAHSUM for FY 1971, Chapter VI: *Social Concerns*, 66.

34. A contemporary brigade-sized unit contained approximately 1,500 service members.

35. By June 1972 enlisted strength climbed to 15.1 percent an historic high. The number of black general officers was increasing from 4 to 9 and the number of colonels had increased from 42 to 93 since the start of 1969. The total overall percentage of black officer strength however had increased only to 3.9 percent from a previous high of 3.5 percent in 1965. See DAHSUM for FY 1972, Chapter 9, *Personnel: Race Relations and Equal Opportunity*, 83–84, and CMH *Integration of the Armed Forces, 1940–1965*, Chapter 22, *Equal Opportunity in the Military Community*, 556–581.

36. See DAHSUM for FY 1974, Chapter 6, Personnel: Equal Opportunity and Minority Recruitment, 61.

37. The Render investigators received complaints that up to 50 percent of the stockade populations were black. "G.I.'s in Germany: Black is Bitter," *New York Times*, November 23, 1970, 1.

38. "U.S. Army in Germany Act to Lift Sagging Morale," *New York Times*, November 29, 1971, 16.

39. "Society: Higher Degree," *Der Spiegel*, June 21, 1971, accessed October 11, 2013, http://www.spiegel.de%2Fspiegel%2Fprint%2Fd-43144257.html.

40. "NAACP Urges Black Lawyers for Negro GIs," *Stars and Stripes*, February 16, 1971, 1.

41. "GI Housing Bias Fought," *Stars and Stripes*, March 21, 1971, 1.

42. "Collins Calls for Better GI Relations," *Stars and Stripes*, May 20, 1971, 2.

43. "Toffler Praises VII Corps Arty on Equal Opportunity Program," *Stars and Stripes*, August 26, 1972, 10.

44. "Racial Progress is Found," *Stars and Stripes*, December 27, 1971, 10.

45. "A Step in the Right Direction," letter to the editor, *Stars and Stripes*, March 13, 1972, 12.

46. "Blacks not Asking for Special Favors," a group of four Letters to the Editor, *Stars and Stripes*, April 3, 1972, 12.

47. Ibid.

48. Ibid.

49. "The New Racism is More Subtle," a group of five Letters to the Editor, *Stars and Stripes*, January 31, 1973, 12.

50. Ibid.

51. Ibid.
52. "Not Enough Time," letter to the editor, *Stars and Stripes*, June 8, 1973, 12.
53. "Blacks not Asking for Special Favors," a group of four Letters to the Editor, *Stars and Stripes*, April 3, 1972, 12.
54. "Army Doing Its Best to Bridge Racial Gap," *Stars and Stripes*, September 9, 1970, 4.
55. Ibid.
56. "G.I.'s in Germany: Black is Bitter," *New York Times*, November 23, 1970, 26.
57. Ibid. Also see Höhn and Klimke, *A Breath of Freedom*, 149.
58. "Society: Higher Degree," *Der Spiegel*, June 21, 1971, accessed October 11, 2013, http://www.spiegel.de%2Fspiegel%2Fprint%2Fd-43144257.html.
59. "Organized Servicemen Abroad Intensify Drive Against Racism," *The New York Times*, November 19, 1971, 14.
60. "Black G.I. Activists in Germany Will Boycott Pentagon Inquiry," *New York Times*, September 28, 1970, 4.
61. "I'll Bleed for Myself, Says Black U.S. Soldier in Europe," *New York Times*, October 11, 1970, 178.
62. Ibid.
63. Ibid.
64. The word *Lumpen* in German means 'the masses.' An exiled branch of the Black Panther Party published the *Voice of the Lumpen* in Algeria. See Klimke's *The Other Alliance: Student Protests in West Germany and the United States in the Global Sixties* (Princeton: Princeton University Press, 2010) for additional details regarding the relationship between the Black Panthers and German and American military activists. For examples of the types of information these releases carried see "G.I. Publications," accessed October 3, 2013, http://www.aavw.org/served/homepage_gipubs.html.
65. "Hunt Angela In Germany," *Daily Defender*, August 24, 1970, 4.
66. "Miss Davis Arrives Here After a Tour of 6 Red Countries," *The New York Times*, October 13, 1972 19.
67. "A Preposterous Proposal," Editorial, *Stars and Stripes*, November 6, 1969, 13 and "Black Panthers Sing Blues in Red Cuba," Editorial, *Stars and Stripes*, July 3, 1969, 13.
68. "Panthers Charged in Detroit Slayings," *Stars and Stripes*, April 17, 1971, 7, "Al Fatah Trains Panthers, But Denies Terror Drills," *Stars and Stripes*, February 1, 1970, 2 and "Militant Groups Hold Gun Drills in Calif. Desert," *Stars and Stripes*, February 17, 1970, 27.
69. "Black Panther Investigation," Letters to the Editor, *Stars and Stripes*, January 24, 1970, 12.
70. "G.I.'s in Germany: Black is Bitter," *New York Times*, November 23, 1970, 1. Comments such as this suggest contemporary efforts at media manipulation by the military hierarchy. This project addresses that troubling subject, which is central to how the Milcom readers viewed their world, later in this chapter.
71. See "Racial Discrimination: The Army Creates a New Negro," and "Society: Higher Degree," *Der Spiegel*, June 21, 1971, accessed October 11, 2013, http://www.spiegel.de%2Fspiegel percent2Fprint percent2Fd-43144257.html and http://www.spiegel.de/spiegel/print/d-43144258.html.
72. "1 Convicted in KKK-Style Cross Burning," *Stars and Stripes*, May 26, 1977, 27 and
73. "Making White Feel Guilty," letter to the editor, *Stars and Stripes*, November 26, 1973, 13.
74. "Complaint on Equal Opportunity," letter to the editor, *Stars and Stripes*, June 22, 1980, 14.
75. Ibid.
76. "On Removal of Klan-Member MPs," letter to the editor, *Stars and Stripes*, February 15, 1981, 13.
77. "GI Chicanos," *Stars and Stripes*, February 28, 1975, 9.
78. "Chicanos Have Proven Loyalty," a group of four Letters to the Editor, *Stars and Stripes*, July 18, 1973, 12.
79. Ibid.
80. "Didn't Make Statement," letter to the editor, *Stars and Stripes*, August 2, 1973, 12.
81. DAHSUM for FY 1974, Chapter 6, *Personnel: Equal Opportunity and Minority Recruitment*, 61.
82. DAHSUM for FY 1977, Chapter 5, *Personnel: Equal Opportunity*, 59.
83. DAHSUM for FY 1978, Chapter 5, *Personnel: Equal Opportunity*, 76.
84. Ibid.
85. "Race, Equal Opportunity Plans," letter to the editor, *Stars and Stripes*, April 12, 1978, 11.
86. "Race Relations," letter to the editor, *Stars and Stripes*, April 20, 1978, 11.
87. "The U.S. Army: A Battle for Survival," *Washington Post*, September 12, 1971, A1.
88. "GI Crime, Violence Climb Overseas," *Washington Post*, September 13, 1971, A1.
89. Ibid.
90. "Race, Drugs, Idleness: An Explosive Combination in the Army," *Washington Post*, September 13, 1971, A1.
91. SASC, Subcommittee on Drug Abuse, 309.
92. Ibid., 429.
93. Ibid., 434.
94. "The Warm-Fuzzies and Other Comments," one of a group of letters to the Editor, *Stars and Stripes*, September 3, 1975, 16.
95. Jeff White (formerly assigned to the 8th Supply and Transportation Battalion, in the Bad Kreuznach Milcom, 1972–1973) in phone interview with author, February 16, 2014.
96. For a description of the struggle for civil rights by black American service members and their families in Germany before and after the war see Höhn and Klimke, *A Breath of Freedom*. Also see Höhn and Moon, *Over There: Living with the U.S. Military Empire from World War Two to the Present*..
97. The reference is to the racial purification efforts of the National Socialist German Workers' Party (Nazi Party) during World War Two. See Höhn and Klimke, *A Breath of Freedom*, 86.
98. See Maria Höhn, *GIs and Fräuleins*, 101–102.
99. The veracity of the article is debatable because the author chose to interview two black soldiers who had deserted from their duty stations. "Racial Discrimination: The Army Creates a New Negro," *Der Spiegel*,

June 21, 1971, accessed October 11, 2013, http://www.spiegel.de/spiegel/print/d-43144258.html.

100. Davison commanded the 8th Infantry Division with headquarters in Bad Kreuznach. The *Stars and Stripes* covered his assumption of command in "F.E. Davison Takes Reins of 8th Inf Div," *Stars and Stripes*, May 24, 1972, 9.

101. "Race Issues: General Davison is no House Negro," *Die Zeit*, October 20, 1972, accessed October 12, 2013, http://www.zeit.de/1972/42/general-davison-ist-kein-hausneger.

102. "Conversation with Max," *Die Zeit*, August 3, 1973, accessed October 12, 2013, http://www.zeit.de%2F1973%2F32%2Fgespraeche-mit-max.

103. "The Country from Which Dream Come: America's Black on the Road to the Middle Class," *Der Spiegel*, January 19, 1976, accessed http://www.spiegel.de/spiegel/print/d-41309563.html.

104. "U.S. Army, Like an Iceberg," *Der Spiegel*, February 6, 1978, accessed October 11, 2013, http://www.spiegel.de/spiegel/print/d-40616663.html.

105. The Institute für Demoskopie Allensbach conducted the poll. Noelle-Neumann, *The Germans: Public Opinion Polls, 1967–1980*, 59.

106. Ibid., 285.

107. Martin Klimke provides an understanding of the German radical students' involvement with the Black Panthers and their cooperative protests against American racism and imperialism in his work *The Other Alliance: Student Protests in West Germany and the United States in the Global Sixties*, 116–22.

108. Martin Klimke, *The Other Alliance*, 123. See also "Ex-GI Given 6 Years in Ramstein Shooting," *Stars and Stripes*, July 13, 1971, 27.

109. "Nixon Needs Language of Gunfire, Panther Says," *Stars and Stripes*, January 24, 1970, 26 and Martin Klimke, *The Other Alliance*, 126.

110. See Martin Klimke, *The Other Alliance*, 126, for a description of how this uncoupling evolved. See also Robert O. Self, *American Babylon: Race and the Struggle foe Postwar Oakland* (Princeton: Princeton University Press, 2003), 215–291, for a description of the contraction of Black Panther political power and influence in the 1970s.

111. "Negroes Face Race Bias in Germany," *Daily Defender*, April 17, 1967, 5.

112. "The Plight of Black GIs," *Daily Defender*, October 22, 1970, 21.

113. "Black Servicemen Protest: Ban Lifted on Housing Agent," *Stars and Stripes*, February 26, 1971, 19 and "Pentagon Studying Capt.'s Request for Inquiry on German Housing Bias," *Stars and Stripes*, March 17, 1971, 28.

114. "2 Black Army Officers Blast Military Base Bias," *Chicago Defender*, November 20, 1971, 1.

115. "Black Servicemen Protest: Ban Lifted on Housing Agent," *Stars and Stripes*, February 26, 1971, 19.

116. "Pentagon Studying Capt.'s Request for Inquiry on German Housing Bias," *Stars and Stripes*, March 17, 1971, 28.

117. The Search for Military Justice, NAACP, 24.

118. "USAREUR Housing Referral Marks First Anniversary," *Stars and Stripes*, December 18, 1971, 9.

119. "These People are Off-Limits," *Stars and Stripes*, December 19, 1972, 9.

120. "Housing Referral: Uncle Sam Turns Real Estate Agent," *Stars and Stripes*, January 5, 1972, 14.

121. "To Be Equal," *Chicago Defender*, October 21, 1972, 16.

122. Housing Wait: Study Shows it Takes Minorities Longer to Find German Quarters," *Stars and Stripes*, August 28, 1982, 9.

123. For a chronology of the women's rights movement in the United States see Ruth Rosen, *The World Split Open: How the Modern Women's Movement Changed America*.

124. In her work *Homeward Bound: American Families in the Cold War Era*, Elaine Tyler May discusses the centrality of home and family to women's lives during the early Cold War years and how they described boundaries of behavior and defined restrictive roles.

125. As Ruth Rosen notes "consciousness-raising" permitted women to interpret the world through their own experiences and so cultivate new identities and "reinvent themselves." See Rosen, *World Split Open*, 114 and 196–201.

126. "Pat Fails to Soothe Ruffled Women," *Stars and Stripes*, June 15, 1970, 27.

127. The positioning of the two pieces is also suggestive of purposeful editorializing by the newspaper's staff.

128. "The Conservative Drive," *Stars and Stripes*, October 29, 1970, 11. Her actions also suggest a bit of contemporary irony as she stepped into the predominantly male arena of politics.

129. 'ERA' is an acronym for the Equal Rights Amendment. "Phyllis Schlafly: the Women Who is trying to Torpedo the ERA," *Stars and Stripes*, January 16, 1976, 12 and "Doonesbury" cartoon, *Stars and Stripes*, December 12, 1977, 15. The cartoon strip centered its comments on Schlafly and the ERA and continued for several days.

130. Phyllis Schlafly's reputation placed her central to the efforts of traditional conservatives whose positions and opinions served as foils against feminist progression. In *Stars and Stripes* alone there are over 100 separate articles that reference her efforts between 1970 and 1990. Carl Rowan was a black journalist and former diplomat who generally wrote liberal editorials. "Schlafly says Rowan Version of Remarks is Incorrect," letter to the editor, *Stars and Stripes*, July 9, 1984, 13.

131. A survey of archived materials reveals that only a handful of articles appearing in *Stars and Stripes* during this period made reference to, or addressed, the more radical aspects of the feminist movement.

132. "NOW Movement's Leading Lady," *Stars and Stripes*, June 5, 1970, 20. Betty Friedan was one of the original founders of the organization in 1966.

133. "The Mother Superior of Women's Lib," Sunday Magazine section, *Stars and Stripes*, January 10, 1970, II.

134. Betty Friedan published *The Feminine Mystique* earlier in 1963. Many sociologists and historians credit it for initiating the second wave of feminism in the United States. It is a non-fiction work that focuses on the unhappiness of the American housewife of the

1950s with the roles of wife and mother that limited her potential and personal power.

135. "The Female Eunuch ... and the Mailer Animal," *Stars and Stripes*, June 9, 1971, 14.

136. Ibid.

137. The Equal Rights Amendment (ERA) was a proposal to amend the Constitution of the United States to guarantee equal rights for women. Feminist Alice Paul wrote and proposed original ERA in 1923. Women's rights groups revived and reintroduced the proposal in 1972. Although it won approval in both houses of Congress, it failed to achieve ratification by the states in 1982. *Roe v. Wade* was a landmark Supreme Court decision supporting women's abortion rights. It passed by a 7–2 decision in January 1973.

138. "Watching the Wall Street Scene," Letters to the Editor, *Stars and Stripes*, November 29, 1968, 8.

139. Ibid. This reference is to the *Overseas Weekly* which did regularly publish photographs of scantily clad young women.

140. "Scantily Clad Young Women," Letters to the Editor, *Stars and Stripes*, June 8, 1970, 12.

141. Ibid.

142. These types of photos however, were still available to Milcom members in issues of the *Overseas Weekly* and in magazines in the PX bookstores.

143. "No Equal Rights," letter to the editor, *Stars and Stripes*, February 5, 1973, 12.

144. Ibid.

145. "Women's Rights: Pro and Con," *Stars and Stripes*, April 16, 1973, 19–20. Regardless of the title the thrust of the article supported the amendment.

146. "Fighting is Fierce on Both Sides of the ERA Battle," Letters to the Editor, *Stars and Stripes*, February 24, 1982, 11.

147. "We Don't Have to be Embarrassed to be Female Athletes Anymore," Daily Magazine Section, *Stars and Stripes*, November 21, 1974, 11 and "Girls Sports Continued to Improve," *Stars and Stripes*, January 1, 1980, 25.

148. The event lost some of its impact however by appearing unobtrusively in a short announcement at the bottom of the second page. "Stripes to Get First Woman Chief," *Stars and Stripes*, March 29, 1979, 2.

149. Colonel Stauber also authored two books prior to her assumption of the editorial post, *The Stars and Stripes in Vietnam* (Columbia: University of Missouri, 1968) and *Freedom and the Military News Media* (Columbia: University of Missouri, 1969).

150. "Women Press for Seat on Top Court," *Stars and Stripes*, October 29, 1979, 4. President Ronald Reagan appointed Sandra Day O'Connor as the first female associate justice to the court in 1981.

151. Elaine Tyler May, *Homeward Bound*, 16–18.

152. This attitude coincided with the termination of conscription in 1973 and the move toward an all-volunteer force. This suggests that the Department of Defense renewed its efforts to increase enlistments of both men and women to maintain its force levels overseas. In 1972 the number of WACs in EUCOM was 473; by 1978 it had increased to 13,671. Morden, *The Women's Army Corps, 1945–1978*, Chapter X: The End of the Draft and WAC Expansion, Table 23, 283, accessed December 6, 2013, http://www.history.army.mil/html/books/030/30-14-1/cmhPub_30-14.pdf.

153. "On Women Joining the Service," letter to the editor, *Stars and Stripes*, September 30, 1979, 14.

154. "She Supports Women in Combat," letter to the editor, *Stars and Stripes*, February 27, 1980, 11.

155. "Thoughts on Women in Combat," letter to the editor, *Stars and Stripes*, October 7, 1985, 11.

156. "Women's Advancements in Military Hailed by General," *Stars and Stripes*, March 12, 1987, 3. According the article BG Foote had commanded the 42nd Military Police Group (Customs) in EUCOM.

157. "ERA Uproar," *Stars and Stripes*, July 13, 1977, 9.

158. "Women's Week: Activities Aim to Remove Barriers that Halt Growth," *Stars and Stripes*, August 26, 1979, 1.

159. "Burning Issues: 275 Women Present VII Corps Officials with Lists of Suggestions at Symposium," *Stars and Stripes*, August 26, 1979, 2.

160. The term 'Ms.' masks the marital status of the user, as opposed to the traditional 'Miss' or Mrs.'

161. "Wives Who Appreciate Privilege," Letters to the Editor, *Stars and Stripes*, October 31, 1974, 12.

162. These groups were the Protestant Women of the Chapel (PWOC) and the Military Council of Catholic Women (MCCW). Both organizations focused on fostering spirituality within the Milcoms although they occasionally supported certain issues such as the selection of a female for a seat on the Supreme Court. See "Group Offers List of Women for High Court," *Stars and Stripes*, September 30, 1971, 7.

163. Elizabeth Heineman provides insight to the burdens placed on the shoulders of German women in the immediate aftermath of the war and how German history remembers that period of time as the 'Hour of the Woman.' Heineman, "The Hour of the Woman: Memories of Germany's 'Crisis Years' and West German National Identity," in Schissler, *The Miracle Years*, 21–56.

164. Hanna Schissler, "Women and the New Women's Movement," in Detlef Junker, *The United States and Germany in the Era of the Cold War*, Vol. 2, 437–38.

165. Ibid. 439.

166. Ibid. 440.

167. It also included the collection, by the group 'Aktion 218,' of 374 signatures of German women: housewives, academics and common workers on a manifesto that protested the government's immutable position. *Stern* magazine published it on June 6, 1971. See Kristina Schulz, "Echoes of Provocation: 1968 and the Women's Movements in France and Germany," in *Transnational Moments of Change: Europe 1945, 1968, 1989*, eds. Gerd-Ranier Horn and Padraic Kenney (New York: Rowman and Littlefield, 2004), 139.

168. Schissler, "Women and the New Women's Movement," 440. German women were unsuccessful in their bid to have the abortion ruling overturned during the 1970s. During the 1980s the German courts permitted it only under special circumstances for health or in cases of rape. It was only after the reunification that in 1992 that the German courts permitted on-

demand abortion. By comparison the 1973 United States Supreme Court ruling in *Roe v. Wade* generally opened the door for abortions in the United States.

169. The rioting included burning figures of conservative church, police, and political figures in effigy. "218 Protest: Taken from Behind," *Der Spiegel*, February 24, 1975, accessed December 6, 2013, http://www.spiegel.de/spiegel/print/d-41575616.html.

170. American feminists lashed out at the Miss America Pageant in 1968 as the symbol of everything they rejected, "woman as spectacle, woman as object, woman as consumer, and woman as artificial image." Their disruptive demonstration included parading onstage with a banner, the crowning of a sheep as Miss America, and the passing out of pamphlets. Rosen, 159–161.

171. For a complete timeline of applicable policy changes and their applicability to overseas Milcoms see "Congressional Research Service: Abortion Services and Military Medical Facilities," January 9, 2013, GPO, accessed February 22, 2014, http://www.law.umaryland.edu/marshall/crsreports/crsdocuments/95387F_01092013.pdf.

172. "Diagnosis of Medical Needs," *Stars and Stripes*, January 13, 1977, 18.

173. "Abortion: It's a Personal Choice," *Stars and Stripes*, August 14, 1982, 7.

174. "Americans Seek Care at European Clinics," *Stars and Stripes*, August 14, 1982, 7.

175. Hanna Schissler recounts how the women's movement in Germany drew heavily from the American authors in "Women and the New Women's Movement," 441. Firestone wrote the *Dialectics of Sex: The Case for Feminist Revolution* in 1979, Hite wrote *Sexual Honesty by Women, For Women* (1974), the *Hite Report on Female Sexuality* (1976), and the *Hite Report on Men and Male Sexuality* (1981).

176. "Year Bestseller 1978," *Der Spiegel*, January 8, 1978, accessed December 5, 2013, http://www.spiegel.de/spiegel/print/d-40351747.html.

177. "Hite Report," *Stars and Stripes*, October 22, 1977, 13.

178. See Kenneth Osgood, *Total Cold War*, 50–51 and 116. Political and military elites on both sides saw propaganda as an important tool in efforts to win the hearts and minds of uncommitted masses particularly in the Third World. Their efforts included information management as well as censorship.

179. "Press Freedom Suffered More Setbacks in 1968," *Stars and Stripes*, January 4, 1969, 8.

180. "A Lid on Pornography?" *Stars and Stripes*, April 9, 1971, 14.

181. "More Care is needed on Censorship," Editorial, *Stars and Stripes*, August 20, 1981, 12.

182. "The Book-Banners at Work in America's Public Schools," *Stars and Stripes*, February 25, 1984, 11.

183. "Writer Charges U.S. News Control in Vietnam," *Stars and Stripes*, April 15, 1970, 8.

184. *Ibid*.

185. "AFRTS Chief Says Broadcasts are Edited," *Stars and Stripes*, January 7, 1970, 2. John C. Broger also served as Deputy Director then Director of the Directorate for Armed Forces Information and Education (Armed Forces Information Service) from 1956 to 1984.

186. "Critics Charge AFRTS Suppression of News," *Stars and Stripes*, October 26, 1970, 8.

187. Zumwalt, 257.

188. "Top Bonn Military Leaders to Discuss General's Ouster," *New York Times*, January 24, 1984, A3, "Kohl, Confers on General's Dismissal," *New York Times*, January 31, A8, "Kiessling Vindicated; Woerner Says," *Stars and Stripes*, February 2, 1984, 2.

189. "Censorship Issue Letters Answered by USEUCOM," Letters to the Editor, *Stars and Stripes*, February 15, 1984, 13.

190. *Ibid*.

191. *Ibid*.

192. *Ibid*.

193. Zumwalt, 258. Ken Zumwalt served as civilian Managing Editor of the European Edition of the *Stars and Stripes* from 1946 until 1955.

194. Zumwalt, 259.

195. GAO/NSIAD-89-60, *Stars and Stripes*, 3. Accessed December 8, 2013, http://gao.justia.com/department-of-defense/1988/12/stars-and-stripes-nsiad-89-60/NSIAD-89-60-full-report.pdf.

196. *Ibid*., 5.

197. *Ibid*., 6.

198. "AFN Controversy," letter to the editor, *Stars and Stripes*, May 21, 1968, 14.

199. "Sound Censorship?" letter to the editor, *Stars and Stripes*, June 18, 1969, 12 and "Radio Censorship," letter to the editor, *Stars and Stripes*, September 13, 1969, 12.

200. *Ibid*.

201. "Freedom to Hear," Letters to the Editor, *Stars and Stripes*, December 5, 1970, 12.

202. "Readers Respond to Criticism of AFN-TV," Letters to the Editor, *Stars and Stripes*, August 25, 1987, 11.

Chapter Eight

1. For example, Mary Nolan describes the "central role" it played during the 1960s as defining a struggle between "national liberation and American imperialism," while David Reynolds and Martin Klimke both emphasize its importance as a vehicle to unify disparate global youth movements. See Nolan, *The Transatlantic Century*, 272, Reynolds, *One World Divisible: A Global History since 1945* (New York: Norton, 2000), 302 and Klimke, *The Other Alliance*, 155.

2. This also presented a unique set of problems for Milcom families remaining behind in Germany when their rights and privileges fell under scrutiny. Military dependents that remained were able to exercise their PX and commissary privileges but were subject to a monthly 19 percent German import duty for goods purchased. Initially there was also a 90-day limit to the support families could receive after the military sponsor departed for a tour in Vietnam. The EUCOM command structure frowned on sponsor-less families who did not return to the United States. See "Husband in Vietnam? You can Use PX in Germany," *Stars and Stripes*, May 4, 1968, 1.

3. By 1968 *Stars and Stripes* began printing commentary from readers in the new 'Letters to the Editor' column. Print archive versions of Milcom member opinions of the war are scarce prior to 1968.

4. In January 1968 Viet Cong guerillas launched a coordinated series of bloody assaults in all the major cities of South Vietnam. This had a lasting psychological effect on U.S. forces and public. The majority of Americans "no longer believed the conflict would end in a U.S. victory" and the anti-war peace movement gained much needed momentum. Isserman and Kazin, *America Divided*, 232–235.

5. "Free Speech v. Intemperate Remarks," B-Bag, *Stars and Stripes*, May 29, 1967, 12.

6. "The Bombing Halt," letter to the editor, *Stars and Stripes*, December 6, 1968, 8. President Eisenhower developed the Domino Theory to describe the consequences of allowing communist forces to seize power in any single nation, as subsequent countries would easily topple under their influence similar to a line of dominoes.

7. "Traitor," letter to the editor, *Stars and Stripes*, December 15, 1969, 12.

8. "Power of the Press," letter to the editor, *Stars and Stripes*, December 15, 1969, 12.

9. "Freedom," letter to the editor, *Stars and Stripes*, December 15, 1969, 12.

10. "Bleeding Hearts," letter to the editor, *Stars and Stripes*, October 11, 1972, 11.

11. "Flaming Angry," letter to the editor, *Stars and Stripes*, May 15, 1973, 12.

12. "Vietnam Solution," letter to the editor, *Stars and Stripes*, May 30, 1969, 12.

13. Isserman and Kazin, *America Divided*, 233.

14. "Dissent," letter to the editor, *Stars and Stripes*, November 18, 1969, 13.

15. "Right to Free Speech," letter to the editor, *Stars and Stripes*, November 18, 1969, 13.

16. "Misjudging the Situation," letter to the editor, *Stars and Stripes*, July 30, 1970, 12.

17. "Vast Sums Wasted in Vietnam," letter to the editor, *Stars and Stripes*, March 31, 1971, 12.

18. "Not President Nixon's War," letter to the editor, *Stars and Stripes*, January 16, 1973, 12.

19. "Priorities," letter to the editor, *Stars and Stripes*, May 12, 1973, 12.

20. "Protest Slight at Dependent Schools," *Stars and Stripes*, October 16, 1969, 28.

21. "Some Facts on the Moratorium Observance at Munich," letter to the editor, *Stars and Stripes*, October 24, 1969, 12.

22. *Ibid.* The Criminal Investigation Division (CID) is an investigative arm of the military that employed undercover agents to investigate crimes and policy violations within the military structure.

23. "The GI Underground," *Stars and Stripes*, May 29, 1969, 14.

24. "War-Foe Coffee House Near Base is Padlocked," *Stars and Stripes*, January 18, 1970, 6, and "Antiwar Ft. Carson GIs Rap with Jane Fonda," *Stars and Stripes*, April 16, 1970, 5. The film *Sir! No Sir!* offers an understanding of the purpose and evolution of the coffee houses as locations for soldiers to gather and discuss their opposition to the Vietnam War. See *Sir! No Sir!* Directed by David Zeigler. 2005. Displaced Films. 2006. DVD. Accessed December 15, 2013, http://www.sirnosir.com/.

25. "Young People find Religion in a Coffee House," *Stars and Stripes*, August 19, 1971, 9, and "This Coffee House Alters Lives," *Stars and Stripes*, December 9, 1971, 10.

26. "Grunts ala Mod," Daily Magazine, *Stars and Stripes*, June 24, 1971, 10.

27. See Chapter 7 this study. Also see Martin Klimke, *The Other Alliance*.

28. "GI Underground Press," *Independent Voices: An Open Access Collection of an Alternative Press*, accessed February 18, 2014, http://www.revealdigital.com/page/titlelist-GIUP/title-list-gi-underground-press.

29. See Chapter 7 this study as well as "Galleries-GI Papers," *Sir, No Sir*, accessed February 18, 2014, http://www.sirnosir.com/archives_and_resources/galleries/cover_pages/fta_with_pride.html.

30. A "Lifer" was a service member who was committed to the ideals of military life and discipline and often made the military a career. These individuals were often at odds with those who protested against the war. "GI Underground Press," *Independent Voices: An Open Access Collection of an Alternative Press*, accessed March 5, 2014, http://www.revealdigital.com/view/11455271/19690401/REVEAL_11455271_19690401_ALTO0001.xml?q=&rskey=1TBlwX.

31. The Federal Bureau of Investigation (FBI), the Central Intelligence Agency (CIA), the Daughters of the American Revolution, and the Ku Klux Klan (KKK). "GI Underground Press," *Independent Voices: An Open Access Collection of an Alternative Press*, accessed February 18, 2014, http://www.revealdigital.com/view/11429452/19721201/REVEAL_11429452_19721201_ALTO0001.xml?q=.

32. "GI Underground Press," *Independent Voices: An Open Access Collection of an Alternative Press*, accessed February 18, 2014, http://www.revealdigital.com/view/27996080/19710301/REVEAL_27996080_19710301_ALTO0001.xml?q=&rskey=quAgNL.

33. Department of the Army Historical Summaries (DAHSUM).

34. *The New Testament* (Schweinfurt Milcom), Issue 2, June 5, 1972, 1.

35. *Ibid.*

36. "Germans and GIs Stage Vietnam War Protest," *Stars and Stripes*, June 6, 1972, 2.

37. *The New Testament* (Schweinfurt Milcom), Issue 3, July 19, 1972, 1.

38. *Ibid.*

39. *The Graffiti* (Heidelberg), Issue 3, November 1969, 12.

40. *FightT bAck* (Heidelberg), Issue 3, November 1972, 12.

41. *FightT bAck* (Heidelberg), Issue 7, April 1973, 10. One legal organization dedicated to providing counsel to service members in Germany was the Lawyers Military Defense Committee (LMDC) located in Heidelberg. Founded in 1970 it advertised free services to soldiers facing legal charges and organized their defense. See "Lawyers Military Defense," *The New York*

Review of Books, June 1, 1972, accessed March 9, 2014, http://www.nybooks.com/articles/archives/1972/jun/01/lawyers-military-defense/?pagination=false.

42. Numerous examples include the *FighT bAck,* Issue 7 (April 1973), 2, *Forward,* Vol. 1, Issue 14 (June 1973), 2 and *Forward,* Vol. 1, Issue 14 (February 1974), 2.

43. "Publications Tell How to Take Safer Trips," *Stars and Stripes,* December 21, 1971, 4.

44. Chapter 47, Title 10, United States Code, "The Uniform Code of Military Justice" (UCMJ) governs the application of disciplinary punishments and corrective measures for all branches of the United States military.

45. *Forward* (West Berlin), Vol. 1, Issue 6 (December 1971), 27.

46. *FighT bAck* (Heidelberg), Issue 13 (November 1973), 10.

47. *Voice of the Lumpen,* Vol. 1, No. 1 (October 1971), 1.

48. "GI Antiwar Paper Editor Gets 6 Months," *Stars and Stripes,* August 10, 1969, 5.

49. *The Graffiti* (Heidelberg), Issue 2, October 1969, 3. The article also referenced punishment of the service man who was editor of *The Bond* newspaper published by the Committee for GI Rights in New York City.

50. DOD Directive 1325.6 Sept 69 (Original) Updated November 27, 2009, Change 1 February 22, 2012 *Subject: Handling Dissident and Protest Activities Among Members of the Armed Forces,* accessed March 3, 2014, http://www.dtic.mil/whs/directives/corres/pdf/132506p.pdf. The Department of Defense distributed the document to the military hierarchy in Europe as early as in May 1969.

51. "Army Sets Rules on Troop Dissent," *New York Times,* September 12, 1969, 1.

52. Ibid.

53. DoD Directive 1325.6 Sept 69, 7.

54. Beginning in 1973 the American military transitioned to an All-Volunteer Force (AVF) after the termination of universal conscription. As a result, military members possessed profiles that generally exhibited higher levels of motivation for military service and higher scores on aptitude and intelligence tests. See "The Evolution of the All-Volunteer Force," Rand Corporation, Research Briefs, accessed March 19, 2014, http://www.rand.org/pubs/research_briefs/RB9195/index1.html.

55. Martin Klimke describes how American military personnel in Germany became the targets of a desertion campaign operated primarily by German student activists during the 1960s and 1970s. See Klimke, *The Other Alliance.*

56. Ibid.

57. "Deserters in Sweden Now Total Nine," *Stars and Stripes,* January 6, 1968, 5.

58. "9 More GIs Get Swedish Asylum," *Stars and Stripes,* May 11, 1968, 23.

59. "58 GI Exiles Quit Sweden," *Stars and Stripes,* April 23, 1969, 14.

60. "GI Desertions Increasing in Foreign Lands," *Stars and Stripes,* January 3, 1970, 6.

61. DAHSUM for 1968, 1969, 1970, 1971, and 1972. Center for Military History, *Department of the Army Historical Summaries,* accessed March 1, 2014, http://www.history.army.mil/html/bookshelves/collect/dahsum.html.

62. DAHSUM for 1969, Chapter IV Personnel, Military Justice, Discipline and Legal Services, 43, accessed March 1, 2014, http://www.history.army.mil/books/DAHSUM/1969/chIV.htm.

63. Paragraph 165, Article 86 of the UCMJ addressed Absent Without Leave (AWOL) as when "any member of the armed forces is through his own fault not at the place where he is required to be at a prescribed time." Paragraph 164, Article 85 addressed Desertion as when a service member "without authority goes or remains absent from his unit, organization, or place of duty with intent to remain away therefrom permanently." The second charge was the more serious and carried options for greater punishment. Generally, after being AWOL for 30 days a unit would list an absent individual as a Deserter in the unit personnel status report.

64. This included the Students for a Democratic Society (SDS), the Association of War Service Objectors, and the Campaign for Disarmament.

65. "Desertion Bate Attracts Few, Army Says," *Stars and Stripes,* January 20, 1968, 4.

66. The underground press did however continually publish articles celebrating those service members who chose to go AWOL and offered opportunities to them for legal counseling, such as the LMDC, and information on how to beat the charges.

67. Two examples of Swedish underground newspapers were the *Paper Grenade* and the *American Exile Newsletter.* The first "devotes itself to the international struggle against the American ruling class," and the second generally provided important contact information to deserters for housing, legal aid, medical emergency, and labor and residency permits.

68. Anni P. Baker, *American Soldiers Overseas,* 77.

69. Ibid.

70. The action drew great criticism from the West Germans. See John Lewis Gaddis, *The Cold War: A New History* (New York: Penguin Press, 2005), 202–203, and Melvyn P. Leffler, *For the Soul of Mankind,* 332, 356. Also see Jeffrey Herf, *War by Other Means,* 165–185.

71. An extract from the meeting memorandum of the NATO allies in Brussels on December 12, 1979. Jussi M. Hanhimäki and Odd Arne Westad, eds., *The Cold War: A History in Documents and Eyewitness Accounts,* 548.

72. See Geisler, "Transatlantic Reflections," in Detlef Junker, *The United States and Germany in the Era of the Cold* War, Vol. 2, 371. In May 1983, German politician and author Erhard Eppler commented, "American planners can engage in reflection over the nuclear holocaust in Europe with a cool head. The Soviets can do less so. We Germans cannot do it at all." In Jeffrey Herf, *War by Other Means,* 178.

73. "Europe Protests Won't Stop Plan for New Missiles," *Stars and Stripes,* October 28, 1981, 1.

74. The same question registered 34 percent declar-

ing they were not in favor and 28 percent undecided. Noelle-Neumann, *The Germans: Public Opinion Polls*, 437.

75. Mary Nolan, *The Transatlantic Century*, 308.

76. LTG (Ret) R.L. "Sam" Wetzel (he served in various key leadership positions as the Executive to the Supreme Allied Commander, Europe, the Deputy Commander in Chief USAREUR, the Commander of the Third Infantry Division in Würzburg, the Commander of the First Infantry Division (Forward) and Commander of the Fifth US Corps in Frankfurt), in correspondence with the author, April 2014. The abbreviation 'C-5's' refers to the Lockheed C-5 model aircraft the military employed as a strategic airlifter for large cargoes during that period. This information is also in his forthcoming book *Frontiers to Frontiers*, due out in 2016.

77. The first shipment of Pershing II missiles arrived in West Germany in 1983. The U.S. military completed the entire shipment of 108 launchers by mid–1985. They were located at kasernes in Neu-Ulm, Mutlangen, and Neckarsulm.

78. "Germans Plan Easter Marches," *Stars and Stripes*, April 9, 1982, 2.

79. *Ibid.*

80. "Anti-Nuke Marches Continue," *Stars and Stripes*, April 12, 1982, 26.

81. Estimates were that 400,000 thousand Germans participated. "Sixty-Mile Human Chain Climaxes Missile Protest," *Stars and Stripes*, October 23, 1983, 1.

82. "West Germans Start Missile Protests," *New York Times*, October 14, 1983, A3 and "Germans Continue Protests Against Missile Deployments," *New York Times*, October 23, 1983, A8.

83. Jeffrey Herf accounts for the large number of German protestors and activists as part of the postwar baby boom that filled the ranks of university students and reached over a million by 1980 and 1.3 million by 1983. See Herf, *War by Other Means*, 68.

84. "West Germans Start Missile Protests," *New York Times*, October 14, 1983, A3.

85. "Sixty-Mile Human Chain Climaxes Missile Protest," *Stars and Stripes*, October 23, 1983, 1.

86. *Ibid.* This event occurred just days prior to a NATO command post exercise (CPX) titled Able Archer 83. This exercise simulated a DEFCON 1 nuclear alert and involved planning for the use of the new Pershing II missiles. Soviet intelligence organizations misinterpreted the CPX as a cover for an actual nuclear strike against the Soviet Union. It was a time of heightened tension that nearly led to an actual nuclear conflict between the superpowers. For additional details see Peter Vincent Fry, *War Scare: Russia and America on the Nuclear Brink* (Westport: Greenwood, 1999).

87. "Groups vow anti-nuke violence, U.S. base blockades," *Stars and Stripes*, September 26, 1983, 8.

88. *Ibid.*

89. "Germans Arrest 188 on U.S. Army Base," *New York Times*, September 29, 1984, 3.

90. Thomas Rehm (former American Army officer stationed in the Neu Ulm Milcom, 1989–1991), in correspondence with the author, September 2013.

91. *Ibid.*

92. Douglas Gaskell (former Army artillery Captain assigned to various nuclear-ready units in West Germany, including the Neu Ulm Milcom, 1981–1984) in correspondence with the author, September 2013.

93. *Ibid.*

94. "Peace Protestors Continue Anti-Nuke Demonstrations," *Stars and Stripes*, April 3, 1983, 24.

95. "200,000 Protest Against N-Arms," *Stars and Stripes* (Pacific Edition), April 5, 1983, 5.

96. "West Europe Says Soviet Arms Move Is Not Last Word," *New York Times*, April 4, 1983, A1.

97. "Protesters Break into Pershing II Base," *Stars and Stripes*, April 23, 1984, 28.

98. "Let's Only Speak from Strength," letter to the editor, *Stars and Stripes*, March 30, 1982, 11.

99. "We Have To React," *Stars and Stripes*, May 17, 1983, 11.

100. "We Must Have Capability to Preserve the Peace," letter to the editor, *Stars and Stripes*, September 5, 1983, 11.

101. *Ibid.*

102. "Analysis of Nuke Protests," letter to the editor, *Stars and Stripes*, November 11, 1983, 11.

103. "Why Use Civilian Guards at Bases?" letter to the editor, *Stars and Stripes*, February 7, 1984, 10.

104. "An Answer to the Belief Americans are not Wanted," letter to the editor, *Stars and Stripes*, November 29, 1983, 11.

105. "…too beautiful to be bombed," letter to the editor, *Stars and Stripes*, April 25, 1982, 14.

106. "Are those of the Peace Movement Unpatriotic?" letter to the editor, *Stars and Stripes*, November 18, 1983, 11.

107. "U.S. Priest, Three Germans Attack Truck," *Stars and Stripes*, December 5, 1983, 28.

108. "More Viewpoints on Anti-Missile Protests in Europe," letter to the editor, *Stars and Stripes*, December 2, 1983, 11.

109. *Ibid.* The letter does not make clear the identity of the Americans as military, civilian, or dependent.

110. "7 Americans Arrested During Missile Protest," *Stars and Stripes*, October 3, 1986, 3. The article does not make clear the identity of all seven Americans as military, civilian, or dependent, except that their group spokesman was an American student at Tübingen University in southern West Germany.

111. *Ibid.*

112. "Turnout Smaller than Expected at German Protests," *Stars and Stripes*, October 21, 1984, 1, 28.

113. "Germany's Anti-Missile Movement Has Lost Its Thrust," *New York Times*, March 11, 1984, E4.

114. "American Soldiers in Germany: Nice, Wasn't It?" *Die Zeit*, March 15, 1985, accessed January 13, 2014, http://www.zeit.de/1985/12/schoen-war-das-nicht.

115. *Ibid.*

116. *Ibid.*

117. These are remembrances of Robert Gelinas a former airman stationed at the Ramstein Air Force Base Communications Center. "A Tale of Two Car Bombs," *American Thinker*, May 8, 2010, accessed January 17, 2014, http://www.americanthinker.com/2010/05/a_tale_of_two_car_bombs.html.

118. Among the injured were American military personnel and German national employees. "Powerful Explosion Injures 15 at USAFE Headquarters," *Stars and Stripes*, September 1, 1981, 1, 28 and "Security Emphasized After Bombing," *Stars and Stripes*, September 1, 1981, 28.

119. This included Germans as well as Americans. Jeffrey Herf, "1968 and the Terrorist Aftermath in West Germany," in *Promises of 1968: Crises, Illusion and Utopia*, ed., Vladimir Tismaneanu (New York: Central European University Press, 2011), 374.

120. Among the groups that operated in Germany were Black September, the Bader-Meinhof Gang, the Red Army Faction (a derivative of the Baader-Meinhof Gang) and the Revolutionary Cells.

121. "Bombs Rock a U.S. Army Base in Frankfurt, Killing a Colonel," *New York Times*, May 12, 1972, 1, and "Blasts at U.S. Base in Germany Kill 3," *New York Times*, May 25, 1972, 3.

122. For background on the Baader-Meinhof Gang see Jeremy Varon, *Bringing the War Home: The Weather Underground, the Red Army Faction, and Revolutionary Violence in the Sixties and Seventies* (Berkeley: University of California Press, 2004), 208–212.

123. "709th MP Battalion," *U.S Army Germany*, accessed February 12, 2014, http://www.usarmygermany.com.

124. "15th MP Brigade," *U.S Army Germany*, accessed February 12, 2014, http://www.usarmygermany.com.

125. "Security Beefed Up at U.S. Installations," *Stars and Stripes*, May 13, 1972, 28.

126. Attacks against German government and police facilities by the Baader-Meinhof Gang had already been ongoing for several years. "German Facilities Struck by Bombs," *Stars and Stripes*, May 13, 1972, 1.

127. "Gang Chief Baader, 2 Others Seized in Frankfurt Shootout," *Stars and Stripes*, June 2, 1972, 1.

128. "MPs, Police Increase Stuttgart Checks," *Stars and Stripes*, June 2, 1972, 28.

129. This was to forestall attacks at places that Americans might congregate. "V Corps Tightens Frankfurt Guard," *Stars and Stripes*, June 2, 1972, 28.

130. Jeff White (formerly assigned to the 8th Supply and Transportation Battalion, in the Bad Kreuznach Milcom, 1972–1973) in phone interview with author, February 16, 2014.

131. The West German *Bundeskriminalamt* (BKA) [Federal Criminal Police Force] printed approximately 6 million copies of the posters displaying them in store windows, train and underground stations, kiosks and on lamp posts throughout the country. The *Baader Meinhof Gang at the Dawn of Terror*, baader-meinhof.com, accessed April 28, 2014, http://www.mustardayonnaise.com/baadermeinhof/gunspeaks/gunintrochapter.html.

132. "Big Four Sign Berlin Accord," *Stars and Stripes*, June 4, 1972, 1.

133. "Jury Acquits Angela," *Stars and Stripes*, June 5, 1972, 1.

134. During the trials of the principal leaders of the group, 1972–1975, younger gang members remained active and staged attacks within Germany. See Stefan Aust and Anthea Bell, *Baader-Meinhof: The Inside Story of the RAF* (New York: Oxford University Press, 2009) and *The Baader-Meinhof Complex*, directed by Uli Edel (MPI Media Group, 2008), DVD.

135. A group of Palestinian terrorists calling themselves 'Black September' gained access to the Olympic Park housing area for athletes. During the unfolding events a number of Israelis and Palestinians died. See "A 23 Hour Drama," *New York Times*, September 6, 1972, 1 and "Arab Terrorists Ambushed at Air Base in and Attempt to Free Israeli Olympians," *Stars and Stripes*, September 6, 1972, 1.

136. Elements of the 709th MP Battalion and the 15th MP Brigade both provided support. See "709th MP Battalion" and "15th MP Brigade," *U.S Army Germany*, accessed February 12, 2014, http://www.usarmygermany.com.

137. During this time American military and civilian personnel in Turkey, Iran, Spain, Columbia, Syria, Greece, Italy and Mexico were targets. See "Lethal Terrorist Actions against Americans, 1973–1985," Threat Analysis Division, Diplomatic Security Service, Bureau of Diplomatic Security, U.S. Department of State, undated.

138. "16 Hurt as Terrorist Bombs Rip 2 Frankfurt V Corps Buildings," *Stars and Stripes*, June 2, 1976, 1.

139. "Arsonists Fire Two Air Force Trucks at Germany Base," *Stars and Stripes*, June 3, 1976, 1 and 28.

140. "Revolutionary Group Takes Credit for Blast, Fire in R-M Officers Club," *Stars and Stripes*, December 3, 1976, 1.

141. "Anarchists Take the Credit for Giessen Blast," *Stars and Stripes*, January 7, 1977, 27.

142. See "Lethal Terrorist Actions Against Americans, 1973–1985," Threat Analysis Division, Diplomatic Security Service, Bureau of Diplomatic Security, U.S. Department of State, undated.

143. DAHSUM 1975, 15.

144. DAHSUM 1977, 65.

145. "Terror Groups," *Stars and Stripes*, November 14, 1977, 11.

146. For a greater understanding of the number and type of attacks against organizations, property and individuals suffered by the Germans see Jeremy Varon's *Bringing the War Home*. Martin Klimke's *The Other Alliance* offers details of the ideologies behind the Red Army Faction as well as its association with other radical groups in Germany such as the Black Panthers.

147. "The Terrorist Question Still is Why?" *Stars and Stripes*, October 27, 1977, 11.

148. Ibid.

149. "Rationale of Terrorists Puzzles the Germans," *Stars and Stripes*, October 31, 1977, 11.

150. Ibid.

151. "Terrorism: The Dilemma of Curbing Violence without Destroying Democratic Freedoms," *Stars and Stripes*, December 29, 1977, 14.

152. "Terror: Almost a Commonplace," *New York Times*, December 30, 1979, DX3.

153. Herf, "1968 and the Terrorist Aftermath in West Germany," in Vladimir Tismaneanu, ed., *Promises of 1968*, 383.

154. Inge M. Queren (German civilian who lived

near several American military communities during the 1960s through the 1980s) in correspondence with the author, February 2014.

155. This was one of the very few letters to the editor that appeared in the *Stars and Stripes* regarding the terrorist threat. This suggests that either few Milcom members chose to write on the subject or that the newspaper editors made a decision to limit the number they printed for other reasons, such as dampening widespread fear and concern. "Opponents of Mideast Peace," letter to the editor, *Stars and Stripes*, December 14, 1977, 11.

156. Although Congressional panels began discussions on dedication of resources and defining policies for protection of American overseas the passage of a bill or resolution was still years off. Among the first to appear was H.R. 6311 (98th Congress) titled "1984 Act to Combat International Terrorism." It received the President's signature on October 19, 1984. See same title accessed March 21, 2014, http://congressional.proquest.com.mutex.gmu.edu/congressional/docview/t53.d54.00098-stat-2706-098533?accountid=14541.

157. An original document appeared in 1976. Subsequent updates followed. See DOD Directive 2000.12, "Protection of Department of Defense Personnel Abroad Against Terrorist Acts," accessed March 17, 2014, http://www.dod.mil/pubs/foi/docs/947.pdf.

158. *Ibid.*

159. Several pages of advice and guidance included specific precautions to take while shopping, driving, walking, or in an office building. It also included advice to avoid kidnapping. See DA Pamphlet 190–52, *Personal Security Precautions Against Acts of Terrorism*, HQs Department of the Army, GPO, Wash, DC, 3–1thru 3–3.

160. "Bomb Wrecks House Used by Army MI Outfit," *Stars and Stripes*, March 30, 1981, 1.

161. "CPO Target of Fire Bomb in Frankfurt," *Stars and Stripes*, March 31, 1981, 1.

162. "Reagan Shot, Wounded; Bullet Punctures Left Lung," *Stars and Stripes*, March 31, 1981, 1.

163. Unknown perpetrators attempted to derail the duty train by using a steel cable stretched across the track. The effort failed. See *Countering Terrorism on US Army Installations*, US Army Military Police School, Fort McClellan, AL, 1984, 153–154.

164. "Powerful Explosion Injures 15 at USAFE Headquarters," *Stars and Stripes*, September 1, 1981, 1.

165. "Fires Set at Housing Area Gut 4 Cars, 1 Motorcycle," *Stars and Stripes*, September 2, 1981, 1.

166. David Kaylor (a former Air Force officer assigned to Kapaun Air Station in the Kaiserslautern Milcom, 1980–1983) in correspondence with the author, June 2014.

167. "3 Bombs Thrown at U.S. Consul's Home in Frankfurt," *Stars and Stripes*, September 14, 1981, 28.

168. Gen. Kroesen Safe as Car is Hit by Terrorist Grenades," *Stars and Stripes*, September 16, 1981, 1.

169. *Ibid.*, 28.

170. "Berlin Images with Scratches," *Die Zeit*, September 18, 1981, accessed January 18, 2014, http://www.zeit.de/1981/39/berlin-bild-mit-kratzern.

171. "Blast Hurts 2 U.S. Soldiers," *Stars and Stripes*, December 8, 1981, 1.

172. "The RAF and their Sympathizers: Break Out of the Isolation," *Die Zeit*, September 11, 1981, accessed January 18, 2014, http://www.zeit.de/1981/38/ausbruch-aus-der-isolation.

173. "Bombs Jolt Four USAREUR Buildings," *Stars and Stripes*, June 2, 1982, 1 and 28.

174. *Ibid.*

175. See "2 MPs Receive Medals for Finding Fire Bomb," *Stars and Stripes*, August 7, 1982, 27, and "Bombs Planted in Two Soldiers' Cars," *Stars and Stripes*, December 15, 1982, 1 and 28.

176. "Two Bombs Damage Air Force Officers Club," *Stars and Stripes*, August 8, 1983, 1.

177. "Security Emphasized after Bombing," *Stars and Stripes*, September 1, 1981, 28.

178. *Ibid.*

179. The reference is to the bombing of USAFE Headquarters a day earlier; *ibid.*

180. "Terrorism and Ways to Combat It," *Stars and Stripes*, September 9, 1983, 9.

181. *Ibid.*

182. *Ibid.*

183. *Ibid.*

184. "Study of Anti-Terrorist Measures in Europe Completed," *Stars and Stripes*, February 23, 1984, 1.

185. *Ibid.*

186. LTG (Ret) R.L. "Sam" Wetzel (served in various key leadership positions as the Executive to the Supreme Allied Commander, Europe, the Deputy Commander in Chief USAREUR, the Commander of the Third Infantry Division in Würzburg, the Commander of the First Infantry Division (Forward) and Commander of the U.S. V Corps in Frankfurt), in correspondence with the author, April 2014. At the time, the Abrams building was the Headquarters of the U.S. V Corps in Frankfurt.

187. "More Anti-US Attacks Feared," *Stars and Stripes*, September 2, 1982, 1.

188. "Taxis and Security at Muenchweiler Casern," letter to the editor, *Stars and Stripes*, April 11, 1982, 14.

189. This letter followed the kidnapping and subsequent release of Brigadier General James L. Dozier by a terror cell in Italy earlier that year. "Anti-Terrorism Takes Brains," letter to the editor, *Stars and Stripes*, June 5, 1983, 13.

190. "Two Cents on Terror," letter to the editor, *Stars and Stripes*, September 26, 1981, 11.

191. "Questions Security Measures Against Terrorism," letter to the editor, *Stars and Stripes*, May 17, 1984, 13.

192. "German Hails NATO Peace Policy," letter to the editor, *Stars and Stripes*, May 11, 1983, 11.

193. "Apology from a German," letter to the editor, Stars and Stripes, February 11, 1983, 11.

194. "Possible Link of GI Killing to Bombing Being Probed," *LA Times*, August 14, 1985, accessed March 20, 2014, http://articles.latimes.com/1985-08-14/news/mn-2719_1_red-army-faction.

195. The report noted that this was the seventh incident of that year directed against NATO and U.S. military installations in Germany. "Car Bomb at Rhein-Main HQ," *Stars and Stripes*, August 8, 1985, 1 and "Car

Bomb Kills 2 on a U.S. Air Base in West Germany," *New York Times*, August 9, 1985, A1.

196. *Ibid.*

197. "Fringe Terrorists Bombed AFN Radio Tower," *Stars and Stripes*, August 18, 1985, 2.

198. "Bomb Debris Checked for Clues," *Stars and Stripes*, November 26, 1985, 1 and 28.

199. *Ibid.*

200. Of the 155 persons injured in the attack 60 were Americans. Investigators traced the origins of the bombing back to Libyan operatives. This precipitated the Reagan administration's ordering of retaliatory air strikes against that nation. "Bomb Blast Rips Berlin Nightclub; GI, Turkish Woman Killed, 155 Hurt," *Stars and Stripes*, April 6, 1986, 1.

201. "U.S. Military No. 1 Terror Target," *Stars and Stripes*, June 11, 1986, 1.

202. Kyle Winward (former dependent family member and DODDS student, Bad Kreuznach Milcom, 1982–1988) in correspondence with the author, July 2014.

203. "1986 Berlin Discotechque Bombing," *Wikipedia*, accessed May 14, 2014, https://en.wikipedia.org/wiki/1986_Berlin_discotheque_bombing.

204. See "Terrorism Chronology: 1981–1986, Incidents Involving U.S. Citizens or Property," Report No. 86–531 F, Congressional Research Service, The Library of Congress, January 29, 1986, accessed March 27, 2014, http://congressional.proquest.com.mutex.gmu.edu/congressional/result/pqpresultpage.gispdfhitspanel.pdflink/http%3A$2f$2fprod.cosmos.dc4.bowker-dmz.com$2fapp-bin$2fgis-congresearch$2f5$2fc$2fc$2f9$2fcrs-1986-fnd-0042_from_1_to_10.pdf/entitlementkeys=1234 percent7Capp-gis percent7Ccongresearch percent7Ccrs–1986-fnd–0042.

205. For details of the Pimental murder see "Possible Link of GI Killing to Bombing Being Probed," *LA Times*, August 14, 1985, accessed March 20, 2014, http://articles.latimes.com/1985-08-14/news/mn-2719_1_red-army-faction.

206. DAHSUM 1983, Chapter 1. *Introduction*, 4, accessed March 10, 2014, http://www.history.army.mil/books/DAHSUM/1983/index.htm.

207. DAHSUM 198, Chapter 2. *The Army and National Security Strategy, International Terrorism and Espionage*, 26, accessed March 10, 2014, http://www.history.army.mil/books/DAHSUM/1989/Index.htm.

208. 1984 Act to Combat International Terrorism, accessed April 2, 2014, http://congressional.proquest.com.mutex.gmu.edu/congressional/docview/t33.d34.98_pl_533?accountid=14541.

209. Report on the Committee of Governmental Affairs, US Senate, *An Act to Combat International Terrorism*, Report No. 95–908, 9th Congress, 2d session, May 23, 1978, 14 and 17, accessed March 25, 2014, http://congressional.proquest.com.mutex.gmu.edu/profiles/gis/result/pqpresultpage.gispdfhitspanel.pdflink/http:$2f$2fprod.cosmos.dc4.bowker-dmz.com$2fapp-bin$2fgis-serialset$2f2$2fc$2ff$2ff$2f13200–4_srp908_from_1_to_433.pdf/entitlementkeys=1234%7Capp-gis%7Cserialset percent7C13200–4_s.rp.908.

210. *Ibid*, 19.

Chapter Nine

1. "GI's Landlady Notes Plight, Reduces Rent," *Stars and Stripes*, August 1, 1973, 9.

2. "Devaluation Hits GIs Hard," *Stars and Stripes*, March 26, 1973, 1.

3. During the 1950s the average annual rate of *per capita* national output in West Germany was 6.5 percent compared to other Western European nations that averaged less than 5 percent growth and its share of world export of manufactured goods rose from 7.3 percent (1950) to 19.3 percent (1960). Much of this was the result of the postwar *Wirtschaftswunder* inspired by the Economic Recovery Plan (Marshall Plan). See Tony Judt, *Postwar: A History of Europe Since 1945* (New York: Penguin, 2005).

4. See Harold James, "The Deutsche Mark and the Dollar," in Detlef Junker, *The United States and Germany in the Era of the Cold War*, Vol. 2, 230.

5. This occurred as European banks sought to exchange their dollars for gold resulting in a draining of American reserves. Judt, *Postwar*, Kindle electronic edition: Chapter XIV, Location 10525. For a fuller explanation of the collapse of the postwar Bretton-Woods economic system and the ensuing re-evaluation of worldwide currencies see Barry Eichengreen, "When Currencies Collapse: Will We Replay the 1930s or the 1970s?" *Foreign Affairs* 91, no. 1 (January/February 2012):117–134.

6. Harold James, "The Deutsche Mark and the Dollar," 230.

7. *Ibid.*, 232.

8. In the immediate aftermath of the Arab-Israeli War of 1973 oil producing nations of the Middle-East (OPEC) raised the price of crude oil by 70 percent a barrel, cut production by 25 percent and placed an embargo on those nations that were closely allied with Israel. By January 1974 these actions had driven oil prices four times higher than they had been in September 1973. See *Slaying the Dragon of Debt: 1973–1974 Oil Crisis*, accessed April 19, 2014, http://bancroft.berkeley.edu/ROHO/projects/debt/oilcrisis.html and Nolan, *The Transatlantic Century*, 284–285.

9. Robert M. Collins, "The Economic Crisis of 1968 and the Waning of the American Century," *American Historical Review* 101, no. 2 (April 1996): 398.

10. "American Soldiers in Germany: The Poor Devil from Overseas," *Die Zeit*, June 29, 1979, accessed May 23, 2014, http://www.zeit.de/1979/27/die-armenteufel-aus-uebersee.

11. "Dollar Down Except in Germany, France," *Stars and Stripes*, August 24, 1971, 1.

12. *Ibid.*

13. *Ibid.*

14. "Pay Raises and Price Hikes," letter to the editor, *Stars and Stripes*, January 17, 1972, 12. EES is the European Exchange System that includes the PX, commissary, and numerous other service operations.

15. *Ibid.*

16. *Ibid.*

17. "Cheated," letter to the editor, *Stars and Stripes*, March 23, 1973, 12.

18. *Ibid.*

19. "Next Mark Rate is 2.81, 2.82," *Stars and Stripes*, March 24, 1973, 28.

20. "American Soldiers in Germany: The Poor Devil from Overseas," *Die Zeit*, June 29, 1979, accessed May 23, 2014, http://www.zeit.de/1979/27/die-armenteufel-aus-uebersee.

21. *Ibid.*

22. *Ibid.*

23. "Devaluation Hits GIs Hard," *Stars and Stripes*, March 26, 1973, 1.

24. *Ibid.*

25. *Ibid.*

26. *Ibid.* By 1973 inflation in West Germany had peaked at 8.0 percent having risen steadily from approximately 1 percent in 1967. After 1973 it began a downward trend to reach 5.2 percent in 1980. "Historic Inflation Germany," *Worldwide Inflation Data*, accessed May 16, 2014, http://www.inflation.eu/inflation-rates/germany/historic-inflation/cpi-inflation-germany.aspx.

27. 100 Pfennings equaled one DM. "Pfennig-Pinching GIs are Hurting," *Stars and Stripes*, July 27, 1973, 2.

28. "But When you can't Afford Things," *Stars and Stripes*, December 19, 1974, 13.

29. Joseph Weber (former U.S. Army enlisted medic assigned to the dispensary at the Amberg Milcom, 1975–1978) in correspondence with the author, May 19, 2014.

30. Soldiers required 'command-sponsorship' to receive full funding for a move overseas. It ensured housing eligibility, travel, household goods shipment, and schooling for dependent children. For a better understanding of command-sponsorship see the sample unit information sheet for the 2nd Armored Cavalry Regiment, accessed May 13, 2014, http://www.2cr.army.mil/Newcomers/COMMAND percent20SPONSORSHIP.pdf.

31. The new USAREUR policy, announced in December 1970, relied on a point system rubric based on time in grade, time-in-service and the date departed the United States for overseas assignment. However, it also took into account special medical needs and availability of government housing with lower enlisted personnel able to occupy no more than 10 percent of the available quarters for any community. Rental housing in urban areas was generally more expensive than that in more remote regions. See "USAREUR Housing to go on Point System," *Stars and Stripes*, December 3, 1970, 1.

32. Military conscription ended in January 1973 but negative feelings regarding the draft may have been lingering and rankled sensitivities of some enlisted personnel who entered the service unwillingly only to live in cramped, high cost housing.

33. This letter was from a soldier living in the Heilbronn Milcom. "Sacrifice to Devaluation," letter to the editor, *Stars and Stripes*, July 24, 1973, 12.

34. This letter was from a soldier living in the Baumholder Milcom and exhibited some hyperbole in that there was no measure to show his rent was twice that of a soldier in government-subsidized quarters; *ibid.*

35. Joseph Weber (former U.S. Army enlisted medic assigned to the dispensary at the Amberg Milcom, 1975–1978) in correspondence with the author, May 19, 2014.

36. Of note is the fact that at the time of its release the COLA index did not include the dependents of WACs. A Supreme Court decision (*Frontiero v. Richardson*) resolved the issue in 1973, for subsequent implementation and ensured that a dependent spouse was eligible to receive the allowance for quarters as well as medical and dental benefits. See DAHSUM, FY 1973, Chapter VI, *Personnel, Special Remuneration Programs*, 69, accessed May 14, 2014, http://www.history.army.mil/books/DAHSUM/1973/chVI.htm. See also "No COLA for WAC," letter to the editor, *Stars and Stripes*, December 22, 1973, 12.

37. The U.S. State Department eventually introduced a COLA rate for civilian Milcom members by February 1978. It offset increased costs of housing and purchases as did the COLA rate for military members. "COLA OKd for Civilians," *Stars and Stripes*, February 17, 1978, 28.

38. "Pioneers: Non-sponsored GIs in Germany Roughing it on the Economy," *Stars and Stripes*, December 15, 1977, 1.

39. *Ibid.*

40. The last reference was to downhill-skiing a popular sport in Europe. "Dollar Plunge Continues," *Stars and Stripes*, December 15, 1977, 1.

41. "Economy Wives," letter to the editor, *Stars and Stripes*, September 3, 1973, 12.

42. "No Official Mark-$ Exchange Rate," letter to the editor, *Stars and Stripes*, November 15, 1976, 12.

43. "Dollar Debacle Leaves GI Families on Economy Eking out a Bare Living," *Stars and Stripes*, December 3, 1977, 1 and 10.

44. *Ibid.*

45. *Ibid.*

46. Randy Tucker (Former U.S. Army Signal Corps technician, stationed at a remote microwave site at Hohenpeißenberg, 1971–1974) in correspondence with the author, May 1, 2014. Hohenpeissenberg is located approximately 35 miles southwest of München.

47. "V Corps Economy Couples Meet," *Stars and Stripes*, June 16, 1971, 8.

48. LTG (Ret) R.L. "Sam" Wetzel (he served in various key leadership positions as the Executive to the Supreme Allied Commander, Europe, the Deputy Commander in Chief USAREUR, the Commander of the Third Infantry Division in Würzburg, the Commander of the First Infantry Division (Forward) and Commander of the U.S. V Corps in Frankfurt), in correspondence with the author, June 2014.

49. "Housing Allowance Raise," letter to the editor, *Stars and Stripes*, April 3, 1973, 11.

50. *Ibid.*

51. "Cost of Housing," *Stars and Stripes*, May 29, 1973, 1 and 10.

52. *Ibid.*

53. *Ibid.* These were generally the non-command-sponsored families of members who were E-4 and below with less than 2 years' time in service. They comprised approximately 54 percent of those living on the economy and 25 percent of total Army families in Germany.

54. *Ibid*. This was in comparison to 9,300 Air Force families in government quarters. Approximately 10 percent of total Air Force families in Germany were living on the economy and not authorized government quarters.
55. "Allowances," *Stars and Stripes*, August 29, 1973, 10.
56. "Germany GIs Due Added Housing," *Stars and Stripes*, May 29, 1973, 10.
57. "1.88 Marks to the Dollar," *Stars and Stripes*, April 13, 1979, 27.
58. "Junior Enlisted Personnel Stationed Overseas," Hearings before the Military Compensation Subcommittee, HASC, 95th Congress, May 10, 1978, page 1, accessed June 4, 2014, http://congressional.proquest.com.mutex.gmu.edu/congressional/docview/t29.d30.hrg-1978-ash-0005?accountid=14541.
59. *Ibid*., 6.
60. *Ibid*., 17.
61. "Veterans Claim Discrimination," letter to the editor, *Stars and Stripes*, May 20, 1973, 27. The reasons for military and civilian government employees to remain in Germany after retirement varied. Many had married and wished to reside there with their families and friends. Others had taken jobs with the U.S government or private American and German corporations. Some simply enjoyed the culture. Regardless, their presence continued to increase during the early postwar years.
62. "Retiree Group," letter to the editor, *Stars and Stripes*, August 30, 1972, 12.
63. *Ibid*.
64. Larry Applebaum (retired Army Lieutenant Colonel residing in Germany and current President of the Solider for Life-Heidelberg Retiree Council) in correspondence with the author, May 11, 2014.
65. "Retirees," letter to the editor, *Stars and Stripes*, September 21, 1972, 12.
66. "Veterans Claim Discrimination," *Stars and Stripes*, May 20, 1973, 27. Military regulations linked the length of a dependent's residence in the Milcom to that of the military or civilian sponsor and were normally set at 24 to 36 months. This was much shorter than that of a retiree who might reside in Germany indefinitely.
67. *Ibid*.
68. "Retiree Group," letter to the editor, *Stars and Stripes*, August 30, 1972, 12.
69. *Ibid*.
70. "VOTERS Meeting Set for Oct. 13 in Nuernberg," *Stars and Stripes*, October 8, 1973, 10. The purpose of the gathering was to establish a charter and discuss the "U.S. military's policy of giving military dependents and local nationals priority over military retirees in employment.
71. "Retiree Office and Hotline Open for USAREUR Area," *Stars and Stripes*, October 4, 1979, 27.
72. "Europe Retirees," *Stars and Stripes*, November 22, 1980, 2.
73. *Ibid*.
74. Larry Applebaum (retired Army Lieutenant Colonel residing in Germany and current President of the Solider for Life-Heidelberg Retiree Council) in correspondence with the author, May 11, 2014.
75. "Attacks Retiree Job Discrimination," letter to the editor, *Stars and Stripes*, July 15, 1982, 11.
76. *Ibid*.
77. *Ibid*. Non-appropriated fund jobs are those that are generally associated with morale-building. They augment funds provided by Congressional programs through operating profits. Examples are child-care providers, bar tenders, custodians, maintenance, librarians, and recreational assistants. These types of positions were generally non-skilled and drew low hourly pay rates.
78. "EES Increases its Gas Prices by as Much as 50 Percent," February 12, 1974, *Stars and Stripes*, 1.
79. *Ibid*.
80. *Ibid*.
81. *Ibid*.
82. "EES Hiking Gas Prices up to 36 percent," *Stars and Stripes*, July 26, 1973, 1.
83. "Conservation Idea," letter to the editor, *Stars and Stripes*, February 26, 1974, 12. For Milcom members living on the economy away from urban centers there was often a scarcity of mass-transportation to rely on as a means to get to work. Where it did exist it did not necessarily match the schedule of military personnel who often had long or erratic hours. This made ownership of a vehicle more critical and more costly with the increase in the price of fuel.
84. "Gasoline," *Stars and Stripes*, July 20, 1974, 1.
85. *Ibid*., 28.
86. "Fueling Around with Your Vacation," Daily Magazine, *Stars and Stripes*, June 25, 1974, 11.
87. "More About Gas Price Hikes," letter to the editor, *Stars and Stripes*, July 29, 1976, 12.
88. *Ibid*.
89. *Ibid*.
90. *Ibid*.
91. *Ibid*.
92. "AAFES Will Start Flexible Gas Price," *Stars and Stripes*, May 21, 1977, 1.
93. "AAFES Plans Second Straight Gas-Price Cut," *Stars and Stripes*, July 9, 1977, 1.
94. *Ibid*. AAFES offered coupon books for the purchase of tax free gasoline to its customers. The coupons were welcome at all AAFES outlets as well as many German gas stations. This benefitted Milcom members who often purchased their fuel near their homes on the economy away from American facilities. Coupons allowed them to purchase gas at AAFES rates not at higher German prices.
95. See "AAFES Gasoline Prices to Inch up in Germany," *Stars and Stripes*, August 10, 1977. 2.
96. Throughout the 1970s gas prices averaged 60–80 cents more per gallon for German consumers than for AAFES' customers. For example, in spring 1974 the AAFES price for a gallon of regular was 53 cents, for the Germans it was $1.20, and in the fall 1976 the AAFES price for a gallon of regular was 60 cents, for the Germans it was $1.40.
97. "New German Tax to Hit Americans as Well," *Stars and Stripes*, January 6, 1968, 4.
98. *Ibid*.

99. *Ibid*.
100. "Tax Hike Bites Retirees," *Stars and Stripes*, April 25, 1968, 4.
101. "Your Tourist Visitors Can Avoid the *Mehrwertsteuer*," *Stars and Stripes*, June 17, 1971, 9.
102. "There's No Way to Escape Tax on Foreign Made Cars," and "German Clarifies the Situation for Americans," *Stars and Stripes*, December 27, 1974, 14.
103. "New German Hunting Agreement," *Stars and Stripes*, February 23, 1973, 26.
104. "Tax Break: How to Save 11 percent on Economy Purchases in Germany," Public Service Report, *Stars and Stripes*, December 18, 1975, 14.
105. *Ibid*. Also see the 1959 NATO SOFA Supplemental Agreement Article 67, *Tax Treatment of a Force and of a Civilian Component*, Para. 3. (a) (i) and (ii).
106. *Ibid*. The relief program applied to all service members, civilians, and dependents assigned to duty in Germany on a permanent or temporary basis. Policy did limit it however only to purchases over DM 225.
107. *Ibid*.
108. "Added-Value-Tax Routine Altered," *Stars and Stripes*, March 11, 1978, 9.
109. "Questions Concerning the VAT," letter to the editor, *Stars and Stripes*, September 29, 1982, 11.
110. "Air Force Says Tax Relief is Working," *Stars and Stripes*, December 29, 1980, 9.
111. "German Tax Increasing to 14 percent," *Stars and Stripes*, June 30, 1983, 2.
112. "Kin in Messes is Working Out Well," *Stars and Stripes*, April 15, 1978, 28.
113. *Ibid*.
114. *Ibid*.
115. "Secret Santa," *Stars and Stripes*, January 6, 1979, 1.
116. *Ibid*.
117. "Americans Active in Black Market Dealing," *Stars and Stripes*, October 5, 1976, 8.
118. *Ibid*.
119. "Black Marketers Reported Active in West Berlin," *Stars and Stripes*, October 6, 1976, 7.
120. "The Flourishing Black Market: The Price is Right," *Stars and Stripes*, December 2, 1975, 18.
121. "Americans Active in Black Market Dealing," *Stars and Stripes*, October 5, 1976, 8.
122. "Europe Black Mart is Big Business—and Yanks are Major Suppliers," *Stars and Stripes*, October 5 1976, 8.
123. *Ibid*.
124. "The Flourishing Black Market: The Price is Right," *Stars and Stripes*, December 2, 1975, 19.
125. Customs Handbook and USAREUR Reg 600-702.
126. "Tips Helps Customs in Making Arrests," *Stars and Stripes*, October 6, 1976, 7.
127. *Ibid*.
128. Military punishments often varied in severity based on the volume and cost of goods involved and could include fines, loss of rank, and imprisonment. All cases did however include repayment of lost tax revenue to the German authorities. See "NCO Gets 4 Years for Thefts, Black Marketing," *Stars and Stripes*, August 15, 1989, 28.

129. "Tips Helps Customs in Making Arrests," *Stars and Stripes*, October 6, 1976, 7.
130. *Ibid*.
131. "Americans Active in Black Market Dealing," *Stars and Stripes*, October 5, 1976, 8.
132. *Ibid*.
133. "Huge Profits," *Stars and Stripes*, October 8, 1976, 7.
134. "The Flourishing Black Market: The Price is Right," *Stars and Stripes*, December 2, 1975, 18.
135. *Ibid*.
136. "Smuggling: Extra Secret," *Der Spiegel*, May 2, 1983, accessed May 24, 2014, http://www.spiegel.de/spiegel/print/d-14022671.html.
137. *Ibid*.
138. *Ibid*.
139. By 1978 there were 67,000 LNs working for U.S. forces in Germany at all levels of employment from skilled maintenance, electrical, communications and industrial work to unskilled labor in recreation, child care, and retail at the PX and commissaries. "Jobs," *Stars and Stripes*, February 17, 1978, 1 and 28.
140. "How Did the Law Come About?" letter to the editor, *Stars and Stripes*, March 24, 1972, 12.
141. *Ibid*.
142. "Hiring Practices for Dependents," Letters to the Editor, *Stars and Stripes*, July 6, 1980, 14.
143. "USAREUR Explains SOFA Agreement, Hiring Rules," letter to the editor, *Stars and Stripes*, January 7, 1986, 11.
144. "How Did the Law Come About?" letter to the Editor, *Stars and Stripes*, March 24, 1972, 12.
145. *Ibid*.
146. "Hiring Practices for Dependents," Letters to the Editor, *Stars and Stripes*, July 6, 1980, 14.
147. That number represented 23 percent of all civilian hire positions. "USAREUR Explains SOFA Agreement, Hiring Rules," letter to the editor, *Stars and Stripes*, January 7, 1986, 11.
148. *Ibid*.
149. The 1959 NATO SOFA Supplementary Agreement outlined the conditions and guidelines of LN employment not the hiring quotas. See Article 56, *Labor*, of the agreement.
150. "USAREUR Explains SOFA Agreement, Hiring Rules," letter to the editor, *Stars and Stripes*, January 7, 1986, 11.
151. "Hiring Practices for Dependents," letter to the editor, *Stars and Stripes*, July 6, 1980, 14.
152. *Ibid*.
153. "Forces Jobs: Limit Set on Putting Yanks in Posts Held for Germans," *Stars and Stripes*, February 17, 1978, 1.
154. *Ibid*. The 5.4 percent average unemployment rate in Germany was one of the lowest in Western Europe at the time. In France it was 7 percent, in Italy 8 percent, and in the UK 9 percent. See Judt, *Postwar*, Kindle electronic edition: Chapter XIV, Location 10595. German unemployment peaked just short of 10 percent in 1982 then declined to approximately 5.5 percent in 1990. See Harold James, "Cooperation, Competition, and Conflict," in Detlef Junker, *The United States and Germany in the Era of the Cold War*, Vol. 2, 189.

155. Ibid.

156. "Currency Comparison Trends" reflect data gathered from *Historical Dollar-to-Marks Currency Conversion Page*, accessed June 10, 2013, http://www.history.ucsb.edu/faculty/marcuse/projects/currency.htm#tables; and Federal Reserve Bank of St. Louis, accessed June 10, 2013, http://research.stlouisfed.org/fred2/data/EXGEUS.txt.

157. Leffler, *For the Soul of Mankind*, 346.

158. For a more comprehensive understanding of Reagan's economic policies, that bore the portmanteau 'Reaganomics,' see William A. Niskanen, "Reaganomics," *Library of Economics and Liberty*, accessed May 28, 2014, http://www.econlib.org/library/Enc1/Reaganomics.html. See also "Reagan Defends Policy in Weekly Radio Address," *Stars and Stripes*, February 6, 1983, 23.

159. "Election Boosts Dollar in Europe," *Stars and Stripes*, November 5, 1982, 1.

160. Ibid.

161. Ibid.

162. German economists showed concern for the sudden resurgence of American economic strength noting that the dollar had reached its "highest level in over 13 years." But central to their fears was America's increasing trade imbalance and its increasing foreign debt. See "The Market Has Gone Crazy," *Der Spiegel*, February 25, 1985, accessed April 2, 2014, http://www.spiegel.de/spiegel/print/d-13513390.html.

163. "The Booming Greenback: Good for Spending, Good for Saving," *Stars and Stripes*, November 2, 1984, 13.

164. Ibid.

165. Military spending increased from $325.1 B in 1980 and $339.6 B in 1981 to a peak of $456.5 B in 1987. "Reagan's Defense Buildup Bridged Military Eras," *Washington Post*, June 9, 2004, E01, accessed May 26, 2014, http://www.washingtonpost.com/wp-dyn/articles/A26273-2004Jun8.html.

166. See "Historical Military Pay Rates," Military.com, Benefits, accessed April 10, 2014, http://www.military.com/benefits/military-pay/charts/historical-military-pay-rates.html. The armed services provided the BAQ for all military members regardless of rank, location, or command-sponsorship. Those who lived in government sanctioned housing in Germany also received the Station Housing Allowance (SHA) and the Cost of Living Allowance (COLA), which increased their pay and provided even more financial leverage.

167. "Americans in Europe on a Car-Buying Spree," Daily Magazine, *Stars and Stripes*, December 28, 1984, 13.

168. Ibid.

169. Ibid.

170. "Strong Dollar Good, Bad for AAFES," *Stars and Stripes*, March 9, 1985, 1.

171. Ibid.

172. Ibid.

173. "Mighty buck Mixed Blessing for U.S. allies," *Stars and Stripes*, February 19, 1985, 9.

174. "1 Year Ago Mighty Dollar was Riding High," *Stars and Stripes*, February 28, 1986, 2.

175. Ibid. These other world powers included West Germany and Japan.

176. Ibid.

177. "Despite Budgeting, Low Buck Still Hurts," *Stars and Stripes*, December 21, 1987, 1 and 2.

178. Ibid.

179. Ibid.

180. "Experts Predict Dollar's Drop to 1.75 Marks," *Stars and Stripes*, October 23, 1988, 18.

181. "Dollar Drops to lowest Mark Rate in Months," *Stars and Stripes*, November 26, 1989, 18.

182. Ibid.

183. "Currency Comparison Trends" reflect data gathered from *Historical Dollar-to-Marks Currency Conversion Page*, accessed June 10, 2013, http://www.history.ucsb.edu/faculty/marcuse/projects/currency.htm#tables And Federal Reserve Bank of St. Louis, accessed June 10, 2013, http://research.stlouisfed.org/fred2/data/EXGEUS.txt.

184. This was the residual effect of a second oil crisis precipitated by the Iranian Revolution. Oil production fell by 4 percent and the price for crude oil rose sharply and remained high. See Philip K. Verleger, Jr., "The U.S. Petroleum Crisis of 1979," *Brookings Paper on Economic Activity*, 2:1979, Brookings Institute, undated, accessed May 30, 2014, http://www.brookings.edu/~/media/Projects/BPEA/1979%202/1979b_bpea_verleger_okun_lawrence_sims_hall_nordhaus.PDF.

185. "Run on Fuel Coupons Brings out Rain Checks," *Stars and Stripes*, January 29, 1987, 2.

186. According to the press the new prices were the result of increases in state taxes and wholesale oil prices. "Gas Price Averages Over $1 a Gallon, *Los Angeles Times*, July 13, 1987, accessed June 2, 2014, http://articles.latimes.com/1987-07-13/business/fi-2231_1_average-price.

Conclusion

1. Van Dyke was a Presbyterian minister. He wrote this poem in 1909 but his more popular *Hymn of Joy* (1907) is better known. The reference in the second stanza to Europe's fixation on the past is central to the concept of American exceptionalism.

2. James Alling (former dependent in the Heidelberg Milcom, 1948–1951) in correspondence with the author, July 2014.

3. "Bye, Bye Heidelberg," *Sonderbeilage, Rhein-Neckar-Zeitung*, 11–12 May 2013.

4. Ibid., 17.

5. "Heidelberger Spring," Thorsten Schmidt, *Sonderbeilage, Rhein-Neckar-Zeitung*, 11–12 May 2013, 6.

6. "A Better Lot," Manfred Lautenschläger, *Sonderbeilage, Rhein-Neckar-Zeitung*, 11–12 May 2013, 5.

7. "A Prelude," Detlef Junker, *Sonderbeilage, Rhein-Neckar-Zeitung*, 11–12 May 2013, 13.

8. "Sixty-Mile Human Chain Climaxes Missile Protest," *Stars and Stripes*, October 23, 1983, 1.

9. See Martin Klimke and Maria Höhn's "The Civil Rights Struggle, African American GIs, and Germany—A Digital Archive," German Historical Institute, accessed July 20, 2011, http://www.aacvr-germany.org.

Bibliography

Archives

National Archives, College Park, MD
Record Group 59, Records of the US Department of State
Record Group 111, Office of the Chief Signal Officer
Record Group 218, Joint Chiefs of Staff
Record Group 260, Records of US Occupation Headquarters
Record Group 306, Records of the United States Information Agency, Research Reports: Part 2, German Public Opinion, 1945–1970
Record Group 466, Records of the US High Commissioner of Germany, 1945–1955
Record Group 549, Records of the United States Army, Europe, 1942–1991
U.S. Army Center of Military History, Fort Leslie J. McNair, Washington, D.C.
U.S. Army Military History Institute, Carlisle, PA
U.S. Department of the Army Historical Summaries

Government Publications

DA *Historical Summary* (DAHSUM) Series FY 1969—FY 1990. Washington, D.C.: US Army Center of Military History, 1973–1990.
Office of the Secretary of Defense, Armed Forces Information and Education Division: *An Introduction to Germany for Occupation Families*. Headquarters, US Forces European Theater, G-1, 1947.
Office of the Secretary of Defense, Armed Forces Information and Education Division: *A Pocket Guide to Germany*. Wash, D.C.: US GPO, 1950.
U.S. Congress. *Congressional Record* 92 (1946) A1834, A3163, A3176, A3180, A3180, A4275–76. (Text from: *Congressional Record Permanent Digital Collection*). Accessed February 12, 2012.
_____. *Congressional Record* 94 (1948) 1812–13, 3067. (Text from: *Congressional Record Permanent Digital Collection*). Accessed February 12, 2012.
_____. *Congressional Record* 106 (1960) A3318–19. (Text from: *Congressional Record Permanent Digital Collection*). Accessed February 12, 2012.
_____. *Congressional Record* 108 (1962) 9664. (Text from: *Congressional Record Permanent Digital Collection*). Accessed February 12, 2012.
_____. *Congressional Record* 113 (1967) 6908–12, 11339–40. (Text from: *Congressional Record Permanent Digital Collection*). Accessed February 12, 2012.
_____. *Congressional Record* 130 (1984) 2685–88. (Text from: *Congressional Record Permanent Digital Collection*). Accessed February 12, 2012.
U.S. Department of the Army, *Information for Dependents Traveling to Overseas Areas*, Wash, D.C.: US GPO, 1959.
U.S. House. Committee on Armed Services. *Hearings on National Defense Authorization Act for Fiscal Year 1990*. (HRG-1989-ASH-0028; 22 February 1989). Text in: ProQuest® *Congressional Hearings Digital Collection*. Accessed 26 January 2012.
U.S. House. Committee on Armed Services. *Special Subcommittee on Non-appropriated Fund Activities within the Department of Defense*. (HRG-1972-ASH-0035; 9 May 1972). Text in: ProQuest® *Congressional Hearings Digital Collection*. Accessed 26 January 2012.
U.S. Senate. Committee on Armed Services. *Special Preparedness Subcommittee on Military Cold War Education and Speech Review Policies, Part 3*. (HRG-1962-SAS-0026; 8 March 1962). Text in: ProQuest® *Congressional Hearings Digital Collection*. Accessed 13 July 2012.
U.S. Senate. Committee on Armed Services. *Special Preparedness Subcommittee on Military Cold War Education and Speech Review Policies, Part 5*. (HRG-1962-SAS-0033; 16 April 1962). Text in: ProQuest® *Congressional Hearings Digital Collection*. Accessed 13 July 2012.

Periodicals, Publications and Newspapers

American Historical Review
Armed Forces and Society
Callalo
Chicago Defender
Crisis
Der Spiegel
Die Zeit
Ebony
Economist
Film History
Foreign Affairs

German Historical Institute Bulletin
Journal of American History
Life
New York Times
Newsweek
Overseas Weekly
Political Studies
Public Opinion Quarterly
Rhein-Neckar-Zeitung
Stars and Stripes (European Edition, 1946–1990)
Time
U.S. Lady
Veritas
Washington Post

Oral History and Interviews by Author

From 2012 to 2014, I advertised in the MOAA (Military Officers Association of America) Magazine and on the U.S. Army Germany website and received input from members of the Lifelong Learning Institute of Chesterfield County, Virginia and the West Point Society of Richmond, Virginia. Between correspondence, telephone calls and interviews I received valuable information for this project from approximately 100 individuals. Listed below are their names. The majority were assigned to West Germany while in the military, some were there as dependents, others were German citizens who interacted with Milcom members during the period studied. Correspondence and recordings of telephone conversations are in the author's possession. Aaron, Bryan; Ables, Tom; Albaugh, Neil; Alling, James; Applebaum, Lawrence; Banner, Greg; Barksdale, Frank; Bierly, Robert; Bradley, Martha; Bullard, Wood; Cadow, Robert; Ceniceros, Leon; Charnquist, Chuck; Chazaud, Lois; Chiste, Ron; Chorazy, Jim; Cipolla, Jack; Cockfield, Mary; Coleman, Tom; Dawes, Jack; Dean, Terry; DeLong, Ed; Dietrich, Steve; Duncan, Jeffrey; Elkins, Walter; Finch, Ken; Fürher, Christian; Gallagher, Keith; Garner, Bruce; Gaskell, Douglas; Gilbert, Timothy; Goldsmith, Kent; Greaney, Denis; Green, Jr., Robert E.; Greenwalt, John; Greyhosky, Gus; Griffin, Eric; Hamrick, Scott; Hanne, Bill; Hollenbaugh, Sally; Harding, Bruce; Hubp, Frank; Isbell-Prieto, Shirley; Johnson, Hank; Kappes, Norman; Kauffman, Tim; Kaylor, David; Kiely, Joe; Laverty, Michael; Lawson, Thomas; Lincoln, Jim; Manning, Larry; McCracken, Norman; McEnery, Kevin; Millstein, Charles; Montgomery, Wes; Moody, Joan; Mulvihill, Jane; Mumma III, Morton; Niles, Russell; Pitre, George; Poitevent, Benjamin; Profitt, Ron; Queren, Inge; Rehm, Thomas; Ryan, Jim; Santens, Michael; Sabulsky, Renate; Schulz, Peter; Schulz, Shirley; Sheeley, Charles; Skelton, Robert; Smith, Mark; Snider, John; Spiller, Winton; Stockmeyer, Neal; Swora, Maria; Tagg, Lawrence; Terry, Bill; Thamm, Erik; Tracy, Tommy; Trottier, Wayne; Tucker, Randy; Veden, Barry; Volz, Arthur; Weber, Joseph; Weekley, Robert; Wetzel, Robert L.; Whitaker, Vivian; White, Jeffrey; Winward, Kyle; Wolf, Jon

Books and Articles

American Exceptionalism

Boorstin, Daniel J. *The Americans: The Colonial Experience*. New York: Random House, 1958.

Committee of Fifteen (Herbert Agar, Frank Aydelotte, G.A. Borgese, Hermann Broch, Van Wyck Brooks, Ada L. Comstock, William Yandell Elliot, Dorothy Canfield Fisher, Christian Gauss, Oscar Jászi, Alvin Johnson, Hans Kohn, Thomas Mann, Lewis Mumford, William Allan Neilson, Reinhold Niebuhr, Gaetano Salvemini). *The City of Man: A Declaration on World Democracy*. New York: Viking Press, 1940.

Gutfeld, Arnon. *American Exceptionalism: The Effects of Plenty on the American Experience*. Portland: Sussex Academic Press, 2002.

Hartz, Louis. *The Liberal Tradition in America: An Interpretation of American Political Thought since the Revolution*. New York: Harcourt, Brace and World, 1955.

Lewis, RWB. *The American Adam*. Chicago: University of Chicago Press, 1955.

Lipset, Seymour M. *American Exceptionalism: A Double-Edged Sword*. New York: Norton, 1997.

———."Still the Exceptional Nation?" *Wilson Quarterly* 24, no.1 (Winter 2000): 31–45.

Potter, David M. *People of Plenty: Economic Abundance and the American Character*. Chicago: University of Chicago Press, 1954.

Schulman, George. "American Exceptionalism Revisited: Taking Exception to Exceptionalism." *American Literary History* 23, no.1 (December 2010): 69–82. doi: 10.1093/alh/ajq076.

Turner, Frederick Jackson. *The Frontier in American History*. Lawrence: Digireads.com, 2010.

American Perspective

Aguilar, Manuela. *Cultural Diplomacy and Foreign Policy*. New York: Peter Lang, 1996.

Allitt, Patrick. *Religion in America Since 1945: A History*. New York: Columbia Univrsity Press, 2003.

Alvah, Donna. *Unofficial Ambassadors: American Military Families Overseas and the Cold War, 1946–1965*. New York: New York University Press, 2007.

Anderson, Benedict. *Imagined Communities*. New York: Verso, 2006.

Baker, Anni *American Soldiers Overseas: The Global Military Presence*. Westport: Praeger, 2004.

Barnhisel, Greg, and Catherine Turner, eds. *Pressing the Fight: Print, Propaganda, and the Cold War*. Amherst: University of Massachusetts, 2010.

Belmonte, Laura A. *Selling the American Way: U.S. Propaganda and the Cold War*. Philadelphia: University of Pennsylvania Press, 2010.

Bergmann, Peter. "American Exceptionalism and German 'Sonderweg' in Tandem." *The International History Review* 23, no. 3 (September 2001): 505–534.

Bogle, Lori L. *The Pentagon's Battle for the American Mind: The Early Cold War*. College Station: Texas A&M Press, 2004.

Browder, Dewey A. *Americans in Post-World War II Germany: Teachers, Tinkers, Neighbors, Nuisances*. Lewiston: Edwin Mellen Press, 1998.

Calder, Kent E. *Embattled Garrisons: Comparative Base*

Politics and American Globalism. Princeton: Princeton University Press, 2007.
Casey, Steven. *Selling the Korean War: Propaganda, Politics, and Public Opinion, 1950–1953*. New York: Oxford University Press, 2008.
Clay, Lucius D. *Decision in Germany*. Garden City, NY: Doubleday, 1950.
Clay, Lucius D., and Jean Edward Smith. *The Papers of General Lucius Clay: Germany, 1945–1949*. Bloomington: Indiana University Press, 1974.
Cook, James W., and Lawrence Glickman, and Michael O'Malley. *The Cultural Turn in U.S. History*. Chicago: University of Chicago Press, 2008.
Cooley, Alexander. *Base Politics: Democratic Change and the U.S. Military Overseas*. Ithaca: Cornell University Press, 2008.
Costello, Matthew J. *Secret Identity Crisis: Comic Books and the Unmasking of Cold War America*. New York: Continuum, 2009.
Craig, Campbell, and Sergey Radchenko. *The Atomic Bomb and the Origins of the Cold War*. New Haven: Yale University Press, 2008.
Davidson, Eugene. *The Death and Life of Germany: An Account of the American Occupation*. Columbia: University of Missouri, 1999.
Davis, Franklin. *Come as a Conqueror: The United States Army's Occupation of Germany, 1945–1949*. New York: Macmillan, 1967.
De Grazia, Victoria. *Irresistible Empire: America's Advance through Twentieth-Century Europe*. Cambridge: Belknap Press, 2005.
Douglas, Susan. *Where the Girls Are*. New York: Three Rivers Press, 1995.
Dudziak, Mary L. Dudziak. *Cold War Civil Rights: Race and the Image of American Democracy*. Princeton: Princeton University Press, 2000.
Edwards, Joe. "Burger King Clinches Landmark Military Deal; Signs Agreement to Build 185 Units over Next 5 Years." CBS Interactive Business Network Resource Library (18 June 1984): 1–3, http://findarticles.com.
Elkin, Frederick. "The Soldier's Language." *American Journal of Sociology* 51, no. 5 (March 1946): 414–22.
Falzini, Mark. *Letters Home: The Story of an American Military Family in Occupied Germany, 1946–1949*. New York: iUniverse, 2004.
Fulbrook, Mary. *The Divided Nation: A History of Germany, 1918–1990*. New York: Oxford University Press, 1991.
Geertz, Clifford. *The Interpretation of Cultures*. New York: Perseus Books, 1973.
Gimbel, John. *A German Community under American Occupation, Marburg, 1945–52*. Palo Alto: Stanford University Press, 1961.
Glaser, Daniel. "The Sentiments of American Soldiers Abroad Toward Europeans." *American Journal of Sociology* 51, no. 5 (March 1946): 433–38.
Grathwol, Robert, and Donita Moorhus. *Berlin and the American Military: A Cold War Chronicle*. New York: New York University Press, 1999.
Gravois, Martha. "Military Families in Germany, 1946–1986: Why They Came and Why They Stay." *Parameters* XVI, no. 4 (Winter 1986): 57–67.

Hämäläinen, Pekka, and Samuel Truett. "On Borderlands." *Journal of American History* 98, no. 2 (September 2011): 338–361.
Harrington, Daniel F. *Berlin on the Brink: The Blockade, the Airlift, and the Early Cold War*. Lexington: University Press of Kentucky, 2012.
Hawkins, John *Army of Hope, Army of Alienation: Culture and Contradiction in the American Army Communities of Cold War Germany*. 2nd ed. Tuscaloosa: University of Alabama Press, 2005.
Haynes, John E. *Red Scare or Red Menace?* Chicago: Ivan R. Dee, 1996.
_____. "A Bibliography of Communism, Film, Radio, and Television." *Film History* 16 (2004).
Herf, Jeffrey. *War by Other Means: Soviet Power, West German Resistance, and the Battle of the Euromissiles*. New York: The Free Press, 1991.
Herzog, Jonathan. *The Spiritual-Industrial Complex: America's Religious Battle against Communism in the Early Cold War*. New York: Oxford University Press, 2011.
Howley, Frank. *Berlin Command*. New York: Putnam's Sons, 1950.
Hubp, Frank. "210th Field Artillery Group," *U.S Army Germany*, accessed February 13, 2014, http://www.usarmygermany.com.
Isaac, Joel, and Duncan Bell, eds. *Uncertain Empire: American History and the Idea of the Cold War*. New York: Oxford University Press, 2012.
Judt, Tony. *Post War: A History of Europe Since 1945*. New York: Penguin Press, 2005.
Kerwick, Jack. "American Exceptionalism and Identity Politics." *American Thinker* (July 17, 2011). Accessed Feb 12, 2012. http://www.americanthinker.com.
Key, Lawrence L. "Cultivating National Will: An Introduction to National Will." *Maxwell Paper* no.5, Air War College, Maxwell Air Force Base, Alabama, 1996
Knox, Jo, and David H. Price. "The Changing American Military Family: Opportunities for Social Work." *Social Service Review* 69, no. 3 (September 1995): 479–497.
Lair, Meredith. *Armed with Abundance: Consumerism and Soldiering in the Vietnam War*. Chapel Hill: University of North Carolina Press, 2011.
Lears, T. J. Jackson. "The Concept of Cultural Hegemony: Problems and Possibilities." *American Historical Review* 90, no. 3 (June 1985): 567–93.
Lemza, John. "Brown v. Board of Education of Topeka, Kansas (1954)." In *The Public Debate over Controversial Supreme Court Decisions*, edited by Melvin I. Urofsky, 197–205. Washington, D.C.: CQ Press, 2006.
Lentz, Richard, and Karla K. Gower. *The Opinions of Mankind: Racial Issues, Press, and Propaganda in the Cold War*. Columbia: University of Missouri Press, 2010.
Loveland, Anne C. *American Evangelicals and the U.S. Military: 1942–1993*. Baton Rouge: Louisiana State University Press, 1996.
Lutz, Catherine. *The Bases of Empire: The Global Struggle against U.S. Military Posts*. New York: New York University Press, 2009.
Malik, Dean. "Identity Politics: The Denial of Ameri-

can Exceptionalism." *American Thinker* (July 10, 2011). Accessed February 19, 2012. http://www.americanthinker.com.

May, Elaine Tyler. *Homeward Bound: American Families in the Cold War Era*. New York: Basic Books, 2008.

McGirr, Lisa. *Suburban Warriors: The Origins of the New American Right*. Princeton: Princeton University Press, 2001.

McGuire, Phillip, ed. *Taps for a Jim Crow Army: Letters from Black Soldiers in World War Two*. Lexington: University Press of Kentucky, 1993.

Merritt, Anna J. ed. *Public Opinion in Semi-Sovereign Germany: The HICOG Surveys, 1949–1955*. Champaign: University of Illinois Press, 1980.

Merritt, Richard. *Democracy Imposed: US Occupation Policy and the German Public, 1945–1949*. New Haven: Yale University Press, 1995.

Meyerowitz, Joanne, ed. *Not June Cleaver: Women and Gender in Postwar America, 1945–1960*. Philadelphia: Temple University Press, 1994.

Naumann, Katja. "Teaching the World: Globalization, Geopolitics, and History Education at U.S. Universities." In *Beyond the Nation: United States History in Transnational Perspective*, edited by Thomas Adam, and Uwe Luebken, 123–140. Bulletin of the German Historical Institute, Supplement 5, 2008.

Njølstad, Olav, ed. *The Last Decade of the Cold War: From Conflict Escalation to Conflict Transformation*. New York: Frank Cass, 2004.

Nolan, Mary. *The Transatlantic Century: Europe and America, 1890–2010*. New York: Cambridge University Press, 2012.

Nye, Joseph, Jr. *Soft Power: The Means to Success in World Politics*. New York: Public Affairs, 2004.

Osgood, Kenneth. *Total Cold War: Eisenhower's Secret Propaganda Battle at Home and Abroad*. Lawrence: University Press of Kansas, 2008.

Palmer, Thomas A. "Why We Fight: A Study of Indoctrination Activities in the Armed Forces." PhD diss. University of South Carolina, 1971. ProQuest (PQDT ID 302549153).

Paul, Roland A. *American Military Commitments Abroad*. Piscataway: Rutgers University Press, 1973.

Pells, Richard. "Is American Culture 'American'?" *eJournal USA*. US Department of State International Information Programs (February 2006). Accessed July 6, 2011. http://seoul.usembassy.gov/uploads/lm/1R/lm1RIU_wiNwj9G5Ylaevyg/The-Challenges-of-Globalization.pdf

_____. *Not Like Us: How Europeans Have Loved, Hated, and Transformed American Culture Since World War II*. New York: Basic Books, 1998.

Pry, Peter Vincent. *War Scare and America on the Nuclear Brink*. Westport: Praeger, 1999.

Reeves, Richard. *Daring Young Men: The Heroism and Triumph of the Berlin Airlift, June 1948-May 1949*. New York: Simon & Schuster, 2010.

Reynolds, David. *One World Divisible: A Global History since 1945*. New York: Norton, 2000.

Ritzer, George. *The McDonaldization of Society*. Newbury Park: Pine Forge Press, 2004.

_____. *The McDonaldization of Society*. Thousand Oaks: Sage Publications, 2013.

Rodgers, Daniel T. "Exceptionalism." In *Imagined Histories: American Historians Interpret the Past*, eds. Anthony Molho and Gordon S. Wood, 21–40. Princeton: Princeton University Press, 1998.

Rosen, Ruth. *The World Split Open: How the Modern Women's Movement Changed America*. New York: Penguin Books, 2006.

Saunders, Frances Stonor. *The Cultural Cold War: The CIA and the World of Arts and Letters*. New York: Free Press, 1999.

Sbardellati, John. *J. Edgar Hoover Goes to the Movies: The FBI and the Origins of Hollywood's Cold War*. Ithaca: Cornell University Press, 2012.

Schulman, Bruce J., and Julian E. Zelizer, eds. *Rightward Bound*. Cambridge: Harvard University Press, 2008.

Schulman, George. "American Exceptionalism Revisited: Taking Exception to Exceptionalism." *American Literary History* 23, no.1 (December 2010): 69–82. doi: 10.1093/alh/ajq076.

Schmoekel, Wolf W. *The Dragoon Story: A History of the 2nd Armored Cavalry Regiment*. Greensboro: Randall Print Company, 1958.

Schneider, Robert A. "AHR Conversation: How Size Matters: The Question of Scale in History." *American Historical Review* 118, no. 5 (December 2013): 1431–1472.

Shaw, Tony, and Denise J. Youngblood. *Cinematic Cold War: The American and Soviet Struggle for Hearts and Minds*. Lawrence: University Press of Kansas, 2010.

Smith, William Gardner. *Last of the Conquerors*. New York: Signet Books, 1949.

Tarr, David. "The Military Abroad." *Annals of the American Academy of Political and Social Science* 368 (November, 1966): 31–42.

Terry, William. "42nd FA BDE," *U.S. Army Germany*, accessed February 12, 2014, http://www.usarmygermany.com.

Tyrrell, Ian. "American Exceptionalism in an Age of International History." *American Historical Review* 96, no. 4 (October 1991): 1031–1055.

Veden, Barry J. "504th Aviation Battalion," *U.S Army Germany* accessed February 12, 2014, http://www.usarmygermany.com.

Von Eschen, Penny. "Globalizing Popular Culture in the 'American Century' and Beyond." In *America on the World Stage: A Global Approach to U.S. History*, eds. Gary W. Reichard and Ted Dickson, 238–252. Champaign: University of Illinois Press, 2008.

Willet, Ralph. *The Americanization of Germany: Post-War Culture, 1945–1949*. London: Routledge, 1992.

Willoughby, John. *Remaking the Conquering Heroes: The Postwar American Occupation of Germany*. New York: Palgrave Macmillan, 2001.

Willoughby, John. "The Sexual Behavior of American GIs during the Early Years of the Occupation of Germany." *The Journal of Military History* 62, no. 1 (January 1998): 155–174.

Wolf, Charlotte. *Garrison Community: A Study of an Overseas Military Colony*. Westport: Greenwood Press, 1969.

Wolfe, John. "66th Engineer Battalion," *U.S Army Germany*, accessed February 18, 2014, http://www.usarmygermany.com.

Zumwalt, Ken. *Stars and Stripes: World War Two and the Early Years.* Austin: Eakin Press, 1989.

German/European Perspective

Aust, Stefan. *Baader-Meinhof: The Inside Story of the R.A.F.* New York: Oxford University Press, 2008.

Berghahn, Volker, Anselm Doering-Manteuffel, and Christof Mauch, eds. "The American Impact on Western Europe: Americanization and Westernization in Transatlantic Perspective." Bulletin 24, Spring 1999:21–33. German Historical Institute, 1999. http://www.ghi-dc.org/publications/ghipubs/bu/024/bulletin_S99.html#Westernization.

Boehling, Rebecca. *A Question of Priorities: Democratic Reform and Economic Recovery in Postwar Germany.* New York: Berghahn Books, 1996.

———. "The Role of Culture in American Relations: The Case of the U.S. Occupation of Germany." *Diplomatic History* 23, no. 1 (Winter 1999): 57–69.

Bredella, Lothar, ed. *Mediating a Foreign Culture: The United States and Germany.* Tubingen: Narr, 1991.

Davis, Belinda, ed. *Changing the World, Changing Oneself: Political Protest and Collective Identities in West Germany and the U.S. in the 1960s and 1970s.* New York: Berghahn Books, 2010.

Diner, Dan. *America in the Eyes of the Germans: An Essay on Anti-Americanism.* Princeton: Markus Wiener, 1996.

Ermath, Michael. *America and the Shaping of German Society, 1945–1955.* 1st ed. Oxford: Berg Publishers, 1994.

Gienow-Hecht, Jessica. *Transmission Impossible: American Journalism as Cultural Diplomacy in Postwar Germany: 1945–1955.* Baton Rouge: Louisiana State University Press, 1999.

Glaser, Elisabeth, and Hermann Wellenreuther, eds. *Bridging the Atlantic: The Question of American Exceptionalism in Perspective.* Washington, D.C.: German Historical Institute, 2002.

Goedde, Petra. "From Villains to Victims: Fraternization and the Feminization of Germany, 1945–1947." *Diplomatic History* 23, no. 1 (Winter 1999): 1–20.

———. *GIs and Germans: Culture, Gender, and Foreign Relations, 1945–1949.* New Haven: Yale University Press, 2002.

Gordon, Adi, and Udi Greenberg. "The City of Man, European Émigrés, and the Genesis of Postwar Conservative Thought." *Religions* 3 (2012): 681–698. Accessed January 15, 2013. doi: 10.3390/rel30306 81.

Grathwol, Robert P., Donita Moorhus, and Douglas J. Wilson. *Oral History and Postwar German-American Relations: Resources in the United States.* Washington, D.C.: German Historical Institute, 1997.

Höhn, Maria. *GIs and Frauleins: The German-American Encounter in 1950s West Germany.* Chapel Hill: University of North Carolina Press, 2002.

Höhn, Maria, and Martin Klimke. *A Breath of Freedom: The Civil Rights Struggle, African American GIs, and Germany.* New York: Palgrave MacMillan, 2010.

Höhn, Maria, and Seungsook Moon, eds. *Over There: Living with the U.S. Military Empire from World War Two to the Present.* Durham: Duke University Press, 2010.

Horn, Gerd-Ranier and Padraic Kenney, eds. *Transnational Moments of Change: Europe 1945, 1968, 1989.* New York: Rowman & Littlefield, 2004.

Junker, Detlef, ed. *The United States and Germany in the Era of the Cold War, 1945–1990: A Handbook, Volumes 1 and 2: 1945–1990.* Washington, D.C.: German Historical Institute and New York: Cambridge University Press, 2004.

Klimke, Martin. *The Other Alliance: Student Protests in West Germany and the United States in the Global Sixties.* Princeton: Princeton University Press, 2010.

Long, Wellington. "The American Presence." *American-German Review* 32, no. 6 (1966): 2–5.

Merkl, Peter H., ed. *The Federal Republic of Germany at Forty.* New York, New York University Press, 1989.

Moeller, Robert G., ed. *West Germany Under Construction:Politics, Society, and Culture, in the Adenauer Era.* Ann Arbor: University of Michigan Press, 1997.

Müller, Christian T. "Foreign Troops in Germany during the Cold War: Experience, Relations, Conflicts." Hamburger Institut für Sozialforschung: Completed Projects. (January 2010). Accessed August 14, 2010. http://www.his-online.de/en/research/completed-projects/211.html.

Ninkovich, Frank A. *Germany and the United States: The Transformation of the German Question Since 1945.* Twayne's International History Series no. 2. New York: Twayne Publishers, 1995.

Noelle, Elisabeth and Erich Neumann, eds. *The Germans: Public Opinion Polls, 1947–1966.* Bonn: Verlag für Demoskopie, 1967.

Poiger, Uta. *Jazz, Rock, and Rebels: Cold War Politics and American Culture in Divided Germany.* Berkeley: University of California Press, 2000.

Ramet, Sabrina, and Gordana Crnkovic, eds. *Kazaaam! Splat! Ploof! The American Impact on European Culture since 1945.* New York: Rowman and Littlefield, 2003.

Rieger, Bernhard. "From People's Car to New Beetle: The Transatlantic Journeys of the Volkswagen Beetle." *Journal of American History* 97, no. 1 (June 2010): 91–115.

Scharnholz, Theodor, ed. *The American Presence and Civil-Military Relations in Germany: A Guide to Sources in American and German Archives.* Washington, D.C.: German Historical Institute, 2002.

Schissler, Hanna, ed. *The Miracle Years: A Cultural History of West Germany, 1949–1968.* Princeton: Princeton University Press, 2001.

Seipp, Adam R. *Strangers in the Wild Place.* Bloomington: University of Indiana Press, 2013.

Stephan, Alexander, ed. *Americanization and Anti-Americanism: The German Encounter with American Culture after 1945.* New York: Berghahn, 2008.

Swett, Pamela E., S. Jonathan Wiesen, Jonathan R. Zatlin, and Victoria De Grazia. *Selling Modernity: Advertising in Twentieth-Century Germany.* Duke University Press, 2007.

Tent, James F. *Mission on the Rhine: Reeducation and Denazification in American-Occupied Germany.* Chicago: University of Chicago Press, 1984.

Tismaneanu, Vladimir, ed. *Promises of 1968: Crises, Illusion, and Utopia*. New York: Central European Press, 2011.

Tolliday, Steven. "Enterprise and State in the West German *Wirtschaftswunder*: Volkswagen and the Automobile Industry, 1939–1962." *The Business History Review* 69, no.3 (Autumn 1995): 273–350.

Turner, Henry Ashby. *Germany from Partition to Reunification*. New Haven: Yale University Press, 1992.

Wagnleitner, Reinhold. "Propagating the American Dream: Cultural Policies as Means of Integration." *American Studies International* 24, no. 1 (April 1986): 60–84.

Wennberg, S.G. "Some Economic Problems of Allied Occupation Policy in Germany." *American Journal of Economics and Sociology* 5, no. 4 (July 1946): 425–447.

Wiesen, S. Jonathan. *West German Industry and the Challenge of the Nazi Past, 1945–1955*. Chapel Hill: University of North Carolina Press, 2001.

Wyman, Mark. *DP: Europe's Displaced Persons, 1945–1951*. Philadelphia: The Balch Institute Press, 1989.

Zimmermann, Hubert. *Money and Security: Troops, Monetary Policy, and West Germany's Relations with the United States and Britain, 1950–1971*. New York: Cambridge University Press, 2002.

Index

Numbers in *bold italics* refer to pages with tables or figures.

A&W 122, 259n6
AAFES (Army and Air Force Exchange System) 124–25, *125*, 215–16, 224, 259n20, 259n23, 276n94
AAP (Affirmative Action Plans) 150
abortion 166–67, 267nn167–169
Absent Without Leave (AWOL) 181, 270n63
ACLU (American Civil Liberties Union) 79, 177
ACS (Army Community Services office) 209
Act to Combat International Terrorism (1984) 199, 273n156
Adams, Alvalee 236n44
Adams, John B. 236n44
ADAPCP (Alcohol and Drug Abuse Prevention and Control Program) 140
Adenauer, Konrad 93, 95, 96–97, 105, 117
ADMs (Atomic Demolition Munitions) 100
Adorno, Theodor W. 48–49, 244n95
affirmative action 150, 157; *see also* racial issues
Affirmative Action Plans (AAP) 150
AFI&E (Armed Forces Information and Education) 17, 237n87
AFIS (Armed Forces Information Service) 251n10
AFN (Armed Forces Network) 20, 26, 43, 238n138
AFRC (Armed Forces Recreation Center) 130
African-Americans: all-black military units 59, 246n43; conflicts between white and black GIs 56–57, 246n21; German attitude towards 46, 243–44n77; German housing discrimination against 160–61; influence of the Black Panthers and 154–55; number of soldiers in Germany 246n20; percentages of soldiers in the Army and Air Force *64*; *see also* racial issues
AFRS (Armed Forces Radio Service) 73, 249n127
AFRTS (Armed Forces Radio and Television Service) 168–69, 238n138
AIPO (American Institute of Public Opinion) 99
Albaugh, Neil 45, 90, 94
Alcohol and Drug Abuse Prevention and Control Program (ADAPCP) 140
All-Volunteer Force (AVF) 270n54
Allensbach Institute 256n17
Alling, James 226
America Soldier's Union 176
American Civil Liberties Union (ACLU) 79, 177
American Daily 249n129
American Institute of Public Opinion (AIPO) 99
American Occupation Women's Voluntary Service 34
American retirees abroad: claims of employment discrimination 212, 213, 276n66; creation of an Army council for 213; formation of VOTERS 213, 276n70; lack of military privileges for 212; motivation for remaining in Germany 276n61; size of the community 212
American Southerners 36, 48, 57, 59, 60, 61, 66, 247n78
American Volunteer Army (VOLAR) 138
American Way of Life (film) 23
American Women's Activities in Germany (AWAG) 70
American Women's Club of Heidelberg 50
Andrew, Jean 16
Andrews, Dana 84
Anti-Terrorism Operations Center 196
Applebaum, Larry 100, 213
Armed Forces Information and Education (AFI&E) 17, 237n87
Armed Forces Information Service (AFIS) 251n10
Armed Forces Network (AFN) 20, 26, 43, 238n138
Armed Forces Radio and Television Service (AFRTS) 168–69, 238n138
Armed Forces Radio Service (AFRS) 73, 249n127
Armed Forces Recreation Center (AFRC) 130
Army and Air Force Exchange System (AAFES) 124–25, *125*, 215–16, 259n20, 259n23, 276n94
Army Community Services office (ACS) 209
Army Retirement Service Office (ARSO) 213
Army Times 249n128
Association of War Service Objectors 270n64
"Atomic Annie" 106
Atomic Demolition Munitions (ADMs) 100
automobiles in Germany: cultural bridge 41; economic contribution 40; new car buying system established by the EES 39–40, 241n16; overseas shipping process 40, 242nn23–25; policy for ownership 40; popularity 39, 241n3; rebound in purchases 224; safety fixation 40–41, 242n26; success of Volkswagen and 108, 111, 256nn25–27; value added tax on 217
AVF (All-Volunteer Force) 270n54

285

AWAG (American Women's Activities in Germany) 70
AWOL (Absent Without Leave) 181, 270n63

"B-Bag" (newspaper column) 27, 239n144
Baader, Andreas 188
Baader-Meinhof Gang 187–88, 190, 198, 199, 272n120, 272n134
Baldwin, Hanson 84
The Bashful Elephant (film) 46
basic allowance for quarters (BAQ) 120, 223–24, 258n89, 278n166
Basic Law, Germany 166
Becker, Frank J. 94, 245n6
Becker, Wolfgang 122, 258n1
Benjamin Franklin (Doren) 47
Bennett, Ivan L. 19–20
Bergmann, Peter 233n4
Berlin Action Council for Women's Liberation 166
Berlin Airlift 13–14
Berlin Blockade 85, 86, 258n77
Berlin Wall 93, 122
Bierly, Robert, Jr. 82, 139
Big Jim McClain (film) 84, 251n12
The Big Picture (film) 22–23, 237nn96-100
The Big Red One (film) 128, 260n48
Bizonia 258n73
Black Action Group 153
Black American Law Students Association 150
Black Baptists 153
Black Defense Group 153
black market: devaluation of the dollar and 219–20, 277n128; impact 220; MCPs and 120; Milcom members participation in 115–16, 117, 257n55
Black Panther Party 153, 154–55, 159, 265n64
Black September 190, 272n120, 272n135
Blackboard Jungle (film) 45
Blacks in Action 153
Bolden, Melvin 264n26
Bonanza (television show) 129
bookmobiles 48, 244n89
Boorstin, Daniel 237n84, 238n109, 241n3, 248n87, 251n13
Borgese, G.A. 250n1
Boy Scouts 34–35, 132, 240n198
Boyle, Joseph 242n39
Brandt, Willi 93, 160
brats 24, 238n121
Bremerhaven Port of Entry (BPE) 40

Brentano, Heinrich von 257n38
Brentano-Trimble Agreement 257n38
A Bridge Too Far (film) 128
Broger, John C. 169, 236n54, 251n10, 268n185
Brooks, Richard 128
Brown, Helen Gurley 161
Brown v. Board of Education of Topeka Kansas 57, 66, 246n40
Buckley, William F. 154
Bundeswehr (Federal Armed Forces) 97–98
Burger King 122, 124–25, **125**, 127, 259n20, 259n23
Burt, Richard 198
Bush, George 183

Caesar, Peter 135
"Call for Justice Day" 153
Call Up! (newspaper) 176
Campaign for Disarmament 270n64
Campbell Barracks, Heidelberg, Germany **4**, **8**
Caniff, Milton 79
Catholics 55
Ceniceros, Leon 147–48
censorship of media: Cold War and 77–78; German public's interest in debates over 79; information management and 168–69; Milcom members' reaction to 169; military leaders' rationale for 169–70; results of a congressional investigation 170; suspicions voiced by *Overseas Weekly* 78, 250nn161-162; value placed on freedom of speech 170–71
Center for Military History (CMH) 13, 235n23
Central Army Group (CENTAG) 98
Challenge of Ideas (film) 21, 84, 237n96
Chambers, Whittaker 86, 251n19, 251n20
The Changed Face of Europe (film) 110, 256n16
Chaplain's Corps 19–20
Charnquist, Charles 53
Chazaud, Lois 56–57, 245n18
Chicago Defender 154
chicken pox 30
Chiste, Ron 101
Christ Chapel, Frankfurt 19
Christian Democrat party 184
Chrysler 39
Churchill, Winston 99
CID (Criminal Investigation Division) 174, 269n22
Cipolla, Jack 28

City of Man 82, 250n1
Civil Rights Act (1964) 161
Civil Rights movement 57, 60, 66, 153, 161, 192
Civilian's Wives Club 70
Clark, Mark W. 234n1
Clark, Mrs. Mark W. 11
Clark, Tom C. 55
Clay, Lucius 12, 13, 35–36, 76, 77, 234n1
Clay, Mrs. Lucius D. 11
Cleaver, Kathleen 154, 159
Clergy and Laymen Concerned About Vietnam 260n51
CMH (Center for Military History) 13, 235n23
Coca-Cola 39, 122, 127, 241nn6-7, 258n2
The Code of Conduct (film) 21
Code of Conduct 16, 21, 235nn42-43
COLA (Cost-of-Living Allowance) 207, **208**, 210, 275nn36-37, 278n166
Cold War: censorship of newspapers and 77–78; Eisenhower's strategy for 15; propaganda use 168, 268n178; start 14–15
Collins, Arthur S. 151
Collisson, Norman H. 109–10
Combat! (film) 128–29
comics in newspapers 79–80, 250n174
Commission on the Status of Women 161
Committee to Combat Anti-Semitism 111
Communism: accusations that a newspaper was pro-communism 76; American public's feelings regarding East-West political developments 96, 253nn83-84; anti-communism message in films 84, **85**, 251nn10-17; anti-communism message in print media 85–86, 251n19; anti-communism offensive in the U.S. 88, 89, 252n31; anti-communism sentiments of West Germans 87, 90, 93, 94, 96–98, 251nn27-28, 252n43; call for American leadership 82–83, 250n1, 250n3; conservative anti-communist backlash in America 17; evacuation drills in Milcom neighborhoods 90, 92, 252n49, 252n63; evangelical movement and 19–20, 237nn80-81; German public's interest in censorship debates 79; impact of political

debates on Milcom members 83; reaction to erection of the Berlin Wall 4; reaction to Kennedy's assassination 95–96; solidarity between the Germans and Americans over 95–98, 254nn92–93; Soviet demands in Berlin 92–93, 95, 253n74; Soviet nuclear weapons capability and 83, 87–88, 251n8; Soviet takeover of Hungary 90, 92; tensions felt by Milcom members 86, 88, 89, 90–92, 93–94, 95; visual and printed references to a communist threat 84–86, 251nn10–20; West German view of McCarthy's anti-communism offensive 88–89
"Communist Myth" (video series) 251n16
Conference on American Women's Activities 34
conscription 138, 180, 186, 206, 267n152, 270n54, 275n32
CONUS (Continental United States) 236n71
Copper Canyon (film) 46
COPW (European Council of Protestant Women) 20, 70
Corporal Missile system 100
Cost-of-Living Allowance (COLA) 207, **208**, 210, 275nn36–37, 278n166
Council of Books in Wartime 47, 244n82
Council of Europe 110
Countering Terrorism and Other Major Disruptions on Military Installations 192
Criminal Investigation Division (CID) 174, 269n22
Cuban Missile Crisis 93
Cultural League for the Democratic Renewal of Germany 49
culture and consumerism, American: American books in Germany 47–48, 244nn82–84; automobiles and 39–41, 241n13, 241n16, 242n26; bookmobiles 48, 244n89; contrast between Germans and Americans 45, 241n3, 243n64; creolization and fusion of languages 51–52, 245n112, 245n117; degree of penetration into German culture 38, 241n2; efforts to teach the German language to Milcom members 52–54, 245n118; exporting of violence and crime (*see* drug use; violence and crime); fast food industry and

(*see* fast food industry in Germany); housing projects' display of consumerism 41–42, **42**, 242n37; influence on German choices 50–51, 245n110; libraries 48; movies and (*see* films, American); music and (*see* music of America); negative cultural attributes (*see* drug use; violence and crime); popularity of the short story 48; in print media 42; propaganda role 41–42, 242nn38–39; sexual stereotyping and 67–69 (*see also* feminism); softening of West German attitudes toward 49, 244n99; West German elites' opposition to cultural Americanization 43–44, 49, 243n47; West Germans' renewed interest in consumer wealth and 49–50, 244nn103–104; young Germans' embracing 39, 49, 51, 242n43
Cuneo, Ernest 154
currency reform: acceptance of the conversion plan 117; black market and 115–16, 117, 120, 257n55; effect of the devaluation of the dollar (*see* devaluation of the dollar); exchange rate 115, **119**; impact on Milcom EES prices 118–19; initiation 115, 257n51; introduction of the Deutsche Mark 115, 116, 257n54, 258n64; Milcom exemption from the VAT 121, 258n90; MPC "scrip" program **118**, 119–20, 258nn82–85; post-1980 uptick in the value of the dollar 223; post–Deutsche Mark change in consumer prices 117; situation for Milcom families living on the economy 120–21, 258n89; workers' demonstrations against economic policies 117, 258n74

DAHSUM (Department of the Army Historical Summaries) 143–44, 149, 180, 190, 199, 260n78, 264n29
Daily American 249n129
Daily Defender 154, 159
Dallas (television show) 129
Dames, Arthur 22
Danish Red Cross 31
"Danke Schön" (song) 52, 245n115
DARE (Drug Abuse Resistance Education) 144

Davis, Angela 154, 189
Davis, Benjamin O., Jr. 246n29
Davison, Frederic E. 158, 266n100
Davy Crockett firing device 100
Dean, Terry 11
death penalty 135–36
Defense Against Enemy Propaganda (film) 21, 237n94
Defense Manpower Data Center (DMDC) 13, 235n23
Defense Race Relations Institute (DRRI) 149–50
DeLong, Ed 33
Department of Defense (DOD) 17, 20, 21, 27, 147, 148, 192, 221, 267n152
Department of Defense Dependents School System (DODDS) 17, 31, **32**, 33, 238n129
Department of Defense Dependents Schools, Europe (DODDSEUR) 261n61
Department of Defense Directive 1325.6 179
Department of the Army Historical Summaries (DAHSUM) 143–44, 149, 180, 190, 199, 260n78, 264n29
dependents: acts of poor behavior by American youths 36; Army's efforts to influence the behavior 20–23; congressional opposition to allowing dependents overseas 94–95, 253n73; defined 235n22; drug use among 140, 143–45, 263n145; employment by fast food companies 124; first dependent arrivals 11; government's impetus for sending families to Germany 12, 234nn9–14; hiring program 221; number of dependents planned for 234n3; number of foreign born **15**; number of military bases and dependents by 1960 12–13, 234nn19–20; overseas dependent population by race **63**; population by 1990 13, **14**, 235n23, 235n26; precautions to protect against terrorism 188; segmentation from German children 31–33; situation when the military member deployed to Vietnam 268n2; spouses' support for the Code of Conduct 16; wives of service members (*see* Milcom wives)
Detroit riots 147
Deutsche Mark (DM) 115, 116, 117, **119**, 202, 257n54, 258n64
devaluation of the dollar: black

market commerce and 219–20, 277n128; COLA adjustments 207, 208f, 275nn36–37; decoupling of the dollar from the gold standard and 202, 203–4; exchange rate *203*, 203–4; fuel price increase in 1986 225, 278n184, 278n186; impact on Milcom members 204–5, 208–9, 210, 275nn36–37; inflation in West Germany 205, 275n26; initiatives to help service members manage economic burdens 209–10; numbers of Milcom members living on the economy 207, 210, 275nn53–54; plight of noncommand junior enlisted 205–8, 275nn30–34; post-1980 uptick in the value of the dollar 223; repeat of in 1986 224–25; suggested adjustments in compensation 211–12
"Dick Tracy" (comic) 80
diphtheria 30
Displaced Persons (DPs) 29, 112, 238n115, 239n166, 242n35
DMDC (Defense Manpower Data Center) 13, 235n23
DOD *see* Department of Defense
DODDS (Department of Defense Dependents School System) 17, 31, *32*, 33, 238n129
DODDSEUR (Department of Defense Dependents Schools, Europe) 261n61
Dollars (film) 128, 260n49
Domino Theory 173, 269n6
Dondero, George A. 76
Doren, Carl van 47
Dozier, James L. 273n189
DPs *see* Displaced Persons
draft *see* conscription
DRRI (Defense Race Relations Institute) 149–50
Drug Abuse Resistance Education (DARE) 144
drug use: among American dependents 140, 143–45, 263n145; anti-drug abuse education program 144; characteristics of a drug abuser 141, 142; degree of attention being paid to the drug problem 143–44, 145; effect of the Vietnam war on 139; German opinions about Americans' drug use 137–38; illegal drugs sources 142; Milcom members' views on the drug problem 141; prevalence 136, 262n95; punishment for 143, 263n145; raids and arrests 140; recovery and rehabilitation programs 140–41; relation to crime 136–37; relation to racial tensions 157; statistics within the Army *137*, *138*; statistics within the German community 142, 263n140; trends in marijuana and hard drug use 139, 144, 262n111, 262n113; underground GI press' role in addressing 178; *see also* violence and crime
Duck and Cover (film) 102
Dulles, John F. 111, 256n25
Dutschke, Rudi 191

Ebony 58
EC (European Command) 27, 237n87
economic challenges (1967–1990): black market commerce 219–20, 277n128; care packages from German neighbors 218–19; changes in the value of the dollar (*see* devaluation of the dollar); dining hall privileges for junior enlisted 218; economic environment in the 1950s and 1960s 202, 274n3; events contributing to an economic decline 202, 274n5, 274n8; hiring of local nationals (*see* employment of local nationals); for military retirees (*see* American retirees abroad); OPEC fuel embargo and (*see* fuel embargo); value added tax (*see* value added tax)
Economic Cooperation Administration (ECA) 109
economic miracle (*Wirtschaftswunder*) 7, 49, 50, 108, 202; *see also* economics of Germany (1947–1967)
economic resurgence (1980–1985): automobile purchases and 224; end 224–25; German economists' concern over the dollar 278n162; new pay raises for service members 223–24; relief felt by Milcom members 223; strong dollar's impact on AAFES 224; uptick in the value of the dollar 223
economics of Germany (1947–1967): aid from the U.S. 110–11, 256n22; America's interest in an economically strong Germany 109, 110, 256n8, 256n10, 256n21; black market and 115–17, 257n55; conclusion of the Marshall Plan 111; conditions immediately after the war 108, 255n4; currency reform and (*see* currency reform); employment of West Germans by the U.S. military (*see* employment of local nationals); polls about Americans' view of the ERP 109–10; polls about West Germans' view of the ERP 109, 110, 256n18, 256nn11–12; propaganda film about the ERP 110, 256n16; provisions of JCS 1067 108, 255n3; situation for Milcom families living on the economy 120–21, 258n89; start of an economic resurgence 109, 255n6; success of Volkswagen and 111, 256nn25–27; value added tax 216–18, 277n106
ECSC (European Coal and Steel Community) 110
EDC (European Defense Community) 97, 105
Eddy, Manton S. 34
Education Act (1972) 164
Edwards, Mrs. M.O. 71, 249n118
EES (European Exchange System) 39–40, 118–19
Eisenhower Administration 4, 15, 17, 34, 55, 269n6
Eisenhower the Soldier (film) 23, 237n106
employment of local nationals (LNs): American dependent hire program and 221; economic boom in towns and 115; employment under EUCOM 112, *113*, 257nn36–38; explanation of the hiring practices 221–22; German government's petition to stop American hires 222; German unemployment rate *222*, 277n154; importance of workers' groups 112–13; job growth outside military employment 114–15; number employed by the U.S. 114, 227n139; perception of preferential hiring 221; positions served by German civilian labor 51, 112; screenings before employment 112, 257n36; shift in responsibility for workers' wages 113–14; unemployment rate *114*, 115; workers' demonstrations against economic policies 117, 258n74
Enlisted Wives Club 70
Eppler, Erhard 270n72

Equal Opportunity Offices 149
Equal Rights Amendment (ERA) 162–63, 266n129, 267n137
Erhard, Ludwig 49, 117, 244n99
Erlanger Tagblatt 133
European Coal and Steel Community (ECSC) 110
European Command (EC) 27, 237n87
European Council of Protestant Women (COPW) 20, 70
European Defense Community (EDC) 97, 105
European Exchange System (EES) 39–40, 118–19
European Motion Picture Service 44
European Nuclear Disarmament 182
European Recovery Plan (ERP) 109–10, 256n16, 256n18, 256nn11–12; *see also* economics of Germany (1947–1967)
exchange rate 115, *119*, *203*, 203–4
Exchange System Automotive Activities Center 39

FAHS (Frankfurt American High School) 33, 90, 174, 240n187
Far East Broadcasting Company 236n54
fast food industry in Germany: accommodation of local tastes 126; arrival 122, 259nn3–4; Burger King's deal with AAFES 124–25, *125*, 259n20, 259n23; cultural penetration 126–27, 260n38; cultural symbolism 122; emerging postwar globalism and 127; employment of Milcom family members 124; franchises establishment 122–23, 259n8; German resistance to 123, 259n9; location choices 122–23, 259n12–14; McDonalds and 123, *124*, 126; popularity 123, 124, 125, 260n32
Faulkner, William 48, 244n93
Federal Aid Highway Act (1956) 242n26
Federal Armed Forces (*Bundeswehr*) 97–98
Federal Bureau of Investigation (FBI) 130
Federal Civil Defense Administration 101
Federal Republic of Germany (FRG) *see* West Germany
Federal Women's Week 164, 165
The Female Eunuch (Greer) 162

The Feminine Mystique (Friedan) 162, 167, 266n134
feminism: changing opinions about women in the military 164–65; debates over the publication of "cheesecake" photos 163; empowerment of women and 165; Equal Rights Amendment and 163–64; protests against the Miss America Pageant 166; struggle between traditionalists and 162–63; women's protests against abortion laws 166; *see also* women's rights
FighT bAck (newspaper) 177–78
films, American: about Germany 21, 22–23; attendance numbers at showings 46–47; centrality to German-American cultural discourse 46; contrast in cultural norms between Germans and Americans 38; German interest in music and films 44, 45–46; impact on German culture 46; pro–American ideology films 21–23; propaganda films about a nuclear threat 101–3; public showings as propaganda 46, 243n72; themes of violence in 128–29, 135–36; West Germans' view 47, 128–29
Firestone, Shulamith 167
Fonda, Jane 175
Foote, Evelyn P. 165
Ford 39
Foreign Nationals (film) 114
Forrestal, James 77
Fort Osage (film) 46
Forward (newspaper) 176, 177, 178
Fourteen Point manifesto 260n55
France 227n154
Frankfurt American High School (FAHS) 33, 90, 174, 240n187
Frankfurt War Objectors 181
Frankfurt Women's Council 166
freedom of speech 170–71, 177
Freedoms Foundation 17–18, 23, 236n50, 237n106
French, Marilyn 167
FRG (Federal Republic of Germany) *see* West Germany
Friedan, Betty 162, 167, 266n132, 266n134
The Friendly Hand (film) 242n39
From Here to Eternity (film) 45
FTA with Pride (newspaper) 176, 177
fuel embargo: change in the price of gasoline 214, 216; fuel price increase in 1986 225, 278n184, 278n186; gas prices in the U.S. versus Germany 214, *215*; impact on Germans 216, 276n96; letters to the editor about high costs 214–15; new AAFES pricing system 215–16, 276n94; resulting hardships for Milcom members 214, 276n83

Gallup 96
GAO (Government Accounting Office) 170
GARIOA (Government Aid and Relief in Occupied Areas) 239n167
Gaskell, Douglas 125, 183–84
Gateway 41
Gelinas, Robert 187
General Patch (ship) 100
Geneva Convention 173
George Washington Honor medal 17–18
German-American bond: American solidarity with German missile protesters 185–86, 271n110; automobiles and 41; bridges between the two cultures 34–35, 36–37, 241n215; cementing of Germany's connection with the U.S. 95; centrality of American films to 46; complexity of German-American political relations 186–87, 229–30; complexity of political relations and 229–30; economics-based 230–31; factors affecting 37; fast food industry in Germany and 126–27, 260n38; Germany's changing relationship with the U.S. 4, 233n8; Germany's political alliance with the U.S. 96–98, 254nn92–93; racial issues and 161; reaction to Kennedy's assassination 95–96; solidarity over Communism 95–98, 254nn92–93; tensions over nuclear weapons (*see* nuclear threat); terrorism and 192, 195, 199–201; tests of (*see* missile protests; terrorism; Vietnam War); women's rights and 166–67
German-American week 46, 49
German Employees Council 112
German Industrial Exhibition 111
German Youth Activity (GYA) 35–36
Germany Today (film) 23, 84, 237n104
GI Joe (Pyle) 47

Gilbert, Tim 11, 36
Gillem, Alvan C., Jr. 247*n*68
Girl Scouts 34, 132
The Godfather (film) 128
Goebbels, Joseph 79
Golden Plague 115
Goldsmith, Kent 33
Goldwater, Barry 103
Good Bye Lenin! (film) 122, 258*n*1
Government Accounting Office (GAO) 170
Government Aid and Relief in Occupied Areas (GARIOA) 239*n*167
The Graffiti (newspaper) 177, 179, 270*n*49
Graham, Billy 19
Green, Robert E., Jr. 94
Green Party 195
Greer, Germaine 162, 167
Gregg, Arthur 214
Gromyko, Andrei 95
Gunsmoke (television show) 129
GYA (German Youth Activity) 35–36

Hambric, Scott 23–24
Handling Dissident and Protest Activities Among Members of the Armed Forces 179
Hanne, Bill 31, 63, 101
Harding, Bruce 139
Hargis, Billy James 18, 236*n*60
Harrell, Wilson 248*n*99
Harriman, W. Averell 110
Hartness, Harlan N. 236*n*50
hashish 137, **138**, 139, 140, 142, 143, 262*n*111
Hatch Act 19
Heflin, Van 84
Heidelberg Housewives Fair 50
Heidelberg Liberation Front 176
Heidelberg Military Post (HMP) German Employees Council 113
Heidelberg Post 40, 41, 113
Heineman, Elizabeth 267*n*163
Henkel Corporation 51
Hepatitis B 140
Heritage Foundation 13, 235*n*23
HICOG *see* U.S. High Commissioner of Germany
Hispanic Milcom members 156
Hiss, Alger 86, 251*n*20
Hite, Shere 167
Hite Report on Female Sexuality (Hite) 167
Hodgdon, A. Dana 71
Hofstadter, Richard 233*n*4
Hollenbaugh, Sally 31
Homeward Bound (May) 242*n*38, 266*n*124

Honest John Missile system 100
Hoover, Herbert 30
Hour of Power (radio program) 237*n*80
House Military Compensation Committee 211
House Sub-Committee on Traffic Safety 242*n*26
House Un-American Activities Committee (HUAC) 76, 83, 88, 89, 251*n*5, 251*n*11
Housing Cost Data Survey 210
Housing Referral Offices (HRO) 160
Howard, Albert 159
Howells-Tierney, Janet 164–65
Howley, Frank 86, 251*n*23
HRO (Housing Referral Offices) 160
Hubp, Frank 99
Hungary 90, 92

Information and Education Overseas (film) 22, 237*n*101
Institut für Demoskopie 110, 256*n*17
Institut für Demoskopie Allensbach 135
International Herald-Tribune 73
International Media Co. 72
International New York Times 249*n*128
An Introduction to Germany for Occupation Families 21, 24, 237*n*89
Iranian Revolution 278*n*184
Irish Republican Army 191
The Iron Curtain (film) 84, 251*n*17
Italy 227*n*154

JAG (Judge Advocate General's Corps) 150–51, 156
Japan 13, 235*n*26
Jászi, Oscar 250*n*1
Jazz 42, 43, 49, 242*nn*42–43, 244*n*102
JCS 1067 108, 255*n*3
Jews 29, 56, 111, 239*n*166
Jim Crow in Germany (cartoon) 58, 246*n*32
Joffe, Bernard 47
John Birch Society 18, 79, 236*n*60
Johnny Belinda (film) 45–46, 243*n*69
Johnson, Hank 24, 34, 90, **91**, 92
Johnson, Lyndon 93, 103
joint religious services 36
Jones, Nathaniel, R. 149, 151
Jorgensen, George 250*n*162
Judge Advocate General's Corps (JAG) 150–51, 156

Kaempfert, Bert 245*n*115
Kaiserslautern American High School 174
Kale, Sam 24, 28, 86
Kappes, Norman 25, 36, 240–41*n*210
Kaufhof stores 126
Kaye, Sammy 44
Kaylor, David 193
Kennan, George 256*n*8
Kennedy, John F. 95, 129, 161
Kennedy, Robert F. 6, 129
Kentucky Fried Chicken (KFC) 122, 127, 259*n*6
Khrushchev, Nikita 41, 92, 242*n*37
Kiely, Joe 26
Kiessling, Günter 169
Kilpatrick, James 168
King, Martin Luther, Jr. 6, 147
"Kitchen Debates" 41, 242*n*37
Klimke, Martin 268*n*1, 270*n*55
Korean War 77, 89
Kroc, Ray 126, 260*n*35
Kroesen, Frederick, J. 195, 199
Ku Klux Klan (KKK) 147, 154, 155

Labor Service Guard Units 112, **113**, 257*nn*37–38
Ladies' Home Journal 46
languages: Creolization and fusion 51–52, 245*n*112, 245*n*117; efforts to teach German to Milcom members 52–54, 245*n*118
Lasky, Victor 154
The Last of the Conquerors (Smith) 58
Lawson, Richard L. 169
Lawyers Military Defense Committee (LMDC) 178, 269*n*41
Lee, C.H. 76
Lewis, R.W.G. 241*n*3
libraries 48
Libya 198, 274*n*200
license plates on American cars 25, 238*n*126
Life (magazine) 72
lifer 269*n*30
Li'l Abner (comic) 80
Linkletter, Art 69, 248*n*99
Little America 25, 33, 34, 41–42, **42**, 63, 79, 210, 231, 242*n*37
LMDC (Lawyers Military Defense Committee) 178, 269*n*41
local nationals (LNs) *see* employment of local nationals (LNs)
London Conference (1948) 115
Luther, Martin King, Jr. 129, 260*n*51
Lynam, Nancy 26

MacDonald, Doris 71
Mad Anthony Wayne's (coffee house) 175
Manchurian Candidate (film) 84
Mann, Thomas 82, 250*n*1, 250–51*nn*4–5
marijuana 137, **138**, 139, 140, 144, 262*n*95, 262*n*111, 262*n*113; *see also* drug use
Marshall, George 109
Marshall, Thurgood 264*n*11
Marshall Plan 109, 111, 255*n*6, 256*n*16
Martin, Thomas E. 236*n*58
May, Elaine Tyler 242*n*38, 266*n*124
May, Karl 127, 260*n*44
McCarthy, Joseph 17, 88, 90, 251*n*11, 252*n*31, 252*n*44
McCollum v. Board of Education 245*n*4
McCracken, Norman 111
MCCW (Military Council of Catholic Women) 20, 70, 267*n*162
The McDonaldization of Society (Ritzer) 260*n*38
McDonalds 123, **124**, 124, 126, 127, 259*n*19
McEnery, Kevin 31
McNamara, Robert 18, 79, 258*n*89
measles 30–31
media *see* Armed Forces Radio Service; films, American; print media
Mehrwertsteuer (MwSt) 121; *see also* value added tax
Meinhof, Ulrike 190
Men of Science in America (Joffe) 47
Miami Vice (television show) 129
Milcom wives: celebrations of in print media 71, 72–73, 249*n*117; displays of consumerism 50, 51, 245*n*110; engagement in welfare work by wives 34; gender-based categorizations 67; gender inequalities in the WACs 70–71; growing empowerment 69–70, 72–73; images of Americanism among 26–27; number of women in the dependent population 71–72; print media's use of sexist stereotypes 67–69, 70, 248*n*96, 248*n*99; stress felt due to devaluation of the dollar 208–9; support for the Code of Conduct 16; *see also* dependents; feminism; women's rights

Milcoms (military communities): change in their role after WWII 4–5, 233*n*8; Code of Conduct and (*see* Code of Conduct); complexity of German-American political relations 186–87, 229–30; demographic composition 63–64, 65, 146, 247*nn*68–69; economic bonds between Germans and Americans 230–31; exporting of violence and crime (*see* violence and crime); family members in Germany (*see* dependents); German economy and (*see* economic challenges [1967–1990]; economic resurgence [1980–1985]; economics of Germany [1947–1967]); information sources for this study 6, 233–34*nn*11–12; "lifer" definition 269*n*30; military leaders' propaganda campaign (*see* propaganda); number of Americans in Germany between 1946 and 1990 231; number of military bases and dependents by 1960 12–13, 234*nn*19–20; penetration into German culture (*see* culture and consumerism, American); political issues and (*see* censorship of media; Communism; freedom of speech; nuclear threat; Vietnam War); religion in (*see* religion in the Milcom); segmentation from Germans (*see* segmentation of communities); societal issues revealed in (*see* drug use; feminism; racial issues; violence and crime; women's rights); steadfastness during the Berlin Airlift 13–14, 235*n*34; tensions challenging the identity 5–6; trans-cultural changes 228–29; travel conditions to Germany 11; unifying characteristics of geographically-distant Milcoms 233*n*9
Militant Liberty: A Program of Evaluation and Assessment of Freedom 18
Militant Liberty program 18, 236*n*58
Military Council of Catholic Women (MCCW) 20, 70, 165
Military Payment Certificates (MPC) **118**, 119–20, 258*nn*82–85
Military Police (MP) 132, 188
Military Wife of the Year contest 69

Millstein, Charles 28
Miss America Pageant 166, 267*n*170
Miss Cheesecake contest 68–69
missile protests: American solidarity with German protesters 185–86, 271*n*110; anti-nuclear protests in Europe 182–83, 271*n*81, 271*n*83; complexity of German-American political relations and 186–87; decline in number 186; focus of anti-missile anger 183, 271*n*86; incidents involving violence by demonstrators 183–84; Milcom members' feeling about 183–84; voices of support for the missile deployments 184–85; West German concern over the presence of nuclear weapons 182, 270*n*70, 270*n*72, 270*n*74
Moorish Church 153
MP (Military Police) 132, 188
Mulvihill, Jane 11, 62–63
Mumford, Lewis 250*n*1
Mumma, Morton C. III 116
Munich-American Peace Committee 186
Münich Olympic Village 190, 272*n*135
Murray v. Curlett 245*n*4
Murrow, Edward R. 22, 84, 237*n*96, 251*n*11
music of America: British rock music and 259*n*5; elites' opposition to American cultural 43–44, 243*n*47; popularity 42, 43, 49, 242*nn*42–43, 244*n*102; responses to criticisms of rock and roll 44–45; youth riots at movies 44
MwSt (*Mehrwertsteuer*) 121; *see also* value added tax (VAT)
My Lai, South Vietnam 129
My Son John (film) 46, 84

National Association for the Advancement of Colored People (NAACP) 149, 150–51, 160, 264*n*11
National Conference of Black Lawyers 151
National Education Association (NEA) 101
National Organization of Women (NOW) 161, 162, 165
National Organization of Women Judges 164
National Security Act (1947) 19
National Security Council (NSC) 15, 235*n*36
National Urban League 151

National Vietnam Moratorium Day 174
NATO 254n113
NEA (National Education Association) 101
Neckarsulm Milcom chapel 19
Negerkinder 57, 246n26, 246n28
NEO (Non-Combatant Evacuation Operation) 99
Neue Zeitung 76, 79, 249n138, 250n170
The New Testament (newspaper) 176, 177
New York Times 75, 77, 154, 183, 186
Newsweek 249n128
Newton, Wayne 52
Niebuhr, Reinhold 250n1
Night and Day (film) 45, 243n69
Nixon, Richard M. 41, 130, 161, 203, 242n37
Nolan, Mary 259n5, 268n1
non-appropriated funds 213, 276n77
Non-Combatant Evacuation Operation (NEO) 99
non-judicial punishment 147, 264n10
Nordhoff, Heinrich 111
North Korea 16
NOW (National Organization of Women) 161, 162, 165
NSC (National Security Council) 15, 235n36
nuclear threat: attitude towards probable use of weapons 104; contrasting discourse about the reality 98–99, 101; deployment of nuclear-capable units 100, 254nn107–108; evacuation drills 99; HUAC and 83; hydrogen bomb development and 104, 255n131; impact of political debates on Milcom members 83; mishaps with bombs 105–6; politics around stationing weapons in Germany 100, 105–6, 255nn139–140; production of propaganda films in the U.S. 101–3; protests against in Germany (*see* missile protests); proximity to populated areas **106**; Soviet capabilities 83, 99–100, 251n8; tensions felt by Milcom members 83, 98–99, 101–2, 105–6, 255nn146–147; training exercises 101; U.S. response to Soviet missile deployments 182, 271n77; U.S. rhetoric about deterrence 99, 100; West German complaints about lack of funding for nuclear shelters 107; West Germany's reluctance to support a reliance on nuclear defense 105; worries about safety and security 105–6, 255nn146–147

OCB (Operations Coordinating Board) 15, 235n37
The Occupation Soldier (film) 59
Occupation Statute 110
Of Soldiers and Altars (film) 19
Office of Military Government, United States (OMGUS) 239n165
Office of Policy Coordination (OPC) 15, 235n37
Officer Candidate School 150
Officers' Wives Club 70
O'Hair, Madalyn Murray 55, 56, 245n8
Oleo Strut (coffee house) 175
Olympic Games (1972) 123
OMGUS (Office of Military Government, United States) 239n165
One, Two, Three (film) 46, 122, 244n79, 258n2
OPC (Office of Policy Coordination) 15, 235n37
OPEC (Organization of Petroleum Exporting Countries) 202, 274n8
Operation Friendly Hand (film) 22–23, 41–42, 237n103
"Operation Golden Flow" 139
Operation Snow White 140
Operations Coordinating Board (OCB) 15, 235n37
O'Reilly, Aubrey J. 19
Organization of Petroleum Exporting Countries (OPEC) 202, 274n8
Organized Crime Control Act 130, 261n58
Ottumwa, U.S.A. (film) 23, 237n105
Our Friend the Atom 102
Overseas Weekly 18, 249n129; comics and 79–80, 250n174; founding 72; publishing of "cheesecake" photos 267n139, 267n142; repercussions of its reporting on an anti-communism program 79; suspicions of censorship 78, 250nn161–162
Oxnam, G. Bromley 55

Paper Grenade (newspaper) 270n67
paperbacks (*Taschenbücher*) 48
Parent Teacher Association (PTA) 132

USS *Patch* 11
Patton, George S. **28**
Paul, Alice 267n137
People of Plenty (Potter) 242n38
People-to-People 16
People-to-People (film) 22, 23, 237n102
Pershing II cruise missiles 182, 195
Persil detergent 51
Personnel Security Precautions Against Acts of Terrorism 192
Pledge of Allegiance 55
Plowshares 186
A Pocket Guide to Germany 21, 36
polio 30
Polk, General 148
Potsdam Agreement 92
Potter, David 242n38
Prayon, Horst 185
Presley, Elvis 42, 44, 242n41
print media: anti-communism message in 85–86, 251n19; celebrations of women's accomplishments in 71, 72–73, 249n117; censorship 168–70; comics and 79–80, 250n174; coverage of radicalization of the race struggle 153–55, 264n64, 265n70; culture and consumerism in 42; efforts to bolster service members' American idealism 17; examples of manipulation by AFRTS 168–69; Milcom members' reaction to censorship 169; *Overseas Weekly* (see *Overseas Weekly*); propaganda use in the Cold War environment 168, 268n178; role in declaring American exceptionalism 26–27; sexist stereotypes in 67–69, 248n96, 248n99; *Der Spiegel* (see *Der Spiegel*); *Stars and Stripes* (see *Stars and Stripes*); tone of publications and films about Germany 21, 22–23; underground press (*see* underground GI press); value placed on freedom of speech by members 170–71; *Die Zeit* (see *Die Zeit*)
Pro-Blue program 79, 236n59
Pro-Familia 167
"Project Plowshares" 102
propaganda: acts of poor behavior by American youths 36; American scouting program and 34–35, 340n198; anti-communism message in films 84, **85**, 251nn10–17; Code of Conduct development 16,

235nn42–43; display of military prowess and 27–28, 239nn153–154; efforts to influence the behavior of dependents 20–23; evangelical movement's participation in 19–20, 236nn69–70, 237nn80–81; fate of an anticommunist indoctrination program 18; films about a nuclear threat 101–3; Freedoms Foundation's initiatives 17–18, 23, 236n50, 237n106; German Youth Activity and 35–36; images of Americanism among Milcom wives 26–27; introduction by the United States 15–16, 235n37; Militant Liberty program 18, 236n58; OMGUS surveys 35, 240n206; print media's efforts to bolster service members' American idealism 17; print media's role in declaring American exceptionalism 26–27; pro-American ideology films 21–23; production of films about a nuclear threat 101–3; public showing of American films and 46, 243n72; role of American consumerism in 41–42, 242nn38–39; selling of the Marshall Plan 110, 256n16; tone of publications and films about Germany 21, 22–23
"Protection of Department of Defense Personnel Abroad Against Terrorist Acts" 192
Protestant Women of the Chapel (PWOC) 165, 267n162
Proxmire, William 170
PSB (Psychological Strategy Board) 15, 235n37
Psychological Strategy Board (PSB) 15, 235n37
Psychological Warfare Branch 47
PTA (Parent Teacher Association) 132
Pyle, Ernie 47

Quartermaster Labor Units 112
Queren, Inge 94, 95, 191–92

Race Relations Council, Mannheim Milcom 147
racial issues: affirmative action initiatives 150, 157; all-black military units 59, 246n43; attempts to diffuse racial tensions 59; attitudes about the level of progress made toward equality 151–52; blind spots to the emerging race reality 147; claims of concern for local opposition to integration 60–61, 62; conflicts between white and black GIs 56–57, 246n21; connection between crime, drugs, and racial conflicts 157; demographic composition of Milcoms 63–64, 65, 146, 246n20, 247nn68–69; designation of a staff officer on Negro affairs 59–60, 245nn45–50; effort to downplay effects of racism in the Milcoms 61–65; emergence of the KKK in EUCOM 147; equality measures enacted 149–50, 264n31; German attitude towards African Americans 58–59, 60, 61, 158–59, 265n97; German media's critiques of American race relations 158; German perception of racial tensions 56, 65–67, 245n13, 247n75, 247n78; grassroots initiatives to confront 147–48; Hispanic Milcom members' experiences 156; housing discrimination against blacks 151, 160–61; impact of births of *negerkinder* 57, 246n26, 246n28; impact of racial segregation on the Milcoms 57–58, 62, 242n29, 242n32; incidents of violence between the races 147; interposition movement 247–48n78; investigations into racial inequities in the armed forces 147, 148–49, 264nn15–16; JAG minority recruiting program 150–51, 156; military's adoption of standard personnel classifications 156; number of black soldiers in Germany 246n20; overseas dependent population by race 63; pattern of bias towards whites 147, 151, 264n37, 264nn10–11; percentages of black soldiers in the Army and Air Force 64; perceptions of racial accord by Milcom members 62–63; positive experiences of some African American GIs 58; pushback against skewed equality 65; race relations in the U.S. in 1960s 146–47, 263n6; racist attitudes of some service members 36, 48, 57, 59, 60, 61, 66, 247n78; radicalization of (*see* radicalization of the race struggle); Render Report 148–49, 151, 153; revisions of regulations 150; segregation in US stateside military bases 62; tenacity of racial tensions 146
Radford, Arthur 18, 235–36n43, 236n50
radicalization of the race struggle: circulation of publications 153–54, 264n64; coverage by the media 154–55, 265n70; demonstrations against racial inequities 152–53, 159; German student's activism 159; influence of the Black Panthers 154–55; influence of the KKK 155; networks and activities of radical GI groups 153; race riots and 152; white soldiers' questioning of equality efforts 155
Radio in the American Sector (RIAS) 43
Radio Luxembourg 43
RAF (Red Army Faction) 187, 191, 192, 195, 198, 272n120
Rambo: First Blood (film) 135
rape prevention program 132–33
Ray, Marcus H. 59–60, 245nn45–50
Reagan, Ronald 44, 193, 223
Red Aid 191
Red Army Faction (RAF) 187, 191, 192, 195, 198, 272n120
Red Brigade 191
Red Scare 89
Rehm, Thomas 125, 139, 183
Reichsmarks 116
religion in the Milcom: change to the Pledge of Allegiance 55; debate over separation of church and state 55–56, 245n4, 245n6; evangelical movement and 19–20, 55, 236nn69–70, 237nn80–81; spirituality and 17, 20, 56, 250n3, 251n13, 251n28, 267n162
Render, Frank W., II 148
Render Report 148–49, 151, 153
Residence Regulation Law, FRG 254n151
Resor, Stanley R. 151
retirees, American: claims of employment discrimination 212, 213, 276n66; creation of an Army council for 213; formation of VOTERS 213, 276n70; lack of military privileges for 212; motivation for remaining in Germany 276n61; size of the community 212

Revolutionary Cells 190, 195–96, 198, 199, 272n120
Revolutionary People's Communication Network 178
Reynolds, David 268n1
Rhein-Main Air Base 198
RIAS (Radio in the American Sector) 43
Richards, Aurelia 26, 249n116
Ridgway, Matthew 76, 249n146
"RIP Corby" (comic) 80
Ritzer, George 260n38
Robeson, Paul 82, 250n4
Rock Around the Clock (film) 44, 45
Rocky IV (film) 135
Roe v. Wade 163, 267n137
Rogers, Bernard 169
Rosen, Ruth 266n125
Rospach, Marion 72, 78
Rowan, Carl 162, 266n130
Ryan, Jim 93, 252n58

Sabulsky, Renate 44
SAODA (Special Action Office for Drug Abuse) 178
Saturday Night Live (television show) 171
Scanlon, Kay 162
Schissler, Hanna 268n175
Schlafly, Phyllis 162, 266n128, 266n130
Schmoekel, Wolf W. 116
School District of Abingdon Township v. Schempp 245n4
Schuller, Robert 20, 237n80
Schulz, Peter 58
scouting program 34–35, 340n198
Scouting Transatlantic Council 35
scrip program *118*, 119–20, 258nn82–85
SDS (Students for a Democratic Society) 178, 270n64
The Search for Military Justice 149, 160
Second Front International 176
segmentation of communities: acts of poor behavior by American youths 36; availability of food and clothing in Germany 23–24, 238n112; bridges between the two cultures 34–35, 36–37, 241n215; comparison to occupying Romans 28; construction of homes and facilities for Americans 25, 41, 238nn127–129, 242n35; differences in everyday routines and 31; due to separation of dependent schools 31–33; emergence of a sequestered lifestyle 25–26, 238nn130–131; establishment of youth groups 34–35; existence of postwar animosity 33–34; German disease outbreaks and 30–31; privileged status of personnel and families 26, 238n140; rationing of food by US forces 29–30, 239n163, 239nn167–170; requisitioning of German properties for Americans' use 24–25, 26, 238nn115–119; tensions with host Germans 28–29, 239n162; total number of American service members, 1946 to 1990 231
Selma, Alabama 147
Sergeant Missile system 100
Servicemen's Wives and Children's Association 234n12
Sex and the Single Girl (Brown) 161
sexual stereotyping 67–69
SHA (Station Housing Allowance) pay 210, 278n166
Sheeley, Charles 140
Signal Corps Pictorial Service 84, 251n10
Sinatra, Frank 84
Singlaub, John K. 144
Sir! No Sir! (film) 269n24
Smith, Dina 241n13
Smith, Margaret Chase 12, 234n13
Smith, William Gardner 58
Snow White II 140
Soderston, Dolores 71
SOFA (Status of Forces Agreement) 26, 121, 212, 217, 238n137, 261n75
Sound Off (film) 46
Soviet Union: Cold War and 14–15; demands in Berlin 92, 95, 253n74; Hungary and 90, 92; nuclear capabilities 83, 99–100, 251n8; pass system in Germany 45, 243n67; sealing off of western Berlin 13; U.S. response to missile deployments in Europe 182, 271n77
Spec-5s 136, 262n99
Special Action Office for Drug Abuse (SAODA) 178
Der Spiegel: about 247n75; on American comics 80; on American segregation 66–67, 158, 265n99; on Americans' violent behavior 44, 129; anti-communism message in 87; on censorship 78; outline of West German anti-communism sentiments 93; reports on anti-missile anger 183; tracking of the cultural penetration of fast food 126, 260n38; view of McCarthy's anti-communism offensive 89
Spiller, Winton, Jr. 63, 89, 101
SS-20 missiles 182
Stars and Stripes: anti-communism message in 85–86, 251n19; on anti-missile protests 184; articles about racial tensions 61; on auto arrivals 39, 241n16; censorship debates 76–78, 79, 168–69; circulation 73–74, 249n129; on the Civil Rights movement 57, 246nn22–23; comics and 79–80, 250n174; contribution to teaching German to Milcom members 53–54; corporate ads in 125, 259n28; crime reports 130; defining of the Milcom wife 67–69, 248n96; on dependent arrivals 11, 234n4; on disease outbreaks 30; economic status of Milcom members 204–5; on the Equal Rights Amendment 163–64, 267n145; evangelical movement support 19, 20; on GI susceptibility to interrogation pressures 16; on the high costs of gas 214–15; initiation of a music column 43; listing of community events 34; Militant Liberty reports 18; on nuclear exercises and deployments 100; popularity 75; post-war changes in 74; press locations 249n130; publication of "cheesecake" photos 163, 267n139, 267n142; on race relations 155, 156; on racial tensions in the States 147, 263n6; readership 239n139; response to criticisms of rock and roll 44; role in propaganda 26; on the struggle between traditionalists and feminists 162–63, 266nn128–137; on terrorism 192, 273n155; tone toward women 70; treatment of race-related news 154–55, 265n70; on the women's rights movement 161–62, 164–65, 266n127
Station Housing Allowance (SHA) pay 210, 278n166
Status of Forces Agreement (SOFA) 26, 121, 212, 217, 238n137, 261n75
Stauber, Ruby R. 164, 267n149

Steinem, Gloria 167
Stennis, John 94
"Steve Canyon" (comic) 79
Stimson, Henry 12
Strump, Felix 236n50
Students for a Democratic Society (SDS) 178, 270n64
Stuttgart Economy Wives Club 120
Stuttgart Post News 17, 71, 249n117
Stuttgarter Vorfälle 117, 258n72
Subcommittee on Drug Abuse in the Military 157
Survey of Drug Use (1971) 157
Sutherland, Donald 175
Swedish Alien Commission 180
Swedish Vietnam Committee 180

Table of Organization and Equipment (TO&E) 254n115
Taschenbücher (paperbacks) 48
Teentime Tunetime 45
terrorism: arrest of Baader 188, 190; attack on Rhein-Main Air Base 198, 273n195; automobiles security suggestions **200**; Baader-Meinhof Gang attacks 187–88; bombing of Frankfurt Milcom 195–96, 198, 273n200; bombing of USAFE headquarters 193; confusion among Germans about terrorism violence 191–92; congressional reaction to 199; establishment of an anti-terrorism center 196; failure to acknowledge all attacks 190–91, 195, 199; German-American bond and 192, 199–201; German challenge of balancing security with personal freedom 191; goal of terrorist groups 187, 272n120; launching of counter-terrorist operations 188, **189**, 272n131; level of protection increases on military installations 196; Milcom members' unease about safety 187, 193, 197–98, 273n189; missile protests and 195; policy guidelines from the DOD 192, 273n156, 273n159; precautions to protect dependent family members 188; RAF attacks 187, 192–94, 195, 272nn118–119, 273n163; Revolutionary Cells attacks 190; sense of complacency and false security among the Milcoms 190, 272nn135–137; timeline of attacks **193–94**

"Terrorism Chronology: 1981–1986" 199
Terry, William 105–6
Terry and the Pirates (comic) 79
Tet offensive, Vietnam 5, 172, 173, 269n4
Thamm, Erik 88
Thamm, Gerhardt 87
Third World 153
USS *Thomas Barry* 11
Thompson, Dorothy 235n37
Thurmond, Strom 236n58
Time 249n128
Title VII, Civil Rights Act 161
Title IX, Education Act 164
TO&E (Table of Organization and Equipment) 254n115
Tomahawk cruise missiles 182
Tracy, Tom 139
Trimble, William C. 257n38
Truman, Henry S 13, 99, 104, 235n29, 256n8
Truman Doctrine 109
tuberculosis 30
Tucker, Randy 209
280-mm atomic cannon 100, 106

UCMJ (Uniform Code of Military Justice) 121, 178, 264n10, 270n44
UFO (coffee house) 175
Ulrich, Pat 71
Umsatzsteuer 216
"Underground" (radio program) 170
underground GI press: anti-war rhetoric 176, 178; directive curtailing dissident activities 179; expressing of radical ideas 178–79; fading out 180; lack of support for desertion in 181; lampooning of military leadership 178; military leaders' efforts to reduce the impact 179; number of and associations 175–76; right to freedom of speech and 177, 179; role in addressing drug abuse 178; types of information carried by 177–78
Uniform Code of Military Justice (UCMJ) 121, 178, 264n10, 270n44
United Black Soldiers 153
United Kingdom 227n154
United Service Organization (USO) 175
USS *United States* 11
United States: American's view of Europe 3, 233n4; changing role of Milcoms 4–5, 233n8; Cold War and 14–15; complexity of German-American political relations 229–30; events influencing national belief systems 5–6; GIs' behavior in Germany 12, 234n9; introduction of psychological warfare 15–16, 235n37; politics and political strategy (*see* Communism; nuclear threat); post–WWII ideology 3–4, 5, 233n1; reports of GIs' susceptibility to interrogation pressures 16, 270n67; trajectory of change 227–28; withdrawal from Heidelberg 226–27
U.S. Army Headquarters in Europe (USAREUR) **9**, 77, 130, 187
U.S. Census Bureau 13, 235n23
U.S. High Commissioner of Germany (HICOG) 12, 46, 60, 90, 96, 103, 104, 109, 117, 239n165, 240n206, 256n11
United States Information Agency (USIA) 235n37
United States Information Services (USIS) 235n37
U.S. Joint Chiefs of Staff Directive 1067 108, 255n3
U.S. Lady (magazine): addressing of opposition to allowing dependents overseas 252n73; Code of Conduct support 16, 26, 239n141; ownership 42, 236n44; recognition of women's accomplishments 71, 248–49n116, 249n120
U.S. Military Academy 150
Unsatisfied Black Soldier group 153, 176
Up Against the Wall (newspaper) 176
USS *Upshur* 11
urinalysis program 139–40, 144, 262n119, 262n122
USIA (United States Information Agency) 16, 235n37
USIS (United States Information Services) 15, 235n37
USO (United Service Organization) 175

V Corps 187, 190
value added tax (VAT): on automobiles 217; impact on Milcom retirees 216–17; Milcom exemption 121; provisions 216; tax relief program 217–18, 277n106
Vance, Mrs. Cyrus 239n141
Van Dyke, Henry 226, 278n1
Veden, Barry J. 95
venereal disease (VD) 12, 234n9

Viet Cong 269n4
Vietnam War: coffee houses featuring anti-war discussion groups 175, 269n24; desertion by Milcom service members 180–81, 270n55; drug use by Americans and 139; German reaction to the My Lai massacre 129; impact on Milcom members in Germany 172, 268n2; increase in dissenting opinions about America's involvement in 173–74; limits to dependent support during 268n2; Milcom members' participation in anti-war events 174–75; Milcom members' support 172–73; prevalence of drug use during 136, 262n95; Tet offensive 5, 269n4; underground GI press and (see underground GI press)
VII Corps 165
violence and crime: crime prevention progress 132; foreign jurisdiction over Americans 134, 261n78; German dismay over the violence in American culture 47, 127, 128–29, 135–36; German opposition to the death penalty 135–36; German reaction to crimes 133, 261nn75–66; German reaction to the My Lai massacre 129; global influences on 127, 260n42; impact on lives of Germans 133; legislation addressing crime in the U.S. 130, 261n58; Milcom members' concerns about crime 130–31; rape prevention program 132–33; rate of violent crime 130, **131**, **132**, 261nn59–60; reports of a devolving of the environment in Milcoms 129–30; tension in the Milcoms due to 133–34; themes of violence in films and television shows 128–29, 135–36; urinalysis program 139–40, 144, 262n119, 262n122; see also drug use
Vogelweh Milcom chapel, Kaiserslautern, Germany 19, 237n76
Voice of America 43
Voice of the European Retirees (VOTERS) 213, 276n70
The Voice of the Lumpen 153, 154, 178–79, 265n64
VOLAR (American Volunteer Army) 138
Volkswagen Beetle 108, 111, 256nn25–27

Vorwärts (newspaper) 76
Vrotsos, Johnny 43

WACs (Women's Army Corps) 70–71, 267n152
Wagnleitner, Reinhold 244n84
Walker, Edwin 18–19, 79, 236n59
Walt Disney studios 102
Ward, Thomas 56
Warsaw Pact 254n113
Washington Post 129, 154
Watts riots 147
Wayne, John 84, 127, 251n12
We Got the Brass (newspaper) 176
Weber, Joseph 205, 207
Weekley, Robert 88, 89, 93, 101, 139
Weinberger, Caspar 182
Wendy's 124
The West Berlin Struggle (film) 23, 84, 251n14
West Germany: Adenauer's anti-communist rhetoric 97; American culture's penetration into 38, 46, 241n2; anti-communism sentiments in 87, 90, 93, 94, 96–98, 251nn27–28, 252n43; cementing of its connection with the U.S. 95; challenge of balancing security with personal freedom 191; changing relationship with the U.S. 4, 233n8; confusion among Germans about terrorism violence 191–92; critiques of American behavior 12, 234n9; death penalty opposition 135–36; drug use within the German community 142, 263n140; economic resurgence [1980–1985]; economics of (see economic challenges [1967–1990]; economics of Germany [1947–1967]); elites' opposition to American culture 43–44, 49, 243n47; employment of locals by the U.S. military (see employment of local nationals); equal rights for women and 73, 166, 167, 249n126; establishment as an independent state 96, 253nn86–87; fast food industry in 126–27, 260n38; German attitude towards African Americans 58–59, 60, 61, 158–59, 160–61, 265n97; German perception of racial issues in the Milcoms 56, 65–67, 245n13, 247n75, 247n78; German student activists' aiding of US

deserters 180–81, 270n55, 270nn66–67; illegal drugs sources 142; inflation in 205, 275n26; memories of Soviet erection of the Berlin Wall 94; Milcom consumerism's influence on 49–51, 244nn103–104, 245n110; nuclear weapons concerns and debates 100, 103–4, 105, 107, 182, 254n125, 254nn107–108, 270n70, 270n72, 270n74; opinions about Americans' drug use 137–38; pace of equality for German women 71, 249n126; political alliance with the U.S. 96–98, 254nn92–93; population 239n164; postwar burden placed on women 166, 267n163; postwar instances of disease 30–31; rationing of food by US forces 29–30, 239n163, 239nn167–170; reactions to Kennedy's assassination 95–96; tone of military publications about 21; uncertainty of the West's ability to deter aggression from the East 96; view of American comics 80; view of Americans' violent behavior 128–29, 260n55; view of McCarthy's anti-communism offensive 88–89; women's protests against abortion laws 166, 267nn167–169; young Germans' embracing of American culture 39, 43, 49, 51, 242n43; youth movement in 1968 6, 233n10
Wetzel, R.L. "Sam" 182, 196–97, 209–10, 271n76
Where It's At (newspaper) 178
White, Jeff 136, 157, 188
whooping cough 30
The Wild One (film) 45
Wilder, Billy 122
Williams, Julius E. 264n26
Wilson, Charles 16, 18
Wilson, Woodrow 129, 260n55
WIN (Women Involved Now) 165
WINTERSHIELD 98
Winthrop, John 20, 237n84
Winward, Kyle 198
Wirtschaftswunder (economic miracle) 7, 49, 50, 108, 202; see also economics of Germany (1947–1967)
wives, Milcom see Milcom wives
Wolf, Charlotte 239n162
Wolfe, Jon 111
Women Involved Now (WIN) 165

Women's Army Corps (WACs) 70–71, 267*n*152

Women's Bureau, Labor Department 161

women's rights: changing of opinions about women in the military 164–65, 267*n*152; debates over the publication of "cheesecake" photos 163, 267*n*139, 267*n*142; expansion of women's athletics in the Milcoms 164; function as a bridge between German and American societies 166–67; grassroots groups' activities 165–66, 267*n*162; initiatives in support of the empowerment of women 165; legislation advancing equal rights for women 69, 163–64; Milcom women's access to abortion 166–67; opportunities for Milcom women to air their grievances 165; pace of equality for German women 71, 249*n*126; protests against the Miss America Pageant 166, 267*n*170; stateside actions and news regarding women's rights 161–62; struggle between traditionalists and feminists 162–63, 266*nn*128–137

Wunder, George 79

Die Zeit: about 247*n*75; on American segregation 66; on Americans' violent behavior 44; commentary on terrorism in Germany 195; concerns and debates over nuclear weapons 103–4; on a decline in antimissile protests 186; on the economic status of Milcom members 204; view of American comics 80; view of McCarthy's anti-communism offensive 89

Zimmermann, Friedrich 198

Zumwalt, Ken 170, 268*n*193

www.ingramcontent.com/pod-product-compliance
Lightning Source LLC
Chambersburg PA
CBHW081541300426
44116CB00015B/2708